INTELLECTUAL DEVELOPMENT

READINGS IN EDUCATIONAL RESEARCH

American Educational Research Association
READINGS IN EDUCATIONAL RESEARCH

Merlin C. Wittrock, EDITOR OF THE SERIES

PHILOSOPHY OF EDUCATIONAL RESEARCH
Harry S. Broudy | Robert H. Ennis | Leonard I. Krimerman

INTELLECTUAL DEVELOPMENT
Pauline S. Sears

SOCIAL DEVELOPMENT AND PERSONALITY
George G. Thompson | Francis J. DiVesta | John E. Horrocks

LEARNING & INSTRUCTION
Merlin C. Wittrock

EDUCATIONAL ORGANIZATION AND ADMINISTRATION
Donald A. Erickson

RESEARCH DESIGN & ANALYSIS
Raymond O. Collier, Jr.

EVALUATION & CURRICULUM DEVELOPMENT
William W. Cooley

INTELLECTUAL DEVELOPMENT

Pauline S. Sears, EDITOR

JOHN WILEY & SONS, INC.
New York · London · Sydney · Toronto

Copyright © 1971 by John Wiley & Sons, Inc.

All rights reserved. Published simultaneously in Canada.

No part of this book may be reproduced by any means, nor transmitted, nor translated into a machine language without the written permission of the publisher.

Library of Congress Catalogue Card Number: 73-146672

ISBN 0-471-76975-4

Printed in the United States of America

10 9 8 7 6 5 4 3 2 1

Series Preface

This book is one of a series entitled "Readings in Educational Research," sponsored and prepared by the American Educational Research Association (AERA). The tentative titles of the seven projected volumes are:

1. Philosophy of Educational Research
2. Intellectual Development
3. Social Development and Personality
4. Learning and Instruction
5. Educational Organization and Administration
6. Research Design and Analysis
7. Evaluation and Curriculum Development

The object of this preface is to state the purposes of the series, to describe briefly the history of its development, and to acknowledge the people who created the series. For several years they donated their time and considerable abilities to its preparation.

The two purposes for publishing the series have in common the liberal theme of building understanding across the different areas and specialties of educational research and of preventing insularity among educators and educational researchers. The major purpose is to promote a systematic development of the quickly growing field of educational research. A multivolume series encompassing different fields of educational research, such as educational administration and research design and analysis, is one appropriate way for AERA to further the cohesiveness of educational research. The second purpose of the series is to make available to students, teachers, researchers, and administrators a comprehensive, useful, and organized set of outstanding published papers representing major fields of educational research.

These two objectives have guided the editors in their selection of the papers and articles that comprise the series. Each paper is included in the series because it contributes to the two purposes mentioned above. Each paper makes important points about significant issues or problems of education and each complements the logical organization of the series and the volume editor's conception of the significant divisions of his field of research.

Lee Cronbach conceived the idea for the series. He is absolved of any inadequacies it may have. When he was president of AERA, he appointed a committee to investigate the advisability and value of having AERA sponsor the series. The members of this committee were John DeCecco, Arthur P. Coladarci, Leland K. Medsker, David G. Ryans, and M. C. Wittrock, chairman.

The committee recommended that the preparation of a multivolume series of readings was an appropriate endeavor for AERA, provided that the series encompassed several major areas of educational research. The series would not then compete with individual researchers' single-volume treatments of their fields of educational research. More important, the series would help to accomplish the objectives mentioned above.

A second committee was then appointed to provide a tentative design for the series and to select a Board of Editors to prepare the series. The second committee consisted of Luvern Cunningham, Ellis Page, Ole Sand, George Thompson, Robert Travers, and M. C. Wittrock, chairman. This committee nominated people to serve as the Board of Editors.

The Board of Editors was then appointed with the responsibility of designing and preparing the seven volumes. This board consisted of nine people, seven of whom each took senior responsibility for preparing a volume: Harry S. Broudy, Raymond O. Collier, William Cooley, Donald Erickson, Pauline S. Sears, George G. Thompson, and M. C. Wittrock. W. W. Charters, Jr. and Robert Travers worked at large with the preparation of all the volumes.

Lack of space allows me to mention only a few of the other people involved in the preparation of the series. Dr. Richard Dershimer and the Central AERA staff were of invaluable help. The successive presidents of AERA, Lee Cronbach, Benjamin Bloom, Julian Stanley, John Goodlad, Roald Campbell, and Robert Gagné, and their respective Association Councils were, without exception, highly supportive of the series and most helpful in its development. The staff members of the Center for Advanced Study in the Behavioral Sciences at Stanford, California also gave extensively of their time to the completion of several manuscripts for the series. Joseph F. Jordan, of John Wiley, was consistently helpful whenever he was needed.

It is my hope that "Readings in Educational Research" helps to accomplish the goals set for it by the Board of Editors. We have prepared it to further the development and organization of educational research and to provide its readers with intellectual stimulation that will warrant its continued use in coming years.

M. C. Wittrock
Editor of the Series
Readings in Educational Research

Preface

Although philosophers and men of science have been fascinated by the mind since the beginning of recorded time, it is only within the past century that a systematic inquiry into the nature and development of intellectual behavior has begun. One consequence of this investigation has been the accumulation of evidence that experience influences the development of intelligence. Thus, education became accepted as necessary for the optimal development of the mind. This is not a new idea, to be sure, but its widespread acceptance has changed the structure and function of schooling in much of the Western world.

Developmental research on intelligence and intellectual processes has stemmed from several widely disparate orientations. The constructs used, the theoretical rationale and, in fact, the very methods of research differ markedly. This volume presents samples from some of the streams of work, and calls attention to points at which these streams may be converging.

The first section gives a brief historical introduction to the *measurement* of "intelligence" and the subsequent use of mental-ability tests in the study of intellectual development. This work started in France with Binet and Simon, whose aim was to identify children that were likely to fail if placed in regular classes. The child's mental age, obtained from comparison of his responses to those of a large group of children of the same age, was contrasted with his chronological age to obtain the intelligence quotient. Development was thought to progress in a regular fashion with age, without qualitative change. The Binet-Simon tests were taken over and transformed into "IQ" tests by Terman and his colleagues in the United States. Scores have been widely used in schools for placement of children and planning of instruction. Within a middle-class segment of society, they have usually proved fairly predictive of later school achievement. IQ measures have been frequently used as an index of the effectiveness of preschool or home environments in fostering intellectual development. Recently the standardized tests have also been used to evaluate Head Start and other educational programs, often with less than perfect satisfaction on the part of the researchers. As other sections of this volume show, intellectual development involves subtle changes in children's ways of thinking, and the attempt to measure a child's intellect by a single score is simplistic. Efforts have been made in Great Britain and the United States to differentiate this single score into a variety of more or less separable abilities. An example is Guilford's proposal in this volume. The global IQ may be a useful general index of development, but it shows little about the process that goes on as children reach more complex and adaptive modes of thought.

The second section considers a basic element in children's intellectual development—the acquisition of generalized concepts of objects, actions, and relationships in the environment. Much of this research has been inspired by Piaget; in contrast to the age-based intelligence-testing research, the aim is to understand the processes or mechanisms underlying growth in conceptual processes. The focus is on individual sequential development without regard for group age norms. Explanations are sought for the changes in modes of thinking as the child develops.

Piaget's theory suggests that cognitive development takes place in a series of *stages*, beginning with rather simple sensory-motor thinking that later evolves into a formal, coplex organization of ideas. The order of these stages is thought to be constant for all children (a fixed sequence), although the rate of development may show individual variations. Intellectual development is seen as an organization and structuring of underlying principles, so that the quality of a child's thinking may be quite different at one stage as compared to another. The progression of stages is hierarchical; a child at a certain level of development can succeed on all problems characteristic of an earlier stage of development. To Piaget, and to some other theorists who consider the development of language, there is a certain logic or necessity to the developmental sequence. Thus, it is argued that educative efforts will be ineffective unless curriculum is organized according to this sequence and unless instruction is geared to the student's developmental capacities.

Some have suggested[1] that there is an optimal educative "match" between

[1] J. McV. Hunt, *Intelligence and Experience*. New York: Ronald, 1961.

a child's level of thinking and the concepts offered to him through school curricula. This match may consist in presenting ideas geared at a level slightly in advance of the point at which the child has complete mastery. Since the stages are sequentially and hierarchically arranged, the next level of development is known. A difficulty here is caused by the fact that the "stages," as now conceived, are too gross to be very useful in matching a student's level to a curriculum sequence.

The systematic development of strategies for solving problems is another basic aspect of intellectual development that has its own tradition, and yet reflects some common issues. Growth in problem-solving abilities has been found to increase with experience. Some find evidence for qualitative shifts in strategies of problem solving, while others maintain that the same variables account for problem-solving behavior at all ages. Reinforcement and instruction of children in careful use of information seems to facilitate the learning of more complex strategies. Olson, in his article on conceptual strategies, suggests that "there is a very large gap between what children conventionally do and what they are capable of doing." The researches here may show some ways in which this gap can be narrowed.

Perhaps the most important component in human intellectual development is the acquisition and elaboration of language. The final chapter of this volume presents evidence that language influences the thinking that children are able to do. And since contemporary education depends heavily on verbal skills, the research described in this chapter has significant implications for teaching.

A difficulty exists in drawing educational implications that have significant consequences for the practitioner (teacher, principal, supervisor, or curriculum builder) from the psychological research reported in this volume as well as in the psychological journals. Much psychological research on intelligence and the intellectual process can be characterized as basic research that was carried out without regard for the immediate applicability of the results to education.

Hilgard and Bower,[2] however, conceive of basic and applied research as forming a continuum of relevance for education. They see three stages of basic research followed by three stages of applied research. These stages are as follows:

1. Research on learning without regard for human education relevance. This often involves the use of animals as subjects, and physiological studies.

2. Research on learning and cognition that uses human subjects but

[2] E. R. Hilgard and G. Bower, *Theories of Learning*, 3rd Edition. Appleton-Century-Crofts, 1966.

nonschool-related materials; for example, studies of memory using nonsense syllables.

3. Research using school-age subjects and investigating cognitive phenomena using school-related materials. Much of the research reported in this volume falls into this category. But the problems were set by the investigator in relation to some theoretical issues and generally did not arise out of the practical needs of education.

4. Research carried out in special laboratory classrooms using special teachers so that optimal conditions are present.

5. Research carried out in the regular classroom with the regular teacher to confirm whether the results obtained in Step 4 hold without optimal conditions necessarily existing.

6. Steps related to general advocacy and adoption of the results of the previous two steps.

Although most of the research reported in this volume was carried out at Step 3, as seems appropriate, significant educational innovations occur only after research at Steps 5 and 6. We cannot meaningfully and validly extrapolate results from basic research and apply them directly to education. Nevertheless, the research reported in this volume represents basic first approaches to educational problems, and suggests hypotheses for Steps 5 and 6

The organization of the volume presented some problems, because of the diversity of approaches to understanding of intellective phonemena and development. The volume might be organized in different ways and the present organization of the book, influenced by the history of the field, is neither exhaustive nor are the divisions mutually exclusive. There are papers in each section which indicate areas of overlap between the various research domains. These suggest possible ways of integrating the field. For example, in the section on conceptual processes, the Kendler paper deals with the facilitating effect of verbal labels on concept attainment; and in the section on language, papers by Carroll and Casagrande and Hess and Shipman suggest important relationships between language and thought. The sections on intelligence and conceptual processes also complement each other. The psychometric approach to intelligence focuses on individual differences in intellective *products*, whereas the conceptual approach attempts to reveal the *processes* involved in building concepts. It seems reasonable that these processes underlie the products revealed in intelligence tests. Correlations as high as .91 have been reported between scores on standard IQ tests and Piaget-type problems. Kohlberg, in an article in the chapter on intelligence, suggests some important links between psychometric intelligence, conceptual processes, and language.

The *criteria* we have used in selecting the readings follow. Not every reading meets each of these criteria, but if it fails on some, it is considered very important on others.

1. The reading is clearly outstanding and is likely to be influential for future work. It is forward looking, provides new perspectives, or solves troublesome problems.

2. The reading can stand alone; it presents theoretical rationale and sufficient discussion of method to be clear as to what was done; it gives proper credit for ideas, and the conclusions are soundly based on results.

3. In the case of research studies, which include the majority of the readings, sound methodology and analyses are required. A very few challenging theory articles are included in which the methodology is not strong or not carefully described.

4. The reading is interesting, clear, and comprehensible to first-year graduate students.

5. The reading suggests educational implications and sheds light on process. It can be related in some degree to other readings in the three other sections.

6. The readings as a whole provide some diversity in content and theoretical approach; for example, one or more readings in each area provide cross-cultural perspective or specification of environmental effects.

7. The reading has not been widely reproduced in other books of readings; however, an exception is made when the paper seems truly a classic. Important "overlooked" papers are included.

8. Each paper presents ideas or evidence on *developmental* phenomena.

The selections for this volume have been made by the four editors with help and advice from distinguished colleagues in the developmental field. Consultants for the *Development of Intelligence* section were Nancy Bayley and Lee Cronbach. For the *Conceptual Processes* section, Celia Lavatelli and Irving Sigel gave counsel. Betsey Gammon did valuable preliminary work on this section. Harold Stevenson, Jan Smedslund, and David Olson reviewed the *Problem Solving Strategies* readings and offered criticism. Courtney Cazden did the same for the *Development of Language* section.

The work was supported by the American Educational Research Association and the Stanford Center for Research and Development in Teaching. The senior editor is grateful for facilities provided by the Center for Advanced Study in the Behavioral Sciences.

PAULINE S. SEARS
SUSAN B. CROCKENBERG
DAVID H. FELDMAN
S. SHIRLEY FELDMAN

Contents

CHAPTER 4

The Development of Language

INTELLECTUAL DEVELOPMENT

CHAPTER 1

The Development of Intelligence

PAULINE S. SEARS, EDITOR

The long history of research on the development of intelligence has involved some exciting issues. The solutions devised for resolving these issues with scientific research make the history a fascinating one indeed. Questions that have arisen repeatedly over the years include the following:

1. *Definition.* What are the basic features of intelligent behavior; that is, how is intelligence to be defined?

2. *Measurement.* Can intelligence be objectively measured, in a standard fashion from subject to subject, so that scores are comparable from different examiners?

3. *Nature-nurture.* To what extent is intelligence genetically determined; to what extent may culture, environment, or education influence it? This is the familiar heredity-environment question, also referred to as nature-nurture.

4. *One ability or many.* Is there a single, global "general intelligence" that, if measured, can be reported as a single score such as the IQ, or are there numerous types of mental abilities, some of which may be independent of one another?

5. *Fixed intelligence.* Is intelligence a more or less fixed quantity that remains constant over time? This is the question of constancy of the IQ.

6. *Factors in change.* If there are marked changes in intelligence over time, what environmental conditions and/or personality correlates are associated with change?

7. *Regular increase with age; age versus stage.* Are there regular quantitative increments in intelligence with age, or does the older child show

qualitatively different processes of thought than the younger child?

8. *Decrements in adulthood.* Which aspects of intelligence show decrements in middle and old age?

9. *Predictive validity.* What is the predictive validity of an intelligence-test score? If we know the IQ of a given child, what can we predict about his adult success in college or an occupation?

Since it is impossible to incorporate readings from all the pioneers who attempted to answer these questions, the following brief historical survey has been prepared.[1] Quotes are given from some of the most outstanding researches. The readings themselves are chosen to illustrate types of strategies used by relatively modern researchers in attempting to answer these questions.

In 1905, two French physician-psychologists, Binet and Simon, published the first of a series of papers calling for objective measurement of intelligence under conditions so standardized that results from two different examiners should be comparable. In 1916, an American psychologist, Terman, refined their tests, greatly increasing the population sample on which age norms were based. His resultant scale is commonly known as the 1916 revision of the Stanford-Binet intelligence test scale. On the work of these three men has been based an enormous movement in the testing of individual differences in the development of intelligence. Many of the later tests of intelligence were evaluated by their relationship to the 1916 Stanford-Binet, or by the 1937 and 1960 revisions. For these reasons, it is of great interest to see how these men *chose the items* that were to make up their scales. What was to be included and what omitted from the concept of general "intelligence," since the choice of items, in effect, constitutes the definition of intelligence?

Binet and Simon (1905) described their strategy this way:[2]

---

[1] There are other much more comprehensive historical surveys. The following are recommended:

Ann Anastasi, *Individual Differences.* New York: Macmillan, 1958.

L. Cronbach, *Essentials of Psychological Testing,* 3rd ed. New York: Harper, 1970.

J. McV. Hunt, *Intelligence and Experience.* New York: Ronald Press, 1961.

J. J. Jenkins & D. E. Paterson, *Studies in Individual Differences: The Search for Intelligence.* New York: Appleton-Century-Crofts, 1961.

H. Jones, *Environmental Influences in the Development of Intelligence.* In L. Carmichael (Ed.), *Manual of Child Psychology.* New York: Wiley, 1954.

W. Kessen, *The Child.* New York: Wiley, 1965.

J. Peterson, *Early Conceptions and Tests of Intelligence.* Yonkers, New York: World Book Co., 1926.

[2] A. Binet & Th. Simon, *The Development of Intelligence in Children* (translated by Elizabeth S. Kite). Baltimore, Maryland: Williams and Wilkins Co., 1916. Reprinted with permission of the publisher. Originally published in *L'Année Psychologique,* 1905, **11,** 163–244.

Our purpose is to evaluate a level of intelligence. It is understood that we here separate natural intelligence and instruction. It is the intelligence alone that we seek to measure, by disregarding insofar as possible, the degee of instruction which the subject possesses. He should, indeed, be considered by the examiner as a complete ignoramus knowing neither how to read nor write. This necessity forces us to forego a great many exercises having a verbal, literary, or scholastic character. These belong to a pedagogical examination. We believe that we have succeeded in completely disregarding the acquired information of the subject. We give him nothing to read, nothing to write, and submit him to no test in which he might succeed by means of rote learning. In fact we do not even notice his ability to read if a case occurs. It is simply the level of his natural intelligence that is taken into account.

But here we must come to an understanding of what meaning to give to that word so vague and so comprehensive, "the intelligence." Nearly all the phenomena with which psychology concerns itself are phenomena of intelligence; sensation, perception and intellectual manifestations as much as reasoning. Should we therefore bring into our examination the measure of sensation after the manner of the psycho-physicists? Should we put to the test all of his psychological processes? A slight reflection has shown us that this would indeed be wasted time.

It seems to us that in intelligence there is a fundamental faculty, the alteration or the lack of which is of the utmost importance for practical life. This faculty is judgment, otherwise called good sense, practical sense, initiative, the faculty of adapting one's self to circumstances. To judge well, to comprehend well, to reason well, these are the essential activities of intelligence. A person may be a moron or an imbecile if he is lacking in judgment; but with good judgment he can never be either. Indeed the rest of the intellectual faculties seem of little importance in comparison with judgment. What does it matter, for example, whether the organs of sense function normally? Of what import that certain ones are hyperesthetic, or that others are anesthetic or are weakened? Laura Bridgman, Helen Keller and their fellow-unfortunates were blind as well as deaf, but this did not prevent them from being very intelligent. Certainly this is demonstrative proof that the total or even partial integrity of the senses does not form a mental factor equal to judgment. We may measure the acuteness of the sensibility of subjects; nothing could be easier. But we should do this, not so much to find out the state of their sensibility as to learn the exactitude of their judgment.

Note that these authors specifically reject the testing of the level of education of the subject. They are here attempting to isolate a level of intelligence independent of what the subject has been taught. Whether this can in fact be done has been and still is an important research question, being particularly relevant to proposals for education of children. (In the references that follow, Ausubel attacks the problem directly.)

Terman (1916) took over many of Binet and Simon's test items. Here he describes another important feature of the scale; namely that intelligence is assumed to *increase with age,* up to a given point, much as height does:[3]

> However, an examination of the scale will show that the choice of tests was not guided entirely by any single formula as to the nature of intelligence. Binet's approach was a many-sided one. The scale includes tests of time orientation, of three or four kinds of memory, of apperception, of language comprehension, of knowledge about common objects, of free association, of number mastery, of constructive imagination, and of ability to compare concepts, to see contradictions, to combine fragments into a unitary whole, to comprehend abstract terms, and to meet novel situations . . . .
>
> In choosing his tests Binet was guided by the conception of intelligence which we have set forth above. Tests were devised which would presumably bring into play the various mental processes thought to be concerned in intelligence, and then these tests were tried out on normal children of different ages. If the percentage of passes for a given test increased but little or not at all in going from younger to older children this test was discarded. On the other hand, if the proportion of passes increased rapidly with age, and if children of a given age, who on other grounds were known to be bright, passed more frequently than children of the same age who were known to be dull, then the test was judged a satisfactory test of intelligence. As we have shown elsewhere, practically all of Binet's tests fulfill these requirements reasonably well, a fact which bears eloquent testimony to the keen psychological insight of their author.

Note that once the scale is constructed according to this principle of increase of intelligence with age, the original assumption, that in fact it does so increase, cannot be tested. Tests that do not show the predicted increase have been eliminated.

Another assumption implicit in the work of Binet and Terman can, on the other hand, be subjected to empirical test: namely, the idea that intelligence is

---

[3] L. M. Terman, *The Measurement of Intelligence.* Cambridge, Mass.: Riverside Press, 1916, pp. 44, 46, 47, 50

a *fixed* or *stable* quantity throughout life. According to this conception, growth in intelligence should be at a rather constant rate, so that the IQ remains the same (within limits of error of the test) when the child is tested at, say, age 3 and age 9.

There have been two research strategies for approaching this question. The first is illustrated by work by Skodak and Skeels (1949): here children of mothers of low intelligence were placed in generally higher-intelligence home environments. The children tested out, on the average, as of higher intelligence than would have been predicted for them had they remained with their biological mothers. They were placed in an environment conducive to enriched experience, and their intelligence developed better than would have been expected under normal parent-child rearing conditions.

Skeels (1966) also did the heroic job of locating adopted and still-institutionalized children after a lapse of twenty-one years. All had been initially judged retarded. As adults, all who had been in adoptive homes were self-supporting, having completed a median of 12th grade education. Some had had college work. Most of the contrast group were still institutionalized.

The second research strategy for testing constancy of intelligence does not involve radical changes in the environment of the child, but rather repeated testings by the longitudinal method of study.[4] This involves following the same children over a period of years, testing them periodically and noting to what extent the IQ remains constant. The paper by Bayley (1965) illustrates this approach. As she shows, there are data for a time span of 25 years in the lives of the subjects.

The longitudinal studies show a fair constancy of the IQ in a majority of subjects. In some cases (Honzik, 1948), a poor or deprived environment was found in children whose IQ's declined over time, but in other children environmental deprivation was not associated with decreased IQ. Classic work on effects over time of nonstimulating environments is reported by Ausubel (1965).

Kagan et al. (1958) show that middle-class boys whose IQ's increase over time, compared to those whose IQ's decrease, also show high need achievement, competitive striving, and curiosity about nature. These characteristics may stimulate them to learn more about their environment, which in turn is reflected in IQ scores.

For educators, this question of effect of cultural, environmental, or personal-

---

[4] The *longitudinal* method of study can be contrasted with the *cross-sectional* method. The latter involves taking a different group of children from each age level, rather than waiting for the single group of children to grow up. Schaie and Strother (1968, in this volume) compromise by testing groups of different ages (cross-sectional) and retesting the same groups 7 years later. They call this method *cross-sequential*. They find decrements in middle age much less striking than those found by cross-sectional samples.

ity factors in increasing or decreasing general intelligence is obviously of first importance. If either home or school environments can be provided that facilitate development of mental ability, then we have a tremendous tool for the improvement of human welfare. Can some of the intellectual deficits found more frequently in economically underprivileged than in privileged children be compensated for by educational procedures?

Basic to this question is another assumption underlying the tests of general intelligence; namely, that any test item purporting to measure intelligence rather than education (as Binet and others have wished) must be a part of the normal culture presented to the child in the course of his growing up. The assumption is that all children have been *exposed* to the idea in question, or have had an opportunity to think about it. If this condition is not met, then success or failure on the test item may be a function of the child's environmental exposure rather than his ability to show intelligent behavior. Culture-bound items will not provide a proper test for persons not exposed to that culture.

That what Binet and Terman called intelligence may be limited to certain cultures has been suggested by Vernon (1965), a British psychologist:[5]

> The group of skills which we refer to as intelligence is a European and American middle-class invention: something which seems to be intimately bound up with puritanical values, the repression of instinctual responses and emphasis on responsibility, initiative, persistence, and efficient workmanship. It is a kind of intelligence which is specially well adapted for scientific analysis, for control and exploitation of the physical world, for large-scale and long-term planning and carrying out of materialistic objectives. It has also led to the growth of complex social institutions such as nations, armies, industrial firms, school systems, and universities, though it has been notably less successful in working out solutions of group rivalries or providing harmonious personal adjustment than have the intelligences of some more primitive cultures. Other cultures have evolved intelligences which are better adapted than ours for coping with problems of agricultural and tribal living. The aboriginal in the Australian desert and the Eskimo in the Far North have many schemata far more efficient than our own. Again subcultures such as our lower working class, or rural groups, develop rather different intelligence.

(See the Maccoby and Modiano paper in the conceptual processes chapter.)

Binet and Terman put together a diverse set of test items, some involving

[5] Philip E. Vernon, Ability Factors and Environmental Influence, *American Psychologist*, 1965, **20**, 723–733. Reprinted with slight abridgement by permission. (In R & A, II.)

memory, some reasoning, and some knowledge of vocabulary or number operations, and came up with *one* score of mental age, or IQ. Global intelligence, then, was thought to be composed of different functions, all of which were related to the total single score. In fact, this was accomplished statistically by rejecting for the intelligence scale any item that did not correlate positively with the total.

Other researchers, such as Thurstone (1926), and Guilford (1956, 1968), have supposed that there are many different mental abilities, all more or less independent of one another. By the statistical method of factor analysis, they look for these "primary mental abilities." Guilford has suggested a model incorporating 120 abilities, including both "convergent" thinking (for problems in which there is one, and only one, right answer) and "divergent" thinking (for problems in which there may be many right answers). Because the idea of divergent thinking, presumably involved in creativity, is an important concept, Guilford's theory is presented in this section despite the fact that he has concerned himself very little with the *development* of intelligence.

Wechsler (1958) developed an individual test of intelligence that has a verbal scale and a performance scale. The latter includes block designs and other problems not involving use of language. These scales prove discriminating in the Witkin et al. (1966) study given here.

Finally, with respect to what *predictive validity* intelligence test scores have, Thorndike presented a good summary in 1921:[6]

> If the boy has had ordinary American opportunities this score (in standardized tests of the Binet or of the group test type) will prophesy rather accurately how well he will respond to intellectual demands in cases of book-learning at the time and for some time thereafter, and very possibly for all his life. It will prophesy less accurately how well he will respond in thinking about a machine that he tends, crops that he grows, merchandise that he sells, and other concrete realities that he encounters in the laboratory, field, shop and office. It may prophesy still less accurately how well he will succeed in thinking about people and their passions and in responding to these.

As instigated by Binet, intelligence tests have always been used as predictors of scholastic aptitude or school success. On this they do fairly well, as school curricula are now constituted. But this type of validity is essentially a static one. *If* we were able to devise new curricula looking toward problem-solving in the modern world, or devise ways of motivating underprivileged youngsters

[6] E. L. Thorndike, Intelligence and Its Measurement: A Symposium. *Journal of Educational Psychology*, 1921, **12**, 124–127.

toward school learning, then it is possible that the predictive validity of current tests would be less than now appears. New tests that tap the potential for new types of problem-solving or "learning to learn" would be required. Jensen's work (1968, 1969) shows that lower-class children of low-tested intelligence performed markedly better than middle-class children in the same range of IQ on a series of rote learning tasks.

The article by Witkin et al. (1966), included here, shows that boys considered "retarded" were in fact weak in verbal comprehension, and their educational future was decided on this basis. They did better on tests involving analytic ability, but this did not prevent their assignment to the "retarded" group.

The later chapters in this volume, on development of conceptual processes and problem-solving strategies, present other types of samples of the research directed to this end. Cronbach (1969), in reply to Jensen's paper (1969), believes that our present criterion of school success is too limited: "We are training people for a *status quo* which is already vanishing" (p. 341). Rather than attempting to raise the IQ by education, we should ask that education promote intrinsically valuable achievement. An example is the development of conceptual learning ability.

The foregoing description of work on development of intelligence has focused on the Binet-Simon conception, emphasizing psychometric measurement of regular progress with age. In a sense, the items selected for intelligence tests have been a hit-or-miss potpourri without much conceptual foundation. The fact that they "work" does not give us much illumination as to the processes of intellectual development as the child matures. Yet educational planning requires knowledge of what influences such development.

During the last ten years there has been in the United States a tremendous surge of interest in the theories of Piaget, a Swiss psychologist. His writings date from 1928, but attention by American psychologists and educators is much more recent. For Piaget, intelligence or cognition is a function by which the organism understands his world. Beginning with birth, cognition proceeds through *stages* of structural reorganization. These stages each represent quite different modes of thinking, are universal (appear in all children), are sequential, and are irreversible. Movement from one stage to another generally occurs naturally as the child interacts with his environment, and specific training so far has not shown very durable effects in promoting such movement.

Research based on Piaget's concepts is presented in the second section of this volume under the rubric of development of conceptual processes. But illustrating the differences between the Binet-Simon approach and the Piagetian is Kohlberg's analysis in this section. This author also contrasts a maturational view, a cultural-training (learning) view, with what he calls the cognitive-developmental or interactional theory of development. Thus Kohlberg's paper presents the leading theories of development of "intelligence," giving consequences of each line of thought to the planning of early education.

The readings selected for this chapter are a sampling of the researches designed to shed light on the questions that were asked at the beginning of this chapter. The reader will not always find clear and unequivocal answers to these complex questions; this appears to be the normal course of events in behavioral-science research. Gradually, over the course of a number of researches, we approach sound and replicable results that begin to reveal the true nature of causal relationships. Recent comprehensive reviews of the field have been made by Bayley (1970) and Cronbach (1970).

READINGS

** Reprinted as reading.
* Quoted in chapter introduction.

A fair proportion of the articles have been reprinted in one or another book of readings. Those used, with the abbreviation which appears on the following list are:

Kuhlen, R. G., & Thompson, G. G. (Eds.). *Psychological Studies of Human Development.* New York: Appleton-Century-Crofts, 1963. (2nd ed.), 1970 (3rd ed.). (K & T.)

Mussen, P. H., Conger, J. J., & Kagan, J. (Eds.). *Readings in Child Development and Personality.* New York: Harper & Row, 1965 (1st ed.), 1970 (2nd ed.). (M, C, & K.)

Palermo, D. S., & Lipsitt, L. P. (Eds.). *Research Readings in Child Psychology.* New York: Holt, Rinehart & Winston, Inc., 1963 (1st ed.) 1970 (2nd ed.). (P & L.)

Rosenblith, Judy, & Allinsmith, W. *The Causes of Behavior: Readings in Child Development and Educational Psychology.* Boston: Allyn & Bacon, 1962 (1st ed.) 1966 (2nd ed.). (R & A, I & II.)

Stendler, C. B. (Ed.). *Readings in Child Behavior and Development.* New York: Harcourt, Brace & World, Inc., 1964. (S.)

References

*Ausubel, D. P. The Influence of Experience on the Development of Intelligence. In M. J. Aschner & C. E. Bish (Eds.), *Productive Thinking in Education.* Washington, D.C.: NEA, 1965, 45–62.

Bayley, N. Consistency and Variability in the Growth of Intelligence from Birth to Eighteen Years. *Journal of Genetic Psychology,* 1949, **75,** 165–196.

Bayley, N. On the Growth of Intelligence. *American Psychologist,* 1955, **10,** 805–818.

Bayley, N. Research in Child Development. *Merrill-Palmer Quarterly,* 1965, **11, 183–208.

*Bayley, N. Development of Mental Abilities. In Mussen, P. L., *Manual of Child Psychology,* 2nd ed. New York: Wiley, 1970.

*Binet, A., & Simon, H. *The Development of Intelligence in Children* (Trans. by Elizabeth S. Kite). Baltimore: Williams & Wilkins, 1916. (In R & A, I & II.)

Bing, Elizabeth. Effect of Child Rearing Practices on Development of Differential Cognitive Abilities. *Child Development,* 1963, **34,** 631–648. (In R & A, II.)

Bloom, B. S. Intelligence. In *Stability and Change in Human Characteristics*. New York: Wiley, 1964. (Chapter 3.)

Bradway, Katherine, & Thompson, Clare. Intelligence at Adulthood: a Twenty-five Year Follow-up. *Journal of Educational Psychology*, 1962, **53**, 1–14.

Cronbach, L. J. Year-to-year Correlations of Mental Tests: a Review of the Hofstaetter Analysis. *Child Development*, 1967, **38**, 283–291.

*Cronbach, L. J. *Essentials of Psychological Testing*. 3rd ed. New York: Harper, 1970.

*Cronbach, L. J. Heredity, Environment, and Educational Policy. *Harvard Educational Review*, Spring 1969, 338–347.

Dennis W., & Dennis, Marsena. Development Under Controlled Environmental Conditions. In W. Dennis, *Readings in Child Psychology*. New York: Prentice-Hall, 1951.

Deutsch, M. Facilitating Development in the Preschool Child: Social and Psychological Perspectives. *Merrill-Palmer Quarterly*, 1964, **10**, 249–263.

Galton, F. *Hereditary Genius: An Inquiry into its Laws and Consequences*. New York: Meridan Books, 1962. (Originally published in 1862.)

Gray, Susan, & Klaus, R. An Experimental Program for Culturally Deprived Children. *Child Development*, 1965, **36**, 887–898.

*Guilford, J. P. The Structure of Intellect. *Psychological Bulletin*, 1956, **53**, 267–294.

Guilford, J. P. Intelligence Has Three Facets. *Science*, 1968, **160, No. 3828, 615–620.

Hall, G. S. The Story of a Sandpile. In *Aspects of Child Life and Education*. New York: Appleton-Century-Crofts, 1907, 142–156.

Hirschenfang, S., & Benton, J. Delayed Intellectual Development in Cerebral Palsied Children. *Journal of Psychology*, 1965, **60**, 235–238.

Honzik, M. P., MacFarlane, J. W., & Allen, L. The Stability of Mental Test Performance Between Two and Eighteen. *Journal of Experimental Education*, 1948, **17**, 309–324. (K & T, 2nd & 3rd.)

Honzik, M. P. Developmental Studies of Parent-Child Resemblance in Intelligence. *Child Development*, 1957, **28**, 215–228. (M, C, & K, 1st.)

Honzik, M. P. A Sex Difference in the Age of the Parent-Child Resemblance in Intelligence. *Journal of Educational Psychology*, 1963, **54**, 231–237.

Honzik, M. P. Environmental Correlates of Mental Growth: Prediction from the Family Setting at 21 Months. *Child Development*, 1967, **38**, 337–365.

Hunt, J. McV. Recapitulation and Conclusion. In *Intelligence and Experience*, Chapter 9. New York: Ronald Press, 1961, 347–365.

*Jensen, A. R. Patterns of Mental Ability and Socioeconomic Status. *Proceedings of the National Academy of Science*, 1968, **60**, No. 4, 1330–1337.

*Jensen, A. R. How Much Can We Boost IQ and Scholastic Achievement? *Harvard Educational Review*, Winter 1969, **39**, No. 1, 1–123.

*Jones, H. The Environment and Mental Development. In Carmichael, L. (Ed.), *Handbook of Child Psychology*. New York: John Wiley, 1954. Chapter 10.

Kagan, J., Sontag, L. W., Baker, C. T., & Nelson, V. L. Personality and IQ Change. *The Journal of Abnormal and Social Psychology*, 1958, **56, 261–266. (M, C, & K, 1st; K & T, 2nd.)

Kagan, J., & Moss, H. A. Parental Correlates of Child's IQ and Height: A Cross Validation of the Berkeley Growth Study Results. *Child Development*, 1959, **30**, 325–332.

Kohlberg, L. Early Education: A Cognitive Developmental View. *Child Development*, 1968, **19, 1013–1062.

Kounin, J. S. Intellectual Development and Rigidity. In R. E. Barker, J. S. Kounin, H. F. Wright (Eds.), *Child Behavior and Development*. New York: McGraw-Hill, 1943, Chapter XI.

Lesser, G., Fifer, G., & Clark, D. H. Mental Abilities of Children from Different Social Class and Cultural Groups. *Monographs of the Society for Research in Child Development*, 1965, **30**, No. 4, (102), 115.

MacKinnon, D. W. The Nature and Nurture of Creative Talent. *American Psychologist*, 1962, **17**, 484–495.

McNemar, Q. Lost Our Intelligence? Why? *American Psychologist*, 1964, **19**, 871–882.

Ojemann, R. H. Development Factors Related to Productive Thinking. In Mary Jane Aschner & C. E. Bish (Eds.), *Productive Thinking in Education*, Washington, D.C.: NEA, 1965.

Schaie, K. W. Age Changes and Age Differences. *The Gerontologist*, 1967, **7**, No. 2, Part I, 128–132.

Schaie, K. W., & Strother, C. R. A Cross-sequential Study of Age Changes in Cognitive Behavior. *Psychological Bulletin*, 1968, **70, 671–680.

Scott, J. P. New Directions in the Genetic Study of Personality and Intelligence. *Eugenical News* (now *Eugenical Quarterly*), 1953, **38**, 97–101. (R & A, II.)

Sheldon, W. H. Constitutional Factors in Personality. In J. McV. Hunt (Ed.), *Personality and the Behavior Disorders*, New York: Ronald Press, 1944, 526–550.

*Skeels, H. Adult Status of Children with Contrasting Early Life Experiences. *Monographs of the Society for Research in Child Development*, 1966, **31**, No. 3, (105), 65.

*Skodak, M., & Skeels, H. M. A Final Follow-up Study of One Hundred Adopted Children. *Journal of Genetic Psychology*, 1949, **75**, 85–124.

Sontag, L. W., Baker, C. T., & Nelson, V. L. Personality as a Determinant of Performance. *American Journal of Orthopsychiatry*, 1955, **25**, 555–562.

Sontag, L. W., Baker, C. T., & Nelson, V. L. Mental Growth and Personality Development: a Longitudinal Study. From Individual and Group Differences in the Longitudinal Measurement of Change in Mental Ability. *Monographs of the Society for Research in Child Development*, 1958, **2**, 1–139. (M, C, & K 1st.)

Spearman, C. *The Abilities of Man.* New York: Macmillan, 1927.

Taba, Hilda. Cultural Deprivation as a Factor in School Learning. *Merrill-Palmer Quarterly*, 1964, **10**, 147–159. (R & A, II.)

*Terman, L. M. *The Measurement of Intelligence.* Cambridge, Massachusetts, Riverside Press, 1916, 45, 46, 47, 50.

Terman, L. M. Intelligence in a Changing Universe. *School and Society*, 1940, **51**, 465–470.

Terman, L. M. The Discovery and Encouragement of Exceptional Talent. *American Psychologist*, 1954, **9**, 221–230. (R & A, I, II.)

*Thorndike, E. L. Intelligence and its Measurement: a Symposium. *Journal of Educational Psychology*, 1921, **12**, 124–127.

*Thurstone, L. L. Theories of Intelligence. *Scientific Monthly*, 1946, **62**, 101–112.

Tyler, Leona. Changes in Children's Scores on Primary Mental Abilities Test Over a Three-year Period. *American Psychologist*, 1953, **8**, 448–449.

*Vernon, P. Ability Factors and Environmental Influences. *American Psychologist*, 1965, **20**, 723–733. (R & A, II.)

Wallach, M. A., & Kogan, N. *Modes of Thinking in Young Children.* New York: Holt, Rinehart & Winston, 1965.

*Wechsler, D. *The Measurement and Appraisal of Adult Intelligence* (4th ed.). Baltimore: Williams & Wilkins, 1958.

Witkin, H. A., Faterson, Hanna, Goodenough, D. R., & Birnbaum, Judith. Cognitive Patterning in Mildly Retarded Boys. *Child Development*, 1966, **37, 301–317.

Wolfle, D. *America's Resources of Specialized Talent.* New York: Harper & Row, 1954.

1. RESEARCH IN CHILD DEVELOPMENT: A LONGITUDINAL PERSPECTIVE[1]

Nancy Bayley*

The longitudinal perspective from which I speak is a personal one, as I had the good fortune to work for many years at the University of California's Institute of Human Development, where the main emphasis in research has been the study of children by repeated measurements as they grew from infancy to adulthood. During most of this period Harold Jones, first as Director of Research (1927–1935) and then as Director of the Institute until his retirement in 1960, was actively involved in these studies. He first initiated there and continued to be a staunch supporter of "The Growth Study as a Psychological Method," as he titled it in a 1935 address. During most of this period, three growth studies were simultaneously in operation at the Institute of Child Welfare—each with a different staff, a different emphasis on the problems to be studied, and with different subject populations, seen over different age spans (Jones, 1960).

The Berkeley Growth Study (Jones and Bayley, 1941), with which I have been identified throughout, was the first of these studies to be started (1928) and the one which covers the longest age span. The second, the more elaborately conceived Berkeley Guidance Study (Macfarlane, 1938), has from its inception been under the direction of Jean Walker Macfarlane. Harold Jones,

SOURCE. *Merrill-Palmer Quarterly of Behavior and Development*, 1965, **11**, 8.

* Institute of Human Development, Edward Chace Tolman Hall, University of California, Berkeley, Calif. 94720.

[1] This paper, slightly revised for publication, was presented as the Fourth Annual Lecture of the Merrill-Palmer Historical Library in Child Development and Family Life, October 23, 1965.

together with Herbert Stolz directed the third, started in 1931 as the Adolescent Study (Jones, 1939), and now known as the Oakland Growth Study. However, even though Dr. Jones devoted much of his time to the last named of these studies, he maintained an active interest in all of them. It was his strong support and his conviction of their basic worth that made it possible to continue all three of the studies through a variety of adverse circumstances. Fortunately, the present Director, Dr. John A. Clausen, sees the continuing value of these growth studies. He is promoting the further analyses of the accumulated data, the current followup of the Berkeley Growth Study cases, and the development of plans for future study of all three groups.

For both the longitudinal method and the knowledge gained from the studies, we owe much to Harold Jones, and to other similarly oriented directors of child research across the country. The maintenance of these programs has not been easy.

The longitudinal method of research in child development has had a history of early optimistic espousal followed by vehement rejection on the part of many investigators, only to be reconsidered more recently as essential for gaining an understanding of the nature of many developmental processes. With this current renewed interest in the method, it seems appropriate to review both the values and the difficulties of this form of research, to try to find ways to circumvent these difficulties, and thus to enhance the values that may be derived from the study of the same individuals over time.

Longitudinal studies were among the first carefully documented records of child growth and behavior. And like other methods of research they have gone through a process of methodological improvement. So far as I know, the earliest longitudinal study to be reported is that of Buffon in 1837, in which he gives heights of one child, measured repeatedly over a period of 17 years from 1759 to 1776. Then there was a series of biographies of infants, in which the scientist observed and recorded behaviors of a single child (usually his own or a close relative) at frequent intervals over periods of one to three years. Included among these biographies are the well-known publications of Tiedeman (1863), Perez (1878), Preyer (1882), Shinn (1893), Moore and Mrs. W. S. Hall in 1896, and Pestalozzi (1899). In all of these individual case reports there was clear evidence of the age-related processes of development. In the very young infant the changes were often evident from one day to the next. In the older child the changes were more gradual. But again at adolescence physical growth, at least, was accelerated for a period, after which growth rates gradually diminished.

Clearly, the next logical step would be to go on from measuring one or two children in one's own family to measuring a larger number of children, and thus to obtain more general information about growth rates and processes. The first of these larger studies, concerned with physical growth, were carried out at Harvard University (Dearborn and Rothney, 1941). The first of the Harvard growth studies, reported by the physiologist Bowditch in 1872, gives the average heights of twelve males and twelve females, measured annually over a period of 25 years. Another physiologist, Porter (1922), in the second Harvard growth study secured monthly heights and weights of a large number of Boston school children over a period of nine years, between 1910 and 1920. Baldwin at Iowa published in 1921 a series of individual curves of several body dimensions and of lung capacity of school children.

From these and other similar studies much of value was learned about the nature of growth in individual children. Also, Baldwin added to his studies the variable of rates of maturing, as observed from measures of X-rays of the carpal bones.

The next most obvious step was to include in the longitudinal studies measures of still other aspects of growth. During the 1920's, with the establishment of a number of child research centers, many interdisciplinary longitudinal growth studies were initiated. The most frequent types of data collected, in addition to body dimensions and skeletal maturing, were measures of intelligence (thanks to Binet, I.Q.'s and mental ages were available). Social and emotional behaviors, and a variety of physiological functions were also included in a number of the studies. Information about socioeconomic status and ethnic background was usually included in all studies for purposes of both classification and comparison.

Populations to be studied varied in size from twenty or so to several thousand. Their starting ages varied from the prematures and normal neonates of Gesell, to the 17-year-olds included among Terman's sample of gifted children. The intervals between measures ranged from a few days or weeks to an occasional retesting after lapses of five or ten years or even longer. The longitudinal span, so far as the age of the subject was concerned, might be a year or eighteen years, or possibly a lifetime. There was some effort to obtain a "normal" sample by selecting an entire first grade in a school, or a "random" subsample of a community or of hospital births. There was also in some studies selection of a special population, such as prematurely born persons, or "gifted" children selected on the basis of I.Q.'s.

The investigators used the best measuring instruments and procedures available. They were careful to set up and follow carefully defined and described procedures for conducting the tests and measurements.

With the data coming in from these carefully measured populations, the investigators set out to answer a variety of questions about the individual processes of growth and the interrelations between the various aspects of growth. But their questions proliferated like the flood of the sorcerer's apprentice. They got many answers to their questions, but no answer ever seemed to be complete. Each effort seemed to terminate in a whole array of new questions which themselves often called for new techniques, new instrumnts, or new samples of populations.

However, this tends to be the nature of practically all research. Each new set of verified, or even potentially verifiable, facts points the way to other possible knowledge and opens up new fields to explore. This kind of continually expanding range of questions for investigation can be exhilarating and sometimes discouraging. But then there is another phenomenon related to the rate of progress in gaining information in a field or method. Although the first fruits of a new method yield a big harvest of the easy-to-find answers, the returns tend gradually to be reduced, until a period is reached when nothing new of any significance can be learned. What is needed at this point is some new breakthrough—some different and better instruments or procedures, or an entirely new perspective.

This was the impasse in which longitudinal research found itself in the 1940's and 1950's, and many people put the blame on the longitudinal method itself. However, the discontent wtih the method was not entirely the result of slow returns in new information. The years of experience with such programs had revealed many difficulties in carrying out the intended projects and many limitations on the extent to which generalizations from the data are possible.

Some of the criticisms leveled at longitudinal studies are concerned with the same problems inherent in most research, but perhaps intensified. Others are peculiar to the method itself. Some criticisms are more devastating to certain types of data; other data may be relatively immune. The criticisms loomed so large that people began to shy away from such research as too difficult, too wasteful, and impossible to conduct with adequate controls. Still, after all of these criticisms were leveled and longitudinal studies were denounced and rejected, it remained evident that certain important theories could not be tested and certain burning questions could not be answered except by careful observation, measurement, and documentation of the same individuals over time as they grew.

In the interests of knowledge and science, then, let us look at these criticisms and see what can be done about them.

The horrible example of the longitudinal study described by its critics is one in which the investigators rushed into a long-term project with no research design: they just started measuring everything they could think of in the hope of finding some significant relations. This I consider to be an irresponsible criticism, usually made by young persons who forget that many of the hypotheses to be tested thirty or forty years ago have long since been proved (or disproved) and are now in the textbooks as common knowledge. Also, these earlier hypotheses were not formulated in the words of the current ritual, which gives at least a semblance of scientific exactitude. What the earlier investigators did was to ask questions that were relevant for testing accepted beliefs, partially verified theories, or even sometimes mere hunches. There is nothing the matter with this procedure in its proper place. When a field of investigation is new, it is necessary to be more exploratory, to make a crude map of the territory in order to get one's bearings, before an exact and detailed map is possible.

The critics also held that longitudinal researchers did not select their cases with care but took a readily available, and often atypical, sample because it was willing and at hand. It might be a captive, institutional population, a clinically biased sample seeking help, or the children of cooperative highly educated parents who understood the "scientific" reasons for the study. But this criticism can be made of many "cross-sectional" studies in which the typical population might, for example, be composed of college sophomores. The captive school population such as that used in the third and best known Harvard Growth Study is probably one of the most representative of a broad general sample to be found among many studies, both longitudinal and other.

In all of the longitudinal samples—but even more so if the sample is carefully selected as generally representative—there is the bugaboo of maintaining sample constancy. This is one of the real limitations of longitudinal research. It is impossible to test every child at every scheduled testing on every item to be tested. Children get sick (one case of measles on the projected testing date could ruin a rigid research design); they become upset and a measure must be omitted; they refuse to comply on some items. Families go on vacations and take the study subject out of town at just the wrong time, or mother forgets the appointment and takes the child shopping; families move away permanently, or refuse to cooperate further in the study, and thus diminish the size of the sample for the older ages. These are certainly problems to be concerned about. If they can not be eliminated, they can at least be acknowledged and designated as limitations on the general applicability of the findings of the study. Sometimes if the original sample is large enough, it is possible to select, for a given age-span, a subsample which meets certain criteria of representativeness.

In the matter of sampling, after the sample is selected, perhaps most important for the investigator who conducts a longitudinal study is the need to find ways to keep the subjects motivated and willing to continue to participate. This requires consideration of the subjects as persons, with rights, needs and values which are not to be violated. Care must be taken to keep records confidential, to maintain a friendly interest in each person, to make adjustments to his preferences and needs whenever these do not defeat the goals of the study, to avoid causing hardship or distress, and whenever appropriate to give some return in the form of information about the study or the value of the subject's contribution to it.

Whether or not the sample is constant, the very fact that the children are tested so many times changes the nature of the behaviors tested. Familiarity with the situation makes a difference. Test-wise children make better scores than the naive children on whom the tests were standardized. The answers to specific test items may be learned through repeated tests—often the very repetitions which are needed to measure growth in intelligence. Or the children grow bored with the same old TAT pictures. But if, in order to avoid familiarity and boredom, you change the test, then how do you evaluate the children's responses? How comparable are the different but similar tests you use? These questions call for such devices as including cross-sectional studies on some aspects of the data. And they often require some specialized statistical procedures.

The problem about the testing instrument doesn't stop here. In the lapse of time during which the study is in process new and better tests are devised. The investigator is faced with the decision whether to stay with the old test and maintain constancy of instrument, or to change to the new and get a more adequate measure. For example, do we measure growth in intelligence by staying with the 1916 Stanford-Binet with which we started, or by changing to the 1937 and then the 1960 revision because they are more up-to-date and have more top at the upper levels? Or do we change to a still different test that has been constructed to measure identified factors of intelligence and thus permit more adequate analyses of mental growth? Or can we add new tests without dropping the old ones, and without overburdening the time and tolerance of the subjects?

If the investigators should get carried away with enthusiasm for new tests, or the potentialities of adding new dimensions of investigation to enrich the already-full program, the study can easily flounder. Not only are they asking too much of their subjects, but they are also overloading the staff who do the testing.

The problem of staff time is often crucial. In growth studies the children keep on having birthdays. The predetermined schedule of testings must be met, if the cells of the design are to be filled, and at the correct re-test intervals. Too much data to collect and to analyze, too many cases to test, often means that there is no time left for analysis and writing up of the data already obtained. Files and files of undigested data accumulate and grow out-of-date for their possible significance. Time may be wasted collecting data that, if studied, could have been dropped from the program if it turned out to be valueless. Furthermore, a schedule of continuous data analysis, writing and publishing not only serves to help weed out useless and unreliable material, it makes for continued productivity of research findings, and maintains staff morale at a high level.

Staff continuity is another real problem in long-term studies. For one thing, it is a large factor in maintaining the cooperation of the sample. When the same persons stay with the study and see the children repeatedly as they grow, bonds of friendship and loyalty are established. A child or an adult will often be more willing to return for measures if he is asked by a person he knows and trusts, and to whom he finds it hard to say "No", than if asked through an impersonal letter or by a complete stranger.

A long-term study may also fall apart with a change in the principal investigators. Such a change characteristically brings investigators with a new set of values, skills, and interests. Much material that had been laboriously collected by one person with certain well-considered goals, may seem to the new investigator to be of little value or outside the range of his skills and interests. Old tests are dropped and new ones instituted, thus producing new discontinuities. It may be that the useful returns of a long-term growth study are in direct proportion to the term of participation of the key persons on the staff. Changes are, of course, inevitable. But they may be buffered, when they can be anticipated, by cooperative programs, with gradual shifts in personnel.

The passage of time is accompanied by many changes that bother the longitudinal researchers. If, as in the Berkeley studies, the entire sample, all approximately the same age, is collected at one time, and then followed, one can not know whether certain changes are inherent in the subjects under study—or whether they are the result of certain environmental factors, all encountered by the subjects at about the same age. War, depression, changing cultures, and technological advances all make considerable impacts. What are the differential effects on two-year-olds of parents with depression-caused worries and insecurities, of T.V. or no T.V., of the shifting climate of the baby-experts' advice from strict-diet, let-him-cry, no-pampering schedules to permissive, cuddling "enriching" loving care? On the other hand, as in some studies, one might eliminate this chronological problem by adding from five to ten newborn infants each year, and then making comparisons according to age of the child and not the calendar year. But then one must wait five years or so to get a large enough sample at any one age for statistical purposes. Over this time, staff, measuring procedures and test instruments may change, making it impossible ever to get enough children for study who are the same age measured in the same way on the same instrument. Furthermore, such a procedure might only obscure significant environmental changes, and introduce uncontrolled variables that would mask significant developmental processes.

No wonder there are impatient people who can not tolerate all of these problems, even when they are reduced with careful planning and, when irreducible, are at least spelled out as limiting conditions. Also, the impatient find the necessarily long wait for results intolerable. One solution that is offered, recurrently, is only a partial solution. This is the short-term longitudinal study, which is a combination of cross-sectional and longitudinal methods, hopefully to be completed in from three to five years' time. Typically, on this method the design calls for the selection of equal numbers of children at each of five or more ages, and the retesting of all children at predetermined intervals, e.g., at intervals of one year for a period of five years.

There is much to be said in favor of such a research design. It will at least reduce the magnitude of many of the problems we have just listed. The shorter the elapsed time of data collection the less will be the attrition of the sample, and the greater the ease of maintaining the same staff and measuring instruments and procedures. Annual increments can still be studied, and the effects of different life experiences can be cancelled out or measured and statistically controlled. As Warner Schaie has recently pointed out (1964), the research can be so designed that data can be collected concurrently for both longitudinal and cross-sectional as well as age-specific comparisons. For example, the growth rates of children between successive one-year intervals can be compared for children born in 1956 and children born in 1960 or 1964. Eight-year-olds tested for the first time can be compared with eight-year-olds tested for the second, third, or fourth time. In addition, one can get quickly (at least once a year) measures on cross-sectional samples of children of different ages all measured at the same time. With these combinations it should be possible to untangle some of the nagging problems of the effects on test scores of differing life experience and of differing testwiseness, and thus to estimate the amount of change due to the growth process itself.

This is all good, so far as it goes. But it still can not give answers to many of the problems we ask of a long-term study of the same individuals. It can not tell us such things as how long the effects of experiences in infancy will last, or how early we can predict a child's adult height or I.Q., or the degree of persistence into adulthood of characteristic response tendencies evidenced in infancy.

At this point it may be helpful if we shift from generalities to actual data. Because I am most familiar with it, the Berkeley Growth Study may best serve me to illustrate some of both the limitations that must be imposed, and the contributions that can be derived from the long-term method.

Some aspects of this program were carefully planned, others just happened. At its inception, I worked with a pediatrician, Dr. Lotte V. Wolff. We started with some general hypotheses but also with some not-too-well defined questions. For example, on the then-believed assumption that the I.Q. is constant we wanted to develop a series of tests of infant behavior-development that could be used in early diagnosis of mental ability. We wanted to test hypotheses that in early life reflexes are correlated with motor coordinations and that over time mental and motor development are correlated with physical growth. In addition, we wished to establish normative data and to study the individual trends in patterns of development in a whole series of body dimensions and proportions, in reflexes indicative of neurological development, in blood-pressure, pulse and breathing rate and temperature, as well as in the mental and motor behaviors. We had prepared record forms for entering the data, as well as procedural plans and directions for obtaining them.

You may be surprised to learn that our project was not planned to be a long-term growth study. We called it the "Intensive Survey," a subsample of a representative "survey" sample of babies born in Berkeley in 1927–29. From this larger group we were to select 125 full-term, hospital-born babies of white, English-speaking parents. The babies were to be observed in the hospital and then by appointment at monthly intervals throughout their first year. At that time, we would probably all have been appalled at the idea that it would turn out to be a 36-year, or possibly longer, study.

Almost from the start certain aspects of our carefully laid plans went out of control. It was impossible to coordinate the selection of survey babies from the official birth records with Dr. Wolff's visits to the hospitals to see infants still under four days of age. Failing in this, she took whatever babies she found on her hospital visits if they met the other criteria for inclusion.

After we had been accumulating and measuring babies for six months, we suddenly realized that the 61 infants then enrolled in the study took up all of our available time on the monthly testing schedule. This hard fact determined the size of our sample.

As for the test data, it soon became evident that the baby's state, including various emotions (Bayley, 1932), wakefulness and hunger, affected our measures. So we hurried to prepare forms for recording and rating these behaviors and to write down any conditions (including maternal behaviors) which seemed to be relevant to the validity of the records.

Fortunately, there was a little time available for working up the data as we went along. We did this in part to reassure ourselves that our procedures were reliable and adequate for our purposes. The results were so interesting to us, and so many of our questions remained unanswered at the end of the first year, that we decided to extend the monthly tests through 15 months and then to continue to test on a three-month schedule. With this breakthrough on the original time limit, another limit was never set. There always remained the lure of questions about what each child would be like as he grew a little older. So the pattern became established of an open-ended, continuing study of growth. The name of the study was changed, accordingly, to the Berkeley Growth Study.

This Topsy-like growth called repeatedly for readjustments, often on short notice. The original schedule of procedures was rapidly outgrown and new, more age-appropriate tests and measures had to be selected or devised. However, the fact that the sample was compact in age (with a range of only six months) made it possible always to test the complete sample on the same schedule at any one age level. Also, eventually the rates of growth slowed and the need for quick changes accordingly became less urgent.

The tests used were varied, in part to reduce practice-effects and in part to reduce boredom in the subjects. Starting at three years with a six-month schedule, intelligence tests, anthropometrics, physicals and X-rays were given on the birthday visits. Varied schedules, which included measures of manual skills, gross motor performance, and projective tests, interest questionnaires, and a variety of incidental records as well as a short physical, were given at the half-year visits. These between-birthday schedules served not only to provide us with a variety of records that might very well be relevant to the basic records on mental and physical growth. They also served as a kind of safety valve. It was at the half-year visit that we could yield with impunity to some of the temptations to add new tests and measures to the schedule. One-shot tests or experimental procedures could be introduced at this time without interfering with the continuity of the original program. Yet these tests often served to enrich the background of information relevant to the interpretation of our basic data.

After the age of 18 years the subjects were seen on a reduced schedule, at 21 years, and again at some time between 25 and 29 years. The present program calls for a repeat at about 36 years of the regular mental and physical examinations, with the addition of independent interviews concerned with the subjects' adequacy as adults, in their interpersonal occupational and intellectual performance and adjustments.

The fact that this kind of adult continuation of a number of these long-term studies is being supported with research funds is a sign of the recent renewal of interest in the longitudinal study, and a recognition of its potential value. Why is this so? If the Berkeley Growth Study is representative of the kinds of incomplete planning and inadequate research design of the longitudinal studies initiated prior to 1940, then what can we find in it that made the effort worth while? I should like to spell out some of the findings from this study. A similar case could be made for each of the other long-term studies. In fact, because several such studies have been in process concurrently, they have in many ways acted independently to cross-validate each other's findings. Thus the charge that such studies are limited by small, restricted samples from which one can not generalize, can be at least reduced in its severity.

As for my own study, the first surprise came in the correlational findings on mental growth in the first three years (Bayley, 1933). It turned out that the infants' I.Q.'s were *not* constant. The tests devised for, and standardized on, these infants had every indication of concurrent validity and reliability. But they had no predictive power beyond a few months lapsed time. Tests given in the first three months correlated —.09 with tests given at three years. Correlations between other intermediate test ages showed a consistent pattern in which the correlations were reduced with increasing time between tests, but were also consistently increased as the age at the first test was increased. The individual children's scores (I.Q.'s) when plotted against age showed a variety of individual patterns of growth, clearly in accord with the pattern of correlations.

These findings initiated a still-continuing investigation into the nature of these early intellectual processes and their correlates. Every few years, with new ages available for inclusion and with new hypotheses about the possible factors involved, further analyses of the data were made (Bayley, 1940a; 1940b; 1949; 1954; 1955; 1956b; 1957). The importance of the findings from these analyses has derived mainly from the fact that the sample involved is relatively constant, and by selection of subsamples can be made completely constant. Although the subjects became test-wise, it is also true that when comparisons are restricted to this sample, then all of them will have had nearly equal opportunities for practice.

Some charts selected from my own published reports, or from those in which I collaborated with Earl S. Schaefer, should help to make clearer various aspects of these long-term studies.[2]

To illustrate the pattern of age changes in the stability of the I.Q.'s over the first 18 years, let us look at Figure 1. Here we have used the children's mean at 16 to 18 years as a standard with which their scores at all earlier ages are correlated. There are two sets of correlations, one each for boys and for girls. The children's scores in the first year are unrelated, or perhaps even negatively related to their scores by the time of high-school graduation. Although some relationship appears by two years, and the correlation has risen to about .6 at four years, the I.Q.'s are not highly stable until about six. Since we found the test-retest correlations to average .82 in the first four years, thus showing adequate reliability, what then is the nature of early mental growth? Why is it so little related to later tested intelligence? Our sample appears to be typical in this respect, as similar trends in age-related correlations have been found in other longitudinal studies (e.g., by Honzik, 1938; Ebert and Simmons, 1943; and J. E. Anderson, 1939). These questions have led us and others to make further analyses.

Some other of the long-term findings from these studies in intelligence may be seen in the following illustrations. Figure 2 presents a curve of the growth of intelligence for the first 21 years (Bayley, 1956b). This curve was con-

[2] Figs. 1, 5, 8, 9, 10 and Fig. 11 are, respectively, from *Monographs of the Society for Research in Child Development* No. 97, 1964 (Bayley & Schaefer) and No. 87, 1963 (Schaefer & Bayley). Figs. 2, 3 and 7 originally appeared in *Child Development*, 1956, Vol. 27, pp. 66, 67 and 70. Fig. 4 is from the *American Psychologist*, 1955, Vol. 10, p. 816; and Fig. 6 from the *Journal of Educational Psychology*, 1954, Vol. 45, p. 11. All are reproduced here with the permission of the journals named.

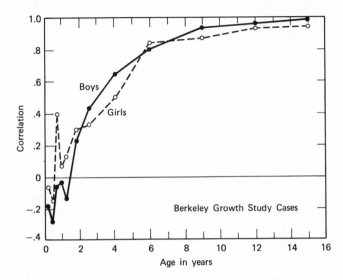

FIGURE 1.   Correlations of earlier mental test scores with 16–18 year scores.

structed after the separate test scores had been converted into an approximation of absolute scale units for this sample. Among other things, it shows continuing growth through 21 years, and generally increasing variability of

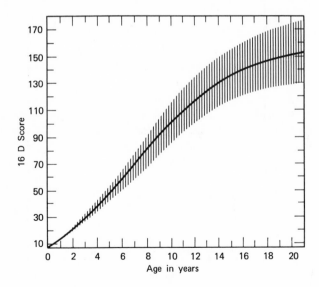

FIGURE 2.   Intelligence by age: 16 D scores.

scores. There is evidence, not clearly shown here, that there are periods at which I.Q.'s in this constant sample are relatively more variable, at around six months and eleven years; and other periods, at one year, at six years, and again at sixteen years, when the variability is greatly reduced. These trends, together with other aspects of the interrelations of scores, have suggested that the nature of intellectual processes changes with growth, probably in accordance with Piaget's theories of cognitive functioning. Further the trends suggest that variability is greatest at periods when there are greater individual differences in rates of change, periods which appear to coincide with rapid changes in the nature of intellectual processes.

Figure 3, showing the growth curves of intelligence for five boys, clearly indicates the individuality of the patterns of growth (Bayley, 1956b). The curves show also that after five or six years, in spite of minor fluctuations and an increasing spread between the low and high scores, these boys' relative positions remain fairly consistent. The curves also demonstrate that growth is continuing through 25 years.

In another study (Bayley, 1955), I have linked the Berkeley curve of intelligence to data from two other longitudinal studies (Terman and Owens) and in this way have constructed a hypothetical curve of intellectual growth when

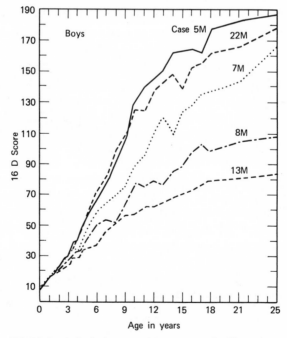

FIGURE 3. Individual curves of 16 D scores (intelligence).

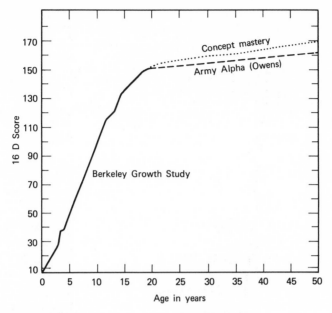

FIGURE 4. A composite age curve of intelligence.

the same population is tested. (See Fig. 4.) Extending from birth to 50 years, it shows some increment throughout this span. These findings have shown the need to re-examine the nature of intellectual change in maturity and old age, and to study the reasons for differences between the longitudinal and cross-sectional data. It may very well be that an intelligence score is to a considerable extent a function of a person's early life history—for example, the quality of his education, both formal and informal (Bayley, 1963).

Relevant to this last question is the finding from the Berkeley study that the relation of mental scores to socioeconomic status changes with age (Bayley and Jones, 1937; Bayley, 1954). In Figure 5 the patterns of correlation are shown for the boys and girls separately, with five criteria of socioeconomic status (Bayley and Schaefer, 1964). The socioeconomic variables are as of the time the children were born. They include family income, father's occupation, education of mother and of father, and a rating of the home and neighborhood. The size of the correlation is indicated by the length of the bar; positive correlations extend to the right, and negative correlations to the left of the vertical line. The correlations for the boys are on the left half of the chart (Fig. 5), for the girls, on the right half. The same five parental variables are correlated with children's I.Q. for each of thirteen successive age-levels of the children's intelligence scores, ages one month to eighteen years. (An age-level score is the average of a child's I.Q.'s for three consecutive test-ages.)

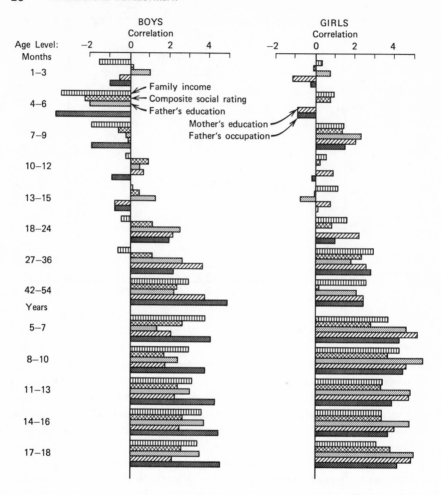

FIGURE 5. Socioeconomic data (1928). Correlations with mental test scores by age.

For the girls (at the right) there is no correlation between I.Q. and parental status during the first two years. After this age, however, the correlations become clearly positive (around .40 to .50), and are largest with mothers' and fathers' education. The pattern of correlations is similar for the boys, except that around four to six months the boys' scores correlate negatively with the parental variables, and for the five to eighteen year range their correlations tend to be lower than those of the girls. Their highest correlations are with fathers' occupation.

The fact that the same children show this marked shift in correlation with parental status calls for further inquiry. We have found, for example, as

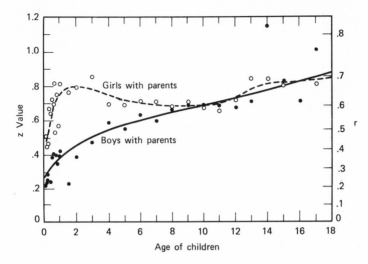

FIGURE 6. Correlations between midparent heights and heights of children.

shown in the next chart (Fig. 6), that children's heights also show increasing correlation with their parents' heights (Bayley, 1954). Again, the relationship is established with the girls at an earlier age than with the boys. These trends may be due, in part, to both individual and sex differences in rates of maturing. However, there are some clear differences between the mental and physical curves.

At this point, let us digress to another kind of comparison which is possible to make only with long-term growth materials. That is, as shown in Figure 7 (Bayley, 1956b), we can rule out individual differences in size and intelligence, and study growth rates by computing for each child the percent of his own adult status attained at each earlier measuring. In this figure the means, by sex, are given for the percent of 18-year stature, and for the percent of 21-year mental 16-D (or "absolute") score. The slopes of the mental and the physical growth curves are very different. Also, there are clear sex differences in growth rates in height, but not in intelligence. Both sexes show spurts of growth in height at adolescence, though at different ages. If there is any similar spurt in intelligence it is much less intense, and earlier, around nine or ten years, with no sex difference in the amount or the timing. From this chart it appears that over most of the first eighteen to twenty-one years physical and mental growth rates are largely independent of each other. This is true, even though there is a correlation between I.Q. and size.

In the area of physical growth this treatment of the 18-year span has had practical usefulness. With individual differences in size ruled out, high correlations were revealed, after nine years of age, between percent of mature

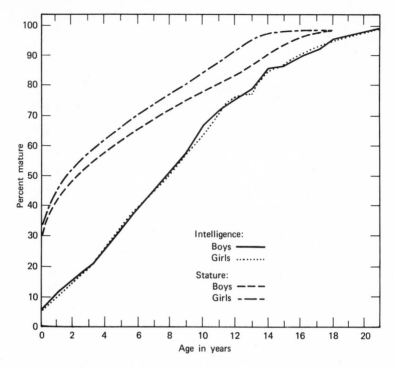

FIGURE 7.   Percent of adult stature and intelligence achieved at successive ages.

height and skeletal age. Thus it was possible, by combining the data from all three growth studies, to develop procedures for predicting with fair accuracy adult height from a child's current height and skeletal age (Bayley, 1946; Bayley and Pinneau, 1952; Bayley, 1962). It was also possible to devise growth curves of height and weight scaled according to physical maturity (Bayley, 1956a).

Even though in this study we found no sex differences in I.Q.'s or mental growth rates, we do find a pervasive sex difference in factors which correlate with the children's intelligence. These differences are illustrated in Figure 8 for a series of correlations between the children's I.Q.'s at ages one to twelve months, and an array of maternal behaviors, as of the children's first three years (Bayley and Schaefer, 1964). The maternal behaviors were developed by Schaefer and Bell (Schaefer, Bell and Bayley, 1959) from the Berkeley Growth Study materials. (These were the notes we took after we realized that the mother's behaviors affected the adequacy of our measures.) The maternal behaviors are listed at the left and are presented in Schaefer's (1959) order of neighboring, with the more highly correlated behaviors adjacent to each other. They start with granting the child autonomy and move through accepting, loving behaviors which gradually become more controlling, then through increasing hostility and decreasing control, to hostility which gradually becomes rejecting and ignoring. There are two principal orthogonal factors here: autonomy-control and love-hostility.

The pattern of correlations in this chart (Fig. 8) indicates that in the first year of life boy babies with what we might call democratic, loving mothers tend to make low scores; those with hostile and rejecting mothers make high scores. For girls on this maternal factor the correlations are just the opposite. Both sexes tend to show positive correlations between I.Q. and maternal controlling behaviors.

Referring next to Figure 9, we see the preschool-age correlations—that is,

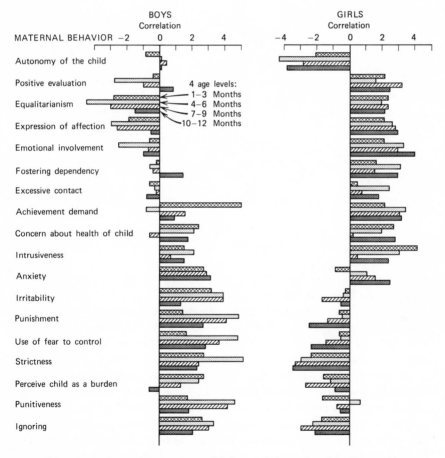

FIGURE 8. Correlations between maternal behavior (0–3 years) and intelligence (4 age levels, 1–12 months).

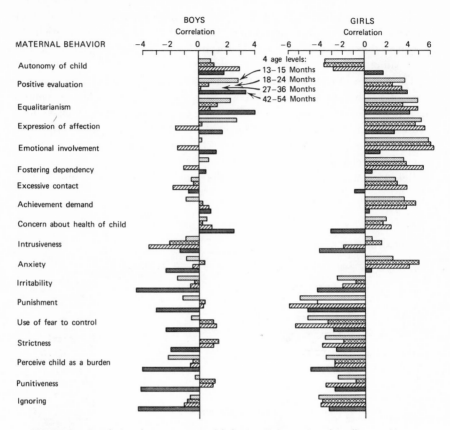

FIGURE 9.   Correlations between maternal behavior (0–3 years) and intelligence (4 age levels, 13–54 months).

for tests at 13 to 15 months. The pattern for the boys is shifting here, becoming at four years more like the girls at three years.

The school-age correlations—five to eighteen years—are shown in Figure 10. Surprisingly, the boys' I.Q.'s are clearly correlated, through 18 years, with the maternal behaviors we observed toward them in infancy. The boys who had loving mothers and who made low scores in infancy now make high scores, while those with hostile, rejecting mothers make low scores. The picture for the girls is very different. Only one type of maternal behavior, intrusiveness, is correlated (negatively) with the girls' school-age I.Q.'s.

From these correlations, it appears that the mothers' treatment of their infants in the first three years had lasting effects on their sons' intelligence, but had little or no perseverative effect on their daughters' intelligence.

Relevant to this is the fact that the early maternal behaviors showed persis-

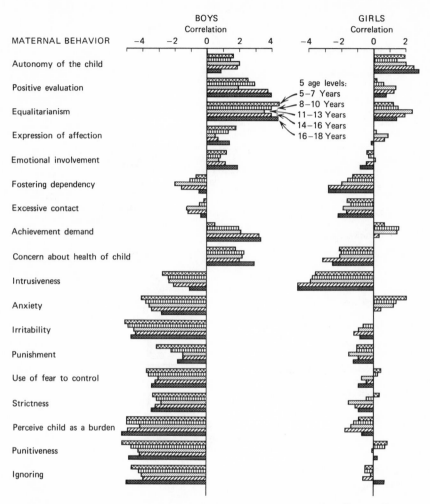

FIGURE 10. Correlations between maternal behavior (0–3 years) and intelligence (5 age levels, 5–18 years).

tent correlations with the boys' but not with the girls' adolescent behaviors (Schaefer and Bayley, 1963). Figure 11 shows that the pattern of the early maternal behaviors characterized as positively evaluating, affectionate, and controlling is related to an intercorrelated group of boys' extraverted adjusted behaviors at adolescence. Figure 12 shows negative correlations of these same maternal behaviors and their sons' introverted adjusted behaviors. The correlations for the girls have not been charted because they are all so close to zero.

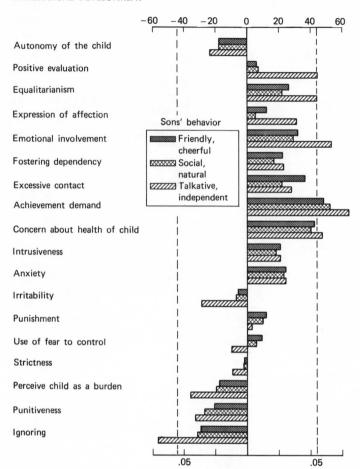

FIGURE 11. Positive correlations between maternal behavior (0–3 years) and sons' adolescent behavior.

Also, as shown in Figure 13 (Bayley and Schaefer, 1964) for ratings of happiness in infancy, we find that the boys' intelligence scores show a trend from negative correlations with happiness in infancy to positive correlations after five years between early happiness and later IQ. Again the girls' correlation trends are just the reverse. For them concurrent ratings of happiness and I.Q. are positive—but the girls' emotional state in infancy is very little, if any, related to their later I.Q.'s. Such predictive value as we have of early emotional tone to school-age I.Q. is clearest for the ratings made at 18 to 30 months.

These findings, together with others on this sample and supporting data

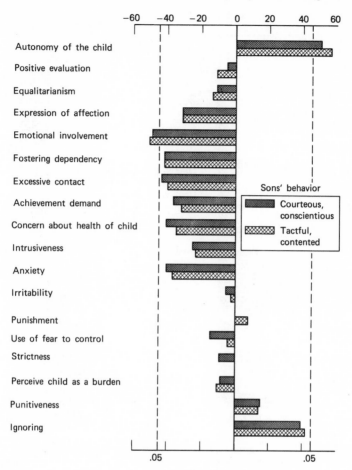

FIGURE 12. Negative correlations between maternal behavior (0–3 years) and sons' adolescent behavior.

from other longitudinal studies (e.g., Kagan and Moss, 1959; Moss and Kagan, 1958; Honzik, 1963) have led me to hypothesize a genetic sex difference in the persistence of the effects of early experience. These effects are evident in emotional behaviors and intellectual functions as well as in physical conditions. The girls' I.Q.'s tend to be more related to parental ability, while the boys' I.Q.'s appear to be related to early maternal behaviors.

I have used these results to demonstrate some of the kinds of information which have been obtained, and could only be obtained, through long-term repeated observations on the same individuals. These illustrations are samples of findings from the Berkeley Growth Study, findings which have been spelled

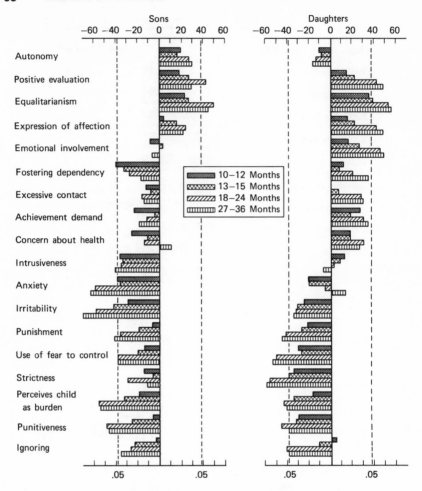

FIGURE 13. Correlations between maternal behavior (0–3 years) and children's happiness at four age levels (10–36 months).

out in detail elsewhere. Other long-term studies are currently producing in a similar way much valuable new information. Often the results of the several studies serve to corroborate each other. To the extent that the different studies with somewhat different methods and populations do obtain similar results, to that extent we are able to generalize our hypotheses and our knowledge.

Although this sketchy presentation of the Berkeley Growth Study material has been undertaken as a justification of longitudinal studies, even the relatively haphazard ones started 30 to 40 years ago, I would not advise that at this time new ones should be designed to replicate exactly the early ones.

We have learned much from the early studies that will help new researchers to avoid many false moves and wasteful procedures.

However, in spite of all precautions, it will not be possible to design and institute in 1964 a longitudinal research program that in 1984 will be judged perfect. Newly-gained techniques, testing instruments, and insights into human behavior will inevitably have served to outmode the 1964 design. Unforeseen and uncontrollable changes in staff and in the study sample will have altered the goals and potentials of the study.

If, however, one starts on a new program knowing something of its inherent limitations he should then be less disturbed over some of the failures. After all, one of the exciting things about a long-term follow-up is to be able to look in new ways at data in old records. Often a new technique can be applied that will extract much hitherto unsuspected information. More attention should be given to the development of means for circumventing or reducing the problems of longitudinal research. Some of these means will be statistical, some will be in sample selection and maintenance, some will be in methods of securing and recording the data to permit later adaptations and reinterpretations. One important procedure will be to plan time and staff and funds to facilitate a continuous process of analyzing, interpreting, and publishing as the data are collected. Short-term follow-ups and cross-sectional studies, as well as the long-term studies, are all valuable. They supplement each other in important ways. There is no reason to denounce any one of the methods as not worth doing. To wait for a perfect design for longitudinal studies is to stifle all research in an area that is of basic importance for theory and practice in the field of growth and development.

References

Anderson, J. E. The limitations of infant and prechool tests in the measurement of intelligence. *J. of Psychol.*, 1939, **8**, 351–379.

Baldwin, B. T. *Physical growth of children from birth to maturity.* Iowa City, Iowa. University Studies in Child Welfare, I, No. 1, 1921.

Bayley, Nancy. A study of the crying of infants during mental and physical tests. *J. genet. Psychol.*, 1932, **40**, 306–329.

Bayley, Nancy. Mental growth during the first three years. A developmental study of sixty-one children by repeated tests. *Genet. Psychol. Monogr.*, 1933, **14**, 1–92.

Bayley, Nancy. Factors influencing the growth of intelligence in young children. In G. M. Whipple (Ed.), Intelligence: its nature and nurture. *Yearb. nat. Soc. Stud. Educ.*, 1940, 39, Part II. Pp. 49–79.

Bayley, Nancy. Mental growth in young children. In G. M. Whipple (Ed.),

Intelligence: its nature and nurture. *Yearb. nat. Soc. Stud. Educ.*, 1940, 39, Part II. Pp. 11–47.

Bayley, Nancy. Tables for predicting adult height from skeletal age and present height. *J. Pediatrics*, 1946, **28**, 49–64.

Bayley, Nancy. Consistency and variability in the growth of intelligence from birth to eighteen years. *J. genet. Psychol.*, 1949, **75**, 165–196.

Bayley, Nancy. Some increasing parent-child similarities during the growth of children. *J. educ. Psychol.*, 1954, **45**, 1–21.

Bayley, Nancy. On the growth of intelligence. *Amer. Psychologist*, 1955, **10**, 805–818.

Bayley, Nancy. Growth curves of height and weight by age for boys and girls, scaled according to physical maturity. *J. Pediatrics*, 1956, **48**, 187–194. (a)

Bayley, Nancy. Individual patterns of development. *Child Develpm.*, 1956, **27**, 45–74. (b)

Bayley, Nancy. Data on the growth of intelligence between 16 and 21 years as measured by the Wechsler-Bellevue Scale. *J. genet. Psychol.*, 1957, **90**, 3–15.

Bayley, Nancy. The accurate prediction of growth and adult height. *Modern problems in Paediatrics*, 1962, **7**, 234–255.

Bayley, Nancy. The life span as a frame of reference for psychological research. *Vita Humana*, 1963, **6**, 125–139.

Bayley, Nancy. Comparison of mental and motor test scores for ages 1 through 15 months by sex, birth order, geographical location and education of parent. *Child Develpm.*, in press.

Bayley, Nancy, & Jones, H. E. Environmental correlates of mental and motor development: A cumulative study from infancy to six years. *Child Develpm.*, 1937, **8**, 329–341.

Bayley, Nancy, & Oden, Melita H. The maintenance of intellectual ability in gifted adults. *J. Geron.*, 1955, **10**, 91–107.

Bayley, Nancy, & Pinneau, S. R. Tables for predicting adult height from skeletal age: revised for use with the Greulich-Pyle Hand Standards. *J. Pediatrics*, 1952, **40**, 423–441.

Bayley, Nancy, & Schaefer, E. S. Correlations of maternal and child behaviors with the development of mental abilities: data from the Berkeley Growth Study. *Monogr. Soc. Res. Child Develpm.*, 1964, **29**, No. 6 (Serial No. 97).

Bowditch, H. P. Comparative rate of growth in the two sexes. *Boston Med. & Surg. Jour.*, 1872, **10**, 434–5.

Buffon, ———. Sur l'accroissement successif des enfants; Gueneau de Montbeillard mesure de 1759 à 1776. *Oevres completes.* Paris: Furne et Cie., 1837.

Dearborn, W. F., & Rothney, J. W. M. *Predicting the child's development.* Cambridge: Sci-Art, 1941.

Ebert, Elizabeth, & Simmons, Katherine. The Brush Foundation study of child growth and development. I. Psychometric tests. *Monogr. Soc. Res. Child Develpm.,* 1943, **8**, No. 2 (Serial No. 35).

Hall, W. S. The first 500 days of a child's life. *Child Study Monthly,* 1896–1897, **2**, 330–342, 394–407, 458–473, 522–537, 586–608.

Honzik, Marjorie P. A sex difference in the age of onset of the parent-child resemblance in intelligence. *J. educ. Psychol.,* 1963, **54**, 5, 231–237.

Jones, H. E. The growth study as a psychological method. *Soc. Res. Child Develpm.,* 1935, (Bulletin).

Jones, H. E. The adolescent growth study. I. Principles and methods. II. Procedures. *J. consult. Psychol.,* 1939, **3**, 157–159, 177–180.

Jones, H. E. (Ed.) *Studies in human development.* Inst. Human Develpm. Res. Bull., No. 20. Berkeley: Univer. California Press, 1960.

Jones, H. E., & Bayley, Nancy. The Berkeley Growth Study. *Child Develpm.,* 1941, **12**, 167–173.

Kagan, J., & Moss, H. A. Parental correlates of child's IQ and height: a cross-validation of the Berkeley Growth Study results. *Child Develpm.,* 1959, **30**, 325–332.

Kagan, J., & Moss, H. A. *Birth to maturity: A study in psychological development.* New York: John Wiley, 1962.

Macfarlane, Jean W. Studies in child guidance. I. Methodology of data collection and organization. *Monogr. Soc. Res. Child Develpm.,* 1938, **3**, No. 6, (Serial No. 19).

Moore, K. C. The mental development of a child. *Psychol. Rev. Monogr. Suppl.,* 1896, No. 3.

Moss, H. A., & Kagan, J. Maternal influences on early IQ scores. *Psychol. Rep.,* 1958, **4**, 655–661.

Perez, B. *Les trois premieres annees de l'enfant de trois à sept ans.* Paris: Balliere et Cie, 1878.

Pestalozzi, J. H. *Sammtlich Werke.* Liegnitz, Seyffarth, 1899–1902.

Porter, W. T. The relative growth of individual school boys. *Amer. J. Physiol.,* 1922, **61**, 311–25; also *Boston Med. & Surg. Jour.,* 1923, **188**, 639–644.

Preyer, W. *Die seele des kindes.* Grieben: Leipzig, 1882.

Schaefer, E. S. A circumplex model for maternal behavior. *J. abnorm. soc. Psychol.,* 1959, **59**, 2, 226–235.

Schaefer, E. S., & Bayley, Nancy. Maternal behavior, child behavior and their intercorrelations from infancy through adolescence. *Monogr. Soc. Res. Child Develpm.,* 1963, **28**, No. 3 (Serial No. 87).

Schaefer, E. S., Bell, R. Q., & Bayley, Nancy. Development of a material behavior research instrument. *J. genet. Psychol.,* 1959, **95**, 83–104.

Schaie, C. W. A general model for the study of developmental problems. Symposium on research methods in developmental psychology. *Amer. Psychologist*, July, 1964, 537.

Shinn, M. W. *The development of the senses in the first three years of life.* Berkeley: Univer. California Publ. in Educ., 1907.

Tiedemann, D. Die vier erste Jahre meiner kinder. *J. gen. d'instruction publique*, April, 1863.

2. INTELLIGENCE HAS THREE FACETS

J. P. Guilford[1]

Many a layman who has taken a psychologist's intelligence test, especially if he did not do as well as he thought he should, has the conviction that a score, such as an IQ, does not tell the whole story regarding intelligence. In thinking so, he is absolutely right; traditional intelligence tests fall far short of indicating fully an individual's intellectual status. Just how far short and in what respects have not been well realized until very recent years during which the whole scope of human intelligence has been intensively investigated.

This is not to say that IQ tests are not useful, for they definitely are, as years of experience have demonstrated. Intelligence-quotient tests were originated more than 60 years ago for the purpose of determining which children could not learn at normal rates. This meant that the content of IQ tests weights heavily those intellectual abilities that are pertinent to school learning in the key subjects of reading and arithmetic, and other subjects that depend directly upon them or are of similar nature psychologically. IQ tests (and also academic-aptitude tests, which are essentially similar) predict less well at educational levels higher than the elementary grades, for at higher levels subject matter becomes more varied. Even at the elementary level, predictions of achievement have been poor in connection with the *initial* stages of learning to read, in spelling, and in the arts. The defender of the IQ test might say that intelligence is not involved in such subjects. But he would not only be wrong, he would also be dodging problems.

SOURCE. Science, 1968, **160**, 615–620.

[1] Dr. Guilford is emeritus professor of psychology at the University of Southern California and director of the Aptitudes Research Project.

ONE INTELLIGENCE, OR MANY ABILITIES?

The father of IQ tests, Alfred Binet, believed firmly that intelligence is a very complex affair, comprising a number of different abilities, and he manifested this conviction by introducing tests of many kinds into his composite scale. He did not know what the component abilities are, although he suggested that there are several different kinds of memory, for example. He went along with the idea of using a single, overall score, since the immediate practical goal was to make a single administrative decision regarding each child.

Test-makers following Binet were mostly unconcerned about having a basic psychological theory for intelligence tests, another example of technology running far in advance of theory. There was some concern about theory in England, however, where Charles Spearman developed a procedure of factor analysis by which it became possible to discover component abilities (1). Spearman was obsessed with a very restricting conception that there is a universal g factor that is common to all tests that have any claim to the label of "intelligence tests," where each test has its own unique kind of items or problems. His research, and that of others in his country, found, however, that correlations between tests could not be fully accounted for on the basis of a single common factor (2). They had to admit the existence of a number of "group" factors in addition to g. For example, sets of tests having verbal, numerical, or spatial material, respectively, correlated higher within sets than with tests in other sets. The extra correlation among tests within sets was attributed to additional abilities each of limited scope.

Factor analyses in the United States have followed almost exclusively the multiple-factor theory of Thurstone (3), which is more general than Spearman's. In Thurstone's conception, a g factor is not necessary but analysis by his methods would be likely to find it if the intercorrelations warrant such a result. It is not necessary to know the mathematics basic to factor theory in order to follow the remaining content of this article, but for those who wish additional insights the next few paragraphs present the minimum essentials of a mathematical basis. To all readers it may be said that factor analysis is a sensitive procedure, which when properly used, can answer the taxonomic questions of *what* intellectual abilities or functions exist and what their properties are.

The basic equation in multiple-factor theory, in matrix form, is $Z = FC$, where Z is a matrix of test scores, of order n by N, where N individuals have all taken n different tests. Z indicates that the scores are in standard form, that is, each element $z = (X - \overline{X})/s_x$, where X is a "raw" score on an arbitrary scale, $\overline{X}$ is the mean of the raw scores in the sample of N individuals, and s_x is the standard deviation. In the basic equation, I stands for the "complete factor matrix," which is of order n by $(r + n)$, where r is the number of *common* factors. The addition of n columns indicates that there are n *specific* factors or components, one for each test. In this matrix, f_{ij} is the loading or weight for test I in connection with factor J. C is of the order $(r + n)$ by N and represents the scores of N individuals on $(r + n)$ factors. The basic equation means that for each individual his standard score z_{ij} in a particular test is a weighted sum of his $(r + n)$ factor scores, each factor score also in standard form. An assumption for this form of the equation is that the factors are orthogonal (uncorrelated) variables.

The factor-analysis problem is to derive the matrix of common-factor loadings, A, given the score matrix for N individuals in n tests. The interest is in only the r common factors. The analysis ordinarily starts with intercorrelations among the n tests. The reduced (specifics ignored) intercorrelation matrix R is mathematically related to the factor matrix A by the equation $R = AA'$, where A represents only the common-factor components in F, and A' is the transpose of A. R can be computed from empirical data by the equation $R = ZZ'/N$. Starting with the computed correlation matrix R, the problem is to find the common-factor matrix A. Methods for accomplishing this operation are described by Harman (4).

Very rarely, indeed, does anyone using the multiple-factor approach find and report a g factor. The reason is that there are too many zero correlations among tests of intellectual qualities, where one genuine zero correlation would be sufficient to disallow a g factor that is supposed to be universal. My examination of more than 7000 intercorrelations, among tests in the intellectual category, showed at least 17 percent of them to be acceptable as zero correlations (5). The multiple factors usually found are each commonly restricted to only a few tests, where we may ignore factor loadings less than .30 as being insignificant, following common practice.

DISCOVERY OF MULTIPLE ABILITIES

Only a few events in discovering factors by the Thurstone approach will be mentioned. In Thurstone's first major study (6) as many as nine common factors were thought to be sufficiently interpretable psychologically to justify calling them "primary mental abilities." A factor is interpreted intuitively in terms of the apparent human resource needed to do well in the set of tests loaded strongly together on the mathematical factor. A distinction between mathematical factors and psychological factors is important. Surface features of the tests in the set may differ, but examinees have to perform well in some unique way in all of them. For example, Thurstone designated some of the abilities as being visual-perceptual, inductive, deductive, numerical, spatial, and verbal. Two others dealt with rote memory and word fluency. Thurstone and his students followed his 1938 analysis with others that revealed a few additional kinds of abilities.

Another major source of identified intellectual abilities was the research of aviation psychologists in the U.S. Army Air Force during World War II (7). More important than the outcome of adding to the number of intellectual abilities that called for recognition was the fact that where Thurstone had found one spatial ability, there proved to be at least three, one of them being recognized as spatial orientation and another as spatial visualization. Where Thurstone had found an inductive ability, there were three reasoning abilities. Where Thurstone had found one memory ability, there were three, including visual memory. In some of these cases a Thurstone factor turned out to be a confounding of two or more separable abilities, separable when more representative tests for each factor were analyzed together and when allowance was made for a sufficient number of factors. In other cases, new varieties of tests were explored—new memory tests, space tests, and reasoning tests.

The third major event was in the form of a program of analyses conducted in the Aptitudes Research Project at the University of Southern California since 1949, in which attention was first concentrated on tests in the provisional categories of reasoning, creative thinking, planning, evaluation, and problem-solving (8). Nearly 20 years later, the number of separate intellectual abilities has increased to about 80, with at least 50 percent more predicted by a comprehensive, unified theory. The remainder of this article is mainly concerned with that theory.

THE STRUCTURE-OF-INTELLECT MODEL

Two previous attempts to put the known intellectual abilities into logical schema had been made by Burt (9) and Vernon (10), with similar results. In both cases the models were of hierarchical form, reminiscent of the Linnaeus taxonomic model for the animal kingdom. Following the British tradition of emphasis upon g, which was placed at the apex of the system, there were broad subdivisions under g and under each subdivision some sub-subcategories, on down to abilities that are regarded as being very narrow in scope.

My first attempts (11) found that the hierarchical type of model had to be discarded for several reasons. First, there had to be a rejection of g itself, for reasons mentioned earlier. Furthermore, most factors seemed to be of somewhat comparable level of generality, where generality is operationally defined in terms of the number and variety of tests found to represent each ability. There did appear to be categories of abilities, some concerned with discovery or recognition of information, memory for information, productive thinking, and evaluation, with a number of abilities in each category, but there are other ways of organizing categories of abilities. The most decisive observation was that there were a number of parallels between abilities, in terms of their common features.

Some examples of parallels in abilities will help. Two parallel abilities differ in only one respect. There was known to be an ability to see relations between perceived, visual figures, and a parallel ability to see relations between concepts. An example of a test item in the first case would be seeing that one figure is the lower-left half of another. An item in the second case might require seeing that the words "bird" and "fly" are related as object and its mode of locomotion. The ability to do the one kind of item is relatively independent of the ability to do the other, the only difference being that of kind of information—concrete or perceived in the one case and abstract or conceived in the other.

For a pair of abilities differing in another way, the kind of information is the same for both. One of the abilities pertains to *seeing* class ideas. Given the set of words *footstool, lamp, rocker, television,* can the examinee grasp the essence of the nature of the class, as shown by his naming the class, by putting another word or two into it, or by recognizing its name among four alternatives? The ability pertains to discovery or recognition of a class concept. In another kind of test we ask the examinee to *produce* classes by partitioning a list of words into mutually exclusive sets, each with a different class concept. These two abilities are relatively independent. The one involves a process of understanding and the other a process of production. These processes involve two psychologically different kinds of operation.

A third kind of parallel abilities has pairs that are alike in kind of information involved and in kind of operation. Suppose we give the examinee this kind of test item: "Name as many objects as you can that are both edible and white." Here we have given the specifications for a class and the examinee is to produce from his memory store some class members. The ability involved was at first called "ideational fluency." The more of appropriate members the examinee can produce in a limited time, the better his score. In a test for a parallel ability, instead of producing single words the examinee is to produce a list of sentences. To standardize his task for testing purposes and to further control his efforts, we can give him the initial letters of four words that he is to give in each of a variety of sentences, for example: W_____ c_____ s_____ d_____. Without using any word twice, the examinee might say, "Why can't Susan dance?," "Workers could seldom deviate," or "Weary cats sense destruction." The ability was first called "expressional fluency." The kind of information in both these tests is conceptual, and the kind of operation is production.

But the kind of operation in the last test is different from that for the classifying test mentioned before. In the classifying test, the words given to the examinee are so selected that they form a unique set of classes and he is so told. The operation is called "convergent production." In the last two tests under discussion, there are many possible responses and the examinee produces alternatives. The operation is called "divergent production." It involves a broad searching or scanning process. Both operations depend upon retrieval of information from the examinee's memory store.

The difference between the two abilities illustrated by the last two tests is in the nature of the things produced. In the first case they are single words that stand for single objects or concepts. The thing produced, the "product," is a *unit* of information. In the second case, the product is an organized sequence of words, each word standing for a concept or unit. This kind of product is given the name of "system."

In order to take care of all such parallels (and the number increased as time went on and experience grew), a matrix type of model seemed called for in the manner of Mendeleev's table of chemical elements. The differences in the three ways indicated—operation (kind of processing of information), content (kind of information), and product (formal aspect of information)—called for a three-dimensional model. Such a model has been called "morphological" (12). The model as finally completed and presented in 1959 (13) is illustrated in Fig. 1. It has five categories of operation, four categories of content, and six categories of product.

It is readily seen that the theory calls for $5 \times 4 \times 6$, or 120, cubical cells in the model, each one representing a unique ability, unique by virtue of its peculiar conjunction of operation, content, and product. The reader has already been introduced to three kinds of operation: cognition (discovery, recognition, comprehension), divergent production, and convergent production. The memory operation involves putting information into the memory store and must be distinguished from the memory store itself. The latter underlies all the operations; all the abilities depend upon it. This is the best logical basis for believing that the abilities increase with experience, depending upon the kinds of experience. The evaluation operation deals with assessment of information, cognized or produced, determining its goodness with respect to adopted (logical) criteria, such as identity and consistency.

The distinction between figural and semantic (conceptual) contents was mentioned earlier. The distinguishing of symbolic information from these two came later. Symbolic information is presented in tests in the form of letters or numbers, ordinarily, but other signs that have only "token" value or meaning can be used.

The category of behavioral information was added on the basis of a hunch; no abilities involving it were known to have been demonstrated when it was included. The basis was E. L. Thorndike's suggestion (14) many years ago that there is a "social intelligence," distinct from what he called "concrete" and "abstract" intelligences. It was decided to distinguish "social intelligence" on the basis of kind of information, the kind that one person derives from observation of the behavior of another. Subsequent experience has demonstrated a full set of six behavioral-cognition abilities as predicted by the model, and a current analytical investigation is designed to test the part of the model that includes six behavioral-divergent-production abilities. In a test for cognition of behavioral systems, three parts of a four-part cartoon are given in each item, with four alternative parts that are potential completions. The examinee has to size up each situation, and the sequence of events, correctly in order to select the appropriate part. As a test for divergent production of behavioral systems, the examinee is given descriptions of three characters, for example, a jubilant man, an angry woman, and a sullen boy, for which he is to construct a number of alternative story plots involving the characters and their moods, all stories being different.

The reader has already encountered four kinds of products: units, classes, relations, and systems, with illustrations. The other two kinds of products are transformations and implications. Transformations include any kind of change: movement in space, rearrangement or regrouping of letters in words or factoring or simplifying an equation, redefining a concept or adapting an object or part of an object to a new use, revising one's interpretation of another person's action, or rearranging events in a story. In these examples the four kinds of content are involved, from figural to behavioral, illustrating the fact that all six kinds of products apply in every content category.

Implied information is suggested by other information. Foresight or prediction depends upon extrapolating from given information to some naturally following future condition or event. If I make this move in chess, my knight will be vulnerable. If I divide by X, I will have a simpler expression. If it rains tonight, my tent will leak. If I whistle at that girl, she will turn her head. The "If . . . then" expression well describes an instance of implication, the implication actually being the thing implied.

SOME CONSEQUENCES OF THE THEORY

The most immediate consequence of the theory and its model has been its heuristic value in suggesting where to look for still undemonstrated abilities. The modus operandi of the Aptitudes Research Project from the beginning has been to hypothesize certain kinds of abilities, to create new types of tests that should emphasize each hypothesized ability, then factor analyze to determine whether the hypothesis is well supported. With hypotheses generated by the model, the rate of demonstration of new abilities has been much accelerated.

At the time this article was written, of 24 hypothesized abilities in the category of cognition, 23 had been demonstrated. Of 24 expected memory abilities,

14 were recognized. In the other operation categories of divergent production, convergent production, and evaluation, 16, 13, and 13 abilities, respectively, were accounted for, and in all these categories 17 other hypotheses are under investigation. These studies should bring the number of demonstrated abilities close to the century mark. It is expected that the total will go beyond the 120 indicated by the model, for some cells in the figural and symbolic columns already have more than one ability each. These proliferations arise from the differences in kind of sensory input. Most known abilities are represented by tests with visual input. A few have been found in tests with auditory input, and possibly one involving kinesthetic information. Each one can also be placed in the model in terms of its three sources of specification—operation, content, and product.

Having developed a comprehensive and systematic theory of intelligence, we have found that not the least of its benefits is an entirely new point of view in psychology generally, a view that has been called "operational-informational." I have elaborated a great deal upon this view elsewhere (15). Information is defined for psychology as that which the organism discriminates. Without discrimination there is no information. This far, there is agreement with the conception of information as viewed by communication engineers, but beyond this point we part company. Psychological discriminations are most broadly and decisively along the lines of kinds of content and kinds of products, from which arise hiatuses between intellectual abilities. Further discriminations occur, of course, within the sphere of a single ability. I have proposed that the 4×6 intersections of the informational categories of the SI (structure of intellect) model provide a psychoepistemology, with 24 subcategories of basic information. I have also proposed that the six product categories—units, classes, relations, systems, transformations, and implications—provide the basis for a psycho-logic (16). Although most of these terms are also concepts in modern logic, a more complete representation appears in mathematics.

The operational-informational view regards the organism as a processor of information, for which the modern, high-speed computer is a good analogy. From this point of view, computer-stimulation studies make sense. In addition to trying to find out how the human mind works by having computers accomplish the same end results, however, it might be useful, also, to determine how the human mind accomplishes its ends, then to design the computer that performs the same operations. Although a psychology based upon the SI concepts is much more complicated than the stimulus-response model that became traditional, it is still parsimonious. It certainly has the chance of becoming more adequate. The structure of intellect, as such, is a taxonomic model; it provides fruitful concepts. For theory that accounts for behavior, we need operational models, and they can be based on SI concepts. For example, I have produced such a model for problem-solving (17).

There is no one problem-solving ability. Many different SI abilities may be drawn upon in solving a problem, depending upon the nature of the problem. Almost always there are cognitive operations (in understanding the nature of the problem), productive operations (in generating steps toward solution), and evaluative operations (in checking upon both understanding and production). Memory operations enter in, to keep a record of information regarding previous steps, and the memory store underlies all.

There is something novel about producing solutions to problems, hence creative thinking is involved. Creative thinking depends most clearly upon divergent-production operations on the one hand, and on transformations on the other. Thus, these two categories have unique roles in creative problem-solving. There is accordingly no one unique ability to account for creative potential. Creative production depends upon the area in which one works, whether it is in pictorial art, music, drama, mathematics, science, writing, or management. In view of the relative independence of the intellectual abilities, unevenness of status in the various abilities within the same person should be the rule rather than the exception. Some individuals can excel in more than one art form, but few excel in all, as witness the practice of having multiple creative contributors to a single motion picture.

The implications of all this for education are numerous. The doctrine that intelligence is a unitary something that is established for each person by heredity and that stays fixed through life should be summarily banished. There is abundant proof that greater intelligence is associated with increased education. One of education's major objectives should be to increase the stature of its recipients in intelligence, which should now mean stature in the various intellectual abilities. Knowing what those abilities are, we not only have more precise goals but also much better conceptions of how to achieve those goals.

For much too long, many educators have assumed, at least implicitly, that if we provide individuals with information they will also be able to use that information productively. Building up the memory store is a necessary condition for productive thinking, but it is not a sufficient condition, for productive abilities are relatively independent of cognitive abilities. There are some revealing findings on this point (18). In a sample of about 200 ninth-grade students, IQ measurements were available and also the scores on a large number of tests of various divergent-production (DP) abilities. Table 1 shows a scatter diagram with plots of DP scores (19) as a function of IQ. The striking feature of this diagram pertains to the large proportion of high-IQ students who had low, even some very low, DP scores. In general, IQ appears to set a kind of upper limit upon DP performance but not a lower limit. The same kind of result was true for most other DP tests.

On the basis of present information, it would be best to regard each intellectual ability of a person as a somewhat generalized skill that has developed

TABLE 1

Scatterplot of Expressional Fluency (One Aspect of Divergent Production) Scores in Relation to CTMM (California Test of Mental Maturity) IQ

DP Score	Intelligence Quotient								
	60–69	70–79	80–89	90–99	100–109	110–119	120–129	130–139	140–149
50–59						1	3		1
40–49					2	4	1		
30–39			2	3	4	11	17	6	2
20–29			1	3	10	23	13	7	
10–19	1	5	3	9	11	19	7	3	1
0– 9	1	3	1	4	10	11	2		

through the circumstances of experience, within a certain culture, and that can be further developed by means of the right kind of exercise. There may be limits to abilities set by heredity, but it is probably safe to say that very rarely does an individual really test such limits. There is much experimental evidence, rough though it may be, that exercise devoted to certain skills involved in creative thinking is followed by increased capability (15, p. 336). Although special exercises have their demonstrated value, it is probably better to have such exercises worked into teaching, whatever the subject, where there are opportunities. Informing individuals regarding the nature of their own intellectual resources, and how they enter into mental work, has also been found beneficial.

There is not space to mention many other problems related to intelligence— its growth and its decline, its relation to brain anatomy and brain functions, and its role in learning. All these problems take on new aspects, when viewed in terms of the proposed frame of reference. For too long, many investigators have been handicapped by using a single, highly ambiguous score to represent what is very complex but very comprehensible.

Without the multivariate approach of factor analysis, it is doubtful whether any comprehensive and detailed theory of the human intellect, such as the model in Fig. 1, could have been achieved. Application of the method uncovers the building blocks, which are well obscured in the ongoing activities of daily life. Although much has already been done by other methods to show the relevance and fruitfulness of the concepts generated by the theory (15), there is still a great amount of developmental work to be done to implement their full exploitation, particularly in education.

SUMMARY

In this limited space I have attempted to convey information regarding progress in discovering the nature of human intelligence. By intensive factor-

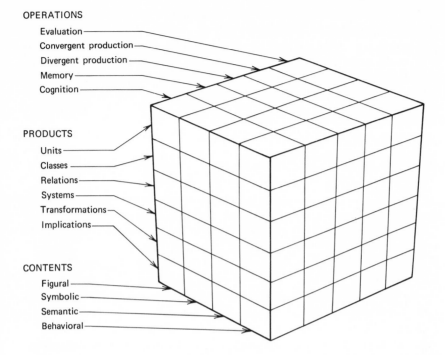

OPERATIONS
  Evaluation
  Convergent production
  Divergent production
  Memory
  Cognition

PRODUCTS
  Units
  Classes
  Relations
  Systems
  Transformations
  Implications

CONTENTS
  Figural
  Symbolic
  Semantic
  Behavioral

FIGURE 1.   The structure-of-intellect model.

analytic investigation, mostly within the past 20 years, the multifactor picture of intelligence has grown far beyond the expectations of those who have been most concerned. A comprehensive, systematic theoretical model known as the "structure of intellect" has been developed to put rationality into the picture.

The model is a cubical affair, its three dimensions representing ways in which the abilities differ from one another. Represented are: five basic kinds of operation, four substantive kinds of information or "contents," and six formal kinds of information or "products," respectively. Each intellectual ability involves a unique conjunction of one kind of operation, one kind of content, and one kind of product, all abilities being relatively independent in a population, but with common joint involvement in intellectual activity.

This taxonomic model has led to the discovery of many abilities not suspected before. Although the number of abilities is large, the 15 category constructs provide much parsimony. They also provide a systematic basis for viewing mental operations in general, thus suggesting new general psychological theory.

The implications for future intelligence testing and for education are numerous. Assessment of intellectual qualities should go much beyond present standard intelligence tests, which seriously neglect important abilities that contribute to problem-solving and creative performance in general. Educational philosophy, curriculum-building, teaching procedures, and examination methods should all be improved by giving attention to the structure of intellect as the basic frame of reference. There is much basis for expecting that various intellectual abilities can be improved in individuals, and the procedures needed for doing this should be clear.

References and Notes

1. C. Spearman, *Am. J. Psychol.* **15**, 201 (1904).

2. For the benefit of the uninitiated, a (positive) correlation between any two tests means that if certain individuals make high (low) scores in one of them they are likely also to make high (low) scores in the other.

3. L. L. Thurstone, *Vectors of Mind* (Univ. of Chicago Press, Chicago, 1935).

4. H. H. Harman, *Modern Factor Analysis* (Univ. of Chicago Press, Chicago, 1967).

5. J. P. Guilford, *Psychol. Bull.* **61**, 401 (1964).

6. L. L. Thurstone, "Primary Mental Abilities," *Psychometric Monographs No. 1* (1938).

7. J. P. Guilford & J. I. Lacey, Eds., *Printed Classification Tests* (Government Printing Office, Washington, D.C., 1947).

8. We are indebted to the Office of Naval Research, Personnel and Training Branch, for continued support, and for additional support at various times from the U.S. Office of Education and the National Science Foundation, Biological and Medical Sciences Division.

9. C. Burt, *Brit. J. Educ. Psychol.* **19**, 100, 176 (1949).

10. P. E. Vernon, *The Structure of Human Abilities* (Wiley, New York, 1950).

11. J. P. Guilford, *Psychol. Bull.* **53**, 267 (1956).

12. F. Zwicky, *Morphological Analysis* (Springer, Berlin, 1957).

13. J. P. Guilford, *Am. Psychologist* **14**, 469 (1959).

14. E. L. Thorndike, *Harper's Magazine* **140**, 227 (1920).

15. J. P. Guilford, *The Nature of Human Intelligence* (McGraw-Hill, New York, 1967).

16. ——, *ibid.*, chap. 10.

17. ——, *ibid.*, chap. 14.

18. —— & R. Hoepfner, *Indian J. Psychol.* **41**, 7 (1966).

19. Expressional Fluency is the sentence-construction test illustrated earlier.

3. A CROSS-SEQUENTIAL STUDY OF AGE CHANGES IN COGNITIVE BEHAVIOR[1]

K. Warner Schaie & Charles R. Strother

Previous cross-sectional and longitudinal studies of age changes over the adult life span have reported contradictory age gradients. The apparent contradiction was assessed by means of a new research design, called the cross-sequential method, which involves the repeated measurement of members of a cross-sectional sample. The SRA Primary Mental Abilities Test (PMA) and Schaie's Test of Behavioral Rigidity (TBR) were administered to a stratified-random sample of 500 Ss with quotas of 25 men and 25 women in each 5-yr. age interval from 20 to 70 yrs. 7 yr. later all Ss who could be located were contacted and 302 Ss were retested. Significant cross-sectional age changes were found for all variables studied, but longitudinal age changes occurred for all cohorts only for those variables where response speed was of importance. Analysis of the comparative age gradients suggests that age changes over time within a given individual appear to be much smaller than differences between cohorts and that the steep textbook age gradients represent no more than the effects of increased environmental opportunity and/or genetic changes in the species. Further implications with respect to revisions in current thinking on adult age changes are discussed.

One of the pervading problems troubling the developmental psychologist

SOURCE. *Psychological Bulletin*, 1968, **70**, 6, 671–680.

[1] This investigation was supported by Public Health Service Research Grant HD-00367-02 from the National Institute of Child Health and Human Development. Acknowledgment is made to Betty Bostrom, Margaret Baltes, Robert F. Peterson, Judy Higgins, and Pat Sand, who assisted in the testing and data analyses.

who is interested in studying age changes over the adult life span has been the consistent reporting of contradictory age gradients found as the result of cross-sectional and longitudinal inquiries. Many cross-sectional studies report peak performance in the early twenties or thirties with steep decrement gradients thereafter (cf. Horn & Cattell, 1966; Jones & Conrad, 1933; Schaie, 1958; Schaie, Rosenthal, & Perlman, 1953). Most longitudinal studies, on the other hand, report no decrement at all. In fact, slight gains in performance are recorded at least into the midfifties (Bayley & Oden, 1955; Owens, 1953). It has been argued that these contradictory findings can be accounted for by systematic sample attrition in the longitudinal studies, which tends to eliminate more subjects of low ability. It has been observed that none of the longitudinal studies has yet reached the sixties and seventies, the age range where the greatest decrement has been noted in the cross-sectional findings (Jones, 1959). The cross-sectional results also have been questioned because of the difficulties in the adequate matching of subsamples over extensive age ranges (Schaie, 1959a). All these criticisms of both the cross-sectional and the longitudinal method are well founded. They are obtuse, however, in that they overlook the methodological problem which is the crux of the difficulty.

It has been shown elsewhere that the conventional cross-sectional and longitudinal methods are simply special cases of a general developmental model (Schaie, 1965). Let us point out here that they can be expected to yield similar age gradients only under very exceptional circumstances. The basis for this statement is the fact that the cross-sectional method compares scores for samples of subjects at different ages who belong to different cohorts (generations) but are measured at the same point in time. Differences between age groups therefore could be a function of actual age differences, or they could be a function of differences between cohorts, or due to both age and cohort differences. In the longitudinal method, one compares scores for a sample of subjects, belonging to the same cohort, measured at different ages, each measure taken at a different point in time. Differences here can be a function of age changes, or of effects of the environment upon the sample over time, or due to both age changes and time differences. It follows that similar age gradients can be obtained from cross-sectional and longitudinal studies only if age differences are due to maturational phenomena alone, unrelated to any genetic or cultural variation. In most instances the cross-sectional method will confound age differences with cohort differences and the longitudinal method will confound age changes and time differences (Schaie, 1967).

It is possible to handle the above-mentioned difficulty by deriving a design which will permit the joint analysis of age, cohort, and time differences. In principle, this design would call for the longitudinal study of successive cohorts over the entire age range of interest. Such a design, of course, is not feasible due to the usual attrition problems as well as the limitations of the investigator's own life span. An efficient design, however, can be suggested which will permit a relatively short-term investigation of the problem. The proposed design will be called the cross-sequential method since it involves the sequential analysis of data from two or more cross-sectional studies. To be precise, the requisite design will involve the reexamination of a cross-sectional sample after a suitable time interval. The repeated-measurement aspect is simply a convenient rather than necessary feature of the cross-sequential method (see Schaie & Strother, 1968b).[2]

The purpose of the cross-sequential design is to obtain two or more measures from each of the cohorts included in the initial cross-sectional study so that it becomes possible to contrast the age changes occurring within generation with the age differences between generations measured at a given point in time. This can be done either by testing random splits of the original sample at successive points in time or, as was done in the present study, by obtaining repeated measures on all retrievable members of the originally measured samples.

---

*Table 1 illustrates the distinctions. It contains a set of six independent random samples, three of which have a common age, three of which have been

TABLE 1

Example of a Set of Samples Permitting All Comparisons Deducible from the General Developmental Model

		Sample 3	Sample 5	Sample 6
	1910	Age 45 $A_1C_3T_1$	Age 50 $A_2C_3T_2$	Age 55 $A_3C_3T_3$
Time of Birth (Cohort)	1905	Sample 2 Age 50 $A_2C_2T_1$	Sample 4 Age 55 $A_3C_2T_2$	
	1900	Sample 1 Age 55 $A_3C_1T_1$		
Time of Testing		1955	1960	1965

A—Age level at time of testing.
C—Cohort level being examined.
T—Number of test in series.

[2] A study with a similar design was proposed but not completed or published some years ago by John C. Flanagan (personal communication, February 29, 1968).

* Material between rules excerpted from K. W. Schaie, Age Changes and Age Differences, *The Gerontologist*, 1967, **7**, 2, 128–132.

given some measure of cognitive behavior at the same point in time, and three of which have been drawn from the same cohort; i.e., whose date of birth is identical. If we compare the performance of samples 1, 2, and 3 we are concerned with *age differences*. Discrepancies in the mean scores obtained by the samples may be due to the difference in age for samples measured at the same point in time. But note that an equally parsimonious interpretation would attribute such discrepancies to the differences in previous life experiences of the three different cohorts (generations) represented by these samples.

If, on the other hand, comparisons were made between scores for samples 3, 5, and 6, we are concerned with *age changes*. Here the performance of the same cohort or generation is measured at three different points in time. Discrepancies between the mean scores for the three samples may represent age changes, or they may represent environmental treatment effects which are quite independent of the age of the organism under investigation. The two comparisons made represent, of course, examples of the traditional cross-sectional and longitudinal methods and illustrate the confounds resulting therefrom.

Lest it be thought that there is no way to separate the effects of cohort and time differences from that of aging, we shall now consider a further set of differences which may be called *time lag*. If we compare samples 1, 5, and 6, it may be noted that the resulting differences will be independent of the organism's age, but can be attributed either to differences among generations or to differences in environmental treatment effects or both.

Any definitive study of age changes or age differences must recognize the three components of maturational change, cohort differences, and environmental effects as components of developmental change; otherwise, as in the past, we shall continue to confuse age changes with age differences and both with time lag. Hence, it may be argued that studies of age differences can bear upon the topic of age changes only in the special case where there are no differences in genetically or environmentally determined ability levels among generations and where there are no effects due to differential environmental impact. It follows, therefore, that findings of significant age differences will bear no necessary relationship to maturational deficit, nor does the absence of age differences guarantee that no maturational changes have indeed occurred.

The cross-sequential design not only permits the evaluation of cross-sectional age gradients at two or more points in time, but it also permits the construction of a composite longitudinal age gradient, each section of which will represent the age change for a given cohort over a constant time interval. Since the effect of environmental change will be constant for all age groups, it may be argued that differences in measured change ought to be due to the effect of maturational variance, and that the composite longitudinal age gradients consequently offer a more appropriate comparison with the cross-sectional findings than gradients which could be derived from a conventional longitudinal study.

Much criticism of developmental studies covering broad age ranges is based on the contention of widely differing initial characteristics of the various age groups. The population base used for the present study is thought to be one of the most representative samples of the adult population ever investigated. Nevertheless, it is obvious that successive generations must have differing characteristics in a dynamic society. The explicit purpose of the cross-sequential design strategy is to differentiate between those components of developmental change which are indeed a function of differences in initial level between generations from those which are attributable to maturational change.

PROCEDURE

The SRA Primary Mental Abilities Test (PMA), the Test of Behavioral Rigidity (TBR), and a socioeconomic status questionnaire were administered to a stratified-random sample of 500 subjects. The population base from which subjects were sampled consisted of the approximately 18,000 members of a prepaid medical plan. The membership of this plan was fairly representative of the census figures for a large metropolitan area (although somewhat curtailed at the lower end of the socioeconomic continuum). Detailed procedures of the sampling plan have been reported elsewhere (Schaie, 1958, 1959a). Quotas of 25 men and 25 women were obtained for each 5-year age interval from 20 to 70 years. Seven years later, all subjects who could be located were contacted, and 302 subjects were retested with the same instruments. The retested subjects were distributed approximately equal by age, with a slight preponderance of female subjects. Comparison of socioeconomic data for the original and attrited sample suggested that the attrition was fairly random and not significantly biased with respect to socioeconomic factors.

The analysis of variance was used to test the significance of the age-cohort (cross-sectional) and age-time (longitudinal) differences and their interaction with sex differences. Results will be reported on the subjects tested on both occasions for variables involving intellectual ability, response tendencies, and attitudes. These include in the area of intellectual abilities the variables of Verbal Meaning, Space, Reasoning, Number, and Word Fluency. Following the PMA manual (Thurstone & Thurstone, 1949), scores were derived also for a general index of intellectual ability ($V + S + 2R + 2N + W$) and an index of educational aptitude ($2V + R$). From the TBR (Schaie, 1955, 1960), data are reported on the variables of Motor-Cognitive Rigidity, Personality-Perceptual Rigidity, Psychomotor Speed, and a scale of Social Responsibility (Gough, McCloskey, & Meehl, 1952; Schaie, 1959b). To facilitate comparisons, all scores were transformed into T scores with means (Ms) of 50 and a standard deviation (SD) of 10, using as a base the first test administration to a sample of 1,000 adult subjects (Schaie & Strother, 1968b).

RESULTS

The results of the analysis of variance, reported in Table 1, yielded cohort differences significant at the .001 level of confidence for all variables except for social responsibility. (Cohort differences for the latter variable, however, were significant at the .05 level of confidence.) The replicability of cross-sectional subsample differences over two administrations for measures of ability and cognitive response style was thereby demonstrated. Quite different findings occurred for the analysis of the longitudinal time differences. If the hypothesis of intellectual decrement with age is justified, then one should expect that over a 7-year interval, decrement will occur at every adult age level and for every cohort followed over such a period of time. Such overall time differences, however, were found to be significant only for two variables, which are primarily measures of response speed and fluency (Verbal Meaning on the PMA and Psychomotor Speed on the TBR), and for the intellectual ability index of which the Verbal Fluency test is a component. It must be concluded, therefore, that the cross-sectional differences for all other variables represent differences between generations rather than age changes.

Matters are not quite as straightforward as they might appear at this point. An account must be rendered for the numerous significant interactions between the time and cohort levels. Such significant interactions imply that there are positive age changes for some cohorts and negative changes for others. Interactions significant at the .001 level of confidence were found for all variables except Space, Word Fluency, and Motor-Cognitive Rigidity.

Additionally, the analysis of variance revealed significant sex differences for Space and Psychomotor Speed. A significant triple interaction between time, cohort, and sex was found for Number. The latter finding suggests that the shape of the age gradient for Number will differ for men and women.

Test-retest reliability estimates also were obtained from the analyses of variance which, as reported in the last column of Table 2, range from .64 for Motor-Cognitive Rigidity to .94 for the PMA estimate of intellectual ability.

Next, we must concern ourselves with the problem of constructing appropriate gradients which will permit comparisons between the cross-sectional and longitudinal findings provided by this study. The combined Ms for both sexes were used to construct the age gradients since none of the sex-time interactions and only one of the sex-time-cohort interactions were found to be significant at or beyond the .01 level of confidence.[3] The cross-sectional estimates were

---

[3] A six-page table of mean scores separately by sex and measurement occasion as well as the estimated average cross-sectional and longitudinal means has been deposited in the American Society for Information Science. Order NAPS Document No. 00160 from ASIS National Auxiliary Publications Service, c/o CCM Information Sciences, Inc., 22 West 34th Street, New York, N. Y., 10001, remitting $1.00 for microfiche or $3.00 for photocopies.

TABLE 2

F Ratios from the Analysis of Variance of Cross-Sectional and Longitudinal Age Differences

Variable	Cohort Difference[ac]	Sex Difference[d]	Cohort × Sex[c]	Time Difference[bd]	Cohort × Time[c]	Sex × Time[d]	Cohort × Sex × Time[c]	r_{tt}
Verbal meaning	14.20**	2.62	—	1.68	3.11*	4.86*	—	.88
Space	13.30**	20.26**	—	1.56	1.30	—	—	.75
Reasoning	20.41**	4.59*	—	4.03*	3.07*	—	—	.93
Number	3.44**	—	1.33	1.44	3.60**	—	2.70*	.91
Word fluency	3.63**	3.41	—	80.61**	1.79	2.19	—	.86
Intellectual ability	13.11**	—	—	14.85**	7.30**	—	1.43	.94
Educational aptitude	17.76**	3.28	1.23	—	4.49**	3.94	—	.92
Motor-cognitive rigidity	15.88**	3.24	—	5.60	—	—	—	.64
Personality-perceptual rigidity	8.35**	—	—	2.67	4.62**	4.95	—	.85
Psychomotor speed	10.13**	25.94**	1.45	132.74**	5.31**	—	1.45	.89
Social responsibility	2.19	—	—	1.55	2.75*	4.40	1.70	.78

Note. The denominator in the first three *F* ratios is based on 282 *df* attributable to the error mean square for the independent observations and the denominator in the remaining *F* ratios is based on 282 *df* attributable to the error mean square for the correlated observations.

[a] Usually called "cross-sectional age differences."

[b] Usually called "longitudinal age differences."

[c] 9 *df.*

[d] 1 *df.*

* p < .01.

** p < .001.

obtained by averaging the two M scores available for each cohort. The longitudinal estimates were obtained by calculating average age changes over a 5-year interval for each age interval in the range covered. To reduce sampling variability, each estimate was based on two cohorts. For example, the longitudinal age change from 25 to 30 was computed by subtracting the M scores for Cohorts 9 and 10 obtained in 1963 from the corresponding M scores in 1956, and then multiplied by 5/7 to adjust for the disparate time span. A composite longitudinal gradient can be constructed then, beginning with the known average base of the cohort. Similar predicted longitudinal gradients could also be constructed for each of the other cohorts by adding or subtracting the longitudinal age changes from their known base.

Figures 1 to 11 provide graphic representations of the various age gradients. Here we compare the age gradients obtained on the basis of the current performance of individuals at different ages who are members of different cohorts with the estimated longitudinal age gradient for a *single* cohort. If the cross-sectional age differences for a given variable are a function solely of maturational change, then one would expect the two gradients to coincide. If, on the other hand, cross-sectional differences include the effects of differential environmental opportunity and/or genetic changes in the species, then one would expect discrepancies between the two gradients. Whenever cohort differences are in the positive direction (i.e., improvement of the species with respect to a given variable) the cross-sectional gradient will have to drop below the longitudinal, since in such case the performance of an older cohort will be below that of a younger one even if there is no maturational age change whatever. Conversely, the longitudinal gradient will fall below the cross-sectional for those variables where there is decrement in ability over generations for the population samples.

In the following paragraphs we shall examine the age gradients for each of the variables included in this study and shall attempt to highlight appropriate inferences to be drawn from these findings.

Verbal Meaning (Figure 1). This is the ability to understand ideas expressed in words. It is important in any activity involving the transmission of verbal or written communication. The cross-sectional data place the peak of this ability at age 35, and suggest a decrement from peak age of as much as $1\frac{1}{2}$ population SDs. The cross-sequential analysis, however, revealed that actual decrement does not occur for any cohort until age 60. The longitudinal data place the peak age for Verbal Meaning at age 55, and indicate that the decrement for the remainder of the range studied is less than half an SD and that the predicted M score at age 70 is still above the M score for age 25. The steep cross-sectional gradient must be attributed to increased level of verbal ability in successive cohorts, presumably due to increasingly favorable environmental experience. It will be noted that the improvement gradient is reach-

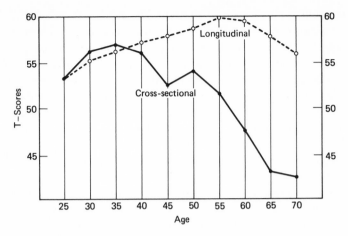

FIGURE 1.   Estimated age gradients for verbal meaning.

ing an asymptote. In fact, Cohorts 8 and 9 (born in the late 1920s and early 1930s) show a more favorable position than the last cohort. Comparison of the two gradients suggests that age decrement on Verbal Meaning within generations is quite mild and probably not seriously disabling until very old age (see Strother, Schaie, & Horst, 1957).

Space (Figure 2).   This is the ability to think about objects in two or three dimensions and is important in being able to see the relations of an arrangement of objects in space. Significant sex differences in favor of males occur for this ability. The age gradients, however, maintain the same shape for both sexes and joint analysis seems warranted. The peak age estimated by the cross-

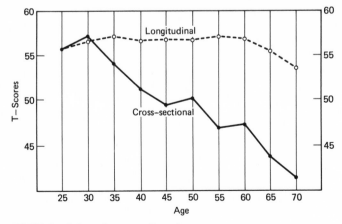

FIGURE 2.   Estimated age gradients for space.

sectional gradient for Space is at 30 years. The decrement from the peak level to age 70 is approximately $1\frac{1}{2}$ *SD*s. The cross-sequential analysis shows an ability plateau from approximately 35 to 55 years. The longitudinal data place the actual peak at age 35, but also show that the age changes over the entire range studied are almost trivial and that the maximum age decrement is less than $\frac{1}{2}$ *SD*. The steep cross-sectional gradient again must be attributed to increasing ability for successive cohorts on Space. Here, too, an asymptote seems to appear with the last two cohorts showing approximately comparable ability. These results may have important implications for retirement practices involving pilots, draftsmen, engineers, and other occupations which require high-level functioning on Space. Older members of such professions have in the past compared unfavorably with their younger peers, in the light of these results, not because their ability had declined, but because the younger generation had greater ability to begin with. If an asymptote has been reached, however, the apparent decrement will be lessened or will no longer appear when the present generation is compared with younger individuals.

Reasoning (Figure 3). This is the ability to solve logical problems, to foresee consequences and to make and carry out plans according to recognizable facts. The peak age for Reasoning is estimated at 25 years by the cross-sectional data and the maximum decrement exceeds $1\frac{1}{2}$ *SD*s. The cross-sequential data show continuing increments until age 35 and a plateau until approximately 45. The longitudinal data place the peak age for this ability at 40 years and do not show any substantial decrement until 60. There is a drop of close to $\frac{2}{3}$ *SD* from peak age, a longitudinal age change which barely reaches significance at the 5% level of confidence. Differences among generations are again much in excess over the decrement within a given generation. The cohort gradient for

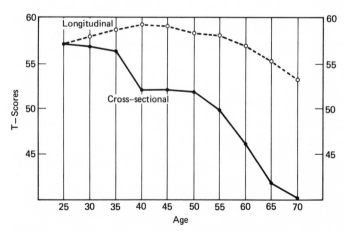

FIGURE 3. Estimated age gradients for reasoning.

Reasoning has not yet reached its asymptote, but it does show leveling off for the last three cohorts. There is some question whether the time limits imposed in this test are too stringent; it is possible that the longitudinal age gradient might flatten out further in a comparable power test.

Number (Figure 4). This is the ability to work with figures and to handle simple quantitative problems rapidly and accurately. The cross-sectional data place the peak for Number at age 50, with an approximate $\frac{1}{2}$ *SD* gain from age 25 and an approximate decrement of $\frac{4}{5}$ *SD* until age 70. Actual gain here occurs until age 65. The longitudinal gradient is considerably flatter than the cross-sectional with the 70-year-old level predicted to be above the performance of the 25-year-olds. The maximum age decrement at age 70 is less than $\frac{1}{4}$ *SD* and probably of no practical consequence. The cohort gradient here is quite curvilinear and suggests that an ability peak was reached by the generation born in the early twenties with a slight but not statistically significant decline for the subsequent cohorts. There are differences in gradients for men and women, with less decrement for the female subjects.

Word Fluency (Figure 5). This is the ability to emit in writing previously learned verbal material. It is measured by asking subjects to write the largest possible number of words beginning with a given letter in a brief period of time. The cross-sectional measures for this attribute place the peak age for Word Fluency at 35 years and note a decrement of approximately 1 *SD*. The cross-sequential analysis, however, notes decrements for every cohort beginning at age 25, at which age the longitudinal analysis would place the peak performance. A highly significant longitudinal age difference is found here which is much in excess of differences between generations. In fact, the longitudinal estimates predict a decrement of $2\frac{1}{2}$ *SDs* within a given cohort. The

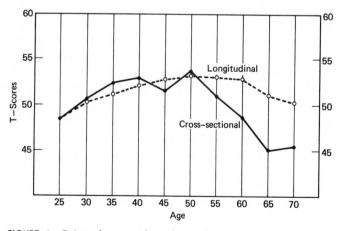

FIGURE 4.   Estimated age gradients for number.

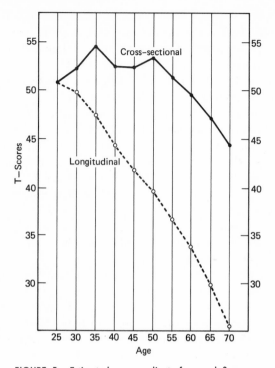

FIGURE 5. Estimated age gradients for word fluency.

cohort gradient for this variable is negative and suggests that we are only about to reach a low asymptotic level. What is the explanation for these findings? Cattell (1963) has argued that differential gradients are to be expected for fluid and crystallized forms of intelligence. Word Fluency is ambiguous in loading on both Gc and Gf, and the latter is said to be subject to decay. On the other hand, it may be suggested that Word Fluency is a highly speeded test which requires a quick response and emission of familiar material. It is well known that reaction time increases as a function of age. Word Fluency perhaps may be a better measure of physiological than psychological response capacity. What about the negative cohort gradient? Just as an enriched environment leads to higher ability levels, so does it obviate the necessity for physical exertion. The present findings certainly suggest decrement in the fluency and response latency of successive generations. Similar investigations with purer measures of speed and response strength will be required, of course, to confirm this inference.

Index of Intellectual Ability (Figure 6). This index is merely a composite of the five PMA variables weighted approximately inversely to their *SD*s. It should give a reasonable estimate of a person's general level of intellectual

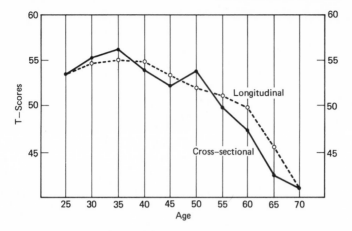

FIGURE 6.   Estimated age gradients for intellectual ability.

function. The cross-sectional data place the peak for this global measure at age 35 and yield a decrement gradient in excess of $1\frac{1}{2}$ SDs. The cross-sequential study shows increment on this measure until age 35 and decrement for all ages thereafter. The longitudinal gradient for this measure is remarkably similar to the cross-sectional gradient. The absolute maximum decrements are almost alike, but the longitudinal gradient is not quite as steep. It appears that inclusion of Word Fluency, with its steep longitudinal decrements at older ages, has the effect of matching the decrement gradient within generations closely to that between generations for a composite measure of intelligence. The meaning for composite measures of intelligence for developmental studies must be viewed, therefore, with great caution.

Index of Educational Aptitude (Figure 7). Thurstone (1958) has advocated that the combination $2V + R$ has been found to be a convenient scholastic aptitude measure which also may be used as a verbal IQ measure similar in meaning to the quotients yielded by tests such as the Otis or Kuhlmann-Anderson. This index does not contain any highly speeded measures, and our findings therefore differ markedly from those given for the global index of intelligence. The cross-sectional gradient again attains a peak at age 35, and the maximum decrement amount to $1\frac{1}{2}$ SDs. Actual age changes, however, show increments up to age 55, the peak estimated by the longitudinal data. The maximum decrement for this index is less than $\frac{1}{2}$ SD, and the estimated level at age 70 is above that found at age 25. The cohort gradient for the index of educational aptitude appears to have reached an asymptote with comparable levels of ability for the last three cohorts. These results have obvious implications for educational policies and point to the ever increasing importance of adult education programs. Moreover, they suggest that future manpower retraining pro-

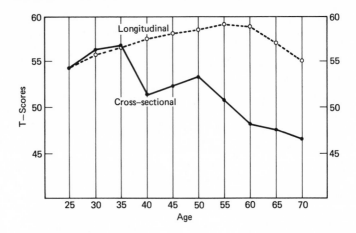

FIGURE 7.   Estimated age gradients for educational aptitude.

grams may be effectively used throughout the adult working force without particular age limitations.

Motor-Cognitive Rigidity (Figure 8).   This measure indicates the individual's ability to shift from one activity to another. It is a measure of effective adjustment to shifts in familiar patterns and continuously changing situational demands. A low score on this variable is in the rigid direction. The cross-sectional gradient for Motor-Cognitive Rigidity peaks at age 25, shows a fairly

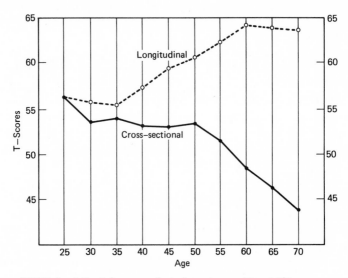

FIGURE 8.   Estimated age gradients for motor-cognitive rigidity.

stable plateau from 30 to 50 years, and then declines steeply, with a maximum decrement of $1\frac{1}{4}$ *SD*s. The cross-sequential study found increments for all cohorts except the next to the oldest group. As a result, the estimated longitudinal gradient shows positive acceleration with a peak at age 60 and a virtual plateau until age 70. This variable shows a predicted longitudinal gain in excess of $\frac{1}{2}$ *SD*. The cohort gradient is correspondingly steep and has not yet reached an asymptote. We find some difficulty in evaluating these unexpected findings. It is conceivable that as a result of life-long practice, people do get more proficient and flexible in dealing with the demands of familiar situations. We are somewhat concerned, however, that there may have been some practice effect on this measure, which involves somewhat unusual tasks which may have been remembered by the subjects. Another problem is the possibility that more careful administration and scoring might have led to some systematic increase in scores obtained for the second testing. Nevertheless, the results are such that at least it should be concluded that there is no Motor-Cognitive Rigidity increase within generations, but that there are highly significant and still ongoing positive shifts in the level of performance on this variable over successive generations.

Personality-Perceptual Rigidity (Figure 9). This measure indicates the individual's ability to adjust readily to *new* surroundings and change in cognitive and environmental patterns. It is a measure of ability to perceive and adjust to *unfamiliar* and *new* patterns and situations. The average cross-sectional peak here is placed at age 25. Personality-Perceptual Rigidity was the only variable for which the peak ages obtained in the cross-sectional gradients differed between the two testing occasions. In 1956, the peak appeared in the 31- to 35-year-old group, but the 21- to 25-year-olds obtained the highest *M*

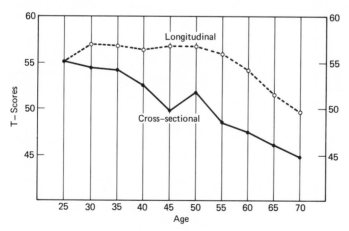

FIGURE 9.   Estimated age gradients for personality-perceptual rigidity.

score in the retest. Maximum increment for Personality-Perceptual Rigidity amounts to slightly above 1 *SD*. The cross-sequential analysis shows increased rigidity beginning with age 35, but there are several reversals, with an increment appearing as late as the next to the oldest cohort. There is no distinct longitudinal peak but, instead, a peak plateau extending from 30 to 50 years. Maximum increment in rigidity is approximately $\frac{2}{3}$ *SD,* indicating that there is some within-generation loss in flexibility in adjusting to unfamiliar patterns. This loss becomes noteworthy only in the late 60s, and even at 70 is predicted to be only approximately $\frac{1}{2}$ *SD* below the status at age 25. The cohort gradient, while significant, is much less steep than for most other variables. It is positively accelerated, however, and has not yet reached its asymptote.

Psychomotor Speed (Figure 10).   This measure indicates the individual's rate of emission of familiar cognitive responses. This measure is the other variable in our battery which is highly speeded, and the resulting age gradients consequently are quite similar to ones obtained for the PMA measure of Word Fluency. The cross-sectional gradient peaks at age 30 with a maximum decrement of 1.2 *SD*s. The within-generation decrement here is larger than the between-generation differences. Decrements over time were noted for every cohort studied. The longitudinal gradient peaks at age 25 and shows a predicted decrement in excess of 2 *SD*s. It appears that the cross-sectional data on Psychomotor Speed underestimate the within-generation decrement and that this is another characteristic where the level of ability for the population has de-

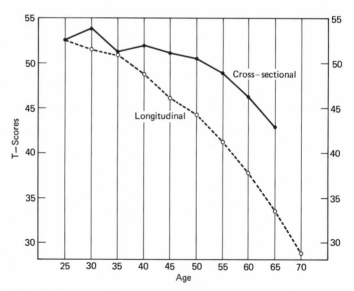

FIGURE 10.   Estimated age gradients for psychomotor speed.

clined for successive generations. The intergeneration decrement curve appears to have reached its asymptote since this ability for the last two cohorts is roughly comparable. Psychomotor Speed shows sex differences in favor of the female subjects. The age gradients, however, are similar for both sexes.

Social Responsibility (Figure 11). The final variable to be examined has slightly different characteristics from the remainder of our measures in that it is strictly an attitude scale. This is the only variable for which cohort differences failed to reach the .01 level of confidence in the variance analysis. However, cohort differences were found to be significant at the 5% level, and the cross-sectional gradient peaks at age 55, with an increment of $\frac{3}{4}$ SD from the youngest age and a decrement of $\frac{1}{2}$ SD until age 70. Increments over time occur for Social Responsibility for all cohorts until age 55. The longitudinal gradient peaks at ages 50 and 55. Increments and decrements are quite similar to the cross-sectional findings, with a somewhat smoother decrement gradient after age 55. We must conclude that the cohort differences for Social Responsibility are adequately accounted for by maturational changes in attitudes, except for the three oldest cohorts where some shift over generations in favor of more responsible attitudes seems to occur.

CONCLUSIONS

The most important conclusion to be drawn from this study is the finding that a major portion of the variance attributed to age differences in past cross-sectional studies must properly be assigned to differences in ability between successive generations. Age changes over time within the individual appear to be much smaller than differences between cohorts, and textbook age gradients may represent no more than the effects of increased environmental opportunity and/or genetic improvement in the species. The findings on longitudinal age changes suggest further that levels of functioning attained at maturity may be

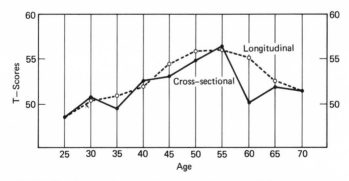

FIGURE 11.   Estimated age gradients for social responsibility.

retained until late in life except where decrement in response strength and latency interferes.[4] The finding that many of the cohort-differences curves appear to reach asymptotic levels suggests many implications for adult education and retirement practices.

There are several serious limitations to the present study. All our estimates are based on two points in time, and it is conceivable that we have selected a particularly atypical time span for our study. The only remedy for this problem is replication over a different time span. The second problem is the possible effect of practice on test performance. A 7-year span appears long enough to resolve this problem, but it cannot be dismissed as being trivial. Moreover, it is conceivable that the subjects whom we retested do not represent a truly random sample of the original population, a problem implicit in any repeated measurement study. The latter problem is currently being dealt with by repeating the present study with an independent sampling design. A new random sample was drawn and tested in 1963, the results from which will be compared with the entire original 1956 sample. These additional data will permit estimation of the effects of practice and contribute further information on the validity of our estimated age gradients (Schaie & Strother, 1968b).

References

Bayley, N., & Oden, M. H. The maintenance of intellectual ability in gifted adults. *Journal of Gerontology*, 1955, **10**, 91–107.

Cattell, R. B. Theory of fluid and crystallized intelligence: An initial experiment. *Journal of Educational Psychology*, 1963, **105**, 105–111.

Gough, H. G., McCloskey, H., & Meehl, P. E. A personality scale for social responsibility. *Journal of Abnormal and Social Psychology*, 1952, **47**, 73–80.

Horn, J. L., & Cattell, R. B. Age differences in primary mental ability factors. *Journal of Gerontology*, 1966, **21**, 210–220.

Jones, H. E. Intelligence and problem solving. In J. E. Birren (Ed.), *Handbook of aging and the individual*. Chicago: University of Chicago Press, 1959.

Jones, H. E., & Conrad, H. S. The growth and decline of intelligence: A study of a homogeneous group between the ages of ten and sixty. *Genetic Psychology Monographs*, 1933, **13**, 223–298.

Owens, W. A., Jr. Age and mental abilities: A longitudinal study. *Genetic Psychology Monographs*, 1953, **48**, 3–54.

---

[4] For a discussion of optimal limits of cognitive function in old age, see Schaie and Strother (1968a).

Schaie, K. W. A test of behavioral rigidity. *Journal of Abnormal and Social Psychology*, 1955, **51**, 604–610.

Schaie, K. W. Rigidity-flexibility and intelligence: A cross-sectional study of the adult life span from 20 to 70 years. *Psychological Monographs*, 1958, 72(9, Whole No. 462).

Schaie, K. W. Cross-sectional methods in the study of psychological aspects of aging. *Journal of Gerontology*, 1959, **14**, 208–215. (a)

Schaie, K. W. The effect of age on a scale of social responsibility. *Journal of Social Psychology*, 1959, **50**, 221–224. (b)

Schaie, K. W. *Examiner manual for the Test of Behavioral Rigidity.* Palo Alto: Consulting Psychologists Press, 1960.

Schaie, K. W. A general model for the study of developmental problems. *Psychological Bulletin*, 1965, **64**, 92–107.

Schaie, K. W. Age changes and age differences. *The Gerontologist*, 1967, **7**, 128–132.

Schaie, K. W., Rosenthal, F., & Perlman, R. M. Differential deterioration of functionally "pure" mental abilities. *Journal of Gerontology*, 1953, **8**, 191–196.

Schaie, K. W., & Strother, C. R. Cognitive and personality variables in college graduates of advanced age. In G. A. Talland (Ed.), *Human behavior and aging: Recent advances in research and theory.* New York: Academic Press, 1968. (a)

Schaie, K. W., & Strother, C. R. The effect of time and cohort differences upon age changes in cognitive behavior. *Multivariate Behavioral Research*, 1968, **3**, 259–294.

Strother, C. R., Schaie, K. W., & Horst, P. The relationship between advanced age and mental abilities. *Journal of Abnormal and Social Psychology*, 1957, **55**, 166–170.

Thurstone, L. L., & Thurstone, T. G. *Examiner manual for the SRA Primary Mental Abilities Test.* Chicago: Science Research Associates, 1949.

Thurstone, T. G. *Manual for the SRA Primary Mental Abilities 11–17.* (3rd ed.) Chicago: Science Research Associates, 1958.

4. COGNITIVE PATTERNING IN MILDLY RETARDED BOYS*
READINGS

Herman A. Witkin, Hanna F. Faterson, Donald R. Goodenough,
& Judith Birnbaum

Two groups of mildly retarded boys (one institutionalized, the other living at home) were given the WAIS and WISC, respectively; tests of perceptual field dependence; and the figure-drawing test. On the Wechsler scales almost all the boys performed extremely poorly on subtests loading a verbal-comprehension factor and relatively much better on subtests loading on analytical factor. The retarded boys showed the discrepancy between these sets of scores significantly more often than two groups of normal boys. Among the retarded, as in normals, measures of field dependence (i.e., analytical competence) and figure-drawing sophistication-of-body-concept scores related significantly to prorated analytical IQ's but not to prorated verbal-comprehension IQ's. The frequent occurrence of cases with relatively high analytical and low verbal-comprehension ability in groups now identified as retarded may be the result of particular emphasis on verbal skills in "routing" children in the school-age period.

SOURCE. *Child Development*, 1966, **37**, 301–317.

* The work described here has been supported by grants from the United States Public Health Service, National Institutes of Health (M-628, MH-K3-16,619). We are deeply indebted to Dr. Isaac N. Wolfson, Director, Letchworth Village, for his generous cooperation in arranging for the Letchworth Village boys to be brought to our laboratory for testing. We are very grateful to Dr. Jacob Cohen, Dr. Samuel J. Messick, Dr. David R. Saunders, and Dr. John P. Van de Geer for their critical reading of this paper. We are also indebted to the staffs of P.S. 238 and J.H.S. 252 in Brooklyn for their aid in recruiting the CRMD (children-with-retarded-mental-development) boys. Witkin's address: Psychology Laboratory, Department of Psychiatry, State University of New York, Downstate Medical Center, Brooklyn, N.Y.

Clinicians and workers in the area of mental retardation have long been aware of the inadequacy of the total IQ both of describing a person's intellectual functioning and for comparing individuals. In a search for more sensitive indicators of intellectual functioning, patterns of subtest scores on standard intelligence tests have been examined. While this approach has proved productive, the kinds of tasks which make up these standard tests limit the intellectual patterns that may be identified; moreover, the processes that underlie achievement in some of these tasks are not yet sufficiently understood. Patterns of subtest scores, it has also long been apparent, are the product of a complex interplay between intellectual and personality variables. Understanding these patterns accordingly requires reference to the personality factors that have helped shape them.

The approach to mental retardation in the study to be reported, stemming from our earlier research on cognitive style with normal persons (Witkin, Dyk, Faterson, Goodenough, & Karp, 1962; Witkin, Lewis, Hertzman, Machover, Meissner, & Wapner, 1954) takes account of the need for a more comprehensive and complex view of intellectual functioning than the IQ provides. First, the emphasis is on patterning. Second, the patterning considered includes not only performance on subtests of standard intelligence tests but perceptual performance as well. The concern is therefore with *cognitive* patterning rather than with intellectual patterns alone. Finally, the components of the pattern to be considered have in past studies been examined in relation to personality.

The present investigation had its origin in a recent series of factor-analytic studies of cognitive functioning in children and adults (Goodenough & Karp, 1961; Karp, 1963). Included in the battery of cognitive tasks used in these studies were perceptual tests and various intellectual tests, among them subtests of the Wechsler Intelligence Scale for Children (WISC) and Wechsler Adult Intelligence Scale (WAIS). One factor identified in these studies encompassed both tasks classically called perceptual and tasks classically called intellectual. Loading on this factor were, among others, tests of perceptual field dependence and the Block Design, Picture Completion, and Object Assembly subtests of the Wechsler scales. The common requirement of all these tests is the ability to experience items as discrete from the organized field of which they are a part—in other words, analytical ability. The Wechsler-scale subtests loading this "analytical factor" have, in past factor-analytic studies of the Wechsler scales, defined a factor sometimes labeled "perceptual organization" (Cohen, 1957; 1959). This is one of the three major factors which apparently account for most of the intercorrelations of Wechsler-scale subtests. A second factor, found both in Cohen's studies of the Wechsler and in the more comprehensive studies by Goodenough and Karp (1961) and Karp (1963), is well defined by the Vocabulary, Information, and Comprehension subtests of the

Wechsler. This factor has been labeled "verbal comprehension."[1] A third factor, again identified in both groups of studies, is usually defined by the Digit Span, Arithmetic, and Coding subtests of the Wechsler scales. This factor has been interpreted as an attention-concentration or memory factor.

Analytical ability, as reflected in the analytical-factor score, has been studied extensively (Witkin et al., 1954; 1962). Developed analytical ability has been shown to be an aspect of an articulated (as contrasted to a global) cognitive style, indicative of a high level of differentiation in cognitive functioning. An articulated cognitive style has, in turn, been related to other characteristics of a high level of differentiation; among these are a differentiated self, reflected particularly in an articulated body concept and a developed sense of separate identity, and the use of structured, specialized defenses. Verbal functioning, in which the verbal-comprehension factor is highly represented, has also been studied widely. Considerable evidence indicates that level of verbal functioning is related to educational accomplishment, occupational pursuits, and many aspects of life adjustment. Because they have been so intensively studied and "carry a message" about pervasive dimensions of personal functioning, the analytical and verbal-comprehension factors are of particular value in the investigation of cognitive patterning. The third factor, the attention-concentration factor, on the other hand, is not as clearly defined nor has it been as widely studied; moreover, its relation to other aspects of personal functioning has not been as thoroughly explored. Therefore, we will not be centrally concerned with this factor in the present report.

As part of a program of research on children who show uneven development in different areas of cognitive functioning and on "deficit children" who grow up under the influence of a serious handicap (as blindness), we have become particularly concerned with children demonstrating a marked discrepancy in level of functioning on the analytical and verbal-comprehension dimensions.

Considering specifically the Wechsler subtests represented on these dimensions, ordinarily we may expect from Wechsler standardization procedures that, in a normal group, persons will perform on the average at approximately the same level on both the analytical and verbal-comprehension clusters. While an even level of subtest performance is the expected group trend, intersubtest variability is of course characteristic of many individual Wechsler profiles and has long been used by clinicians in evaluating an individual's intellectual functioning. Moreover, in groups selected on the basis of extremely high or extremely low total IQ's, group averages might be expected to show discrepant

---

[1] "Verbal comprehension" is a factor name and is not to be confused with the verbal IQ or with the comprehension subtest of the Wechsler.

profiles. Since verbal comprehension is heavily weighted in total Wechsler scores, a group with high total IQ's ought to have higher scores on verbal-comprehension subtests than on other subtests; and because of the phenomenon of statistical regression toward the mean, they should have relatively lower scores on analytical subtests. Similarly, a group selected for low total Wechsler IQ's ought to have lower scores on verbal-comprehension subtests than on other subtests and relatively higher analytical-subtest scores. While these group patterns might be expected on a priori ground, discrepancies between the analytical- and verbal-comprehension-subtest clusters, with which we are particularly concerned here, have not been investigated.

An intensive study we made of several retarded boys alerted us to the possibility that it may be of particular value to consider discrepant functioning between the analytical and verbal-comprehension clusters in conceptualizing problems of mental retardation. These boys, with a total IQ in the 60's, scored very low on the verbal-comprehension cluster but close to average on the analytical cluster. Corresponding to their average performance on the analytical cluster of Wechsler subtests they also scored about average on tests of perceptual field dependence, which, as noted, load the same factor as the Wechsler analytical subtests. These preliminary observations raised the question of whether such a cognitive picture is characteristic of most mildly retarded persons and the further question of the developmental significance of this pattern.

We have not been able to find in the literature on the retarded a specific breakdown of Wechsler performance into the analytical and verbal-comprehension clusters. Our examination of several reports in which subtest scores were given showed, however, that in the retarded the sum of scores for the Block Design, Picture Completion, and Object Assembly subtests, which constitute the analytical cluster, tends to run higher than the sum of scores for the Vocabulary, Information, and Comprehension subtests, which constitute the verbal cluster. In the 22 retarded groups we were able to locate in the literature for which a Wechsler-subtest breakdown was reported, we found only 1 group that reversed this trend; in 6 groups there was no difference in scores for the two clusters. Both boys and girls were used in these studies, suggesting that this picture is characteristic of retarded boys and retarded girls (see, e.g., Baroff, 1959; Cutts & Sloan, 1945; Fisher, Dooley, & Silverstein, 1960; Hays, 1951; Mathews & Reitan, 1963; Sandercock & Butler, 1952; Stacey & Carleton, 1955; Vanderhost, Sloan, & Bensberg, 1953; Wechsler, Israel, & Balinski, 1941).

The present study was designed to explore systematically the cognitive pattern observed in the several retarded boys we had studied. It was hypothesized, first, that in the mildly retarded, as in normals, measures of perceptual field dependence and of related functions would correlate highly with analytical-subtest scores of the Wechsler scales but not with verbal-comprehension-subtest scores. It was further hypothesized that the retarded would show a relatively high level of performance on tests of analytical ability (both Wechsler subtests and tests of perceptual field dependence) and a relatively low level of performance on tests of verbal comprehension.

METHOD

Two groups of retarded boys served as subjects in this study. From previous studies comparison data are available for two groups of normal boys.

The first group of 29 retarded boys came from Letchworth Village, a New York State institution for the retarded. They constituted a complete cottage unit of "teachable" mildly retarded boys. Their ages ranged from 16 to 21 years, with a mean of 18.4 years. Because of the possibility that the institutional environment may have had a particularly adverse effect on these boys' verbal development, a second group of 30 retarded boys was added. These boys were living at home and attending special classes for children with retarded mental development (CRMD classes) in local New York City public schools. Almost all the boys in three CRMD classes of two schools participated. The age range of this group was from 11 to 16 years, with a mean age of 13.7 years. These children came from schools which drew upon predominantly middle-class Jewish families, a subculture in which verbal skills tend to be relatively highly developed (see, e.g., Levinson, 1958).

The 59 boys came to our laboratory for testing. The test battery included tests of perceptual field dependence; the WISC and WAIS for the CRMD and Letchworth groups, respectively; and the figure-drawing test.

For the Letchworth group the perceptual tests used were the rod-and-frame test (RFT), the body-adjustment test (BAT), and the embedded-figures test (EFT).[2] The CRMD group was given a special children's version of the embedded-figures test (CHEF) only. These tests are described briefly below.

In the RFT the subject is seated in a completely darkened room facing a luminous square frame, which can be tilted clockwise or counterclockwise. Within the frame, and pivoted at the same center, is a luminous rod which can be tilted in similar fashion, independently of the frame. With rod and frame tilted at the outset of each trial (28° left or right), the subject's task is to direct adjustment of the rod to a position he perceives as vertical, while the frame remains at its initial position of tilt. Relatively field-dependent performance in carrying out this task is reflected in a tendency to align the rod with the tilted frame, and relatively field-independent performance in a

[2] See Witkin et al. (1962) for a more detailed account of these tests.

tendency to adjust the rod close to the true upright, regardless of frame position and with reference to body position. The subject's score is the mean degrees absolute deviation of the rod from the upright for eight trials of the test. A low score reflects ability to overcome the influence of the field (frame) or to perceive in a field-independent, analytical fashion.

In the BAT the subject is seated in a chair within a specially constructed room. Room and chair can both be tilted left or right, separately or together. At the beginning of each trial, subject (with eyes closed) and room are tilted to set positions (room 35° and chair 22°, left or right). The subject's task, after opening his eyes, is to direct adjustment of his chair (and thus of his body) to the vertical, while the room remains at its initial position of tilt. The subject's score is the mean degrees absolute deviation of the body from the upright for the six trials of the test. Again, the score reflects extent of field dependence or of ability to keep an item (the body) separate from an organized perceptual field (the room).

Finally, both the EFT (which with normal children is applicable at ages 10 and above) and the CHEF (which is more appropriate for children below age 10) require location of a simple figure within a complex organized figure designed to obscure it. The EFT consists of 12 pairs of simple and complex geometrical figures, each figure on a separate card. The subject's score is the mean time taken to locate the simple figure within the complex one.[3] The CHEF, described in detail elsewhere (Goodenough & Eagle, 1963), was designed to provide an EFT-like situation particularly suitable for children in the 5- to 9-year age range.[4] The CHEF was designed to make the task interesting and comprehensible to young children, to avoid any requirement for sustained attention, and to reduce frustration due to failure. The complex figures of the CHEF are large multicolored "jigsaws." All are representations of meaningful figures, in order to insure that they are initially perceived as organized wholes. Each complex figure is composed of several sections, one of which is the sought-after simple figure. Several of these sections have knobs attached to them, but only the simple figure, obscured by the overall organization of the total, can be removed by pulling the knob. The subject's score is the number of correct first choices of simple figures in a series of 18 complex figures.

The CHEF was given to the CRMD group, tested after work with the Letch-

[3] In the present study, the score employed was the per cent of the total time allotted actually used by the child in locating the simple figures. Total time was computed at 5 minutes per figure, the maximum time allowed. This procedure was followed since the test was discontinued before the full set of 12 figures was completed with children who consistently failed the first few figures and for whom it seemed a strain to go on.

[4] Since this study was carried out, another more easily administered children's version of the embedded-figures test has been developed (Karp & Konstadt, 1963).

worth group had been completed. Standardization of the CHEF had not yet been finished when the Letchworth group was tested; and experience with the Letchworth group suggested that, in view of its special treatment of problems of interest and motivation, the CHEF would be particularly appropriate for the CRMD boys who were chronologically younger.

The scores for both the EFT and CHEF again reflect ability to perceive an item as discrete from an organized field—that is, extent of field dependence or analytical ability.

Administration of the perceptual tests was specially adapted for the retarded boys to insure their understanding of procedure.

To obtain figure drawings the subject was simply asked to draw a person and then to draw a person of the opposite sex. The figure drawings were rated on a five-point sophistication-of-body-concept scale, developed for our earlier studies (Witkin et al., 1962). This scale evaluates the extent to which the figures drawn are relatively articulated or relatively global; a low score reflects more global drawings. Previous studies with both children and adults have shown that sophistication-of-body-concept scores relate highly to measures of field dependence. A global way of perceiving (indicated by field-dependent performance in the perceptual tests) and a global body concept (indicated by drawings of human figures with such features as little detail, a lack of sex characteristics, and unrealistic proportioning) have both been conceived to reflect limitedly developed psychological differentiation.

The psychologist who rated figure drawings according to the sophistication-of-body-concept scale had never seen the children and had no information about their other test results.[5]

For the Wechsler scales, the usual total IQ, Verbal IQ, and Performance IQ were determined; and, in addition, subtotals were computed of the scaled scores for the analytical cluster of subtests—Block Design (BD), Picture Completion (PC), and Object Assembly (OA); for the verbal-comprehension cluster—Information (I), Comprehension (C), and Vocabulary (V); and for the attention-concentration cluster—Digit Span (DS), Coding (Cod), and Arithmetic (A). To facilitate comparisons, each subject's scaled scores for the analytical and verbal-comprehension clusters were transformed into prorated IQ's.[6] This was done for the WISC by multiplying the mean of the three scaled

---

[5] We are indebted to Dr. Hanna Marlens for rating these drawings.

[6] For the WAIS the IQ's, but not the scaled scores, are age-corrected. Prorated IQ's were therefore used for the WAIS and, to make scores for the two scales comparable, for the WISC as well. Because of the possibility that standard prorating procedures may lead to IQ distributions for the verbal-comprehension and analytical clusters which have unequal standard deviations, we also computed the IQ's from the two clusters by converting standard scores to a distribution with a mean of 100 and a standard deviation of 15, i.e., deviation IQ's as they are usually defined. Using these measures, the outcome was essentially the same as with IQ's prorated in the usual manner.

scores in each cluster by 10 (the number of scales in the full test) and treating this value as the sum of scaled scores, obtaining an IQ from the full-scale conversion table. For the WAIS, which has 11 subtests, a multiplier of 11 was used.

RESULTS

Patterns of Interrelations among Test Scores

Our first hypothesis was that the patterning previously observed in normal subjects (Goodenough & Karp, 1961; Karp, 1963) would be found in the retarded as well. The matrix of intercorrelations in Table 1 for the Letchworth

TABLE 1

Intercorrelations Among Test Scores for Letchworth Village Group

	EFT	BAT	Ana-lytical IQ[a]	Figure-Drawing	Verbal-Compre-hension IQ[a]	Attention Concen-tration IQ[a]	Full-Scale IQ
RFT[b]	.45*	.04	—.67**	—.16	—.26	—.32	—.59**
EFT	—	.05	—.74**	—.58**	—.30	—.26	—.62**
BAT	—	—	—.10	.02	.16	.06	.11
Analytical IQ[a]	—	—	—	.43*	.25	.47*	.79**
Figure-drawing	—	—	—	—	.05	—.05	.28
Verbal-comprehension IQ[a]	—	—	—	—	—	.51**	.65**
Attention-concentration IQ[a]	—	—	—	—	—	—	.81**

[a] WAIS prorated IQ's based on factor scores.

[b] Lower scores on the RFT, EFT, and BAT represent a more field-independent or analytical performance, whereas for the analytical prorated IQ higher scores represent greater analytical ability. For the figure-drawing scale, lower scores reflect a more articulated body concept, ordinarily associated with field independence or analytical ability.

* Significant at .05 level.

** Significant at .01 level.

boys, the group studied first, gives substantial support to this expectation. The measures of analytical ability are all significantly intercorrelated, except for the BAT measure.[7] The intercorrelations among RFT scores, EFT scores, and prorated analytical IQ's for the WAIS (based on BD-, PC-, and OA-subtest scores) are .45, .67, and .74, all significant. Again paralleling the finding for

---

[7] We have no hypothesis to account for the failure of BAT scores to relate to other field-dependence measures in the retarded as they do in normals.

normal subjects, figure-drawing sophistication-of-body-concept ratings tend to be related to scores for the analytical tests; two of the four correlations between figure-drawing- and analytical-test scores are significant. Finally, once more as with normals, correlations between analytical-test scores and figure-drawing scores, on the one hand, and prorated verbal-comprehension IQ's (based on V, I, and C WAIS-subtest scores), on the other hand, are generally much lower than correlations among scores for tests of analytical functioning and the figure-drawing test, and none is significant.

The picture that emerges from these data, with the single exception of the BAT, is entirely consistent with the picture previously observed in normals. The findings for the Letchworth retarded boys are supported by the results for our second retarded group, the CRMD boys, presented in Table 2. Here again

TABLE 2

Intercorrelations Among Test Scores for CRMD Group

	Analytical IQ[a]	Figure-Drawing	Verbal-Comprehension IQ[a]	Attention-Concentration IQ[a]	Full-Scale IQ
CHEF[b]	.50**	.45*	.16	.26	.51**
Analytical IQ[a]	—	.36*	.41*	.26	.82**
Figure-drawing	—	—	.18	.01	.33
Verbal-comprehension IQ[a]	—	—	—	.13	.59**
Attention-concentration IQ[a]	—	—	—	—	.57**

[a] WISC prorated IQ's based on factor scores.

[b] *Higher* scores on the CHEF represent a more field-independent or analytical performance, whereas for the analytical prorated IQ *higher* scores represent greater analytical ability. For the figure-drawing scale, *higher* scores reflect a more articulated body concept, ordinarily associated with field independence or analytical ability.

* Significant at .05 level.

** Significant at .01 level.

scores for a test of perceptual field dependence (the CHEF) relate significantly to WISC prorated analytical IQ's but not to WISC prorated verbal-comprehension IQ's. The figure-drawing scores also relate significantly to CHEF scores and WISC prorated analytical IQ's, although the correlation is not significant.

The patterns of interrelationships in Tables 1 and 2 were not altered when partial correlations were computed with age controlled. Also, partialling out verbal-comprehension scores had only a trivial effect on the correlations between various cognitive measures. Nor did the data support the hypothesis that the pattern of interrelations observed might be a consequence of differences in restriction of the range for the individual subtests.

In general, the findings support the conclusion from previous studies that the ability to overcome an embedding context, or to deal with cognitive tasks analytically, is involved in particular Wechsler subtests as well as in tests of perceptual field dependence; and they extend this conclusion to retarded persons, reflecting on its generality. These findings also confirm and extend the observation that analytical cognitive functioning, which we have interpreted to be indicative of developed differentiation, tends to occur in association with a differentiated body concept.

Discrepancy in Level of Functioning on the Analytical and Verbal-Comprehension Dimensions

The data bearing on our second hypothesis, that retarded children would be disproportionately poorer on verbal-comprehension than on analytical tests, are to be found in Table 3. Table 3 presents mean prorated IQ's for the Letchworth and CRMD groups for each of the three major factors of the Wechsler scales. The means for the Wechsler total, Verbal, and Performance IQ's, as conventionally computed, are also given.

TABLE 3

Mean IQ's for Selected Wechsler Components for Letchworth and CRMD Retarded Groups

	Letchworth (N = 30)	CRMD (N = 29)
	Mean Prorated IQ's Based on Factor Scores	
Verbal-comprehension IQ	61.2	60.5
Analytical IQ	80.8	73.4
Attention-concentration IQ	71.3	63.4
	Mean Conventional IQ's	
Verbal IQ	71.1	67.1
Performance IQ	76.3	70.5
Full-Scale IQ	71.7	65.5

Though both retarded groups, on the average, are lower than normals on *all* the measures in Table 3, it is clear, in keeping with our expectations, that they are not equally retarded in all areas of functioning. Both groups do most poorly on verbal-comprehension tests and relatively better on analytical tests. The discrepancy in cognitive functioning of these retarded subjects emerges more sharply when the verbal-comprehension and analytical prorated IQ's are compared than when the conventional Verbal and Performance IQ's are compared. For example, for the Letchworth group, the mean difference between the Verbal and Performance IQ's is only 5 points, whereas the difference between the mean prorated verbal-comprehension and mean prorated analytical IQ's is 20 points.

The pattern of factor-score IQ's evident in Table 3 is confirmed when individual cases are examined in detail. Of the 59 boys in the two retarded groups, 20 have prorated analytical IQ's of 85 or above, that is, in the dull-normal or better range; 6 of these 20 have analytical IQ's of 95 or above. In contrast, individual prorated verbal-comprehension IQ's are at a uniformly low level. Only a single boy (in the CRMD group) has a verbal-comprehension IQ above 85.

This picture of discrepancy between verbal-comprehension and analytical functioning is further highlighted when the retarded are compared to normals. For this comparison we have data for two normal groups from previous studies. One group consisted of 30 10-year-old boys recruited from an elementary school near the laboratory for our studies of psychological differentiation. Their total IQ's on the WISC ranged from 84 to 138, with a mean of 115.9, and their mean prorated verbal-comprehension and analytical IQ's were 126.5 and 105.2, respectively. The second normal group consisted of 20 12-year-old boys recruited from a free dental clinic, attended by economically deprived families. The prorated total WISC IQ's of these boys ranged from 82 to 115, with a mean of 91.5.[8] Their mean prorated verbal-comprehension and analytical IQ's were 90.3 and 92.7, respectively.

Comparison of the normal and retarded groups shows a sharp difference between them. While there is a high frequency of cases with relatively low verbal-comprehension IQ's and relatively high analytical IQ's among the retarded, a very few such cases are to be found among the normal boys studied. In fact, when a marked discrepancy does occur between these two measures in the normal boys, it tends to be in the opposite direction. Twenty-six of the 29 Letchworth boys and 25 of the 30 CRMD boys have higher analytical than verbal-comprehension IQ's, as compared to only 4 of 30 elementary school boys and 9 of 20 dental-clinic boys. When each of the two retarded groups was compared with each of the two normal groups for incidence of higher analytical than verbal-comprehension IQ's, the differences all proved significant (by χ^2, $p < .01$).[9]

---

[8] Only the six subtests making up the verbal-comprehension and analytical clusters were given to these boys.

[9] The mean scores for the tests of perceptual field dependence have not been considered in this report. Although results obtained with these perceptual tests typically are consistent with results for the analytical subtests of the Wechsler scales, there do not yet exist for the perceptual tests standardization data comparable to those available for the

DISCUSSION

This study confirms the repeated observation that the mildly retarded tend to do better on the Performance part than on the Verbal part of standard intelligence tests. Our results, however, have made it possible to go beyond this observation in two ways.

First, the areas of Wechsler performance in which the retarded show particularly marked disability and relative competence have been pinpointed more specifically. Almost all the retarded subjects we studied did extremely poorly on the verbal-comprehension subtests of the WISC and WAIS and relatively well on the analytical subtests.[10] This breakdown shows more clearly the marked unevenness that exists in the intellectual functioning of high-grade retardates than does the usual Verbal-Performance breakdown.[11]

Second, analytical competence of the retarded on Wechsler subtests that evaluate this ability has been linked to analytical competence in perceptual functioning and to sophistication of body concept. These characteristics have been found to show a similar association in normals, where they have been further linked to other characteristics not examined in the present study. This self-consistency in mode of cognitive functioning may be taken as evidence of a cognitive style that exists in the retarded as well as in normals. The particular cognitive style with which we are dealing involves, at one extreme, a tendency to experience in relatively global fashion and, at the other extreme, a tendency to experience in relatively articulated fashion. In our past studies with normals we have accumulated evidence that suggests that a more global or a more articulated mode of cognitive functioning is indicative of relatively limited or relatively developed psychological differentiation. The global-articulated cognitive-style dimension cuts across areas conventionally identified as intellectual functioning (performance on standard intelligence tests), perception (performance in tests of perceptual field dependence), and personality (nature of body concept projected in figure-drawings). The application of this dimension to the retarded provides a broad framework for studying them. Moreover, the

Wechsler scales. Effective comparison of the retarded and normal groups in patterns involving tests of perceptual field dependence is therefore not possible.

[10] The same pattern has been found recently by Jacques M. van Meel (personal communication, 1964) with a group of Dutch retarded boys. Forty-one of 46 boys in this group had a higher analytical than verbal-comprehension score. In contrast, in a comparison group of normal Dutch boys of about the same mental age, only 19 of 46 children had a higher analytical score.

[11] In the present study boys only were used. As noted earlier, our examination of studies in the literature, which used girls as well as boys, showed a similar picture. Also, in the study by van Meel cited in n. 10, the discrepancy between verbal-comprehension- and analytical-subtest scores was found for retarded girls as well as for retarded boys. Thus, our findings for retarded boys seem to hold for retarded girls as well.

framework is one that has a conceptual base arrived at through extensive past investigations.

The question inevitably arises as to why, in the retarded subjects we studied, the analytical versus verbal-comprehension discrepancy went so consistently in one direction. The answer may lie in the heavy emphasis placed upon verbal skills, both in society and in test construction, with the result that verbal competence may play a particularly decisive role in routing children through life, to the relative disregard of other kinds of ability.

We may speculate about the way in which this emphasis on verbal competence may affect the routing of the mildly retarded. It is reasonable to imagine that cognitive abilities exist in a variety of patterns in children and that some patterns involve deficits in one or more cognitive areas. We may further suppose that children who show a deficit in the verbal area, whatever other cognitive strengths they may have, are more likely to be recognized as suffering a deficit than children with other kinds of cognitive deficits who are functioning at the same overall level. Because verbal ability is an early and readily evident indicator of "intelligence," such children are likely to be identified by their parents as "not quite all right." In school, again—where the emphasis, especially at the outset, is so strongly on verbal abilities, such as speech, reading, etc.—their difficulty will also be readily noted. Such children are therefore likely to be referred for special testing. Moreover, these children are particularly penalized on standard intelligence tests. In the standardization of these tests one of the criteria of validity has been school achievement, which rests heavily on verbal competence. This, in turn, is reflected in the greater emphasis on subtests involving verbal skills in the total IQ. Such a situation exists not only in the Wechsler scales but, even more, in the various Binet versions, with their predominantly verbal content. Thus, the verbally handicapped child is not only more likely to be referred for testing than children with other cognitive deficits but, when tested, he is likely to earn a low IQ, with the prospect of being classified as retarded. In light of all this it need not be surprising that children in retarded groups as now constituted should have extremely low verbal-comprehension-subtest scores but show a regression toward the norm on analytical-subtest scores which are only slightly related to verbal-comprehension performance and at a relatively low level to total test performance.

Children who show other kinds of cognitive deficit, functioning at a similar overall level, may be routed quite differently. For example, the child with particular impairment in the analytical area, but with relatively better verbal-comprehension competence, not only may escape the selection filter which leads to classification as retarded but may even be considered "a good child" by his teachers. We know from our studies that field-dependent children, low in analytical ability, are often conforming to adult authority. This characteristic, together with their ability to "talk nicely," is apt to be particularly pleasing to teachers. Even if such children should be referred for testing, their analytical deficit is not as likely to make for a low IQ (especially if a Binet-type test is used), and so they may avoid the "retarded" label. There is every reason to believe that children with such cognitive patterns do exist but are now likely to pass unnoticed. They could best be located through a large-scale, systematic testing program, preferably utilizing a broad battery of cognitive tests, each devised on the basis of a theoretical rationale. It is likely that these children, though fitting more easily into the school situation, later in life are more handicapped than those now classified as retarded, particularly in work situations. Jobs for which the retarded may be considered suitable are more likely to call for analytical skills, which these children lack, than for verbal skills.

Consistent with our concept of routing is the statement by Levine and Dysinger (1964): "We suggest that Ss who score better on verbal than on non-verbal tests do not appear mentally retarded to the lay person or school teacher and therefore are generally not referred to a home for the Mentally Retarded. . . . it might be important—both theoretically and for humanitarian reasons —to locate the lost grcup: the Ss with overall scores in the borderline or even mildly retarded range, but whose verbal scores are higher than their non-verbal scores" (p. 786).

The existence of cases with the kinds of cognitive discrepancies that have been considered calls into question the practice of using verbal tests alone as "quickie" intelligence tests.

The routing concept that has been proposed may also be applied to the repeated observation that more boys than girls are referred for testing because of suspected mental subnormality. Thus, the Onondega County survey showed a two-to-one ratio (N.Y. State Department of Mental Hygiene, 1955). A common explanation of the sex difference in reported retardation at the adult level has been that retarded men are not as likely to "get by," since the demands upon them—to earn a livelihood, to get along in a job situation—are greater, and therefore their handicap is more likely to be noted. Such an explanation, however, cannot be applied to children. Lemkau (1956) has offered an interesting hypothesis to account for the sex difference in incidence of reported retardation in children. He suggests that the sex difference may be "due primarily to characteristics of the male that are well recognized: first, his retardation in comparison with the female as regards communication skills and, second, his greater aggressiveness that tends to lead to lower grades in deportment, reflecting his greater capacity to 'make trouble' and thus to have his defect discovered in the course of a fundamentally unrelated investigation. These two factors are not themselves uncorrelated, as any remedial reading teacher can testify" (p. 69). Again, deficiency in verbal skills is indicated as important in the routing of children toward classification as retarded.

The findings of a consistent discrepancy between the verbal-comprehension and analytical areas in the retarded has raised provocative questions for research about the development of this group. Identification of discrepancies between these areas, in other contexts of cognitive and personality functioning, may open further directions of research on the development of cognitive patterning at various levels of overall intellectual functioning. That this may be so is suggested by observations reported by Shafer (1962) for a group of girls with Turner's syndrome.

The Turner syndrome is now known to be caused by a genetic abnormality; of the normal female complement of two X chromosomes, one is missing. Turner girls fail to develop normal genitalia and secondary sex characteristics at puberty. They are also usually short, and there has been some suggestion that they may show a variety of cognitive anomalies. Often their abnormality is not detected until they reach teenage.

In a study of 20 girls with Turner's syndrome Shafer found a normal average total IQ (98.8), but their Performance IQ was considerably lower than their Verbal IQ. If the verbal-comprehension and analytical triumvirate of Wechsler subtests are considered, the discrepancy is even more marked.[12] Their prorated verbal-comprehension IQ is 112.5 and their prorated analytical IQ is 84.0. As a group these girls are thus of dull-normal status on the analytical dimension and of bright-normal status on the verbal-comprehension dimension. The discrepancy in level of functioning between these two areas is found consistently when individual cases are considered. Eighteen of the 20 Turner girls showed a discrepancy in favor of the verbal-comprehension IQ. In a number of cases, the prorated analytical IQ was clearly in the retarded category, whereas the prorated verbal-comprehension IQ was about average. The pattern of discrepancy in the Turner girls is opposite to that of the Letchworth and CRMD groups, although the Turner girls are functioning at a higher overall level than the other two groups.

Of particular theoretical interest is the possibility that we have in the Turner cases a cognitive pattern that is to some extent at least under the influence of the sex chromosomes. Without more knowledge about how the girls in Shafer's group were selected, we cannot say whether the essential characteristic of the Turner cognitive pattern is a deficit in analytical functioning, an advantage in verbal-comprehension ability, or a combination of both. In any case, the possibility of a linkage between sex chromosomal makeup and cognitive characteristics (whatever the mechanism by which the chromosomes exert their influence on cognitive development) is of special interest in view of the repeated finding that men are consistently superior to women in analytical abil-

[12] We are indebted to Dr. Shafer for making the original Wechsler records of these girls available to us for this analysis.

ity (Witkin et al., 1962) and that women are consistently superior to men in verbal ability (Tyler, 1956). Investigation of Turner and other cases with sex-chromosome anomalies has obvious potential for exploring the possible genetic basis of patterns of cognitive development and of sex differences in these patterns.

References

Baroff, G. S. WISC patterning in endogenous mental deficiency. *Amer. J. ment. Defic.*, 1959, **64**, 482–485.

Cohen, J. The factorial structure of the WAIS between early adulthood and old age. *J. consult. Psychol.*, 1957, **21**, 283–290.

Cohen, J. The factorial structure of the WISC at ages 7–6, 10–6, and 13–6. *J. consult. Psychol.*, 1959, **23**, 285–299.

Cutts, R. A., & Sloan, W. Test patterns of adjusted defectives on the Wechsler-Bellevue test. *Amer. J. ment. Defic.*, 1945, **50**, 98–101.

Fisher, G. M., Dooley, M. D., & Silverstein, A. B. WAIS performance of familial and undifferentiated mental subnormals. *Psychol. Rep.*, 1960, **7**, 268.

Goodenough, D. R., & Eagle, Carol J. A modification of the embedded-figures test for use with young children. *J. genet. Psychol.*, 1963, **103**, 67–74.

Goodenough, D. R., & Karp, S. A. Field dependence and intellectual functioning. *J. abnorm. soc. Psychol.*, 1961, **63**, 241–246.

Hays, W. A comparison of scatter patterning for mental defectives on the Wechsler forms I and II. *Amer. J. ment. Defic.*, 1951, **55**, 264–268.

Karp, S. A. Field dependence and overcoming embeddedness. *J. consult. Psychol.*, 1963, **27**, 294–302.

Karp, S. A., & Konstadt, Norma. Manual for the children's embedded-figures test. Cognitive tests. Unpublished manuscript. Authors, P. O. Box 4, Vanderveer Station, Brooklyn, N.Y. 11210, 1963.

Lemkau, P. V. Epidemiological aspects. In *The evaluation and treatment of the mentally retarded child in clinics.* New York: National Association for Retarded Children, 1956.

Levine, D., & Dysinger, D. W. Patterns of intellectual performance and the outcome of institutionalization in the mentally retarded. *Amer. J. ment. Defic.*, 1964, **68**, 784–788.

Levinson, B. M. Cultural pressures and WAIS scatter in a traditional Jewish setting. *J. genet. Psychol.*, 1958, **93**, 277–286.

Mathews, C. C., & Reitan, R. M. Relationship of differential abstraction ability levels to psychological test performances in mentally retarded subjects. *Amer. J. ment. Defic.*, 1963, **68**, 235–244.

New York State Department of Mental Hygiene, Mental Health Research Unit. *Technical report.* Syracuse, N.Y.: Author, 1955.

Sandercock, Marian G., & Butler, A. J. An analysis of the performance of mental defectives on the Wechsler Intelligence Scale for Children. *Amer. J. ment. Defic.*, 1952, **57**, 100–105.

Shafer, J. W. A specific cognitive deficit observed in gonadal aplasia (Turner's Syndrome). *J. clin. Psychol.*, 1962, **18**, 403–406.

Stacey, C. L., & Carleton, F. O. The relationship between Raven's Colored Progressive Matrices and two tests of general intelligence. *J. clin. Psychol.*, 1955, **11**, 84–85.

Tyler, Leona E. *The psychology of individual differences.* (2nd ed.) New York: Appleton-Century-Crofts, 1956.

Vanderhost, Leonette, Sloan, W., & Bensberg, G. J., Jr. Performance of mental defectives on the Wechsler-Bellevue and the WISC. *American Journal of mental Defic.*, 1953, **57**, 481–483.

Wechsler, D., Israel, M., & Balinski, B. A study of the subtests of the Bellevue Intelligence Scale in borderline and mental defective cases. *Amer. J. ment. Defic.*, 1941, **45**, 555–558.

Witkin, H. A., Dyk, Ruth B., Faterson, Hanna F., Goodenough, D. R., & Karp, S. A. *Psychological differentiation.* New York: Wiley, 1962.

Witkin, H. A., Lewis, Helen B., Hertzman, M., Machover, Karen, Meissner, Pearl B., & Wapner, S. *Personality through perception.* New York: Harpers, 1954.

5.   PERSONALITY AND IQ CHANGE[1]

Jerome Kagan, Lester W. Sontag, Charles T. Baker,
& Virginia L. Nelson

Research on mental development during the last twenty years has indicated that a child's IQ score does not necessarily remain constant with age (2, 3, 4, 10). Several reports (9, 10, 12) suggest that changes in environmental conditions can depress or raise IQ level and it is sometimes implied that these changes may be explained by recourse to personality variables. The purpose of this paper is to demonstrate that changes in IQ during childhood are correlated with certain personality predispositions as inferred from projective test data. The personality variables under study include (a) need for achievement, (b) competitive strivings, (c) curiosity about nature, and (d) passivity.

Performance on an IQ test is assumed to be a function of at least two major variables; the variety of skills and abilities the person brings to the test situation and his motivation to perform well on the test (2, 6). Since the IQ scores of some children change markedly during the school years, it seems plausible to assume that those children who show marked increases in IQ have a very strong motivation to acquire or develop the various intellectual skills tapped by an IQ test and to perform well in a testing situation. It is suggested that need for achievement, competitive strivings, and curiosity about

SOURCE. *The Journal of Abnormal and Social Psychology*, March 1958, **56**, 2. Copyrighted 1958 by American Psychological Assoc.

[1] This investigation was supported in part by a research grant (PHS M 1260) from the National Institute of Mental Health of the National Institutes of Health, United States Public Health Service. The writers wish to thank Dr. Seymour B. Sarason for his critical reading of the manuscript.

nature motivate the acquisition and improvement of cognitive abilities and by so doing facilitate increases in tested IQ.

The social environment often awards praise and recognition for intellectual accomplishment, and school age children with a high need for achievement might seek to gratify this need through intellectual activity. Thus it was predicted that children showing marked increases in IQ would produce more achievement imagery on the TAT than those with minimal gains in IQ.

Secondly, the school environment emphasizes competitive intellectual activity, and children with strong competitive needs would be highly motivated to acquire the intellectual skills which result in successful competition with one's classmates. Thus it was predicted that children showing IQ gains would show more competitive strivings than children displaying minimal gains in IQ. In choosing an index of competitive strivings, besides the related measure of TAT achievement fantasy, it was decided to use aggressive content on the Rorschach. The bases for this choice rested on the assumptions that (a) incidence of aggressive imagery reflected degree of aggressive motivation and (b) competition was a socially accepted form of aggressive behavior. For in competition, as in aggression, the child desires to defeat another individual and assert his superiority over him. The population of children in this study is predominantly middle class and apt to place strong inhibitions on direct, overt expression of aggression. Therefore, there would be a tendency for the individual with high aggressive motivation to seek socially accepted channels for aggressive expression such as competitive activity with peers. Thus it was predicted that children showing IQ gain would report more Rorschach aggressive content than those with minimal gain because of their greater competitive predisposition.

A third motive that might facilitate a child's acquisition of knowledge and skills in dealing with the environment could be curiosity about nature. Interest in birth, death, sexual anatomy, and other processes of nature is a frequent phenomenon in young children. It is suggested that the more intense this curiosity the greater the motivation to acquire the habits which would gratify this motive. Since reading, questioning, and manipulating the environment are effective behavioral methods of gratifying one's curiosity, it might be expected that the highly curious child would be more likely to develop these skills and therefore apt to gain in IQ score. The TAT measure used to evaluate curiosity was presence of themes of interest in nature and its phenomena. For the Rorschach, it was hypothesized that concern with the body might reflect, in part, heightened interest in natural processes, and it was suggested that anatomy content might be more frequent for children who showed marked IQ gains than for those with minimal increases in IQ. It is recognized that many clinical psychologists regard anatomy content in adults as indicative of psychopathology. This study is concerned with the correlates of IQ gain rather than psychopathology, and it is not implied that children who show increases in IQ are completely free of conflict. Secondly, it was felt that the determinants of anatomy content for children might be different from those which produce this content in adults.

A final prediction dealt with the predisposition to behavioral passivity. The children who show IQ gains have been characterized as having high need achievement, competitive strivings, and curiosity about the environment. This constellation of motives implies that when these children are confronted with a problem, they would have a tendency to attack and attempt to solve the problem rather than withdraw from the situation or seek help. On this basis, it was predicted that children who showed IQ gains would be less likely than those with minimal IQ increases to characterize their TAT heroes as passive in attitude or behavior.

The Fels Research Institute is uniquely equipped to test these ideas about IQ change since it has continuous longitudinal information on the development of a sample of normal children. These data include intelligence and projective tests, observations of the children, and reports on the parent-child interaction. In a recent study, Sontag, Baker, and Nelson (11) related personality information on a sample of children with changes in IQ and found that those children who showed marked increases in IQ were rated as more competitive, more likely to display self-initiated behavior and less passive than those who showed decreases in IQ. The TAT and Rorschach protocols were not utilized in making these personality ratings, and the results from this study served as a major stimulus for the present investigation.

METHOD

A sample of 140 Fels subjects (Ss), 70 of each sex, were chosen for study because a fairly complete record of test information was available on them. From ages $2\frac{1}{2}$ to 6, the Stanford-Binet intelligence test (1916 or 1937 revision) was administered to most Ss twice yearly, on their birthdays and six months after their birthdays. From ages 6 to 12, most Ss received alternately Form L or Form M of the 1937 revision annually on or near each S's birthday. All of the tests were administered by one of the authors (VLN). The mean IQ of the Fels population is near 120, with standard deviation varying from 14 to 20 IQ points.

In order to obtain groups of Ss who showed the most change in IQ score from ages 6 to 10, a smoothed longitudinal plot of each S's IQ was prepared by averaging the mean of three consecutive test scores around each age. This procedure is explained in detail in other reports (1, 10, 11). This technique tends to eliminate erratic variations in IQ and hopefully furnishes a more valid measure of IQ changes. Then each S's smoothed IQ at age 6 was subtracted from his smoothed IQ at age 10, and this distribution of differences, positive if S gained in IQ and negative if S lost in IQ, was divided into quartiles. This report deals with the projective test information on those Ss in the two extreme groups; those who increased and those who decreased the most in IQ score. These will be called Group A, the IQ ascenders, and Group D, the IQ descenders, respectively. There was no significant difference between the mean IQ of the two extreme quartiles at age six, the means being 119 and 116 for Groups A and D respectively. The average amount of increase in IQ for Group A was larger (plus 17 points) than the corresponding decrease for the members of Group D (minus 5 points) and while 46 per cent of Group D lost five or more points, every child in Group A gained 10 or more points during the years 6 through 10. The mean IQ of the entire sample of 140 tends to increase slightly from ages 6 to 10, probably as a result of practice effects with the same test. Since every S in Group D showed a decrease in IQ, it might be inferred that the members of Group D did not benefit from practice and familiarity with the test, and it is probably more accurate to view Group D Ss in this light rather than as Ss who showed marked decreases in IQ score.

The projective tests used in the analysis were the Rorschach and selected TAT pictures. Two factors governed the choice of the TAT cards which were analyzed. Because the protocols were gathered over a period of years, there was not complete comparability for all Ss for the number of cards administered. Secondly, the specific hypotheses of the study dictated the cards chosen for analysis and Cards 1, 3 BM, 3 GF, 5, 6 BM, 12 F, 14, and 17 BM were selected for analysis. The age at which the TAT protocols were administered ranged from 8–9 to 14–6 with median at 11–6 and 80 per cent of the protocols obtained between the ages of 11 and 12. The age at which the Rorschachs were administered ranged from 6–5 to 13–6 with median at 10–5 and 63 per cent of the sample having had the test between ages 10 and 11. Since the Rorschach and TAT were administered by different examiners there was no comparability with respect to inquiry or probing. Thus, the analysis of both the Rorschach and TAT was restricted to the S's spontaneous verbalization to the stimulus before any questions or inquiry were conducted by the examiner. The protocols were scored for the following fantasy categories.

1. *Need Achievement on the TAT.* Achievement imagery on the TAT was scored according to the definition of McClelland et al. (8) ; and themes involving a reference to competition with a standard of excellence were scored achievement imagery.

2. *Rorschach Aggression.* The definition of aggressive content on the Rorschach included (*a*) people, animals, or creatures engaged in physical or verbal aggression, e.g., fighting or quarreling, (*b*) explosive objects or explosions, e.g., volcanoes, bombs exploding, fireworks, and (*c*) objects or

animal parts normally regarded as instruments of aggression, e.g., spears, rifles, clubs, guns, knives, horns, and claws.

3. *Intellectual Curiosity About Nature.* For the TAT, curiosity was defined in terms of themes in which someone is interested in the processes or phenomena of nature. Curiosity on the Rorschach was restricted to anatomy or X-ray responses of internal organs or boney parts, e.g., stomach, backbone, ribs.

4. *Passivity.* Because of the limited amount of thematic material in the spontaneous performance, themes of passivity were limited to stories in which the central figure was described as sleepy, tired, or resting.

The fantasy categories were independently scored by the senior author and an assistant without knowledge of the *S*'s IQ score.[2] Reliability was very high because of the limited amount of content scored for each response and the objectivity of the definitions. Percentage of agreement for the three TAT categories was 95 per cent and for the two Rorschach categories 99 per cent.

RESULTS

Although there was a total of 70 *S*s in the two extreme quartiles, not all of the *S*s had Rorschach or TAT data for the age range under study. Table 1

TABLE 1

Distribution of *S*s by Sex and Direction of IQ Change Used in the Analysis of the TAT and Rorschach

Group	TAT		Rorschach	
	Boys	Girls	Boys	Girls
Group A	22	11	22	10
Group D	10	20	9	18
Both groups	32	31	31	28

shows the distribution of *S*s, by sex and direction of IQ change, for the TAT and Rorschach analyses. Because there are approximately twice as many boys as there are girls in Group A, all comparisons were first made separately by sex and results were only combined if the direction of the result for both boys and girls in the same IQ group was in the predicted direction.

1. *Need Achievement.* All achievement themes, save one, occurred to Cards 1 and 17 BM. The typical achievement story to Card 1 concerned a

[2] The writers wish to thank Mary Schnurer for her assistance in assessing the reliability of the scoring.

boy who wanted to master the violin and/or become a famous violinist, while the typical achievement theme to 17 BM involved competitive activity with regard to rope climbing. Table 2 shows the percentage of Ss in each group

TABLE 2

Percentage of Ss Reporting Achievement Imagery to Cards 1 and 17 BM

TAT Card	Group A			Group D		
	Boys	Girls	Boys and Girls	Boys	Girls	Boys and Girls
Card 1	36.4	50.0	40.6	27.3	15.0	19.4
Card 17 BM	36.4	30.0	34.4	0.0	15.0	9.7
Cards 1 and 17 BM	22.7	10.0	18.8	0.0	0.0	0.0

reporting achievement imagery plots to Cards 1, 17 BM, and to both pictures.

For both Cards 1 and 17 BM, more male and female Ss in Group A report achievement imagery than the boys or girls of Group D. For Card 1, the difference between Group A and Group D girls is reliable at the .03 level; the difference for boys is in the predicted direction but not significant. For Card 17 BM, the difference between Group A and Group D boys is significant $(P = .03)$ and in the predicted direction for girls. All P values are for one tail and were evaluated using the exact method suggested by Fisher (5). When the sexes were pooled, comparisons between Groups A and D were significant not only for Cards 1 and 17 BM separately but also for the number of Ss telling achievement imagery to both Cards 1 and 17 BM $(P < .10, .03,$ and .01 respectively). Thus, the Ss who showed increases in IQ were more prone to structure Cards 1 and 17 BM in terms of achievement oriented behavior than the Ss in Group D.

2. *Aggressive Content on Rorschach.* There was no significant difference between Groups A and D or between boys and girls with respect to the mean number of responses per protocol, and the mean for the entire sample was 27 responses. These was no difference between Group A and Group D girls with respect to percentage of each group reporting one or more aggressive responses per protocol (30.0 per cent for Group A versus 33.0 per cent for Group D). However, the difference between Group A and D boys approached significance with 59.1 per cent of the former and 22.2 per cent of the latter reporting one or more aggressive images $(P = .07)$. Thus, the prediction of a correlation between IQ increase and aggressive imagery held only for the boys. Because of the tentativeness of this result and the more speculative nature of the hypothesis relating competitive striving and aggressive content, an attempt was made to validate this finding by analyzing a later Rorschach protocol for

the boys in Groups A and D. Not all of the boys had Rorschachs administered to them at a later age, and only 15 Ss in Group A and five in Group D were available for analysis. The median ages at the time of administration were 13-8 and 15-0 for Groups A and D respectively, and there was no significant difference in the lengths of the protocols of the two groups. The results were in the same direction for 86.7 per cent of Group A, and 20.0 per cent of Group D reported one or more aggressive images, and this difference is highly significant ($P = .01$).

3. *Intellectual Curiosity.* The only TAT card eliciting curiosity plots was Card 14, and the typical theme described a person gazing at or interested in the stars or the heavens. Table 3 shows the percentage of each group telling such themes to Card 14.

Both the boys and girls in Group A told more themes of interest in the stars or heavens than the males and females in Group D ($P = .14$, $P = .10$, respectively) and combining of the sexes yielded a highly significant difference between Groups A and D ($P < .01$).

4. *Anatomy and X-ray Responses on the Rorschach.* There was no differ-

TABLE 3

Percentage of Ss Reporting Themes of Curiosity to Card 14

Sex	Group A	Group D
Boys	40.9	18.2
Girls	30.0	5.0
Boys and girls	37.5	9.7

TABLE 4

Percentage of Ss Reporting Themes of Passivity to Card 3 BM

Sex	Group A	Group D
Boys	9.1	27.3
Girls	10.0	45.0
Boys and girls	9.4	38.7

ence between Group A and Group D girls reporting one or more anatomy responses (30.0 per cent versus 38.9 per cent for Groups A and D respectively). For the boys, 31.8 per cent of Group A and 0.0 per cent of Group D reported anatomy or X-ray imagery, a difference that approached significance ($P = .06$). This finding was also validated on the same sample of 20 boys that was used to check the differences in aggressive content. The results were in the same direction with 60.0 per cent of Group A and 20.0 per cent of Group D reporting anatomy content ($P = .15$).

5. *Passivity.*   Card 3 BM accounted for most of the passivity themes and the groups were compared with respect to the incidence of stories to Card 3 BM in which the central figure was sleepy, tired, or resting. Table 4 shows the percentage of each group telling such themes. Both the boys and girls in Group D showed more passivity themes than the boys and girls in Group A. Although only the difference for the girls was significant ($P = .06$), when the sexes were pooled the difference was highly reliable ($P < .03$).

Cards 3 GF, 5, 6 BM, and 12 F did not furnish data relevant to the hypotheses under test and these results are not summarized.

DISCUSSION

In the main, the hypotheses about the differences between Groups A and D have been verified. Boy and girl ascenders produced more TAT achievement imagery and curiosity about nature than Group D children and male ascenders displayed more aggressive content on the Rorschach than the boys in Group D. The higher incidence of aggressive imagery for the boys who gained in IQ was interpreted as reflecting stronger competitive motivation. Finally, the Ss in Group D were presumed to have a more passive orientation since they were more likely to perceive the ambiguous figure on Card 3 BM as sleeping or tired. The relation between Rorschach anatomy content and IQ gain was the most tentative finding.

The results are interpreted as indicating that high motivation to achieve, competitive strivings, and curiosity about nature may motivate the acquisition of intellectual skills and knowledge which, in turn, facilitates increases in tested IQ. If one accepts the generally assumed notion that boys are more competitive and achievement oriented than girls, the fact that there were twice as many boys in Group A as there were girls supports the present interpretation. A recent study using the Edwards Personal Preference Schedule found that high school boys obtained higher need achievement scores than high school girls (7).

These results are not interpreted as indicating that strong achievement, competitive, and curiosity motives are the only variables involved in producing gains in IQ. The Ss in this study are all average or above in IQ and there is not adequate sampling of children with lower IQ levels. One would not expect Ss with low IQs or language handicaps to suddenly show an interest in reading despite achievement needs or intellectual curiosity. The child who spends increased time reading because of a heightened interest in natural processes must have already learned the basic reading skills so that this behavior is not a difficult or unlikely choice for him.

Similarly, needs for achievement and successful competition should only motivate attempts at improvement of intellectual abilities in a social milieu where praise, recognition, and superior status are awarded for such accomplishment. That is, achievement-oriented children from homes in which intellectual activity was praised would probably be more likely to master intellectual skills than achievement-oriented children from homes in which such accomplishment was not rewarded. In a cultural environment where athletic ability, fighting prowess, or success with the opposite sex was highly valued, one might expect the child to choose these behavioral channels to gratify his achievement and competitive needs. The parents in the Fels population are predominantly middle class and tend to place importance on intellectual accomplishment. A large majority of the parents have attended college, and since enrollment in the Fels program is voluntary it might be inferred that only parents who valued knowledge and scientific pursuits would be predisposed to become part of the research population. Thus, the children under study tend to come from homes which value intellectual ability.

Study of the educational attainment of the parents of the Ss in Groups A and D revealed no significant difference between the groups with respect to the percentage of families in which both parents attended college (57.1 per cent for Group A versus 42.9 per cent for Group D; $P > .30$). Although there is a slight difference favoring the educational level of Group A families, the difference was not dramatic. There may be important differences between Groups A and D with respect to the differential encouragement of intellectual achievement, but measurement of these differences would probably require variables more refined than educational level of the parents. However, even though parental emphasis on intellectual activity may increase the child's desire to improve his cognitive skills, the child's predisposition to adopt or rebel against parental values should selectively influence his motivation to strive for intellectual accomplishment. Thus, the type of relation between parent and child may be an important factor in this process.

Finally, there is the possibility that genetic and/or constitutional variables may play a role in facilitating marked IQ changes. There is considerable data indicating that genetic factors influence general IQ level but less evidence relevant to the role of these variables in producing childhood increases in IQ score. For most of the children in our population, IQs tend to level off during the ages 6–10 and most of the marked changes in level occur during the preschool years. However, the exact relationship between genetic variables and IQ change has yet to be determined. The phenomenon of IQ increase during the school years is admittedly complex and it is not implied that the child's motives are the major factor. However, it is suggested that personality needs may influence this process. Perhaps the most accurate generalization is that for middle-class children with average or above IQ levels, strong achievement, competitive, and curiosity needs may facilitate IQ gains by motivating the child to master intellectual skills.

A final implication of these findings is that they add indirect evidence for the usefulness of the Rorschach and TAT as research instruments. Validation of a predicted relationship between TAT achievement imagery and IQ gain increases one's confidence in the hypothesis that TAT plots can serve as an index of achievement-oriented tendencies. The results of the Rorschach analysis suggest that aggressive content may be an index of an individual's aggressive predispositions but not necessarily a measure of his tendency to express direct, physical aggression. Although Sontag, Baker, and Nelson (11), using behavioral observations, rated the boys in Group A as more competitive than those in Group D, there was no difference between these groups with respect to intensity or incidence of direct verbal or physical aggression or destruction of property. We have assumed that competition is a socially approved form of aggressive behavior and the higher incidence of aggressive content for Group A boys was presumed to be a result of their more intense competitive strivings. Some clinicians who use projective tests are too prone to focus on predictive statements about direct, physical aggression when confronted with a protocol containing aggressive content. One is apt to overlook the fact that the individual may have alternative behavioral channels for expression of aggressive motives.

SUMMARY

For a group of 140 boys and girls in the Fels Research population on whom continuous Binet IQ data were available, a distribution of IQ change was obtained by subtracting each S's smoothed IQ at age 6 from his smoothed IQ at age 10. This distribution of differences was divided into quartiles, and the Rorschach and TAT protocols of the upper (maximum increase in IQ) and lower (maximum decrease in IQ) quartiles were analyzed and compared. The results showed that in comparing the Ss who showed IQ increases with those showing IQ decreases, the former had, on the TAT, significantly more (a) achievement imagery on Cards 1 and 17 BM and (b) themes of curiosity about nature on Card 14, and significantly fewer themes of passivity on Card 3 BM. For the boys only, more of the Ss who increased in IQ had anatomy responses and aggressive imagery on the Rorschach. The results were interpreted as indicating that high need achievement, competitive striving, and curiosity about nature are correlated with gains in IQ score because they may facilitate the acquisition of skills that are measured by the intelligence test.

References

1. Baker, C. T., Sontag, L. W., & Nelson, Virginia L. Specific ability in IQ change. *J. consult. Psychol.*, 1955, **19**, 307–310.

2. Bayley, Nancy. Mental growth in young children. *Yearb. Nat. Soc. Stud. Educ.*, 1940, **39**, (II), 11–47.

3. Bayley, Nancy. Consistency and variability in the growth in IQ from birth to eighteen years. *J. genet. Psychol.*, 1949, **75**, 165–196.

4. Bradway, Katherine. IQ constancy on the Revised Stanford-Binet from the preschool to the junior high school level. *J. genet. Psychol.*, 1944, **65**, 197–217.

5. Fisher, R. A. *Statistical methods for research workers.* (5th ed.) Edinburgh: Oliver & Boyd, 1934.

6. Haggard, E. A., Davis, A., & Havighurst, R. J. Some factors which influence performance of children on intelligence tests. *Amer. Psychol.*, 1948, **3**, 265–266.

7. Klett, C. J. Performance of high school students on the Edwards Personal Preference Schedule. *J. consult. Psychol.*, 1957, **21**, 68–72.

8. McClelland, D. C. Atkinson, J. W., Clark, R. A., & Lowell, E. L. *The acvhievement motive.* New York: Appleton-Century-Crofts, 1953.

9. Richards, T. W. Mental test performance as a reflection of the child's current life situation: A methodological study. *Child Develpm.*, 1951, **22**, 221–233.

10. Sontag, L. W., Baker, C. T., & Nelson, Virginia L. Personality as a determinant of performance. *Amer. J. Orthopsychiat.*, 1955, **25**, 555–562.

11. Sontag, L. W., Baker, C. T., & Nelson, Virginia L. Mental growth and personality development. *Monogr. Soc. Res. Child Develpm.*, in press.

12. Wellmann, Beth L., & McCandless, B. R. Factors associated with Binet IQ changes of preschool children. *Psychol. Monogr.*, 1946, **60**, No. 2 (Whole No. 278).

6. EARLY EDUCATION: A COGNITIVE-DEVELOPMENTAL VIEW*

Lawrence Kohlberg

This paper reviews the implications of the cognitive-developmental theories of Baldwin, Dewey, Piaget, and Vygotsky for preschool education. The conception of cognitive stage basic to these theories is analyzed, and the connection of a stage conception to an interactional (as opposed to a maturationist or environmentalist-training) view of the origins of mental structure is analyzed. Emperical studies are reviewed supporting the validity of this conception of intellectual development. Preschool programs of academic and linguistic training or stimulation are examined from this point of view. The conception of the preschool period as a critical period for the environmental stimulation of general intelligence is examined, considering general intelligence in both psychometric and Piagetian terms. It is concluded that the theories reviewed do not so much imply an emphasis upon specific forms of preschool intellectual stimulation as they do imply a systematic formulation of the cognitive-developmental components of the play, constructive, aesthetic, and social activities which have traditionally been the heart of the preschool.

A glance over the field of early education in America at the time of Jean Piaget's seventieth birthday reveals a curious contrast. While Piaget's ideas

SOURCE. *Child Development*, 1968, **39**, 1013–1062. Abridged with author's permission.

* This paper was written while the author was at the University of Chicago. The research of the author and his colleagues on the factorial structures of Piagetian tasks and their relations to psychometric tasks and to cultural deprivation has been supported by an Office of Education grant to the Early Education Research Center of the University of Chicago.

100

are salient wherever research is done on early cognitive development, their salience in formulations of goals and processes in early education is much less widespread. Enthusiasts for early cognitive stimulation often make reference to Piaget's ideas but adapt them to a viewpoint different than that held by him. Bruner (1960, 1966), Bruner, Oliver, and Greenfield (1966), and Hunt (1961, 1964) interpret Piaget's ideas as consistent with the notion that intelligence is a set of acquired information-processing skills and that any intellectual content can be taught early if the teaching is adapted to the child's cognitive level. On the opposite pole, the "child-development" tradition of preschool education has appealed to Piaget's ideas as part of a body of maturational theory including Freud (in Kessen, 1965), Gesell (1954), Isaacs (1933), and Spearman (1930). In this context, Piaget's ideas have been viewed as consistent with the notion that preschool educators should just let cognitive abilities grow and that the educator should concentrate upon helping the child to adjust and develop emotionally.

This ambiguity is not surprising in light of the fact that "if one looks carefully through Piaget's writings, one seldom, if ever, finds an attempt to deal with concrete problems of pedagogy or childrearing" (Elkind in Piaget, 1967, p. xvi). More fundamentally, however, the ambiguity is due to Piaget's rejection of traditional dichotomies implicit in much controversy about early cognitive learning. In the first place, Piaget discards the dichotomy between maturation and environmentally determined learning. He insists that cognitive processes emerge through a process of development which is neither direct biological maturation nor direct learning in the usual sense, since it is a reorganization of psychological structures resulting from organism-environment interactions (Elkind, 1967b; Flavell, 1963; Hooper, 1968; Piaget, 1964; Wallace, 1965). In the second place, Piaget discards the dichotomy between the cognitive (usually considered as a set of intellectual skills) and the social emotional. According to Piaget, social development, play, and art all have large cognitive-structural components and contribute to, and are contributed to by, cognitive development in the narrower sense.

Piaget's rejection of the maturation-learning and the cognitive-emotional dichotomies is part of a general intellectual tradition out of which Piaget's work grows. This tradition has been variously labeled the "functional-genetic" (Baldwin, 1906–1915; Dewey, 1930), the "symbolic interactionist" (Mead, 1934), and the "cognitive-developmental" (Kohlberg, 1966a, 1968b). In addition to Piaget and the American genetics functionalists, Werner (1948) and Montessori are also in part representatives of this tradition (Elkind, 1967b; Kohlberg, 1968a).

As we elaborate in the following sections, there are three broad streams of educational thought which vary from generation to generation in their statement, but which are each continuous in starting from the same assumptions.

The first stream of thought commences with Rousseau (in Kessen, 1965) and is contemporarily represented in the ideas of followers of Freud and Gesell. This maturationist stream of thought holds that what is most important in the development of the child is that which comes from within him and that the pedagogical environment should be one which creates a climate to allow inner "goods" (abilities and social virtues) to unfold and the inner "bad" to come under the control of the inner good, rather than to be fixated by adult cultural pressures. The extreme of this view is presented by Neill (1960). The second "cultural training" stream of thought assumes that what is important in the development of the child is his learning of the cognitive and moral knowledge and rules of the culture and that education's business is the teaching of such information and rules to the child through direct instruction. This stream of thought can be traced from John Locke to Thorndike and Skinner (cf. Kessen, 1965). The clearest and most thoughtful contemporary elaboration of this view in relation to preschool education is to be found in the writing of Bereiter and Engelman (1966).

The third stream of thought, the "cognitive-developmental" or "interactional" view is based on the premise that the cognitive and affective structures which education should nourish are natural emergents from the interaction between the child and the environment under conditions where such interaction is allowed or fostered. More specifically, the basic postulates of this approach are:

1. The terms "cognition," "thought," or "intelligence" basically refer to adaptive actions upon objects or internalizations of such actions. Mature or adequate cognition is defined by an equilibrium or reciprocity between action and object. Cognition is defined as function (as modes of action) rather than as content (as sets of words, "verbal responses," associations, memories, etc.) or as a faculty or ability (a power of producing words, memories, etc.). The encouragement of cognitive development, then, is the provision of opportunities for activities of an organized or equilibrated form.

2. Cognition proceeds through stages of structural reorganization. While cognitive functions are present from birth, cognitive structures are radically different from one stage to the next.

3. The implication of structural reorganization in development is that the source of cognitive structure and of cognitive development is to be found neither in the structure and maturation of the organism nor in the teaching structures of the environment but in the structure of the interaction between organism and environment.

4. The optimal conditions for such structural organization entail some optimal balance of discrepancy and match between the behavior structures of the child and the structure of his psychological environment.

5. From birth, there are inherent motives for cognitive activities, but these motives too undergo structural change in development.

6. Both the "cognitive" and the "affective" are functions, not psychic contents or structures. Cognitive and affective development are parallel aspects of the structural transformations undergone in development.

While all of the above ideas are common to all writers in the cognitive-developmental tradition, Piaget's work has been the first to apply these assumptions to children's behavior in logically precise and empirically specified form. The implication of Piaget's work for education, then, may best be understood as giving greater precision to the general functional-genetic approach to education, presented in its most comprehensive form by Dewey (1913, 1930, 1938, 1965).

In the present paper, we shall first summarize the Piagetian (or cognitive-developmental) position and some exemplary research as it bears upon two related topics central to preschool education: first, the general role of experience in cognitive development, and, second, the issue of whether preschool cognitive experience defines a special or "critical" period in intellectual development. In the course of this discussion, we shall attempt to consider its implications for the introduction of various types of cognitive "curricula" into the preschool. In a forthcoming book (Kohlberg & Lesser, in press) we use this viewpoint to analyze the contributions of play, art, and social interaction to the child's development.

Part of the purpose of this paper is to examine some of the implications of Piaget's rather difficult notions of cognitive development for the concrete concerns of the preschool educator, because it may be of some practical use for educational policy. In part, it also seems of use for the clarification of theory itself. Piagetian theory must take account of research on early education as well as "pure" research on cognitive development if it is to undergo the elaboration and refinement required of a viable theory. Accordingly, this paper attempts to both elaborate the position and to review some of the findings which make it plausible. Such a review of a broad range of findings somewhat tangentially related to Piaget's ideas is bound to be somewhat cursory and superficial, but it will at least suggest areas where current findings and Piagetian theory must confront one another.

I. THE COGNITIVE-DEVELOPMENTAL APPROACH AND THE CONCEPT OF STAGE

We have suggested that the basic characteristics of the cognitive-developmental approach may be best grasped by contrasting them with theories of innate patterning and maturation on the one hand and theories of environmental associationistic learning on the other. As opposed to either set of theories, cognitive-developmental theories are "interactional," that is, they assume that basic mental structure is the product of the patterning of the interaction between the organism and the environment rather than directly reflecting innate patterns or patterns of event-structures (stimulus contingencies) in the environment.

The distinction between theories stressing the innate and theories stressing the acquired has often been thought of as a contrast in quantitative emphasis on hereditary biological factors as opposed to environmental stimulation factors in causing individual differences. When the problem is posed in such a fashion, one can be led to nothing but a piously eclectic "interactionism" which asserts that all concrete behavior is quantitatively affected by both hereditary and environmental factors. The theoretical issues are quite different, however. They are issues as to type of theory, that is, between conceptions of basic mental structure and the location of the principles producing this structure within or without the organism.

The statement just made presupposes a distinction between behavior differences in general and mental structure. Structure refers to the general characteristics of shape, pattern, or organization of response rather than to the rate or intensity of response or its pairing with particular stimuli. According to cognitive-developmental theory, all mental structure has a cognitive component (and all cognition involves structure). Many cognitive theories do not employ structural concepts. As an example, Baldwin (1968) terms a number of theories (including his own) "cognitive" because (a) they postulate a coding or representational process intervening between stimulus and response, and (b) they postulate that the learning of representations or maps may occur without any overt response and without any definite reinforcement for this learning. In addition to these more general assumptions, cognitive-developmental theory assumes that "cognitions" are internally organized wholes or systems of internal relations, that is, structure. Cognitive structures are rules of processing information or for connecting experienced events. Cognition (as most clearly reflected in thinking) means putting things together, relating events, and in cognitive theories this relating is assumed to be an active connecting process, not a passive connecting of events through external association and repetition. The process of relating events depends upon general categories which represent the modes of relating common to any experienced events, for example, causality, substantiality, space, time, quantity, and logic (i.e., the identities, inclusions, or implications of classes and propositions).

The awareness that the child's behavior has a cognitive structure or organizational pattern of its own which needs description independently of the degree of its correspondence to the adult culture is as old as Rousseau, but this awareness has only recently pervaded the actual study of cognitive development. Two examples of the revolution resulting from defining the structure of the child's mind in its own terms may be cited. The first is that of Piaget, whose first psychological effort was to classify types of wrong answers on the Binet test. By moving beyond an analysis of intellectual development in terms of number of right answers to an analysis in terms of differences in structure, Piaget transformed the study of cognitive development. The second example comes from the study of children's language, which was for a generation based on counting nouns and verbs as defined by conventional adult grammar. In the last decade, psychologists have approached children's grammar with the methods of structural linguistics, as if the child's language were that of an exotic tribe. While the implications of the Piagetian revolution in cognition and the structuralist revolution in language are far from clear, they have made the conception of mental structure a reality accepted even by associationistic S-R psychologists of cognition (cf. Berlyne, 1965).

It is evident, then, that general questions as to the origins and development of mental structure are not the same as questions regarding the origins of individual differences in behavior. As an example, the fact that one 6-year-old child may pass all the 6-year items on the Binet test and another fail them all might be attributed purely to hereditary differences in general intelligence, while the patterns of behavior involved in the child's actual test performance (knowing the word "envelope") may be purely culturally learned behavior. Because many American psychologists have been peculiarly concerned with individual differences rather than developmental universals, and because they have failed to understand the distinction between behavior differences in general and behavior structure, they have frequently misinterpreted European theories of development. It is because of this confusion that some American writers have misinterpreted Piaget's stages as "maturational" and have thought that he claimed intelligence is unaffected by environment, while others have correctly interpreted Piaget's stages as being based on the assumption of organism-environment interactions, but takes this assumption as indicating that individual differences in intellectual performance are less hereditary than was long believed. In fact, there is nothing in Piaget's theory which suggests that individual differences in speed of development through his stages is not largely due to the hereditary factors which seem to account for at least half of the variance in the usual IQ tests.

Maturational theories, then, are not theories based on quantitative assumptions about the role of heredity. In terms of quantitative role, maturational or nativistic theories, like those of Gesell (1954) or Lorenz (1965), recognize the importance of environmental stimulation in modifying genetically grounded behavior patterns. In a similar sense, associationistic learning theorists, like Hull (1943) or Pavlov (1928), recognize the quantitative role of hereditary traits of temperament and ability in causing individual differences in personality and in rate and type of learning. The difference between the two types of theories is not in the recognition of both innate and environmental causal factors in development but in the belief about which set of factors are the source of basic patterning.

The contrast between the quantitative and structural roles awarded to experience becomes clear with regard to the issue of critical periods. Most research on the effects of experience upon development has postulated "critical periods" in which the individual is especially sensitive to environmental influence in a given domain. Yet this notion of extreme quantitative sensitivity depends upon a maturational or nativistic theory. The existence of a fixed time period, during which a certain amount of stimulation is required to avoid irreversible developmental deficits, presupposes an innate process of growth with an inner time schedule and an inner pattern which can be arrested or distorted by deficits of stimulation.

In the nativistic view, stimulation may be needed to elicit, support, and maintain behavior patterns, but the stimulation does not create these patterns, which are given by templates in the genotype. In fact, learning or environmental influence itself is seen as basically patterned by genetically determined structures. Learning occurs in certain interstices or open places in genetic patterns, and the structuring of what is learned is given by these patterns (Lorenz, 1965). As an example, "imprinting" represents a type of learning, a determination of response by environmental stimulation. However, the "learning" involved represents a specific sensitivity or open spot in a genetically patterned social-sexual response, phylogenetically determined to produce a tie to others of the species. As another example, an insect or bird may learn a specific "map" of the geography of its home place, but this map is structured by an innate organization of space in general (Lorenz, 1965).

In dealing with developmental changes, nativistic theories such as Gesell's (1954) have stressed the notion of unfolding maturational stages. The patterning of these age-specific behavioral forms, their order and timing, is believed to be "wired into" the organism. The organism grows as a whole so that the effort to teach or force early maturation in one area will either be ineffective or will disrupt the child's total pattern and equilibrium of growth.

In contrast to nativistic theories, learning theories may allow for genetic factors in personality and in ease of learning of a complex response, but they assume that the basic structure of complex responses results from the structure of the child's environment. Both specific concepts and general cognitive structures, like the categories of space, time, and causality, are believed to be reflections of structures existing outside the child, structurings given by the physical and social world.

Almost of necessity, the view that structure of the external world is the source of the child's cognitive structure has led to an account of the development of structure in associationistic terms. From John Locke to J. B. Watson and B. F. Skinner (Kessen, 1965), environmentalists have viewed the structure of behavior as the result of the association of discrete stimuli with one another, with responses of the child, and with experiences of pleasure and pain.

At its extreme, this conception of mental structure has the following implications for early education:

1. Mind or personality is a set of specific responses to specific stimuli in the environment. Cognitive development is the result of guided learning, of recurrent associations between specific discriminative stimuli in the environment, specific responses of the child, and specific reinforcements following these responses.

2. "Cognition" is a matter of discrimination and generalization learning. Conceptual development occurs through learning overt or covert verbal labeling responses to discriminated and generalized classes of stimuli. Training in discrimination of the stimulus attributes implied by cultural concepts and generalization of response to these attributes leads to concept learning.

3. The child is born with very little patterning of personality or of mind. Accordingly, it is possible to teach a child almost any behavior pattern, provided one teaches in terms of the laws of association learning and provided one starts at an early age before competing response patterns have been learned.

4. It is important to start education early because early learning, if appropriate, facilitate later learning, while if they are inappropriate they impede later learning.

It is important to recognize that all these educational postulates of environmentalist theories of learning are not inconsistent with the innate determination of IQ or other traits of ability or temperament. These postulates do, however, suggest that teaching can go on without much prior understanding of the structure of a given desired behavior pattern as it "naturally" develops and as it relates to prior organismic behavior structures. Teaching instead requires primarily a careful statement of a behavior pattern considered desirable (e.g., a skill such as reading or arithmetic) in terms of specific responses. This pattern is then to be taught in accordance with general laws of learning believed applicable to the learning of all organisms (old or young, human or nonhuman) and to the learning of all behavior patterns.

In general, such a program implies a plan for shaping the child's behavior by successive approximation from responses he is now making to the desired end responses. At every step, immediate feedback or reward is desirable and immediate repetition and elaboration of the correct response is used. A careful detailed programing of learning is required to make sure that (a) each response builds on the preceding, (*b*) incorrect responses are not made since once made they persist and interfere with correct responses, and (*c*) feedback and reward are immediate.

We have constructed the maturationist assumption that basic mental structure results from an innate patterning with the learning theory assumption that basic mental structure is the result of the patterning or association of events in the outside world. In contrast, the cognitive-developmental assumption is that basic mental structure is the result of an interaction between certain organismic structuring tendencies and the structure of the outside world, rather than reflecting either one directly.

This interaction leads to cognitive stages, which represent the transformations of simply early cognitive structures as they are applied to (or assimilate) the external world and as they are accommodated to or restructured by the external world in the course of being applied to it.

The core of the cognitive-development position, then, is the doctrine of cognitive stages. Cognitive stages have the following general characteristics (Piaget, 1960):

1. Stages imply distinct or qualitative differences in children's modes of thinking or of solving the same problem at different ages.

2. These different modes of thought form an invariant sequence, order, or succession in individual development. While cultural factors may speed up, slow down, or stop development, they do not change its sequence.

3. Each of these different and sequential modes of thought forms a "structured whole." A given stage-response on a task does not just represent a specific response determined by knowledge and familiarity with that task or tasks similar to it; rather it represents an underlying thought-organization. An example is the stage of "concrete operations," which determine responses to many tasks which are not manifestly similar to one another on the "ordinary" dimensions of stimulus generalization. According to Piaget, at the stage of concrete operations, the child has a general tendency to maintain that a physical object conserves its properties on various physical dimensions in spite of apparent perceptual changes. This tendency is structural; it is not a specific belief about a specific object. The implication is that both conservation and other aspects of logical operations should appear as a consistent cluster of responses in development.

4. Cognitive stages are hierarchical integrations. Stages form an order of increasingly differentiated and integrated *structures* to fulfil a common function. The general adaptational functions of cognitive structures are always the same (for Piaget the maintenance of an equilibrium between the organism defined as a balance of assimilation and accommodation). Accordingly, higher stages displace (or rather reintegrate) the structures found at lower

stages. As an example, formal operational thought includes all the structural features of concrete operational thought but at a new level of organization. Concrete operational thought or even sensorimotor thought does not disappear when formal thought arises but continues to be used in concrete situations where it is adequate or when efforts at solution by formal thought have failed. However, there is a hierarchical preference within the individual, that is, a disposition to prefer a solution of a problem at the highest level available to him. It is this disposition which partially accounts for the consistency postulated as our third criterion.

In contrast, if structural stages do define general ontogenetic sequences, then an interactional type of theory of developmental process must be used to explain ontogeny. If the child goes through qualitatively different stages of thought, his basic modes of organizing experience cannot be the direct result of adult teaching or they would be copies of adult thought from the start. If the child's cognitive responses differed from the adult's only in revealing less information and less complication of structure, it would be possible to view them as incomplete learnings of the external structure of the world, whether that structure is defined in terms of the adult culture or in terms of the laws of the physical world. If the child's responses indicate a different structure or organization than the adult's, rather than a less complete one, and if this structure is similar in all children, it is extremely difficult to view the child's mental structure as a direct learning of the external structure. Furthermore, if the adult's mental structure depends upon sequential transformations of the child's mental structure, it too cannot directly reflect the current structure of the outer cultural or physical world.

If stages cannot be accounted for by direct learning of the structure of the outer world, neither can they be explained as the result of innate patterning. If children have their own logic, adult logic or mental structure cannot be derived from innate neurological patterning because such patterning should hold also in childhood. It is hardly plausible to view a whole succession of logics as an evolutionary and functional program of innate wiring.

It has just been claimed that it is implausible to view a succession of cognitive stages as innate. This claim is based on an epistemological assumption, the assumption that there is a reality to which psychology may and must refer, that is, that cognition or knowing must be studied in relation to an object known.

The invariant sequences found in motor development (Ames, 1937; Shirley, 1931, 1931–1933) may well be directly wired into the nervous system. The fact that the postural-motor development of chimpanzees and man proceed through the same sequence suggests such a maturational base (Riesen & Kinder, 1952). The existence of invariant sequence in cognition is quite a different matter, however, since cognitions are defined by reference to a world. One cannot speak of the development of a child's conception of an animal without assuming that the child has experience with animals. Things become somewhat more complicated when we are dealing with the development of categories, that is, the most general modes of relating objects such as causality, substance, space, time, quantity, and logic. These categories differ from more specific concepts, for example, the concept of "animal," in that they are not defined by specific objects to which they refer but by modes of relating any object to any other object. Every experienced event is located in space and time, implies or causes other events, etc.

The interactional account assumes that structural change in these categories depends upon experience. The effects of experience, however, are not conceived of as learning in the ordinary sense, in which learning implies training by pairing of specific objects and specific responses, by instruction, by modeling, or by specific practices of responses. Indeed, the effects of training are determined by the child's cognitive categories rather than the reverse. If two events which follow one another in time are cognitively connected in the child's mind, it implies that he relates them by means of a category such as causality, for example, he perceives his operant behavior as causing the reinforcer to occur. A program of reinforcement, then, cannot directly change the child's causal structures since it is assimilated to it.

If cognitive development occurs in terms of stages, then, an understanding of the effect of experience upon it requires three types of conceptual analysis customarily omitted in discussions of learning.

In the first place, it requires an analysis of universal structural features of the environment. While depending on structural and functional invariants of the nervous system, cognitive stages also depend upon universal structures of experience for their shape. Stages of physical concepts depend upon a universal structure of experience in the physical world, a structure which underlies the diversity of physical arrangements in which men live and which underlies the diversity of formal physical theories held in various cultures at various periods.

In the second place, understanding cognitive stages depends upon a logical analysis of orderings inherent in given concepts. The invariance of sequence in the development of a concept or category is not dependent upon a pre-patterned unfolding of neural patterns; it must depend upon a logical analysis of the concept itself. As an example, Piaget postulates a sequence of spaces or geometrics moving from the topological to the projective to the Euclidean. This sequence is plausible in terms of a logical analysis of the mathematical structures involved.

In the third place, an understanding of sequential stages depends upon analysis of the relation of the structure of a specific experience of the child to the behavior structure. Piaget (1964) has termed such an analysis an "equilibration" rather than a "learning" analysis. Such an analysis employs such notions as "optimal match," "cognitive conflict," "assimilation," and "accommodation." Whatever terms are used, such analyses focus upon discrepancies between the child's action system or expectancies and the experienced event, and hypothesize some moderate or optimal degree of discrepancy as constituting the most effective experience for structural change in the organism.

In summary, an interactional conception of stages differs from a maturational one is that it assumes that experience is necessary for the stages to take the shape they do as well as assuming that generally more or richer stimulation will lead to faster advances through the series involved. It proposes that an understanding of the role of experience requires (a) analyses of universal features of experienced objects (physical or social), (b) analysis of logical sequences of differentiation and integration in concepts of such objects, and (c) analysis of structural relations between experience-inputs and the relevant behavior organizations. While these three modes of analysis are foreign to the habits of associationistic learning theorists, they are not totally incompatible in principle with them. While associationistic concepts are clumsy to apply to universal objects of experience or to the logical structures of concepts and to the problem of match, it can be done, as Berlyne (1961, 1965) has demonstrated. As yet, however, such associationistic analyses have not led to the formulation of new hypotheses going beyond translations of cognitive-developmental concepts into a different language.

II. RESISTANCE OF SEQUENTIAL COGNITIVE DEVELOPMENTS TO SPECIFIC TEACHING: EXPERIMENTS ON CONSERVATION

In the preceding section, we outlined an interactional theory of the role of experience which shares with maturationism a pessimism about the effect of specific teaching on cognitive-structural development. In a practical sense, the interactional view suggests that limited specific training experiences cannot replace the massive general types of experience accruing with age. Both views then agree in the factual importance of age-readiness but disagree in their interpretation of this fact. An example of evidence used for the maturational view is the finding of Gesell and Thompson (Gesell, 1954) that an untrained twin became as adept at tower building and stair climbing after a week of practice as was the trained twin who had been given practice in tower building and stair climbing over many weeks. As Hunt (1964) convincingly argues, while this finding shows the limited value of *specific training*, it does not show that the function in question does not depend upon *general experience*. The untrained twin was not just "maturing," he was walking and climbing on other objects than stairs; he was placing and manipulating other objects than block towers, etc. While the developmental and the maturational view may practically agree on the relative futility of early specific training of a function, the developmental view sees specific training as failing primarily because it cannot make up for the age-linked general experiential lacks of the young child rather than because it cannot make up for his neurological immaturity.

As an example, preschool children advanced in verbal knowledge and information are still almost as immature in level of development of the dream concept as are less verbally knowledgeable preschool children. Thus, Jack, a bright verbal child (Stanford-Binet MA = 6 yr., 10 mo.), age 5 years, 2 months, responds as follows to the dream task: "Dreams come from God. God makes the dreams and puts them in balloons. The balloons float down from heaven and enter a dream bag under your stomach. In the dream bag there are some little men and a sergeant. They have a cannon that shoots the dream-balloons up into your head where they burst into pictures outside your head."

Jack here is much closer in developmental level to his chronological age-mates than to his mental age-mates. Yet his creative thinking and his possession of verbal concepts are high. Ongoing research by DeVries (in preparation) and others (Goodnow & Bethon, 1966) suggests that in general mildly retarded children are more advanced in Piaget concepts than younger average children of the same psychometric mental age and that average children are in turn more advanced than younger bright children of the same psychometric mental age. Our interpretation is not that Piaget stages represent age-fixed maturational unfoldings independent of psychometric ability but that cognitive-structural development depends upon massive general experience, a requirement which the "innately" bright child cannot short circuit. The psychometrically bright child is adept at organizing or "educing relations and correlates" in a cognitive field (Spearman, 1930), but the logical structure of the relations which are induced demands massive experience for its reorganization.

Much more comprehensive evidence to support the notion that specific training cannot substitute for age-linked general experience comes from the numerous experiments designed to teach conservation of mass, weight, or number to young children (Sigel & Hooper, 1968). These studies suggest that direct teaching of conservation through verbal instruction and reinforcement or through provision of observations of examples of conservation (e.g., weighing masses changed in shape on a balance) do not lead to the formation of a general or stable concept of conservation. Little change is induced by such methods.[1]

---

[1] A general review is presented by Sigel and Hooper (1968). Some exceptions to our

If specific experimental teaching seems to have only limited value for the attainment of conservation, general formal schooling appears to have no influence at all upon conservation. Conservation of number, mass, weight, and volume appears at the same age in schooled and unschooled subjects when other relevant variables are controlled. Probably the most definitive study on this question is that of Mermelstein (Mermelstein, 1964; Mermelstein & Shulman, 1967). Mermelstein compared the conservation responses on a number of tasks (including number) of 6- and 9-year-old Negro children of Prince Edward County who had been deprived of schooling with northern urban Negro children who had attended school. No significant differences were found between the two groups. An equally careful study by Goodnow showed no difference between unschooled Hong Kong children and comparable IQ schooled children in various types of conservation (Goodnow & Bethon, 1966). Price-Williams (1961) found that African Tiv children without schooling attained conservation on several tasks including number at about the same age Western children achieve conservation. Greenfield (1966) found some retardation on conservation in nonschooled Senegalese children, but this retardation disappeared when an appropriate form of the conservation task was used which eliminated set effects due to beliefs about magical attributes of white authorities. Kohlberg (1968a) hypothesized that Montessori schooling for young children might accelerate conservation and transitivity because the Montessori training tasks are directed at sensorimotor experiences of quantitative measurement and comparison. While Montessori schooling over 9 months did significantly raise Stanford-Binet IQ, it failed to have any effects upon Piaget conservation tasks.

While the resistance of conservation to specific instruction is noteworthy, it is more significant to note that the conditions under which instruction does change conservation are those expected by cognitive-developmental theory. In the first place, the approach distinguishes between reversible situational

generalizations are reported in some studies, e.g., Sullivan's (1967) findings of partially generalized conservation induced through film instruction and Gelman's (1967) findings of partially generalized conservation induced through generalized discrimination learning set training. The only way in which the writer can integrate these findings with others is suggested by the older age (6 to 8) of Sullivan's experimental subjects. Using methods minimizing verbal complications, I find that the large majority of children this age possess conservation concepts. It seems likely that Sullivan's procedure led to the application of the conservation concept to new situations rather than to its formation. The same comment applies to the results of other studies in which conservation responses are increased by training the child to ignore irrelevant cues, to redefine the meaning of words like "bigger," etc. These studies are not studies indicating the possibility of early teaching of a conservation concept but rather indicating the possibility of its somewhat earlier elicitation by clarifying its situational relevance. Finally, rote-learning effects are probably responsible for some of the change reported.

learning and structural development. An associationistic theory of learning typically assumes that any learning is situation-specific (i.e., under the control of situational discriminative stimuli and reinforcers) and is reversible (i.e., can be extinguished). In the operant conditioning paradigm, the demonstration of reversibility (extinction and subsequent relearning) is part of the demonstration that the researcher has isolated the variables controlling behavior change. In contrast, both common sense and cognitive-developmental theory hold that cognitive development is generalized and irreversible. This constitutes the root meaning of the notion of cognitive structure. If the child has developed a concept of conservation, we expect that he will not lose it even in the face of contrary stimulation or social pressure. We also expect that he will invoke or apply the concept under conditions appropriate to the meaning of the concept rather than in terms of situational and sensory parameters extraneous to its meaning. It is obvious that insofar as structural change can be induced such change should take precedence over reversible situational learning as a focus of educational effort. There is no particular reason to expect that preschool teaching of a reversible situation-specific type can have any lasting effect upon the child.

There is ample evidence that "naturally" developing conservation concepts have the structural properties mentioned. They typically cannot be reversed by trick demonstrations of nonconservation nor by social pressure from the experimenter (Kohlberg, 1963; Smedslund, 1961a). While some forms of conservation are more difficult than others, the order of difficulty tends to be regular (constituting a Guttman-scaled "horizontal decalage," e.g., conservation of mass, weight, and volume), and children showing conservation on a given task are likely to show it on others, that is, to generalize or transpose the concept in comparison to children of the same chronological or mental age who do not show conservation on that given task (Uzgiris, 1968).

In contrast, most of the effects of specific instruction in inducing conservation do not have the structural properties mentioned. Artificial acceleration of conservation seems to be limited in generalization. While generalizing across specific objects, training of number conservation does not seem to lead to acceleration of other forms of conservation (Gruen, 1968). Apparent attainment of conservation so obtained seems to be partly or wholly reversible. Exposure to trick conditions suggesting nonconservation leads to loss of belief in conservation where conservation has been taught rather than developing naturally (Smedslund, 1961b).

We have stated that conservation responses are resistant to direct instruction and that often when they are not resistant (i.e., where conservation is induced) the response changes do not represent a genuine acquisition of conservation in the sense of an irreversible generalized belief in conservation. However, it also appears that some genuine acceleration conservation may be induced if the instruction methods used follow from the conceptions of cognitive structure and of conflict and match implied by Piaget's theory. In the first place, successful induction of conservation is contingent upon the match in the sense that the child must already be near the level of attainment of conservation in terms of chronological and mental age. In the second place, some successful induction of conservation is achieved through stimulation of the development of the logical prerequisites of conservation defined by Piaget (e.g., the ability to make double classifications or to consider two dimensions simultaneously [Sigel, Roeper, & Hooper, 1968] or the stimulation of imaginative reversal [Wallach & Sprott, 1964]). In the third place, some successful induction of conservation results from creation of experiences in which nonconserving expectations lead to certain conditions of conflict (Langer, 1967; Smedslund, 1961a, 1961b).

In addition to the experimental findings mentioned, naturalistic studies support the notion that acquisition of conservation is contingent upon a background of general experience. Some degree of retardation in conservation appears in some semiliterate non-Western cultures, regardless of schooling (Greenfield, 1966; Hyde, 1959; Kohlberg, unpublished data on the Taiwan Atayal). Preliminary findings indicate that lower social class and "culturally disadvantaged" (Aid to Dependent Children) groups matched with middle-class subjects on Stanford-Binet mental age do more poorly on conservation tasks (Kohn, in preparation).

It seems unlikely that the "general experience" effects of social class and culture upon conservation are primarily or directly linguistic. The fact that conservation development is not directly contingent on language development is indicated by findings on the deaf (Furth, 1966). While these findings indicate some retardation of conservation among the deaf, this retardation is not marked, in spite of the fact that most of the deaf children studied have almost no facility with verbal language in any form. Much more marked deficits have been found in blind children of normal verbal IQ who do not appear to attain most forms of conservation reached by normal children at ages 5 to 7 until ages 9 to 11 (Nordan, 1967). The findings seem to be in line with Piaget's notions of the visual-motor roots of "concrete operations."

In summary, the conservation findings clearly demonstrate that conservation is not a strict maturational product but is the product of interactional experience between organismic structure and environment. On the practical side, however, they do not give much support to the notion that development on basic Piaget-type cognitive functions can be markedly accelerated by deliberate intervention of a schooling variety, since such acceleration tends to be limited, specific, and contingent upon a narrow time gap between the intervention experience and the child's natural readiness. This readiness is determined by age, IQ, and the richness of the child's general background of stimulation.

III. PRESCHOOL CURRICULUM: SPECIFIC INTELLECTUAL INSTRUCTION

While differing in theory with the maturational view held by traditional "child development" preschool educators, the cognitive-developmental analysis just presented practically agrees with the maturationists that specific early training of cognitive functions is often useless. It should be noted that this conclusion holds for sequential age development in conceptual structures of a spontaneous sort, such as concepts of conservation. Many preschool behavior changes associated with age are not of this type; some are primarily maturational (e.g., early motor development), while other behavior changes are more directly the result of instruction and reinforcement by socializing agents. We must now consider the relative contributions of specific instruction and of natural structural change to the preschool child's total cognitive development, in their implications for preschool programs.

Our viewpoint suggests that the speeding up of cognitive-structural change is extremely difficult to achieve but is likely to have long range general effects, since invariant sequence implies that advance in one step of development may lead to advance in the next step. In contrast, specific learnings are more easily achieved but are unlikely to have long range developmental effects. As an example, it is relatively easy to teach culturally disadvantaged preschool children to discriminate and name animals, but it is difficult to "teach" them conservation. Naming and discriminating unfamiliar animals may lead to some temporary rise in the Stanford-Binet in terms of vocabulary and picture-discrimination items. It is unlikely, however, in itself to lead to any future cognitive development which might lead to higher "general intelligence" some years later. By grade school, the children will have "spontaneously" picked up the labels and discriminations involved in any case. In contrast, "teaching" the children conservation might lead to an accelerated general development of arithmetical and classificatory operations.

We have contrasted structural change in natural concepts like conservation with specific information learning as objectives of preschool education. Many cognitive developments are neither one nor the other, however, but represent an organic mixture of structural and informational changes. These have been termed "scientific" as opposed to "spontaneous" concepts by Vygotsky (1962). The dream concept is a spontaneous concept, because while it requires some learning of cultural labels it is primarily organized around the child's direct experience of dreams and related experiences involving differentiation of the mental-subjective from the physical-objective. In contrast, the concept of electricity depends upon verbal instruction for its organization and development. The child's experience of lightning, electric motors, etc. does not naturally lead to the organization of a structural concept of electricity. The development of such "scientific" concepts is obviously a major goal of elementary and high school education. It is not clear, however, that preschool children are capable of developing scientific concepts, that is cognitive organizations based on symbolic definitions of new concepts as opposed to being able to "fill in" verbal labels with their own natural conceptual organization. It seems likely that the "natural science" and "social studies" information given the preschool child is assimilated into the organization represented by the child's natural concepts. Concepts of life, death, birth, economic and occupational role, sex role, and many others appear to develop naturally through Piaget-type stages, regardless of preschool "scientific" informational input (Kohlberg, 1966a, 1968b). While teaching may contribute specific information at the preschool level, it is unlikely to lead to much in the way of "scientific" conceptualization. The acquisition of information about physical and social objects and events (preschool "natural and social science") does not itself produce the school-age capacity for classificatory and causal thought required for understanding natural and social events. Insofar as preschool "science" is the teaching of specific information without new cognitive organization, it seems somewhat similar to vocabulary teaching, an area of learning by children which does not require specific programed teaching by adults.

The most obvious example of mixed or "scientific" conceptual structure relevant to preschool are mathematical and arithmetic concepts. Piaget's theory stresses almost exclusively the natural components of number development "logical and arithmetical operations therefor constitute a single system that is psychologically natural, the second resulting from generalization and fusion of the first" (Piaget, 1952, p. viii). According to Piaget's theory, arithmetical operations (addition, multiplication, etc.) correspond to more general operations of thought which are internalizations of the child's actions upon concrete operations in the external world. In the field of arithmetic, operations presuppose (and lead to) conservation of number, that is, the invariance of number through all changes in spatial arrangement, etc. These operations, according to Piaget, are developing at around the same age (6 to 7) at which arithmetic is commonly taught, and the teaching of most phases of arithmetic depends upon the natural development of the cognitive structures of concrete operations and of conservation. The findings on the development and teaching of number conservation previously discussed as well as findings of natural sequence in arithmetical development (Dodwell, 1968; Kofsky, 1968; Wohlwill, 1968) related to sequence in the development of classification suggest that Piaget's view of the natural developmental base of arithmetic learning appears to be largely correct. Insofar as this view is correct, it suggests that the early teaching of arithmetic will lead only to rote learning of habits with no conceptual base.

An example of an opposed point of view is that of the "new math" curriculum, which, like Piaget, stresses understanding rather than the rote learning of habits, but which structures arithmetic teaching in logical sequences in an artificial symbolic language. Bereiter and Engelmann have adapted this approach to the preschool level, stating that "the extent to which arithmetic and everyday language share assumptions is the extent to which arithmetic can be taught as a foreign language" (1966, p. 123). While the cognitive-developmental approach agrees that linguistic-grammatical development reflects a process of developmental transformations of structure reminiscent of thought development, it stresses that the actual structural developments involved are quite different, as indicated by the fact that grammatical development is relatively complete in middle-class children at an age (4) at which they are not yet capable of concrete operational thought. Accordingly, the Piagetian is disposed to be skeptical of claims of teaching arithmetical understanding to children below the age (6 to 7) of concrete operations.

With specific regard to the Bereiter and Engelmann program, it is important to note that it has been successful in bringing preschool children to first-grade level according to the standards of arithmetic achievement tests (Bereiter, 1967). However, first-grade scores on arithmetic achievement tests can be readily achieved by rote knowledge of counting and very simply rote knowledge of addition and subtraction. Such scores can be achieved without the least genuine capacity to order quantitative relations. As an example, in our studies of conservation we ask children to pick the "more candy" for themselves, six pieces in a long row as opposed to seven pieces in a short row. Some preschool children count each row correctly but are unable to answer "Which is more, six or seven?" Others respond to the verbal question of "more" correctly, that is, they say seven is more than six, but when asked to pick the "more candy" for themselves pick the long row with six candies. Unsystematic observation by the writer indicated that some children in the Bereiter program made both the previous errors, although they had learned verbal series such as "six plus two equal eight," or "four plus zero equal four." It is difficult to know what such verbal learning indicates in the way of arithmetical thought in the absence of the underlying concrete operations which are presumably involved.

While the early teaching of arithmetic encounters the block of a lack of development of the concrete operational base required for mathematical understanding, it is not clear that it is useless for the child's later cognitive development in the sense in which specific vocabulary teaching of a random set of words may be said to be useless. It is obvious that some counting (and adding and subtracting) experiences are a prerequisite to arithemetical operations. It is also obvious that detailed skill in use of arithmetical operations requires the information and skill teaching customarily given in elementary school after the "natural" concrete operational base of arithmetic has already developed. It seems likely that the child may emerge from an early arithmetic program with a sense of interest and competence with numbers and with an ability to attend to arithmetic instruction, which allows him to retain his "headstart" throughout elementary school arithmetic programs. It should be noted, however, that such long-range effects of an early arithmetic program might be "artificial," in that they are based on a competitive advantage of the child who has had such a program. Such a finding could occur, and yet exposure of all children to preschool programs might lead to the same average performance at a later age as occurred without early instruction.

In any case, it is clear that mathematical learning is the learning of a set of concepts and skills with an extremely important natural base. This is reflected in the Piagetian elementary school math curriculum of Dienes (1963, 1965) and Lovell (1966) and partially in the Montessori math curriculum (Kohlberg, 1968a). The extent to which a mathematics curriculum which recognizes this natural base should orient to the preschool period is not at all clear.

So far we have discussed the issue of earlier teaching of portions of the elementary school curriculum involving logical, mathematical, and scientific concepts. Other portions of the elementary school curriculum, however, do not appear to be necessarily dependent upon the cognitive-structural changes typically occurring at ages 4 to 6. Learning the mechanics of reading and writing need not depend heavily on the development of new levels of cognitive structure (categories of relation), although it may depend on the development of perceptual structure (Elkind, 1967a). Compared to the cognitive-structural transformations required for development of spoken language at age 2 or 3, the cognitive-structural requirements in tying together spoken and written signs seems modest. It is true that conventional methods of teaching reading ordinarily require considerable cognitive-structural capacity, just as they require considerable psychomotor maturity. It appears, however, that methods of teaching reading and writing can shortcut many requirements of both visuo-motor coordination and of cognitive-conceptual structurings and promote early learning on a simple discrimination-and-association basis. This is essentially what Moore (1968) has succeeded in doing with a number of preschool children. Moore's electric typewriter method bypasses both maturing motor skills (e.g., those involved in handwriting) and cognitive structurings by focusing on elementary active phonic sound-sight associations and the further association of these schemata into words.

Given the possibility of early teaching of reading and writing, is it desirable? Here it appears that the considerations suggested by Durkin

(1965) are eminently sound. The major reason for such a program is that usually if a skill can be easily learned earlier it is more enjoyable for the child to learn it early. A good deal of learning to read and write in the elementary school is a tedious task for the 6- to 8-year-old, requiring drill, repetition, self-correction, and considerable insecurity in comparing the child's own performance with that of other children in the classroom. Because reading and writing (especially reading) are relatively low-level sensorimotor skills, there is nothing in the cognitive structure of the reading task which involves any high challenge to the older child. In contrast, the identification of letters and words (as well as repetitive pounding of Moore's typewriters) may be challenging fun for younger children. Many preschool children and kindergarten children have considerable desire for learning "big-kid" or adult skills such as reading, and find school a much more interesting place if there is opportunity for such learning. Thus, regardless of its effect on later abilities, the interest principle suggests that there is something to be gained by optional, relaxed, and well-thought-out programs of early reading.

It is important to recognize that the basic value to an approach like Moore's does not derive from the principle that earlier learning leads to greater general cognitive development but derives from the principle of optimal developmental match between the challenge of a task and the child's skills and interests.[2]

The second reason for an early reading program is, of course, to free the child's time in elementary school for cognitively more valuable activities than the mastery of the mechanics of reading and writing. This reason, of course, presupposes massive changes in the elementary schools. As long as the child goes to public schools in which the teaching of reading and writing are the primary content of the first three grades, early reading programs tend to leave the child doomed to boredom. Given such a change, however, the child would enter first or second grade not only with reading skills but with the cognitive capacity to make use of this skill, since the normal middle-class 6-year-old child is able to enjoy story or informational reading if he has the sensorimotor skills to do it.

While various forms of early stimulation and learning have value, then, they do not justify teaching things earlier that will come later with less effort, whether these be the standard school skills or whether they be intelligence or mental age type tasks as such. The cognitive-developmental approach agrees

---

[2] This same principle, suggesting that novel techniques may allow early learning of reading to be more enjoyable than later learning, also suggests that conventional methods of teaching reading might be better commenced at a later age than usual with the culturally disadvantaged. The contrast between the interest and the rate of learning of culturally disadvantaged adults in literacy programs and of disadvantaged children in school suggests thinking of such a possibility.

with maturationism in viewing the preschool period as one in which cognitive development is not sufficiently advanced for the traditional forms of intellectual instruction. The approach sees the preschool period as one in which the child has a qualitatively different mode of thought and orientation to the world than the older child, one in which he is prelogical, preintellectual or not oriented to external truth values. Cognitive-developmental theories and findings suggest that certain shifts in cognitive functioning occur around the ages of 5 or 6 which justify the traditional practice of starting formal intellectual training at about age 6. From this point of view, school starts at age 6, because it is at about that age that children attain the "concrete operations" which are necessary for so much of elementary school learning and thinking.[3] In a sense, these facts are especially limiting for early education for the disadvantaged. As discussed earlier, presumably because of generalized deficits in organized physical and social stimulation, disadvantaged children tend to be retarded in cognitive-structural development as much or more than they are in Binet-test "verbal" performance. For this and other reasons, it is even less possible to use traditional intellectual instruction techniques with disadvantaged preschool children than it is with middle-class preschool children. The notion that academic intellectual instruction can remedy the cognitive-structural retardation of culturally disadvantaged children, then, has little plausibility. Thus, the objectives of preschool programs for the disadvantaged must be phrased in other terms.

IV. PRESCHOOL CURRICULUM: LANGUAGE STIMULATION

The most common definition of preschool cognitive objectives has been in terms of language abilities or aptitudes. This interest in preschool language stimulation has arisen largely because of the obvious linguistic deficiencies of culturally disadvantaged children. Most persons focusing on preschool language stimulation have assumed that advances in language will cause advances in cognition. There is no direct experimental demonstration of this assumption, nor is there as yet any evidence that language-focused preschool programs are of any greater value than any other preschool programs in leading to improved cognitive functioning. The assumption, however, follows from so many different points of view that it seems extremely plausible.

---

[3] It should be noted that the view that age 5 to 7 is a watershed in cognitive development is one which is not contingent upon Piaget's particular description of this watershed in terms of "concrete operations." White (1965) has summarized a wide range of basic shifts occurring in the years 5 to 7 in areas of perception, discrimination, transposition and probability learning, and concept formation. All may be loosely characterized as shifts from associative to cognitive-conceptual modes of functioning. The attainment of Piaget's conservations, on its face a rather minor cognitive achievement, is found to correlate with a quite wide variety of attainments in the area of abstract-conceptual thought.

One source of this hypothesis is S-R verbal mediation theory, which points to the role of implicit verbal labeling in processes of discrimination learning, concept attainment, and transposition learning (Berlyne, 1965; Reese, 1962; White, 1963). As Flavell and others have pointed out, the notion of verbal mediation must be broken down into (a) possession of the verbal sign, (b) spontaneous production of the verbal sign in a cognitive task, and (c) effective usage of the produced sign to mediate the task. A multiplicity of evidence suggests that mere knowledge of verbal labels does not in itself lead to effective verbal mediation in cognitive tasks. This evidence supports cognitive-developmental distinctions between knowledge of verbal labels (vocabulary) and their cognitive use in concept attainment or classification tasks. As an example, preschool children when asked to "put together the dolls that go together" characteristically do not separately group together all the boy dolls and all the girl dolls (categorical sorting) but rather put together a boy and a girl "because they play together" (relational sorting). By age 5 or 6 almost all normal children make such categorical sorts (Kohlberg, 1963; Stodolsky, 1965). The failure of preschool children to make use of categorical concepts is not directly due to ignorance of verbal labels, then, since the preschool children are able to group the male dolls together if explicitly told to do so. Instead it seems to be related to various Piaget concrete operations, as evidenced by the fact that categorical sorting forms a scale point in a sequence of Piaget operations (Kofsky, 1968; Kohlberg, 1963).

Flavell, Beach, and Chinsky (1966) have proposed that young children's cognitive deficits in many tasks are due to a generalized failure of children to spontaneously produce verbal signs in cognitive tasks, even though these signs are in their repertoire. Evidence for this hypothesis from studies by Flavell, Kohlberg, Luria, Vygotsky, and others is reviewed in Kohlberg, Yaeger, and Hjertholm (1968). The studies indicate that:

1. Older children engage in more private or self-directed speech on tasks than do younger children.

2. Bright young children engage in more private speech in tasks than do average young children.

3. Middle-class children use more private speech than do culturally disadvantaged children.

4. Children who use self-directed speech on some tasks do better than those who do not.

5. An experimental condition requesting self-directed speech leads to more self-directed speech and consequent improvement in performance.

6. Experimental prompting of self-directed speech does not, however, engender continued use of self-directed speech in situations where no prompt-

ing occurs. Spontaneous use of self-directed speech in memory tasks appears to be a relatively stable characteristic among children of a given age.

While these studies clearly indicate relations between private speech performance and cognitive functioning, the exact causal direction of this relation is not clear. The fact that older, brighter, and more culturally advantaged children engage in more private speech may indicate that cognitive advance is the cause rather than the effect of private speech production. While the studies of Flavell and his colleagues indicate improved performance after prompting of private speech, they also indicate improved performance if pointing (to the self) rather than talking (to the self) is experimentally prompted. These results are understandable because the task used was a serial memory rather than a cognitive-inferential task.

The findings, then, suggest that cognitive mediation requires something more than the possession and spontaneous production of verbal signs, though these latter may be necessary or facilitating conditions for the former. One line of thought has suggested that the structural-grammatical development of speech (rather than the possession and production of verbal labels) is largely responsible for the massive development of cognitive mediation in the preschool and early school years. This line of thought has been particularly influenced by Bernstein's (1961) characterization of social class differences in linguistic codes. In Bernstein's view, in addition to a "restricted code" shared by both classes, the middle class makes use of an "elaborated code" having distinctive stylistic and syntactical features as well as more cognitively abstract referential functions. The absence of exposure to this code in the lower class and the disadvantaged is believed to be influential in causing the poorer tested performance of the lower class in a number of intellectual tasks.[4]

This conception has been particularly influential in the approaches to early education of the culturally disadvantaged, elaborated by Bereiter and Englemann (1966), Deutsch (1965), and Hess and Shipman (1965). In particular, the Bereiter and Englemann program focuses upon teaching the grammatical

---

[4] With regard to class differences in language, Schatzman and Strauss (1955) describe social class differences in language in terms similar to Bernstein's, but present a Piagetian view that failure to use an elaborated code in impersonal situations represents a certain "egocentricity" of perspective, i.e., a restriction of role-taking of the perspective of the listener and a failure to differentiate it from that of the self or other intimates. Following Mead (1934) they hold that the greater opportunities for participation and role-taking available to the middle class lead to a broader or more generalized perspective in communication. From this point of view the language form itself is less a directly transmitted subcultural entity than it is a reflection of a social perspective or cognitive orientation, and the educational problem is not to teach a syntactic code but to create opportunities for communication and role-taking at the level which will stimulate the development of a generalized perspective.

speech of the "elaborated code" as a "second language" to the culturally disadvantaged. (In this connection it may be pointed out that a goal of teaching standard English as a second language may best be achieved by exposing disadvantaged children to middle-class models in an integrated program [Kohlberg, 1967]).

While Bernstein's portrayal of parallels between cognitive and grammatical-stylistic aspects of language is intuitively convincing, the Piaget viewpoint suggests a number of qualifications as to the notion that the linguistic-grammatical aspects of the "elaborated code" are primary and determinative of the cognitive orientations involved. In Piaget's (1967, p. 98) view, "language is only a particular form of the symbolic function and as the individual symbol is simpler than the collective sign, it is permissible to conclude that thought precedes language and that language confines itself to transforming thought by helping it attain its forms of equilibrium by means of a more advanced schematization and a more mobile abstraction. . . . The structures that characterize thought have their roots in action and in sensori-motor mechanisms deeper than linguistics. The more the structures of thought are refined, the more language is necessary for the achievement of this elaboration. Language is thus a necessary but not sufficient condition for the construction of logical operations. Language and thought are linked in a genetic circle where each necessarily leans on the other in interdependent formation. In the last analysis, both depend on intelligence itself, which antedates language and is independent of it."

Research support for Piaget's view comes from a recent study by Sinclair (1967). Sinclair found a marked association between success on conservation tasks and certain modes of language. Training increasing usage of these language modes, did not, however, lead to much greater success on the conservation tasks. With regard to the "concrete operations" which may be considered the primary structural achievement in the preschool beginning school period, we have noted that these develop without complex structural language in the deaf but seem markedly retarded in the blind. We also noted that the major features of grammatical language typically develop some years before "logical" concrete operational thought, so that development of linguistic structure is not sufficient for the development of cognitive structure. All these findings suggest that particular linguistic developments are not necessary conditions for cognitive-structural development.

The Piagetian view, than, holds that neither increased verbal labeling nor increased grammatical structuring are causally responsible for the basic cognitive developments of the later preschool years. It does hold that language may aid in "transforming thought by helping it attain its forms of equilibrium by a more advanced schematization and a more mobile abstraction." One way in which this may occur is suggested by Luria (1961) and

Vygotsky (1962). Vygotsky believes that thought and speech have independent ontogenetic roots, that they "fuse" early in development and that the subsequent fate of thought is determined by the fact that thought in the older child (over 5 or 7) is a structure of interiorized speech. As we had noted, his suggestion that private speech is a way station between overt speech and interiorized inferential thought has received considerable support (Kohlberg, Yaeger, and Hjertholm, 1968). From this point of view, the shift from associative to conceptual modes in the years 4 to 7 can be seen as the result of the interiorization of language occurring in this period (Kohlberg, 1963). We cited earlier the fact that possession of verbal labels did not in itself lead the preschool child to use categorical class concepts. In Vygotsky's view however, this conceptual failure of the preschool child may be due to his failure to use linguistic labels in an interiorized form. When the preschool child sorts objects, verbal labels seem to be "outside" the child as one of many perceptual attributes of the object, for example, the doll has a red necktie, it is big, and it is also called a boy. The label "boy" is not, however, an internal response subsuming all other external characteristics of the doll. For the older child, "boy" represents not one of many perceptual attributes of the doll but something over and above these individual attributes used to organize them. This may be because an internal verbal mediator organizes the concept, rather than acting as an external stimulus. In a similar spirit, Bruner et al. (1966) have suggested that the development of Piagetian conservation is related to the internalization of speech which frees the child from dominance by the immediate perceptual aspects of the situation. The Vygotsky analysis of internalization just discussed comes close to Piaget's view of concrete operations as the internalization of action. Whether "linguistic internalization" or "internalization of action" is stressed, however, it is clear that the stimulation of cognitive development involves something much more refined than the focus upon verbal labeling and grammar characterizing current preschool language-stimulation programs.

To summarize, cognitive-developmental theorists like Piaget and Vygotsky are in broad agreement as to the parallel and interdependent nature of the development of thought and speech. This parallelism of language and thought is most grossly reflected in the high correlations between measures of verbal development or knowledge and cognitive measures (like the Raven matrixes) which do not obviously depend upon verbal development. These correlations need not be interpreted as indicating that language development is the causal foundation of cognitive development, however. A more plausible interpretation is that the more basic cognitive abilities contributing to nonverbal tasks also contribute to language achievements (and, to some extent, vice versa).

The fact that the preschoolers' cognitive ability and development is correlated with vocabulary scores does not mean that intervention to increase vocabulary will increase cognitive ability or development. A child's success in defining "envelope" correlates with general performance on the Stanford-Binet, but teaching him the word "envelope" will not increase his cognitive functioning. If this is true for a single word, it is true also for a dozen or a hundred. Theories such as Vygotsky's suggest sensitive points at which language development and cognitive development intersect. As these points come to be studied, we will probably find ways in which language stimulation can serve cognitive development. For the present, however, it must be stressed that language achievements should not be confused with general cognitive development. It is evident that the education of language achievement may have definite values apart from its effect upon general cognitive development, but it is unfortunate if educational thought is based upon a theoretical confusion between the two.

V. PRESCHOOL AS A CRITICAL PERIOD IN THE DEVELOPMENT OF PSYCHOMETRIC GENERAL INTELLIGENCE

We have suggested that age-linked structural change in the preschool period is necessary before the child is open to many forms of cognitive training. This does not imply a biological critical period, however. As we suggested earlier, the most extreme "critical period" notions of the importance of preschool cognitive stimulation rest as much upon a theory of maturational unfolding as do notions that early stimulation is unnecessary for later development because intelligence is innate.[5] This is because critical period concepts imply a biologically timed unfolding of a certain type of behavior, with a corresponding biologically based period of sensitivity to, or need for, normal supporting stimulation.

Although Hunt's (1961, 1964) use of Piaget in developing his own views sometimes suggests it, Piaget's theory does not imply critical periods in intellectual development, insofar as the critical period concept implies (a) sensitivity to stimulation at a definite chronological time span, (b) greater sensitivity to stimulation at earlier than at later periods of development, or (c) irreversibility of the effects of early stimulus deprivation. The Piaget position holds that there are developmental phases of sensitivity, but these are tied to the child's behavioral level, not to chronological age. The position does hold that there are special sensitivities to stimulation at definite stages of development, and it implies that the effectiveness of stimulation is contingent upon its match

---

[5] While associationistic learning theorists often stress the importance of early learning, they provide little rationale for the notion that early learnings (or learning deficits) are critical or irreversible. While Hebb (1949, 1955) has distinguished between primary (irreversible and general) learning and secondary learning, this distinction has never been incorporated into a general learning theory nor operationalized in human research.

with a given level of development. The child's perception of the world is determined by his stage of cognitive organization, and a stimulus is only a stimulus if it can match or be assimilated to already developed schemata. This was illustrated by the experimental work on training conservation cited earlier. "Teaching" of conservation was only found to be effective in children close in chronological mental age to the normal age of spontaneous attainment of conservation.

Not only does the position hold that stimulation is only effective under conditions of match but it holds experience at a given period of appropriate match is sufficient for development of a specific structure and does not require continual supplementation throughout life. Stages imply that cognitive structures are irreversible, that is, they are not subject to regression or extinction in the absence of the stimulation which originally facilitated their formation. (In this way Smedslund [1961a] was able to experimentally differentiate the cognitive-structural development of conservation from its "conditioned" imitations.)

While the cognitive-developmental position implies the developmental phase specificity and irreversibility of effective stimulation, it does not imply that such stimulation must occur at a given point in time. Sensitivities to a stimuli are not determined by a chronological age or a maturational period but by the actual level of the child's cognitive structures, so that effectiveness of stimulation for conservation involves a match to mental, not chronological, maturity. (It might even be argued from the cognitive-developmental position that certain cognitive-enrichment programs should be timed later for culturally disadvantaged children because of cognitive retardation, rather than attempting to provide enrichment programs for these children at the age at which more advanced middle-class children are presumed to be receiving parallel stimulation.) The position does not imply that retarding stimulus deficits at an early time point are not reversible by compensating stimulation at a later time point. The stimulation necessary for normal development from one stage to the next should be effective in moving a retarded child to the next stage, even if the child has chronologically missed the time at which normal children received this stimulation.

Cognitive stages, then, do not imply chronologically determined and irreversible sensitive periods for stimulation. They also do not imply that earlier levels of development are generally more sensitive to critical stimulation than are later periods. Piaget's theory suggests that the child's sensitivity to environmental stimulation tends to increase rather than to decrease with development. Each level of cognitive development represents the capacity to be stimulated by, or to experience, something new. The child can only be stimulated by events or stimuli which he can partly assimilate, that is, fit into his already existing cognitive structures or schemata. The newborn baby is simply not sensitive to most of the events in the world around him. According to Piaget (cf. Hunt, 1961), the infant at first (Stage 1) responds only to those stimuli in the outside world which are directly related to his own activities, which fit innate reflexes. He next (Stage 2) responds to stimulus events which are associated with these reflexes, but only if he "perceives" them as caused by, or associated with, his own activity. Still later (Stage 4) he becomes interested in new events which he does not feel that he has directly caused, and, finally (Stage 5), he directly seeks to produce novel events. There is, then, a progression of stimulation to which the child becomes sensitive and which is required at succeeding levels of development. Even in a culturally deprived home, the kind of minimal simple stimulation that the infant requires is probably present, the kind of stimulation which will allow the exercise of sensorimotor schemata of one sort or another. As the child gets older and develops further he requires successively more complicated forms of stimulation so that the effects of stimulus deprivation would be expected to become more critical as the child develops further and further.

The claim that early stimulus deprivation leads to irreversible cognitive deficit must be viewed with great caution. As increasingly careful work has been done in the effects of early deprivation in infants, the impressionistic conclusions of Spitz and Bowlby as to massive irreversible cognitive and developmental retardation due to maternal and stimulus deprivation in infancy have come increasingly under question (Robinson, 1968; Yarrow, 1964). A number of studies (Dennis & Najarian, 1957; Rheingold & Bayley, 1965) indicate that some observed retardation due to infant institutional deprivation, and some observed compensation by infant enrichment programs, wash out in later development.

The major factual considerations leading to the notion of a preschool critical period in cognition derive from neither animal nor institutionalization studies. The real basis for stressing preschool cognitive programs comes from the belated recognition by educators that differences in the child's educational achievement are primarily due to the characteristics of the child and of his home environment rather than to the child's elementary schooling as such. This point has been ably documented by Bloom (1964). According to Bloom, longitudinal studies indicate that about 50 per cent of the child's final intelligence and about 33 per cent of his performance on school achievement tests is predictable from measures of his intelligence before he enters school. While the fact that later achievement is quite predictable from intelligence test functioning at school entrance is unquestionable, the implication that the preschool era is a "critical period" for the environmental stimulation of intellectual development and that raising the IQ in this period is a practical and feasible goal for preschool programs is questionable.

The critical-period interpretation of test stabilization data starts from the finding that tests administered in the first year of life do not predict adult intelligence scores, that tests administered at school entrance sizably do predict these scores, and that there is only a small increase in predictability found if tests are administered later than school entrance. The critical-period interpretation of this large increase in predictability from age 1 to age 6 is due to the fact that environmental stimulation has "fixed" intellectual growth and functioning during this period. This interpretation, as elaborated by Bloom (1964), is based on two assumptions. The first is that the degree of predictability from a childhood test to an adult ability test is a function of the proportion of the pool of adult knowledge and skills tested which has developed at the childhood age. The second assumption is that the filling in of the ability pool between the two time points is largely a function of differential environment. Neither assumption seems tenable in light of other known findings concerning intelligence. The stability of intelligence tests after age 6 is not necessarily due to the completion of development at age 6 of half the elements composing adult ability but may be due to the continuing stable influence of both heredity and environment after this age. With regard to stabilization due to the environment, it should be recognized that the stimulation potential of home and neighborhood are more or less constant throughout childhood. The fact that low IQ of 6-year-olds from culturally deprived homes predicts to low IQ in adolescence does not necessarily indicate that the effect of environment on adult intelligence occurred primarily in the preschool years. The deprivation of the environment is fairly constant and continues to operate throughout the childhood years and accordingly contributes to the predictability of the preschool IQ to later intelligence.

With regard to stabilization due to heredity, there is also no reason to assume that this factor is completely manifest in early infancy or in the preschool years.

The major reason the hereditary contribution to stability of intelligence scores has been questioned recently is that infant tests do not predict to adult status, and it has been assumed that a hereditary factor should be manifested at birth. In fact, however, baby tests simply do not measure the same dispositions as do later intelligence tests, whether these dispositions be viewed as due to heredity or to environment. Baby tests were not constructed to measure cognition (i.e., eduction of relations and categories) but to record the age of appearance of sensory and motor responses.[6] Factor analytic studies indicate very little overlap between the content of baby tests and the content of intelligence tests, whereas they indicate something like a general cognitive factor in intelligence tests given after age 4.

[6] This assumption is not clearly implausible, however, for the cognitive baby tests patterned after Piaget's baby observations, developed by Uzgiris and Hunt (1964) and by this writer (Kohlberg, 1961).

Accordingly, the hereditary components of adult intelligence are not manifested in baby tests, which represent hereditary (and environmental) factors quite different than those influencing school-age or adult intelligence test functioning. Because of this, much of the difference between the adult predictive power of infant tests and of school entrance tests is due to the fact that only the latter tap the hereditary contribution to adult intellectual status. This is demonstrated by the studies of Skodak, Skeels, and Honzik, reviewed by Jones (1954), which indicate a regular rise up until age 5 in the correlations between the IQ of children in foster homes and the education of their real mothers; this almost exactly parallels the rise in infant-mother correlations found for home-reared children. These correlations, then, cannot be attributed to stimulation by the real parents themselves. Rather, they indicate that the cognitive abilities of the adults (reflected in educational status or test performance) represent hereditary factors, which influence later cognitive performance of their children and are quite different from the hereditary factors influencing baby test performance.

We have claimed that neither cognitive-developmental theory nor empirical findings support the notion that the preschool period is a specially open period for stimulating general intelligence or general cognitive development. These conclusions are strengthened by the rather disappointing findings concerning the actual effects of preschool cognitive stimulation upon performance on psychometric tests of general intelligence. Morrisett (1966) summarizes reviews of the literature (Fowler, 1968; Robinson, 1968) as well as unpublished work suggesting "that there is no compelling evidence for the long-term effectiveness of short-term educational intervention at the preschool level. Many preschool programs for disadvantaged children have shown that they make relatively large gains in intelligence test performance during the first year of the program; but this characteristic acceleration in intellectual growth is not always maintained during a second preschool year or when the children enter first grade." As one of many examples of such findings, we may cite a study of our own (Kohlberg, 1968a). An integrated Montessori program for Head-start children aged 3 and 4 led to a mean 14-point increase in Stanford-Binet IQ in the first 6 months. No significant further increase in IQ was found during the remaining $1\frac{1}{2}$ years in which the children were in the program. The initial IQ increases could not be considered actual increases in general cognitive-structural development, since they were not paralleled by any significant increases in performance upon Piaget cognitive-structural tasks. The primary cause of the IQ increase was an improvement in attention and rapport with adults. Increases in rated attention in the classroom (as well as in the test situation) were marked during the first 6 months, and individual improvement in rated attention correlated .63 with improvement in Stanford-Binet IQ's during this period. In addition to attention, verbalization showed a sharp initial spurt related to improvement on IQ performance. In summary, then, it appears that the IQ changes were more a result of changes in cognitive motivation than a change in cognitive capacity. These changes in turn had a ceiling rather than moving continuously upward, and the motivational changes themselves did not lead to a later increase in cognitive capacity because of increased general learning.

VI. PIAGET CONCEPTS AND MEASURES OF PRESCHOOL INTELLECTUAL GROWTH

In the preceding section, we concluded that studies using psychometric tests indicate a heavy hereditary determination of intelligence and suggest that the effects of programs of preschool stimulation upon intelligence are rather minor and transient. We must now consider Hunt's (1961) suggestion that these conclusions may be specific to the concepts and methods employed by psychometric tests and might be revised by work with the newer concepts of methods of studying intelligence developed by Piaget.

It is not surprising to find that psychometric tests include a core of performance due to general cognitive ability of a partially hereditary nature, when this core constituted the rationale for their construction. The rationale of the general intelligence test of Binet, Spearman, and Wechsler (Spearman, 1930) is that of measuring a fixed biological capacity, as is implied in the division of performance into "g" (general ability) and "s" (specific experience) factors. Experience factors are largely consigned to "specificity" rather than to general intelligence. This rationale led to the construction of tests designed to wash out experience effects, partly by providing novel tasks and partly by providing a random and heterogeneous sample of tasks. Such tests lead to a sum score in which individual differences in experience with specific tasks might be expected to balance out. Stated differently, the Binet-Spearman approach has avoided defining basic cognitive achievements except in highly general terms ("eduction of relations and correlates") applicable to any task. Any item or achievement is a good intelligence test item if it elicits individual differences relating to other ability items. The more the item fails to correlate generally with all other items the worse or the more "specific experience loaded" the item is assumed to be.

There can be no question that this approach has yielded longitudinally stable and situationally general measures, which predict to all sorts of good outcomes in personality adjustment and in general problem solving as well as in scholastic achievement. However, the Spearman-Binet-Wechsler approach is not the only approach to yielding longitudinally stable and situationally general measures of cognitive development. In contrast to the psychometric approach to intelligence, the Piaget approach attempts to specify the basic concepts or operations characterizing each developmental era. It does not range over a wide variety of developmental items in order to wash out specific experience effects and leave a general rate of learning or development factor. Instead, it attempts to theoretically define some general cognitive operations and restricts items to those which may elicit such operations.

In a sense, then, Piaget's definition of intelligence or intellectual development is an a priori theoretical one, and it is irrelevant to him whether or not it leads to measures of situationally general and longitudinally stable individual differences. However, it is obvious that cognitive age-development as defined by Piaget's conceptions and cognitive age-development as defined by the Binet sampling approach must have some relation to one another. In fact the correlations between summed scores on Piaget tests and Binet scores are in the .70's for children of a given age (Kohlberg, 1966b; DeVries, in preparation). These findings seem to accord with Piaget's view that psychometric tests of intelligence get at the same thing as his tests, but in less pure and conceptually understandable form (1947, p. 154):

> It is indisputable that these tests of mental age have on the whole lived up to what was expected of them: a rapid and convenient estimation of an individual's general level. But it is no less obvious that they simply measure a "yield," without reaching constructive operations themselves. As Pieron rightly pointed out, intelligence conceived in these terms is essentially a value-judgment applied to complex behavior. Inhelder was able to distinguish moronism from imbecility by the presence of concrete groupings and slight backwardness by an inability to reason formally. This is one of the first applications of a method which could be developed further for determining level of intelligence in general.

In this spirit, Pinard and Laurendeau (1964) have been developing a standardized method of assessing general intelligence or mental age with the Piaget procedures.

The writer's own view on this problem is somewhat different than that expressed by Piaget. My interpretation is that there is a hereditary general ability component of psychometric tests, a general "eduction of relations and correlates" or "rate of information-processing" factor, which contributes, along with other factors, to general cognitive-structural development as defined by Piaget. As I stressed earlier, the insistence of Piaget that *universal cognitive structures* are the result of interaction and are not pre-formed or maturational does not constitute a denial of the quantitative influence of heredity upon *individual differences in rate* of formation of these structures. It might be found that the rate at which experience was assimilated to create new cognitive structures was largely a function of genetic factors, and yet these structures would still be said to depend upon experiences as long as it was found that every child who developed the structures had had certain universal physical or social experiences.

While hereditary factors may enter into Piaget level, Piaget's theory also provides a definite rationale for the existence of item-general and longitudinally predictive differences in cognitive level based on differential amounts of general experience. The Piaget approach allows experiential effects to define general rather than specific differences in performance. General effects of experience are revealed in manner of handling a familiar object, specific effects in familiarity with the object itself. This focus is supported by the assessment of presence or absence of a level of thought or an intellectual operation, not assessment of speed and facility in its use. Piaget procedures treat the high school boy and Einstein as alike in possession of formal operations, though they differ greatly in their use. The generality of intellectual level in the Piaget view results from the fact that cognitive stages are structured wholes rather than from an innate rate factor. Intellectual performance is general because it rests on general operations which develop as total structures, not because it represents a general biological factor intersecting with specific experience or learnings (Smedslund, 1964).

In similar fashion, Piaget's theory may be used to account for the stability of intelligence without postulating an innate rate of growth factor. Longitudinal stability of cognitive level is implied by the existence of invariant sequences in cognitive development which has been found for many Piaget-type tasks (Sigel, 1964; Sigel & Hooper, 1968). Attainment of a given level of development implies successive attainment of all the preceding levels of development. Accordingly, relative cognitive maturity at a later age should be predictable from maturity at an earlier age without the assumption of an innate rate factor. If all children must go through an invariant sequence in cognitive development, children at a lower level at an earlier time point must go through more intervening stages and therefore will be relatively low at a later time point.

The writer and his colleagues (DeVries, in preparation; Kohlberg, 1963; Kohn, in preparation) have been engaged in research comparing psychometric and Piaget intellectual measures at ages 4 to 7 with regard to the following hypotheses derived from the framework just stated:

1. There should be a "general factor" among Piaget tests greater than that found among general psychometric items, but largely accounting for the general factor in the psychometric items.

2. Relative level on the Piaget tasks should be more longitudinally stable in the years 4 to 7 than would be expected from the stability of psychometric intelligence in this period.

3. Piaget items should depend more on general experience, and hence chronological age, than psychometric items. Accordingly, older average children should be more advanced on Piaget tasks than younger bright children matched for psychometric mental age.

4. Mere chronological aging should not, however, lead to greater development on Piaget items if the environment is very deprived. Culturally disadvantaged children, then, should show more retardation on nonverbal Piaget tasks than control children matched for psychometric mental age.

While much of the data from this research program has not yet been processed, some preliminary findings are available. While correlating with the Binet, Piaget tasks also hang together after Binet and other psychometric intellectual factors are removed. Presumably the intertask consistency of Piaget level represents a "general factor" independent of any innate rate factors entering into the Binet. The fact that chronological age correlates with the Piaget factor, with Binet mental age controlled, but that this correlation does not hold under conditions of cultural deprivation, gives additional support to the notion that the Piaget "factor" represents a general and longitudinally predictive residue of effects of experience upon cognitive development.

The logic and preliminary findings just mentioned suggest a number of reasons why Piaget measures might reflect general increments in cognitive development due to natural or educational experience better than do psychometric measures. In principle they resolve the paradox of the Binet, which almost forces us to view any educational increments as specific contents or as motivational sets not truly reflecting cognitive-structural development.[7] Insofar as Piaget measures of intelligence define general and sequential (longitudinally predictive) structural effects of general experience, they should be valuable in assessing the effects of various types of general cognitive-stimulation programs, whether or not these programs define accelerating Piagetian intellectual development as explicit objectives.

[7] This was our interpretation of Binet increments in the Montessori program. We claimed they were due to attentional and verbalization factors rather than to general or cognitive-structural development, since the changes were not reflected in increments in Piaget performance. The study also suggested that this was not due to any failure of the Piaget tasks to assess general cognitive level. It was found that Piaget tests were more stable than the Binet tests, i.e., they yielded test-retest reliabilities between a 2- and 4-month period in the 90's. It was also found that when a child was initially high on the Piaget tests and low on the Binet tests, he would increase markedly on the Binet test at the later period. In other words, the Piaget tasks were more situation-free measures of cognitive capacity. Using nonverbal techniques (choice of lengths of gum, glasses of Coca Cola) to indicate possession of the conservation concept, the Piaget tasks elicited evidence of cognitive maturity masked by distractibility or shyness in the Binet situation. The Piaget tests, then, seemed to eliminate some "noncognitive" situational and verbal factors due to experience.

The possibility that Piagetian measures will detect some general and stable effects of preschool cognitive-stimulation programs more clearly than do psychometric measures does not, however, change the fundamental caution about preschool stimulation of general intelligence or cognitive development reflected in the previous section. The findings on acceleration of Piaget concrete operations indicate that such acceleration is neither easy nor does it typically generalize, either to other Piaget tasks or to Binet mental age tasks. With regard to the critical-period issue, it also does not appear that a wave of longitudinal, twin, and experimental studies using Piagetian measures would lead to radically different conclusions than those of the psychometric studies as to the role of heredity and of preschool experience upon long-range intellectual development. The fact that Piagetian and psychometric measures correlate as well as they do seems to preclude this possibility.

VII. CONCLUSIONS AS TO PRESCHOOL COGNITIVE OBJECTIVES

This paper has elaborated a view of preschool intellectual development as one of sequential structural change equipotentially responsive to a variety of specific types of experience but reflecting differences in the effects of general amount and continuity of organized experiences in the preschool age range. I have argued that specific types of preschool academic and linguistic training, even if immediately successful, are unlikely to have long-run general beneficial effects and that programs directed toward raising general psychometric intelligence are unlikely to have marked success. I have claimed that a Piagetian conception of methods of accelerating intellectual development (employing cognitive conflict, match, and sequential ordering of experience), a Piagetian focus upon basic intellectual operations, and a Piagetian procedure of assessment of general intellectual development might generate somewhat more general and long-range cognitive effects than would other approaches.

Basically, however, the Piaget approach does not generate great optimism as to the possibility of preschool acceleration of cognitive development (or of compensation for its retardation) nor does it lead to a rationale in which such acceleration (or compensation) is especially critical during the preschool years.

The cognitive-developmental approach suggests both modesty in the hopes of creators of preschool stimulation programs and modesty in the claims that one program of stimulation will differ markedly from another in its general impact upon the child. Cognitive-developmental theory, itself, is broadly compatible with a diversity of specific cognitive-stimulation programs, ranging from Moore to Montessori, insofar as all these programs define their cognitive goals developmentally and center on relatively active and self-selective forms of cognitive stimulation for the child (Kohlberg, 1968a). The compatibility of the cognitive-developmental view with a variety of programs is based first on its definition of cognitive advance in terms of natural lines of development rather than in terms of specifically taught "content." Second, this compatibility is based upon a concern with general forms of active experience, in terms of which a variety of specific types of stimulation are more or less functionally equivalent for cognitive development.

More generally, cognitive-developmental theory does less to suggest or support radical new preschool cognitive stimulation programs than it does to clarify the child-centered developmental approach to education expressed in its broadest form by John Dewey. The approach departs more from traditional child development concerns in providing a systematic analysis of the cognitive-structural and cognitive-interest implications of the play, aesthetic, constructive, and social activities which form the heart of the preschool than in suggesting narrowly "cognitive" activities in the preschool. Recent American Piagetian research on the preschool child has focused almost exclusively on children's quantitative and logical classificatory concepts, as indicated by Sigel and Hooper's (1968) anthology. It should be recalled, however, that Piaget and his followers have systematically studied the development of preschool children's play, their conversations with one another, their conceptions of life, of death, of reality, of sexual identity, of good and evil. The implications of these and other themes for the broader definition of preschool objectives are taken up elsewhere (Kohlberg & Lesser, in preparation).

References

Ames, L. B. The sequential patterning of prone progression in the human infant. *Genetic Psychology Monograph,* 1937, **19,** 409–460.

Baldwin, A. Cognitive theory and socialization. In D. Goslin (Ed.), *Handbook of socialization.* New York: Rand McNally, 1968.

Baldwin, J. M. *Thoughts and things or genetic logic.* Vol. 3. New York: Macmillan, 1906–1915.

Bereiter, C. Progress report on teaching the disadvantaged. Urbana, Ill.: Institute for Research on Exceptional Children, 1967, mimeographed.

Bereiter, C., & Engelmann, S. *Teaching disadvantaged children in the preschool.* Englewood Cliffs, N.J.: Prentice-Hall, 1966.

Berlyne, D. *Conflict, arousal and curiosity.* New York: McGraw-Hill, 1961.

Berlyne, D. *Structure and direction in thinking.* New York: Wiley, 1965.

Bernstein, B. Social class and linguistic development: a theory of social learning. In A. Halsey, J. Floud, & C. Anderson (Eds.), *Education, economy, and society.* New York: Free Press, 1961.

Bloom, B. *Stability and change in human characteristics.* New York: Wiley, 1964.

Bruner, J. *The process of education.* Cambridge, Mass.: Harvard University Press, 1960.

Bruner, J. *Toward a theory of instruction.* Cambridge, Mass.: Harvard University Press, 1966.

Bruner, J., Olver, R., & Greenfield, P. *Studies in cognitive growth.* New York: Wiley, 1966.

Dennis, W., & Najarian. Infant development under environmental handicap. *Psychological Monographs*, 1957, **71**, (7, Whole No. 436).

Deutsch, M. The role of social class in language development and cognition. *American Journal of Orthopsychiatry*, 1965, **35**, 78–88.

DeVries, R. Performance of bright, average, and retarded children on Piagetian concrete operation tasks. Unpublished monograph, University of Chicago, Early Educational Research Center, in preparation.

Dewey, J. *Interest and effort in education.* Boston: Houghton Mifflin, 1913.

Dewey, J. Experience and conduct. In C. Murchison (Ed.), *Psychologies of 1930.* Worcester, Mass.: Clark University Press, 1930.

Dewey, J. *Experience and Education.* New York: Collier, 1963 (originally written in 1938).

Dewey, J. In R. Archambault (Ed.), *Dewey on education, a selection.* New York: Modern Library, 1965.

Dienes, Z. P. *An experimental study of mathematics.* London: Hutchinson, 1963.

Dienes, Z. P. *Modern mathematics for young children.* Harlow, England: Educational Supply Association, 1965.

Dodwell, C. Development of number concepts. In I. Sigel & F. Hooper (Eds.), *Logical thinking in children.* New York: Holt, Rinehart & Winston, 1968.

Durkin, D. Some issues in early reading. Unpublished paper, University of Illinois, Urbana, 1965.

Elkind, D. Reading, logic and perception. In J. Hellmuth (Ed.), *Educational therapy.* Vol. 2. Washington, D.C.: Special Child Publication, 1967. (a)

Elkind, D. Piaget and Montessori. *Harvard Educational Review*, 1967, **37**, No. 4. (b)

Flavell, J. *The developmental psychology of Jean Piaget.* New York: Van Nostrand, 1963.

Flavell, J., Beach, D., & Chinsky, J. Spontaneous verbal rehearsal in a memory task as a function of age. *Child Development*, 1966, **37**, 283–299.

Fowler, W. The early stimulation of cognitive development. In R. Hess &

R. Bear (Eds.), *Preschool education: Theory, research and action.* Chicago: Aldine, 1968.

Furth, H. *Thinking without language; psychological implications of deafness.* New York: Free Press, 1966.

Gelman, R. Conservation, attention and discrimination. Unpublished doctoral dissertation, University of California, Los Angeles, 1967.

Gesell, A. The ontogenesis of infant behavior. In L. Carmichael (Ed.), *Manual of child psychology.* New York: Wiley, 1954.

Goodnow, J., & Bethon, G. Piaget's tasks: The effects of schooling and intelligence. *Child Development,* 1966, **37,** 573–582.

Green, B. A method of scalogram analysis using summary statistics. *Psychometrika,* 1956, **21,** 79–83.

Greenfield, P. On culture and conservation. In J. Bruner et al. *Studies in cognitive growth.* New York: Wiley, 1966.

Gruen, G. E. Experience affecting the development of number conservation in children. In I. Sigel & F. Hooper (Eds.), *Logical thinking in children: Research based on Piaget's theory.* New York: Holt, Rinehart & Winston, 1968.

Guttman, L. The basis for scalogram analysis. In S. A. Stouffer et al. *Measurement and prediction.* Princeton, N.J.: Princeton University Press, 1954.

Hebb, D. *Organization of behavior.* New York: Wiley, 1949.

Hebb, D. The mammal and his environment. *American Journal of Psychiatry,* 1955, **111,** 1–9.

Hess, R., & Shipman, V. Early experience and the socialization of cognitive modes in children. *Child Development,* 1965, **36,** 869–886.

Hooper, F. Piagetian research and education. In I. Sigel & F. Hooper (Eds.), *Logical thinking in children: research based on Piaget's Theory.* New York: Holt, Rinehart & Winston, 1968.

Hull, C. *Principles of behavior.* New York: Appleton-Century, 1943.

Hunt, J. McV. *Intelligence and experience.* New York: Ronald, 1961.

Hunt, J. McV. The psychological basis for using pre-school enrichment as antidote for cultural deprivation. *Merrill-Palmer Quarterly,* 1964, **10,** 209–248.

Hyde, D. M. An investigation of Piaget's theories of the development of number. Unpublished doctoral dissertation, University of London, 1959.

Isaacs, S. *Social development in young children.* London: Routledge, 1933.

Jones, H. Environmental influences in the development of intelligence. In L. Carmichael (Ed.), *Manual of child psychology.* New York: Wiley, 1954.

Kaplan, B. The study of language in psychiatry. In S. Arieti (Ed.), *American handbook of psychiatry*. Vol. 3. New York: Basic Books, 1966.

Kessen, W. (Ed.) *The child*. New York: Wiley, 1965.

Kofsky, E. A scalogram study of classificatory development. In I. Sigel & F. Hooper (Eds.), *Logical thinking in children: research based on Piaget's theory*. New York: Holt, Rinehart & Winston, 1968.

Kohlberg, L. A schedule for assessing Piaget's stages of sensorimotor development in infancy. Unpublished schedule, Yale University, 1961, mimeographed.

Kohlberg, L. Stages in children's conceptions of physical and social objects in the years 4 to 8—a study of developmental theory. Unpublished monograph, 1963, multigraphed (in preparation for publication).

Kohlberg, L. A cognitive developmental analysis of children's sex-role attitudes. In E. Maccoby (Ed.), *Development of sex differences*. Stanford, Calif.: Stanford University, 1966. (*a*)

Kohlberg, L. Cognitive stages and preschool education. *Human Development*, 1966, 9, 5–19. (*b*)

Kohlberg, L. Assessment of a Montessori program. Paper delivered at American Education Research Association, New York, February, 1967.

Kohlberg, L. The Montessori approach to cultural deprivation. A cognitive-development interpretation and some research findings. In R. Hess & R. Bear (Eds.), *Preschool education, theory, research and action*. Chicago: Aldine, 1968. (a)

Kohlberg, L. Stage and sequence: The developmental approach to socialization. In D. Goslin (Ed.) *Handbook of socialization*. New York: Rand McNally, 1968. (b)

Kohlberg, L., & Lesser, G. *What preschools can do: theories and programs*. Chicago: Scott, Foresman, in press.

Kohlberg, L., Yaeger, J., & Hjertholm, E. Private speech: four studies and a review of theory. *Child Development*, 1968, 39, 691–736.

Kohlberg, L., & Zigler, E. The impact of cognitive maturity upon the development of sex-role attitudes in the years four to eight. *Genetic Psychology Monograph*, 1967, 75, 89–165.

Kohn, N. The development of culturally disadvantaged and middle class Negro children on Piagetian tests of concrete operational thought. Doctoral dissertation, University of Chicago, in preparation.

Langer, J. The role of cognitive conflict in development. Paper delivered at meetings of Society for Research in Child Development, New York, March 21, 1967.

Linden, J. The performance of schizophrenic children upon a series of Piagetian tasks. Doctoral dissertation, University of Chicago, in preparation.

Lorenz, K. *Evolution and the modification of behavior.* Chicago: University of Chicago Press, 1965.

Lovell, K. Concepts in mathematics. In H. Klausmeier & C. Harris (Eds.), *Analyses of concept learning.* New York: Academic, 1966.

Luria, A. R. *The role of speech in the regulation of normal and abnormal behavior.* New York: Liveright, 1961.

Mead, G. H. *Mind, self, and society.* Chicago: University of Chicago Press, 1934.

Mermelstein, E. The effect of lack of formal schooling on number development, a test of Piaget's theory and methodology. Unpublished doctoral dissertation, Michigan State University, 1964.

Mermelstein, E., & Shulman, L. S. Lack of formal schooling and the acquisition of conservation. *Child Development,* 1967, **38**, 39–52.

Moore, O. K. Teaching young children to read. In R. Hess & R. Bear (Eds.), *Preschool education; theory, research, and action.* Chicago: Aldine, 1968.

Morrisett, L. Report of a conference on preschool education in *Items of the Social Science Research Council,* June, 1966.

Neill, A. S. *Summerhill.* New York: Hart, 1960.

Nordan, R. The development of conservation in the blind. Unpublished minor research paper, University of Chicago, 1967.

Pavlov, I. P. *Lectures on conditioned reflexes.* New York: Liveright, 1928.

Piaget, J. *The child's conception of the world.* New York: Harcourt Brace, 1928.

Piaget, J. *The psychology of intelligence.* London: Routledge, Kegan Paul, 1947.

Piaget, J. *The child's conception of number.* London: Routledge, Kegan Paul, 1952.

Piaget, J. The general problem of the psychobiological development of the child. In J. M. Tanner & B. Inhelder (Eds.), *Discussions on Child Development.* Vol. 4. New York: International Universities Press, 1960.

Piaget, J. Cognitive development in children. In R. Ripple & V. Rockcastle (Eds.), *Piaget rediscovered, a report on cognitive studies and curriculum development.* Ithaca, N.Y.: Cornell University, School of Education, 1964.

Piaget, J. *Six psychological studies.* D Elkind (Ed.). New York: Random House, 1967.

Pinard, A., & Laurendeau, M. *Causal thinking in children.* New York: International Universities Press, 1964.

Price-Williams, D. R. A study concerning concepts of conservation of quantity among primitive children. *Acta Psychologica,* 1961, **18**, 297–305.

Reese, H. W. Verbal mediation as a function of age level. *Psychology Bulletin*, 1962, **59**, 502–509.

Rheingold, H., & Bayley, N. The later effects of an experimental modification of mothering. In C. B. Stendler (Ed.), *Readings in child behavior and development*. New York: Harcourt, Brace & World, 1965.

Riesen, A. Plasticity of behavior; psychological aspects. In H. F. Harlow & C. N. Woolsey (Eds.), *Biological and biochemical bases of behavior*. Madison: University of Wisconsin Press, 1958.

Riesen, A., & Kinder, E. *The postural development of infant chimpanzees*. New Haven, Conn.: Yale University Press, 1952.

Robinson, H. The problem of timing in preschool education. In R. Hess & R. Bear (Eds.), *Preschool education: theory, research and action*. Chicago: Aldine, 1968.

Rosenzweig, M. Experimental complexity and cerebral change in behavior. Paper delivered at American Association for the Advancement of Science, Washington, D.C., December 30, 1966.

Schatzman, L., & Strauss, A. Social class and modes of communication. *American Journal of Sociology*, 1955, **60**, 329–338.

Shirley, Mary M. The sequential method for the study of maturing behavior patterns. *Psychological Review*, 1931, **38**, 501–528.

Shirley, Mary M. *The first two years, a study of twenty-five babies*. Minneapolis: University of Minnesota Press, 1931–1933. 2 vols.

Sigel, I. The attainment of concepts. In M. Hoffman & L. Hoffman (Eds.), *Review of child development research*. Vol. 1. New York: Russell Sage, 1964.

Sigel, I., & Hooper, F. (Eds.), *Logical thinking in children: research based on Piaget's theory*. New York: Holt, Rinehart & Winston, 1968.

Sigel, I. E., Roeper, A., & Hooper, F. H. A training of procedure acquisition of Piaget's conservation of quantity. In I. Sigel & F. Hooper (Eds.), *Logical thinking in children: research based on Piaget's theory*. New York: Holt, Rinehart & Winston, 1968.

Sinclair, H. *Acquisition du langage et development de la pensee*. Paris: Dunod, 1967.

Smedslund, J. The acquisition of conservation of substance and weight in children, III: Extinction of conservation of weight acquired normally by means of empirical control as a balance. *Scandinavian Journal of Psychology*, 1961, **2**, 85–87 (reprinted in Sigel & Hooper, 1968). (a)

Smedslund, J. The acquisition of conservation of substance and weight in children, V: Practice in conflict situations without external reinforcement. *Scandinavian Journal of Psychology*, 1961, **2**, 156–160, 203–210 (reprinted in Sigel & Hooper, 1968). (b)

Smedslund, J. Concrete reasoning: A study of intellectual development. *Monographs of the Society for Research in Child Development*, 1964, **29**, (2, Serial No. 93), 3–39.

Spearman, C. The psychology of "g." In C. Murchison (Ed.), *Psychologies of 1930*. Worcester, Mass.: Clark University Press, 1930.

Stodolsky, S. S. Maternal behavior and language and concept formation in Negro pre-school children: an inquiry into process. Unpublished doctoral dissertation, University of Chicago, 1965.

Sullivan, E. Acquisition of conservation of substance through film modeling techniques. In D. Brison & E. Sullivan (Eds.), *Recent research on the acquisition of substance* (Educational Research Series No. 2). Ontario: Ontario Institute for Studies of Education, 1967.

Thompson, W., & Heron, W. Environmental restriction and development in dogs. *Canadian Journal of Psychology*, 1954, **17**, No. 8.

Uzgiris, I. Situational generality of conservation. In I. Sigel & F. Hooper (Eds.), *Logical thinking in children: research based on Piaget's theory*. New York: Holt, Rinehart & Winston, 1968.

Uzgiris, I., & Hunt, J. McV. A scale of infant psychological development. Unpublished manuscript, University of Illinois, 1964.

Vygotsky, L. *Thought and language*. New York: Wiley, 1962.

Wallace, J. G. *Concept growth and the education of the child*. The Mears, Upton Park, Slough, Bucks: National Foundation for Education Research in England and Wales, 1965.

Wallach, L. & Sprott, R. Inducing number conservation in children. *Child Development*, 1964, **35**, 1057–1071.

Werner, H. *The comparative psychology of mental development*. Chicago: Wilcox & Follett, 1948.

White, S. Children's learning. In H. Stevenson (Ed.), *Child psychology: sixty-third yearbook of the National Society for the Study of Education*. Chicago: University of Chicago Press, 1963.

White, S. Evidence for a hierarchical arrangement of learning processes. In L. Lipsett & C. C. Spiker (Eds.), *Advances in child development and behavior*. Vol. 2. New York: Academic, 1965.

Wohlwill, J. A scalogram analysis of the number concept. In I. Sigel & F. Hooper (Eds.), *Logical thinking in children: research based on Piaget's theory*. New York: Holt, Rinehart & Winston, 1968.

Yarrow, L. Separation from parents during early childhood. In M. L. Hoffman (Ed.), *Review of child development research*. Vol. 1. New York: Russell Sage, 1964.

CHAPTER 2

Conceptual Processes

S. SHIRLEY FELDMAN, EDITOR

The ability to form concepts is basic to thinking, problem solving, and all forms of cognitive functioning. How concepts are formed and maintained is therefore a crucial psychological question. Vinacke (1952) indicates that the following are the basic issues in studying concept formation. The first issue pertains to the *process* of concept formation and concerns how an individual attains a particular concept and the conditions related to concept formation. The second problem is to determine the concepts that characterize various stages in the development of the child's thinking and acting. For this question the *content* or the outcome of the active process of concept formation is relevant. The third issue concerns the organization and structure of the conceptual system, and the complex interrelations among concepts. From the viewpoint of education, the first of these questions, concerning the actual processes involved in developing concepts, is the most important. The majority of the readings reported in this section have therefore been chosen to focus on this issue.

A distinction should be drawn between *concept formation,* which Bruner, Goodnow, and Austin (1956, p. 232) call "the inventive act by which classes are constructed," and *concept attainment,* which refers to the search for and testing of attributes that can be used to distinguish exemplars from nonexemplars. Concept formation thus appears to refer to how concepts are originally acquired, whereas concept attainment (sometimes called concept identification) refers to a translation process in which a concept already in the person's repertoire is associated with a new name or symbol. This distinction between concept formation and concept attainment has not always been made in the

143

literature, perhaps because the two processes are not completely independent. In this section processes involved in both formation and attainment of concepts will be represented in the studies. However, more stress will be placed on those having to do with concept formation, since these have greater relevance for education.

Another issue that is important in studying conceptual processes concerns the continuity or discontinuity of these processes. The question is whether a more abstract level of functioning in the conceptual domain is only a quantitative extension of a more concrete level, or whether there are qualitative differences between the two levels of conceptual functioning. In the work of those who study concept attainment there is often the implicit assumption that the various levels of conceptual activity are continuous, whereas many of those who study concept formation usually assume that there is some discontinuity between the processes. The educational implications of these positions are clear: for the continuity theorists, similar educational techniques should be effective for teaching concepts to children of different ages, whereas for the discontinuity theorists, different methods for inducing concept formation are appropriate at different stages of the child's development.

There are presently two major orientations to the study of conceptual processes, the behavioristic and the cognitive. The word "concept" has different connotations for each of these orientations, and consequently they use different research techniques. Anderson (1966) notes that in behavioristic terms, "concept" refers to the contingency in which a common response is evoked by a class of stimuli. A concept is acquired when a response emitted in the presence of the discriminative stimulus is differentially reinforced. On the other hand, the cognitive theorists generally stress central organizing processes, with recognition that these processes become partially autonomous and result in the organism becoming an actor upon rather than a reactor to its environment.

THE BEHAVIORIST VIEW OF CONCEPTUAL PROCESSES

There are in fact two different behavioristic views of conceptual processes: one, the simple behavioristic view, is interested in concept attainment, and the other, the intervening or mediating processes view, studies concept formation. Both behavioristic orientations to conceptual processes are concerned with the role of the stimulus and the response in the formation of concepts.

Hull (1920), using a simple behavioristic orientation, was the first to use experimental methods to study concept attainment. He presented twelve series of Chinese symbols paired with nonsense syllables. Unknown to the subjects, part of the Chinese character (called a radical) was paired with a given nonsense syllable while other details of the Chinese character were varied. The task of the subject was to anticipate the nonsense syllable associated with the Chinese character. Hull found that the fewer the irrelevant elements in the stimuli, the easier the task. This effect was increased if the relevant radical was made more salient.

Heidbreder (1946) modified Hull's procedure by pairing nonsense syllables with drawings of three types of familiar objects or concepts: concrete objects, patterns, and specific numbers of things. Subjects learned most easily the concepts of concrete objects, then abstract forms, and finally numbers. Heidbreder claimed that concept attainment was a special case of perception, and that the order of learning the concepts resulted because of the greater perceptual salience of concrete objects. It was necessary to abstract the recurrent feature from all the instances, and then generalize it to new instances. It is the process of abstraction and generalization, inferred from the ability to name new instances correctly, that is called concept attainment.

Welch (1947) claimed that concept learning was based on the conditioning of a response to a stimulus trace. He hypothesized that with repeated presentation of the stimulus, the overt naming response to that stimulus became associated with the criterial attributes of the concept. Welch built this model to account for the learning of hierarchical concepts such as horse, animal, and living things. In a very carefully designed study reported in this chapter, Long and Welch (1942) show that 8- to 11-year old children are able to use concepts of objects (boy, lion, pear, corn, bus, rowboat, and the like) most easily, and that the more inclusive higher-order concepts (humans, subhumans, vegetables, and land and water vehicles) were significantly more difficult. A second-order hierarchy (animals, foods, vehicles) proved still more difficult.

Hunt (1962) points out that an analysis that considers only conditioning to stimulus elements does not explain concept learning, in which the correlation between the elements of the stimulus and the presence or absence of a particular name is not perfect. Such a situation occurs when a conjunctive or disjunctive concept (such as green *and* square) is learned. Yet such learning is possible, as Bruner, Goodnow, and Austin (1956) have shown for adults, and Furth and Youniss (1965) have shown for children.

This brings us to the second behavioristic orientation, that of mediation, which attempts to deal with such data. Much of the contemporary research on conceptual processes carried on by behaviorists includes references to covert behavior—frequently language behavior—that is said to mediate between observable stimuli and observable responses. An excellent example of this approach is found in the work of the Kendlers (Kendler and Kendler, 1959, 1961, 1963). In this chapter a reading by Kendler (1964) is presented. This reading tests the hypothesis that for children who employ verbal mediation, a reversal shift, in which the initially relevant dimension (for example, size) remains the same and only the attribute within the dimension changes (large to small), is easier than a nonreversal shift, in which the relevant dimension changes (size to color). In a series of experiments, most 3- and 4-year olds made nonreversal shifts when they were given a choice, while 50 percent of the 6- to 7-year olds made reversal shifts. From this the Kendlers concluded that different paradigms characterize learning at different ages. Apparently, before a certain age children do not use verbal mediating responses.

In general, those who study mediation are interested in concept formation rather than attainment, and believe that early and later conceptual processes are discontinuous. They claim that two different processes enter into concept formation at different stages of the child's development. At an early age associative factors linking responses to stimuli are important, whereas at a later age the learning of concepts is short circuited by the child's ability to produce and spontaneously use verbal labels.

THE COGNITIVE VIEW OF CONCEPTUAL PROCESSES

The cognitive position on conceptual processes is not unitary, and two representative positions will be discussed here: the first is the information-theory approach, and the second is the approach of Piaget and his collaborators. In general, the research based on information theory is concerned with concept attainment, whereas the research of Piaget and those stimulated by his theory is concerned with concept formation.

Hovland (1952) made a thorough analysis of the amount of information transmitted by positive and negative instances of a concept. In a theoretical analysis he determines precisely the minimum number of each type of instance required to communicate correctly the characteristics of a concept to subjects who know the nature of the concept model and the number and types of dimensions that are to be considered. A representative of this information-processing approach is a reading by Huttenlocher (1964) included in this section. Huttenlocher shows that in a concept-attainment task younger children are less able than older to hold in mind a number of intellectual steps as they form concepts.

Perhaps the most influential theory pertaining to conceptual processes has been proposed by Jean Piaget, who has been concerned with the development of stages in the acquisition of concepts of subject matter such as number, space, and time as well as with the processes involved in such acquisitions.

Piaget believes there are four stages in cognitive development. The sensorimotor period occupies approximately the first two years of life, in which development of understanding in the infant is based on the child's own activity. The infant begins life with reflexes that are modified from the start by the child's encounter with the environment. During this period the child establishes relations between his own body and objects in the environment, and comes to recognize the permanence of objects.

The preoperational period begins with the use of signs and symbols, particularly language. There are two substages: the first consists of language development, symbolic play, and imitation of others. The second substage is called the period of intuitive thought and occurs between the approximate ages of four and seven. During this period the child uses intuition, that is, immediate apprehension without reasoning, and consequently is misled by perceptual configurations.

The concrete operational period occurs between approximately seven and twelve years of age. It is a time of acquiring a certain basic stock of concepts and organizing them into coherent systems. Logic is applied to concrete objects, and the child is able to handle operations such as classification and seriation, and to construct the fundamental operations of elementary logic, mathematics, and physics.

The period of formal operations, beginning at about twelve, heralds the development of a stable system of thought that can be applied to categories and propositions as well as objects. Ability to form hypotheses and deduce consequences from them characterize this period.

The reader should be aware that while Piaget's work could well be called studies in the development of intelligence, his research was developed quite independently of the work on standardized tests described in the previous section. His conception does not presuppose regular increments with age of the same functions. Rather there are distinct phases, with development of later phases contingent on the incorporation and reorganization of an earlier mode of thought.

An important concept in Piaget's theory is conservation, which refers to the ability of an individual, based on previously acquired skills and structures, to realize the invariant aspects of properties of objects in the face of transformations. The ability to conserve is shown, for example, when the child grasps the mathematical idea that number is not changed when a set of objects is partitioned into subgroups or heaped together, and the physical idea that mass or substance does not change when the shape or appearance of an object is altered. Conservation depends on the child's ability to multiply relations in order to understand that changes in length, for example, are compensated by changes in width. The child must also grasp the notion that the operation that altered the appearance of the materials is reversible (or potentially reversible), that is, can be undone, so that the materials are returned to the state they were in initially. Furthermore, comprehension at conservation is aided if the child understands that nothing has been added or subtracted to the original amount, and consequently the amount has not been changed despite appearances.

Until the child can conserve, his world is in a state of flux, altering from moment to moment according to perception and resulting in grave inconsistencies in thought. With the achievement of conservation the child is able to separate appearances from reality, and on the basis of a lawful and stable world can begin to reason about his surroundings.

It is impossible to adequately summarize Piaget's theory in a few paragraphs, and the interested reader is directed to more comprehensive accounts of this theory. Many of Piaget's books are now available in English (Inhelder & Piaget, 1964; Piaget, 1950, 1956, 1965; and many others). An excellent presentation of Piaget's theory and review of his prolific research is found in Flavell (1963). For those interested in shorter accounts, the following are recommended: Baldwin (1967), Furth (1969), Hunt (1961), and Phillips (1969). For capsule summaries of his theory the reader is directed to Wallach (1963) and Berlyne (1957).

Piaget's theory and the research it has stimulated have important educational implications, as Flavell (1963), Hooper (1968), and Sigel (1969) indicate. One of the most popular justifications for the relevance of developmental research to education is that education will be effective only when it is geared to the individual's level of development. Presumably if a teacher knows what a child is capable of doing at a given age, she can gear her teaching, both method and content, to that level. When direction of development is specified, as in Piaget's sequential approach, then the match that is optimal for stimulating further cognitive growth must be in a particular direction, and failure to match curriculum with level of development may have gross motivational consequences. In other words, Piaget's sequence suggests that the introduction of a new concept or new topic in a curriculum should be geared at a level slightly in advance of the point at which the individual has complete mastery, and since the stages are sequentially and hierarchically arranged, the next level of development is known.

Furthermore, in a stage notion where underlying principles, processes, and structures account for the unity of the stage, curriculum innovations can be analyzed to determine the underlying principles involved, and then introduced at the stage of development when that process or principle is being mastered. Thus Piaget's stage notion of development suggests new directions for education.

A stage notion of development also implies that some process or principle underlies a range of relatively specific learning tasks. Piaget's theory suggests that a core of basic underlying operations such as multiplicative classification, relations, and reversible transformations exist that influence the child's performance on a wider variety of tasks. Thus, education designed to develop these cognitive structures or processes should facilitate the rate at which a child masters the specific tasks that define the stage. However, this is an issue to be decided only by careful empirical studies.

Piaget's work also has relevance for teaching strategy. Piaget (1964, p. 4) notes, "Experience is always necessary for intellectual development. . . . The subject must be active, must transform things, and find the structure of his own actions on the objects." This places Piaget with Montessori and Dewey in his stress on self-discovery and activity. Since activity is a prerequisite of cognitive development, opportunities to manipulate objects and ideas should facilitate development. Dienes (1965) has devised a mathematics curriculum of advanced concepts that involves action and various concrete aids, and that seems to have been inspired by Piaget.

Finally, Piaget-type tasks can be used as concept-readiness measures, since they probe beneath the verbal surface, and assess important conceptual components necessary for the use of a concept. Dodwell (1961) has successfully used Piaget's tests of number to indicate arithmetic readiness in school children.

Several papers in this section deal with the preoperational and concrete operational periods when important concepts are acquired and applied. Elkind (1961), in a replication of Piaget's research on conservation of mass, weight, and volume, confirms Piaget's theory that conservation of different types develops at different times. He shows that the order of attaining conservation for different attributes is mass, then weight, and finally volume.

Dodwell's paper (1960) sets out to test Piaget's claim that before number conservation can be achieved the child must be able to deal with objects in a one-to-one correspondence and also to deal with transitive relations. The results provide support for Piaget's "global," "intuitive," and "concrete" operational stages, but the age trends differ with different test situations.

Shantz (1967), in her paper on logical multiplication, tests Piaget's claim that cognitive abilities are interrelated. Three abilities, multiplication of classes, of asymmetrical relations, and of spatial relations, are chosen because in Piaget's theory these show a close interdependence of logical structures, and according to the theory similarities of structure should be revealed in children's thinking. The results offer only moderate support for Piaget's theory.

In order to shed some light on the conditions, both in the child and in the environment, that influence the acquisition of concepts, a number of training studies have been undertaken in which attempts are made to teach children such concepts as conservation. The pioneering work was done by Smedslund (1961, a, b, c, d, e), who compared and contrasted a number of different training procedures designed to hasten conservation. In this section, a paper by Gruen (1965) is presented in which he provides two types of training—one related to Piaget's theory, and the other based on reinforcement theory, with knowledge of results as the reinforcement. He also examines whether pretraining on relational terms (such as "longer than," "more than") influences the acquisition of number conservation. The combination of verbal pretraining with cognitive-conflict training (which stems from Piaget's theoretical model) resulted in learning the concept. Gruen also evaluates the transfer of training from number conservation to length and substance conservation.

Bruner (1964) in a paper presented in this section appears to combine aspects of both types of cognitive theory discussed here—the information processing and the Piagetian. Bruner believes that concepts are formed in a process in which "transformations" are imposed on the data by the child. He cites several different studies, which can be found reported in greater detail in Bruner (1966). Bruner also claims that with age there is a growth of strategies that make it possible for simpler processing of information.

Maccoby's research extends the concept of equivalence, discussed in Bruner's paper (1966), to a cross-cultural situation, and thereby reveals the influence of environment. Equivalence, the ability to abstract common properties of objects in order to form a concept, was studied first in Mexican and American children from five to seventeen and then in Mexican children of two different age groups and from two environments.

As a concluding note to this introduction, the reader's attention is drawn to a number of excellent books and papers on conceptual processes. Hunt (1962) reviews the evidence on concept learning, primarily based on research with adults, and proposes an information-processing model. Pikas (1967) reviews the evidence on abstraction and concept formation from many different psychological frames of reference. White (1965) is more concerned with developmental changes in cognitive processes, and integrates the data on conceptual processes into a general cognitive model. An excellent book of readings edited by Sigel and Hooper (1968) contains thirty-two papers based on Piaget's theory.

READINGS

** Recommended to reprint as reading.
* Quoted in Introduction.

*Anderson, R. C. Concept Formation. Introduction in R. C. Anderson & D. P. Ausubel (Eds.) *Readings in the Psychology of Cognition*. New York: Holt, Rinehart & Winston, 1966.

*Baldwin, A. *Theories of Child Development*. New York: Wiley, 1967.

*Berlyne, D. E. Recent Developments in Piaget's Work. *British Journal of Educational Psychology*, 1957, **27**, 1–12.

Bruner, J. S. The Course of Cognitive Growth. *American Psychologist*, 1964, **19, 1–15.

*Bruner, J., Goodnow, J., & Austin, G. *A Study of Thinking*. New York: Wiley, 1956.

Davies, C. M. Development of the Probability Concept in Children. *Child Development*, 1965, **36**, 779–788.

*Dienes, Z. P. *Modern Mathematics for Young Children*. Harlow, England: Educational Supply Association, 1965.

Dodwell, P. C. Children's Understanding of Number and Related Concepts. *Canadian Journal of Psychology*, 1960, **14, 191–205.

*Dodwell, P. C. Children's Understanding of Number Concepts: Characteristics of an Individual and a Group Test. *Canadian Journal of Psychology*, 1961, **15**, 29–36.

Elkind, D. Children's Discovery of the Conservation of Mass, Weight and Volume: Piaget Replication Study II. *Journal of Genetic Psychology*, 1961, **98, 219–227.

Elkind, D. Discrimination, Seriation and Numeration of Size and Dimensional Differences in Young Children: Piaget Replication Study VI. *Journal of Genetic Psychology*, 1964, **104**, 275–296.

*Flavell, J. H. *The Developmental Psychology of Jean Piaget*. New Jersey: Van Nostrand, 1963.

*Furth, H. G. *Piaget & Knowledge*. Englewood, New Jersey: Prentice-Hall, 1969.

*Furth, H. G., & Youniss, J. The Influence of Language and Experience on Discovery and Use of Logical Symbols. *British Journal of Psychology*, 1965, **56**, 381–390.

Griffiths, J. A., Shantz, C. U., & Sigel, I. E. A Methodological Problem in Conservation Studies: The Use of Relational Terms. *Child Development*, 1967, **38**, 841–848.

Gruen, G. E. Experiences Affecting the Development of Number Conservation in Children. *Child Development*, 1965, **36, 963–979.

*Heidbreder, E. The Attainment of Concepts: Terminology and Methodology. *Journal of General Psychology*, 1946, **35**, 173–189.

*Hooper, F. H. Piagetian Research and Education. In I. E. Sigel & F. H. Hooper (Eds.), *Logical Thinking in Children*. New York: Holt, Rinehart, and Winston, 1968.

*Hovland, C. I. A Communication Analysis of Concept Learning. *Psychological Review*, 1952, **59**, 461–472.

*Hull, C. L. Quantitative Aspects of the Evolution of Concepts. *Psychological Monographs*, 1920, **28** (Whole No. 123).

*Hunt, E. B. *Concept Learning*. New York: Wiley, 1962.

*Hunt, J. McV. *Intelligence and Experience*. New York: Ronald, 1961.

Huttenlocher, J. Development of Formal Reasoning on Concept Formation Problems. *Child Development*, 1964, **35, 1233–1242.

Inhelder, B. Cognitive Development and Its Contribution to the Diagnosis of Some Phenomena of Mental Deficiency. *Merrill-Palmer Quarterly*, 1966, **12**, 299–319.

*Inhelder, B., & Piaget, J. *The Early Growth of Logic in the Child: Classification and Seriation*. New York: Harper & Row, 1964.

*Kendler, H. H., & Kendler, T. S. Effect of Verbalization on Reversal Shifts in Children. *Science*, 1961, **134**, 1619–1620.

*Kendler, T. S. Development of Mediating Responses in Children. In J. C. Wright & J. Kagan, Basic Cognitive Processes in Children. *Monographs of Society for Research in Child Development*, 1963, **28**, (Whole No. 86).

Kendler, T. S. Verbalization and Optional Reversal Shifts Among Kindergarten Children. *Journal of Verbal Learning and Verbal Behavior*, 1964, **5, 428–436.

*Kendler, T. S., & Kendler, H. H. Reversal and Non-reversal Shifts in Children. *Journal of Experimental Psychology*, 1959, **58**, 56–60.

Kingsley, R. C., & Hall, V. C. Training Conservation Through the Use of Learning Sets. *Child Development*, 1967, **38**, 1111–1126.

Kofsky, E. A Scaleogram Analysis of Classificatory Development. *Child Development*, 1966, **37**, 191–204.

Lee, C. L., Kagan, J., & Rabson, A. Influence of a Preference for Analytic Categorization Upon Concept Acquisition. *Child Development*, 1963, **34**, 433–442.

Long, L., & Welch, L. Influence of Levels of Abstractness on Reasoning Ability. *Journal of Psychology*, 1942, **13, 41–59.

Lovell, K., & Ogilvie, E. A Study on the Conservation of Substance in the Junior School Child. *British Journal of Educational Psychology*, 1960, **30**, 109–118.

**Maccoby, M., & Modiano, N. On Culture and Equivalence: I. in J. S.

Bruner, *Studies in Cognitive Growth*, New York: Wiley, 1966, 257–269.

Osler, S. F., & Shapiro, S. L. Studies in Concept Attainment: The Role of Partial Reinforcement as a Function of Age and Intelligence. *Child Development*, 1964, **35**, 623–633.

Osler, S. F., & Trautman, G. E. Concept Attainment II: Effect of Stimulus Complexity Upon Concept Attainment at Two Levels of Intelligence. *Journal of Experimental Psychology*, 1961, **62**, 9–13.

*Phillips, J. L. Jr. *The Origins of Intellect*: Piaget's Theory. San Francisco: W. H. Freeman & Co., 1969.

*Piaget, J. *The Psychology of Intelligence*. New York: Harcourt, 1950.

*Piaget, J. Three Lectures. In R. E. Ripple & V. N. Rockcastle (Eds.), *Piaget Rediscovered*. Ithaca, New York: Cornell University Press, 1964.

*Piaget, J. *The Child's Conception of Number*. New York: Norton, 1965.

*Pikas, A. *Abstraction and Concept Formation*. Scandinavian University Press, 1967.

Pratoomraj, S., & Johnson, R. C. Kinds of Questions and Types of Conservation Tasks as Related to Children's Conservation Responses. *Child Development*, 1966, **37**, 342–353.

Shantz, C. V. A Developmental Study of Piaget's Theory of Logical Multiplication. *Merrill-Palmer Quarterly*, 1967, **13, 121–137.

Shantz, C. V., & Smock, C. D. Development of Distance Conservation and the Spatial Co-ordinate System. *Child Development*, 1966, **37**, 943–948.

*Sigel, I. E. The Piagetian System and the World of Education. In D. Elkind & J. H. Flavell (Eds.), *Studies in Cognitive Development: Essays in Honor of Jean Piaget*. New York: Oxford University Press, 1969.

*Sigel, I. E., & Hooper, F. H. (Eds.), *Logical Thinking in Children*. New York: Holt, Rinehart & Winston, 1968.

*Smedslund, J. The Acquisition of Conservation of Substance and Weight in Children. I. Introduction. *Scandinavian Journal of Psychology*, 1961, **2**, 11–20 (a).

*Smedslund, J. The Acquisition of Conservation of Substance and Weight in Children. II. External Reinforcement of Conservation of Weight and the Operations of Addition and Subtraction. *Scandinavian Journal of Psychology*, 1961, **2**, 71–84 (b).

*Smedslund, J. The Acquisition of Conservation of Substance and Weight in Children. III. Extinction of Conservation of Weight Acquired "Normally" and by Means of Empirical Controls on a Balance Scale. *Scandinavian Journal of Psychology*, 1961, **2**, 85–87 (c).

*Smedslund, J. The Acquisition of Conservation of Substance and Weight in Children. IV. An Attempt at Extinction of the Visual Components of the Weight Concept. *Scandinavian Journal of Psychology*, 1961, **2**, 153–155 (d).

*Smedslund, J. The Acquisition of Conservation of Substance and Weight in Children. V. Practice in Conflict Situations Without External Reinforcement. *Scadinavian Journal of Psychology*, 1961, **2**, 156–160 (e).

*Smedslund, J. The Acquisition of Conservation of Substance and Weight in Children. VI. Practice on Continuous Versus Discontinuous Material in Conflict Situations without External Reinforcement. *Scandinavian Journal of Psychology*, 1961, **2**, 203–210 (f).

Spiker, C. C., Gerjuoy, I. R., & Shepart, W. O. Children's Concept of Middle-Sizedness and Performance. *Journal of Comparative Physiological Psychology*, 1956, **49**, 416–419.

Stendler, C. B. Intellective Processes in Children. In C. B. Stendler (Ed.), *Readings in Child Behavior and Development*. New York: Harcourt, 1964, 319–332.

7. INFLUENCE OF LEVELS OF ABSTRACTNESS ON REASONING ABILITY* [1]

Louis Long & Livingston Welch

A. PROBLEM

According to Spearman one of the fundamental characteristics of the capacity for cognition is the power to discover the relationships which exist between two or more ideas, facts, or other items of mental content (7). For example, the relationship of comparative size may be established from a knowledge of the number five and the number seven. Many factors operate, however, to influence the ease and facility with which a relation between two or more fundaments is educed. Some of these which have received consideration are the intelligence and mental set of the cognizing organism and the familiarity and the abstractness of the material to be cognized.

The relationship between reasoning and intelligence has been investigated by Burt (1), Sells (6), and Wilkins (10). Correlations between scores on syllogistic and intelligence tests vary from 0.58 to 0.81. Results from other studies (3, 9) suggest that for the solution of any standardized reasoning problem a minimal level of development or maturation must have been attained in abilities which are only partially measured by standard intelligence tests.

SOURCE. *The Journal of Psychology*, 1942, **13**, 41-59.

* Received in the Editorial Office on October 24, 1941, and published immediately at Provincetown, Massachusetts. Copyright by The Journal Press.

[1] From the Institute for Research in Child Psychology at Hunter College. This work has been aided by a grant from the American Philosophical Society. The authors are indebted to Miss Ruth Leder and to Mr. Robert Chin for their valuable assistance with many parts of this research project.

The operation of a particular type of mental set, viz., atmosphere effect, on syllogistic reasoning was studied by Sells (6) and Woodworth and Sells (11). This effect is defined as a set to complete a task with that one of several responses which is most similar to the general trend or tone of the whole situation (6, p. 7). The operation of this effect caused a spread of the implication from the two premises of the syllogism to the conclusion. For example, two universal affirmative premises (all A's are B's) suggested a universal affirmative as a conclusion.

Another approach to the problem of mental set has been made by Maier in his study of direction (4, 5). This term is defined as the "selective and integrative processes involved in the reorganization of isolated experiences in such a manner that a goal is achieved" (5, p. 44). The presence or absence of "direction" in a reasoning problem is not determined by a knowledge of the elements to be integrated for it has been shown that such knowledge is not of itself sufficient to solve a problem (4). Stated in this way, the conclusion is experimentally justified but at the same time it appears that, other things being equal, the more knowledge one has about the elements the more likely will be the occurrence of a solution. Some experimental evidence for this statement can be found in the analyses of hypotheses used by children in solving reasoning problems (3, 9). An extension of the problem of the effect of the presence or absence of knowledge on reasoning may be made through an investigation of the effect on reasoning of varying degrees of familiarity with the material employed.

Meaningful words, nonsense syllables, and letters of the alphabet have been utilized in presenting the propositions of the syllogisms. It has been found that the difficulty of applying a principle of reasoning increases as the meaningfulness of the terms decreases (6, 10). Long and Welch (3) have reported that the efficacy of applying principles learned with three dimensional materials diminishes when the same type of reasoning problem is presented in pictures, words, or letters. The subjects in this last experiment were children who had been in school only a year or two and who were relatively more familiar with three dimensional material than with words and letters.

The process of generalization may involve a transfer from three dimensional material to pictures or words as in the study cited above (3), or it may involve applying the same principle to various hierarchical levels. The latter type of generalization was the main concern of the present project. The extent to which a child would be able to generalize a principle which was discovered at the object level to the first and second hierarchy levels was the main problem under investigation. A subdivision of this problem was possible since some of the subjects needed assistance in finding the principle. Consequently the generalization scores of those children needing assistance on the object level test were compared with those of the children who discovered the principle with-

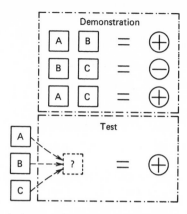

FIGURE 1. Schematic drawing of arrangement of blocks in joint method problems.

out assistance. Another aspect of the problem is the relationship between performance at the various hierarchical levels and the ability to verbalize the principle at each. Finally the influence of chronological and mental ages on finding and generalizing the principle was investigated.

B. PROCEDURE AND MATERIAL

The apparatus of the present experiment was very similar to that of previous studies (3, 9). A schematic drawing of the apparatus is presented in Figure 1. The squares with letters represent blocks on the tops of which were small photographs. The circles with a plus or minus sign represent light bulbs; the presence of a light is indicated by a plus, the absence, by a minus.

Eighteen different photographs were used, representing the objects listed in Table 1. The classification presented in this table served as the basis for the tests of generalization to be described below. The discussion of the procedure can be facilitated by dividing the experiment into two parts: the initial test which was concerned with whether or not the principle of reasoning could be discovered by the child; and the generalizing tests which investigated the extent to which this principle could be generalized on the same level of abstractness as well as on higher ones.[2]

1. Discovering the Principle

a. Object Level Test, Sub-Human Only. Only the blocks with photographs of sub-human animals were presented in this part of the experiment (to be

[2] It is realized that generalization is involved in discovering the principle, but for convenience the terminology of discovering and generalizing the principle will be used throughout the paper.

TABLE 1

Classification of the 18 Objects Used as Stimuli

		Level of Classification			
		Second Hierarchy			
Animals		Foods		Vehicles	
		First Hierarchy			
Humans	Sub-humans	Fruits	Vegetables	Land	Water
		Object Level			
Boy	Lion	Pear	Corn	Bus	Rowboat
Man	Camel	Apple	Beans	Truck	Sailboat
Woman	Horse	Banana	Carrot	Passenger car	Battleship

referred to as the object level test, sub-human only). The first three pairs of blocks (see Figure 1) were placed by the experimenter. As each pair was placed the child's attention was called to the presence or absence of the light in that particular row. When the experimenter had placed the six blocks (two of each of the sub-human animals), he presented the subject with three additional blocks—one of each of the three sub-human animals already placed. The child was told to select the block he thought would make the fourth light go on. This light would go on only if the type of block (indicated by "A" in Figure 1) opposite the two lighted bulbs was selected. The child was given only one choice; consequently, he worked with knowledge of correctness versus incorrectness, but if the response was of the latter type he did not know which of the two remaining blocks was the correct one. As soon as the subject had made his selection the apparatus was removed from his field of vision and the experimenter then prepared the apparatus for the next trial. To rule out the possibility that the problem was being solved by some principle other than the one indicated above many elements of the situation were varied in a chance order; for example, the position of the causal block in both columns and rows, the rows with lights, and the position of the three blocks presented to the child. The test continued until 30 trials were completed or until 10 consecutive correct selections were made. If this criterion of 10 consecutive correct responses was fulfilled, the child was asked to explain his selection on the last criterion trial. If the criterion was not fulfilled the same test was presented on the following day and the procedure was the same, except that a standardized hint was given after each incorrect response. This procedure continued for another 30 trials or until 10 consecutive correct responses were made.

2. Generalizing the Principle

a. Object Level Test, Six Species. When the child fulfilled the criterion, with or without hints, he was immediately presented with the second situation. This was introduced to test his ability to apply the same principle to a variety of data on the same level of abstractness. Photographs representing members of the following classes were introduced: sub-human animal, human, land vehicle, water vehicle, vegetable, and fruit. As in the first test, three species (for example, horse, lion, camel) of a single class (sub-human animal) were used in each trial. The members of each class occurred in triplets—two on the board and one presented to the child. In the object level test, sub-human only, the stimuli for all trials were members of the class sub-human animals, whereas in the object level test, six species, the stimuli were drawn from any one of the six classes listed above. A standard random order was followed in determining which class would be presented on any particular trial. The child did not receive hints in this test and he worked with the same knowledge of correctness as in the first test. The second test continued until 10 consecutive correct responses were made. On the last trial the child was asked to explain his selection.

b. First Hierarchy Test. The second generalization situation made use of more abstract concepts. In the first two tests which have been described above the child was required to perceive that the rows with the lighted bulbs always contained a common block (for example, a lion, or "*A*" in Figure 1). In the present test the child was required to perceive that the two rows with lighted bulbs always contained two different species of the same class (for example, a camel and a lion). The child was required to group the blocks into classes corresponding to first hierarchy concepts; consequently this situation will be referred to as the first hierarchy test. In each trial three different classes are represented by two species from each. The child had, up to this point, selected the block which was identical with the one he thought was making the light go on. He was now forced to select one from a group of three made up of the remaining member of each of the three classes used on that trial. The combination of classes to be used from trial to trial was determined beforehand by a standard chance order, as were the species to be placed by the experimenter. In this situation the child worked without knowledge of error since any selection he made would cause the fourth light to go on. The child was given 10 trials regardless of the correctness of his responses. An explanation of the selection was requested on the tenth trial.

c. Second Hierarchy Test. The final test of generalization involved the second hierarchy level and necessitated the use of the second hierarchy concepts. It will, therefore, be referred to as the second hierarchy test. From Table 1 it will be observed that the six classes of the first hierarchy test can be combined to form three second hierarchy classes: animal, vehicle, and food. For each trial two members of each of the three second hierarchy concepts were selected in such a way that each sub-division of the second hierarchy was represented by one block. The six blocks were placed by the experimenter so that that two species of any second hierarchy group were in different rows. As in the previous tests the lights in two rows went on as the blocks were placed. The child was then presented with three blocks; each of the second hierarchy concepts were represented, but duplicates of the six blocks already used were avoided. An illustration will clarify the set-up:

Row 1:	woman	auto	light on
Row 2:	pear	lion	light on
Row 3:	battleship	corn	light not on
Extra blocks:	bus, bean, camel		

In the above example the camel is the correct response since a woman and a lion appear in the first two rows where the lights are on. All of these are contained in the second hierarchy concept "animal." Bus and bean cannot be correct because a battleship and corn appear in the row where the light is not on. The blocks to be used in any trial were selected by a random order procedure; the positions they were to occupy were also varied in a chance fashion. Ten trials were presented, regardless of the correctness of the response. The child worked without knowledge of error since any block selected would cause the light to go on.[3] An explanation of the selection was requested on the tenth trial.

The final task was a classification problem. Eighteen blocks, one for each of the objects used in the various experiments (see Table 1) were presented to the child in a mixed order. He was first asked to name all of the blocks. He was then told to group the blocks ("put those together which you think belong together"). If further instructions were necessary he was told to put the blocks together in groups of three's. Finally, he was asked to consolidate the six groups into three groups. After each classification the child was instructed to name the groups and to explain his grouping.

C. SUBJECTS

These tests were administered to 40 children enrolled in the Hunter Elementary School. The subjects were also given the *Stanford-Binet Intelligence Test* (revised) and the Pintner *Aspects of Personality Test*. The age range of the subjects was from 8 to 11½ years. The children were divided into four age

---

[3] Needless to say the child also worked without knowledge of this fact.

groups: 8, 9, 10, and 11 years. The range of each age group was ± 6 months; for example, the 11-year group included children from 10 years 7 months to 11 years 6 months of age. The average chronological age, mental age, intelligence quotient, and percentile rating on the emotionality scale of the Pintner test for the four age groups will be found in Table 2. The average *IQ*'s indi-

TABLE 2

Group Data on Chronological Age, Mental Age, Intelligence, and Emotionality

Age Groups	Number of S's	Average CA (Months)	Average MA (Months)	Average IQ	Average Percentile Rating on Emotionality
8 years	10	98.0	130.1	132.7	33.6
9 years	10	106.9	139.3	130.1	77.5
10 years	10	120.1	154.0	128.2	68.4
11 years	10	133.4	160.2	120.9	88.0
Average		114.60	145.90	127.98	66.88
SD		13.62	18.05	12.74	28.19

cate that the children of the various groups differed to some extent in relative intelligence. Since the performance of the groups was to be compared it was hoped that the *IQ*'s of the children of the several groups would not differ greatly. That is to say, a homogeneous group was desired. A test of heterogeneity was made by comparing the variability between the groups with that found within the groups. This analysis of the variance indicated more variation between group than within but the preponderance was not great enough to assume that the population was heterogeneous ($P > 0.05$). In addition to this over-all comparison each group was individually paired with every other one. This analysis indicated that the *IQ*'s of the children in the 11-year group were significantly different from those of the 8- and 10-year groups, but in all other instances the differences were unreliable. Consequently in the ensuing discussion it should be remembered that the children of the oldest group were not as bright for their chronological age as were those of the two youngest groups. The three youngest groups can, however, be assumed to form a homogeneous group as far as relative brightness is concerned.

D. RESULTS

1. Comparison of Performance of Children at Various Age Levels

On the object level test, sub-human only, the child was given an opportunity to discover the principle for himself. It was found that 21 children were able

TABLE 3

Number of Subjects Passing Object Level Test With and Without Hints

	Age Groups (Years)			
	8	9	10	11
No. S's passing with hints	9	4	4	2
No. S's passing without hints	1	6	6	8

to make 10 consecutive correct responses within 30 trials, whereas 19 others were unable to do so and were assisted by standardized hints. From Table 3 it is evident that as age increases the number of children solving the problem without hints definitely increases. That this increase is significant is clear, but the impossibility of ruling out spurious factors in such a table calls for a more detailed analysis of the relationships between discovering the principle and chronological age. Consequently, the bi-serial correlation technique was used to obtain an estimate of the amount of this relationship as well as the relationship between discovering the principle and mental age. When the mental age and discovering the principle are correlated an r of 0.52 $(SD = 0.16)$ is obtained; if chronological age is partialled out the r is reduced to 0.23. Practically the same results are obtained when mental age is held constant in the correlation between chronological age and discovering the principle $(r = 0.36)$. The relationship indicated in Table 3 is the result of increases in both CA and MA.

The influence of CA and MA can also be observed in the tests of generalization. The averages for these three tests will be found in Table 4. It will be observed that there is an indication that as age increases the average scores on

TABLE 4

Average Scores for Three Tests of Generalization

	Age Groups (Years)			
Tests	8	9	10	11
Object level, six species	9.9	9.8	10.0	9.8
First hierarchy	5.5	7.7	9.2	8.6
Second hierarchy	5.2	6.4	6.9	7.3

each of these tests increase. For the most part, the changes are relatively small. The fluctuations in the scores of the object-level test, six species, were found to be of a chance order, as were those of the second hirarchy test. But in the case of the first hierarchy test a reliable difference was found when the average score of the 8-year group was compared with the average scores of the 10- or 11-year groups. In all other cases the differences were unreliable.

2. Effect of Different Levels of Abstractness on Generalization

From the averages of Table 4 it is evident that the children generalized from the object level test, sub-human only, to the object level test, six species. These tests are on the same level of abstractness and the fact that all except four children made perfect scores (10 correct out of 10 trials) gives positive evidence that the children could solve such problems at this level. The scores for the two tests at higher levels of abstractness are consistently lower than those for the object level test, six species. The scores of the object level test, six species, were found to be significantly higher than those for the first hierarchy test in the case of two age groups (8 years and 10 years). When the scores of the object level, six species, were compared with those for the second hierarchy test a reliable difference was found for all age groups. The scores from the two abstract tests were found to be similar for all except the 10-year group. In this case the scores on the first hierarchy test were significantly greater than those on the second hierarchy test. These findings may be summarized by stating that as the level of abstractness is increased the ability of the child to generalize a known principle decreases. The higher level of abstractness causes the scores to drop off enough for the shift to be statistically significant for all age groups. In addition it might be mentioned that the scores on the highest level of abstractness were lower than those on the abstract test at a lower level, but this difference is not significant in most cases.

3. Comparison of Performance of Children Discovering Principle without Hints with That of Children Needing Hints

The question arises as to whether the children who needed hints on the initial test differed in their performance on the tests involving generalization from those who did not need hints. The average for the object level tests, six species, was higher for the children who received hints, but their averages for the other two tests were lower. The difference between all three pairs of averages was found to be too small to be considered statistically significant, but the difference in the case of the second hierarchy approaches significance ($P = .08$). A second statistical procedure suggests that the group receiving no hints did better on this test of generalization. It was found that a significantly greater number of children from the group receiving hints made scores below the median score for all 40 subjects. There is consequently an indication that the children who discovered the principle for themselves were more efficient in applying it to abstract material. This does not, however, necessarily imply a causal relationship between discovering and applying a principle since these two activities may depend upon common traits or characterictics. For example, it was pointed out above that the subjects who found the principle without assistance tended to be more advanced both chronologically and mentally. Such developmental superiority might very well be responsible for the higher scores on the generalization tests.

In the discussion thus far a dichotomy has been made between children who discovered the principle and generalized, and children who needed help in discovering the principle. A further subdivision can, however, be made: (*a*) children who discovered the principle without assistance and generalized; (*b*) children who discovered the principle without assistance and did not generalize; (*c*) children who discovered the principle after assistance was given and then generalized; and (*d*) children who discovered the principle after assistance was given and did not generalize. Since the terms used above are relative, it is appropriate to indicate how they will be employed in this report. "Discovering the principle without assistance" indicates that the child satisfied the criterion of 10 consecutive correct responses within 30 trials, whereas "discovering the principle after assistance was given" means that the child was given 30 trials but failed to satisfy the criterion until hints were given. A child was considered to have generalized if his score on any of the tests of generalization was above the median score of the group.

There is no a priori reason to suppose that because the child discovers the principle by himself he will be able to generalize it to higher levels of abstraction; nor is it necessary to assume that if the child needs assistance in discovering the principle he will have difficulty in generalizing. The processes of discovering and generalizing principles are psychologically very different in many essential respects and a person may conceivably excel in one and not in the other. That such was found to be the case in this experiment can be seen from Table 5. It will be noted that in both the first and second hierarchy tests sizeable portions of the group scored above the median but needed hints, or scored below the median and did not need hints. It can, therefore, be

TABLE 5

Relationship Between Performance on First and Second Hierarchy Tests
And Giving of Hints on Object Level Test

	First Hierarchy Test		Second Hierarchy Test	
	Number of S's Given Hints	Number of S's Given No Hints	Number of S's Given Hints	Number of S's Given No Hints
Number of S's scoring above median	9.5	9.5	6	14
Number of S's scoring below median	9.5	11.5	13	7

concluded that on the basis of the criteria used herein for determining the ability to discover and to generalize a principle some subjects were distinctly superior in one process and inferior in the other. This conclusion is supported by data from both hierarchy tests, but it is more striking in the data from the first hierarchy test. The distribution in Table 5 for this test does not differ significantly from chance. The indication is that a child who discovers the principle by himself is just as apt to score above as below the median on the first hierarchy test. The distribution for the second hierarchy test (Table 5) is, however, significantly different from a chance distribution. The likelihood of a child scoring above the median of this test is greater if the child discovers the principle on the object level test, subhuman only, by himself, than it is if he needs assistance on the initial test.[4] That there is only a tendency for this to be true is indicated by the fact that in one-third of the cases the positive relationship between these two tests is absent.

4. Classification of the Objects by the Children

In an experiment concerned with testing the subject's generalization of a principle it is desirable to have evidence indicating whether the material with which the subject is working is familiar to him. The present study investigated the extent to which the child's ability to use a reasoning principle would be affected by varying the level of abstractness. It is essential to show that the failures on the abstract tests did not result from ignorance of the concepts employed in these tests. An attempt was made to obtain information on this by having each child name and classify the objects. All but two of the photographs of the objects were correctly named by the 40 children. Six children gave names to the photograph of the beans which would place this object in some category other than a vegetable. One child in response to the photograph of a carrot said only that it was to be eaten. While this classification was considered correct, it should be noted that the concept of vegetable was not mentioned. In all other instances the subjects named the objects correctly. Consequently, it can be assumed that the objects were recognizable and familiar to the children.

Each child was also asked to sort the blocks into groups of three's. A name for each group was requested. Only four children failed to give names similar to the first hierarchy concepts listed in Table 1. Three children had trouble with the concept vegetable or fruit, while one child placed a land vehicle in the group of water vehicles and a water vehicle in the group of land vehicles. In all other instances correct groupings were made and the first hierarchy

---

[4] This is in line with Katona's findings that retention of the solution of a problem is greater if the person originally solved the problem without assistance than if he needed help (2).

concept was mentioned. It can therefore be assumed that the majority of the children knew the first hierarchy classification and the corresponding concepts.

Finally, each child was told to place the six blocks together that he believed belonged together. In three cases the groupings indicated in Table 1 were not given. One child did not see how the sub-human animals and the humans could be placed together. Another child placed the vegetables and the sub-human animals in one group, while the humans and the fruits were placed in another. The third child placed the humans and the cars in one group, while the boats and the sub-human animals were placed in another. Most of the children gave rational explanations of their groupings, but the main concern here is to point out that the structures of the hierarchies presented in Table 1 were known to most of the subjects.

5. Explanations of the Principle Given by the Subjects

As each child satisfied the criterion of a test he was asked to explain the selection made on the last trial. Thirty-two of the 40 children gave complete explanations (i.e., mentioned the presence of the causal factor in the rows with lights and its absence in the row without a light) in the first object level test, sub-human only. Complete explanations were received from 31 of these children on the object level test, six species, and from 27 on the first hierarchy test, and from 10 on the second hierarchy test.

Partial explanations, mentioning *either* the presence of the causal factor in the rows with lights *or* the absence of the causal factor in the row with no light were obtained from eight children in the object level test, sub-human. Only two of these continued to give explanations of these types on succeeding tests.

The most interesting feature of these data is the fact that all explanations for the two object level tests can be placed into the two categories, complete and partial; whereas when the explanations of the two abstract tests were classified only 32 of the first hierarchy test and 14 of the second hierarchy test fell into these categories. In the remaining explanations factors irrelevant to the principle were mentioned. This is further evidence of the greater difficulty of the more abstract tests for the subjects. The scores dropped and the previously verbalized principle failed to be applied as the abstractness of the tests was increased.

6. Relationship between Scores and Explanations

In addition to the 10 children who gave complete explanations and the two who gave partial explanations on all three generalizing tests, it was found that two other subjects gave either complete or partial explanations in all three instances. The scores on the three tests for these 14 children were found in all cases to be more than seven correct responses in 10 trials. This record was equalled by only six of the remaining 26 children. All of these six subjects responded with complete or partial explanations in all problems, except at the second hierarchy level.

Of the 20 children who made seven or less correct responses none gave complete or partial explanations on all three tests. Such explanations were, however, found for one or two of the tests. Either a partial or complete explanation was given by all subjects in the second object level test, six species, and no score was below nine. The verbalizations of 12 children fall into one of these categories on the first hierarchy test and their average score was 8.8, two scores being below 8. The average score of the remaining eight children who mentioned factors irrelevant to the principle in their explanations was 2.1. In the second hierarchy test partial or complete explanations were not received from any of these 20 children. The average score was 3.9 and all scores were below eight.

This comparison of the types of explanations with the scores demonstrates the close relationship between actual performance and ability to verbalize the principle of reasoning employed in the different experimental situations. The probability that a child will make eight correct responses in 10 trials by chance alone is remote. When such a record was obtained it was taken to indicate that the child was working with a definite hypothesis. It was, therefore, gratifying to find verification of this assumption in the verbalizations given by the subjects. If a child makes eight or more correct responses in 10 trials it can be assumed that he has grasped the principle since the probability of his being able to verbalize the principle is great. Similarly, if his score is below eight it can usually be assumed that the child did not understand the principle, because he will probably not be able to verbalize it.

7. Several Causes of Failure on the Reasoning Problems

No attempt will be made at this time to list all of the factors that caused incorrect responses in this battery of reasoning situations. Some factors can, however, be mentioned. Although many of them are very obvious, they are nevertheless important insofar as they prevent the child from grasping the problem.

It often happened that the child at first focused his attention on the extra blocks rather than on the board. If the problem is to be solved, attention to the board is essential. In some instances 15 or 20 trials were given before this shift from the choice blocks to the set-up on the board took place. During these early trials the child often used position hypothesis; i.e., he selected the choice block on his left, right, or in the middle. In other cases a preference hypothesis operated; that is, he chose the same block on succeeding trials. In several instances children developed position and preference hypotheses during the second hierarchy test.[5]

Another factor that caused errors to be made is related to the classifications used in the hierarchy tests. Decreases in the scores of the second hierarchy test were sometimes caused by cross classifications of the first hierarchy concepts; for example, a bus might be picked as the causal factor because a man rides in an automobile, the lights being on in the rows containing these two blocks. The correct solution would be a row boat because the automobile and the battleship are in rows with lights, whereas the selection of the choice block of the boy would be incorrect because a horse is in the row without a light. To judge from the verbalizations of the principle, this type of crossed classification seems to have operated from time to time in the performance of 16 children. Six of these, however, made scores of 8 or more in this test.

8. Relationship between the Battery of Tests Presented as Three Dimensional Material and the Same Battery Presented as Printed Material

Sixteen of the 40 children who received the tests of this experiment were subsequently presented with a paper and pencil test. The latter included nine different situations and among these were the object level test, six species; first hierarchy test; and second hierarchy test. The blocks with pictures were replaced by words naming the object represented, and the presence or absence of a light was indicated by a plus or a minus sign. The number of trials was the same for both experiments: i.e., 10 for each test of the experiment. The average scores for the two experiments are presented in Table 6. The difference between the average scores of the experiment using three dimensional material and the experiment using printed material was found to be unreliable for all three tests. When the total scores for the two tests are correlated an r of 0.81 ($SD \pm 0.09$) is obtained. The conclusion indicated is that the performance on the paper and pencil test was not different from that on the three dimensional

TABLE 6

Comparison of Performance on Tests of Generalization When Presented in Two Different Media

	Average Scores	
	Three Dimensional	Printed
Tests	Material	Material
Object level, six species	9.81	9.13
First hierarchy	8.50	8.38
Second hierarchy	7.44	7.81
Average total score (all three tests)	25.75	25.31

[5] These hypotheses have been discussed in detail elsewhere (3, 9).

material. This is an indication of another type of generalization, not involving levels of abstractness of the concept but rather the medium of presentation. Such changes have been found in some cases to cause performance to drop (3, 9). The discrepancy is probably due to the difference in amount of experience with printed material. The decrease found by Long and Welch (3, 9) was obtained with younger children, many of whom were just entering school. In the present experiment the children were all over eight years of age.

E. DISCUSSION OF RESULTS

A stimulus for the present experiment was supplied by observations made in two previous research projects concerned with the effect of abstractness on performance (3, 8). In one experiment the ability to learn and use concepts of varying degrees of abstractness was studied by a technique which was largely verbal (8). It was found that children could learn three object level concepts much quicker than they could learn three concepts of a first hierarchy. Furthermore their ability to use the object level concepts was greater. The level of abstractness involved in a test situation is therefore an important factor in determining the use that can be made of the concepts.

In the second experiment the abstractness of the test was increased by changing the type of material used as a medium of presentation. The effect of this change on the child's ability to solve problems was discussed above and has been reported in detail elsewhere (3). Briefly this type of increase in abstractness also caused a decrease in the performance.

The main conclusion of the two experiments suggests that either type of increase in abstractness will affect performance, but since the general plan of the two experimental situations differed considerably, the present investigation was designed to allow for direct comparison. The similarity between the problem to be solved and the procedure of the experiment is now great enough to warrant a closer study of the relationship between the effect of these two types of abstractness on reasoning ability. Obviously this comparison cannot be made directly, but it can be pointed out that in each reasoning experiment the child learned a principle and was then given an opportunity to generalize it to a very similar situation as well as to others differing in abstractness. In both experiments generalization to the situation of the same degree of abstractness was practically complete, whereas increase in abstractness reduced the amount of generalization. The statistical treatment indicates that the average performance on the test of the same degree of abstractness was superior to that on the tests involving a greater degree. Therefore it can be concluded that increasing the abstractness, either by varying the medium of presentation or by varying the hierarchy level, will affect adversely the child's ability to apply a principle of reasoning.

F. SUMMARY AND CONCLUSIONS

An investigation of the relationship between reasoning and levels of abstractness was the concern of the present experiment. Forty children, varying in age from 8 to 11½ years, were presented with four reasoning problems, all of which were solvable by the same general principle. The battery of tests included two series at the same minimum level of abstractness (object level) and two series at higher levels of abstractness. One of the latter series involved first hierarchy concepts while second hierarchy concepts were used in the other.

The subjects were tested first on one of the object level tests and when the criterion of passing (10 consecutive correct responses) was fulfilled the three tests of generalization were presented. It was found that generalization to the test of the same level of abstractness was almost perfect. The performance on the first and second hierarchy tests was, however, definitely below that on the object level test. The scores at the first hierarchy test were above those of the second hierarchy, but the differences were not significant in most cases.

The fact that some children needed assistance in discovering the principle made it possible to contrast the performance on the tests of generalization of the children who discovered the principle without hints with the performance of those needing hints. The results indicate that the likelihood of a child scoring above the median on the second hierarchy test is greater if the child discovers the principle on the initial test by himself. This does not, however, necessarily imply a causal relationship between discovering and applying a principle since these activities may depend on common traits. For example, subjects who found the principle without assistance tended to be more advanced both chronologically and mentally. This developmental superiority is undoubtedly conducive to better generalizing.

References

1. Burt, C. Mental and Scholastic Tests. London: King, 1922. Pp. xv + 432.

2. Katona, G. Organizing and Memorizing. New York: Columbia Univ. Press, 1940. Pp. xii + 318.

3. Long, L., & Welch, L. Reasoning ability in young children. *J. of Psychol.*, 1941, **12**, 21–44.

4. Maier, N.R.F. Reasoning in humans: I. On direction. *J. Comp. Psychol.*, 1930, **10**, 115–143.

5. ———. A further analysis of reasoning in rats. *Comp. Psychol. Monog.*, 1938, **15**, No. 1. Pp. 85.

6. Sells, S. B. The atmosphere effect: An experimental study of reasoning. *Arch. of Psychol.*, 1936, No. 200. Pp. 72.

7. Spearman, C. The Abilities of Man. New York: Macmillan, 1927. Pp. vi + 415.

8. Welch, L., & Long, L. The higher structural phases of concept formation of children. *J. of Psychol.*, 1940, 9, 59–95.

9. ————. Comparison of the reasoning ability of two age groups. *J. Genet. Psychol.* (In press).

10. Wilkins, M. C. The effect of changed material on the ability to do formal syllogistic reasoning. *Arch. of Psychol.*, 1928, No. 102. Pp. 83.

11. Woodworth, R. S., & Sells, S. B. An atmosphere effect in formal reasoning. *J. Exper. Psychol.*, 1935, 18, 451–60.

8. VERBALIZATION AND OPTIONAL REVERSAL SHIFTS AMONG KINDERGARTEN CHILDREN[1]

Tracy S. Kendler

The purpose of this research was to test the expectation that instructing children to represent verbally the cues in a discrimination problem would increase the probability that, when given an option, they would execute a reversal shift. In order to account for the fact that older children and adults execute a reversal shift more easily than an extradimensional shift (previously referred to as a nonreversal shift), a mediational mechanism that encourages responses to an entire dimension rather than to a specific stimulus value has been proposed (Kendler and Kendler, 1962). Since this mechanism operates in adults and older children (e.g., Buss, 1953; Harrow and Friedman, 1958; Kendler and D'Amato, 1955) and not in infrahuman animals and younger children (e.g., Brookshire, Warren, and Ball, 1961; Mackintosh, 1962; Kendler, Kendler, and Learnard, 1962; Kendler, Kendler, and Wells, 1960) it seems reasonable to assume that mediating is related to some response system characteristic of the former but not the latter. Language is such a system. Consequently it is hypothesized that as humans mature the tendency to make covert verbal representational responses increases, and these in turn mediate the relatively rapid execution of a reversal shift. If it can be assumed that *overt* representational responses affect the learning of young children in the same way that the hypothetical *covert* representational responses affect more mature humans, then

SOURCE. *Journal of Verbal Learning and Verbal Behavior*, 1964, **3**, 428–436.

[1] This research was supported by a grant from the National Science Foundation. The author is grateful for the cooperation of Sylvia Mark, who conducted Experiment I, and Margaret Woerner, who conducted Experiment II.

supplying young children with overt representational responses should increase the relative ease with which they make a reversal as compared to an extradimensional or inconsistent shift.

EXPERIMENT I

Method

Each S learned two successive discriminations followed by a test series (see Fig. 1). The initial discrimination was between stimuli that differed simultaneously on two dimensions, brightness (B) and shape (S), only one of which was relevant for any given S. During this discrimination experimental Ss learned to precede each choice response with a sentence that labelled the correct and incorrect stimulus of the relevant dimension. Control Ss were not instructed to verbalize. In the second discrimination, the optional shift, only one of the two pairs of stimuli used during the initial discrimination was presented and the reinforcement pattern was changed. Both dimensions were now relevant and redundant. The S could attain criterion by responding in a reverse manner to the previously relevant dimension, or in an extradimensional manner to the previously irrelevant dimension, or in a nonselective manner to both stimulus dimensions. Which kind of shift occurred was inferred from which member of the test pair S chose during the test series that followed the optional shift. The basic comparison was between the percentage of Ss in the Verbalization (V) Group and Control (C) Group who made optional reversal shifts as defined by their behavior in the test series.

Subjects. The Ss were 49 kindergarten children of both sexes drawn from two public schools in Berkeley, California. One S was eliminated because he could not learn the initial discrimination within 200 trials. The remaining Ss were randomly assigned to the V and C Groups, 24 to each. The mean CA's and IQ's of the V and C Groups were 69.5 and 69.7 months and 105.8 and

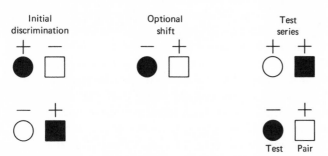

FIGURE 1.   Illustration of one of the arrangements of stimuli and reinforcements used in the experiments.

102.1, respectively. Neither the age nor IQ difference was statistically significant.

Apparatus. The discrimination apparatus, described in more detail in Kendler, Kendler, and Learnard (1962) was a gray aluminum structure 17 inches high and 10 inches wide. Symmetrically arranged on its front surface were two apertures for the presentation of stimuli, two steel rods which pointed toward the apertures, and two slots for the delivery of rewards. The S made a choice by pushing one of the metal rods. When the rod that pointed to S+ was pressed a marble was automatically released into the slot below that rod.

The discriminanda consisted of four pasteboard cards covered with mid-gray (Color-Vu No. 7) paper. Mounted on two of these were circles 1.25 inches in diameter, one black and one white; on the other two were squares with sides of 1.06 inches, one black and one white. The discriminanda were presented two at a time and paired so as to vary simultaneously on two dimensions. The white circle (WCi) was always paired with the black square (BSq), and the black circle (BCi) with the white square (WSq).

Additional equipment included a wooden marble board with spaces for 50 marbles, and vari-colored glass marbles which served as reinforcers during the learning but which were returned to E at the completion of the experimental session.

Procedure. Each S was run individually. All correct responses were rewarded with a marble. After each incorrect response S not only failed to receive a marble but also had to return one of the marbles already acquired.

During the initial discrimination both pairs of stimuli (WCi and BSq, BCi and WSq) were presented alternately in a prearranged sequence designed so that (1) each pair appeared equally often but no more than twice in succession and (2) the correct stimulus appeared equally often on the right and left but no more than twice in succession in either position. In order to discourage position habits, the stimuli were not changed until a correct response was made. Each response, correct or incorrect, was regarded as a trial. For any given S, responses to only one stimulus value, i.e., B or W, or Sq or Ci, were rewarded. Each stimulus value was correct for one quarter of the Ss. Thus, for half of the Ss in each group, brightness was relevant in the initial discrimination. For the other half shape was relevant.

After the criterion of 9 correct out of 10 successive responses was reached on the initial discrimination, the optional shift discrimination was presented with no ostensible break in the procedure. Only one pair of discriminanda was presented and the previous reinforcement pattern was reversed. Thus the stimuli still differed on the same two dimensions but both of them were now relevant. In the illustration (Fig. 1) S could reach criterion on the optional shift discrimination by responding to W, Sq, or both.

The test series followed immediately after S reached the criterion of learning (9 correct out of 10 successive responses) on the optional shift discrimination. Both pairs of stimuli were presented, 10 times each, in the same prearranged order used in the initial discrimination. A response to either member of the pair of stimuli that had *not* appeared in the optional shift discrimination was reinforced. Responses to this test-pair served to indicate the basis of response during the optional shift, since for this pair the critical aspects of the previously redundant stimulus values were separated. For example (Fig. 1), if S learned the optional discrimination on a reversal-shift basis, i.e., by shifting from B to W, he would respond primarily to WCi in the test series. When S responded in this manner eight or more times, his shift was classified as a *reversal*. If he learned the second discrimination by making an extradimensional shift, i.e., by shifting from B to Sq, he would respond primarily to BSq. If S made this response eight or more times his shift was classified as *extradimensional*. A shift was classified as being *inconsistent* if S did not choose eight or more times either the stimulus that indicated a reversal shift or the one that indicated an extradimensional shift. The stimulus pair used during the optional shift discrimination, with the same reinforcement pattern, was interspersed in the test series to help keep S responding as he had during the optional shift.

All Ss were trained and tested in the above manner except that those in the V Group were told at the outset of the initial discrimination to precede each choice with the sentence, "The _____ is the winner and the _____ is the loser." The blank spaces were filled in with adjectives that described S+ and S— for that particular S, e.g., "The black is the winner and the white is the loser," or "The square is the winner and the circle is the loser." After S learned to precede his choice with the relevant sentence in the initial discrimination no further instructions about verbalization were given at any point in the training. The Ss in the C Group were given no instructions about verbalization.

If a S did not attain criterion on the initial discrimination within 50 trials for any given day, the session was terminated and resumed as close to the next day as possible. Once criterion was reached on the initial discrimination, the remainder of the experimental procedure was completed in the same session for all Ss. Thirty-seven Ss completed the experiment in one session. Seven Ss required two, and four Ss required three, sessions. All but one of these Ss who required more than one session were in the C Group.

An IQ score was obtained by individually administering the Peabody Picture Vocabulary Test (Dunn, 1959) to each S immediately after termination of the test series.

RESULTS

Table 1 shows that verbalization facilitated learning the initial discrimination of both dimensions. A rank test for paired replicates (Wilcoxon, 1949)

TABLE 1

Number of Trials to Criterion on Initial and Optional Shift Discriminations

| | Brightness | | | | Shape | | | |
| | Initial Discrimination | | Optional Shift | | Initial Discrimination | | Optional Shift | |
Group	Median	Range	Median	Range	Median	Range	Median	Range
V	0.0	0–6	5.5	1–18	0.0	0–34	3.5	1–26
C	7.0	0–86	6.5	0–25	41.5	0–151	3.0	0–35

indicated that the difference between the V and C Groups is significant for both brightness ($N = 8$, $LRT = 1$, $p < 0.02$)[2] and shape ($N = 9$, $LRT = 3$, $p = 0.02$). On the other hand the same test indicated that the negligible differences between the V and C Groups for the number of trials to learn the optional shift was not significant for either dimension.

The major result of the experiment, as shown in Table 2, is that verbalization significantly increased the proportion of optional reversers on both di-

TABLE 2

Percentage of Ss Responding in Each Category During Test Series

| | Brightness | | | Shape | | |
Group	Reversal	Extra-dimensional	Incon-sistent	Reversal	Extra-Dimensional	Incon-sistent
V	83.3	0	16.7	75.0	16.7	8.3
C	41.7	33.3	25.0	25.0	50.0	25.0

mensions. A multiple-contingency χ^2-analysis (Sutcliffe, 1957) was applied to the corresponding frequencies with the following results: (1) the difference between the V and C Groups is significant ($\chi^2 = 10.232$, $df = 1$, $p < 0.005$), (2) neither the difference between the dimensions ($\chi^2 = 0.762$, $df = 1$), nor (3) the interaction between dimension and verbalization ($\chi^2 = 0.083$, $df = 1$) is significant. In this analysis the frequencies in the extradimensional and inconsistent categories were combined to increase the N in these cells sufficiently to meet the assumptions of the χ^2-test.

The results thus far reported are in good accord with the hypothesis that

[2] In the rank test for paired replicates N refers to the number of replicates to which ranks are assigned. When a zero difference is obtained between two members of a pair, that comparison is ignored in assigning rank numbers. In the 12 pairs of replicates referred to above 4 had a zero difference, hence $N = 8$. LRT refers to the lower rank total.

when an overt representational verbal response occurs it mediates the behavior of kindergarten children in two significant ways. The verbal response facilitates initial learning and increases the transfer within the relevant stimulus dimension more than between dimensions.

However, before confirmation can be claimed, there is another set of results, quite unexpected, whose possible effects should be considered. As the experiment progressed, it was observed that some Ss continued throughout the optional shift to say the sentence they were instructed to say during the initial discrimination. This was surprising because, since the reinforcement pattern had been changed, the verbalization was no longer appropriate to the choice behavior. Thus, for example, a child who made no adjustment in the words he spoke would be saying "Black is the winner and white is the loser," while he consistently chose the white square. In order to quantify this observation the record of each S's verbalizations during his last five criterion trials was re-examined. On these five trials, 10 Ss (42%) continued with the instructed sentence; an equal number adjusted their verbalizations to suit their choice; one S adjusted his verbalization on some trials and continued with the instructed sentence on others; and three Ss stopped verbalizing. No S labeled the previously irrelevant dimension. Those who adjusted the sentence merely transposed the winner and loser words thus making them appropriate to their choice. Although no pattern relating verbal perseveration to choice behavior emerged, it is possible that the type of optional shift S made would be affected by the perseveration of the instructed sentence. Therefore, conclusions about the major results were postponed until this possibility was experimentally investigated in Exp. II.

EXPERIMENT II

This experiment had two purposes. One was to see whether the results of Exp. I could be replicated, including the unexpected verbal behavior on the part of Ss in Group V. The other was to determine whether encouraging Ss to adjust their verbal behavior to their instrumental responses during the optional shift would influence their tendency to make optional reversal shifts.

Three groups were included, two of which were intended, with minor modifications, to replicate the V and C Groups of Exp. I. The third group, Group VP, received the same treatment as Group V except that the VP Ss were prompted by E to make their words consistent with their choice behavior during the optional shift.

Method

Subjects. The Ss were 81 kindergarten children of both sexes drawn from two public schools in Bergenfield, New Jersey, and were randomly assigned to three groups. Of these, seven Ss were eliminated because they failed to learn the initial discrimination within 200 trials. Two other Ss were eliminated because they did not reach criterion on the optional shift within 100 trials. All of the nine eliminated Ss were from Group C. Note that the number of Ss eliminated from Group C in this experiment is considerably greater than in Exp. I where only one S was dropped for failure to learn.

Each group consisted of 24 Ss who completed all phases of the experimental procedure. The mean CAs of the V, VP, and C Groups were 66.3, 67.2, and 67.2 months, respectively. The corresponding IQ's were 107.1, 104.9, and 107.0. No significant differences existed among the groups on either measure.

Apparatus. The apparatus was the same as used in Exp. I.

Procedure. The procedures used with Groups V and C were similar to those used in Exp. I, except for what were believed to be three small improvements. In order to reduce the tendency for Ss to adopt an alternating position habit the procedure of keeping a given stimulus arrangement unchanged until a correct choice occurred was discontinued. On occasion the correct stimulus appeared as many as three times in succession in one position, unlike in Exp. I where the limit was two. These two changes probably increased rather than decreased the difficulty of the task, resulting in the loss of many more Ss than in Exp. I. The third change was that the sentence spoken by the V Group was simplified as follows, "_____ wins and _____ loses." The word "round" was substituted for "circle" because many children made this substitution spontaneously in Exp. I.

The initial training for Groups V and VP was identical. During the optional shift their training differed in that Group VP was given additional instructions to make their verbalizations coincide with their choices, without suggesting what either should be. After S made two consecutive correct responses, if he had not spontaneously changed his words, the stimuli were left in place and E asked, "Which one wins?" If S described the stimulus that was presently being reinforced according to either or both of the two dimensions that were now relevant he was told, "From now on I want you to tell me the one that you think will win, and then point to it." If S's verbal response was inappropriate, additional questions were asked such as "Which one did you point to?", "Did that one win the marble?", etc., until the correct verbal description of the winner was elicited. After this the sentence beginning with "From now on . . . " was repeated as often as necessary until S spontaneously preceded his choices with words that corresponded with his subsequent choice.

RESULTS

Table 3 shows the results for the three groups in learning the initial and optional shift discriminations.

TABLE 3

Number of Trials to Criterion on Initial and Optional Shift Discrimination

| | Brightness | | | | Shape | | | |
| | Initial Discrimination | | Optional Shift | | Initial Discrimination | | Optional Shift | |
Group	Median	Range	Median	Range	Median	Range	Median	Range
V	0.0	0	3.0	1–93	0.0	0–16	6.5	0–61
VP	0.0	0–27	4.0	1–22	0.0	0–224	10.0	1–96
C	12.0	0–191	6.0	1–94	0.0	0–60	8.0	0–48

Since Groups V and VP learned the initial discrimination under identical conditions, their learning should not differ significantly. According to the rank test for paired replicates, there was no significant difference in trials to criterion for each dimension taken separately. Consequently the initial learning scores of the V and VP Groups were combined and compared with Group C in a Mann-Whitney U-test. The result was that for the brightness dimension the initial learning of the combined V and VP Groups was significantly faster than that of the C Group ($z = 2.84$, $p < 0.01$). There was, however, no corresponding difference in learning for the shape dimension ($z = 0.78$), probably because the C Group for which shape was relevant learned so rapidly that there was little room for improvement. Fifty-eight % of this group reached criterion with no errors and an additional 17% made only one error. A conservative interpretation of these findings is that if verbalization has any effect on learning, it is to facilitate it and can therefore be considered at least a partial corroboration of the previous findings.

When the optional-shift learning of the V and VP Groups was compared on the rank test for paired replicates, no significant difference was obtained for either dimension. Since there was a difference in the treatment of these V and VP Groups during the optional shift each of the following comparisons was made on the rank test for paired replicates: VB vs. CB, VPB vs. CB, VS vs. CS, and VPS vs. CS. In each case the result was insignificant. In other words, as in Exp. I, there is no evidence that verbalization affected the number of trials required to learn the optional shift. Moreover, there is no evidence that prompting S to adjust his words to his choice facilitated, or interfered, with learning.

Turning now to the results of the test series, the first question was whether encouraging Ss to adjust their verbalization appropriately during the optional shift affected the kind of optional shift they made. It can be seen from Table 4 that the choice behavior of Groups V and VP was remarkably similar for both dimensions. Apparently once Ss are instructed to verbalize during the

TABLE 4

Percentage of Ss Responding in Each Category During Test Series

	Brightness			Shape		
Group	Reversal	Extra-dimensional	Incon-sistent	Reversal	Extra-dimensional	Incon-sistent
V	100	0.0	0.0	66.7	33.3	0.0
VP	100	0.0	0.0	66.7	25.0	8.3
C	66.7	25.0	8.3	58.3	41.7	0.0

initial discrimination, whether they adjust their words to their behavior during the optional shift has little or no effect on the kind of shift they make.

The next question was whether the instructions to verbalize significantly increased the tendency to make reversal shifts. Since there were no significant differences between the V and VP Groups their combined optional shift choices were compared with those of the C Group in a χ^2 multiple-contingency analysis with the following results: (1) the difference between the V and C Groups is significant ($\chi^2 = 3.936$, $df = 1$, $p < 0.05$), (2) the difference between the two dimensions is significant ($\chi^2 = 6.184$, $df = 1$, $p < 0.025$), and (3) there is no significant interaction between dimension and verbalization ($\chi^2 = 1.20$, $df = 1$). As in Exp. I, the frequencies of the extradimensional and inconsistent categories were combined for the multiple-contingency analysis.

The high proportion of reversers in the C Group of this experiment relative to Exp. I is probably due to the greater degree of selective elimination for failure to learn. Since slow learners are less likely to make reversal shifts than fast learners (Kendler and Kendler, 1959; Kendler, Kendler, and Learnard, 1962), elimination of Ss based on failure to learn within the required trials could be expected to increase the proportion of reversers in the C Group of Exp. II.

When the verbal behavior of the V Group during their last five criterion trials was analyzed, it was found that 15 Ss (62%) continued with the instructed sentence, 4 Ss adjusted their verbalizations to suit their choice, 2 Ss adjusted their words on some trials and not on others, and 3 Ss stopped verbalizing. Once again no S verbalized the stimuli of the initially irrelevant dimension. In line with this was the finding that all Ss in the VP Group also verbalized only stimuli on the initially relevant dimension.

These results suggest that the overt choice behavior weakens more rapidly than the linguistic behavior that precedes it. Once the overt choice changes the reinforcement resumes. At this point S is reinforced for saying the instructed but now inappropriate sentence. Under these circumstances many children calmly go on saying one thing while they do another. Note, however, that this inconsistency applies primarily to the win and lose words rather than to the stimulus labels. All reversal Ss continued to label the appropriate stimulus dimension. Only Ss who made extradimensional shifts and continued to use the instructed sentence could be said to have clearly applied the wrong stimulus labels. In the present experiment there were 4 Ss who made extradimensional shifts. In Exp. I there were 2 such Ss. Of these 6 Ss, 5 continued with the instructed sentence and one stopped verbalizing.

DISCUSSION

These experiments were intended to test and supplement a model of concept formation that can be summarized as follows: (1) Relatively mature humans are likely to respond to discrimination-learning or concept-formation situations by making covert responses that mediate both learning and transfer. (2) When the mediation is relevant to the task, learning is likely to be rapid and transfer is more likely to take the form of a reversal than of an extradimensional or inconsistent shift. (3) When the mediation does not occur, learning, which then depends on the gradual accretion of differential habit strengths, is likely to be relatively slow and the subsequent transfer is less likely to take the form of a reversal shift. (4) In human Ss the mediators are likely either to be verbal or to be somehow activated by verbal responses.

Experimental support for this model was obtained in previous research which showed that requiring 4- and 7-year-old children to label a stimulus according to the to-be-relevant dimension during the initial discrimination decreases the number of trials to learn a reversal shift while labelling the stimulus according to the to-be-irrelevant dimension increases them (Kendler and Kendler, 1961). The present results lend further credence to the model by showing that requiring kindergarten Ss to say a sentence that labels S+ and S— of the relevant dimension facilitated initial learning and increased the proportion of Ss who made a subsequent optional reversal shift. Apparently at this developmental stage overt verbalization has the same effect that the model ascribes to covert verbalization among more mature human Ss. This is consonant with the finding that for college students there is no significant difference in the effect of overt and covert verbalization on shift learning (Lachman and Sanders, 1963).

Having demonstrated that verbalization increases optional reversals does not preclude the possibility that other experimental operations, for example those designed to manipulate perceptual variables, could produce similar effects. (Note the indication in the present research that the dimension is a significant variable.) It does not even preclude the possibility that the verbalization was effective because it activated a perceptual response, nor is such a possibility incompatible with the theoretical model in its present stage. The results do, however, demonstrate experimentally that there is a close connection in young children among verbal representation, mediation, and reversal shifts. They also open the way for further investigation and theorizing about the nature and development of mediating processes.

As represented within an S-R framework, the simplest mediation process requires that three different events occur in sequence. The first event is the evocation of a representational response by a stimulus (Bousfield, 1961; Osgood, 1963). The second event is the production of a distinctive cue by the representational response. In the third event the response-produced cue leads to an overt act. If no mediation occurs it could be due to the omission of any one or more of the three events since each of these events may be determined by a different set of conditions. The occurrence of one event does not necessarily mean that the others also have occurred or will occur.

When an optional reversal shift occurs it is assumed that all three events have occurred in the proper sequence. Thus, for example, the 48% of the control Ss who made optional reversals (both experiments combined) are assumed to have generated a covert representational response to the discriminative stimulus which did lead to the other two events. Conditions for the Ss in the Verbal Groups differed from the control Ss in that only the first event was made to occur. But apparently this was enough to spark the rest of the sequence for the 82% of the children in the V groups (both experiments combined) who made optional reversals. From these data it can be inferred that about 34% (82 — 48) of these children would not ordinarily make representational responses to the discriminative stimuli, but would have their overt behavior guided by such responses if they did occur. It can also be inferred that for the remaining 18% either the stimulus was not sufficiently distinctive or, as is more likely, it did not exercise a controlling influence on their overt choice.

The three groups described above can represent three stages in the development of mediational responding similar to those proposed by Luria (1961). In the first stage are the Ss who do not make reversal shifts even with overt verbalization. The verbal labels as yet exert relatively little or no control over behavior. In the second stage, represented by Ss who make reversal shifts only when instructed to verbalize, the relationship between the labels and the ensuing choice behavior is established. The child has learned to respond to the directions of others and transfers these associations to overt directions he gives himself. It is, however, only in the third stage that he both generates his own verbal representations of the external stimulation and these representations provide cues for overt behavior. If these stages can be identified by the use of optional reversals, the conditions or events that lead to their evolution can be experimentally investigated.

SUMMARY

Previous research has found that the proportion of children who make optional reversal shifts increases with age. One explanation offered for this result is that as children get older they are more likely to respond to discrimination-learning situations by making covert mediating responses. These responses are of such a nature that they facilitate transfer from S+ to S—. In human Ss it is further assumed that these covert mediators are themselves verbal representational responses. The present research was designed to determine whether instructing kindergarten children overtly to label S+ and S— would have the effect assigned to the hypothetical covert response.

Two experiments were performed in which children were presented with an initial discrimination involving a relevant and irrelevant dimension. After criterion was attained, a second discrimination was presented in which both dimensions were present and relevant and the reinforcement pattern was changed. This discrimination was called the optional shift because S had the option of reaching criterion on the basis of a reversal shift, an extradimensional shift, or a nonselective (inconsistent) shift. A test series which followed the attainment of criterion on the optional shift provided the means of inferring the basis of the optional shift.

In each of the experiments one group of children was instructed to precede their choices during the initial discrimination with a sentence that labelled S+ and S— (V Group). Another group was run on the same discrimination but were given no instructions about verbalization (C Group). The major finding was that the V Group had significantly more optional reversers in both experiments.

It was concluded that among kindergarten children overt verbal representation has a function similar to that assigned to the hypothetical covert mediating response. A three-stage analysis of the development of the mediation chain was proposed.

References

Bousfield, W. A. The problem of meaning in verbal learning. In Cofer, C. N. (Ed.), *Verbal learning and verbal behavior*. New York: McGraw-Hill, 1959.

Brookshire, K. H., Warren, J. M., & Ball, G. G. Reversal and transfer learning following overtraining in rat and chicken. *J. comp. physiol. Psychol.*, 1961, **54**, 98–102.

Buss, A. H. Rigidity as a function of reversal and nonreversal shifts in the learning of successive discriminations. *J. exp. Psychol.*, 1953, **45**, 75–81.

Dunn, L. D. *Peabody Picture Vocabulary Test (PPVT)*. Nashville, Tenn.: American Guidance Service, 1959.

Harrow, M., & Friedman, G. B. Comparing reversal and nonreversal shifts in concept formation with partial reinforcement controlled. *J. exp. Psychol.*, 1958, **55**, 592–597.

Kendler, H. H., & D'Amato, M. F. A comparison of reversal shifts and nonreversal shifts in human concept formation behavior. *J. exp. Psychol.*, 1955, **49**, 165–174.

Kendler, H. H., & Kendler, T. S. Effect of verbalization on discrimination reversal shifts in children. *Science*, 1961, **134**, 1619–1620.

Kendler, H. H., & Kendler, T. S. Vertical and horizontal processes in problem solving. *Psychol. Rev.*, 1962, **69**, 1–16.

Kendler, T. S., & Kendler, H. H. Reversal and nonreversal shifts in kindergarten children. *J. exp. Psychol.*, 1959, **58**, 56–60.

Kendler, T. S., Kendler, H. H., & Learnard, B. Mediated responses to size and brightness as a function of age. *Amer. J. Psychol.*, 1962, **75**, 571–586.

Kendler, T. S., Kendler, H. H., & Wells, D. Reversal and nonreversal shifts in nursery school children. *J. comp. physiol. Psychol.*, 1960, **53**, 83–87.

Lachman, R., & Sanders, J. A. Concept shifts and verbal behavior. *J. exp. Psychol.*, 1963, **65**, 22–29.

Luria, A. R. The role of language in the formation of temporary connections. In B. Simon (Ed.), *Psychology in the Soviet Union.* Stanford Univ. Press, 1957, Pp. 115–129.

MacKintosh, N. J. The effects of overtraining on a reversal and a nonreversal shift. *J. comp. physiol. Psychol.*, 1962, **55**, 555–559.

Osgood, C. E. *Method and theory in experimental psychology.* New York: Oxford Univ. Press. Ch. 16.

Sutcliffe, J. P. A general method of analysis of frequency data for multiple classification designs. *Psychol. Bull.*, 1957, **54**, 134–137.

Wilcoxon, F. Some rapid approximate statistical procedures. New York: American Cyanamid Co., 1949.

9. DEVELOPMENT OF FORMAL REASONING ON CONCEPT FORMATION PROBLEMS[1,2]

Janellen Huttenlocher*

This experiment investigates development of ability to solve simple concept formation problems on the basis of different sequences of positive and/or negative instances. Earlier analysis of information processing on such problems had suggested that the number of intellectual steps required for problem solution varied with the type sequence. Since abilities of small children to carry out such steps seem particularly limited, it was predicted that the accuracy of these Ss' conclusions should suffer most on sequences requiring the greatest number of steps. The results were completely consistent with these predictions.

In this study, the development of formal reasoning in children has been investigated with puzzles similar to those used in several studies of concept formation in adults, e.g., by Hovland and Weiss (4), Bruner, Goodnow, and Austin (1), and Glanzer, Huttenlocher, and Clark (3). These puzzles may be described as follows: They involve highly schematized materials consisting of

SOURCE. *Child Development*, 1964, **35**, 1233–1242. © Society for Research in Child Development, Inc., 1964.

[1] This study was supported in part by the National Institute of Mental Health, United States Public Health Service, under Research Grant MH-06626, and in part by a grant to the Harvard Graduate School of Education from the Higgins Fund.

[2] The author wishes to thank the staff of the Concord Public Schools and especially Miss Jean Nelson, Director of Guidance, for their aid in obtaining the subjects for this study.

* Center for Cognitive Studies, Harvard University, Cambridge 38, Massachusetts.

a finite number of clearly identifiable attributes (e.g., geometric figures), each of which can assume a limited number of values (e.g., colors). An array of these attributes, each in a particular value, is called an instance. *S*s encounter a set of instances that vary from one another in certain respects. Information is given as to membership or nonmembership of each instance in a particular class; a class member is called a positive instance and a nonmember a negative instance. *S*s' task is to use a set of instances to discover the principle on which the classification was based. It is possible to present a set of instances that defines the answer exactly and without redundancy. There are often several alternative sets of instances that may do this.

Studies with adults indicate that efficiency of isolating the answer in such puzzles depends on the sequence of instances presented. One important factor is whether or not the instances are members of the critical class, i.e., are positive or negative. Hovland and Weiss (4) found that on conjunctive concept problems sequences of positive instances were easiest, sequences of negative instances most difficult, and mixed sequences of intermediate difficulty. In view of the fact that with conjunctive concepts each positive instance transmits more information about an answer than each negative instance, it was not possible to control the amount of information from single positive and negative instances in this study. Using binary attributes, if the answer involves only a single attribute, the amount of information available from individual positive and negative instances is equivalent. The author carried out an experiment of this sort in which each problem was made up of only two instances and all four possible combinations of positive and negative instances were studied (5).

The order of difficulty for the four types of problems was as follows: a negative instance followed by a positive instance (— +) was easiest, either a positive instance followed by a negative instance (+ —) or two positive instances (+ +) were of intermediate difficulty, and two negative instances (— —) were most difficult.

Studies such as these have been the basis for analyses of information processing in the formation of concepts. Glanzer, Huttenlocher, and Clark (3) have suggested that, at least on this schematic type of problem, *S*s proceed as follows: They attempt to remember the initial instance. Later instances are then compared with this initial one and attributes that have changed value are examined to determine whether they are relevant to the answer. This manner of processing information has been called "focusing" and is a common strategy in experiments where *S*s determine their own sequence of instances (1).

Extending this general approach, the author proposed an analysis of the information processing steps required in the simple puzzles in her experiment. These can best be followed by examining Figure 1 while considering the steps.

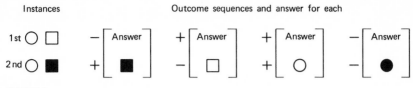

FIGURE 1.

One should bear in mind that the two instances were presented successively rather than simultaneously. After seeing the two instances Ss must: (a) Determine the relevance or irrelevance of the changed attribute. On mixed sequences ($+$ $-$ and $-$ $+$) it can be inferred that the changed attribute is the answer. On sequences where both outcomes are the same ($+$ $+$ and $-$ $-$) a simple step is necessary, i.e., attributes that change are irrelevant and thus the remaining attribute must be the answer. (b) Determine the correct value for the relevant attribute. If the final instance is positive it can be inferred that the relevant attribute is in the appropriate value. If the final instance is negative a simple step must be taken, i.e., the attribute must be in the other value. In terms of this analysis, the number of steps required to obtain answers varies with the sequence in a way that parallels findings on efficiency of performance: $-$ $+$ sequences require the minimum number of steps, and $-$ $-$ sequences require the maxiumum number of steps (5).

This analysis suggested repetition of the original experiment with children of varying ages. Small children appear to have particular difficulty in holding on to a set of items or carrying through a series of inferential steps. Such difficulties would seem to result from limited memory span and poorly developed symbolic processes that prevent the child from talking solutions through to himself. Given this difficulty, and the accuracy of the above analysis, certain predictions can be made about the development of ability to draw inferences from different sequences. Young children should be able to use sequences requiring a minimal number of steps before they can use others, and the accuracy of conclusions should be more contingent on type of sequence in younger than older children.

The present experiment is thus designed to determine whether children's obvious intellectual limitations can explain in part the types of difficulties they would encounter on specific conceptual problems. These puzzles are of special interest for such a study since the four types of sequences exemplify in simple concrete form Mill's methods of inductive reasoning: $+$ $-$ and $-$ $+$ sequences representing the method of difference, and $+$ $+$ and $-$ $-$ sequences the method of agreement. Just as Mill's methods elaborate the meaning of causal relations under certain restricted conditions, these puzzles would seem to test Ss' understanding of such simple causal relations.

METHOD

Subjects

*S*s were 300 children from the Concord public schools. There were 25 boys and 25 girls from each of the first, third, fifth, seventh, ninth, and eleventh grades.

Apparatus

A cut-out board 12 by 42 inches was mounted at a 30-degree angle in an open-backed box 16 by 12 inches. This box had doors mounted on hinges at the sides that could close over the cut-out board. The area above the cut-out board and below the top of the box was open so that the experimenter could reach her hand through to the front of the cut-out board.

Eight different figures were cut out of the board, each approximately 2½ inches square. Molding was mounted above and below the figures 4 inches apart; 4-inch square pieces of plywood could be placed over any number of figures so as to allow for presentation of problems involving less than eight figures. A light was mounted above the upper molding on the cut-out board. Batteries and a bell were mounted behind the cut-out board. A switch behind the cut-out board activated the light and bell simultaneously.

Blocks of 1-inch thick plywood shaped to fit the cut-outs were painted black on one side and white on the other. (See Figure 2.)

Design

Each of the blocks (i.e., heart, square, etc.) represented a single attribute. The black and the white sides of the blocks were the two possible values

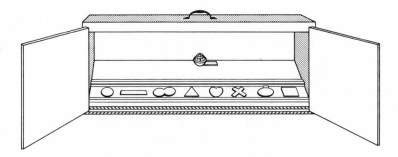

FIGURE 2. Apparatus.

each attribute could assume. Each instance of a concept consisted of an array of the same group of blocks varying with respect to whether these appeared in black or white. Activation of light and buzzer signaled a positive instance. The answer to each problem involved one block in one particular color (e.g., a white square, or a black heart). Each concept was defined in exactly two instances. Before presentation of the initial instance S could infer that the answer might involve any single block in either color. The initial instance, whether positive or negative, eliminated half of the possible answers. If the initial instance (e.g., black triangle and white circle) was positive, S could infer that the answer involved one of the blocks in the color showing (e.g., either black triangle or white circle); if the initial instance was negative, S could infer that the answer involved one of the blocks in the color not showing (e.g., either white triangle or black circle). The second instance was always so arranged that it eliminated all other hypotheses except the answer.

Performance was compared on the following four types of problems:

1. Positive instance followed by a positive instance $(+ +$ sequence)
2. Positive instance followed by a negative instance $(+ -$ sequence)
3. Negative instance followed by a positive instance $(- +$ sequence)
4. Negative instance followed by a negative instance $(- -$ sequence)

In order to obtain reliable information on the difficulty of these four types of sequences, six problems of each of the four types were used. Thus, there was a total of 24 problems. All Ss were run on all problems. Two factors previously shown to affect difficulty of forming concepts (3) were varied systematically within each set of six problems: (a) the number of irrelevant attributes; on two of the problems there was one irrelevant attribute (i.e., two blocks were exposed), on two of the problems there were two irrelevant attributes (i.e., three blocks were exposed), and on two of the problems there were three irrelevant attributes (i.e., four blocks were exposed); (b) the homogeneity of color of attributes on initial instances.

The answer was randomly selected for each problem. The blocks exposed on each problem were adjacent on the cut-out board, but the position of the block on the left was selected randomly so that different blocks were exposed in different problems. The order of the 24 problems was randomized with the restriction that there were three problems of each of the four types in the first set of twelve problems and similarly in the second set of twelve problems. Because Ss were not run individually the same order of problems was used for all Ss.

Procedure

An instance was presented to Ss by opening the doors of the apparatus and exposing the array of blocks. Two seconds after the doors were opened the light and buzzer were presented for half a second if the instance was a positive one. Doors were closed after ten seconds of exposure and the second instance was presented ten seconds later.

The following instructions were given to Ss:

> You will be given a set of puzzles. Let me tell you about them. This box contains a cut-out board and a set of blocks that fit the different holes. Each block can be put in so that it faces up white or black. There are also a light and a buzzer in this box. They go on together like this. For each puzzle you will have to figure out which block in which color makes the light and buzzer go on. Let us do an example problem. Here is a black circle and the light and buzzer go on like this. Now I will show you another example from the same problem. Here the circle is white and the light and buzzer do not go on. This means that on this particular problem the black circle made the light and buzzer go on. On the first page of your booklet draw a circle and fill it in. That is how you will indicate your answer on each problem. Draw the figure that made the light and buzzer go on. If it had to be white leave the figure blank, if it had to be black then fill the figure in.
>
> Here is another example problem. Here is a black $\times$. The light and buzzer did not go on. That means that the $\times$ had to be white to make the light and buzzer go on. On the next page draw an $\times$ and don't fill it in. Now, in the puzzles you will do there will be more than one block and you will have to figure out which block in which color makes the light and buzzer go on. On each puzzle you will be given enough information to solve the problem without guesswork. However, the problems are difficult and if you aren't sure of the answer then guess. You will see each puzzle twice. Each time you draw the answer. Don't look back at your first answer the second time through because you should know it better after the second chance. I will give you the answer to each problem after the second time through it.

Ss were run in groups of three or four. Groups were run for two sessions, each of approximately 50 minutes.

RESULTS AND CONCLUSIONS

Scores for each concept formation problem were made up as follows: each answer was scored either right or wrong, and, since each problem was presented twice, the score for a problem was zero if the answer was wrong both times, one if it was correct once, and two if it was correct both times. There was a total of 24 problems (so the maximum score for each S was 48) and six problems of each of the four types (so the maximum score for each S for a problem type was 12).

The average scores for Ss in the different grades are presented in Table 1. The mean number of successful responses per S was 33.2, increasing from

TABLE 1

Mean Number of Correct Responses for All Grades

	Grade in School					
	1	3	5	7	9	11
Average score	15.0	26.0	33.3	40.5	42.8	41.3

15.0 in the first grade to 41.3 in the eleventh grade. Scores increased through the seventh grade (when Ss were 12½ to 13 years of age) and then leveled off. Extrapolation of accuracy scores suggests that groups younger than the youngest group used in this experiment (first graders of 6½ to 7 years of age) would not perform above chance levels. The total chance score for these problems is 8.7. (Chance scores are discussed later in this section.)

Since the mean number of successful responses per S across grades for the entire set of 24 problems was 33.2, the mean would be 16.6 for each of the first and second sets of 12 problems if there were no learning. Actually the mean for the first set of 12 problems was 15.0 and for the second set was 18.2. Thus learning was slight and the entire set of problems contributed to error scores.

The means for each of the four categories of problems are presented in Table 2. The order of difficulty was the same as in the original experiment:

TABLE 2

Mean Number of Correct Responses for the Four Categories of Problems for All Grades

	++	+−	−+	−−	Mean
Grade 1	4.2	2.9	6.8	1.2	3.8
Grade 3	7.5	6.5	8.8	3.3	6.5
Grade 5	8.8	8.6	10.6	5.2	8.3
Grade 7	10.1	10.5	11.3	8.7	10.2
Grade 9	10.9	10.6	11.7	9.6	10.7
Grade 11	10.6	10.6	11.1	9.0	10.3
Mean	8.7	8.3	10.5	6.2	

− + sequences were easiest (10.5), + + and + − sequences were of intermediate difficulty (8.7 and 8.3 respectively), and − − sequences were most difficult (6.2). Despite the marked differences in efficiency on different types of problems, performance on each type leveled off at the seventh grade, as with total scores, increasing slightly in the ninth grade and decreasing again slightly in the eleventh.

The means for the four types of problems for the six different age groups paralleled in each case those for the entire group. A separate analysis of variance was carried out for each of the grades. These analyses are presented in Table 3. For each grade the differences between means for the four types of problems were significant far beyond the .001 level (F for problem type had to be 5.42 for significance at .001). To compare the significance of the differences between individual means for problem type in each grade, use was made of the least significant difference (lsd) (2). The lsd for first-grade scores was .6 and for third-grade scores was .7, so that all the means were significantly different from one another in both grades. In the fifth grade where the lsd was .6, the — + problems were significantly easier than all others, and the — — problems were significantly more difficult; the difference between the + + and the + — problems was insignificant. The relation between problem type and performance remained approximately the same in the seventh, ninth, and eleventh grades as in the fifth, although the differences in means for the different types of problems decreased in magnitude. The lsds in these grades were .5, .4, and .3, respectively.

The chance score for a problem type for an S can be calculated as follows: On the problems with two blocks showing there were four possible answers so that the probability of getting the correct answer by chance was $\frac{1}{4}$; on the problems with three blocks there were six possible answers so the probability of getting the correct one by chance was $\frac{1}{6}$; on the problems with four blocks there were eight possible answers so the probability of getting the correct one by chance was $\frac{1}{8}$. For each type of problem the total possible score was 12, a possible score of 4 each in two-, three-, and four-block problems. Thus the chance score for a problem type was $(4)\frac{1}{4} + (4)\frac{1}{6} + (4)\frac{1}{8}$, or 2.17.

Children in the first grade performed above chance on all problems except the — — ones where performance was clearly below chance, suggesting that — — sequences were misleading to these Ss. (This is discussed below.) On the other hand, first graders did over half of the — + problems correctly.

The relative dependence on the particular sequence was, as predicted, considerably greater in the younger than in the older groups. Table 3 indicates that the mean square for problem type in the first grade (282.73) was seven times as great as the mean square for problem type in the eleventh grade (40.75). Statistical comparison of variability in different age groups should be evaluated with caution: it is doubtful that the scale is completely linear, e.g., that it is equally difficult to improve one's score from 2 to 4 and from 10 to 12; it should also be noted that scores have a ceiling of 12, thus possibly

TABLE 3

Analysis of Variance for Four Categories of Problems for All Grades
(Separate Two-Way Analysis for Each Grade)

Source	df	Mean Square	F
Grade 1			
Subjects	49	10.89	3.08
Problem type	3	282.73	79.87
Error	147	3.54	
Grade 3			
Subjects	49	29.41	7.52
Problem type	3	275.45	70.45
Error	147	3.91	
Grade 5			
Subjects	49	19.59	5.85
Problem type	3	252.96	75.51
Error	147	3.35	
Grade 7			
Subjects	49	16.99	7.79
Problem type	3	60.77	27.88
Error	147	2.18	
Grade 9			
Subjects	49	3.35	2.99
Problem type	3	37.61	33.58
Error	147	1.12	
Grade 11			
Subjects	49	10.43	6.60
Problem type	3	40.75	25.79
Error	147	1.58	

attenuating differences in older groups. A rough measure of the significance of changes with age is provided by comparing differences between problem types with the highest and lowest average scores ($-+$ and $--$ problems) in the first and eleventh grades. This difference was 5.6 in the first grade and 2.1 in the eleventh grade, a difference of 3.5 (see Table 2). The standard error of the difference based on the difference scores in the first and eleventh grades was .52. The standard deviate score was 6.7, and the probability of chance occurrence so diminutive as to be quite convincing despite the reservations mentioned above.

Accuracy of inferences from each type of sequence increased gradually. Even on $--$ sequences, where scores increased most rapidly with age, there was no indication of sudden shifts in accuracy of inferences. Reaction of children to these $--$ sequences provides an example of how development proceeded. First graders either answered at random or they offered the wrong answer with some assurance. This generally resulted from their carrying out one of the two required steps and totally ignoring the other. For example, they often gave the right attribute in the wrong value, saying that the answer wasn't the changing attribute(s) so it had to be the remaining one, but failing to notice the necessary transformation of value. Third-grade children occasionally identified the answer by plan rather than chance. This involved the appearance of great effort. A child might correctly answer one such problem and get lost in the process on another such problem. No fifth-grade children were sure of wrong answers, but many still got confused. As indicated in Table 2, even eleventh graders missed about 25 per cent of the answers. Thus accuracy of conclusions seemed to depend on a gradually evolving ability to hold on to the information necessary to get through the problem.

Results are completely consistent both with the proposed analysis of information processing and with the notion that small children are unable to carry out a sequence of intellectual steps. That is, in summary, the number of accurate inferences from — + sequences far exceeded that from — — sequences in small children; and the importance of type of sequence for accuracy was greater in younger than older children. So far as ability to solve these puzzles indexes understanding of simple causal relations, the results indicate that certain aspects are more difficult than others; e.g., that demonstration of irrelevance of an attribute cannot be handled as early as direct demonstration of its relevance; and that ability to cope with such relations may develop gradually, perhaps in correspondence with the evolution of prerequisite skills, rather than in sudden shifts.

It must be noted that while the results are perfectly consistent with the notion that inability to carry out a consecutive sequence of inferential steps prevented complete grasp of these causal relations, another explanation is also plausible. Lack of understanding of causal relations could have made it difficult for children to carry out the inferential steps rather than vice versa. One argument that could be advanced in favor of the latter interpretation is that those sequences postulated to demand maximum processing, — — ones, are unfamiliar as a basis for inference and thus would be expected to be relatively more difficult for small children in any case.

References

1. Bruner, J. S., Goodnow, J. J., & Austin, G. S. *A study of thinking.* Wiley, 1956.
2. Federer, W. T. *Experimental design: theory and application.* Macmillan, 1955.

3. Glanzer, M., Huttenlocher, J., & Clark, W. H. Systematic operations in solving concept problems: a parametric study of a class of problems. *Psychol. Monogr.*, 1963, 77, No. 1 (Whole No. 564).

4. Hovland, C. I., & Weiss, W. Transmission of information concerning concepts through positive and negative instances. *J. exp. Psychol.*, 1953, 45, 175–182.

5. Huttenlocher, J. Some effects of negative instances on the formation of simple concepts. *Psychol. Rep.*, 1962, 11, 35–42.

10. CHILDREN'S DISCOVERY OF THE CONSERVATION OF MASS, WEIGHT, AND VOLUME: PIAGET REPLICATION STUDY II*

David Elkind[1]

A. INTRODUCTION

This study is the second[2] in a series devoted to the systematic replication of experiments originally performed by the Swiss psychologist, Jean Piaget. For its starting point the present study takes one of Piaget's (1940) investigations dealing with the ages at which children discover the conservation of mass, weight, and volume. Piaget assumes that concepts develop and that the discovery of conservation earmarks the final stage of their development. By studying children's responses to demonstrations of the conservation of mass, weight, and volume Piaget sought to uncover the genetic stages in the formation of these concepts. The present study differs from Piaget's investigation in its standardization of his procedures and in its use of statistical design.

In his investigation Piaget tested for the conservation of mass, weight, and volume by means of the "sausage" experiment. The purpose of this experiment was to determine whether the child could tell that a quantity remained the same (was conserved) after it was changed in appearance. For example, in testing for the conservation of mass Piaget showed the child two clay balls

SOURCE. *The Journal of Genetic Psychology*, 1961, **98**, 219–227.

* Received in the Editorial Office on July 6, 1959.

[1] This study was carried out while the writer was a Staff Psychologist at the Beth Israel Hospital in Boston. The writer is indebted to Dr. Greta Bibring, the head of Beth Israel's Dept. of Psychiatry, and to the members of the research committee for granting him the time to make the study.

[2] For a report of the first study cf. Elkind (1961).

identical in size, shape, and weight. After the child agreed that both balls had equal clay, Piaget made one of the balls in to a sausage. Then he asked the child to judge whether the ball and the sausage contained the same amount of clay. Piaget also asked the child to predict—while both pieces of clay were shaped as balls—if they would be the same were one made into a sausage and to explain his judgments and predictions.

Using the sausage experiment to test 5–12 year-old children, Piaget found that discoveries of conservation followed a regular order that was related to age. The conservation of mass was discovered at ages 7-8; the conservation of weight was discovered at ages 9-10; and the conservation of volume was discovered at ages 11 and 12. These findings, together with his theoretical interpretations, Piaget reported with the aid of a great many illustrative examples but without statistics.

Starting from Piaget's procedures and results the present study was designed to test the hypotheses that, other things being equal, (a) the number of conservation responses does not vary significantly with the Type of Response (prediction, judgment, and explanation) required; (b) the number of conservation responses varies significantly with the Type of Quantity (mass, weight, and volume) ; (c) the number of conservation responses varies significantly with Age Level; (d) the number of conservation responses varies significantly with the joint effect of Type of Quantity and Age Level (the statistical test of Piaget's age-order of discovery finding). In addition children's explanations were categorized for comparison with the explanations given by Piaget's subjects.

B. METHOD

1. Subjects

One hundred and seventy-five children attending the Claflin School[3] in Newton, Mass., were tested. Twenty-five children were randomly selected from each of the grades from kindergarten to sixth. The mean age and standard deviation for each grade were: Kindergarten, M = 5:8, SD = 3.0; Grade 1, M = 6:8, SD = 3.9; Grade 2, M = 7:7, SD = 3.6; Grade 3, M = 8:6, SD = 3.8; Grade 4, M = 9:7, SD = 3.0; Grade 5, M = 10:7, SD = 2.5; Grade 6, M = 11:9, SD = 5.56 months. Hereafter the grades will be referred to by their age level.

For 125 children at the five oldest age levels, Kuhlmann-Anderson Intelligence Test scores were available. The mean IQ for this group was 109 and the SD was 11.0 points. Most of the children came from middle to upper-middle class homes.

[3] The writer is grateful to the principal, Dr. Harry Anderson, and teachers of the Claflin School whose friendly cooperation made the study not only possible but enjoyable.

2. Procedure

Each *S* was seen individually and questioned three times on each type of quantity. For each quantity *S* was asked first to predict, next judge, and then explain his conservation or non-conservation responses. The order of the questions and the order of presenting the quantities—mass, weight, volume—was the same for all *S*s. A fixed order of presentation was used to provide a more rigorous test of Piaget's findings. Any practice effects resulting from the fixed order should have worked against the differences Piaget found. On the other hand if differences were developmentally determined, as Piaget assumes, then the minimal practice effect over a brief time span should have had little effect.

3. Tests

In the test for the conservation of mass, two clay balls identical in size, shape, and weight were on the table. *E*, "Do both balls have the same amount of clay, is there as much clay in this ball as in this one?" *S* was encouraged to "make them the same," if he doubted the equality of the balls. When *S* agreed that the two balls were equal *E* asked, "Suppose I roll one of the balls out into a hot dog, will there be as much clay in the hot dog as in the ball, will they both have the same amount of clay?" (Prediction question.)

After *S*'s prediction *E* actually made one of the balls into a hot dog while *S* looked on. *E*, "Is there as much clay in the ball as in the hot dog, do they both have the same amount of clay?" (Judgment question.) Then *E* asked "Why is that?" to *S*'s response. (Explanation question.)

Exactly the same procedure was used to test for the conservation of weight and volume. To test for the conservation of weight *E* asked, "Do they both weigh the same, do they both have the same amount of weight?" etc. And to test for the conservation of volume *E* asked, "Do they both take up the same amount of space, do they both take up as much room?" etc. On each test the child was initially given the opportunity to handle the balls and to add or subtract clay as he liked to "make them the same."

4. Scoring

Each conservation response was scored 1 and all non-conservation responses were scored zero. For each *S* there was a total possible conservation score of 9 and for each Type of Quantity and Type of Response there was a total possible score of three.

5. Statistical Analyses

To test for the effects of Type of Response an analysis of variance design described by Lindquist (1953, Ch. 6) was used. In this design chance differences between subjects were controlled by testing all subjects on all types of response.

To test for the separate and combined effects of Age Level and Type of Quantity a different analysis of variance design was used (Lindquist, 1953, pp. 267-273). In this design chance differences between subjects were controlled, for the Type of Quantity variable only, by testing all subjects on all types of quantity.

C. RESULTS

1. Type of Response

In his investigations Piaget used children's predictions, judgments, and explanations interchangeably as signs of conservation or non-conservation. In the present study the F for Type of Response was NS and did not approach significance. This finding agreed with Piaget's use of these three types of response as equivalent signs of conservation.

2. Type of Quantity

Piaget found that, other things being equal, the conservation of mass was easiest to discover, the conservation of weight was of intermediate difficulty, and the conservation of volume was the most difficult discovery of all. The F for Type of Quantity obtained in the present study was 255.55 and was significant beyond the .01 level. Individual t tests for the Type of Quantity means revealed that the mean for each type of quantity was significantly different than every other. For all subjects the average number of conservation responses given for mass was 2.08, the average number given for weight was 1.75, and the average number of conservation responses given for volume was 0.25. The order of difficulty obtained in the present study was the same as the order that Piaget observed.

3. Age Level

The Swiss children tested by Piaget showed that, other things being equal, their conservation responses increased with age. For the children in the present study the same held true. The F for Age Level was 14.38 and was significant beyond the .01 level. Individual t tests of Age Level means showed that the magnitude of the Age Level means increased significantly with age in agreement with Piaget's finding.

4. Type of Quantity-Age Level Interaction

Piaget's illustrative examples indicated that age group differences varied with the type of quantity in question. For mass there was a marked difference between the 5–6 and the 7–12 year-old groups; for weight there was a marked difference between the 5–8 and the 9–12 year-old groups; and for volume there was a marked difference between the 5–10 and the 11–12 year-old groups in their number of conservation responses.

In the present study the variations in the differences between age groups for each type of quantity appeared as the interaction effect of Type of Quantity and Age Level. This interaction F was 6.93 and was significant beyond the .01 level. Individual t tests for age group differences showed that: (a) For mass the 5–6 and the 7–11 year-old groups differed significantly; (b) for weight the 5–8 and 9–11 year-old groups differed significantly; and (c) for volume the 5–10 and the 11 year-old groups differed significantly from each other in number of conservation responses given. These findings agreed with expectations based on Piaget's results.

In Piaget's early studies (1951a) he assigned different tests to the age level at which the per cent passing was 75.[4] Although he gave no percentages for the conservation experiments one can assume that he used the same criterion for assigning the conservation of mass to ages 7-8; the conservation of weight to ages 9-10; and the conservation of volume to ages 11-12. The results of the present study were converted into percentages for comparison with Piaget's criterion and these are presented in Table 1.

TABLE 1

Per cent[a] of Conservation Responses for Mass, Weight, and Volume at Successive Age Levels ($N = 25$ at Each Age Level)

Type of Quantity	Age Level						
	5	6	7	8	9	10	11
Mass	19	51	70	72	86	94	92
Weight	21	52	51	44	73	89	78
Volume	0	4	0	4	4	19	25

[a] Of 75 possible responses.

Table 1 shows that the 70 per cent point for mass was reached at the seven year level but that the 75 per cent point was not reached until age nine. For weight the 73 per cent was reached at age nine and the 75 per cent point by age 10. In this study the 75 per cent point for volume was not reached at the 11 year level.

The slight discrepancies between Piaget's results and those in Table 1 for weight and mass could easily be due to the small size of the samples used in the present study. The relatively low number of conservation responses

[4] For a test oriented approach to the replication of Piaget's work cf. Laurendeau & Pinard (1957).

at the 11 year level may be due to the fact that Piaget used a somewhat different procedure in his test for the conservation of volume. Piaget had his subjects say whether the ball and the sausage would displace the same amount of water. As a check the same procedure was used with some of the subjects of the present study (after the other testing was completed) and conservation seemed easier to discover by means of the displacement problem.

5. Children's Explanations

When Piaget interpreted the results of his investigation he made use of children's explanations without categorizing or quantifying them as he did in early studies (Piaget, 1951a). In the present study four types of explanation were distinguished. Two of these were explanations of non-conservation: (a) Romancing (Piaget, 1951b, introd.), it's more because "My uncle said so;" (b) Perceptual, it's more because it's "longer, thinner, thicker, wider, etc." The two types of explanation given for conservation were: (c) Specific, "You didn't add any or take any away," "You can roll it back into a ball and it will be the same," and "The hot dog is longer but thinner so the same;" (d) General, it's the same because "No matter what shape you make it into it won't change the amount." Table 2 shows the per cent for each type of explanation given at each age level.

TABLE 2

Per Cent for Each of Four Types of Explanation Given at Successive Age Levels ($N = 25$ at Each Age Level)

Type of Explanation	Age Level						
	5	6	7	8	9	10	11
Romancing[a]	4	3	7	7	0	1	0
Perceptual[a]	85	64	53	57	36	32	33
Specific[b]	11	33	40	36	60	51	49
General[b]	0	0	0	0	4	16	18

[a] Explanation of non-conservation.
[b] Explanation of conservation.

Table 2 shows that Romancing and Perceptual explanations decrease with age while Specific explanations first increase and then level off with age. Piaget noted the same types and age trends in the explanations given by his subjects. The explanations are one type of evidence Piaget takes for his theory that as the child's thinking develops, it frees itself from its earlier domination by immediate perception. One step in this liberation is the interpretation of a perceptual effect as the result of a specific action which can be reversed (you can roll it back into a ball). A later step is to interpret a perception as but one of a great many possible instances (no matter what shape you make it into it will always be the same). The results in Table 2 agreed with the observations upon which Piaget builds his theory of the developmental changes in the relation between thought and perception.

D. DISCUSSION

The results of the present study agreed with Piaget's findings regarding the ages at which children discover the conservation of mass, weight, and volume. In both studies: the conservation of mass did not usually appear before the ages 7-8; the conservation of weight did not usually appear before the ages 9-10; and the conservation of volume did not in most cases appear before the age of 11. The discussion will briefly summarize Piaget's interpretation of the results.

Piaget's theory[5] is that concepts of quantity develop in three stages with the final stage ear-marked by the discovery of conservation. Children at the first stage have only a general impression of quantity but are capable of judging crude weight, volume, and mass differences. In the sausage experiment they give non-conservation responses because to their general impression the sausage is different than the ball. When they are forced to break down this impression, by the explanation question, then they judge quantity by single dimensions which they are unable to coordinate one with the other.

Those children who are at the second stage have a differentiated impression of quantity and are unable to judge quantity differences two by two (long-wide, long-narrow, etc.) which Piaget calls *logical multiplication*. Children at this stage give non-conservation responses in the sausage experiment because to their differentiated impression the sausage is both more (in length) and less (in width) than the ball. They are unable to resolve the contradiction, as one child expressed it, "It's more and it's less, I'll take one of each." When these children are forced to explain their non-conservation answers they also judge quantity by single dimensions.

At the third stage children have an abstract quantity concept and judge quantity in unit terms. In the sausage experiment they immediately predict and judge conservation. Their explanations indicate either that the perceived transformation can be cancelled (the sausage can be rolled back into a ball) or that the perceived differences can be equated (what the sausage gained in length it lost in width) and therefore the quantity is the same.

According to Piaget the *equation of differences* results in the formation of ratios and fixed units and underlies abstract quantity and number (Piaget,

[5] For more complete presentations of Piaget's theory cf. Piaget (1950; 1957; 1958).

1952) concept formation. On the perceptual plane the equation of differences enables the child to discover that an object which changes in appearance can still be the same in quantity. Piaget's theory is that once conservation is discovered it is immediately externalized and the subject has the impression that conservation is a perceptually given property of the object.

The initial appearance of the conservation of mass at ages 7-8 Piaget attributes to the development by that age of logical multiplication and equation of differences which he speaks of as *mental operations*. The time lag before the discovery of the conservation of weight at ages 9-10 and the even greater lag before the conservation of volume at ages 11-12 Piaget attributes to the quantities themselves. He argues that a quantity is difficult to conceptualize, and so to conserve, to the degree that it is associated with the subject's own action. Length, for example, was more easily dissociated from the child's action than was weight. In Piaget's theory, therefore, the discovery of conservation is limited both by the maturational level of the subject and by the properties of the object and in this sense it is both a nature *and* a nurture theory.

E. SUMMARY

One hundred and seventy-five children were asked to predict, judge, and explain the conservation of mass, weight, and volume in a systematic replication of Piaget's investigation. Analysis of variance showed that the number of conservation responses varied significantly with: Age Level; Type of Quantity; Age Level–Type of Quantity Interaction; but not with Type of Response. Romancing and Perceptual non-conservation explanations decreased, while Specific and General conservation explanations increased, with age.

The results were in close agreement with Piaget's finding of a regular, age related order in the discoveries of the conservation of mass, weight, and volume. Briefly presented was Piaget's theory that quantity concepts develop through three stages with the final stage ear-marked by the discovery of their conservation.

References

1. Elkind, D. The development of quantitative thinking: A systematic replication of Piaget's studies. *J. Genet. Psychol.*, 1961, **98**, 37–46.
2. Inhelder, B., & Piaget, J. The growth of logical thinking from childhood to adolescence. New York: Basic Books, 1958.
3. Laurendeau, M., & Pinard, A. Une méthode rationelle de localization des testes dans échelles d'age. *Canad. J. Psychol.*, 1957, **11**, 33–47.

4. Lindquist, E. F. Design and Analysis of Experiments in Psychology and Education. Cambridge, Mass.: Riverside, 1953.

5. Piaget, J., & Inhelder, B. Le développement des quantités chez l'enfant. Paris: Delachaux and Niestle, 1940.

6. Piaget, J. The Psychology of Intelligence. London: Broadway, 1950.

7. ———. Judgment and Reasoning in the Child. London: Routledge, 1951.

8. ———. The Child's Conception of the World. London: Routledge, 1951.

9. ———. The Child's Conception of Number. London: Routledge, 1952.

10. ———. Logic and Psychology. New York: Basic Books, 1957.

11. CHILDREN'S UNDERSTANDING OF NUMBER AND RELATED CONCEPTS[1]

P. C. Dodwell

Some years ago an English translation of Piaget's *"La Genèse du nombre chez l'enfant"* was published (Piaget, 1952a). Unlike some of his earlier work on children's language and thinking (e.g., Piaget, 1926; 1929), this study of number concepts and children's ability to use numerical operations has not produced very great interest, acclaim, or criticism; nor, to judge by published reports, has it stimulated much research by independent investigators. This is surprising, since the work is an improvement on Piaget's earlier studies in at least two respects. First, the theoretical background is much more precise, but at the same time more elaborate than his earlier theories of cognitive development, and secondly the empirical investigations are more objective, described in sufficient detail to be essentially repeatable, and not open to the earlier criticisms of too heavy a reliance on interpretation of verbal statements and the possibility of "projecting" the experimenter's ideas into these interpretations (Hazlitt, 1930; McCarthy, 1930). This is not to say that the later experiments are above criticism; Piaget usually fails to specify the number of subjects used in any one investigation, frequently bases a generalization (apparently) on the behaviour of but one or two children, and does not say whether a particular type of observed behaviour is universal, typical, or merely found occasionally, at any particular age or stage of development.

SOURCE. *Canad. J. Psychol.*, 1960, **14**, 3. Abridged by permission of the author.

[1] This investigation was supported by a grant from the Arts Research Committee of Queen's University, whose assistance is gratefully acknowledged. Thanks are due also to students in the Department of Psychology who took part in the investigation, and to the Inspector of Public Schools in Kingston and the teachers who made it possible.

One study (Estes, 1956) reports findings which claim to refute completely Piaget's statements about young children's responses to problems involving numerical concepts. It would appear that this refutation should be taken seriously since the test situations used were, ostensibly, the very situations which Piaget himself describes. Even though the number of subjects used was not too small (52), the generally inimical tone of the paper tends to raise a doubt in the reader's mind, especially since it appears that Estes was not familiar with the main body of Piaget's work on number concepts. Having supervised several small-scale projects (unpublished) which on the whole tended to support Piaget's statements, I felt that a more thorough investigation was called for. Such an investigation, based on study of some 250 children, is reported below.

PIAGET'S THEORY

Piaget's theory of the development of number concepts is a particular application of his general theory of intelligence (Piaget, 1950). The central idea is that rational behaviour, and in particular the production of rational (operational) solutions to problems involving number, develop from a more primitive form of thinking which is syncretistic and egocentric; that is, which does not operate with categories and relations which are well defined, articulated, and self-consistent, and also does not apply rules which are independent of the "viewpoint" of the operator. Piaget considers this type of thought as being not merely a poor attempt at the thinking which is characteristic of the rational adult, but rather as having positive properties of its own, which are both characteristic for a particular stage of cognitive development, and limit the type of understanding which is possible at that stage. Piaget describes a number of stages of cognitive development; the present study is concerned with but three of them. At about the sixth year, when most children display a spontaneous interest in numbers, and have already learned to count, Piaget claims that they have only a vague notion of what the concept of "number" is. This can be demonstrated in a variety of ways, some of which will be described below. At this stage judgments about problems involving numbers are to a large extent determined by what the child *perceives*, so that if a perceived configuration is changed, the numerical judgments made about the situation will be likely to change. The same considerations apply to judgments about quantities; quantity for a young child turns out to be determined by perceived characteristics, rather than a logical notion which obeys laws of conservation, etc. This stage, which is clearly egocentric (bound to a particular perceptual point of view), is called by Piaget the stage of "global comparisons."[2] It is followed, accord-

[2] The labelling of stages here used is the standard nomenclature of the English translation of *The Child's Conception of Number* (Piaget, 1952).

ing to Piaget, by an "intuitive" stage in which the child starts to realize that judgments of quantity and number cannot be made simply in terms of perceived attributes; it starts to grasp, fleetingly and unclearly, that quantity and number are attributes of objects, or sets of objects, which remain invariant under perceptual transformations. One might say that the child starts to emancipate itself from the purely perceptual field, although its cognitive activity is still bound to judgments about objects in the perceptual field. The third stage, in which judgment becomes completely "operational"—no longer bound to perceived patterns, and not egocentric—is called by Piaget the stage of "concrete operations." Operations and judgments start to manifest stability, self-consistency, and "reversibility,"[3] but can still only be performed on perceived objects, not in the abstract.

Specifically, operations which are necessary conditions of an understanding of numbers are, according to Piaget, the ability to deal with the equivalence of cardinal classes in terms of one-to-one correspondence, and the ability to deal with transitive relations such as "greater than" and "less than." This suggests that in order to understand what a number is, a child must be able to manipulate and make judgments about perceived objects in such a way that (a) the order, or perceived pattern, of elements in a group of objects does not influence judgments about the number of objects present, and (b) the child should be able to arrange objects in series according to some obvious criterion such as size, and should be able to deal with ordinal correspondence between different series (i.e., judgments involving relative position in the series). This is, according to Piaget, the psychological parallel of the fact that number, as a concept, can be reduced to the logically more primitive notions of order, one-to-one correspondence, etc., as Frege, Russell and others have shown (Russell, 1919).

The second (intuitive) and third (operational) stages are held to occur for most children in about the seventh and eighth years, although individual variations are considerable. Piaget has a good deal to say about the transition from one stage to another, but the details of the transitions need not be elaborated here: more complete descriptions of Piaget's theories are to be found in his own writings, and in an article of the present writer (Piaget, 1950, 1952a; Dodwell, 1957).

PIAGET'S EVIDENCE

The evidence Piaget produces consists mainly in demonstrations that young children make inconsistent judgments about numerosity, even when they can

---

[3] An operation is reversible, in Piaget's terminology, if the child understands that it has an inverse operation which cancels the original one; for example, "add two" has the inverse "subtract two," and if a child understands this, the operation of addition is said to be reversible for the child.

count, and that the attainment of consistency follows on the "realization" of the nature of one-to-one correspondence and ordinal equivalence in series.

Weaknesses in Piaget's evidence have been pointed out above; further objections can be raised, on the ground that Piaget does not indicate how *consistent* children are in the types of response they make, nor does he put forward evidence which shows that the stages follow each other in the order required by the theory, in all children.

The test situations used by Piaget involve different types of material (beakers and liquid, counters, eggs and eggcups, dolls, sticks, cards of different sizes, etc.) and all involve the subjects in making judgments about quantities or numbers, and usually also involve manipulation of the materials. A catalogue of these situations will not be given here; the test situations and techniques used in the present investigation were taken over with comparatively little modification from Piaget's work, and their description below will serve to illustrate the sorts of evidence on which Piaget's claims are based.

PROCEDURE

Aim

The aim was to assess the generality of the types of behaviour described by Piaget for children between the ages of about 5 and 8 years old, to examine age trends, the consistency of behaviour at any particular age, and to assess these factors as evidence for a theory of cognitive development in terms of the three stages described above.

Method and Materials

Five persons took part in the investigation, four of them as testers, three (including two testers) as scorers. The subjects—250 of them—were all children in Kingston public schools. They were tested individually with the test to be described below. They were in five different schools, were all in Kindergarten, Grade I or II, and their ages ranged from 5;1 to 10;1 years. No I.Q.'s were available for kindergarten children, but ratings of "above average," "average," and "below average" were obtained from the teachers. For Grade I and II pupils, I.Q.'s were available, measured on a group test; an attempt was made to have the I.Q. proportions in each grade reflect population proportions, at least approximately. No very careful fitting was attempted, for two reasons: first, the number of children available for selection was limited, and secondly, the I.Q.'s available were not particularly accurate measures. In the samples the means were somewhat too heavily represented, at the expense of the extremes, as Table 1 demonstrates. Since the aim of the investigation is to assess the generality of Piaget's findings for "normal" children, this over-representation of the middle categories is hardly a serious defect. The age distributions within each grade were not symmetrical: the distribution for kindergarten was —as one might expect—positively skewed, with a range from 5;2 to 6;8 and mode of 5;5. The Grade I age distribution was also positively skewed, but to a smaller extent, and had a larger range (6;0 to 8;8), with the mode at 6;9. Grade II ages were fairly evenly distributed in the range 7;3 to 8;7, plus a few stragglers at the upper end, with no clear mode. With the numbers of children available it was not possible to match age and I.Q. to obtain symmetrical I.Q. distributions at age, rather than at grade levels. The five schools were in different parts of the city, and all socio-economic levels were represented.

In Piaget's method of investigation the experimenter is to a great extent free to question the child, follow up ambiguous replies and so on, as the situation demands; the argument in favour of this method is that it is the only way of

TABLE 1

Distributions of I.Q. in Sample

	I.Q.				
	−85	86–95	96–105	106–115	116+
Population I.Q. proportions[a]	0.16	0.21	0.26	0.21	0.16
Sample I.Q. proportions					
(Grade I, N = 110)	0.05	0.26	0.34	0.28	0.08
(Grade II, N = 55)	0.07	0.24	0.33	0.25	0.1
Kindergarten (N = 85)					
Below average: 0.23					
Average: 0.53					
Above average: 0.24					

[a] Population I.Q. proportions are calculated on a normal distribution with mean of 100, standard deviation of 15.

gaining a comprehensive insight into the mental processes of the child. One can object to it on the grounds that, however careful the experimenter, different sorts of questions, and different sequences of questions, may influence the sorts of reply given and the behaviour manifested, and hence raise the variability of behaviour. This is not desirable if one wishes to compare performances of children at different ages, estimate norms, etc. For this reason the form of the present investigation was kept fairly standardized. Five different types of test material were used, four of them very similar to materials used by Piaget (see Table 2).

First, the child was asked to count out 12 beads, picking up two at a time (one in each hand) and placing them in two similar glass beakers, six beads in each. It was asked, "Are there the same number of beads in each glass?" and then, "How do you know?" Answers were recorded on a standard test

TABLE 2

Test Subgroups: Situations and Materials[a]

Subgroup	Situation	Materials
I	Relation of perceived size to number	Beakers and beads
II	Provoked correspondence	Eggs and eggcups
III	Unprovoked correspondence	Red and blue poker chips
IV	Seriation	Dolls and canes of graded size
V	Cardination and ordination	Wooden cubes and doll

[a] For description of procedure, see text.

blank. Only three answers are possible to the first question (Yes, No, Don't know), but a number of different answers could be given to the second. The most common answers were: "I counted the beads out," "the beads look the same," "they are the same height in the two beakers," "don't know." If an answer substantially different from one of these was given, it was written out; otherwise the investigator ticked a box on the test blank for the relevant answer. The beads from one beaker were then poured into a taller, narrower beaker, and the child was asked: "Are there the same number of beads in each glass now?", and if the child answered "No" it was asked: "Which has more?" and "Why?" The most frequent answers to the last question were: "This looks higher," "This looks more," or "Don't know," and again if a substantially different answer was given, it was written out. The child was then asked to count out eight pairs of beads into dissimilar beakers, and was asked: "Are there the same number in each glass?" Whether the child answered yes or no, it was asked why it had judged the two numbers to be the same or different. Again common categories of answers were listed on the test blank; other answers were written down. The beads from the narrower beaker were then poured into a beaker similar to the first, and the child was asked again to say whether there were the same number in each, and responses were recorded as before.

The second situation involved what Piaget calls "provoked correspondence," in this case correspondence between a set of eggs and eggcups ("provoked" because there is an obvious perceptual—and utilitarian—relation between the egg and the cup). Six eggcups were placed in a row and the child was asked to put one egg in each cup, then asked: "Are there the same number of eggs and cups?" with if necessary, subsidiary questions. The eggs were then laid out in front of their cups, thus maintaining a clear perceptual relation between the two sets. The child was again questioned about the number of eggs and cups. The eggs were then bunched up together, destroying the perceptual correspondence, and the child was questioned. Whether the child said there were or were not the same number of eggs and cups, it was asked how it arrived at its answer. Finally, the child was asked to replace the eggs in the cups, and asked if there were now equal numbers again. Children who had thought the bunched up eggs different in number from those in the cups were asked to reconsider their decision ("So were there as many eggs as cups when the eggs were all bunched up here? . . . Why not?").

The third situation involved "unprovoked correspondence." The experimenter laid out six blue poker chips in a row, gave the child a box of red chips and said: "Can you put out another row like this one?" Nearly all children put out six red chips in a similar row close to the originals. They were then asked to count the numbers in the two rows, and to say whether both rows had the same number of pieces. The blue chips were then spread out, but still in a straight line, and the child was asked: "Which row has more pieces in it now?" (One leading question out of more than 40 was held to be not excessive. It would of course be interesting to find out what effect the form of the question has on the judgments given.) Whatever the answer, the child was asked: "Can you make as many in your row as there are here?" The almost universal response, even among those who thought the rows of unequal length contained equal numbers, was to shift the red counters out, thus reforming the perceptual correspondence between the sets. Some of the younger children added more pieces to their own row, until the two sets were of equal length. The blue pieces were then put back in their original positions, and the questions were repeated: "Are there the same number in each row now?" and "Can you make the rows the same again, with the same number of pieces in each?"

The fourth situation involved judgments about series of objects of different sizes. The investigator placed eight plywood dolls on the table, in a line from smallest to largest, explaining to the child what he was doing. He then produced some canes, also of different sizes, and placed the two smallest in line with the two smallest dolls, but closer to the child, with appropriate verbal explanation: "Each man has a stick to walk with; a small one for the smallest man, a larger one for the next. . . . I want you to put down the stick which belongs to each man in front of him." The number correctly placed by the child was recorded. The row of dolls was spread out, and the child asked which stick belonged to the smallest doll; the second from largest; the fourth from smallest. The dolls were not mentioned, but pointed to, as the experimenter asked his questions. The child was then asked how he had decided which stick belonged to a particular doll. Answers were recorded in the same way as before.

The fifth and final situation involved building a "staircase" with 2 in. wooden cubes; finding out what the child understands of the process should elucidate its grasp of the relation between ordinal and cardinal numbers. Piaget made use of a similar situation, except that he used rectangular cards of different shapes which could be laid flat on a table to form a "staircase." It was felt that, apart from providing a more realistic situation, the relationship between ordinal and cardinal properties (first—one; second—two, etc.) would be clearer if each class (column of blocks forming a stair) could be seen as composed of individual and separate blocks. The investigator demonstrated by building the first two stairs, and asked the child to build the next one. Then he asked: "Which stair is it? . . . This is the first, this is the second, and this is the . . .?" The child was then asked to build the next two steps, being helped if necessary. It was asked: "What would be the next step? . . . How many blocks would there be in it?" Then, pointing to the third stair: "How many steps will the man have climbed to get here? . . . How many has he still to go?" The third step was removed, and the child was asked how many blocks it had contained, then it was asked to build that stair, but not in its position in the staircase. The last three questions, of a more abstract and hypothetical character were: "If I built 10 steps, how many blocks would there be in the highest step?" "What would the next step be called?" and "How many blocks would there be in it?"

Altogether, 54 questions were listed on the test blanks as "standard questions,"[4] and were always used except in a few cases. For instance, children who obviously knew that the number of eggs and cups did not change when the eggs were bunched up were not all asked the subsidiary questions about how they arrived at their judgments. On the other hand "non-standard" subsidiary questions were occasionally introduced if a child's response had been ambiguous. A small degree of flexibility was thought to be desirable in the administration of the test, despite the arguments mentioned above in favour of standardization.

RESULTS

It was found that, for all subgroups of the test, some children gave answers which were "non-operational" in Piaget's sense, even though they had some idea of what a number is, would count, and appeared to understand the questions. Thus, many children, after counting equal numbers of beads into dissimilar beakers would judge, on *looking* at the beakers, that the numbers in each were not the same. Similarly, in manipulating the chips, judgments about number were frequently changed when the perceived configuration changed, although such children might realize that counting was an operation relevant to their judgments. A distinction could be drawn between children who only made judgments in terms of what was perceived (Piaget's first stage) and those who, whilst realizing the inadequacy of judgments in this vein, were not

---

[4] It was decided not to spell out all 54 questions in this paper; anyone interested in a complete record can obtain one of the test blanks by writing to the author.

able to apply the operations of counting, ordering, etc., in a consistent fashion (Piaget's second stage). These children could again be distinguished from those in the third, fully operational stage. The methods used for discriminating the stages more precisely are given below.

The test blanks were scored in two ways. First, a simple point score for the number of questions answered correctly and a number of items correctly performed was obtained. This measure, as one might expect, is positively correlated with age. Table 3 shows various correlations and partial correlations of this score with other measures.

TABLE 3

Correlations of Point Score and A Score with Measures

	Point score	A score
Age	0.52	—0.56
I.Q.[a]	0.28	—0.24
A score	—0.71	—
Age[a] (I.Q. constant)	0.62	—0.63
I.Q.[a] (Age constant)	0.44	—0.44

[a] Grades I and II only, $N = 165$.
Note. All correlations significant, $p < 0.005$ or better.

A more important measure, as far as the present investigation is concerned, is the "A score." For convenience, Piaget's three stages—of global comparisons, intuitive judgments, and concrete operations—were labelled A, B, and C. Any response made which indicated that a child was in stage A was called an "A response," and the "A score" was simply the number of A responses made. The highest possible number of A responses was ten. In arriving at this number, the following factors were considered: first, only one A response was possible for any one test situation, so that if a child said twice in the same situation that he had judged numbers of beads by their relative heights in the beakers, this was considered one A response. If, however, the child said this in two different situations involving the same material (e.g., when the beads were *poured* into dissimilar beakers, and when they were *counted* into dissimilar beakers), it was counted as two A responses. An A response was one which clearly indicated that the child was basing its judgment on perceived characteristics alone, and this criterion was applied without difficulty, with agreement between different scorers. The A score is obviously not independent of the point score, and one expects a negative correlation between them. Table 3 shows correlations between A score and various other measures.

Unfortunately, the investigation of the effects of length of schooling on ability to deal with number concepts was beyond the scope of the present study.

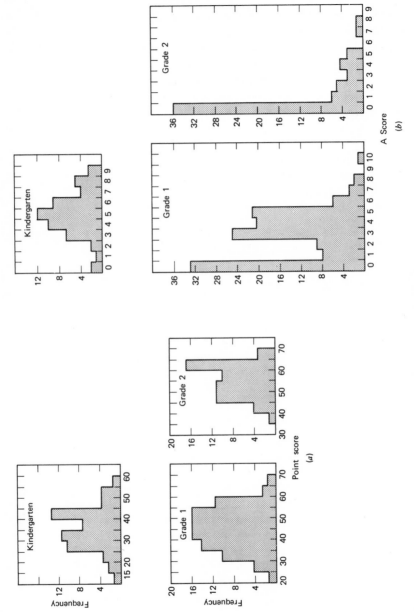

FIGURE 1. (a) Relation of point score to grade. (b) relation of A score to grade.

This factor may be important since a child's ability to deal with numbers might well be determined in part by the amount of formal instruction he has had, and his familiarity with play materials available in school. Clearly, the older children, and those in higher grades, do better than younger children, and better than those in kindergarten (cf. Table 2, Figure 1). The two factors are confounded in the present study; to separate them, it would be necessary to compare the abilities of groups of children, matched for age and I.Q., who have been in school for different lengths of time.

Although no difficulty was experienced in classifying an answer as an "A response" or not, it was not so easy to decide whether, over-all, a child was in stage A, B, or C. Moreover, it appears that a child may be in stage A for one type of material and situation, and in stage B or even C for another. This, of course, does not mean that a theory of stages is untenable, but it does suggest that a child may acquire the set of operations necessary for dealing consistently with one type of material and situation without simultaneously being able to deal consistently with all apparently similar situations. The following procedure was therefore adopted: the child's stage was assessed separately for the five different subgroups of the test (Table 2). If all the answers in a subgroup indicated judgments based on perceived characteristics, the category assigned was A; if all the answers were operational, the stage assigned was C; if there was a mixture of types of answers or uncertainty about whether responses were fully operational, the category B was used. There were some disagreements between scorers, principally as to whether a child was in stage A or B; however, inter-scorer reliability was over .95.

Figure 2 shows percentages of children in the different stages for three test

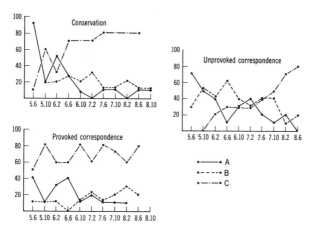

FIGURE 2. Percentages of children at different ages falling into the three stages for three test subgroups; A = global comparison stage, B = intuitive stage, C = operational stage.

subgroups. Quite clearly it would be impossible to state a "typical" age for the attainment of concrete operational activity: whereas 80 per cent of children aged 5 years and 10 months showed concrete operations when dealing with provoked correspondence, none could deal in this fashion with unprovoked correspondence, and only 60 per cent with conservation. Another interesting fact is that there appears to be no change in the percentage of children in stage C for provoked correspondence, between the ages of 5;6 and 8;6, but for conservation and unprovoked correspondence there are very marked changes. There are very few children in stage B for provoked correspondence, but stage B represents, over-all, the largest category in unprovoked correspondence. (It is possible that this may have been partly a function of the questions asked—this point would bear further investigation.) The graphs for the other subgroups—seriation and cardinal-ordinal properties—are not so neat as those shown in Figure 2. As one might expect, seriation showed, on the average, more C responses than cardinal-ordinal properties, but neither showed a very clear age trend. Therefore, although a child can be assigned with a fair degree of assurance to one of the three categories for each test subgroup, there is no consistency of stages within individuals, nor are the age trends similar for the different subgroups. There remains the question of whether ability to operate with serial relations and cardinal properties are necessary conditions of being able to deal with numbers (constructs which entail both these properties). If Piaget's thesis is correct, then it should be the case that a child who can deal operationally with cardinal-ordinal properties is also in stage C for unprovoked correspondence and seriation, and, conversely, that a child in stage C for these latter two should have a high probability of being able to deal operationally with cardinal-ordinal properties.

TABLE 4

Relations Between Stages for Test Subgroups III, IV, and V[a]

$$\frac{P(CIII + CIV)}{(CV)} = 0.56 \qquad\qquad \frac{P(AIII)}{(CV)} = 0.06$$

$$\frac{P(CIII)}{(CV)} = 0.8 \qquad\qquad \frac{P(AIV)}{(CV)} = 0.00$$

$$\frac{P(CIV)}{(CV)} = 0.56 \qquad\qquad \frac{P(BIII)}{(CV)} = 0.13$$

$$\frac{P(CV)}{(CIII + CIV)} = 0.62 \qquad\qquad \frac{P(BIV)}{(CV)} = 0.45$$

[a] The measures are conditional probabilities. Letters identify stages, Roman numerals identify test subgroups. Thus P(CIII + CIV)/(CV) reads: the conditional probability that a subject is in stage C for subgroups III and IV, given that he is in stage C for subgroup V.

A random sample of 100 was drawn from the original 250 test papers. Of these, 15 showed stage C responses for cardinal-ordinal properties. Table 4 shows the conditional probabilities associated with the states of affairs mentioned above. Clearly, Piaget's thesis would require all the conditional probabilities in column I of the table to be unity, or close to it, and those in column II to be 0. A number of the conditional probabilities depart rather markedly from the predicted values. That is, it seems that some children can deal operationally with cardinal-ordinal properties before they can so deal with either classes or series separately, and that ability to deal with classes and series separately does not entail ability to deal with numbers as constructs combining ordinal and cardinal operations.

DISCUSSION

The findings here reported confirm in a general way Piaget's statements concerning young children's ideas about number and related concepts, yet they also show that conceptual development does not follow the neat and regular pattern which his theory prescribes. Estes (1956) notwithstanding, children do confuse operations on sets of objects with "global", perceptual attributes of those sets, and this leads them into making inconsistent judgments.

The types of response described by Piaget for all three stages were found in the present study, and his "intuitive" stage was quite prevalent, especially for some situations (Figure 2). Perhaps the most striking response in this category, given by several children, was to count the poker chips when one of the two rows was extended, but still to judge that there were different numbers of chips in the two rows. Thus, counting per se is no guarantee that a child grasps what the concept "cardinal number" is, or how it applies to a concrete situation.

The evidence here produced confirms Piaget's contention that young children do not fully understand the concept of number, even though they may be able to count. The sorts of behaviour described by Piaget are typical for children between the ages of five and eight. However, there is inconsistency in the type of response made in different situations, and great variability from child to child, at a particular age level, in the sorts of response made. Intelligence, as well as age, is an important factor (Table 3). The stages do not always follow in the sequence Piaget's theory requires (Table 4). Piaget pays scant attention to the part learning may play in the development of number concepts, and points to the fact that children in stages A and B do not understand when one tries to explain to them why their judgments are wrong. But one might suggest that a single explanation cannot be effective since, in Piaget's terminology, the assimilation of the concept explained takes time (Piaget, 1952b, 1954). Churchill (1958) has shown that training with number games over a period of weeks leads to improved understanding of the concept of number. It could be that the variability in types of response from one test subgroup to another is due to incomplete assimilation of a newly learned concept; or, to use Piaget's term again, that the child requires time to accommodate his responses in a novel situation. This could be the case where correct operations have been attained, but not yet integrated into a logical structure, or grouping of operations (Piaget, 1953). Unfortunately, it would be difficult to test this hypothesis, except in an intensive longitudinal study of the development of number concepts, and further progress in this field will necessitate such studies. It seems reasonable to suggest, in the absence of evidence on the point, that the variability in stages, and the absence of strong sequential dependencies predicted from Piaget's theory, is a function of learned responses to particular situations without complete assimilation, or to use a more familiar term, a function of learning without adequate response generalization.

SUMMARY

A study of number concepts in 250 children between 5 and 8 years old showed that the three stages of cognitive development described by Piaget as "global," "intuitive," and "concrete operational" occur. There are considerable variations in type of response given at any age level, and the type of response may vary from one test situation to another for a child. There are age trends; older children tending to give more "operational" judgments, but these trends differ from different test situations. Intelligence, as measured on a standard group I.Q. test, is also a factor in number concept attainment.

The findings do not yield unequivocal support for Piaget's theory of cognitive development. Possible reasons for this are discussed, and a strategy for further research suggested.

References

Churchill, E. M. The number concepts of the young child. *Researches and Studies, University of Leeds Inst. of Educ.*, 1958, **17**, 34–49.

Dodwell, P. C. The evolution of number concepts in the child. *Mathematics Teaching*, 1957, **5**, 5–11.

Estes, B. W. Some mathematical and logical concepts in children. *J. Genet. Psychol.*, 1956, **88**, 219–222.

Hazlitt, V. Children's Thinking. *Brit. J. Psychol.*, 1930, **20**, 354–361.

McCarthy, D. Language development of the preschool child. *Inst. Child Welf. Monogr. No. 4.* Minneapolis: Univ. of Minnesota Press, 1930.

Piaget, J. *The language and thought of the child.* New York: Harcourt, 1926.

Piaget, J. *The child's conception of the world.* New York: Harcourt, 1929.

Piaget, J. *The psychology of intelligence.* London: Routledge and Kegan Paul, 1950.

Piaget, J. *The child's conception of number.* London: Routledge and Kegan Paul, 1952.

Piaget, J. *The origins of intelligence in children.* New York: International Univer. Press, 1952.

Piaget, J. *Logic and psychology.* Manchester: Manchester Univer. Press, 1953.

Piaget, J. *The construction of reality in the child.* New York: Basic Books, 1954.

Russell, B. *Introduction to mathematical philosophy.* London: Allen & Unwin, 1919.

12. A DEVELOPMENTAL STUDY OF PIAGET'S THEORY OF LOGICAL MULTIPLICATION[1]

Carolyn Uhlinger Shantz*

Intensive investigation of children's thinking has led Piaget to propose that there is a substantial correspondence between certain logico-mathematical structures and the organization of children's practical and cognitive actions. In order to model most accurately the structure and limitations of thought processes during the age span of 7 to 11, approximately, Piaget invented a structure called the grouping, which combines properties of structures in modern mathematics. The grouping is composed of one operation (addition or multiplication) applied to certain elements (classes, logical relations, or space) and the relations between elements (symmetrical or asymmetrical). The child's actions of combining, ordering, disassociating, etc., represent the type of thought operations which Piaget holds to be identical to logical operations within a given logical system. Following Bourbaki, Piaget believes it is necessary to analyze separately structures dealing with classes, logical relations, and space.

SOURCE. *Merrill-Palmer Quarterly*, 1967, **13**, 121–137.

[1] A modified version of this paper was read at the American Psychological Association meeting in New York City, September, 1966. This paper is based on research reported in a dissertation submitted in partial fulfillment of requirements for the Ph.D. degree at Purdue University. The author is greatly indebted to Dr. Charles D. Smock for his direction and assistance as major professor. The author's appreciation is also extended to Sisters Frieda and Therese Eileen, principals of St. Lawrence and St. Mary's Schools, respectively, in Lafayette, Indiana, for their generous cooperation.

* Center for Developmental Studies in Cognition, Merrill-Palmer Institute, 71 East Ferry Avenue, Detroit, Michigan 48202.

The correspondence between logical and psychological structures may be supported by two phenomena: contemporaneous emergence of formally similar structures and the close relationship of these structures throughout development in middle childhood. Piaget has asserted in several works that the multiplication of classes, logical relations, and spatial relations evidence these two phenomena as a reflection of their formal similarity (1952, p. 240–243; 1960, p. 145; Inhelder and Piaget, 1964, p. 282, 290).

The data which Piaget marshalls in support of his hypothesis are the similarity in ages of emergence and improvement with age of each ability. In all cases each ability was assessed in different groups of children. Lunzer (1960), in particular, has noted the hazard of Piaget's position: the only methodologically defensible procedure for testing the hypothesis that logical interrelatedness of two or more structures reflects their psychological relatedness is the assessment of relevant abilities in the same group of children.

It is the purpose of this study to investigate the degree of relationship among the three multiplicative groupings within the same individuals at a given age level and to determine the extent to which this relationship and level of performance vary among age groups. The particular groupings under study were selected for their importance within Piaget's theory, as well as providing a test of the general hypothesis. In contrast to the more familiar and specific numerical connotation of "multiplication," the term is defined as the simultaneous combination of two or more elements such as two class attributes ("red and square"), two asymmetric logical relations ("longer and darker"), or two asymmetric spatial relations ("above and to the left of . . ."). Such concepts are identical to the more well-known "conjunctive concepts."

The importance of these multiplicative structures resides in the position they hold as precursors to adolescent systems of combination, in the case of class multiplication; and, as processes underlying some of the most complex concepts attained in the concrete-operational stage—conservation, in the case of asymmetric logical relations, and, Euclidean space concepts in the case of asymmetric spatial relations.

Concrete class multiplication is exemplified by the combination of all class attributes of one series with all attributes of another series, such that red and blue are combined with circle and square to produce four subclasses of red squares, red circles, blue squares, and blue circles. Each subclass is defined by the simultaneous presence of two attributes. Piaget views such combinatorial ability as the forerunner of adolescents' ability to systematically find all combinations and permutations of variables, as in the scientific method.

The second ability under study, multiplication of asymmetric logical relations, is thought by Piaget to be involved in conservation concepts (Flavell, 1963). The experimental paradigm for conservation is the following: given two tall, thin glasses A and B filled with equal amounts of water, and the contents of B poured into a short, wide glass C, the question is posed as to the equality of water in A and C. Piaget contends that as the child is able to consider the relation of C to A ("wider than" *and* "shorter than" A), i.e., as he sees the relations as compensatory, he asserts equality (conserves amount). Multiplication of asymmetric relations, like class multiplication, is the joint consideration of elements within two or more series. In this case, the series are continuous dimensions (e.g., length, shade of color, size) and elements within the dimensions are values.

The third ability, spatial multiplication, also involves continuous dimensions, in this case the spatial dimensions of the horizontal and vertical axes rather than logical dimensions. The joint consideration of sites along two dimensions, when combined, defines a point on a surface. Euclidean space is thought to be based upon the child's ability to locate objects and sites in space in terms of the intersects of three dimensions (right-left; before-behind; up-down).

There have been no correlational data presented by Piaget in support of his hypothesis of a close relationship among the three multiplicative abilities. To date the major supporting evidence is Smedslund's study (1964) of several Piagetian processes, among which were the multiplication of classes and logical relations. He found that children tended either to pass both class and relational multiplication tasks (43%) or fail both (41%).

In view of the significance of the hypothesis of close relationship among groupings for Piaget's operational theory, the present study was undertaken. If the abilities to multiply classes, logical relations, and spatial relations develop in close association, it would be expected that within each age group a high correlation in performance would hold among the three multiplication tasks. It would also be expected that the three abilities would improve with increasing age.

METHOD

Subjects

Ss were 24 children, 12 boys and 12 girls, at each of three age levels, $7\frac{1}{2}$, $9\frac{1}{2}$, and $11\frac{1}{2}$ ($N = 72$). At each age level, Ss were within three months of the half year (e.g., 7 years, 3 months to 7 years, 9 months). This age criterion resulted in Ss within one age level coming from two grades: the $7\frac{1}{2}$ year olds were about equally divided between first- and second-grades; about one-third of the $9\frac{1}{2}$-year-olds were in the third grade, and the remaining in the fourth-grade; all of the $11\frac{1}{2}$-year-olds were in combined fifth- and sixth-grade classes. Ss were drawn from a total of 13 classes.

Each teacher selected children from her class who evidenced "average achievement" *for their age*. The mean intelligence scores for each age group,

TABLE 1

Intelligence Test Data on a Portion of the Study Sample ($N = 58$)

Age Level	N	Intelligence Test	Mean I.Q.	SD
7½ years	11	Kuhlmann-Anderson	113.2	5.3
9½ years	24	Kuhlmann-Anderson	108.3	5.8
11½ years	11	Kuhlmann-Anderson	106.2	7.0
11½ years	12	Otis Quick-Scoring Mental Ability Test	107.5	6.2

based on 58 Ss for whom tests were available, are presented in Table 1. All Ss were drawn from two parochial schools representing primarily lower middle-class families in a small midwestern town.

Experimental Measures

Multiplication of classes was assessed by the revised children's form of the Raven's Progressive Matrices Test (1956). A typical matrix problem requires the selection of one design from six alternatives which combines two class attributes, such as circle vs. square and stripes vs. solid interior, in order to complete the matrix. The index of multiplicative ability was the total number of correctly solved matrices out of 36.

A multiple relations test (MRT) was specially constructed to assess the multiplication of asymmetric logical relations. As in the Raven's test, S's task was to fill in one intersect of a matrix. However, the entire matrix was not presented, as it is in the Raven's test. Instead, only the diagonal of a "conceptual" matrix was used, i.e., that part of a matrix presenting the one-to-one changes along both dimensions. For clarity, the term "matrices" will be used to refer to the tasks rather than the more exact "diagonals of matrices."

The matrices were constructed from various combinations of five continuous dimensions: orientation (A), amount of border (B), shade of color (C), size (D), and degree of emptiness (E). Each of these continuous dimensions was divided into five ordered values, e.g., C ordered from black, to dark gray, medium gray, medium light gray, and light gray.

A total of 15 matrices were constructed, five of which were labeled "control" matrices, five "redundant" matrices, and five "irrelevant" matrices. Each of the control matrices was made from two dimensions (specifically, AB, CD, EA, BC, DE). The values of both dimensions were systematically ordered, e.g., in the CD matrix, values becoming progressively lighter (C) and larger (D). Each of the redundant matrices was constructed from three systematically ordered dimensions (ABC, CDE, EAB, BCD, DEA), the third dimension being considered as redundant information. Each of the irrelevant matrices had two systematically ordered dimensions with the third dimension presented in

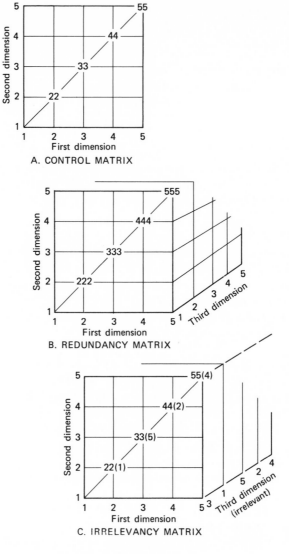

FIGURE 1. Structure of complete matrices for each type of information upon which MRT is based. Numbers represent ordered values within each dimension.

randomly ordered values, labeled irrelevant information (see Fig. 1).[2] The combinations of dimensions for these five matrices were ABD, CDA, EAC, BCE, and DEB.

[2] An analysis of the effects of these information parameters on the ability to multiply

The task was presented in the form of a strip of five cells, the first cell combining the first values of both dimensions in a design, the second cell combining the second values, etc. The fourth cell was blank for S to insert the correct choice from 12 alternatives presented on a choice board. The geometric designs used as vehicles for value combinations differed among all matrices.

The 12 choices offered represented only a small portion of the total possible

TABLE 2

Combinations of Values for Matrices and Choice Boards for Each Type of Information[a]

Type of Matrix Information	Value Combinations of Each Matrix	Value Combinations on Each Choice Board		
Control	1–1	1–4	3–4	4–4
	2–2	2–3	4–1	4–5
	3–3	3–2	4–3	5–4
	5–5	3–3	4–4	5–5
Redundance[b]	1–1–1	1–4–2	3–4–3	4–5–5
	2–2–2	2–3–5	4–3–3	5–1–4
	3–3–3	3–2–1	4–3–4	5–5–4
	5–5–5	3–3–3	4–4–4	5–5–5
Irrelevancy[c]	1–1–3 (1)	1–4–2	3–4–3	4–4–4
	2–2–1 (2)	2–3–5	4–1–4	4–5–5
	3–3–5 (3)	3–2–1	4–3–3	5–4–5
	5–5–4 (5)	3–3–3	4–4–3	5–5–5

[a] The first number or each pair of triplet represents the value of the first dimension, the second number is the value of the second dimension, etc. For example, 3–2 represents the third value of the first dimension combined with the second value of the second dimension.

[b] Correct choices are 4–4–4 and 4–3–4; other correct combinations, 3–4–4 and 4–4–3, were not included among the choices.

[c] The third number in each *matrix* triplet is the value of the irrelevant dimension which appeared in the cells ranked 1, 2, 3, 5 (in parentheses); the third number in each *choice* triplet is the cell rank.

combinations and were selected to clarify the frequency of different types of errors children make in such a task. Types of errors were defined, generally, by the amount of distance from the correct intersect (4–4). Table 2 presents the specific combination of values in the matrices and choice boards. The frequencies of each type of choice among the 12, illustrated with the control

logical relations indicated, briefly, that redundant information did not have significant facilitative effects, but irrelevant information did have the predicted detrimental effects (Shantz, in press).

matrices, were as follows: two choices were correct (4–4) ; two choices combined the correct value on one dimension with a very deviant value on the second dimension (1–4, 4–1) ; two choices combined one correct value and a third value (3–4, 4–3) ; two choices combined one correct value and fifth value (5–4, 4–5) ; two choices were incorrect on both dimensions, one of which was fairly deviant (2–3, 3–2) ; and two choices, also incorrect on both dimensions, were adjacent to the correct intersect (3–3, 5–5). The 12 choices were presented in four staggered rows on each board, and the positions of choices randomized across all boards.

The total 15 matrices were presented in three standard orders, the primary limitation upon random ordering being the condition that no two matrices were presented sequentially which would allow S to use similar dimensions for correct response, e.g., BC and BCE.

After initial administration of the 15 matrices, "limits testing" was done on those redundant and irrelevant matrices which S had failed: E pointed to particular choices and asked whether the combination was acceptable or not to complete the matrix. Those combinations which S accepted were "pitted" against one another to the point where S designated the "best" choice, or in some cases, best choices to complete the matrix.

The two major indices of ability to multiply logical relations were (1) the total number of correctly solved matrices on initial testing, and (2) the number of correctly solved matrices in limits testing added to the initially correct number.

The multiplication of spatial relations was assessed by a modified version of Piaget's landscape task (1956). Two identical landscapes of open country were employed (see Fig. 2). Four rather wedge-shaped quadrants were formed by the intersection of a road and stream; two houses, a group of trees, a hill, and bridge were located on identical points on each landscape. Two dolls, a boy and girl, were placed by E at five standard pairs of positions facing various directions as shown in Fig. 2. S's task was to place two identical dolls in the same positions and facing the same direction as E's dolls, but with S's landscape rotated 180°. S's landscape was made on a styrofoam base to allow for puncturing a paper beneath the landscape for each doll placement; both landscapes were covered with non-drying clay to allow each puncture to be rubbed out. E visually estimated gaze direction after each pair of placements.

S's ability to combine simultaneously the reversed horizontal and vertical dimensions was measured by both doll placement and direction of gaze. The latter was measured in 5° units such that a gaze of 17°, for example, was scored 15°. Exact measurement appeared unwarranted in view of the manner in which responses were initially obtained. The scoring systems used for the two measures are presented in Table 3. In both cases scores could range from

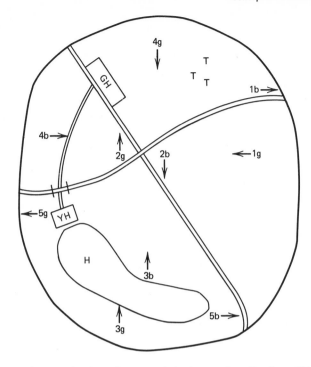

FIGURE 2. Schematic drawing of unrotated landscape. Key: T = tree; GH = green house; YH = yellow house; H = hill; g = girl doll; b = boy doll; ← = gaze direction; and 1–5 = pairs of positions.

a perfect performance of 10, to 50. The total spatial performance index was the sum of placement and gaze scores. Since doll placement presumably required simultaneous use of two reversed dimensions and gaze only one, analyses were done on gaze and placement scores separately as well as together.

TABLE 3

Scoring Systems for Responses to Landscape Task

	Position Responses	Gaze Responses
Score	Placement within circle of:	Deviation from correct direction
1	1-inch diameter around correct location	0°–5°
2	¾-inch diameter beyond the first circle	10°–15°
3	¾-inch diameter beyond the second circle	20°–25°
4	¾-inch diameter beyond the third circle	30°–35°
5	Placement beyond 3¼-inch diameter circle	40° and beyond

Procedure

*S*s were tested individually on the MRT and landscape tasks in one session which averaged approximately 50 minutes. The Raven's test (RPM) was administered with standard instructions (1956) to groups of eight *S*s; the time elapsing between individual testing and RPM testing varied from one week to one month. Individual testing for 60 *S*s was done in a mobile laboratory, and the remaining *S*s were tested under similar conditions in one of the schools.

Each *S* was randomly assigned to two order conditions: the sequence of MRT and landscape tasks, and one of the three standard MRT orders.

Prior to administration of MRT, five seriation pre-tests were presented in random order to each *S* in which each of the five dimensions was presented singly so as to familiarize *S* with the dimensions, the values within dimensions, and the basic task of ordering values. *S* described the dimension presented and the value he thought would complete the order of four cells, the third being blank. When the description was incorrect, *E* briefly described the dimension in a standard manner with emphasis upon the transformation of values from one cell to the next. The choice board of six alternatives was presented, *S* made his selection, and was told whether it was correct or not. If *S* erred, the correct choice was designed by *E* and the standard description reiterated.

Then the 15 matrices were introduced with the following instructions:

> Now I'll show you some puzzles that are a little harder. There is more than one thing changing in these new puzzles, so you must look carefully at everything that is changing. This time I won't ask you any questions first. You look at the puzzle (*E* points to stack of matrices faced down) to figure out the things that are changing. Then look at the big board (*E* points to stack of choice boards faced down) and find the picture that goes in the puzzle as quickly as you can. Point to it as soon as you find it. I am going to time you, but take enough time to be sure you've found the best one to fit in the puzzle. All right? Do you understand?

Each matrix with its choice board was presented on vertical stands in front of *S* while *S*'s eyes were closed, and timing began from the moment *S* opened his eyes until he indicated his choice.[3] The reason for each choice was asked. At no time was the adequacy of the choice or reason indicated by *E*. Upon completion of the MRT, *E* tested limits without timing as previously described.

[3] The latency measure was employed as an index of "information-processing time." An analysis indicated that several combinations of independent variables were significant sources of variation of the latency data (Shantz, in press).

The two landscapes were presented initially in the same orientation, the similarity of objects on both pointed out, and S was given two practice trials. A screen was inserted between the landscapes and S's landscape slowly rotated 180° while S watched. After E placed two dolls, S was told to "figure out" where to place his dolls on his landscape so they would be standing near the same landscape objects and right at the same spot as E's dolls, and looking at the same things. As E placed each doll, she referred to position as "standing here" and gaze as "looking this way" regardless of position and gaze direction so as not to verbally differentiate for S changes in gaze and position. The references to position and gaze were alternated sequentially in an effort to direct S's attention equally to both aspects of the task. S was free to view E's landscape as often as he wished. The order of pairs of positions was randomized for all Ss. After each pair of placements, S's responses were recorded.

RESULTS

It was hypothesized that there would be a high correlation among the three multiplicative tasks within each age level. Since the landscape data did not meet the requirements of parametric correlational statistics, the degree of correlation was evaluated by the coefficient of concordance, W. The following measures were intercorrelated: RPM total score (multiplication of classes); TS, total space score on the landscape task (multiplication of spatial relations); and, two measures of MRT performance (multiplication of logical relations)—the number of correctly solved matrices on initial testing (IT) and that number plus additional correctly solved matrices on limits testing (LT).[4] There was a significant association among all three tasks for each set of data for the 7½-year-olds: RPM, TS, IT ($W = .54$, $X^2 = 37.23$); and, RPM, TS, LT ($W = .56$, $X^2 = 38.71$), $p < .05$ in each case. Likewise, the 9½-year-olds' performance correlated significantly for both sets of data: RPM, TS, IT ($W = .62$, $X^2 = 42.44$); and, RPM, TS, LT ($W = .69$, $X^2 = 47.33$), $p < .01$ in both cases. For the oldest group, however, correlations among tasks only approached the lower level of significance: RPM, TS, IT ($W = .51$, $X^2 = 35.05$); and RPM, TS, LT ($W = .50$, $X^2 = 34.71$), $p < .10$ in both cases.

The rank-order correlations between pairs of tasks for each age group are presented in Table 4. For the youngest group, correlations between MRT and the space task, as each was variously measured, were significant beyond the .05 level. All correlations which were not significant involved the relation-

---

[4] The IT data were obtained under timed conditions, whereas the LT data were not. The latter measure represents maximal performance and is confounded, to a greater degree than IT data, with sequence effects.

TABLE 4

Rank-Order Correlations Among Tasks for Each Age Level ($N = 24$)

	Age Levels		
Tasks	7½ years	9½ years	11½ years
Total space, IT	.42*	.38*	.25
Total space, LT	.58**	.50**	.24
Total space, RPM	.30	.43*	.18
Position, IT	.36*	.29	.13
Position, LT	.50**	.43*	.19
Position, RPM	.38*	.50**	.15
Gaze, IT	.34*	.37*	.29
Gaze, LT	.52**	.46*	.17
Gaze, RPM	.07	.31	.22
RPM, IT	.24	.48*	.37*
RPM, LT	.20	.69**	.42*

* $p < .05$ (rho $= .343$)
** $p < .01$ (rho $= .485$)

ship of the multiple classification test (RPM) to other tasks. The data for the 9½-year-olds indicate fairly uniform correlations among all tasks, the primary difference with the youngest group being the significant correlations of RPM to other tasks. The oldest group evidenced consistently low correlations between the space task and other tasks, the only significant correlations involving the RPM and MRT.

It was also expected that all multiplicative abilities would improve with increasing age. The mean (or median) performance of each group on all tasks is presented in Fig. 3, and reveals an almost linear trend in performance as a function of age. For clarity, the total space score is not presented but falls between the position and gaze scores for each group. All differences between age groups were significant ($p < .05$ and $< .01$) with one exception: landscape placement scores for the 7½- vs. 9½-year-olds did not reach the lower level of significance.

The effects of two independent variables, order for tasks and sex, for each of the three multiplication tasks were analyzed and neither was found significantly ($p < .05$) to influence performance.

Since Piaget's theory is a theory of intelligence, measures of "products" of reasoning would be expected to show a moderate association with tests of operations. Although this was not an explicit hypothesis of the study, one-tailed tests were employed on the correlations between intelligence measures and the three experimental tasks (see Table 5). The MRT measures are the total number of matrices solved in initial testing, and, for the landscape task, the total space scores. The latter scores required the

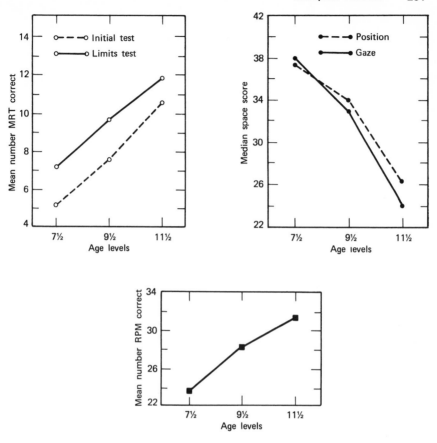

FIGURE 3. Mean (or median) scores on each task for each age level. (Higher scores indicate poorer performance on space task.)

use of the non-parametric correlation statistic, rho. The correlations were not significant for the youngest and oldest groups; however, RPM and space scores correlated significantly ($p < .05$ and $p < .01$, respectively) with intelligence scores for the 9½-year-olds.

The response alternatives offered in each of the three multiplicative tasks allowed for an analysis of types of errors, particularly in terms of errors on two dimensions as compared to one dimension in the RPM and MRT. On the RPM, the percent of choices which were errors on *both* dimensions was 4%, 8% and 1% for 7½-, 9½- and 11½-year-olds, respectively. In contrast, errors on one dimension only accounted for 20%, 13%, and 7% of the choices for each age group. Similar trends were found for the MRT: of all choices, 22%, 13%, and 6% were errors on both dimensions of the two-

TABLE 5

Correlations of Intelligence Scores with Each Task

			RPM	MRT IT	Total Space
Age	N	Intelligence Test	r	r	rho
7½ years	11	Kuhlmann-Anderson	−.23	+.38	−.32
9½ years	24	Kuhlmann-Anderson	+.40*	+.20	+.52**
11½ years	11	Kuhlmann-Anderson	+.42	+.42	−.04
11½ years	12	Otis Quick-Scoring Mental Ability Test	+.06	+.13	+.19

One-tailed tests:
$N = 11$, * $p < .05$ ($r = .521$; rho $= .519$); ** $p < .01$ ($r = .685$; rho $= .735$)
$N = 12$, * $p < .05$ ($r = .497$; rho $= .506$); ** $p < .01$ ($r = .658$; rho $= .712$)
$N = 24$, * $p < .05$ ($r = .344$; rho $= .343$); ** $p < .01$ ($r = .472$; rho $= .485$)

dimensional matrices for 7½-, 9½-, and 11½-year-olds, respectively. Errors on one dimension only were 36%, 27%, and 17% of total choices for each age group. The percentages of various choices on RPM and MRT cannot be compared directly since the RPM offers other types of choices, such as incorrect orientations, irrelevancies, and incomplete patterns. In summary, for each test, two-dimensional errors were less frequent than one-dimensional errors for each age group, and, with one minor exception, both types of errors decreased with increasing age.

Landscape performance, for which there is a scarcity of data in the published literature, was evaluated first by Piaget's criteria of successful performance. That is, incorrect placements are those in the wrong quadrant or on the wrong side of a nearby object; all other placements are considered correct, regardless of the amount of distance error within the correct quadrant. The medium number of correct placements for 7½-, 9½-, and 11½-year-olds were 6.8, 8.6, and 9.7, respectively, of a possible 10. The amount of distance error in placements and gaze deviations were incorporated in the scoring system developed for this study, and provide a second measure of landscape performance. The median scores for each age group, presented in Fig. 3, indicate that placement and gaze responses were quite similar within age levels although no attempt was made to "equate" the two scoring systems. Prior to applying the scoring system, gaze deviations were plotted and revealed an interesting phenomenon in the youngest group: a tendency to make more errors in the 90°-100° range. That is, Ss tended to make quarter-rotations, possibly through confusion of horizontal and vertical axes or mere incomplete rotations.

The final analysis of landscape performance dealt with the relative difficulty of particular positions and gaze directions as shown in Fig. 2. First, all age groups found certain positions and gaze directions difficult, reflected in significant correlations among the three age groups of frequency of position errors ($W = .89$) and frequency of gaze errors ($W = .94$), $p < .01$ in both cases. There was substantial variation in the relative difficulty of particular positions across ages, poorest performance generally being on 3g and 4g (see Fig. 2). The former error appeared to be a constant error induced by the curvature of the hill, and the second error due to placement of the doll on the incorrect horizontal side of the trees. The easiest positions were 4b and 5b. The least accurate gaze orientations, as assessed by summed scores, were on 3g and 3b. Again, the curvature of the hill and edge of the landscape seemed responsible; Ss made the dolls' gaze perpendicular to the hill rather than themselves. The easiest gaze reversal was on 4b.

DISCUSSION

The results of this study appear to have some important theoretical implications and raise some complex methodological problems. The general hypothesis stated that the three multiplicative abilities would be closely associated within each age level. First, there were significant correlations (W) among the three tasks in the younger two groups, but in the oldest group the obtained correlations were significant only at the .10 level. The correlations for pairs of tasks within each age level indicated that correlations among tasks (W) were a function of different task relationships. In the youngest group, correlations between the space task and MRT were consistently greater than correlations of RPM to other tasks. In the 9½-year-old group, all three tasks appeared to have fairly similar degrees of relationship. In contrast to the youngest group, the 9½-year-olds had some of the highest correlations with cross-classification and spatial tasks, relationships which continued in the 11½-year-old group. Most pairs of tasks in the oldest group, however, did not correlate more than would be expected by chance. These correlations between pairs of tasks, as well as among tasks, in the oldest group raise a question: Does the association among multiplicative abilities decrease with increasing age or are the lower correlations in the oldest group dependent upon other factors? The higher correlations among all tasks for the 9½-year-olds compared to the youngest group are suggestive of greater, not lesser, association with age. Likewise, the relative lack of variability of performance on most tasks for the 11½-year-olds, i.e., near-perfect performance, has the statistical effect of limiting the size of correlations (Guilford, 1956). Relevant data would tend to support this conclusion. In the oldest group, the mean number of correct matrices on initial testing was nearly 11 of a possible 15 with a standard deviation (SD) of 2.4; mean number of correct gaze and position responses (scores 1–4) was 16.4 of a possible 20, SD of 3.7; and RPM mean score was 32 of a possible 36, *SD* of 3.4. Such low variability essentially disallowed a clear test of the general hypothesis for the oldest group.

Two questions arise in relation to Piaget's hypothesis. First, to what degree are the correlations among the three tasks greater than those which might occur among other unrelated abilities of the same individuals? This is a question of discriminative validity, primarily, and research designed to define "multiplication" in terms of what it is not would be an important extension of study on the hypothesis. In this regard, the intelligence test data which were available do not provide a clear means of establishing discriminative validity. As noted previously, a moderate correlation might be expected between intellectual operations and concepts measured on intelligence tests. This is particularly true in the case of the Kuhlmann-Anderson Test which includes subtests requiring spatial concepts and ordering, both of which would tend to increase the correlations with the experimental tasks. Nevertheless, it is noteworthy that several of the correlations between intelligence test scores and the experimental tasks were as great, or greater, than correlations between experimental tasks. These correlations suggest that a "general intelligence" factor can account for some of the variability in performance on the experimental tasks.

Second, to what degree do the results of this study support Piaget's hypothesis that a *close* relationship exists among multiplicative abilities? The magnitude of the correlations appear to provide only moderate support for the hypothesis. Although the correlations between tasks differed significantly from zero, for the most part in the younger groups, a more meaningful comparison would be the difference in degree of association between these tasks and some minimal correlation which might be expected between dissimilar tasks given to the same individuals. Moreover, the correlations between tasks seldom account for more than 25% of the variance.

There are also several methodological issues raised in the present study. As noted previously, the landscape task and MRT, as each was variously measured, correlated significantly in the youngest group. The degree to which these correlations indicate association of abilities or shared method variance is an important consideration. The methods used to assess multiplication of logical relations and spatial relations are quite different. The MRT presented stimuli in a fairly structured manner, whereas the landscape task did not; in fact, the degree to which children actually construct a cognitive matrix to solve the landscape problem is moot. The location of a doll on a rotated surface and consideration of the relative values of color and size have some "face validity" as quite independent methods. The extent to which these differences constitute "independence" of methods would determine in part the degree to which correlations could be viewed as relations of abilities.

On the other hand, the differentiation between logical relations and spatial relations as elements is relatively unclear in the experimental tasks of this study, which is also the case with Piaget's tasks (Inhelder and Piaget, 1964). Specifically, the MRT appears to be a quasi-logical relations task in that the majority of dimensions used may be conceived of as primarily spatial: orientation, length of border, spatial area (size), and ratio of filled to unfilled area ("emptiness"). These are similar to the types of relations Piaget refers to as logical, e.g., height and width of containers (1952). This lack of clarity may be due in part to the difficulty of representing logical relations in concrete stimuli. For example, Piaget typically uses kinship relations when discussing the theoretical nature of groupings with logical relations; yet, in his most direct assessment of multiplying logical relations, he employed shades of color and size (Inhelder and Piaget, 1964). In summary, then, the higher relationships between MRT and space tasks found in the younger two groups are limited somewhat by the fact that spatial elements appeared in both tasks.

It is important to note that several major hypotheses in Piaget's theory are similar to the one studied here. For example, Piaget hypothesizes that *addition* of classes, logical relations and spatial relations emerge simultaneously and develop in close association throughout middle childhood, and further, that addition and multiplication of classes, for example, evidence the same phenomena (Inhelder and Piaget, 1964, pp. 282–290). It appears that testing these hypotheses may well entail some of the same methodological problems raised in the present study.

In conclusion, there is a growing body of research relevant to multiplicative skills which bears mentioning. As outlined previously, Piaget has hypothesized that the multiplication of relations, in particular, underlies conservation concepts. It would be his contention that if one wished to teach a particular concept, such as conservation, the most likely method to use would be one which induced or "activated" the requisite operations (in terms of his theory). Yet a review of the conservation training literature suggests that training in the past has been quite specific to the type of conservation studied and by such methods as direct reinforced practice, verbalized rules, or confrontation with the "empirical facts," for the most part resulting in "remarkably little success" in inducing conservation (Flavell, 1963, p. 377). Recently, however, a pilot study by Sigel, Roeper, and Hooper (1966) indicated that training on multiplication of classes, multiplication of relations, and reversibility was effective in producing quantity conservation in four or five children in a training group compared to a control group. This finding was replicated in a slightly larger group by the same authors. Sonstroem (1966) also found training on multiplication of relations with manipulation of materials, compared to reversibility training, an effective procedure for eliciting quantity conservation. Although the hypothesis concerning the relationship among multiplicative abilities bears further study, particularly longitudinal study, it may be that determining whether these abilities are necessary and/or sufficient for conservation concepts will provide a more fruitful means of understanding their role as intellectual processes.

SUMMARY

Piaget's theory of intellectual development proposes a close relationship between structures described by logic and the organization of thought processes. Thus, Piaget hypothesizes that multiplication of classes, of logical relations, and of spatial relations are closely related from ages 7 to 11, approximately. The present study, in contrast to previous research, tested the three multiplicative abilities in the same children (ages $7\frac{1}{2}$, $9\frac{1}{2}$, and $11\frac{1}{2}$). Matrix-type tasks were used requiring classification on double attributes, seriation on two continuous dimensions, and location of objects on a rotated surface. Significant correlations were found among the three tasks for the younger two groups, and these appeared to be a function of association among different pairs of tasks for each age group. It was concluded that the magnitudes of the task intercorrelations provide moderate support for Piaget's hypothesis. Several methodological issues were raised in relation to the hypothesis, as well as to several similar hypotheses in Piaget's theory.

References

Flavell, J. H. *The developmental psychology of Jean Piaget.* New York: Van Nostrand, 1963.

Guilford, J. P. *Fundamental statistics in psychology and education.* New York: McGraw-Hill, 1956.

Inhelder, Barbel, & Piaget, J. *The early growth of logic in the child: classification and seriation.* New York: Harper & Row, 1964.

Lunzer, E. A. Some points of Piagetian theory in the light of experimental criticism. *J. child psychol. Psychiat.*, 1960, 1, 191–202.

Piaget, J. *The child's conception of number.* London: Routledge & Kegan Paul, 1952.

Piaget, J. *The psychology of intelligence.* Paterson, N.J.: Littlefield, Adams & Co., 1960.

Piaget, J., & Inhelder, Barbel. *The child's conception of space.* London: Routledge & Kegan Paul, 1956.

Raven, J. C. *Guide to using the coloured progressive matrices.* London: Lewis, 1956.

Shantz, Carolyn U. Effects of redundant and irrelevant information on children's seriation ability. *J. exp. child Psychol.*, in press.

Siegel, I. E., Roeper, Annamarie, & Hooper, F. H. A training procedure for acquisition of Piaget's conservation of quantity: a pilot study and its replication. *Brit. J. educ. Psychol.*, 1966, **36**, 301–311.

Smedslund, J. Concrete reasoning: a study of intellectual development. *Monogr. Soc. Res. Child Develpm.*, 1964, **29**, No. 2 (Serial No. 93).

Sonstroem, Anne M. On the conservation of solids. In J. S. Bruner, Rose R. Olver, & Patricia M. Greenfield (Eds.), *Studies in cognitive growth.* New York: Wiley, 1966. Pp. 208–224.

13. EXPERIENCES AFFECTING THE DEVELOPMENT OF NUMBER CONSERVATION IN CHILDREN*

Gerald E. Gruen

The experiment was conducted in two sessions over two successive days on 90 children with a mean age of 5·1. All Ss were given pretests and posttests of conservation of number, length, and substance. Half were given pretraining on the verbal discrimination of length and number, and half were not. One-third of the Ss in each of the pretraining groups were given direct training on number conservation, one-third were exposed to situations designed to produce "internal cognitive conflict," and one-third received no training on number conservation. Subjects in the conflict-plus-verbal pretraining group outperformed Ss in the control group without verbal pretraining. There was very little transfer of training from number conservation to other kinds of conservation.

A considerable amount of interest in cognitive development has been generated by Piaget's (1950) theory of intellectual development. Much of the resulting research has been concerned with the transition in cognitive processes that occurs as the child advances from preoperational reasoning to reasoning at the concrete-operational level. One of the most important

SOURCE. *Child Development*, 1965, **36**, 963–979.

* This experiment is adapted from a paper submitted in partial fulfilment of the requirements for the Ph.D. degree at the University of Illinois. The author wishes to thank the directors and teachers of the following kindergarten and nursery schools for their cooperation in making Ss available: The Playtime Nursery School, the Busy Bee Nursery School, the ABC Nursery School, and Westview Kindergarten in Champaign, Illinois; and the Maryville kindergarten in Granite City, Illinois. Author's address: Psychology Department, Worcester State Hospital, Worcester 1, Mass.

components of this transition is the acquisition of various "conservations." The term "conservation" refers to the realization that a particular dimension of an object may remain invariant under changes in other, irrelevant dimensions. For example, a child is said to conserve number when he realizes that the numerical equality between two collections of objects remains unchanged following a change in the spatial arrangement of the objects, provided no objects are added or taken away.

Piaget (1957) theorizes that the transition from nonconservation to conservation occurs through the "equilibration process," an internal process heavily dependent upon activity and experience. According to Smedslund (1961a), equilibration theory "differs radically from that of learning theory, since practice is not assumed to act through external reinforcements, but by a process of mutual influence of the child's activities on each other. Logical inferences are not derived from any properties of the external world, but from the placing into relationship (mise-en-relation) of the subjects' 'own activities.' " For a fuller discussion of equilibration theory see Flavell (1963).

Several investigators have attempted to test Piaget's equilibration theory by determining the kinds of experiences that facilitate conservation (Greco, 1963; Morf, 1963; Smedslund, 1961b; 1961c; 1961d; 1961e; Wohlwill & Lowe, 1962). Smedslund (1961b), investigating conservation of weight, and Wohlwill and Lowe (1962), investigating conservation of number, have compared the relative effectiveness of training procedures derived from Piaget's equilibration model and a more conventional learning-through-reinforced-practice model. Neither of these experimenters found either kind of procedure to be significantly superior to the other in inducing conservation. Nor did they find that the children subjected to these special training techniques outperformed their respective control groups. In a later experiment, however, Smedslund (1961e) found that it was possible to induce conservation of substance in children by means of a training procedure designed to induce "cognitive conflict," which is, according to Smedslund, an essential condition for the development of conservation in the child. Cognitive conflict supposedly induces a reorganization of the child's intellectual actions, which proceeds along the lines postulated by Piaget's equilibration theory. This reorganization then leads to the conservation strategy. Children exposed to this type of training were found to outperform their no-training control group on a posttest of substance conservation, but their performance was not directly compared to a group of children receiving reinforced practice on conservation.

In the present investigation of number conservation, an attempt is made to compare directly the relative effectiveness of training procedures derived from Smedslund's (1961d; 1961e) cognitive-conflict hypothesis and a conventional learning-through-reinforced-practice hypothesis. The training procedures derived from the former hypothesis are designed to induce internal cognitive conflict that will bring about conservation of number. However, they do not permit the kind of external feedback that the training procedures derived from the learning-through-reinforced-practice hypothesis do. The latter provide external feedback, through the process of counting, of the relative number of elements in two collections of elements. The "reinforcement" involved in this procedure is strictly a "knowledge-of-results" kind of reinforcement, no external rewards being given until the end of the experiment. In this respect, the procedure is more comparable to Smedslund's (1961b) procedure with conservation of weight than it is to Wohlwill and Lowe's (1962) procedure with conservation of number. The purpose of this study is not to discover a procedure that will permit early conservation training but, rather, to isolate some of the variables that may play a role in the acquisition of conservation.

The present investigation has one further purpose. The majority of the investigators interested in the acquisition of various Piagetian thought forms have used verbal techniques. Typically, the experiments of these investigators have shown agreement with the findings of Piaget (1950) and Piaget and Inhelder (1948) that conservation and other concrete-operational thought forms do not appear in children until they reach the age of 7 or 8 years. Braine and Shanks (in press, a; in press, b), however, using nonverbal assessment techniques have found several kinds of conservation in children 4.5–5.5 years old. Their findings suggest that a child may have the ability to perform a given operation, such as conservation, without having the verbal skill necessary to adequately comprehend and respond to verbal techniques of assessing conservation.

In the present experiment, a verbal-assessment technique is used, but an attempt is made to insure that all Ss understand the key words that E uses in this verbal assessment. The key words involved are "more" and "same." Half of the Ss in each of the experimental and control groups are pre-set to interpret these words to mean more or same in number, and only in number, and not to associate these words with length, a variable that typically shows substantial correlation with number. The other Ss receive no pretraining on these terms. It is expected that those Ss receiving the verbal pretraining will outperform the other Ss on a posttest of number conservation.

METHOD

The experiment was conducted in two sessions over two successive days. Table 1 shows the order of procedure on each day.

The general design of the experiment was the classical transfer of training paradigm consisting of (a) pretests of conservation of number, length, and

TABLE 1

Order of Procedure

Order	First Day	Second Day
1	Pretest	Refresher pretraining trials (10–13)
2	Pretraining trials (1–9)	Training trials (17–32)
3	Training trials (1–16)	Posttests

substance; (*b*) verbal pretraining; (*c*) the major training for conservation (involving two experimental groups trained on conservation of number and one no-training control group); and (*d*) posttests of conservation of number, length, and substance. There were three training conditions and two pretraining conditions (verbal pretraining vs. no verbal pretraining). Thus, the experiment was a 3×2 factorial design.

Subjects

Subjects for this study were 90 nursery-school and kindergarten children, 50 girls and 40 boys, between the ages of 4·6 and 6·4. The mean age of the *S*s in each of the six experimental conditions varied between 5·0 and 5·2, the over-all mean age being 5·1. These *S*s were selected from a total of 210 children who were given pretests of addition/subtraction and conservation of number (see below). Any child who demonstrated his ability to count from 1 to 9 and who also had a rudimentary understanding of addition/subtraction, but lacked the ability to conserve number, was selected for participation in the experiment. Of the 120 *S*s who were excluded from further participation in the study, 17 were excluded because they were unable to count from 1 to 9, 73 were excluded because they failed the addition/subtraction pretest, and 30 were excluded because they passed the number-conservation pretest. Selected *S*s were assigned at random to the six experimental conditions.

Apparatus

The materials necessary for the pre- and posttest were six plasticine balls of approximately equal weight and volume; nine white and nine blue poker chips; two yellow sticks, both 12 in. long; and four V-shaped figures of black cardboard pasted on a 28×22 in. sheet of white cardboard. The arms of the V-shaped figures formed an angle of approximately 50°. The arms were $4\frac{1}{2}$ in. long and $\frac{3}{8}$ in. wide. Two of the four V-shaped figures were placed with their apexes 12 in. apart and their arms pointing outward, and the other two were placed with their apexes 12 in. apart and their arms pointed inward. This was intended to produce the Muller-Lyer (M-L) illusion.

Blocks of wood of various sizes were the only materials necessary for verbal pretraining. These were 12 $1 \times 1 \times \frac{3}{4}$-in. blocks, 10 $2 \times 1 \times \frac{3}{4}$-in. blocks, 4 $3 \times 1 \times \frac{3}{4}$-in. blocks, and 2 $5 \times 1 \times \frac{3}{4}$-in. blocks. Half of the blocks of each size were painted black, and half were painted white.

The apparatus used in the training of each of the experimental groups consisted of two crisscrossing, scissors-like devices which were parallel to each other. These devices were attached to metal handles that could be pushed and pulled to lengthen and shorten them. Corks were mounted on pegs located at the junctions of the crisscrossing devices. The corks could be easily removed from, and replaced on, these pegs. This apparatus permitted lengthening or shortening of each row of corks independently, while maintaining an approximately equal distance between the corks within a particular row. Trinkets for charm bracelets and M&M chocolate candies were used as rewards.

Procedure

S was seated at a table directly opposite *E* and told that he was going to play a number of games.

Addition/Subtraction Pretest. Two piles of nine poker chips each, one pile made up of white chips and the other of blue chips, were placed on the table before *S*. *E* announced to *S* that both piles contained the same number of chips. Then *E* took a chip away from one of the piles and placed it on the table where it was plainly visible to *S*. The standard conservation questions (Q)[1] was then asked: "Do you think there are more blue chips in this pile, the same number of blue chips and white chips, or more white chips in this pile?" After *S* answered Q, *E* always asked: "Why do you think so?" Following this, the chip was placed back on the pile from which it had been removed, and these questions were repeated. *E* then added a chip to the other pile, and finally, removed it again, asking these same two questions after both the addition and the subtraction.

S had to answer all four of these items correctly and explain his answers in terms of the operations that *E* had performed on the piles of chips (e.g., "you took one chip away from this pile," or "you put a chip back on that pile," etc.) before he was permitted to continue in the experiment.

Conservation Pre- and Posttests. Immediately following the addition/subtraction pretest, *S* was tested for conservation of number, length, and substance, in that order.

---

[1] This same general question is also used to get at conservation of number, length, and substance. It is modified to make it appropriate for each kind of conservation. Hereafter, it will be referred to as Q.

A. Number.[2] Two rows of seven chips each, one blue and the other white, were placed parallel to each other so that both rows were of the same length, and the chips in one row were directly opposite those in the other. *Experimenter* then directed S to count the number of chips in each row. Following this, E deformed one of the rows of chips and asked Q plus the question, "Why do you think so?"

The following three deformations were repeated two times each, making a total of six items which were administered in a random order; the row of blue chips was deformed on one-half of the trials and the row of white chips on the other half: (1) E extended one row of the chips in both directions to a length about twice that of the other row; (2) E subdivided one row of chips into two rows of four and three chips placed parallel to the other row of seven chips; (3) E placed one row of chips in a vertical pile in front of the other row.

B. Length. Two 12-in. yellow sticks were held upright and close together with their lower ends on the table directly before S. After S had seen that the two sticks were equal in length, E slowly laid the sticks down on the M-L figures previously described, creating a perceptual illusion in which one stick appeared longer than the other. Experimenter then asked Q plus the question, "Why do you think so?"

This same procedure was repeated three times. For one-half the Ss the M-L illusion was varied so that first the stick on E's right looked longer, then the one on E's left, and then the one on E's right again. For the other half of the Ss the order was left-right-left.

C. Substance. Experimenter presented S with two balls of plasticine, equal in weight and volume, and told S that they contained the same amount of clay. If S did not think that the two balls looked as though they contained the same amount of clay, he was instructed to make them equal by subtracting from one ball and/or adding to the other. After S was satisfied that the two balls were equal, E rolled one of the balls into another form saying: "Now I change this one into a —— [sausage, ring, or cross]." After each of the three deformations, Q plus the question, "Why do you think so?" were asked.

Verbal Pretraining. On the first experimental day, one-half of the Ss were given nine verbal pretraining items, each item beginning with two rows of wooden blocks placed parallel to each other. For six of these nine items, one row contained a greater number of blocks than the other row but was shorter in length. This was accomplished by using longer blocks in the row with the least number of blocks. The items having an unequal number of blocks

---

[2] The procedures used in the number conservation pre- and posttests were adapted from procedures used by Wohlwill & Lowe (1962), with slight modifications.

in each row were the following: eight 1-in. blocks versus two 5-in. blocks; seven 1-in. blocks versus three 3-in. blocks; and six 1-in. blocks versus four 2-in. blocks. These three items were given, in random order, twice. On half the trials the front row had the greater number of blocks, and on half the back row had the greater number. For the remaining items, the two rows contained the same number of blocks and were equal in length. These three items had either five 1-in. blocks, six 1-in. blocks, or four 2-in. blocks in each row. On the second experimental day, S was again given the three items having an unequal number of blocks in each row and an item having five 1-in. blocks in each row.

On each item S was directed to count out loud the number of blocks in each row. Then Q was asked. If S responded incorrectly, E directed him to count out loud the number of blocks in each row again and then said, for example, "Yes, there are seven blocks in this row and three blocks in that row, so this row has more blocks than that row." Following this, E asked, "Now, which row is longer, this one or that one?" If S responded incorrectly, E said, "No, you see this row sticks out further this way and that way, so it is longer."

Those Ss who did not receive verbal pretraining were given another task that involved about the same amount of interaction between S and E as the verbal-pretraining task. In this task, S was asked to take from a number of blocks placed before him a certain number that were to be placed on an 8-in. $\times$ 11-in. sheet of white paper that E had before him. The number of blocks that S was asked to place on the white paper varied from 2 to 10. On each trial, after S had placed what he thought to be the correct number of blocks on the paper, E asked him to count the blocks to see if he was correct. As in the verbal-pretraining conditions, nine trials were given on the first day and four on the second.

Training for Conservation.   The two experimental groups and the control group all received training on the apparatus, previously described, that permitted the lengthening or shortening of parallel rows of corks.

A. DIRECT-TRAINING GROUP. The apparatus was placed on the table before S with the two horizontal rows running parallel to the front of the table. Experimenter held up a bag of prizes (trinkets) and told S that if he did really well in this game he would receive some prizes at the end of the game. He was instructed to do his very best.

While the rows were in the starting position, E directed S to count the number of corks in each row. The experimenter then lengthened or shortened one of the rows of corks by manipulating the metal bar attached to one end of the apparatus. After each deformation Q was asked. Experimenter neither confirmed nor corrected S's response to Q. After he responded S was directed to count the number of corks in each row a second time. The only external feedback S got as to whether his response to Q was correct or incorrect was the knowledge he obtained through counting. If S counted correctly the number of corks in each row, E confirmed that he had done so by saying, "That's right." If S counted incorrectly the number of corks in each row, E corrected him.

On half the trials there was an equal number of corks in each row, while there was an unequal number (one row having one more cork than the other) on the remaining trials, thus requiring the conservation of inequality. This was necessary in order that these trials would not be too easy and to prevent response stereotypy.

The items used are shown in Table 2. Starting-position A refers to the row nearest S, B to the row farthest from S. Each of these eight items were

TABLE 2

Direct-Training Items

Items	Starting Position	Transformation
1	A = B	A elongated
2	A = B	B elongated
3	A > B	B elongated
4	B > A	A elongated
5	A = B	A shortened
6	A = B	B shortened
7	A > B	A shortened
8	B > A	B shortened

used four times, and the order of their occurrence was randomized. These are not the only transformations possible, but in each there is an inconsistency between length of row and number of corks in a row. Thus, it is necessary for S to make a conserving response in order to answer Q correctly.

B. CONFLICT GROUP. The procedure in this group was identical to that in the direct-training group except that every item consisted of one deformation, followed by Q, and then, rather than a recount of the number of corks in each row, a number of subtractions from the row which S believed to have more corks. Each time E subtracted a cork he asked, "Now which row has more corks, this row or that row?" In order to insure that a conflict between the operation of the deformation and the operation of subtraction had actually occurred, E continued to subtract corks until S changed his answer to this question.

When subtracting a cork, E always removed the third cork from the end of the row first (the corks are numbered from 1–9, beginning at the end of the row on E's left). If more subtractions were necessary E then removed the seventh cork; next, the fifth, fourth, sixth, second, and eighth, in that order. This left only one cork at each end of the row. No S required this many subtractions before he changed his answer as to which row had more corks. When a cork was taken away it was always placed nearby on the table where it was plainly visible to S. Between the trials, E was careful to shield the apparatus from the view of S with a 10-in. $\times$ 22-in. sheet of cardboard while the corks were placed back on the pegs from which they had been removed and the lengths of the rows were adjusted to make them even. This procedure was necessary to insure that S did not receive any external feedback as to the correctness of his response to Q.

The number of corks (nine) in each row and the length of the rows on the apparatus were made identical at the beginning of each item. This made possible only 4 transformations: lengthening or shortening either the front or back row. These 4 items were repeated 8 times in random order, making 32 items altogether.

C. CONTROL GROUP. The rows of corks remained at their minimal spread on all trials for Ss in this group. The corks were removed from both rows, and nine corks were placed directly in front of S and nine in front of E. On each trial E placed a number of corks on the pegs sticking up in row B, the row nearest E. E always placed the first cork on the peg at the end of row B and continued placing the other corks on adjacent pegs. After E had finished placing the appropriate number of corks on row B, he said, "See if you can place as many of these corks on that row as I have placed on this row." This procedure was repeated for 32 trials, with the number of corks used on each trial varying between two and nine. As in the other training groups, Ss in this group were told that they could win prizes if they did well in the game.

RESULTS

Classification of the Children's Explanations

The pre- and posttests of conservation called for an explanation in addition to a response to the conservation question. These explanations were divided into three categories: (1) conserving explanations—those clearly indicating conservation; (2) nonconserving explanations—those clearly indicating nonconservation; and (3) ambiguous explanations—those not clearly indicating either conservation or nonconservation. Experimenter attempted to get Ss to elaborate and give further explanation of ambiguous explanations by interjecting some neutral statement, such as, "Tell me more," following each such response.

The explanations actually given by the Ss were recorded on tape and transcribed. Two scorers then scored the explanations given as either con-

serving, nonconserving, or ambiguous responses. An estimate of the reliability with which these responses could be categorized was then obtained.
A total of 1,080 responses were involved, 540 for number conservation and
270 each for length and substance conservation. The two judges agreed on
1,063, or 98 per cent, of their classifications. A ϕ correlation coefficient of .96
was obtained as an estimate of the overall interjudge reliability. The separate interjudge-reliability coefficients for the number, length, and substance
data, respectively, were: .97, .96, and .88.

Addition/Subtraction

A total of 193 Ss were given the addition/subtraction pretest. Of these,
120 Ss answered all four of the items correctly, while 33 Ss failed all four
items. Of the remaining 40 Ss, 31 passed the first two items but failed the
last two. The first two items consisted of subtracting one chip from one
of two piles of chips, followed by replacing that chip back on the pile from
which it had been removed $(- +)$. Conversely, the last two items consisted
of adding one chip to one of two piles of chips, followed by subtracting that
same chip from the pile to which it had been added $(+ -)$. Only 3 Ss
passed the last two items $(+ -)$ after they had failed the first two $(- +)$.
Five Ss passed one of the first two items $(- +)$ but failed both of the last
two $(+ -)$, and one S failed one of the first two items $(- +)$ and one of
the last two items. None of the 30 Ss who were excluded from the study
because they had passed the number-conservation pretest failed any of the
four addition/subtraction items.

Verbal Pretraining

The 45 Ss in the verbal-pretraining condition were given 13 verbal-
pretraining trials, 9 on the first day and 4 on the second day. The mean
number of trials on which no errors were made for each S was 10.42. Only
one S made errors on as many as 7 trials, and only 4 Ss made errors on the
second experimental day.

Number Conservation

The scores on the number posttest ranged from 0 to 6, with 49 of the
90 Ss making scores of 0 and 12 Ss making scores of 6. Forty-one of the 90
Ss made at least one conserving response, and 31 made three or more conserving responses. Table 3 shows the mean number of conserving responses
per S for each of the six experimental conditions.

A plot of the deviations of the scores within each group from their
group means revealed that the data were positively skewed and bimodal.
Therefore, only nonparametric analyses of the data were considered appropriate.

A Kruskal-Wallis one-way analysis of variance (Siegel, 1956) of the posttest data revealed a significant difference among the six experimental groups $(H = 12.09, 5 \ df, p < .05)$. Using the Mann-Whitney U test (Siegel, 1956), it was found that this difference was due to the greater number of

TABLE 3

Mean Number of Number-Conservation Responses per S for the Experimental Groups

	Training Groups		
	Control	Direct Training	Conflict
Pretraining groups:			
Verbal pretraining	2.00	1.40	3.33
No verbal pretraining	0.67	1.80	1.60

conserving responses made by Ss in the conflict-plus-verbal-pretraining group than by Ss in the control group with no verbal pretraining $(U = 49, p < .02)$. None of the other differences among the six experimental groups was significant.

In order that an estimate of the effect of the verbal-pretraining variable could be obtained, the three groups that had received verbal pretraining were combined and compared with the three groups that had not received verbal pretraining. A Mann-Whitney U test revealed that this variable was not significant $(Z = 1.39, p = .16)$. However, when all Ss who received conflict training were combined and compared with all Ss who received direct training and all Ss in the control condition, a Kruskal-Wallis one-way analysis of variance did reveal a significant difference among the training groups $(H = 7.20, 2 \ df, p < .05)$. This difference was due to the greater number of conserving responses made by Ss in the conflict group than by Ss in the control group, as was shown by the Mann-Whitney U test $(Z = 1.92, p = .05)$.

One other analysis was performed on the number-posttest data. This was a χ^2 analysis of the frequency with which Ss in each of the six groups reached a criterion of three or more (50 per cent) conserving responses. This analysis did not yield a statistically significant difference between the groups although significance was approached $(\chi^2 = 10.28, 5 \ df, .05 < p < .10)$. The frequencies are presented in Table 4.

Length Conservation

Table 5 shows the number of Ss who conserved length on the pretest and posttest. Although there was no significant over-all improvement in length

TABLE 4

Number of Ss Who Made Three or More Conserving Responses on the
Number-Conservation Posttest

| | Training Groups | | |
| | | Direct | |
	Control	Training	Conflict
Verbal pretraining	5	4	10
No verbal pretraining	2	5	5

TABLE 5

Number of Ss Who Conserved Length on Pretest and Posttest

| | Posttest | |
	Nonconservers	Conservers
Pretest:		
Conservers	8	21
Nonconservers	50	11

conservation from pretest to posttest, a Kruskal-Wallis one-way analysis of
variance did reveal significant differences among the groups in their change
scores from pretest to posttest ($H = 11.56$, 5 df, $p < .05$). The Mann-Whitney U test showed that the only group to improve significantly more than
the control group without verbal pretraining from pretest to posttest was the
conflict-plus-verbal-pretraining group ($U = 26$, $p < .02$). The mean improvement score for Ss in the conflict-plus-verbal-pretraining group was 0.6,
while that for Ss in the control group without verbal pretraining was 0.2.

Substance Conservation

Table 6 shows the number of Ss who conserved substance on the pretest
and posttest. As with the length-conservation data, there was no significant
overall improvement in substance conservation from pretest to posttest. How-

TABLE 6

Number of Ss Who Conserved Substance on Pretest and Posttest

| | Posttest | |
	Nonconservers	Conservers
Pretest:		
Conservers	4	5
Nonconservers	71	10

ever, a Kruskal-Wallis one-way analysis of variance did reveal significant differences among the groups in their change scores from pretest to posttest $(H = 23.18,\ 5\ df,\ p < .001)$. The Mann-Whitney U test revealed that the only group to improve significantly more than the control group without verbal pretraining from pretest to posttest was the conflict group without verbal pretraining $(U = 63,\ p < .05)$. The mean improvement score for Ss in the conflict group was 0.47, while that for Ss in the control group was —0.07. The negative improvement score of the control group indicates that they did slightly poorer on the posttest of substance conservation than they did on the pretest.

Transfer of Training

The primary reason the tests of conservation of length and substance were included in this study was to provide a means of assessing the generalizability of laboratory-induced conservation. Specifically, in this study it is of interest to know the extent to which those Ss who acquired the ability to conserve number also acquired the ability to conserve length and/or substance. Table 7 provides this information. Columns (1) and (2) include only those Ss who

TABLE 7

Number of Ss Acquiring Number Conservation Who Incidentally Acquire Other Conservations

	Length[a]		Substance[b]	
	Nonconservers (1)	Conservers (2)	Nonconservers (3)	Conservers (4)
Number:				
Conservers	17	10	26	9
Nonconservers	33	1	45	1

[a] The 29 Ss who made conserving responses on the pretest of length conservation are not included.

[b] The nine Ss who made conserving responses on the pretest of substance conservation are not included.

made no conserving responses on the pretest of conservation of length. The 29 Ss who conserved on the pretest of conservation of length are not included because they were already able to conserve length when the experiment began and did not acquire this ability during the experiment. Similarly, columns (3) and (4) include those Ss who made no conserving responses on the pretest of conservation of substance. Of course, none of the Ss made conserving responses of the pretest of number conservation.

Columns (1) and (2) show that 10, or 37 per cent, of these 27 Ss who acquired conservation of number also acquired conservation of length, while only 1, or 3 per cent, of the 34 Ss who did not acquire conservation of number during the experiment acquired conservation of length. Fisher's exact-probability test (Siegel, 1956) reveals that the difference in these two proportions is highly significant ($p = .0007$). Columns (3) and (4) show that 9, or 26 per cent, of those 35 Ss who acquired conservation of number also acquired conservation of substance, while only 1, or 2 per cent, of the remaining 46 Ss who did not acquire conservation of number during the experiment acquired conservation of substance. Applying Fisher's exact-probability test to these data reveals that the difference in these two proportions is also highly significant ($p = .002$). Thus, there appears to be some tendency for those Ss who acquire conservation of number during the experiment to also acquire conservation of length and/or substance.

DISCUSSION

In one sense, the most obvious conclusion one might draw from the data of this experiment is that neither confronting the child repeatedly with the invariance of numerical values in the face of irrelevant perceptual changes nor devising situations to induce internal cognitive conflict is particularly effective in inducing number conservation. Over one-half of the Ss who received one of these two kinds of training did not make even one conserving response on the posttest of number conservation.

Nevertheless, there were a substantial number of Ss who acquired conservation of number during this experiment. The overall improvement becomes more impressive when it is compared with the improvement in conservation that occurred in previous studies that have attempted to induce conservation in children experimentally (Smedslund, 1961b; 1961c; 1961d; 1961e; Wohlwill & Lowe, 1962).

If we compare those Ss who received only direct training with those Ss who received only training designed to produce internal cognitive conflict, there is little to choose between them. There was approximately the same amount of improvement in both groups. However, if all the Ss (both those who received verbal pretraining and those who did not) who received direct training are compared with all the Ss in the cognitive-conflict condition, it can be seen that the Ss exposed to cognitive conflict outperformed those given direct training, although the difference between these two groups did not reach statistical significance. Thus, although it may not be definitely concluded from these data that either direct external feedback or internal cognitive conflict was more effective in inducing number conservation in these children, the direction of the results tends to support Smedslund's (1961d) equilibration-through-internal-cognitive-conflict hypothesis.

It should be remembered, however, that the direct-training procedure used in this study involved reinforcement of the "knowledge-of-results" kind. Thus, it differed from a similar procedure used by Wohlwill and Lowe (1962), who, in an attempt to induce number conservation by reinforced practice, rewarded correct responses to the conservation question with chips that could be exchanged at the end of the experiment for toys. It also differed from their procedure in that theirs involved a match between a given collection of elements and the corresponding symbolically indicated number, whereas the direct-training procedure of the present study involved a comparison of the *relative* number of elements in two collections. Since the posttest of number conservation in both studies involved the comparison of the relative number of elements in two collections, it would be interesting to see what effect direct confirmation of responses to the conservation question by external rewards would have on a training procedure such as the one used in this study.

Since there was a significant difference between the two conflict groups combined versus the two control groups combined, it seems clear that number conservation can be acquired without any kind of direct external feedback if one can induce appropriate cognitive conflict in a child.

However, the verbal pretraining alone was about as effective as either direct training or cognitive conflict in the inducement of number conservation. Table 3 shows that the mean number of conserving responses for Ss in the control-plus-verbal-pretraining group was 2.00, while that for Ss in the direct training (without verbal pretraining) group was 1.80, and that for Ss in the conflict (without verbal pretraining) group was 1.60. This indicates that an experimenter who uses a verbal test of conservation must be certain that Ss understand the language he is using. Otherwise, a child capable of conserving may be deemed a "nonconserver" erroneously.

The most interesting characteristic of the verbal pretraining, however, was the facilitative effect it had in inducing conservation when it was combined with the cognitive-conflict training. One possible reason for this effect of verbal pretraining follows from the fact that the child in the conflict situation hears the word "more" quite often. Having been given the verbal pretraining, the child supposedly understands that the word "more" refers to the relative number of elements in two collections of elements. He is not likely to lose this understanding if his verbal pretraining is followed by training in the conflict situation, because in that situation he is exposed to, and must respond to, the word "more" repeatedly. Using the word "more" a great number of times places a great emphasis on the *relation* between the two rows of elements involved. It is interesting to note that the children in the training groups other than the conflict group do not have so much emphasis placed on this relation. Thus, they are not as likely to make direct comparisons of the number of elements in the two rows. Focusing one's attention on the relation between two sets of elements may very well be an important aspect of the acquisition of conservation of number.

Generally speaking, training the children on conservation of number did little to increase their ability to conserve length and substance. This seems to indicate either that the process of conserving is acquired for each concept separately and independently and is not a general ability which, once acquired, can operate for all concepts and materials, or, alternatively, that the ability to conserve number, when it is acquired in the laboratory over a few days, may not have as much depth or generality as conservation acquired "naturally" over a long period of time. Both these statements are probably true. Previous studies indicate that the acquisition of conservations of various sorts will appear at different ages in the same child (Elkind, 1961), and Smedslund (1961c) has shown that the ability to conserve weight, when acquired through laboratory training, will extinguish faster than will "naturally" acquired conservation of weight.

Finally, the findings of this study seem to support Smedslund's (1964) finding that the $-+$ operation is easier and appears developmentally earlier than the $+-$ operation. Further, the fact that none of the 30 Ss who had number conservation on the pretest failed any of the four addition/subtraction items, while 90 Ss had addition/subtraction but not conservation, is empirical evidence to support the hypothesis that the addition/subtraction operation logically and developmentally precedes conservation.

References

Braine, M. D. S., & Shanks, B. L. The conservation of a shape property and a proposal about the origin of the conservations. *Canad. J. Psychol.*, in press. (a)

Braine, M. D. S., & Shanks, B. L. The development of conservation of size. *J. verb. Learn. verb. Behav.*, in press. (b)

Elkind, D. Children's discovery of the conservation of mass, weight and volume: Piaget Replication Study II. *J. genet. Psychol.* 1961, **98**, 219–227.

Flavell, J. H. *The developmental psychology of Jean Piaget.* Princeton, N.J. Van Nostrand, 1963.

Greco, P. L'apprentissage dans une situation a structure operatoire concrète: les inversions successives de l'ordre lineaire par les rotations de 180°. Cited by J. H. Flavell, *The developmental psychology of Jean Piaget.* Princeton, N.J.: Van Nostrand, 1963. Pp. 375–376.

Morf, A. Les relations entre la logique et le langage lors du passage du raisonnement concret au raisonnement formel. Cited by J. H. Flavell, *The developmental psychology of Jean Piaget.* Princeton, N.J. Van Nostrand, 1963. P. 375.

Piaget, J. *The psychology of intelligence.* Trans. M. Piercy and D. E. Berlyne. London: Routledge & Kegan Paul, 1950.

Piaget, J. Logique et équilibre dans les comportements du sujet. In L. Apostel, B. Mandelbrot, & J. Piaget, *Etudes d'épistémologie génétique.* Vol. 2. *Logique et équilibre.* Paris: Pr. Univer. de France, 1957. Pp. 27–117.

Piaget, J., & Inhelder, B. Le role des operations dans le développement de l'intelligence. *Proc. 12th int. Congr. Psychol.,* 1948. Pp. 102–103.

Siegel, S. *Nonparametric statistics for the behavioral sciences.* New York: McGraw-Hill, 1956.

Smedslund. J. The acquisition of conservation of substance and weight in children. I. Introduction. *Scand. J. Psychol.,* 1961, **2**, 11–20. (a)

Smedslund, J. The acquisition of conservation of substance and weight in children. II. External reinforcement of conservation of weight and of the operations of addition and subtraction. *Scand. J. Psychol.,* 1961, **2**, 71–84. (b)

Smedslund, J. The acquisition of conservation of substance and weight in children. III. Extinction of conservation of weight acquired "normally" and by means of empirical controls on a balance scale. *Scand. J. Psychol.,* 1961, **2**, 85–87. (c)

Smedslund, J. The acquisition of conservation of substance and weight in children. VI. Practice on continuous vs. discontinuous material in conflict-situations without external reinforcement. *Scand. J. Psychol.,* 1961, **2**, 203–210. (d)

Smedslund, J. The acquisition of conservation of substance and weight in children. V. Practice in conflict situations without external reinforcement. *Scand. J. Psychol.,* 1961, **2**, 156–160. (e)

Smedslund, J. Concrete reasoning: a study of intellectual development. *Monogr. Soc. Res. Child Develpm.,* 1964, **29**, No. 2.

Wohlwill, J. F., & Lowe, R. C. An experimental analysis of the development of the conservation of number. *Child Develpm.,* 1962, **33**, 153–167.

14. THE COURSE OF COGNITIVE GROWTH

Jerome S. Bruner[1]

I shall take the view in what follows that the development of human intellectual functioning from infancy to such perfection as it may reach is shaped by a series of technological advances in the use of mind. Growth depends upon the mastery of techniques and cannot be understood without reference to such mastery. These techniques are not, in the main, inventions of the individuals who are "growing up"; they are, rather, skills transmitted with varying efficiency and success by the culture—language being a prime example. Cognitive growth, then, is in a major way from the outside in as well as from the inside out.

Two matters will concern us. The first has to do with the techniques or technologies that aid growing human beings to represent in a manageable way the recurrent features of the complex environments in which they live. It is fruitful, I think, to distinguish three systems of processing information by which human beings construct models of their world: through action, through imagery, and through language. A second concern is with integration, the means whereby acts are organized into higher-order ensembles, making possible the use of larger and larger units of information for the solution of particular problems.

Let me first elucidate these two theoretical matters, and then turn to an examination of the research upon which they are based, much of it from the Center for Cognitive Studies at Harvard.

SOURCE. *American Psychologist*, 1964, **19**, 1, 1–15.

[1] The assistance of R. R. Olver and Mrs. Blythe Clinchy in the preparation of this paper is gratefully acknowledged.

On the occasion of the One Hundredth Anniversary of the publication of Darwin's *The Origin of Species,* Washburn and Howell (1960) presented a paper at the Chicago Centennial celebration containing the following passage:

> It would now appear . . . that the large size of the brain of certain hominids was a relatively late development and that the brain evolved due to new selection pressures *after* bipedalism and consequent upon the use of tools. The tool-using, ground living, hunting way of life created the large human brain rather than a large brained man discovering certain new ways of life. [We] believe this conclusion is the most important result of the recent fossil hominid discoveries and is one which carries far-reaching implications for the interpretation of human behavior and its origins. . . . The important point is that size of brain, insofar as it can be measured by cranial capacity, has increased some threefold subsequent to the use and manufacture of implements. . . . The uniqueness of modern man is seen as the result of a technical-social life which tripled the size of the brain, reduced the face, and modified many other structures of the body [p. 49 f.].

This implies that the principal change in man over a long period of years—perhaps 500,000 thousand—has been alloplastic rather than autoplastic. That is to say, he has changed by linking himself with new, external implementation systems rather than by any conspicuous change in morphology—"evolution-by-prosthesis," as Weston La Barre (1954) puts it. The implement systems seem to have been of three general kinds—*amplifiers of human motor capacities* ranging from the cutting tool through the lever and wheel to the wide variety of modern devices; *amplifiers of sensory capacities* that include primitive devices such as smoke signaling and modern ones such as magnification and radar sensing, but also likely to include such "software" as those conventionalized perceptual shortcuts that can be applied to the redundant sensory environment; and finally *amplifiers of human ratiocinative capacities* of infinite variety ranging from language systems to myth and theory and explanation. All of these forms of amplification are in major or minor degree conventionalized and transmitted by the culture, the last of them probably the most since ratiocinative amplifiers involve symbol systems governed by rules that must, for effective use, be shared.

Any implement system, to be effective, must produce an appropriate internal counterpart, an appropriate skill necessary for organizing sensorimotor acts, for organizing percepts, and for organizing our thoughts in a way that matches them to the requirements of implement systems. These internal skills, represented genetically as capacities, are slowly selected in evolution. In the deepest sense, then, man can be described as a species that has become specialized by the use of technological implements. His selection and survival have depended upon a morphology and set of capacities that could be linked with the alloplastic devices that have made his later evolution possible. We move, perceive, and think in a fashion that depends upon techniques rather than upon wired-in arrangements in our nervous system.

Where representation of the environment is concerned, it too depends upon techniques that are learned—and these are precisely the techniques that serve to amplify our motor acts, our perceptions, and our ratiocinative activities. We know and respond to recurrent regularities in our environment by skilled and patterned acts, by conventionalized spatioqualitative imagery and selective perceptual organization, and through linguistic encoding which, as so many writers have remarked, places a selective lattice between us and the physical environment. In short, the capacities that have been shaped by our evolution as tool users are the ones that we rely upon in the primary task of representation—the nature of which we shall consider in more detail directly.

As for integration, it is a truism that there are very few single or simple adult acts that cannot be performed by a young child. In short, any more highly skilled activity can be decomposed into simpler components, each of which can be carried out by a less skilled operator. What higher skills require is that the component operations be combined. Maturation consists of an orchestration of these components into an integrated sequence. The "distractability," so-called, of much early behavior may reflect each act's lack of imbeddedness in what Miller, Galanter, and Pribram (1960), speak of as "plans." These integrated plans, in turn, reflect the routines and subroutines that one learns in the course of mastering the patterned nature of a social environment. So that integration, too, depends upon patterns that come from the outside in—an internalization of what Roger Barker (1963) has called environmental "behavior settings."

If we are to benefit from contact with recurrent regularities in the environment, we must represent them in some manner. To dismiss this problem as "mere memory" is to misunderstand it. For the most important thing about memory is not storage of past experience, but rather the retrieval of what is relevant in some usable form. This depends upon how past experience is coded and processed so that it may indeed be relevant and usable in the present when needed. The end product of such a system of coding and processing is what we may speak of as a representation.

I shall call the three modes of representation mentioned earlier enactive representation, iconic representation, and symbolic representation. Their appearance in the life of the child is in that order, each depending upon the previous one for its development, yet all of them remaining more or less intact throughout life—barring such early accidents as blindness or deafness or cortical injury. By enactive representation I mean a mode of representing past events through appropriate motor response. We cannot, for example, give an adequate description of familiar sidewalks or floors over which we habitually walk, nor do we have much of an image of what they are like. Yet we get about them without tripping or even looking much. Such segments of our environment—bicycle riding, tying knots, aspects of driving——get represented in our muscles, so to speak. Iconic representation summarizes events by the selective organization of percepts and of images, by the spatial, temporal, and qualitative structures of the perceptual field and their transformed images. Images "stand for" perceptual events in the close but conventionally selective way that a picture stands for the object pictured. Finally, a symbol system represents things by design features that include remoteness and arbitrariness. A word neither points directly to its referent here and now, nor does it resemble it as a picture. The lexeme "Philadelphia" looks no more like the city so designated than does a nonsense syllable. The other property of language that is crucial is its productiveness in combination, far beyond what can be done with images or acts. "Philadelphia is a lavendar sachet in Grandmother's linen closet," or $(x + 2)^2 = x^2 + 4x + 4 = x(x + 4) + 4$.

An example or two of enactive representation underlines its importance in infancy and in disturbed functioning, while illustrating its limitations. Piaget (1954) provides us with an observation from the closing weeks of the first year of life. The child is playing with a rattle in his crib. The rattle drops over the side. The child moves his clenched hand before his face, opens it, looks for the rattle. Not finding it there, he moves his hand, closed again, back to the edge of the crib, shakes it with movements like those he uses in shaking the rattle. Thereupon he moves his closed hand back toward his face, opens it, and looks. Again no rattle; and so he tries again. In several months, the child has benefited from experience to the degree that the rattle and action become separated. Whereas earlier he would not show signs of missing the rattle when it was removed unless he had begun reaching for it, now he cries and searches when the rattle is presented for a moment and hidden by a cover. He no longer repeats a movement to restore the rattle. In place of representation by action alone—where "existence" is defined by the compass of present action—it is now defined by an image that persists autonomously.

A second example is provided by the results of injury to the occipital and temporal cortex in man (Hanfmann, Rickers-Ovsiankina, & Goldstein, 1944). A patient is presented with a hard-boiled egg intact in its shell, and asked what it is. Holding it in his hand, he is embarrassed, for he cannot name it. He makes a motion as if to throw it and halts himself. Then he brings it to his mouth as if to bite it and stops before he gets there. He brings it to his ear and shakes it gently. He is puzzled. The experimenter takes the egg from him and cracks it on the table, handing it back. The patient then begins to peel the egg and announces what it is. He cannot identify objects without reference to the action he directs toward them.

The disadvantages of such a system are illustrated by Emerson's (1931) experiment in which children are told to place a ring on a board with seven rows and six columns of pegs, copying the position of a ring put on an identical board by the experimenter. Children ranging from 3 to 12 were examined in this experiment and in an extension of it carried out by Werner (1948). The child's board could be placed in various positions relative to the experimenter's: right next to it, 90 degrees rotated away from it, 180 degrees rotated, placed face to face with it so that the child has to turn full around to make his placement, etc. The older the child, the better his performance. But the younger children could do about as well as the oldest so long as they did not have to change their own position vis-à-vis the experimenter's board in order to make a match on their own board. The more they had to turn, the more difficult the task. They were clearly depending upon their bodily orientation toward the experimenter's board to guide them. When this orientation is disturbed by having to turn, they lose the position on the board. Older children succeed even when they must turn, either by the use of imagery that is invariant across bodily displacements, or, later, by specifying column and row of the experimenter's ring and carrying the symbolized self-instruction back to their own board. It is a limited world, the world of enactive representation.

We know little about the conditions necessary for the growth of imagery and iconic representation, or to what extent parental or environmental intervention affects it during the earliest years. In ordinary adult learning a certain amount of motoric skill and practice seems to be a necessary precondition for the development of a simultaneous image to represent the sequence of acts involved. If an adult subject is made to choose a path through a complex bank of toggle switches, he does not form an image of the path, according to Mandler (1962), until he has mastered and overpracticed the task by successive manipulation. Then, finally, he reports that an image of the path has developed and that he is now using it rather than groping his way through.

Our main concern in what follows is not with the growth of iconic representation, but with the transition from it to symbolic representation. For it is in the development of symbolic representation that one finds, perhaps, the greatest thicket of psychological problems. The puzzle begins when the child first achieves the use of productive grammar, usually late in the second year of life. Toward the end of the second year, the child is master of the single-word, agrammatical utterance, the so-called holophrase. In the months following, there occurs a profound change in the use of language. Two classes of words appear—a pivot class and an open class—and the child launches forth on his career in combinatorial talking and, perhaps, thinking. Whereas before, lexemes like *allgone* and *mummy* and *sticky* and *bye-bye* were used singly, now, for example, *allgone* becomes a pivot word and is used in combination. Mother washes jam off the child's hands; he says *allgone sticky*. In the next days, if his speech is carefully followed (Braine, 1963), it will be apparent that he is trying out the limits of the pivot combinations, and one will even find constructions that have an extraordinary capacity for representing complex sequences—like *allgone bye-bye* after a visitor has departed. A recent and ingenious observation by Weir (1962 on her 2½-year-old son, recording his speech musings after he was in bed with lights out, indicates that at this stage there is a great deal of metalinguistic combinatorial play with words in which the child is exploring the limits of grammatical productiveness.

In effect, language provides a means, not only for representing experience, but also for transforming it. As Chomsky (1957) and Miller (1962) have both made clear in the last few years, the transformational rules of grammar provide a syntactic means of reworking the "realities" one has encountered. Not only, if you will, did the dog bite the man, but the man was bitten by the dog and perhaps the man was not bitten by the dog or was the man not

FIGURE 1.   Array of glasses used in study of matrix ordering (Bruner & Kenney, in press).

bitten by the dog. The range of reworking that is made possible even by the three transformations of the passive, the negative, and the query is very striking indeed. Or the ordering device whereby the comparative mode makes it possible to connect what is *heavy* and what is *light* into the ordinal array of *heavy* and *less heavy* is again striking. Or, to take a final example, there is the discrimination that is made possible by the growth of attribute language such that the global dimension *big* and *little* can now be decomposed into *tall* and *short* on the one hand and *fat* and *skinny* on the other.

Once the child has succeeded in internalizing language as a cognitive instrument, it becomes possible for him to represent and systematically transform the regularities of experience with far greater flexibility and power than before. Interestingly enough, it is the recent Russian literature, particularly Vygotsky's (1962) book on language and thought, and the work of his disciple, Luria (1961), and his students (Abramyan, 1958; Martsinovskaya undated) that has highlighted these phenomena by calling attention to the so-called second-signal system which replaces classical conditioning with an internalized linguistic system for shaping and transforming experience itself.

If all these matters were not of such complexity and human import, I would apologize for taking so much time in speculation. We turn now to some new experiments designed to shed some light on the nature of representation and particularly upon the transition from its iconic to its symbolic form.

Let me begin with an experiment by Bruner and Kenney (in press) on the manner in which children between 5 and 7 handle a double classification matrix. The materials of the experiment are nine plastic glasses, arranged so that they vary in 3 degrees of diameter and 3 degrees of height. They are set before the child initially, as in Figure 1, on a 3×3 grid marked on a large piece of cardboard. To acquaint the child with the matrix, we first remove one, then two, and then three glasses from the matrix, asking the child to replace them. We also ask the children to describe how the glasses in the columns and rows are alike and how they differ. Then the glasses are scrambled and we ask the child to make something like what was there before by placing the glasses on the same grid that was used when the task was introduced. Now we scramble the glasses once more, but this time we place the glass that was formerly in the southwest corner of the grid in the southeast corner (it is the shortest, thinnest glass) and ask the child if he can make something like what was there before, leaving the one glass where we have just put it. That is the experiment.

The results can be quickly told. To begin with, there is no difference between ages 5, 6, and 7 either in terms of ability to replace glasses taken from the matrix or in building a matrix once it has been scrambled (but without the transposed glass). Virtually all the children succeed. Interestingly enough, *all* the children rebuild the matrix to match the original, almost as if they were copying what was there before. The only difference is that the older children are quicker.

Now compare the performance of the three ages in constructing the matrix with a single member transposed. Most of the 7-year-olds succeed in the transposed task, but hardly any of the youngest children. Figure 2 presents the results graphically. The youngest children seem to be dominated by an image of the original matrix. They try to put the transposed glass "back where it belongs," to rotate the cardboard so that "it will be like before," and sometimes they will start placing a few glasses neighboring the transposed glass correctly only to revert to the original arrangement. In several instances, 5- or 6-year-olds will simply try to reconstitute the old matrix, building right over the transposed glass. The 7-year-old, on the other hand, is more likely to pause, to treat the transposition as a problem, to talk to himself about "where this should go." The relation of place and size is for him a problem that requires reckoning, not simply copying.

Now consider the language children use for describing the dimensions of the matrix. Recall that the children were asked how glasses in a row and in a column were alike and how they differed. Children answered in three distinctive linguistic modes. One was *dimensional,* singling out two ends of an attribute—for example. "That one is higher, and that one is shorter." A second was *global* in nature. Of glasses differing only in height the child says, "That one is bigger and that one is little." The same words could be used equally well for diameter or for nearly any other magnitude. Finally, there was *confounded* usage: "That one is tall and that one is little," where

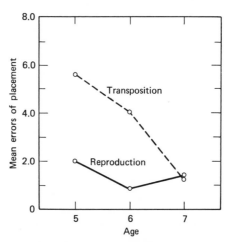

FIGURE 2. Mean number of errors made by children in reproducing and transposing a 3 × 3 matrix (Bruner & Kenney, in press).

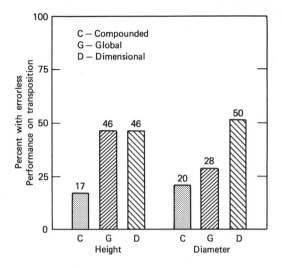

FIGURE 3. Percentage of children (aged 5–7) using different language patterns who reproduced transposed matrix errorlessly (Bruner & Kenney, in press).

a dimensional term is used for one end of the continuum and a global term for the other. The children who used confounded descriptions had the most difficulty with the transposed matrix (Figure 3). Lumping all ages together, the children who used confounded descriptions were twice as likely to fail on the transposition task as those who used either dimensional or global terms. *But the language the children used had no relation whatsoever to their performance in reproducing the first untransposed matrix.* Inhelder and Sinclair[2] in a recent communication also report that confounded language of this kind is associated with failure on conservation tasks in children of the same age, a subject to which we shall turn shortly.

The findings of this experiment suggest two things. First, that children who use iconic representation are more highly sensitized to the spatial-qualitative organization of experience and less to the ordering principles governing such organization. They can recognize and reproduce, but cannot produce new structures based on rule. And second, there is a suspicion that the language they bring to bear on the task is insufficient as a tool for ordering. If these notions are correct, then certain things should follow. For one thing, *improvement* in language should aid this type of problem solving. This remains to be investigated. But it is also reasonable to suppose that *activation* of language habits that the child has already mastered might improve performance as well—a hypothesis already suggested by the findings of Luria's

[2] Bärbel Inhelder and Mimi Sinclair, personal communication, 1963.

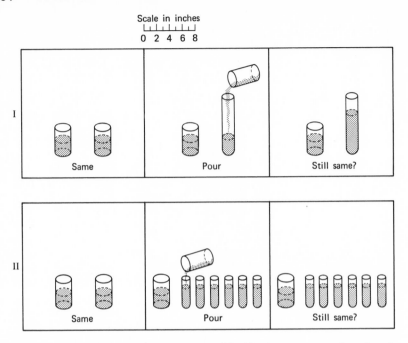

FIGURE 4. Two Geneva tests for conservation of liquid volume across transformations in its appearance (Piaget & Inhelder, 1962).

students (e.g., Abramyan, 1958). Now, activation can be achieved by two means: One is by having the child "say" the description of something before him that he must deal with symbolically. The other is to take advantage of the remoteness of reference that is a feature of language, and have the child "say" his description in the absence of the things to be described. In this way, there would be less likelihood of a perceptual-iconic representation becoming dominant and inhibiting the operation of symbolic processes. An experiment by Françoise Frank (in press) illustrates this latter approach—the effects of saying before seeing.

Piaget and Inhelder (1962) have shown that if children between ages 4 and 7 are presented two identical beakers which they judge equally full of water, they will no longer consider the water equal if the contents of one of the beakers is now poured into a beaker that is either wider or thinner than the original (Figure 4). If the second beaker is thinner, they will say it has more to drink because the water is higher; if the second beaker is wider, they will say it has less because the water is lower. Comparable results can be obtained by pouring the contents of one glass into several smaller beakers. In Geneva terms, the child is not yet able to conserve liquid volume across transformations in its appearance. Consider how this behavior can be altered.

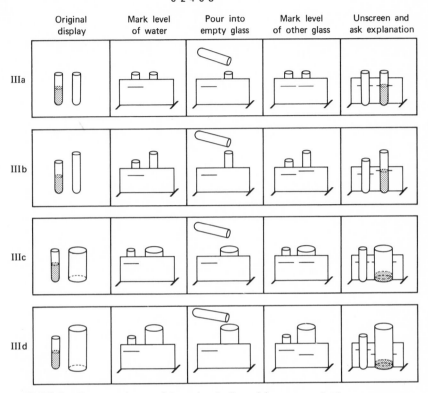

Scale in inches

0 2 4 6 8

FIGURE 5. One procedure used in study of effect of language activation on conservation (Frank, in press).

Françoise Frank first did the classic conservation tests to determine which children exhibited conservation and which did not. Her subjects were 4, 5, 6, and 7 years old. She then went on to other procedures (Figure 5), among which was the following. Two standard beakers are partly filled so that the child judges them to contain equal amounts of water. A wider beaker of the same height is introduced and the three beakers are now, except for their tops, hidden by a screen. The experimenter pours from a standard beaker into the wider beaker. The child, without seeing the water, is asked which has more to drink, or do they have the same amount, the standard or the wider beaker. The results are in Figure 6. In comparison with the unscreened pretest, there is a striking increase in correct equality judgments. Correct responses jump from 0% to 50% among the 4s, from 20% to 90% among the 5s, and from 50% to 100% among the 6s. With the screen present, most children justify

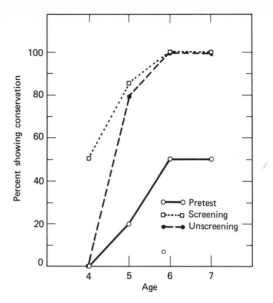

FIGURE 6. Percentage of children showing conservation of liquid volume before and during screening and upon unscreening of the displays (Frank, in press).

their correct judgment by noting that "It's the same water," or "You only poured it."

Now the screen is removed. All the 4-year-olds change their minds. The perceptual display overwhelms them and they decide that the wider beaker has less water. But virtually all of the 5-year-olds stick to their judgment, often invoking the difference between appearance and reality—"It looks like more to drink, but it is only the same because it is the same water and it was only poured from there to there," to quote one typical 5-year-old. And all of the 6s and all the 7s stick to their judgment. Now, some minutes later, Frank does a posttest on the children using a tall thin beaker along with the standard ones, and no screen, of course. The 4s are unaffected by their prior experience: None of them is able to grasp the idea of invariant quantity in the new task. With the 5s, instead of 20% showing conservation, as in the pretest, 70% do. With both 6s and 7s, conservation increases from 50% to 90%. I should mention that control groups doing just a pretest and posttest show no significant improvement in performance.

A related experiment of Nair's (1963) explores the arguments children use when they solve a conservation task correctly and when they do not. Her subjects were all 5-year-olds. She transferred water from one rectangular clear plastic tank to another that was both longer and wider than the first. Ordinarily, a 5-year-old will say there is less water in the second tank. The

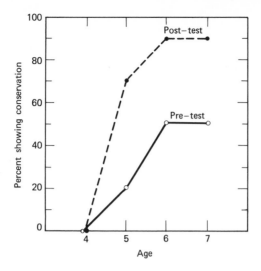

FIGURE 7. Percentage of children showing conservation of liquid volume in identical pretest and posttest run after completion of experiment (Frank, in press).

water is, of course, lower in the second tank. She had a toy duck swimming in the first container, and when the water was poured into the new container, she told the child that "The duck was taking his water with him."

Three kinds of arguments were set forth by the children to support their judgments. One is perceptual—having to do with the height, width, or apparent "bigness" of the water. A second type has to do with action: The duck took the water along, or the water was only poured. A third one, "transformational" argument, invokes the reversibility principle: If you poured the water back into the first container, it would look the same again.[3] Of the children who thought the water was not equal in amount after pouring, 15% used nonperceptual arguments to justify their judgment. Of those who recognized the equality of the water, two-thirds used nonperceptual arguments. It is plain that if a child is to succeed in the conservation task, he must have some internalized verbal formula that shields him from the overpowering appearance of the visual displays much as in the Frank experiment. The explanations of the children who lacked conservation suggest how strongly oriented they were to the visual appearance of the displays they had to deal with.

[3] Not one of the 40 children who participated in this experiment used the compensation argument—that though the water was lower it was correspondingly wider and was, therefore, the same amount of water. This type of reasoning by compensation is said by Piaget and Inhelder (1962) to be the basis of conservation.

Consider now another experiment by Bruner and Kenney (in press) also designed to explore the border between iconic and symbolic representation. Children aged 5, 6, and 7 were asked to say which of two glasses in a pair was fuller and which emptier. "Fullness" is an interesting concept to work with, for it involves in its very definition a ratio or proportion between the volume of a container and the volume of a substance contained. It is difficult for the iconically oriented child to see a half-full barrel and a half-filled thimble as equally full, since the former looms larger in every one of the attributes that might be perceptually associated with volume. It is like the old riddle of which is heavier, a pound of lead or a pound of feathers. To make a correct judgment of fullness or emptiness, the child must use a symbolic operation, somewhat like computing a ratio, and resist the temptation to use perceptual appearance—that is, unless he finds some happy heuristic to save him the labor of such a computation. Figure 8 contains the 11 pairs of glasses used, and they were selected with a certain malice aforethought.

There are four types of pairs. In Type I (Displays 4, 9a, and 9b), the glasses are of unequal volume, but equally, though fractionally, full. In Type II (Displays 2, 7a, and 7b) again the glasses are of unequal volume, but they are completely full. Type III (Displays 3, 8a, and 8b) consists of two glasses of unequal volume, one filled and the other part filled. Type IV consists of identical glasses, in one case equally filled, in another unequally (Displays 1 and 5).

All the children in the age range we have studied use pretty much the same criteria for judging *fullness*, and these criteria are based on directly observable sensory indices rather than upon proportion. That glass is judged fuller that has the greater apparent volume of water, and the favored indication of greater volume is water level; or where that is equated, then width of glass will do; and when width and water level are the same, then height of glass will prevail. But now consider the judgments made by the three age groups with respect to which glass in each pair is *emptier*. The older children have developed an interesting consistency based on an appreciation of the complementary relation of filled and empty space—albeit an incorrect one. For them "emptier" means the glass that has the largest apparent volume of unfilled space, just as "fuller" meant the glass that had the largest volume of filled space. In consequence, their responses seem logically contradictory. For the glass that is judged fuller also turns out to be the glass that is judged emptier—given a large glass and a small glass, both half full. The younger children, on the other hand, equate emptiness with "littleness": That glass is emptier that gives the impression of being smaller in volume of liquid. If we take the three pairs of glasses of Type I (unequal volumes, half filled) we can see how the judgments typically distribute themselves. Consider only

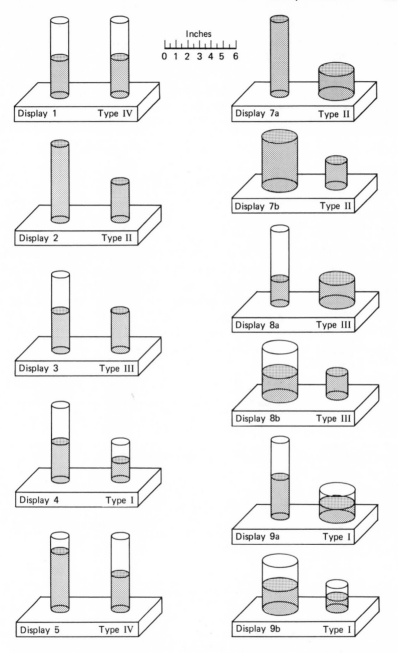

FIGURE 8. Eleven pairs of glasses to be judged in terms of which glass is fuller and which emptier (Bruner & Kenney, in press).

TABLE 1

Percentage of Erroneous Judgments of Which of Two Glasses Is Emptier Based on Two Criteria for Defining the Concept

Judgment	Age		
Criterion for "Emptier"	5	6	7
Greater empty space	27%	53%	72%
Smaller volume of liquid	73%	47%	28%
	100%	100%	100%
Percentage correct	9%	8%	17%
N =	30	30	30

Note. Criteria are greater volume of empty space and lesser volume of water. From Bruner and Kenney (in press).

the errors. The glass with the larger volume of empty space is called emptier by 27% of the erring 5-year-olds, by 53% of the erring 6-year-olds, and by 72% of erring 7-year-olds. But the glass with the smallest volume of water is called emptier by 73% of the 5-year-olds who err, 47% of the 6s, and only 28% of the 7s. When the children are asked for their reasons for judging one glass as emptier, there is further confirmation: Most of the younger children justify it by pointing to "littleness" or "less water" or some other

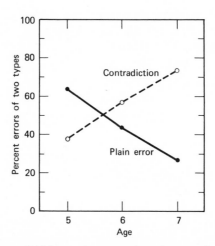

FIGURE 9. Percentage of children at three ages who make contradictory and plain errors in judging which of two glasses is fuller and which emptier. (A contradictory error is calling the same glass both fuller or emptier or calling them equally full but not equally empty or vice versa. A plain error is calling one glass fuller and the other emptier, but incorrectly. From Bruner & Kenney, in press.)

aspect of diminutiveness. And most of the older children justify their judgments of emptiness by reference to the amount of empty space in the vessel.

The result of all this is, of course, that the "logical structure" of the older
children seems to go increasingly awry. But surely, though Figure 9 shows
that contradictory errors steadily increase with age (calling the same glass
fuller and emptier or equally full but not equally empty or vice versa), the
contradiction is a by-product of the method of dealing with attributes. How
shall we interpret these findings?—Let me suggest that what is involved is
a translation difficulty in going from the perceptual or iconic realm to the
symbolic. If you ask children of this age whether something can be fuller
and also emptier, they will smile and think that you are playing riddles. They
are aware of the contrastive nature of the two terms. Indeed, even the very
young child has a good working language for the two poles of the contrast:
"all gone" for completely empty and "spill" or "tippy top" for completely full.
Recall too that from 5 to 7, there is perfect performance in judging which
of two identical beakers is fuller and emptier. The difference between the
younger and the older child is in the number of attributes that are being
attended to in situations involving fullness and emptiness: The younger child
is attending to one—the volume of water; the older to two—the volume of
filled space and the volume of empty space. The young child is applying a
single contrast pair—full-empty—to a single feature of the situation. The
older child can attend to two features, but he does not yet have the means
for relating them to a third, the volume of the container per se. To do so
involves being able to deal with a relation in the perceptual field that does
not have a "point-at-able" or ostensive definition. Once the third term is introduced—the volume of the glass—then the symbolic concept of proportion
can come to "stand for" something that is not present perceptually. The older
child is on the way to achieving the insight, in spite of his contradictions.
And, interestingly enough, if we count the number of children who justify
their judgments of fuller and emptier by pointing to *several* rather than a
single attribute, we find that the proportion triples in both cases between age
5 and age 7. The older child, it would seem, is ordering his perceptual world
in such a way that, shortly, he will be able to apply concepts of relationship
that are not dependent upon simple ostensive definition. As he moves toward
this more powerful "technology of reckoning," he is led into errors that
seem to be contradictory. What is particularly telltale is the fact, for
example, that in the Type III displays, younger children sometimes seem to
find the judgment easier than older children—pointing to the fuller by placing their finger on the rim of the full member and pointing to the emptier
with the remark that "It is not to the top." The older child (and virtually
never the younger one) gets all involved in the judgment of "fuller by
apparent filled volume" and then equally involved in the judgment of "emptier

by apparent empty volume" and such are his efforts that he fails to note his contradiction when dealing with a pair like Display 8b.

Turn now to a quite different experimental procedure that deals with the related concept of equivalence—how seemingly different objects are grouped

TABLE 2

Percentage of Children Who Justify Judgments of "Fuller" and "Emptier" by Mentioning More Than a Single Attribute

Age	"Fuller" Judgments	"Emptier" Judgments	N
5	7.2%	4.1%	30
6	15.6%	9.3%	30
7	22.2%	15.6%	30

into equivalence classes. In the two experiments to be cited, one by Olver (1961), the other by Rigney (1962), children are given words or pictures to sort into groups or to characterize in terms of how they are alike. The two sets of results, one for words, the other for pictures, obtained for children between 6 and 14, can be summarized together. One may distinguish two

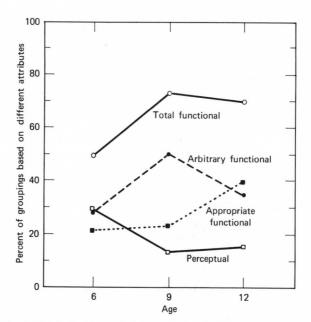

FIGURE 10. Features of objects used by children of different ages as a basis for placing the objects in equivalence groups (Olver, 1961).

aspects of grouping—the first has to do with the features or attributes that children use as a criterion for grouping objects: *perceptual features* (the color, size, pattern, etc.), *arbitrary functional features* (what I can do with the objects regardless of their usual use: You can make noise with a newspaper by crumpling it and with a book by slamming it shut, etc.), *appropriate functional features* (potato, peach, banana, and milk are characterized "You can eat them"). But grouping behavior can also be characterized in terms of the syntactical structure of the equivalence sets that the child develops. There are, first, what Vygotsky (1962) has called *heaps*: collections put together in an arbitrary way simply because the child has decided to put them together that way. Then there are *complexes*: The various members of a complex are included in the class in accordance with a rule that does not account uniformly for the inclusion of all the members. Edge matching is one such rule: Each object is grouped into a class on the basis of its similarity with a neighboring object. Yet no two neighboring pieces may be joined by the same similarity. Another type of complexive grouping is thematic: Here objects are put together by virtue of participating in a sentence or a little story. More sophisticated is a key ring in which one organizing object is related to all others but none of those to each other. And finally, considerably more sophisticated than heaps and complexes, there are *superordinate concepts,* in which one universal rule of inclusion accounts for all the objects in the set—all men and women over 21 are included in the class of voters provided they meet certain residence requirements.

The pattern of growth is revealing of many of the trends we have already discussed, and provides in addition a new clue. Consider first the attributes or features of objects that children at different ages use as a basis for forming equivalence groups. As Figure 10 indicates, the youngest children rely more heavily on perceptual attributes than do the others. As they grow older, grouping comes to depend increasingly upon the functional properties of things—but the transitional phase is worth some attention, for it raises anew the issue of the significance of egocentrism. For the first functional groupings to appear are of an arbitrary type—what "I" or "you" can do to objects that renders them alike, rather than what is the conventional use or function to which objects can be put. During this stage of "egocentric functionalism," there is a corresponding rise in the use of first- and second-person personal pronouns: "I can do thus and so to this object; I can do the same to this one," etc. Gradually, with increasing maturity the child shifts to an appropriate and less egocentric form of using functional groupings. The shift from perceptual to functional groupings is accompanied by a corresponding shift in the syntactical structure of the groups formed. Complexive groupings steadily dwindle; superordinate groupings rise, until the latter almost replace the former in late adolescence. It is difficult to tell which is the pacemaker in this growth—syntax or the semantic basis of grouping.

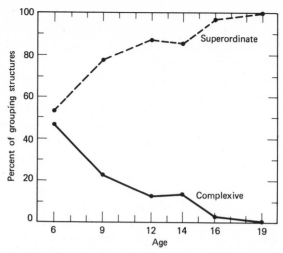

FIGURE 11. The use of two rules of equivalences grouping found in children of different ages (Olver, 1961).

Rigney reports one other matter of some interest. Her young subjects formed groups of any size they wished, choosing pictures from a display board of several dozen little water colors. She observed that the most perceptually based groups and the ones most often based on complexive grouping principles were pairs. A count of these revealed that 61% of all the groups made by 6-year-olds were such pairs, 36% of those made by 8-year-olds, and only 25% of the groupings of 11-year-olds.

On the surface, this set of findings—Olver's and Rigney's alike—seems to point more to the decline of a preference for perceptual and iconic ways of dealing with objects and events, particularly with their grouping. But closer inspection suggests still another factor that is operating. In both cases, there is evidence of the development of hierarchical structure and rules for including objects in superordinate hierarchies. Hierarchical classification is surely one of the most evident properties of the structure of language—hierarchical grouping that goes beyond mere perceptual inclusion. Complexive structures of the kind described earlier are much more dominated by the sorts of associative principles by which the appearance of objects leads to their spontaneous grouping in terms of similarity or contiguity. As language becomes more internalized, more guiding as a set of rules for organizing events, there is a shift from the associative principles that operate in classical perceptual organization to the increasingly abstract rules for grouping events by the principles of inclusion, exclusion, and overlap, the most basic characteristics of any hierarchical system.

We have said that cognitive growth consists in part in the development of systems of representation as means for dealing with information. The growing child begins with a strong reliance upon learned action patterns to represent the world around him. In time, there is added to this technology a means for simultanizing regularities in experience into images that stand for events in the way that pictures do. And to this is finally added a technology of translating experience into a symbol system that can be operated upon by rules of transformation that greatly increase the possible range of problem solving. One of the effects of this development, or possibly one of its causes, is the power for organizing acts of information processing into more integrated and long-range problem solving efforts. To this matter we turn next.

Consider in rapid succession three related experiments. All of them point, I think, to the same conclusion.

The first is by Huttenlocher (in press), a strikingly simple study, performed with children between the ages of 6 and 12. Two light switches are before the child; each can be in one of two positions. A light bulb is also visible. The child is asked to tell, on the basis of turning only one switch, what turns the light on. There are four ways in which the presentations are made. In the first, the light is off initially and when the child turns a switch, the light comes on. In the second, the light is on and when the child turns a switch, it goes off. In the third, the light is on and when the child turns a switch, it stays on. In the fourth and final condition, the light is off and when the child turns a switch, it stays off. Now what is intriguing about this arrangement is that there are different numbers of inductive steps required to make a correct inference in each task. The simplest condition is the off-on case. The position to which the switch has just been moved is responsible for the light going on. Intermediate difficulty should be experienced with the on-off condition. In the on-off case, two connected inferences are required: The present position achieved is rejected and the original position of the switch that has been turned is responsible for lighting the bulb. An even larger number of consecutive acts is required for success in the on-on case: The present position of the turned switch is rejected, the original position as well and the present position of the *other* switch is responsible. The off-off case requires four steps: rejecting the present position of the turned switch, its original position, and the present position of the other switch, finally accepting the alternative position of the unturned switch. The natures of the individual steps are all the same. Success in the more complex cases depends upon being able to integrate them consecutively.

Huttenlocher's results show that the 6-year-olds are just as capable as their elders of performing the elementary operation involved in the one-step case: the on-off display. They, like the 9s and 12s, make nearly perfect scores. But in general, the more inferential steps the 6-year-old must make, the poorer

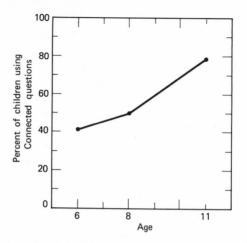

FIGURE 12. The proportion of children at different ages who use connected questions in a Twenty Questions game (Mosher, 1962).

his performance. By age 12, on the other hand, there is an insignificant difference between the tasks requiring one, two, three, or four connected inferences.

An experiment by Mosher (1962) underlines the same point. He was concerned with the strategies used by children from 6 to 11 for getting information in the game of Twenty Questions. They were to find out by "yes-no" questions what caused a car to go off the road and hit a tree. One may distinguish between connected constraint-locating questions ("Was it nighttime?" followed up appropriately) and direct hypothesis-testing questions ("Did a bee fly in the window and sting the man on the eye and make him go off the road and hit the tree?"). From 6 to 11, more and more children use constraint-locating, connected questioning. Let me quote from Mosher's account.

> We have asked children . . . after they have played their games, to
> tell us which of two questions they would rather have the answer to, if
> they were playing the games again—one of them a typical
> constraint-seeking question ("Was there anything wrong with the
> man?") and the other a typical discrete test of an hypothesis ("Did
> the man have a heart attack?"). All the eleven-year-olds and all the
> eight-year-olds choose the constraint-seeking question, but only 29%
> of the six-year-olds do [p. 6].

The questions of the younger children are all one-step substitutes for direct sense experience. They are looking for knowledge by single questions that provide the answer in a finished form. When they succeed they do so by a lucky question that hits an immediate, perceptible cause. When the older child receives a "yes" answer to one of his constraint-locating questions, he most often follows up by asking another. When, on the rare occasions that a younger child asks a constraint question and it is answered "yes," he almost invariably follows it up with a specific question to test a concrete hypothesis. The older child can accrete his information in a structure governed by consecutive inference. The younger child cannot.

Potter's (in press) study of the development of perceptual recognition bears on the same point. Ordinary colored photographs of familiar scenes are presented to children between 6 and 12, the pictures coming gradually into focus. Let me sum up one part of the results very briefly. Six-year-olds produce an abundance of hypotheses. But they rarely try to match new hypotheses to previous ones. "There is a big tower in the middle and a road over there and a big ice cream cone through the middle of the tower and a pumpkin on top." It is like a random collage. The 9-year-old's torrent of hypotheses, on the other hand, shows a sense of consistency about what is likely to appear with what. Things are in a context of likelihood, a frame of reference that demands internal consistency. Something is seen as a merry-go-round, and the child then restricts later hypotheses to the other things to be found in an amusement park. The adolescent operates under even more highly organized sequential constraints: He occasionally develops his initial hypotheses from what is implied by the properties of the picture, almost by intersection—"It is red and shiny and metallic: It must be a coffee-pot." Once such constraints are established, the order of hypotheses reflects even more the need to build up a consistent world of objects—even to the point of failing to recognize things that do not fit it.

What shall we make of these three sets of findings—that older children are able to cumulate information by asking questions in a directed sequence leading to a final goal, and that they are capable of recognizing visual displays in a manner governed by a dominating frame of reference that transcends momentary and isolated bits of information? Several points seem apparent. The first is that as children mature, they are able to use indirect information based on forms of information processing other than the act of pointing to what is immediately present. They seem, in short, to make remote reference to states and constraints that are not given by the immediate situation, to go beyond the information given. Second, and this is a matter that has already been discussed, they seem to be able to cumulate information into a structure that can be operated upon by rules that transcend simple association by similarity and contiguity. In the case of Twenty Questions, the rule is best described as implication—that knowing one thing implies certain other things and eliminates still others. In the experiments with the light switches, it is that if the present state does not produce the effect, then there is a system for tracing back to the other states that cause the light to go on. Where perceptual recognition is concerned, the rule is that a piece of information from one part of the display implies what other parts might be. The child, in sum, is translating redundancy into a manipulable model of the evironment that is governed by rules of implication. It is this model of the environment that permits him to go beyond the information before him. I would suggest that it is this new array of cognitive equipment that permits the child to transcend momentaneity, to integrate longer sequences of events.

Let me urge, moreover, that such a system of processing environmental events depends upon the translation of experience into symbolic form. Such a translation is necessary in order for there to be the kind of remoteness of reference as is required when one deals with indirect information. To transcend the immediately perceptual, to get beyond what is vividly present to a more extended model of the environment, the child needs a system that permits him to deal with the nonpresent, with things that are remote in space, qualitative similarity, and time, from the present situation. Hockett (1959), in describing the design features of language includes this feature as crucial. He is referring to human speech as a system of communication. The same point can be made about language as an instrument of thought. That humans have the *capacity* for using speech in this way is only part of the point. What is critical is that the capacity is *not* used until it is coupled with the technology of language in the cognitive operations of the child.

The same can be said for the models of the environment that the child constructs to go beyond present information. This is not to say that nonverbal animals cannot make inferences that go beyond the present stimulus: Anticipatory activity is the rule in vertebrates. But the models that the growing child constructs seem not to be anticipatory, or inferential, or probabilistic-frequency models. They seem to be governed by rules that can more properly be called syntactical rather than associative.

My major concern has been to examine afresh the nature of intellectual growth. The account has surely done violence to the richness of the subject. It seems to me that growth depends upon the emergence of two forms of competence. Children, as they grow, must acquire ways of representing the recurrent regularities in their environment, and they must transcend the momentary by developing ways of linking past to present to future—representation and integration. I have suggested that we can conceive of growth in both of these domains as the emergence of new technologies for the unlocking and amplification of human intellectual powers. Like the growth of technology, the growth of intellect is not smoothly monotonic. Rather, it moves forward in spurts as innovations are adopted. Most of the innovations are transmitted to the child in some prototypic form by agents of the culture: ways of responding, ways of looking and imaging, and most important, ways of translating what one has encountered into language.

I have relied heavily in this account on the successive emergence of action, image, and word as the vehicles of representation, a reliance based both upon our observations and upon modern readings of man's alloplastic evolution. Our attention has been directed largely to the transition between iconic and symbolic representation.

In children between 4 and 12 language comes to play an increasingly powerful role as an implement of knowing. Through simple experiments, I have tried to show how language shapes, augments, and even supercedes the child's earlier modes of processing information. Translation of experience into symbolic form, with its attendant means of achieving remote reference, transformation, and combination, opens up realms of intellectual possibility that are orders of magniture beyond the most powerful image-forming system.

What of the integration of intellectual activity into more coherent and interconnected acts? It has been the fashion, since Freud, to see delay of gratification as the principal dynamism behind this development—from primary process to secondary process, or from assimilation to accommodation, as Piaget would put it today. Without intending to question the depth of this insight, let me suggest that delay of immediate gratification, the ability to go beyond the moment, also depends upon techniques, and again they are techniques of representation. Perhaps representation exclusively by imagery and perceptual organization has built into it one basic operation that ties it to the immediate present. It is the operation of pointing—ostensiveness, as logicians call it. (This is not to say that highly evolved images do not go beyond immediate time and given place. Maps and flow charts are iconic in nature, but they are images that translate prior linguistic and mathematical renderings into a visual form.) Iconic representation, in the beginning, is built upon a perceptual organization that is tied to the "point-at-able" spatioqualitative properties of events. I have suggested that, for all its limitations, such representation is an achievement beyond the earlier stage where percepts are not autonomous of action. But so long as perceptual representation dominates, it is difficult to develop higher-order techniques for processing information by consecutive inferential steps that take one beyond what can be pointed at.

Once language becomes a medium for the translation of experience, there is a progressive release from immediacy. For language, as we have commented, has the new and powerful features of remoteness and arbitrariness: It permits productive, combinatorial operations in the *absence* of what is represented. With this achievement, the child can delay gratification by virtue of representing to himself what lies beyond the present, what other possibilities exist beyond the clue that is under his nose. The child may be *ready* for delay of gratification, but he is no more able to bring it off than somebody ready to build a house, save that he has not yet heard of tools.

The discussion leaves two obvious questions begging. What of the integration of behavior in organisms without language? And how does language become internalized as a vehicle for organizing experience? The first question has to be answered briefly and somewhat cryptically. Wherever integrated behavior has been studied—as in Lehrman's (1955) careful work on integrated instinctive patterns in the ringdove, it has turned out that a sustaining external stimulus was needed to keep the highly integrated behavior going. The best way to control behavior in subhuman species is to control the stimulus situation. Surely this is the lesson of Lashley's (1938) classic account of instinctive behavior. Where animal learning is concerned, particularly in the primates, there is, to be sure, considerable plasticity. But it too depends upon the development of complex forms of stimulus substitution and organization—as in Klüver's (1933) work on equivalence reactions in monkeys. If it should seem that I am urging that the growth of symbolic functioning links a unique set of powers to man's capacity, the appearance is quite as it should be.

As for how language becomes internalized as a program for ordering experience, I join those who despair for an answer. My speculation, for whatever it is worth, is that the process of internalization depends upon interaction with others, upon the need to develop corresponding categories and transformations for communal action. It is the need for cognitive coin that can be exchanged with those on whom we depend. What Roger Brown (1958) has called the Original Word Game ends up by being the Human Thinking Game.

If I have seemed to underemphasize the importance of inner capacities— for example, the capacity *for* language or *for* imagery—it is because I believe that this part of the story is given by the nature of man's evolution. What is significant about the growth of mind in the child is to what degree it depends not upon capacity but upon the unlocking of capacity by techniques that come from exposure to the specialized environment of a culture. Romantic clichés, like "the veneer of culture" or "natural man," are as misleading if not as damaging as the view that the course of human development can be viewed independently of the educational process we arrange to make that development possible.

References

Abramyan, L. A. Organization of the voluntary activity of the child with the help of verbal instruction. Unpublished diploma thesis, Moscow University, 1958. Cited by A. R. Luria, *The role of speech in the regulation of normal and abnormal behavior.* New York: Liveright, 1961.

Barker, R. G. On the nature of the environment. Kurt Lewin Memorial Address presented at American Psychological Association, Philadelphia, September 1963.

Braine, M. D. On learning the grammatical order of words. *Psychol. Rev.,* 1963, **70**, 323–348.

Brown, R. *Words and things.* Glencoe, Ill.: Free Press, 1958.

Bruner, J. S., & Kenney, Helen. The development of the concepts of order and proportion in children. In J. S. Bruner, *Studies in cognitive growth.* New York: Wiley, in press.

Chomsky, N. *Syntactic structures.* S'Gravenhage, Netherlands: Mouton, 1957.

Emerson, L. L. The effect of bodily orientation upon the young child's memory for position of objects. *Child Develpm.,* 1931, **2**, 125–142.

Frank, Françoise. Perception and language in conservation. In J. S. Bruner, *Studies in cognitive growth.* New York: Wiley, in press.

Hanfmann, Eugenia, Rickers-Ovsiankina, Maria, & Goldstein, K. Case Lanuti: Extreme concretization of behavior due to damage of the brain cortex. *Psychol. Monogr.,* 1944, **57**(4, Whole No. 264).

Hockett, C. F. Animal "languages" and human language. In J. N. Spuhler, *The evolution of man's capacity for culture.* Detroit: Wayne State Univer. Press, 1959. Pp. 32–39.

Huttenlocher, Janellen. The growth of conceptual strategies. In J. S. Bruner, *Studies in cognitive growth.* New York: Wiley, in press.

Klüver, H. *Behavior mechanisms in monkeys.* Chicago: Univer. Chicago Press, 1933.

La Barre, W. *The human animal.* Chicago: Univer. Chicago Press, 1954.

Lashley, K. S. Experimental analysis of instinctive behavior. *Psychol. Rev.,* 1938, **45**, 445–472.

Lehrman, D. S. The physiological basis of parental feeding behavior in the ring dove (*Streptopelia risoria*). *Behavior,* 1955, **7**, 241–286.

Luria, A. R. *The role of speech in the regulation of normal and abnormal behavior.* New York: Liveright, 1961.

Mandler, G. From association to structure. *Psychol. Rev.,* 1962, **69**, 415–427.

Martsinovskaya, E. N. Research into the reflective and regulatory role of the second signalling system of pre-school age. Collected papers of the Department of Psychology, Moscow University, undated. Cited by A. R. Luria, *The role of speech in the regulation of normal and abnormal behavior.* New York: Liveright, 1961.

Miller, G. A. Some psychological studies of grammar. *Amer. Psychologist,* 1962, **17,** 748–762.

Miller, G. A., Galanter, E., & Pribram, K. H. *Plans and the structure of behavior.* New York: Holt, 1960.

Mosher, F. A. Strategies for information gathering. Paper read at Eastern Psychological Association, Atlantic City, N.J., April 1962.

Nair, Patricia. An experiment in conservation. In Center for Cognitive Studies, *Annual Report.* Cambridge, Mass.: Author, 1963.

Olver, Rose R. A developmental study of cognitive equivalence. Unpublished doctoral dissertation, Radcliffe College, 1961.

Piaget, J. *The construction of reality in the child.* (Trans. by Margaret Cook) New York: Basic Books, 1954.

Piaget, J., & Inhelder, Bärbel. *Le développement des quantités physiques chez l'enfant.* (2nd rev. ed.) Neuchâtel, Switzerland: Delachaux & Niestlé, 1962.

Potter, Mary C. The growth of perceptual recognition. In J. S. Bruner, *Studies in cognitive growth.* New York: Wiley, in press.

Rigney, Joan C. A developmental study of cognitive equivalence transformations and their use in the acquisition and processing of information. Unpublished honors thesis, Radcliffe College, Department of Social Relations, 1962.

Vygotsky, L. S. *Thought and language.* (Ed. & trans. by Eugenia Hanfmann & Gertrude Vakar) New York: Wiley, 1962.

Washburn, S. L., & Howell, F. C. Human evolution and culture. In S. Tax, *The evolution of man.* Vol. 2. Chicago: Univer. Chicago Press, 1960.

Weir, Ruth H. *Language in the crib.* The Hague: Mouton, 1962.

Werner, H. *Comparative psychology of mental development.* (Rev. ed.) Chicago: Follett, 1948.

15. ON CULTURE AND EQUIVALENCE: I

Michael Maccoby & Nancy Modiano[1]

The study reported in this chapter has been undertaken to examine how general is the account of the growth in equivalence transformation found in the work of Olver and Hornsby (1966). Beyond that objective there is yet another. Surely the manner in which a child goes about abstracting equivalence should reflect the nature of his society. In most instances the equivalences imposed on one's environment have much wider limits of option than, say, such things as physical judgments do; for example, do two containers hold the same amount to drink? Whether objects are considered as food, for example, does not depend on their nutritional value alone, but also on custom and dietary taboo. To the Christian, beef and pork are two meats, different in taste but equivalent in function and formal classification. But Orthodox Jews and Moslems would not group the two as food, nor would they meet the Hindus' equivalence requirements. In these instances, cultural training puts an affective brake on functional and formal equivalence.

Nor should the matter be restricted to determination by cultural *content*— whether in a semantic sense two things are conventionally grouped or not. One might expect that certain cultural traits would extend to the kinds of attributes preferred for equivalence grouping or, indeed, the kind of grouping rules employed. It is surely reasonable to expect, for example, that a "rational" or technically sophisticated culture would place an early and strong

SOURCE. J. S. Bruner, *Studies in Cognitive Growth*. New York: Wiley, 1966, pp. 257–269.

[1] We would like to thank Ing. Sergio Beltran of the Centro de Calculo Electronico of the National Autonomous University of Mexico and Dr. Nathan Jaspen of New York University for their generous assistance.

emphasis upon the use of functional and formal categories, the better to acculturate its young to the requirements of a technology they would be called on to master.

The first opportunity to explore cultural differences in this kind of activity grew out of broader studies being undertaken in rural Mexico; studies that aimed at elucidating the character structure of Mexican villagers (Maccoby, Modiano, Galvan, 1963). At that time we undertook a pilot study (using the Olver-Hornsby procedure for studying equivalence) to compare North American suburban children with their rural Mexican counterparts.

The task assigned the children was much like that developed by Olver (1961). Items were presented in a series and, as each item was shown, the child was asked to tell in what way it was different from the preceding items and in what way the items were alike. Each item was presented on a small white card which was read by the investigator. Once an item was presented, it was placed in front of the child so that all previous items in the array could be seen at once. The array used by Olver for the North American children she studied was the familiar one: *banana, peach, potato, meat, milk, water, air, germs, stones.* For the Mexican children, *naranja* was substituted for peach, *frijol* for potato, and *lumbre* for germs. In the testing procedure, the first two items (banana and peach) were shown, and the child was asked, "How are banana and peach alike?" After he answered, the next item, potato, was given with the question, "How is potato different from banana and peach?" And then, "How are banana, peach, and potato all alike?" The parallel procedure in Mexico continued in this way, with the exception of the final item, stones, when the child was asked to tell only the difference.

The child's responses in both settings were scored in terms of five main classes, which describe the kind of attributes he used in order to group or differentiate objects: (1) perceptible characteristics, either intrinsic, such as shape, color, size, or extrinsic, such as the position of the object in time and space; (2) functions of the object, either what it can do (intrinsic functions) or what one can do with it (extrinsic functions); (3) moral or affective labels, indicating that an object is good or bad, liked or disliked; (4) nominal characteristics, abstractions learned by the child, such as the fact that an object is a liquid or a solid, a fruit, or a food; and (5) a grouping not by attribute but by decree; the child merely states, for example, "All these are similar." In the Mexican scoring we noted separately whether or not a child employed a particular form of grouping in his attempt at differentiation (analysis) or synthesis. We also judged his analysis or synthesis as successful or not on the basis of (1) the understandable differences in six out of seven cases, and (2) the synthesis of at least those items having to do with ingestion.

The Mexican children numbered fifty-seven, from age five to seventeen, living in a *mestizo* village in rural Mexico with a population of some eight hundred people. These children are compared with fifty American children from age six to seventeen, drawn from a suburban metropolitan school near Boston, the sample of children reported in Olver and Hornsby (1966).

This comparison was undertaken as a pilot study, and it is here reported as a preliminary to the main investigation that will concern us in this chapter—a comparison of rural and urban children in Mexico, where considerations of language could be held constant. Yet it is instructive as just that, for it raises many interesting questions. To begin with, the youngest children of both cultures, from age six to eight, are more similar than any other parallel age groups in their responses to the task. Both Mexican and North American children of this age group are able to differentiate between objects, but they show little or no ability to synthesize. Of ten North American children from age six to eight, six were able to analyze well, but only one could synthesize; of twenty-three Mexican children, 52 percent scored well on analysis, and 13 percent on synthesis. In both samples, the children employed mainly perceptible attributes such as color and form in order to separate objects (80 percent of the Mexicans, 90 percent of the North Americans). It appears as though they were examining the things in their minds and describing the variations they saw. However, purely perceptible attributes do not serve well for synthesizing a diverse array of objects. To do this the child must be able to employ more abstract concepts.

Even in children of six or seven we can note some important differences between the two samples. The North American children tend to use formal, nominal categories. They are more likely to analyze in terms of what one can do with objects (70 percent of the North Americans versus 26 percent of the Mexicans).

These differences, though they have little effect on the relative performances of the younger children, are the seeds of much greater differences to come. At ages nine and ten, while performance at the task of analysis was still similar (seven out of ten North Americans and 63 percent of nineteen Mexican children could analyze successfully), half of the North American children could synthesize well in comparison to only one of the nineteen Mexicans.

The reason for this disparity is not difficult to see. The American children are learning to handle abstract concepts of use, such as the idea that a group of objects all "are necessary for human life." Such concepts in themselves are a synthesis between the child's interest in both the use and "goodness" or "badness" of the objects. The six-year-old may decree that germs are bad; his older brother is more likely to state that they are bad because they cause sickness and so harm people. Similarly, an eight-year-old may say that banana, peach, potato, meat, milk, water, and air are good for you and that these are foods one eats; while the ten or eleven-year-old would more likely comment that these things are necessary for the maintenance of life, thus implying both use and an objective moral standard.

The Mexican child, rather than move in this direction, continues to employ concrete attributes. His perceptual observations become finer and finer. He may note, for example, that a banana and a bean are both crescent-shaped like the moon, or that one fruit tastes both better and more mealy than another, and so forth. He also becomes more and more concerned with the concrete use of objects, such as different ways to cook or eat them. However, he does not employ abstract concepts and, if he gets stuck in trying to explain why a group of things are similar, he is likely to declare them similar or not simply by decree, and leave it at that. This trend showed no relationship with the children's intelligence, as measured both by the block form of Raven's Matrices, and by the Draw-A-Man Test. Nor was there any significant difference between the performances of boys and girls, the girls scoring slightly higher, in accordance with their more rapid rate of maturation.

These differences in style are remarkably consistent in both groups. Even at the age of sixteen or seventeen the Mexican adolescent seldom abstracts, even formally, while the North American develops increasing facility with abstract functions and formal equivalencies, whether at the expense of perceptible and concrete qualities or not.

In general terms, we would contrast the development of North American and Mexican children as follows: the North American child starts out by seeing objects in terms of perceptible and concrete characteristics, but he soon begins to consider them in the light of what he can do with them. Also, he starts to pay attention to abstract qualities and to similarities between objects. At first he may note the "goodness" or "badness" of things, repeating culturally determined labels; but later, as he reasons more, the good objects are those useful to man. By the age of eleven or twelve, seven of ten North American children, in contrast to none of ten Mexicans, employed concepts such as these. At best the North American child develops an interest in theory, in the abstract equivalencies and differences among objects. At worst he merely manipulates things in a formal and increasingly reductionist manner. In fact, a few of the older children completely lose the ability to analyze, because the concrete attributes of objects have become buried beneath formal and abstract notions.

In contrast, the Mexican child of six or eight is far more similar to his older brothers in terms of intellectual approach. Both are most concerned with concrete perceptible attributes. The difference is that the older child looks more closely at the object and begins to consider more concrete ways to use it. At best he demonstrates a rich interest in, and relation to, the object as an individual thing; he expresses and describes his experience, although he has no interest in theory or abstraction. At worst he merely perceives in terms of concrete but narrow attributes, and when he is in doubt he arbitrarily declares that objects are similar or different by decree.

The American child is taught to abstract, to manipulate concepts, to control things. He is a member of a culture that prides itself on its power over nature. Almost as soon as he learns what things are, he is taught what he can do with them and where they can be found. One American child saw the similarity between banana, peach, potato, meat, and milk, as all very common things which you might easily get at the supermarket. On the other hand, the child from rural Mexico has little or no contact with so large a commercial enterprise as a supermarket. His experience is rather one in which he plants the beans, sees them grow, harvests, and then eats them. His experience is with nature, and it continues for as long as he remains in a farming community. He is more passive than the North American, and his education is more authoritarian, so that, as we have observed in this village, children often isolate the school experience from the rest of life. Actually, no relationship could be established between success at analysis or synthesis and academic achievement. Those children who judge things to be similar or different by decree may be reflecting the attitudes of the adults in their lives; things are so because a parent or possibly a teacher has said so.

On a more general cultural level, the schools are in themselves reflections of larger cultural traits. In a highly industrial and diversified economy such as that of the United States, abstraction is a necessity. Time and money must be equated. Children must at an early age learn the "values" of things, not just whether they taste good or are pleasing, but in terms of money. For the rural Mexican money is less important. He often barters things as needed, or produces his own food, shelter, and clothing. In his mind, time has little relation to money. We are now investigating these differences more rigorously with a test we have constructed, in order to learn more exactly the villagers' ideas of time and value.

Looked at from the point of view of the general theory of development set forth in this book, the relativity of culture depends on the extent to which any culture shapes skills and preferences beyond the first stages of enactive representation. American and Mexican six-year-olds are not strikingly different in their emphasis on perceptible properties, but with growth, the Mexican child moves toward greater perceptual subtlety, and the North American toward more abstraction. Before this divergence occurs, the principal impact of either culture is probably affective, reflecting child-rearing practices and the like. Only when the child is capable of sufficient mastery of the symbolic forms of his culture can there be a divergence to the fullest limit. In this case, the divergence of the two cultures consists of quite different conceptions of man and society and their reciprocal relations.

A CLOSER LOOK AT DIFFERENCE

A comparison of rural Mexican and North American suburban children, while dramatic enough, involves too many things such as language, technology, culture, and so on. The second part of the present study, then, concentrates on a limited comparison of rural and urban Mexican children and seeks to discern in what measure urban culture makes its impact on the growth of intellect.

The sample included fifty-two children from the village already mentioned and one hundred two children from a housing development in Mexico City. Within each population, two age groups were tested, children from eight to ten and from twelve to thirteen. In the city this included a complete third-grade class (forty-nine children), and a sixth-grade class (fifty-three children). In the village there was a wide variation in the ages of children within specific grades, so the children chosen by random means were not necessarily in the same grade at school. Table 1 contains the vital statistics.

The same list as had been used with the rural Mexican group was used for both these groups to test for equivalence. In the village, the children were tested individually with the items printed on cards and read out by the tester. The child's responses were taken down verbatim. In the city, the test was group-administered, with the tester reading out the items and the child writing down his responses.

The bases on which the equivalence and difference judgments were made were classified within the categories mentioned earlier in this reading (p.

TABLE 1

Composition of Sample

	Age Eight through Ten			Age Twelve and Thirteen		
	Boys	Girls	Total	Boys	Girls	Total
Village	18	15	33	9	10	19
Mexico City	27	26	53	24	25	49

284). As before, we also noted the differences and the equivalence responses separately. The protocols were also classified in terms of success and failure in both the equivalence and the differentiation tasks. Success on the differentiation task was considered to be achieved if six out of seven possible differences given were comprehensible. For the equivalence task, a successful performance constituted getting all the food words plus *air* and *water* into a group. The criteria for success at the equivalence task are similar to those used by Olver and Hornsby (1966) in classifying superordinate-groupings structures, except that sometimes we allowed complexive groupings which were logical and not too all-inclusive. The scoring for success at formulating differences was less problematic, since any attribute that distinguishes the new attribute from the others was considered adequate, even if the other items were defined only by exclusion (for example, "This is red and one of the others are red.").[2]

By about age nine, the difference is plain. More than twice as many urban as rural children succeed at the equivalence task. By twelve, the difference has become fourfold (Table 2 and Figure 1).

TABLE 2

Percent of Children Succeeding on Equivalence and Difference Tasks

	Age		
	6–7	8–10	12–13
Equivalence			
Mexican village	13[a]	16	26
Mexico City	—	44	82
Boston suburb[b]	10	60	80
Difference			
Mexican village	52[a]	84	95
Mexico City	—	79	96
Boston suburb[b]	60	70	80

[a] This group includes twenty-three children.
[b] Each American group comprises ten children.

We are struck by how much closer Mexico City is to Boston than to a *mestizo* village. Data on the younger groups mentioned in the pilot study are also included. One might well assume that, had we selected a group of six-year-olds in Mexico City, they would have been much like the others. While the urban sample shows a superiority in formulating equivalences, the two

[2] As a reliability check on the food list, the children were also given another array of concepts including: *horse* and *cow, chicken, lion, snake, mosquito, man, tree,* and *mountain.* An analysis of the attributes used showed no significant differences between the reactions to the two tests as measured by the use of perceptible, functional, and formal attributes. The two lists appear only slightly different in difficulty. For example, of the total village sample 51 percent passed the equivalence test on the food list and 48 percent on the animal list. Of the urban sample, 73 percent were scored as passing on the food list and 67 percent on the animal list.

groups are similar in their ability to describe differences. Indeed, at age nine the village children show a slight though nonsignificant superiority.

What causes this difference in the ability to formulate equivalences? Note what kinds of attributes are demanded by the task. While successful equivalence must relate the items of the list, it must not be senselessly inclusive ("All these things are found in the world") or so arbitrary as to contain no principle of including anything more ("I like all these things"). Equivalence on the basis of such shared perceptible attributes as color and shape is easy enough up to a point, but the more a list becomes thus diverse, the more this method becomes powerless to cope, and it leads to the kind of complexive groupings that can easily become arbitrary or overinclusive. Adequate superordinate groupings call for the use of functional and formal attributes.

Though functional extrinsic attributes ("I can eat all of these") are more powerful than perceptible ones for formulating equivalence, they too break down on items such as *air* and *fire*. The same is true of such nominal classifications as "foods" or "solids." Some children who seem particularly wedded to formal classification turn to part-whole equivalence when the simple nominal classification no longer serves. Thus they may say that all the other objects contain air. However, many children would reject such a solution as inelegant, and they would seek a more powerful conceptualization, one which would serve for the inclusion of new items and imply a deeper understanding of the relationship among the concepts, beyond the mere fact that they can

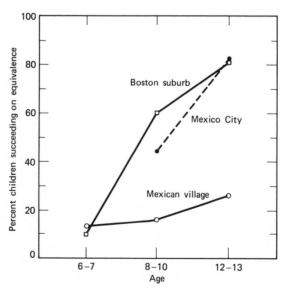

FIGURE 1.   Percent children succeeding on equivalence.

be arbitrarily acted on. The child might, for example, describe the array of items as being "necessary for life" or "used by man to stay alive." To be able to make such a classification, the child must go beyond both sensory impressions (perceptual attributes) or his own personal experience (extrinsic functional) to a general, abstract, and theoretical statement which in fact represents a new capacity in grasping truth. The children who remain on a concrete level of equivalence classifications, whether perceptual or functional, succeed less often in uniting the items, whereas those able to make more abstract or generalized classifications are more likely to find similarities.

A comparison of the urban and village children in Figure 2 reveals how few village children use either nominal or intrinsic functional bases in the equivalence task. Even the older village children continue using perceptible or extrinsic functional attributes. In contrast, urban children are already on their way toward functionalism and formalism by the ninth year.

The over-all picture is quickly summarized. Village children show a strong increase in extrinsic functional grouping and in nominal ones, as well as a small increase in the use of perceptible bases. City children show a sharp drop in the use of perceptual attributes and a sharp rise in both intrinsic functional and nominal groupings. The rural child at age twelve is perceptually oriented or, when functional, very concretely so. He asks what something is used for

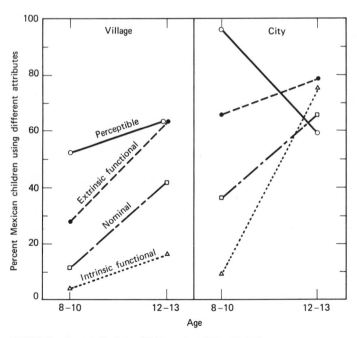

FIGURE 2.   Percent Mexican children using different attributes.

without regard to its abstract properties. The urban child is more sophisticated linguistically, more abstract. Consider now the attributes used by children in characterizing differences (Table 3).

The difference between the younger children of village and city virtually
disappears as one shifts from equivalence judgments to judgments of difference. By age twelve, however, there is a striking contrast: again the village
children fall far behind in the two more abstract bases for grouping—nominal and intrinsic functional. And the falling behind is highly reliable statistically.

There is still a puzzle encountered in comparing Figure 2 and Table 3.
There are rural children who, on the task of finding differences, use attributes that they then do not use in formulating equivalence. For example, 64
percent of rural children from age eight to ten use extrinsic functional attributes to characterize differences, but only 28 percent use them in formulating equivalence. Or, at age twelve, the difference on the the same attribute is
84 percent and 63 percent. In other words, there appears to be a group of
village children who have the ability to use attributes but resist using them
for the equivalence task. Formulating equivalence judgments may depend
more on cultural traits than on individual capabilities.

TABLE 3

Percent of Children Who Use Various Attributes in Formulating Differences

	Age			
	Eight to Ten		Twelve and Thirteen	
	Village	City	Village	City
Perceptible	92	94	90	80
Extrinsic functional	64	68	84	85
Nominal	8	21	26	71
Intrinsic functional	0	9	5	47

In a word, then, there is indeed a patterning of growth going on in the
child between eight and twelve with respect to his approach or resistance
to equivalence judgments, his preference for attributes, and the manner of
specialization in his use of mind. The perceptual, concrete, difference-
sensitive, organically oriented, village child is by age twelve in sharp contrast
to the more abstract, functional, similarity-sensitive, cosmopolitan city child
of the same age.

SOME INFERENCES ABOUT INTELLIGENCE

Unfortunately, growth data are not available on the children with respect to
intelligence and other characteristics. But the older group of children were

tested for intelligence by using the relatively language-free Raven's Progressive Matrices Test. Intelligence, though related to school achievement ($r = 0.50$, $p < 0.01$) was unrelated to success in the equivalence task or in the use of attributes. Incidentally, success on the equivalence task proved to be unrelated to school achievements (a type of achievement based more on a child's ability to memorize and obey authority than to think).

It would seem, and strikingly so, that we are dealing here with a matter of culturally derived preference, preference which through habit becomes finally a personal style. It is reasonable to suppose that within the context of a cultural style one can find variations in the effectiveness with which a child operates. It is doubtful, however, whether the kinds of intelligence tests now available are designed to elucidate such matters.

CULTURE AND ABSTRACTION

A city child coming from an industrial society starts by dealing with objects in terms of their perceptible, concrete characteristics. He soon comes to consider them in the light of what he can do with them. In time, he is led to more abstract formulations as to how things are, how they are alike and how different. Some go so far that they lose the sense of the concreteness of things and become buried in a dry nominalism. They are like people who see a painting immediately in terms of its style, period, and influences, but with no sense of its uniqueness.

Peasant children do not change that much. They are much more similar to their older brothers: they both look. The older one looks at things more closely and considers more concrete ways to use them. While the older peasant child can say how things are alike, he feels more at home with their differences, for that is where reality lies for him. He does not think in generalities. At his best he shows a rich interest in and relation to individual people, individual objects, or particular events. At his poorest he sees only the concrete and the particular and walls himself off from anything beyond immediate experience.

Essentially, such cognitive styles reflect the demands of a culture. The modern industrialized world demands abstractions by its very arrangements, its stimuli, its contrasts, its laws of justice and exchange. What is demanded of the peasant, on the other hand, is that he pay attention to his crops, the weather, and the particular people around him.

The culture is reflected in its institutions—school, family, or work group. The child in an urban school is more likely to learn to manipulate concepts, to use his knowledge beyond school. In an industrialized society, when a child learns what things are, he is taught what he can do with them and where they can be found. In a peasant village, schooling does not get you a better job or even necessarily make you a better farmer. Some boys who do best at school lack the money to continue their education. The urban child can both live at home and advance to higher schools.

The villager tends to be more concrete and more authoritarian in moral outlook. His values are traditional and conservative, and economic scarcity reinforces moral realism. Traditional authoritarianism is rooted in work relations and in the family, where children are taught to obey without question. Unlike the urban world, the small village offers no alternatives to the influence of the family. Even those games by which an industrial society teaches reciprocity and abstract rules of justice are not played within the village (Maccoby, Modiano and Lander, 1964). Observers have noted that many a villager who migrates to the city feels freer when liberated from the restraints of village life (Lewis, 1959)

If the peasant child is not dulled by village life, he will experience the uniqueness of events, objects, and people. But as the city child grows older, he may end by exchanging a spontaneous, less alienated relationship to the world for a more sophisticated outlook which concentrates on using, exchanging, or cataloguing. What industrialized, urban man gains in an increased ability to formulate, to reason, and to code the ever more numerous bits of complex information he acquires, he may lose in a decreased sensitivity to people and events.

References

1. Lewis, O. *Children of Sanchez*, New York, Random House, 1959.
2. Maccoby, M., Galvân, Isidro, & Modiano, N., "Abstraction and Culture," *VII Congreso Interamericana de Psicologia*, Sociedad Interamericana de Psicologia, Mexico, D.F., 1963, pp. 82-86.
3. Maccoby, M., Modiano, Nancy, & Lander, P., "Games and Social Character in a Mexican Village," *Psychiatry*, 26:150-62, 1964.
4. Olver, Rose, R. A developmental study of cognitive equivalence. Unpublished doctoral dissertation, Radcliffe College, 1961.
5. Olver, Rose R., & Hornsby, Joan R. On equivalence. In J. Bruner et al., *Studies in Cognitive Growth*, New York, Wiley, 1966.

CHAPTER 3

The Development of Problem-Solving Strategies

DAVID H. FELDMAN, EDITOR

In this chapter we are primarily concerned with the mental strategies one uses in dealing with problems, and with the systematic development of these strategies over time. We are also interested in applications of research in this area to educational problems, such as the problem of providing a match between the strategy a student uses to solve a problem and the method by which he is taught. These aims are to be distinguished from those of the more traditional problem-solving literature, which focuses on the internal processes involved in problem solving or the external parameters of problems. Specifically, this earlier literature concerns itself with the distinction between learning (or acquisition) and thinking (or mediation). For the reader interested in exploring this fascinating literature, the following may be of interest: Thorndike's cat-in-a-puzzle-box experiments (see Thorndike, 1949); Kohler's *The Mentality of Apes* (1925); Dunker's *On Problem Solving* (1945); and Maier's functional-fixedness experiments (1929). The present chapter grows out of studies such as these, but is equally influenced by more recent cognitive and developmental research.

The readings presented reflect a number of issues and approaches to problem-solving strategies and their development. Readings by Weir and by Olson, for example, reflect two approaches to a single issue: Do problem-solving strategies change systematically over time? Weir's approach to the question is relatively behavioristic; that is, he tends to keep speculation about internal processes to a minimum. Olson's experiment reflects the cognitive approach of Professor Jerome Bruner, in whose laboratory Olson's research was done. The authors come to similar conclusions, despite their differing approaches, thus lending support to the notion that strategies do indeed change systematically over time. Olson describes these behavioral changes as qualitative shifts in problem-solving strategies, calling them simultaneous scanning, successive scanning, and focusing.

In contrast to studies demonstrating the *existence* of problem-solving strategies by showing differences in behavior for children of different age groups, Susan Harter's study sheds some light on the process of *acquisition* of strategies. She explored the contribution of measured intelligence (mental age and IQ) to the ease with which children acquire the use of a learning set. Although fairly technical in design and procedures, this study is well worth reading as a model of careful, well-executed research, as well as for its substantive results.

That children younger than age 5 may not be able to solve problems because they cannot achieve an adequate representation of the problem's "end state" is proposed and tested by Bem (1970). Training on comprehension of "when is the problem solved?" helped these youngsters to solve the new problems for which the end state representation "aha" was not provided.

Sex differences in problem-solving behavior were investigated by G. A. Milton, who used the methods of personality assessment to investigate the influence of the psychoanalytic concept of sex-role identification in problem-solving ability. Milton found that in general boys were better problem solvers than girls, but that subjects with strong male identification performed better regardless of their biological sex. The author speculated that important antecedents of problem-solving skill are to be found in childhood and that improvements in problem-solving skill may be achieved through modification of influences on the identification process. Milton's conclusions, therefore, support Harlow's belief that problem-solving strategies are learned.

Kjell Raaheim, of the University of Bergen, provides additional support for the argument that past experience influences present problem-solving ability. He suggests that only "some of the elements in a given (problem) situation deviate from what the individual is familiar with from past experience." Raaheim's experiments test subjects' ability to generate verbal solutions to a problem that is familiar but has a "gap." The notion of a gap ties Raaheim's work to the earlier "insight" studies of Kohler, Harlow, and others. An issue not raised by Raaheim but of great importance is the relationship between fluency in the use of language and problem-solving ability. This issue is part of a more general question concerning the relationship between language and thought, which is discussed in another chapter.

The digital computer provides another approach to the study of problem-solving strategies, an approach that differs most markedly from previous methods. The computer offers the opportunity to study simultaneously the "internal" process (the printout) and the strategy (the program) involved in solving a problem, and thus may help give us a more comprehensive view of problem solving. A detailed presentation of research and theory in computer simulation is offered by Newell, Simon, and Shaw in their "Elements of a Theory of Human Problem Solving."

Despite the diversity of approaches and impressive findings, the amount of *applied* research on the development of problem-solving strategies is disappointingly small. A great deal more applied work is needed, and the example presented in this section provides an enticing glimpse at the possibilities in this field. Hilda Taba in "The Teaching of Thinking" presents a model for raising classroom interaction from lower to higher cognitive levels. Dr. Taba sees the development of thinking as the primary purpose of instruction, and her methods are aimed at producing better thinking and problem solving in students.

The readings in this chapter represent a few examples of a vast and growing field in the psychology of intellectual development. The reader is reminded that these studies illustrate a number of approaches and issues concerning the development of problem-solving strategies, but do not represent an exhaustive set of readings on the subject. For a more comprehensive view of the trends in problem-solving research, as well as some interesting comments on newer approaches, see *Problem Solving: Research, Method and Theory* (New York: Wiley, 1966), edited by Benjamin Kleinmuntz.

READINGS

Anderson, Richard C. Individual Differences and Problem Solving. In R. M. Gagné (Ed.), *Learning and Individual Differences*. Columbus, Ohio: Charles E. Merrill, 1967.

Anderson, Richard C., & Ausubel, D. P. (Eds.). *Readings in the Psychology of Cognition*. New York: Holt, Rinehart and Winston, 1965.

Ausubel, David P. The Use of Advance Organizers in the Learning of Meaningful Verbal Material. In J. F. Rosenblith and W. Allinsmith (Eds.), *The Causes of Behavior, I*. Boston: Allyn and Bacon, Inc., 1962.

Barron, Frank. Complexity-Simplicity as a Personality Dimension. *Journal of Abnormal and Social Psychology*. 1953, **48**, (2), 163–172.

Bem, Sandra. The role of comprehension in children's problem solving. *Developmental Psychology*, 1970, **1**, 351–359.

Bieri, J. Parental Identification, Acceptance of Authority, and Within-Sex Differences in Cognitive Behavior. *Journal of Abnormal and Social Psychology*, 1960, **60**, 76–79.

Bieri, J. Cognitive Complexity and Personality Development. In O. J. Harvey (Ed.), *Experience, Structure and Adaptability*. New York: Springer, 1966.

Birch, H. G. The Relation of Previous Experience to Insightful Problem Solving. *J. Comp. Psychol.*, 1945, **38**, 367–383.

Birch, Herbert G., & Rabinowitz, Herbert S. The Negative Effect of Previous Experience on Productive Thinking. In Rosenblith and Allinsmith (Eds.), *The Causes of Behavior, I*. Boston: Allyn and Bacon, Inc., 1962.

Bruner, J. S., Goodnow, J. J., & Austin, G. A. *A Study of Thinking*. New York: Wiley, 1956.

Bruner, J. S., Olver, Rose R., & Greenfield, Patricia M. *Studies in Cognitive Growth*. New York: Wiley, 1966.

Duncan, Carl P. Recent Research on Human Problem-Solving. *Psychol. Bull.*, 1959, **56**, 397–429.

Duncan, Carl P. Attempts to Influence Performance on an Insight Problem. *Psychol. Rep.*, 1961, **9**, 35–42.

Duncan, Carl P. (Ed.). *Thinking: Current Experimental Studies*. Philadelphia: J. B. Lippincott Co., 1967.

Dunker, K. On Problem-Solving. (L. S. Lees, Trans.). *Psychol. Monogr.*, 1945, **58**, No. 270, (5).

Forgays, P. G., & Forgays, Janet W. The Nature of the Effect of Free Environment Experience in the Rat. *J. Comp. Physiol.*, 1952, **45**, 322–328.

Gagné, R. M. Problem Solving and Thinking. *Annual Rev. Psychol.*, 1959, **10**, 147–172.

Gagné, R. M. Problem Solving. In A. W. Melton (Ed.), *Categories of Human Learning*. New York: Academic Press, 1964, 293–317.

Gelernter, H. L., & Rochester, N. Intelligent Behavior in Problem Solving Machines. *IBM J. Res. Developm.* **2**, 1958, 336–345.

Getzels, J. W., & Jackson, P. W. The Highly Intelligent and the Highly Creative Adolescent. In *The Third (1959) Univ. of Utah Research Conference on the Identification of Creative Scientific Talent.* Salt Lake City: Univ. of Utah Press, 1959, 46–57.

Gonzales, R. C., & Ross, S. The Basis of Solution by Preverbal Children of the Intermediate-Sized Problem. *Amer. J. Psychol.*, 1959, **71**, 742–746.

Hebb, D. O. A Neuropsychological Theory. In S. Koch (Ed.), *Psychology: A Study of a Science.* Vol. 1. New York: McGraw-Hill, 1959, 622–643.

Harlow, H. F. The Formation of Learning Sets. *Psychological Review*, 1949, **56**, 51–65.

Harlow, H. F., & Harlow, M. K. Learning to Think. *Scientific American*, 1949, pp. 3–6.

Harter, Susan. Discrimination Learning Set in Children as a Function of IQ and MA. *Journal of Experimental Child Psychology*, 1965, **2**, 31–43.

Hovland, Carl I. Computer Simulation of Thinking. *American Psychologist*, 1960, **15**, 687–693.

Hudgins, Bryce B., & Smith, Louis M. Group Structure and Productivity in Problem-Solving. *Journal of Educational Psychology*, October 1966, **57**, (5), 287–296.

Hunt, J. McV. *Intelligence and Experience.* New York: Ronald Press, 1961.

Katona, G. *Organizing and Memorizing.* New York: Columbia Univ. Press, 1940.

Kendler, H. H., & Kendler, T. S. Vertical and Horizontal Processes in Problem Solving. *Psychol. Rev.*, 1962, **69**, 1–16.

Klausmeier, H. J., & Loughlin, L. J. Behavior During Problem Solving Among Children of Low, Average and High Intelligence. *Journal of Educational Psychology*, 1961, **52**, 148–152.

Kleinmuntz, Benjamin (Ed.). *Problem Solving: Research, Method and Theory.* New York: Wiley, 1966.

Kohler, W. *The Mentality of Apes.* New York: Harcourt, 1925.

Luchins, A. A. Mechanization in Problem Solving. *Psychol. Monogr.*, 1942, **54**, (248).

Maier, N. R. F. Reasoning in White Rats. *Comp. Psychol. Monogr.* **6**, 1929 (29).

Maier, N. R. F. Reasoning in Humans. *J. Comp. Psychol.*, 1931, **12**, 181–194.

Maltzman, I. Thinking: From a Behavioristic Point of View. *Psychol. Rev.*, 1955, **62**, 275–286.

Maltzman, I. On the Training of Originality. *Psychol. Rev.* **67**, 1960, 229–242.

Manis, Melvin. *Cognitive Processes.* Belmont, California: Wadsworth, 1966.

Merrifield, P. R., Guilford, J. P., Christensen, P. R., & Frick, J. W. The Role of Intellectual Factors in Problem Solving. *Psychol. Monogr.*. 1962, **76**, 10 (Whole No. 529).

Miller, G. A., Galanter, E., & Pribram, K. H. *Plans and the Structure of Behavior.* New York: Holt, Rinehart and Winston, 1960.

Milton, G. A. The Effects of Sex-Role Identification Upon Problem-Solving Skill. *J. Abn. and Soc. Psychol.*, 1957, **55**, 208–212.

Moore, O. K., & Anderson, S. B. Search Behavior in Individual and Group Behavior Problem Solving. *Amer. Sociol. Rev.*, 1953, **19**, 702–714.

Neimark, Edith D., & Lewis, Nan. The Development of Logical Problem Solving Strategies. *Child Developm.*, 1967, **38**, 107–117.

Newell, A. Simon, H. A., & Shaw, J. C. Elements of a Theory of Human Problem Solving. *Psychol. Review*, 1958, **65**, 151–166.

Olson, David R. On Conceptual Strategies. In Bruner, J., *et al. Studies in Cognitive Growth.* New York: Wiley, 1966.

Osler, S. F., & Shapiro, S. L. Studies in Concept Attainment. IV. The Role of Partial Reinforcement as a Function of Age and Intelligence. *Child Developm.*, 1964, **35**, 623–633.

Osler, S. F., & Trautman, G. E. Concept Attainment. II. Effect of Stimulus Complexity Upon Concept Attainment at Two Levels of Intelligence. *J. Exp. Psychol.*, 1961, **62**, 9–13.

Pribram, Karl. Neocortical Function in Behavior. In H. F. Harlow & C. Woolsey (Eds.), *Biological and Biochemical Bases of Behavior.* U. Wisconsin Press, 1958.

Raaheim, Kjell. Problem-Solving and Past Experience. In Mussen, Paul (Ed.), *European Research in Cognitive Development*, SRCD Monogr. **30** (2), 1965.

Reese, Hayne W. Verbal Mediation as a Function of Age Level. *Psychological Bulletin*, 1962, **59** (6), 502–509.

Schulz, R. W. Problem Solving Behavior and Transfer. *Harvard Educ. Rev.*, 1960, **30**, 61–77.

Sieber, Joan E. Problem Solving Behavior of Teachers as a Function of Conceptual Structure. *Journal of Research in Science Teaching*, 1964, **2**, 64–68.

Staats, A. W. Verbal and Instrumental Response Hierarchies and Their

Relationship to Problem Solving. *Amer. J. Psychol.*, 1957, **70**, 442–446.

Stern, Carolyn, & Keisler, Evan R. Acquisition of Problem Solving Strategies by Young Children, and its Relation to Mental Age. *Amer. Educ. Resch. J.*, 1967, **4**, (1), 1–12.

Taba, Hilda. The Teaching of Thinking. *Elementary English*, May 1965, 534–542.

Taba, Hilda, & Elzey, Freeman F. Teaching Strategies and Thought Processes. *Teachers College Record*, March 1964, **65**, 524–534.

Taylor, D. W. Decision Making and Problem Solving. In J. G. March (Ed.), *Handbook of Organizations*. Chicago: Rand McNally, 1965.

Thorndike, E. L. The Law of Effect. In *Selected Writings from a Connectionist's Psychology*. New York: Appleton-Century-Crofts, Inc., 1949.

Torrance, E. P. Scientific Views of Creativity. *Daedalus*, Summer 1965, 663–681.

Wallach, M. A., & Kogan, Nathan. A New Look at the Creativity-Intelligence Distinction. In Rosenblith and Allinsmith, *The Causes of Behavior, II*. Boston: Allyn and Bacon, Inc., 1966.

Weir, Morton W. Developmental Changes in Problem Solving Strategies. *Psychol. Review*, 1964. **6**, 473–490.

Wertheimer, Max. *Productive Thinking*. New York: Harper and Brothers, 1945.

Wittrock, M. C. Replacement and Non-Replacement Strategies in Children's Problem Solving. *Journal of Educational Psychology* 1967, **58**, 69–74.

16. DEVELOPMENTAL CHANGES IN PROBLEM-SOLVING STRATEGIES[1]

Morton W. Weir

An analysis of the performance of Ss at a number of age levels, from 3 yr. to 20 yr., in a problem-solving task. Dependent variables include terminal level of correct response, rate of rise to terminal level of response, patterns of response, and performance as a function of a preceding correct or incorrect response. A U-shaped relationship between age and terminal level of correct response is reported, while age and simple patterns of response bear an inverted U relationship to one another. Younger Ss show a more rapid rise to terminal level of response than do older Ss. In addition, differential effects of reinforcement and nonreinforcement are noted among the age groups, and differential changes occur in these effects as the task progresses. Data from a number of other studies are discussed in relation to these findings, and an attempt is made to consolidate various sources of evidence to provide support for the mechanisms which are assumed to underlie certain of the developmental changes reported. Differential growth of the ability to generate hypotheses and employ strategies and the ability to process the information Ss gain from their own responding is suggested to account for the major developmental differences reported.

SOURCE. *Psychological Review*, November 1964, **71**, 6.

[1] This research was supported by a grant from the National Institute of Mental Health, United States Public Health Service, Grant Number M-5577, and by funds from the University of Illinois Graduate Research Board. I thank the directors and parents of Playtime Nursery and Kindergarten and the University of Illinois Child Development Laboratory for their cooperation, and John Thompson and Gerald Gruen for their aid in data tabulation and analysis. I also thank J. C. DeFries for his statistical advice.

The psychological literature on problem solving and related topics such as concept formation is vast and appears to be growing exponentially. Attempts to adequately review this literature (e.g., Chown, 1959; Duncan, 1959) have been hampered by the noticeable absence of systematic research programs which attempt to isolate important variables influencing this type of behavior. Even more scarce are developmental analyses of problem solving and related topics. Most studies which include children as a part of their sample use only a limited age range, and the resulting comparisons across ages are sketchy and incomplete (cf. Russell, 1956). There are some notable exceptions, however. Piaget, in a number of works (e.g., Piaget, 1937; Piaget, 1945; Inhelder & Piaget, 1958), has provided modern developmental psychology with invaluable descriptions and speculations as to the nature of intellectual development from early childhood to adulthood. Excellent reviews of his work may be found in Hunt (1962) and Flavell (1963).

The work of the Kendlers (e.g., Kendler & Kendler, 1962; Kendler, 1963) represents a point of view toward developmental research on problem solving considerably different from that of Piaget. The problem situations which Piaget presents to his subjects generally take the form of laboratory versions of real-life situations. The Kendlers, on the other hand, prefer to use less complex situations in an effort to discover basic mechanisms which they presume will also be important determiners of behavior in more complex, real-life situations.

While this paper is not a defense of either of these approaches, the data to be presented here were gathered from a task which fits the Kendler approach much more closely than it does that of Piaget. A considerable number of studies by other investigators have direct relevance to many of the findings which will be reported here. For the most part, however, these studies make use of a variety of tasks and reinforcement conditions, and utilize only a limited age range. As a consequence, any attempt to review them at the beginning of this paper might make the aggregate appear chaotic and unrelated. For this reason, the results and conclusions of the most pertinent of these studies will be discussed later in the context of the results of the present experiment to which they seem most closely related. An attempt will be made to show that there is considerable agreement among the results of these diverse studies, and that they give support, for the most part, to the developmental data and its interpretation which will be presented in this paper.

METHOD

Subjects

The subjects were 290 children, adolescents, and adults ranging in age from 3 years to 20 years. Preschool children were obtained from private nursery schools, and both elementary and secondary school children were obtained from private and public schools. As far as could be ascertained, these children were from neighborhoods consisting of middle- and upper middle-class families. The data to be reported represent, for the most part, the performance of subjects who had been a part of a number of earlier studies, all of which contained groups receiving the same task and instructions (e.g., Gruen & Weir, 1964; Stevenson & Weir, 1959; Stevenson & Weir, 1963). The adult data were collected from college students as a part of an introductory psychology course.

Apparatus

The apparatus has been described in detail previously (Stevenson & Zigler, 1958). It consisted of a yellow panel containing a horizontal row of three knobs. Above the knobs was a signal light and below the knobs was a delivery hole for marbles. The marbles fell into an enclosed plastic container.

Procedure

Subjects were run individually. Each subject was seated in front of the apparatus and was told that he was to play a game, and that when the signal light went on he was to press one of the three knobs. He was also told that if he was correct, a marble would fall into the enclosed plastic container. The subjects were not allowed to handle or keep the marbles, but the younger children were told that if they won enough marbles they would win a prize which they could keep. Since appropriate prizes are difficult to find for adults and adolescents, this part of the instructions was omitted for these groups. It might be argued that the resulting differences in incentive may have affected performance, but so far as the experimenters were able to tell, motivation at all ages was high. All subjects were instructed that the object of the game was for them to win as many marbles as possible. The subjects were given a total of 80 trials each.

For all subjects, only one of the three knobs ever paid off, and that only part of the time. Two reinforcement percentages for the payoff knob were used, 33% and 66%. Choices of the other two knobs never resulted in the delivery of a marble. For each of the two percentage conditions, the subject was reinforced a certain percentage of the times he actually chose the payoff knob. For example, in the 33% condition reinforcement was delivered on 33% of the subject's choices of the payoff knob, rather than on 33% of the total trials in the task. For each subject, one of the three knobs (either left, middle, or right) was designated as the correct knob. Equal numbers of subjects were tested with each of the three knobs. In each percentage condition, subjects from a number of age levels were included. Table 1 shows the mean

TABLE 1

Mean Ages and *N*s for Subjects in the Two Percentage Conditions

33%		66%	
X̄ age	N	X̄ age	N
3.6	10	3.6	10
5.5	27	5.5	35
7.0	31	7.3	20
9.2	15	9.1	15
10.8	26	13.3	10
14.8	26	18.0	30
18.0	35		
Total	170	Total	120

ages of all the age groups in the two percentage conditions, as well as the number of subjects within each of these age groups.

This is a deceptive task. It appears quite simple on the surface, but in fact has no solution—at least not the kind of solution that most subjects seem to expect (Stevenson & Weir, 1963; Weir, 1962). It will not, for example, allow any solution which will yield 100% reinforcement. It will not even allow accurate prediction of when a marble will be delivered and when it will not, since the partial reinforcement schedule is randomized. Because the task does not provide a solution acceptable to most subjects, it makes possible examination of problem-solving strategies over a long series of trials. The solution which will yield the greatest number of marbles is 100% choice of the payoff knob. This behavior, which will be referred to as maximization, will be seen to occur as a predominant strategy only in certain age groups.

RESULTS AND DISCUSSION

Terminal Level of Response

The per cent choice of the payoff knob during trials 61-80 as a function of age and reinforcement percentage condition is shown in Figure 1. (For the sake of brevity, choices of the payoff knob will be referred to in the remainder of this paper as *correct* responses, regardless of whether or not the choice actually resulted in the delivery of a marble.) Examination of each of the two percentage conditions separately revealed a significant difference among the age groups in both the 33% condition ($F = 6.60$, $df = 6/163$, $p < .001$) and the 66% condition ($F = 2.48$, $df = 5/114$, $p < .05$). Due to unequal and disproportionate subclass numbers, both percentage conditions were not included in a single analysis of variance. A t test comparing number of correct responses made by subjects in the two percentage condi-

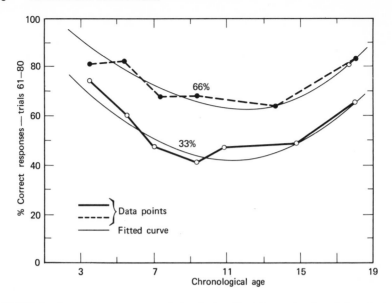

FIGURE 1.   Percent correct responses during the last 20 trials as a function of chronological age and percentage of reinforcement. (Both data points and fitted curves are shown.)[2]

tions indicated that the terminal level of response of subjects in the 66% condition was significantly higher than that of subjects in the 33% condition ($t = 8.18$, $df = 288$, $p < .001$).

The terminal level of response across age groups, shown in Figure 1, appears to be U-shaped in both percentage conditions. A curvilinear regression analysis was performed in order to test the linear and quadratic components of the two percentage curves. Since exact age data were not available for all subjects in some age groups, the mean age of each group (estimated from available age data) was used in a method similar to that suggested by Snedecor (1946, pp. 383-384). From this analysis, the variance due to linear and quadratic components was computed, and the resulting F's showed the quadratic component of the 33% curve to be highly significant ($F = 26.28$, $df = 1/167$, $p < .001$). The quadratic component of the 66% curve was also significant ($F = 10.12$, $df = 1/117$, $p < .01$). The linear component

[2] Equations for the two fitted curves are as follows:
33% condition:
$$\hat{Y} = 99.95 - 10.20X + .455X^2$$
66% condition:
$$\hat{Y} = 114.15 - 8.85X + .395X^2$$
where: $\hat{Y} =$ predicted per cent correct
   $X =$ chronological age.

of neither the 33% nor the 66% curve approached significance ($F < 1$ in both cases). Also plotted in Figure 1 is the line of least squares derived from the linear and quadratic components of the regression analysis. In both percentage conditions, these least squares lines appear to fit the data quite well. (For the remainder of the paper, these least squares lines will be referred to as the "fitted" curves.)

One interesting aspect of this U-shaped relationship is that 3-year-olds, 5-year-olds, and college students all show similar levels of performance after 80 trials in this task. There is no question that different processes must have led to this final level for groups so discrepant in age. An examination of the learning curves of the various age groups in the two percentage conditions may provide one indication that markedly different processes are operating.

Group Learning Curves

Figures 2 and 3 present the mean number of correct choices per block of 10 trials for the various age levels in the two percentage conditions. From these two figures it may be seen that the performance of the 3- and 5-year-olds is characterized by a rapid rise to asymptote, while that of the older subjects either shows little change or a slower rise to terminal level of performance.

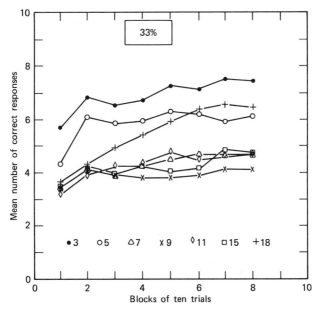

FIGURE 2. Mean number of correct responses per block of 10 trials for the seven age groups in the 33% condition.

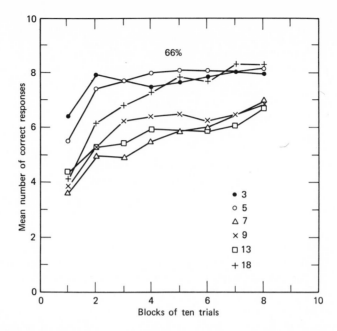

FIGURE 3. Mean number of correct responses per block of 10 trials for the six age groups in the 66% condition.

The percentage of subjects in each of the age groups displaying maximizing behavior (i.e., choosing the payoff knob at least 18 out of 20 trials) during the final 20 trials in the task may be seen in Table 2.

One possible explanation for these differences in trends may be the man-

TABLE 2

Percentage of Subjects Maximizing During the Final 20 Trials

33% Condition		66% Condition	
CA	Per Cent Maximizing	CA	Per Cent Maximizing
3.6	50	3.6	70
5.5	33	5.5	66
7.0	0	7.3	25
9.2	0	9.1	20
10.8	0	13.3	20
14.8	4	18.0	50
18.0	17		

Note. The subject was scored as a maximizer if he chose the payoff knob 18 or more times out of the last 20 trials.

ner in which subjects at different ages approach this task. It is likely that the 3- and 5-year-olds are drawn to the payoff button on the basis of a simple reinforcement notion only. Their tendency to respond to the payoff button is strengthened by each reinforcement, and the tendency to respond to the other two buttons extinguishes rapidly in the face of several nonreinforcements. In order to invoke this explanation of the behavior of younger children, it is necessary to postulate that they do not entertain complex hypotheses involving patterns of response, nor are they particularly disturbed by the partial reinforcement schedule. That is, they may expect neither complex nor "perfect" solutions in a task of this sort, and behave accordingly. A similar result has been reported for children of about this age by Kendler and Kendler (1962). They conclude: "it was possible to infer that as a child matures he makes a transition from responding on the basis of a single unit S-R mechanism to a mediational one." It may be that the single unit S-R mechanisms present in the younger subjects provide an inadequate base for complex strategies. Jones and Liverant (1960) report that younger subjects (4 to 6 years) showed more utilization of "pure" strategy (more maximization) in a two-choice task than did older subjects (9 to 11 years). In addition, their data clearly indicate a more rapid rise in choices of the more frequently reinforced stimulus for the younger than for the older children. In this case, as with the present data, it appears that a pure strategy occurring early in performance is indicative of fairly primitive problem-solving behavior.

Older subjects, particularly adults, enter this task with a strong expectancy that there is a solution which will yield 100% reinforcement, or at least 100% predictability of when a reinforcement will be delivered and when it will not, and employ complex strategies based on complex hypotheses concerning the nature of the task and the reinforcement schedule (Stevenson & Weir, 1963). Younger children, on the other hand, are not concerned with, or more likely not capable of, such complex mediating mechanisms, and do not respond on this basis.

This expectancy for solution that adult subjects show so strongly was encountered by Hyman and Jenkins (1956) who report that it was much more difficult to convince subjects that a sequence was random than it was to convince them that it was structured. A number of investigators have attempted to manipulate this solution set in adult subjects by varying type of task or instructions. Goodnow (1955) found less maximizing behavior in a problem-solving than in a gambling (chance) task, and Morse and Runquist (1960) report that matching behavior (nonmaximizing) is more common in a task which the subject believes to have been pre-scheduled by the experimenter, while more maximizing behavior was noted among subjects who knew that the series was random. A similar finding has been reported by Gruen and

Weir (1964) using instructional sets concerning randomness or nonrandomness.

It is interesting to note that in the studies mentioned above, as well as the present experiment, the belief by older subjects that there is a complex solution actually results in fewer choices of the most frequently reinforced alternative. As a consequence, those subjects behaving in the most complex fashion actually receive a lower frequency of reinforcement than do subjects who are behaving in a less complex fashion. The finding that older subjects tend to expect complex solutions, and are hampered in their problem solving by this set, is not without precedent. Kendler (1963) has reported her belief that in certain tasks, older subjects make the problem more complex than it really is, with this unnecessary complication leading to lowered performance. The same interpretation has been given to results of other studies using several age groups (Stevenson, Iscoe, & McConnell, 1955; Weir & Stevenson, 1959). Goodnow and Pettigrew (1956) propose a "response-hypothesis orientation" to account for a similar difficulty in simple pattern learning. According to them,

> The Ss use their choices as direct tests of specific hypotheses rather than as tools for data gathering with hypothesis testing held in abeyance. As a result, the information gathered is related to a specific hypothesis, and if the latter should prove to be wrong, it is only with difficulty that the information can be transformed and made relevant to another hypothesis. As a rule, Ss do not transform information but start from scratch again with their next hypothesis [p. 385].

In the present task it appears that even though the adult subjects may have been hampered by such complex hypotheses and strategies early in the task, they were nevertheless able to eventually arrive at a high terminal level of performance. There is little doubt that the frequency of correct responses in this oldest group would have continued to increase had they been given additional trials. It seems reasonable to assume, then, that the older subjects (the 18-year-olds, for example) enter this task with complex hypotheses concerning solution, employ complex strategies, systematically reject these strategies when they do not provide a solution which meets their expectation, and finally arrive at something very close to an actual game solution. That is, they eventually begin to realize that two of the buttons have nothing to do with the game and begin to maximize their choice of the only alternative that ever pays off. But this maximizing strategy comes about as the consequence of a vastly different process than does the maximization shown by the 3- and 5-year-olds.

The data and speculations presented above provide at least some manner of explanation for the behavior of the younger children (3- and 5-year-olds) and for the eventual maximizing tendency of the adults. It does not, however, provide much of a clue as to what is occurring in the age groups between the two ends of the age continuum. These "middle-aged" children are characterized by fairly low terminal levels of correct response and only slight increases in performance across trials (see Figures 1, 2, and 3). More light might be cast on the behavior of this middle age range by examining directly some of the strategies which subjects use in this task.

Response Patterns

Previous experimental findings (Weir, 1962) have indicated that the most common response pattern used in this task (at least for some ages) involves some variant of a left, middle, right (LMR) or a right, middle, left (RML) scheme. This type of pattern represents a simple progressive search across the three response buttons. Figure 4 presents the mean number of such patterns made, during the course of the experiment for the various age levels in the two percentage conditions, as well as the fitted curves for the two percentage conditions. Again, due to unequal and unproportional subclass n's, the two percentage conditions were not combined in a single analysis. An analysis of variance performed separately on the two percentage conditions revealed a significant difference among the age groups for both the 33% condition ($F = 4.83$, $df = 6/163$, $p < .001$) and the 66% condition ($F = 5.07$, $df = 5/114$, $p < .001$). A t test comparing mean number of patterns for all 33% groups with all 66% groups indicated that subjects in the 33% condition made significantly more pattern responses of an LMR and RML nature than did subjects in the 66% condition ($t = 6.10$, $df = 288$, $p < .001$).

Again, as with terminal level of performance, a curvilinear relationship between age and performance is indicated. In the case of LMR and RML patterns, however, this relationship takes the form of an inverted U. A curvilinear regression analysis indicated that the relationship between age and performance in the 66% condition is indeed in the form of an inverted U, as the quadratic component was highly significant ($F = 15.45$, $df = 1/117$, $p < .001$), while the linear component did not approach significance ($F = 1.26$). For the 33% condition, however, the linear component was significant ($F = 13.40$, $df = 1/167$, $p < .001$), while the quadratic component did not approach significance ($F < 1$). A Duncan's range test performed on the 33% data revealed the 3-year-old group to differ significantly from the 5-, 7-, and 9-year-olds. This drop at the 3-year level was not sufficient to result in a significant quadratic component, however.

From the statistical analysis presented above and from Figure 4, it seems clear that patterns of this simple LMR and RML nature are less likely to occur during the 80 trials in the younger and older groups than they are

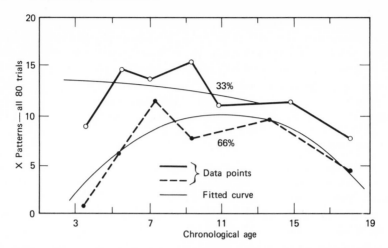

FIGURE 4. Mean number of pattern (LMR and RML) responses made during the task as a function of age and percentage of reinforcement. (Both data points and fitted curves are shown.)[3]

in the middle age ranges. The number of patterns made as each group progressed in the task was examined, and from this it appears that the 3-year-olds virtually *never* use these types of patterns; the older subjects use them some at the beginning of the task, but they then drop out, and the subjects in the middle age groups tend to use these patterns rather consistently throughout the entire task. This indicates that the very young children do not respond in this patterned way at all, and the older subjects, as was suggested earlier, are able to discard these simple patterns after the first time or two they are unsuccessful.

The LMR and RML pattern data begin to throw some light on the performance of the children in the middle age ranges. Children approximately 7 to 10 years of age respond in a highly stereotyped fashion in this task, employing large numbers of these simple patterns throughout the task. At least two explanations for this stereotyped responding appear possible. Either these middle-aged children do not have more complex patterns to use when the simple ones fail, or they are for some reason unable to reject these simple

[3] Equations for the two fitted curves are as follows:
33% condition:
$$\hat{Y} = 13.24 + .144X - .023X^2$$
66% condition:
$$\hat{Y} = -5.97 + 3.00X - .136X^2$$
where: $\hat{Y}$ = predicted number of pattern responses
X = chronological age.

patterns when they do not pay off and continue to respond in a fairly stereotyped fashion.

It is possible that both of these factors are at least partially responsible for the behavior of the children in the middle age ranges. The first explanation, in effect, assumes a severe limitation on the hypothesis formation ability of the child in the middle age range, while the second indicates that this middle-aged child may be capable of complex hypotheses, but he is unable to make full use of the information available from his own responding. This latter explanation would suggest that, in this task, the 7- to 10-year-old is at a point in development where his ability to generate complex hypotheses and employ complex search strategies is growing at a faster pace than his information-processing ability, which catches up only at a later age. Some support for this notion can be found by examining the results of other investigators using similar tasks.

Pattern Responding and Terminal Level of Responses—Data from Other Studies

Most of the information from other studies which can be used for comparison purposes involves decision tasks using only two choices, both of which are partially reinforced. In this type of task, patterns of an LMR or RML nature are clearly impossible, and investigators report that simple alternation is the most frequently encountered response pattern. If alternation in the two-choice task can be looked upon as the analogue of LMR and RML patterns in the three-choice task, then some developmental comparison is possible by combining findings from several recent studies.

Information on alternation behavior is available for the two-choice task for 3- and 4-year-olds from Kessen and Kessen (1961), 5-, 9-, and 13-year-olds from Craig and Myers (1963), 6-, 9-, and 11-year-olds from Gratch (1959), 10-, 13-, and 15-year-olds from Ross and Levy (1958), and some recent data on 3- and 4-year-olds from our laboratory. Although each of these experiments used different tasks, and in most cases, different reinforcement percentages, it is possible to examine the ordering among age groups within each of these studies as far as alternation behavior is concerned. Combination of these relative orderings may then give some picture of developmental differences in alternation behavior in the two-choice task.

When the data are combined in this fashion, an inverted U function between age and number of alternations is revealed. The shape of this curve is quite similar to that reported in the present study for LMR and RML patterns, with one important exception: the apex of the inverted U for alternations appears to be at about 6 to 9 years of age, while that for the LMR and RML patterns is at 9 to 11 years of age (see fitted 66% curve, Figure 4). If this difference in the apexes of the two curves proves to be a replicable one, it may indicate that as the task gets less complex (reduces from three to two choices), the age at which maximum stereotypy appears also decreases. This would provide support for the notion of differential growth of hypothesis formation ability and information-processing capacity. In other words, the 10- and 12-year-olds are capable, in the two-choice task, of processing the information they are receiving from the outcome of their alternation behavior and consequently reject alternation as a solution. In the three-choice task, however, the increasing complexity involved in series of LMR and RML patterns may take them beyond their capacity to make use of the information they are gaining from their own responses. This inability to make maximum use of their previous response patterns may be mainly a function of insufficient memory for fairly long series of responses and their outcomes which denote the success or failure of such a series. If recall of long series is not possible, subjects may return to the basic pattern in the series for a new attack, and this consistent return may produce the pattern stereotypy noted. If inadequate recall is responsible for this stereotypy, allowing subjects of this age to record and keep track of previous responses and their outcomes should considerably reduce the number of stereotyped response patterns.

If the above analysis is correct, the data from the two-choice task should reveal a U-shaped relationship between age and terminal level of performance, with the lowest point of the curve occurring at a younger age than was the lowest point of the U-shaped curve found in the three-choice task. Combining terminal level of response data from the studies mentioned above, with the addition of a study by Crandall, Solomon, and Kellaway (1961), reveals this to be the case. The lowest point of the terminal level of response curve for the two-choice data appears to be at about 5 to 7 years of age, while Figure 1 shows the lowest point of the two fitted curves representing terminal level of correct response to be at 11 to 12 years of age.[4]

It should be noted at this point that the two response measures which have been discussed thus far—terminal level of correct response and patterns of response—are not necessarily independent of one another. If the subject maximizes his choice of the most frequently reinforced alternative, he will be showing no LMR or RML patterns. Conversely, if he is showing a large amount of pattern behavior, his terminal level of correct response will be

---

[4] Results of a study by Jones and Liverant (1960) appear to be slightly out of line with the findings just presented. They found maximizing by a group of subjects 4.5 years of age, while children of 9 to 11 years of age tended to probability match. The finding of matching in the older children is in accord with the results of Craig and Myers (1963), but the maximizing tendency of the younger children is in contradiction to the findings of Kessen and Kessen (1961), and recent results from our own laboratory. One reason for this discrepancy may be that Jones and Liverant used a task much different from those of the other investigators, which may have affected the performance of the younger children.

low. An attempt was made to take this into account by examining the amount of response variability accounted for by LMR and RML patterns and expressing this as a fraction of the total amount of response variability. In doing this, it was possible to examine only the responses subjects made which were not a part of a maximizing strategy and determine what proportion of those variable responses were taken up by patterns. In other words, if a subject maximized completely during the entire last half of the task, this measure of patterning would take into account only the first half, and would indicate the amount of patterning the subject was showing when he *did* vary his responses.

A variable response was scored any time the subject chose an alternative on Trial $n + 1$ which was different from his choice on Trial n. For each subject, the total number of variable responses was computed as well as the number of variable responses which were a part of LMR or RML patterns. When the ratio of variable responses in patterns to total variability was examined, curves nearly identical to those in Figure 4 were the result. This indicates that the pattern of response data presented here does add information to that provided by the terminal level of response data, since the same inverted U relationship between age and performance was found irrespective of the amount of maximization.

Effects of Reinforcement and Nonreinforcement

Thus far, examination of performance in this task has taken into account number of correct responses and patterns of response, and no mention has been made of the effect of a reinforcement or a nonreinforcement on the subjects' behavior. If hypotheses and strategies differ as a function of age, then the effect of a reinforcement or a nonreinforcement should also differ with age. A reinforcement for example, may be reacted to quite differently by a subject who is in the process of going through a complex pattern than it would by a subject who was not using a pattern strategy. In order to assess the immediate effect of a reinforcement or a nonreinforcement, the performance of subjects on the trial following a reinforcement or nonreinforcement was examined. Each subject was scored, on each choice of the correct knob, as having either repeated that choice on the next trial or having switched to another knob. This tabulation was performed for the payoff knob only.

Several types of strategies may be reflected in these data. For example, a subject who maximized his choice of the correct knob early in the task and continued this maximazation would show repeated response to the correct knob following *both* reinforcement and nonreinforcement. This would be termed a win-stay, lose-stay strategy. On the other hand, a subject who was in the process of checking out a fairly complex sequential hypothesis might be virtually unaffected by the occurrence of a single reinforcement or non-reinforcement, and might show any of a number of behaviors, depending on the nature of the sequential hypothesis involved. Other types of strategies such as win-stay, lose-shift, or win-shift, lose-shift, etc., would, if encountered, provide information concerning the effects of reinforcement and nonreinforcement on strategies used in this task.

For each subject, the per cent response repetition was computed for all trials following either a reinforcement or a nonreinforcement. The average per cent response repetition for each of the age groups in the 33% condition is plotted in Figure 5. In this graph, any point above the 50% line reflects a tendency to repeat the previous response, while any point below the 50% line is indicative of a tendency to switch to another choice.

A Lindquist Type I analysis of variance was performed on the data presented in Figure 5. The results of this analysis point up several interesting features of these data. First, the main effect due to age is significant ($F = 7.49$, $df = 6/163$, $p < .001$). There is also a tendency through age 9 for the groups to show more response repetition following a reinforcement than following a nonreinforcement, while at age 11 and beyond, this tendency is reversed. This reversal between ages 9 and 11 is reflected in the analysis of variance by a significant age $\times$ reinforcement-nonreinforcement interaction

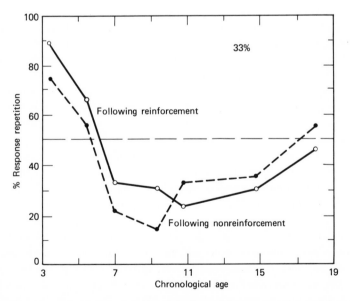

FIGURE 5. Per cent response repetition following reinforcement and nonreinforcement for the seven age groups in the 33% condition (all 80 trials).

($F = 6.86$, $df = 6/163$, $p < .001$). The main effect due to reinforcement-nonreinforcement was not significant ($F < 1$).

It appears then, that the younger children (3- and 5-year-olds) show evidence of a maximizing strategy, with a tendency to repeat their previous response regardless of whether it was correct or incorrect. This is especially true of the 3-year-olds. The 7-, 9-, 11-, and 15-year-olds, however, show a tendency toward a win-shift, lose-shift strategy. This probably comes about as a result of their previously noted stereotyped pattern responding, during which the occurrence or nonoccurrence of a reinforcement would have little effect on their behavior. It also indicates that their pattern responding does not contain a large amount of repetition on the payoff knob, but instead is best represented by some sequence of responses involving the other two knobs to a large degree. A strategy employing LMR and RML patterns would fit this definition and yield a win-shift lose-shift outcome.

The greater tendency to repeat the previous response following a reinforcement than following a nonreinforcement for children through age 9 is in agreement with results reported by Brackbill, Kappy, and Starr (1962) and Stevenson and Odom (1963). The reversal in this behavior which occurs at age 11 and older may reflect the fact that older subjects are adopting a rather subtle strategy based on the absence of long runs of reinforcement in the 33% condition. Since this knob pays off on the average of only one out of every three times, following a nonreinforcement a payoff becomes more likely to occur on the next trial. Conversely, if it has just paid off, a nonreinforcement is more likely to occur on the next trial than is a reinforcement. This type of strategy may be too complex to be adopted by the younger children. Goodnow and Pettigrew (1955) report a similar finding with adults trained in a two-chioce task with only short runs of reinforcement possible. Their subjects showed a marked tendency to persist with an unsuccessful choice. The same tendency has been reported by Jarvik (1951).

In order to examine changes which might occur in the effects of reinforcement and nonreinforcement as the task progressed, per cent response repetition during the first and last blocks of 10 trials only was computed, and is presented in Figure 6. Although all groups reflect at least some tendency to increase response repetition following both reinforcement and nonreinforcement as the task progressed, the greatest change is shown by the adult group. In order to test for the significance of this and other changes, difference scores were computed for each subject by subtracting the per cent response repetition during the first half of the task from per cent response repetition during the last half. A Lindquist Type I analysis of variance was then performed on these difference scores. This analysis was performed on first and last half of the task rather than on first and last block of 10 trials in order to include a greater number of responses for each subject from which the

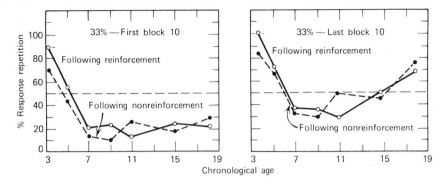

FIGURE 6.   Per cent of response repetition following reinforcement and nonreinforcement for the seven age groups in the 33% condition. (Graph on left is first block of 10 trials; graph on right is last, eighth, block of 10 trials.)

percentage figures were computed. In the case of the 33% condition, this analysis revealed a significant change in response repetition associated with age $(F = 3.56, df = 6/163, p < .01)$, indicating all ages did not change the same amount during the task. The change in response repetition from first to last half of the task was also different for responses following reinforcement than it was for those following nonreinforcement $(F = 5.12, df = 1/163, p < .05)$. The interaction between age and reinforcement-nonreinforcement was not significant $(F < 1)$.

Figure 7 presents percentage of response repetition following both reinforcement and nonreinforcement for the six age groups of the 66% condition. As in the 33% condition, the difference among the age groups was highly significant $(F = 4.29, df = 5/114, p < .001)$. From Figure 7 it can be seen that the tendency to repeat the previous response was greater following reinforcement than nonreinforcement for all ages. This difference accounts for the significant F associated with reinforcement-nonreinforcement $(F = 28.95, df = 1/114, p < .001)$. This tendency is considerably greater for the 7-, 9-, and 13-year-olds than it is for the other ages, resulting in a significant age $\times$ reinforcement interaction $(F = 2.61, df = 5/114, p < .05)$.

As with the 33% condition, the 3- and 5-year-olds and adults in the 66% condition showed an overall tendency to continually choose the payoff button. The same strategy has been reported for adults by DeSoro, Coleman, and Putnam (1960). They found adult subjects to show more win-stay than lose-stay, but also report a predominant tendency to stick with the most frequently reinforced alternative after either a win or loss. Hyman and Jenkins (1956) report a similar finding. The adults may be adopting this strategy

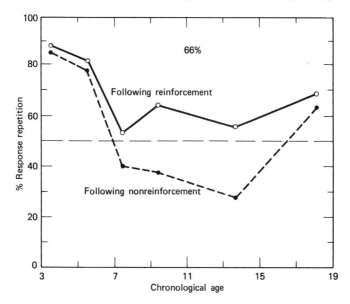

FIGURE 7. Per cent of response repetition following reinforcement and nonreinforcement for the six age groups in the 66% condition (all 80 trials).

in response to the fairly long runs of reinforcement which occur in the 66% condition. Goodnow and Pettigrew (1955) were able to train this sort of strategy into their subjects by means of a reinforcement schedule characterized by long runs. The same sort of behavior has been described by Anderson (1960) and by Derks (1963).

The finding of a win-stay, lose-shift strategy on the part of the children in the middle age ranges agrees with the results of Brackbill, Kappy, and Starr (1962) and Stevenson and Odom (1963). Since the LMR and RML pattern data have indicated that these same subjects are responding in a fairly stereotyped fashion, it appears that they not only display pattern stereotypy, but also, during their pattern sequences, tend to repeat the previously reinforced response following a reinforcement, and to shift following a nonreinforcement. A careful check of individual data sheets shows this to be the case. One discrepant finding has been reported by Cohen and Hansel (1955). They report that 6- to 8-year-olds show more win-shift, lose-stay strategy, while older subjects (10 to 11 years of age) were not affected by the outcome of their previous response. The source of this discrepancy in results is not clear.

As with the 33% condition, response repetition following both reinforcement and nonreinforcement in the 66% condition was computed for the first and last block of 10 trials separately in order to examine changes in

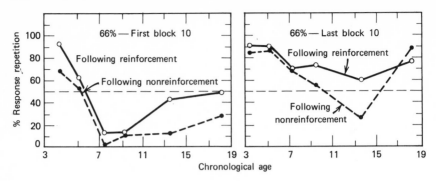

FIGURE 8.   Per cent of response repetition following reinforcement and nonreinforcement for the six age groups in the 66% condition. (Graph on left is first block of 10 trials; graph on right is last, eighth, block of 10 trials.)

strategy as the task progressed. These are presented in Figure 8. Again, there is a general tendency for response repetition to increase from first to last block for all ages. Certain of the age groups show more change than others, particularly the 7- and 9-year-olds and adults, who change most drastically in the direction of maximization. The differential change among the age groups is the source of a significant F associated with age in the analysis of change scores from the first to the last half of the task ($F = 2.66$, $df = 5/114$, $p < .05$). No other significant differences were revealed by this analysis.

One other performance measure seems worthy of comment. In order to assess the degree of tendency toward response repetition which subjects bring with them into this task, the proportion of subjects at each age level who repeated their previous response after the *first* reinforcement or nonreinforcement was calculated. These proportions are plotted in Figure 9. These are first trial data only (or, more precisely, second trial data, since they represent what the subject did following his first reinforcement or nonreinforcement), and represent the sets and tendencies the subjects bring with them to the experimental situation or arrive at through the instructions given. These data present a remarkably similar picture to those presented in Figures 5 and 6, indicating that the 33% reinforcement schedule may not have been sufficient to produce much change in the strategies involving reinforcement and nonreinforcement. It should be noted that the data presented in Figure 9 are not strictly comparable to those in Figures 5 and 6. The data in the latter two figures represent per cent response repetition shown by groups of subjects summed over a series of trials, while the data in Figure 9 are simply proportions of subjects within each of the age groups who show response repetition.

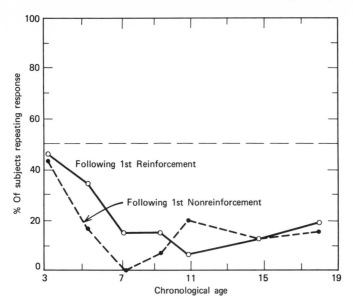

FIGURE 9.   Percentage of subjects repeating same response following first reinforcement or nonreinforcement. (All percentage conditions combined.)

Concluding Remarks

This paper has been an attempt to analyze in a fairly extensive fashion the performance of subjects at various age levels in a problem-solving task, and to compare these findings with those of other investigators who have used comparable tasks. Throughout, it has been assumed that differences in performance at different age levels or at different points during the task reflect hypotheses and strategies on the part of the subjects. Since these hypotheses were not measured directly, they can only be inferred in a general way from the performance data, and their actual existence remains to be demonstrated by further research. This may be impossible for the younger subjects, who are notoriously uncommunicative. Unfortunately, these subjects also represent an age range in which it appears that the greatest changes, probably associated with rapid language development, are taking place. However, by manipulating such variables as type of instruction, pretraining, or incentive condition, it should be possible to demonstrate predictable changes in performance which would be stronger indicators of hypotheses and strategies.

Another limitation to the data which have been presented in this paper is that the strategies discussed were derived from information based on group performance. Obviously, not all subjects within each of the age groups went about solving this problem in the same fashion. However, further research which would include such individual difference variables as intelligence and certain measures of parent-child interaction should make the prediction of individual performance in this task possible.

References

Anderson, N. H. Effect of first-order conditional probability in a two-choice learning situation. *J. exp. Psychol.*, 1960, **59**, 73–93.

Brackbill, Yvonne, Kappy, M. S., & Starr, R. H. Magnitude of reward and probability learning., *J. exp. Psychol.*, 1962, **63**, 32–35.

Chown, S. M. Rigidity—A flexible concept. *Psychol. Bull.*, 1959, **56**, 195–223.

Cohen, J., & Hansel, C. E. M. The idea of independence. *Brit. J. Psychol.*, 1955, **46**, 178–190.

Craig, Grace J., & Myers, J. L. A developmental study of sequential two-choice decision making. *Child Develpm.*, 1963, **34**, 483–493.

Crandall, V. J., Solomon, D., & Kellaway, R. A comparison of the patterned and nonpatterned probability learning of adolescent and early grade school-age children. *J. genet. Psychol.*, 1961, **99**, 29–39.

Derks, P. L. Effect of run length on the "gambler's fallacy." *J. exp. Psychol.*, 1963, **65**, 213–214.

DeSoto, C. R., Coleman, E. B., & Putnam, P. L. Predictions of sequences of successes and failures. *J. exp. Psychol.*, 1960, **59**, 41–46.

Duncan, C. P. Recent research on human problem solving. *Psychol. Bull.*, 1959, **56**, 397–429.

Flavell, J. H. *The developmental psychology of Jean Piaget.* Princeton, N.J.: Van Nostrand, 1963.

Goodnow, J. J. Determinants of choice-distribution in two-choice situations. *Amer. J. Psychol.*, 1955, **68**, 106–116.

Goodnow, J. J., & Pettigrew, T. F. Effect of prior patterns of experience upon strategies and learning sets. *J. exp. Psychol.*, 1955, **49**, 381–389.

Goodnow, J. J., & Pettigrew, T. F. Some sources of difficulty in solving simple problems. *J. exp. Psychol.*, 1965, **51**, 365–392.

Gratch, G. The development of the expectation of the nonindependence of random events in children. *Child Develpm.*, 1959, **30**, 217–227.

Gruen, G. E., & Weir, M. W. The effect of instruction, penalty, and age on probability learning. *Child Develpm.*, 1964, **35**, 265–273.

Hunt, J. McV. *Intelligence and experience.* New York: Ronald Press, 1961.

Hyman, R., & Jenkins, N. W. Involvement and set as determinants of behavioral stereotypy. *Psychol. Rep.*, 1956, **2**, 131–146.

Inhelder, Bärbel, & Piaget, J. *The growth of logical thinking from child-*

hood to adolescence: An essay on the construction of formal operational structures. (Trans. by Anne Parsons & S. Milgram) New York: Basic Books, 1958.

Jarvik, M. E. Probability learning and a negative recency effect in the serial anticipation of alternative symbols. *J. exp. Psychol.*, 1951, **41**, 291–297.

Jones, M. H., & Liverant, S. Effects of age differences on choice behavior. *Child Develpm.*, 1960, **31**, 673–680.

Kendler, Tracy S. Development of mediating responses in children. *Monogr. Soc. Res. Child Develpm.*, 1963, **28** (No. 2) 33–48.

Kendler, H. H., & Kendler, Tracy S. Vertical and horizontal processes in problem solving. *Psychol. Rev.*, 1962, **69**, 1–16.

Kessen, W., & Kessen, Marion L. Behavior of young children in a two-choice guessing problem. *Child Develpm.*, 1961, **32**, 779–783.

Morse, E. B., & Runquist, W. N. Probability-matching with an unscheduled random sequence. *Amer. J. Psychol.*, 1960, 73, 603–607.

Piaget, J. *The construction of reality in the child.* (Orig. publ. 1937) (Trans. by Margaret Cook) New York: Basic Books, 1954.

Piaget, J. *La formation du symbole chez l'enfant.* (Orig. publ. 1945) [*Play, dreams, and imitation in childhood*] (Trans. by C. Gattegno & F. M. Hodgson) New York: Norton, 1951.

Ross, B. M., & Levy, N. Patterned predictions of chance events by children and adults. *Psychol. Rep.*, 1958, **4**, 87–121.

Russell, D. H. *Children's thinking.* Boston: Ginn, 1956.

Snedecor, G. W. *Statistical methods.* Ames: Iowa State College Press, 1946.

Stevenson, H. W., Iscoe, I., & McConnell, C. A developmental study of transposition. *J. exp. Psychol.*, 1955, **49**, 278–280.

Stevenson, H. W., & Odom, R. D. Children's behavior in a probabilistic situation. *J. exp. child Psychol.*, in press.

Stevenson, H. W., & Weir, M. W. Variables affecting children's performance in a probability learning task. *J. exp. Psychol.*, 1959, **57**, 403–412.

Stevenson, H. W., & Weir, M. W. The role of age and verbalization in probability learning. *Amer. J. Psychol.*, 1963, **76**, 299–305.

Stevenson, H. W., & Zigler, E. F. Probability learning in children. *J. exp. Psychol.*, 1958, **56**, 185–192.

Weir, M. W. Effects of age and instruction on children's probability learning. *Child Develpm.*, 1962, **33**, 729–735.

17. ON CONCEPTUAL STRATEGIES

David R. Olson

Most studies of problem solving in children characterize the behavior of the preschool child as receptive or respondent to stimuli, while the behavior of the older child appears to be determined far more by the plans or hypotheses the child generates rather than by immediate stimuli. The transition, we have urged, depends upon the development of representational systems. And one of the important aspects of such developments is the shift to symbolic or linguistically mediated representation. Luria (1961, p. 22) puts it well: "Once taken into the system of verbally formulated links the stimulus becomes not a mere signal but an item of generalized information, and all subsequent reactions depend more on the system it is taken into than on its physical properties."

In previous chapters it has been suggested that the child's cognitive development involves the successive appearance of more powerful modes of representing experience, beginning with the enactive and later augmented by ikonic and symbolic systems, and that these permit the child to move increasingly beyond the stimulus to the nature of the setting of the stimulus in a broader domain.

Particularly with the development of symbolic representation the child masters "higher order techniques for processing information by consecutive inferential steps that take one beyond what can be pointed at" (Bruner [1964] p. 14). The appearance of such symbolic representation has enor-

SOURCE. Jerome S. Bruner et al. (Eds.), *Studies in Cognitive Growth*. New York: John Wiley & Sons, 1966.

mous effects, as we have seen in the preceding chapters, on the way children tackle problems. Indeed, there is interesting evidence presented in passing in those chapters that the strategies employed by children change drastically as the more powerful tools of symbolic representation become available to them.

The present chapter deals directly with the issue of strategies and their development. A decade ago, Bruner, Goodnow, and Austin (1956) first examined the nature of strategies in some detail—the nature of the sequence of decisions made by a subject in attempting to delimit a concept. The solution of concept-attainment problems, it turned out, could be more clearly understood as a systematic sequence of hypotheses than it could in terms of specific, single responses. The three major strategies described in that work were: (1) *simultaneous scanning,* in which subjects attempted to deal with the task of attaining a concept by generating and evaluating all possible hypotheses at once and at each presentation of new information; (2) *successive scanning,* in which subjects worked on a single hypothesis at a time and examined subsequent presentations only in terms of that hypothesis; and (3) a *focusing* strategy, in which subjects dealt not with specific hypothesis but rather with constraints on the features that a correct hypothesis would have to take into account.

When a subject is accumulating information to solve a problem, the questions he asks or the hypotheses he tests are determined by several considerations. Among these are the complexity of the problem, the amount of certainty required, the "pay-off" or cost involved in each question, and, as we have seen in preceding chapters, the person's basic orientation to problem solving.

Surely the child's mode of representation should affect his strategy, that is, the pattern of hypotheses or decisions he makes en route to problem solution. The strategy used by a child who represents his world ikonically should be qualitatively different from that of a child capable of symbolic representation. One would expect, for example, that the more ikonic child would test hypotheses "directly," in the sense of checking whether an instance "pointed" to the correct solution. He would be likely to test one image at a time as to what the correct solution is. As in the Kuhlman (1960) experiments mentioned in the first chapters, we would expect such a child to operate, so to speak, in an "image space" rather than in a conceptual one.

As symbolic representation comes to be handled more competently by the child, we should expect that information would be less tied to specific instances or images, that a "conceptual space" would replace (or augment) the earlier "image space," and that encounters with new instances would be used to decide among alternative hypotheses rather than to check the "correctness" of a single image.

That is all we need consider by way of introduction. The significance of the forms of representation will become more precise in the context of the experiments to be reported.

AN EXPERIMENT

Some ninety-five children served as our subjects, about equally divided into threes, fives, sevens, and nines. About half of them came from the Boston suburban area, the other half from Halifax, Nova Scotia. They were assigned at random to two experimental groups, as will presently be explained. The relevant vital statistics about the children are contained in Table 1.

TABLE 1

Number and Ages of Children in the Experiment

Age	Free Condition			Constrained Condition		
	Number	Mean Age	Standard Deviation, Months	Number	Mean Age	Standard Deviation, Months
3	10	3:10	3	10	3:9	4
5	10	5:3	4	15	5:2	5
7	10	7:7	4	15	7:7	3
9	10	9:3	6	15	9:3	7

The task set the children involved determining which one of several alternative patterns on a board was "correct." To understand how "correctness" was defined we must say a word about the apparatus. It was a "bulb board" consisting of five rows and seven columns of red light bulbs, each one-half inch in diameter and set one-half inch apart. The bulbs were mounted on a uniform gray surface. Normally the bulbs were off and in that state were a dark red color. If a bulb were part of a prearranged pattern on the board, it would light up when pressed, and go off again when released. When lit, the bulb was a brilliant "instrument-panel" red. Bulbs that were not part of the prearranged pattern remained dark even when pressed. Manual switches at the rear of the board made it possible to set any pattern desired. Each time a bulb was pressed, the fact was recorded on an Esterline-Angus recorder. Masks could be placed over the bulb board to reduce the size of the matrix of bulbs from 5 by 7 to any alternative numbers of bulbs—in this case to matrices of 5 by 5, 3 by 3, and 1 by 4. A drawing of the apparatus appears in Figure 1.

Each child (they were tested individually) was presented at each trial with one, two, or more alternative models or diagrams mounted above the bulb board. The models contained possible patterns of lighting bulbs on the board.

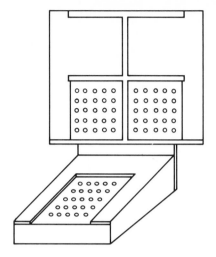

FIGURE 1. Apparatus used in the experiments.

The child's task was to determine which was correct or, in the case of the single model, whether it was correct. Bright red circular spots corresponded to the bulbs that would light up when pressed; dark gray spots represented the bulbs that would remain unlighted. The dimensions of the models were always identical to those of the bulb board itself. On each trial, only one of the alternative models correctly represented the pattern that would light up when pressed.

The children were introduced to the task by being shown first the correspondence between a single model and the bulb board. Then a series of problems were presented in which two diagrams at a time were mounted in front of the child and he was required to choose, with a minimum number of presses, which of the two models corresponded to the bulb board. They worked at each task until they had solved the problem or until, in the judgment of the experimenter, they were making no progress toward solution. If a child appeared to be guessing or showing signs of doubt, the experimenter reminded the child what the task was and urged him to work for the correct answer. Since our major concern is with the strategies or the sequences of bulbs pressed, the eventual solution of the problems was only indirectly relevant. The atmosphere of the task was to encourage the children to keep trying.

Of the various problems set the children, three have been selected for detailed analysis here to show as clearly as possible the differences between children of different ages. Others will also be treated, but not in such fine detail.

Problem A was given on the 3 by 3 board and involved two alternative models, one resembling an inverted T, the other a single bar across the bottom of the board. The inverted T was always correct. Using X to indicate the illuminated bulbs and O the others, the patterns were as follows (the one on the left being correct):

```
O  X  O                              O  O  O
O  X  O              and              O  O  O
X  X  X                              X  X  X
```

Problem B was given on the 5 by 5 board, again with two alternatives. One was an upright T and the other a horizontal row at the top of the board. The latter was always correct.

```
X  X  X  X  X                    X  X  X  X  X
O  O  O  O  O                    O  O  X  O  O
O  O  O  O  O        and         O  O  X  O  O
O  O  O  O  O                    O  O  X  O  O
O  O  O  O  O                    O  O  X  O  O
```

Problem C was presented on the 5 by 5 matrix and required the selection of one of three alternatives: an upright T, an inverted T, and a ⌐ which "shared" the midcolumn and one-half the top and bottom rows with the alternative diagrams. This last alternative was the correct one.

```
X  X  X  O  O      O  O  X  O  O      X  X  X  X  X
O  O  X  O  O      O  O  X  O  O      O  O  X  O  O
O  O  X  O  O      O  O  X  O  O      O  O  X  O  O
O  O  X  O  O      O  O  X  O  O      O  O  X  O  O
O  O  X  X  X      X  X  X  X  X      O  O  X  O  O
```

All three problems involve overlapping patterns. We can distinguish in each problem three kinds of bulbs. There are those that are off the pattern of any of the alternative models; these we shall refer to as "off-pattern" positions; they are redundant, carrying no useful information. Of those positions that fall on the alternative set of patterns, we can distinguish redundant positions that go on for all the alternative models, and informative positions that go on or stay off on only some of the alternative models. In short, then, there are *off-pattern redundant positions, on-pattern redundant positions, and on-pattern informative positions*.

A correct solution to a problem with two alternatives requires a minimum press of one informative bulb, and for a three-alternative problem, a minimum of two informative bulbs.

The same set of problems was presented to all the children. The children were equally divided between two experimental conditions: one did the problems under "free" conditions, the other under "constraint." The children who went "free" were permitted an unrestricted choice of bulbs to solve the problem, provided that "you find the correct answer with as few trials as necessary and that you point to the correct answer as soon as you know it." Children were, in effect, free to use any strategy or approach they preferred. The "constrained" children were permitted to press only one bulb at a time. After each press the experimenter asked, "Now do you know which of the pictures is the correct one?" If the child did not, the experimenter asked, "Would you like to press one more bulb to find out for sure which is the correct picture?" The procedure was designed, of course, to encourage the most economical or informative strategy of which a child was capable. The "constrained" children were permitted to press one bulb at a time until they had located enough information to solve the problem and had pointed to the correct diagram. In principle, two conditions were employed to determine the difference between what children at various age levels *would* do if left free and what they *could* do when pressed.

THE EMERGENCE OF STRATEGIES

We shall examine the results in two ways. One is in terms of *achievement*— how well the children succeeded in solving the problems, how success relates to age, and so on. Such analyses are based, of course, on grouped data and averages and provide useful if limited information. A second approach emphasizes the *process* of problem solving: the strategies employed by individual children on individual problems. Of necessity, there are aspects of such an analysis that are more "subjective" or arbitrary, for it is not always completely apparent what a child has in mind over a series of presses.

We shall necessarily move back and forth between these two approaches. We begin with an analysis of the bulbs pressed by the children while attempting to solve the problems. Inferences regarding strategies may be drawn from these results. If, for example, the children press bulbs that fall on pattern more often than could be expected by chance, we can infer that the children are at least following the models. The question would be which ones of the on-pattern bulbs do they favor? And in what order? From data such as these, strategies can be reconstructed.

Consider first the primitive approach of the youngest children, the *Search Strategy*. It can be described as a quasi-systematic search of the board for bulbs that will light up. The search of any particular child can be shown to be nonrandom, for not all the bulbs are pressed with equal frequency. Edge bulbs predominate. There are, moreover, two ways to show the systematic search pattern of these children. There is first, the occurrence of runs of from four to over fifteen neighboring bulbs in a sequence that could hardly be random. On Problem B, for example, nineteen out of twenty of the youngest children made such runs ranging from three to twenty-seven consecutive presses, with a median of six per run. If, moreover, the bulbs were being pressed at random, we would not find such a high predominance of corner bulb presses followed by the pressing of an adjacent bulb: in fact, the frequency of such adjacent sequence is wildly beyond chance. Children, in short, even young ones, are poor random generators. But we call their performance "quasi-systematic" because it has nothing to do with the nature of the patterns to be found.

What the three-year-olds are doing is best described as a somewhat orderly search of the board for bulbs that will light. As we shall see, the search is conducted quite independently of the diagrams mounted in front of the child. The plan for gathering information, in sum, does not emerge from the models presented the child. Let it be said at once that the older the child, the less likely he is to use this primitive approach—of which more presently. For the three-year-olds who use the strategy, a successful solution is infrequent, but before that matter can be pursued we had best examine some of the other strategies.

By five years of age, a striking and pervasive change occurs in the children's mode of responding, particularly when their choices are "free." While the younger subjects have searched the board in a manner independent of the alternative models, the five-year-old tried out each model successively, independently of what he had tested before or would test next, and he tried it out in its entirety against the bulb board to see which one matches. We call this the *Successive Pattern-Matching Strategy*. Its salient feature is its almost total concentration upon on-pattern bulbs, redundant and informative alike. When a Search Strategy is in force, on-pattern bulbs are pressed no more frequently than off-pattern ones (save for the tendency of some three-year-olds to return to a row that lights up). In successive matching (and a still more sophisticated strategy to be described) off-pattern bulbs are rarely pressed. One would expect by rule of chance that about a third of the bulbs pressed on Problem A would be on-pattern, and a bit over a half on Problem B. For children five and over, these figures are always in excess of eight in ten, and often over nine in ten (Figure 2).

Another marked change begins around seven. What appears now is the *Information-Selection Strategy*. It develops first in response to the constraint imposed on bulb-pressing in one of the two conditions. Recall that the children in this condition are told to select one bulb that will tell which alternative is correct. Only if he is unable to choose the correct model with certainty is he permitted his next choice of a bulb. Information Selection shares with

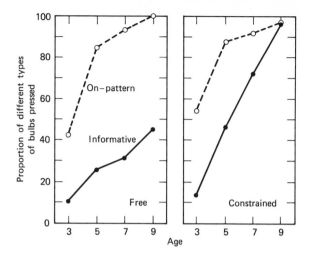

FIGURE 2. Proportion of different types of bulbs pressed on single problems (free and constrained).

Pattern Matching a preoccupation with on-pattern bulbs. But increasingly, these are informative on-pattern bulbs. It is not age alone, however, that accounts for this increased power of strategy; rather, it is the response of older children to the conditions in the constrained procedure. This is also plain in Figure 2.

The difference between constrained and free conditions is nowhere better illustrated than in the speed with which each condition leads subjects to their first informative bulb. The data are set forth graphically in Figure 3. The two conditions produce virtually no overlap in their distributions of responses.

There is still another fairly direct way of checking on the advent of Information Selection. It is by determining whether a child, once he has pressed his first informative bulb, does in fact now have the information in a form that he can use to solve the problem. The data for both our problems are summarized in Figure 4. In effect, the older the child, the more likely he is to solve the problem directly upon achieving the minimum information necessary for that solution. And as before, constraint improves this likelihood strikingly. Note too that, to put it figuratively, a five-year-old operating with constraints imposed will perform in an informationally more efficient fashion than will a seven-year-old operating freely. This suggests (although it is a speculative matter) that perhaps the effect of years is to internalize informational constraints. It may be that at the base of such internalization is a sort of hierarchical structure.

One final matter before we turn to the detailed analysis of individual per-

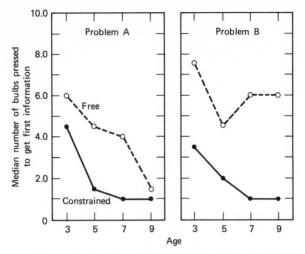

FIGURE 3.   Median number of bulbs pressed to get first information.

formance: the amount of time required by children of different ages in choosing bulbs to press. This suggests some interesting things about the issue of "internal" and "external" constraints. For one thing, there is not much by way of change in time required choosing the bulbs as far as the free condition is concerned (Figure 5). It either declines slightly, or remains

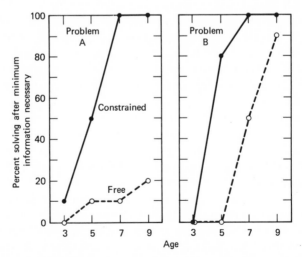

FIGURE 4.   Percent of children solving problems after obtaining the minimum informa-tion necessary for solution.

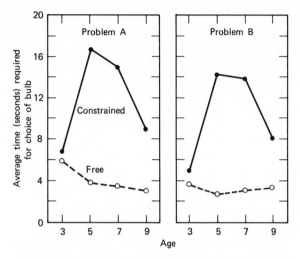

FIGURE 5.   Average time (seconds) required for choice of bulb.

rather constant. The sharp change is under conditions of imposed constraint, in the time needed to choose a next bulb that may be the last. Between three and five there is almost a tripling in the time taken. But interestingly enough, while the three-year-old takes just about the same amount of time to choose, whether free or constrained, the five-year-old requires more than four times as much time under the constrained condition than when he is free to choose. The same thing holds for the seven-year-old. By age nine, however, the difference between constrained and free choice (for this set of problems) begins to diminish very strikingly. For now the nine-year-old is already operating with internal constraints, which are thoroughly mastered; these internalized operations ran off as smoothly and effectively as the externalized ones employed by the "free" nines.

The three patterns—that of the threes, of the fives and sevens, and of the nines—provide vignettes of the strategies: Search, Successive Pattern Matching, and Information Selection. In Search, with no guidance from the alternative models, time is no consideration. One searches, and the time needed is simply the time to pick a handy bulb to press. In Pattern Matching, the free condition is simply a matter of choosing bulbs that are on-pattern, and this the fives and sevens have mastered. Constraint forces them to use a strategy which they control rather poorly and do not use habitually. But by age nine Information Selection has become second nature enough, and the times required under both free and constrained conditions are again within a close range.

INDIVIDUAL STRATEGIES

Consider the three strategies in detail as we find them, not in "average data," but in the behavior of individual children. Each strategy can be described in terms of certain hallmarks.

Search:

a. bulb presses are independent of the model provided;

b. off-pattern bulbs are as likely to be pressed as on-pattern ones;

c. since no particular bulbs are recognized as informative, this strategy frequently fails to lead to a solution.

Successive Pattern Matching:

a. bulbs are pressed that are part of the pattern suggested by one or both of the models;

b. on-pattern presses are no more likely to be informative than redundant, and the one type is no more likely to come first than the other;

c. subjects begin by pressing bulbs of one pattern, whether or not these bulbs will permit discrimination between diagrams;

d. an attempt is usually made to trace out the entire pattern;

e. if a pattern is tried and found to work it may be selected even without considering the alternative;

f. because the entire pattern is tested, subjects require a larger number of trials to solution;

g. because the problem is externalized, the time required per trial is relatively small.

Information Selection:

a. bulbs on-pattern are pressed more than those off-pattern;

b. on-pattern informative bulbs are pressed earlier and oftener than on-pattern redundant ones;

c. because the problem is internalized, the amount of time required per trial is relatively large.

Using these criteria, we sorted the children into three categories according to their strategies on the two problems: Search, Pattern Matching, and Information Selection. Because eighty-five of our ninety-five subjects followed the same strategy on the two problems (itself a rather striking tribute to their strategic consistency) there was little difficulty in classification. For the others, their entire protocols, involving all problems, were examined by two independent judges using the criteria to determine the prevailing strategy. They agreed 94 percent of the time in classifying one hundred eighty problems done by subjects. In the few cases of disagreement, the protocols were re-examined until an agreement was reached.

The picture that emerges is very much in congruence with what came from the analysis of group data. There are plainly marked and reliable changes that occur with growth (Figure 6). One of the most striking changes takes place between three and five, as we have already noted, and it is closely related to the growth of Pattern Matching. But there are also some striking changes between five and seven, best illustrated by the peaking and decline of Pattern Matching around the fifth year and the surge forward of Information Selection (under constraint) at age seven.

There is a striking oppositeness about Pattern Matching as the strategy of the free-choice condition and of Information Selection under constraint. Among the fives, for example, all those who used Pattern Matching in the free situation succeeded, though it just begins to appear at this age. And among the sevens, when Information Selection makes its first appearance under constrained conditions, all who use it also succeed.

In sum, then, the close study of individual records gives a realistic concreteness to the picture of strategies we have been drawing. The strategies are there; they are programs for finding and using information in certain specified ways: by encounter, by the search for matching images, and by the analysis of information (in the information-theory sense of that word).

STRATEGIES ON A COMPLEX PROBLEM

The performance of children on the more complex problem (Problem C) should provide some indication of the viability of the three strategies. Recall

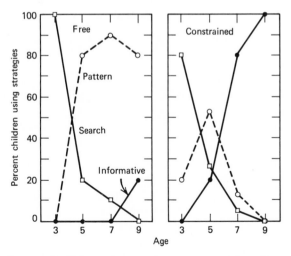

FIGURE 6. Percent of children using search, pattern, or informative strategies on simple problems.

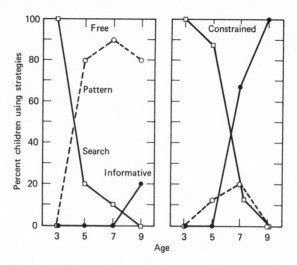

FIGURE 7. Percent of children using search, pattern, or informative strategies on complex problem.

that Problem C presented three alternatives, in which all the models partially overlap one another. At least two decisions in selecting bulbs are needed for a correct solution.

Using the criteria already described, we classified the individual protocols on Problem C according to strategy. Performance on this problem was very similar to that on simpler problems, the only difference being that fewer younger subjects develop Information Selection in response to the constraint condition (Figure 7). In the main, the children do about as well as on the simpler problems—all over five reaching a solution under free conditions, and none under that age. Pattern Matching, interestingly enough, leads to the solution of the complex problem just as well as it did for the simpler problems. But the Information-Selection strategy used under constraint fares less well: at age five only 30 percent reach the solution of the complex problem under constraint, as compared to 70 percent under comparable conditions with the simpler problems (Table 2). Pattern Matching, once developed, seems sufficiently viable to deal with more complex problems. The Information Selection, on the other hand, is somewhat easily swamped by our increasing the number of sequential decisions necessary for solution. This finding suggests in what measure the strategy of Information Selection is not yet consolidated among the middle groups of children.

As might be expected from this result, the complex problem produces much the same kind of on-pattern responding at the different ages (Figure 8), again underlining the viability of Pattern Matching under complex conditions. Again, what suffers is the Information-Selection strategy, and this can

TABLE 2

Percent of Children Solving Problems and the Median Number of Bulbs
Pressed before Solution

Age	Condition	Problem A		Problem B		Problem C	
		Trials	Percent of Success	Trials	Percent of Success	Trials	Percent of Success
9	Free	5.0	100%	6.0	100%	9.5	100%
	Constrained	1.0	100%	1.0	100%	2.0	93%
7	Free	5.5	100%	9.0	100%	11.5	100%
	Constrained	1.0	100%	1.0	100%	4.0	93%
5	Free	8.0	100%	11.0	100%	15.0	100%
	Constrained	4.0	80%	7.0	70%	—	30%
3	Free	—	40%	—	30%	—	0%
	Constrained	—	30%	—	20%	—	0%

be seen on the same figure in the failure of the fives to concentrate their on-
pattern choices on the informative bulbs.

The difficulty of Information Selection is illustrated by one child who
looked at the three alternative models and selected an informative bulb on
the first press. This bulb provided the information that the correct answer
must be M1 or M2. He then selected a second informative bulb, this one providing the information that either M2 or M3 was correct. But the child had

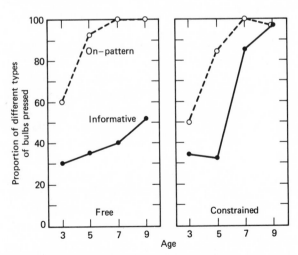

FIGURE 8.   Proportion of different types of bulbs pressed that are "on-pattern" or informative on the complex problem.

now forgotten that his first bulb press had already led him to exclude M3. His inability to combine the information from the two presses led him to press four other informative bulbs before he solved the problem. Again, it would seem that the location and utilization of information might best be considered independently. One is struck, moreover, by the self-same difficulty of children working a two-step information problem such as this one, and that of children trying to use the information obtained in playing the game of Twenty Questions. The structure for combining information sequentially is either not yet developed or it is simply not well enough managed.

SOME OBSERVATIONS AND CONCLUSIONS

One is struck, looking at the behavior of our children in the large, by the fact that there is a very large gap between what children conventionally do and what they are capable of doing. Constraining the children to a more careful use of information leads them to far more sophisticated strategies than we would have anticipated from observing their behavior in the absence of this constraint. It is hard to find problems that are impossible for a child, given some coaching and some external aids.

What did the strategies require? The first requisite for the development of any appropriate strategy was the ability to "map" alternative models on the bulb board. Doing this may be more complex than simply seeing the correspondence between a model and the board. Could children have an image of the model that they could impose on the board without verbally encoding it? To some extent, yes, but to a limited degree. If a model is set near the board, those children not capable of mapping will press the bulb closest to a red mark on the model. The result can be a reversal: a red mark at the *bottom* of a model *over* the board may lead a young child to press the nearest bulb at the *top* of the board. Mapping itself is something of a skill, as we know from Piaget's work (1962). But coaching can help the child, though seemingly through the intervention of language. If a three-year-old can be led to say "These are at the bottom," in describing the model, he can move to the bottom of the bulb board without error. Parts of the model that are easily encoded in terms of "top" or "bottom" or "this side" can then be handled, even if the model is set at some distance from the board. With this aid, the child on occasion can even copy the model, though it has been presented and then removed. It is interesting that children have an easier time finding patterns that are inscribed on the outer border of the bulb board than located in interior columns and rows—suggesting the extent to which they use such landmarks.

It seems, then, that the child must learn some way of abstracting a model of a thing from the real thing—must learn to use a "diagram" to guide his action. Minskava (Luria [1961], note p. 36) has shown that three- and four-year-olds can do tasks requiring the practical manipulation of simple levers to reach a goal inaccessible directly. When the whole system is presented in picture form, however, the children are helpless. And there is ample evidence, too, that diagrams and even pictures require practice before they can be used as substitutes for the "real thing."

A child may grasp correspondence between board and model and yet be unable to press the bulbs depicted in the model. One four-year-old was shown a model having a T-pattern. He correctly identified the places on the model that stood for light and those that did not. Asked to press the bulbs on the board that would light up, he was not guided at all by the model. When the experimenter asked, "Do these come on?" indicating a row on the model, the child would say, "I'll see," and he would press the indicated bulbs. Indeed, we have cases where the child can clearly discriminate whether a model corresponds or does not correspond to the pattern of lights on the bulb board—with all the relevant lights lit up simultaneously or successively. Yet, the child is unable to *reproduce* the pattern depicted on the model. Obviously (as in speech) there is a striking difference between *recognition* and *reproduction*. (Indeed, it is particularly noteworthy with a diagonal pattern which young children cannot reproduce until around the fifth year. The reasons for this lag are currently being studied in detail by the present author.)

So there must obviously be not only the achievement of recognition of correspondence between a model and its referent, but also an achievement of the ability to reproduce. Both of these seem necessary if the child is to go from Search to Pattern Matching. To put it in the language of the opening chapters, there must develop some interplay between the image and the action it must guide and this interaction does not come automatically.

To move on to Information Selection requires, as we have already seen, a large step forward. Specifically, it involves being able to deal not with one image at a time, but rather with the properties or features of several images simultaneously. Such a step corresponds to the development in the Twenty Questions game when children are able to ask "indirect" questions about constraints, rather than testing hypotheses directly. Each depends on two achievements—the first being the mastery of hierarchical organization, the second being "feature analysis." Of the first much has already been said. To deal with a set of patterns "informationally," the child must conceptualize them in terms of the properties that distinguish between members of the set. Such a conceptualization is necessarily hierarchical, for information that leads one to accept one subset and reject another then leads one to the use of a feature to distinguish further among the remaining alternatives.

To understand the construction of such a hierarchy, one must also consider the question of "distinctive features." When a child begins to use Information Selection, he is also beginning to select distinguishing features that can discriminate between a set of alternatives. To construct a hierarchy, he must isolate the defining features that fit its structure. It is at this point that the child's mental processes can be said to be guided *not* by individual events but by the ensemble of possibilities of which they are members. E. R. Gibson (1966) and Garner (1966) take it for granted that this is characteristic of cognitive processes generally. We take the position here that it is a mode of functioning that develops only gradually and only when ikonic representation has been buttressed by the kinds of symbolic processes we have discussed here. It requires conceptualization of the domain of alternatives.

A word, too, about the importance of externally imposed constraints in leading children to improve their strategies, particularly to adopt Information Selection. It appears that intellectual or informational efficiency is willingly sacrificed for economy of effort. It is misleading to assume a close relation between what a child tends to do and what his mind is capable of. Note, however, that this tendency to economy leaves adequate reserve for sudden complexities, such as required in our Problem C, whereas the more efficient but demanding strategy was easily swamped by added complexity. The mind appears automatically to break the information into "chunks" sized appropriately to its level of development. Crutchfield's (1964) success in training children to use information ("clues") suggests, however, that there are many educational implications of this issue.

Finally, then, the component skills of mapping, locating, and utilizing information change with the growth of the child's powers of representation. It is their orchestration that produces a shift with growth from Search, through Pattern Matching, to Information Selection, a development that bears striking resemblance to performance in earlier experiments—to the hypothesis testing and constraint locating in Twenty Questions, and to the progress from pure guessing, through estimated guessing, to constraint guessing in the perceptual tasks. What is plain, however, is that while the component skills of mapping, locating, and using information are orchestrated, they seem to have an independent course of development that remains to be studied.

References

Bruner, J. S. The course of cognitive growth. *American Psychologist*, 1964, **19**, 1–15.

Bruner, J. S., Goodnow, J. J., & Austin, G. A. *A study of thinking.* New York: Wiley, 1956.

Crutchfield, R. Instructing children in creative thinking. Paper read at 72nd Annual Convention, American Psychologists Association, Los Angeles, 1964.

Garner, W. R. To perceive is to know. *American Psychologist*, 1966, **21**, 11–19.

Gibson, Eleanor J. Perceptual development and the reduction of uncertainty. Paper read at Int. Congress of Psychol., Moscow, U.S.S.R., 1966.

Kuhlman, C. Visual imagery in children. Unpublished doctoral dissertation, Harvard University, 1960.

Luria, A. R. *The role of speech in the regulation of normal and abnormal behavior*. New York: Pergamon, 1961.

Piaget, J., & Inhelder, B. *Le développement des quantités physiques chez l'enfant* (2nd revised edition). Neuchâtel, Switzerland: Delachaux & Niestlé, 1962.

18. DISCRIMINATION LEARNING SET IN CHILDREN AS A FUNCTION OF IQ AND MA[1]

Susan Harter

In order to examine the relative contribution of IQ and MA to learning set (LS) formation in children, a factorial design with three levels of IQ (70, 100, 130) and three levels of MA (5, 7, 9) was employed. All Ss were given the ten 4-trial object discrimination LS problems daily until they reached criterion. Significant (p < 0.001) independent effects were discovered for both IQ and MA, indicating that the higher the level of both MA and IQ, the more rapid the LS formation; however, the relationship between CA and LS was negligible. The findings emphasize the need to employ some combination of IQ and MA as the best predictor of LS performance. In general, developmentalists have focused on the role of MA and have failed to appreciate the significance of the IQ. A theoretical interpretation of the role which both of these variables play in learning performance is offered, and it is suggested that the complex nature of the LS

SOURCE. *Journal of Experimental Child Psychology*, 1965, **2**, 31–43.

[1] This study was carried out while the author was an NIMH Fellow, and was partially supported by research grant MH-06809 from NIMH, United States Public Health Service. The author would like to thank Edward Zigler for his critical advice and assistance during every phase of this study. She would like to express further appreciation to Billey Levinson for her encouragement, her insightful comments, and her sponsorship of the author at EPA, 1963, where an earlier version of this paper was presented. Thanks are extended to the following school administrators for their cooperation: Miss Eveline Omwake, Director of the Yale Child Study Center Nursery School; Miss Evelyn Eastman, Director of Leila Day Nurseries; Mr. John Wesolowski, Principal of Scranton School; Miss Iannitti, Whitney Day Nursery; and Mrs. Janet Swibelius, Director of the Woodbridge Association for Retarded Children.

342

solution makes this task ideal for the simultaneous investigation of both IQ and MA effects.

Since Harlow's (1949) initial investigations of learning set (LS), the phenomenon has received considerable attention from comparative psychologists. Research has revealed phylogenetic as well as ontogenetic differences in a variety of infrahuman species. From both types of evidence, Harlow (1959) has concluded that LS learning is dependent upon capacity factors transcending those needed for single-problem learning.

More recently, child psychologists have begun to explore the developmental implications of LS phenomena. Early studies were directed towards the demonstration that children could form a learning set (Kuenne, 1949; Hayes, Thompson, and Hayes, 1953; Shepard, 1957). Subsequent investigations related LS formation to such often employed indicators of cognitive functioning as CA, MA, and IQ (Barnett and Cantor, 1957; Ellis, 1958; Ellis and Sloan, 1959; Girardeau, 1959; House and Zeaman, 1958; Kaufman and Peterson, 1958; Koch and Meyer, 1959; Levinson and Reese, 1963; Stevenson and Swartz, 1958; Wischner, Braun, and Patton, 1962). For the most part, these studies compared normal and retarded populations and verified that LS formation is superior in *S*s having higher mental ability as defined by either MA or IQ. A shortcoming of these studies has been their failure to assess the relative contribution of MA and IQ. The built-in interdependence of these variables has made it difficult to determine whether they influence LS formation independently.

Typically LS performance has been related to MA, the most frequently employed measure of the child's level of cognitive functioning, while IQ has been relatively ignored. Recent investigators (Girardeau, 1959; House and Zeaman, 1960) have emphasized the need for exploring the relationship between IQ and MA in the LS process. However, no study has yet employed a design in which both IQ and MA were varied independently, a procedure which is possible, provided one is unconcerned with the relationship which each of these variables has to CA. The present study is an attempt to evaluate the relative effects of IQ and MA, as well as their interaction, in LS formation.

The utilization of institutionalized retardates in studies employing retarded and normal populations has led to the confounding of level of cognitive functioning and institutionalization effects. Recent studies have indicated that institutionalization is a significant variable in the performance of the retarded (Kaufman, 1963; Lyle, 1960; Stevenson and Zigler, 1957; Zigler, 1963; Zigler and Williams, 1963). In order to avoid any such confounding effects, the present study employed only children living with their parents. In order to provide a broader range for the IQ variable, the design also included a high IQ level. The performance of such children on LS tasks has not been investigated systematically.

METHOD

Design. The 3×3 factorial design is represented in Fig. 1. The actual characteristics of the nine groups are presented in Table 1. Within such a

		IQ Level		
		70	100	130
MA Level	5	CA = 7	CA = 5	CA = 3½
		X̄ = 51.8	X̄ = 30.9	X̄ = 18.8
	7	CA = 10	CA = 7	CA = 5
		X̄ = 38.2	X̄ = 23.8	X̄ = 16.0
	9	CA = 13	CA = 9	CA = 7
		X̄ = 18.1	X̄ = 18.2	X̄ = 10.8

FIGURE 1. Experimental design, approximate CA, and mean criterion score for each group.

design IQ and MA are uncorrelated, and CA varies across IQ and MA levels. As can be seen in Fig. 1, not only can main effects of IQ and MA be determined, but selected comparisons can also be made between groups that are equated on CA but differ on MA and IQ.

Subjects. Each group contained nine Ss. Of the 81 Ss, 42 were boys and 39 were girls. The 100 IQ and 130 IQ Ss were obtained from nursery and public schools in New Haven, Connecticut. Their IQ's were based on scores obtained from the Ammons Picture Vocabulary Test, Form A. The three low IQ groups were also from the New Haven school system but attended special classes. Stanford-Binet scores were available for these Ss. All of the low IQ Ss would be conventionally categorized as familial retardates.

Apparatus. The apparatus was a modification of the Wisconsin General Testing Apparatus. It consisted of a 24×13-inch tray having two wells ½ inch deep and 8 inches apart. An opaque screen was lowered to conceal the tray from the S between trials.

The stimulus objects were a collection of 200 "junk" stereometric objects that were assigned to 100 pairs by a random procedure. One object of each pair was arbitrarily designated as the "correct" object. Marbles served as token rewards and were placed in one of the two wells concealed by the stimulus object. A 6×12-inch 30-hole marble board was used by the Ss

TABLE 1

Characteristics and Criterion Scores of the Nine Groups

Group[a]	N		IQ		MA		CA		Criterion score	
	Boys	Girls	Mean	SD	Mean (years)	SD	Mean (years)	SD	Mean	SD
L-5	4	5	71.4	8.9	4.9	0.63	7.0	0.26	51.8	10.37
L-7	5	4	68.9	7.7	7.0	1.17	10.1	0.77	38.2	10.23
L-9	5	4	70.0	8.7	9.1	0.93	13.2	1.55	18.1	10.11
N-5	5	4	103.9	6.2	5.2	0.44	5.0	0.69	30.9	6.22
N-7	5	4	104.2	4.8	7.2	0.25	6.9	0.36	23.8	11.05
N-9	4	5	102.3	9.7	9.3	0.67	9.1	0.40	18.2	4.20
H-5	4	5	137.1	7.1	4.8	0.46	3.4	0.39	18.8	8.75
H-7	5	4	135.7	8.9	6.7	0.69	4.9	0.36	16.0	4.64
H-9	5	4	132.8	2.9	9.4	0.27	7.1	0.33	10.8	5.24

[a] L, N, and H refer to low, normal, and high IQ levels, respectively, and 5, 7, and 9 refer to the MA levels.

to hold the marbles they found. This marble board was placed to the left of the apparatus. Colored decals were used as prizes. Children in the three youngest CA groups were given the decal of their choice to take with them, while the older children put their decal opposite their name on a "good-player chart."

Procedure. Children were taken individually from the classroom to a small experimental room which contained a table and two chairs. The *S* was seated in front of the apparatus and the *E* sat behind it. With the opaque screen raised so that the *S* could see both the *E* and the tray, he was instructed as follows:

> See these two holes? (*E* points.) I am going to hide a marble in *one* of them, and then cover up each hole with blocks. So you can't see where I am hiding it, I am going to bring this down. (*E* demonstrates how the screen is raised and lowered.) I will hide the marble and then raise this. You may look under one block each time. We are going to do this several times so you will have many chances. When you find a marble you may take it out of the hole here and put it in one of these other holes in this board. (*E* demonstrates and then lets the *S* do it.) See, they just fit! Now I want you to find as many marbles as you can. If you find enough, you may choose one of these pretty stickers to keep. (The older children were told that if they found enough marbles, they could put the sticker opposite their name on a good-player chart.)

The first trial began when the opaque screen was raised and the *S* was presented with the two stimulus objects on the tray.

A standard discrimination LS procedure was employed. A series of four-trial discrimination problems was presented to each *S* daily until he reached criterion. Each problem involved a separate pair of objects. Within each four-trial problem one object was designated as the positive stimulus, and a correct choice was indicated by the presence of a marble under this object. The position of the correct object was varied from left to right in a prede-termined balance sequence. Of the 16 possible left-right sequences for a four-trial problem, two of these, RRRR and LLLL, were omitted. The remaining sequences were randomly ordered into five ten-problem blocks. A noncorrec-tion procedure was used, and the trial was terminated by lowering the opaque screen after the *S* had displaced one of the objects.

Daily sessions of ten problems (40 trials) were continued until the *S* reached the criterion for LS formation: five successive problems in which no more than one error was made on trials 2, 3, and 4 of all five problems, i.e., 93% correct responding over those 15 trials.

RESULTS

No S required more than 7 days to reach criterion. Preliminary analyses revealed no significant sex effects; for the purpose of clarity, the sex variable is not included in the following analyses.

Nature of Acquisition of Learning Set

The acquisition curves of the nine groups are presented on the left in Fig. 2. These group curves suggest that LS is acquired gradually with performance improving over successive blocks of problems. These curves are actually misleading since they do not reflect the nature of the acquisition of LS by individual Ss. An examination of the acquisition curves of individual Ss generally reveals chance or slightly above chance performance on the early problems and then an abrupt rise to criterion. The nature of this acquisition can be seen if the group data are plotted as backward learning curves (Hayes, 1959). These curves, presented on the right in Fig. 2, are obtained by plotting performance backward from the criterion rather than forward to criterion. They reflect the two-stage acquisition process found in individual subject curves. Furthermore, they reveal that the accelerated rate of learning as Ss near criterion is similar for all groups. The differences between groups are reflected in the length of the initial phase where the rate of improvement is exceedingly slight. The discontinuity of learning reflected in these curves is obscured in typically plotted mean performance curves such as those on the left in Fig. 2.

Analysis of Number of Problems to Criterion

The mean values of problems to criterion, given in Fig. 1, are plotted as a family of curves in Fig. 3. On the left in Fig. 3, mean problems to criterion are presented as a function of IQ level. As the IQ level increases, LS acquisition is accelerated, and generally this effect is demonstrated at each MA level. These curves are similar to those generated as a function of MA level, presented on the right in Fig. 3. (Employing errors to criterion rather than problems to criterion resulted in almost identical curves.)

An IQ $\times$ MA analysis of variance of problems to criterion revealed significant IQ ($F_{2/72} = 37.84$, $p < 0.001$) MA ($F_{2/72} = 28.60$, $p < 0.001$), and interaction ($F_{1/72} = 5.55$, $p < 0.001$) effects. As can be seen in Fig. 3, the interpretation of the significant interaction depends on whether one focuses on the MA level or the IQ level. If one focuses on the MA, the significant interaction is due to the fact that the differences between MA groups at the 70 IQ level is greater than the difference at the other two IQ levels. If one focuses on the IQ, the significant interaction would be attributed to the smaller difference between IQ groups found at the 9-year MA level as compared to the other two MA levels. In either case, this interaction is primarily due to the fact that the performance of the group with an IQ of 70 and an MA of nine is better

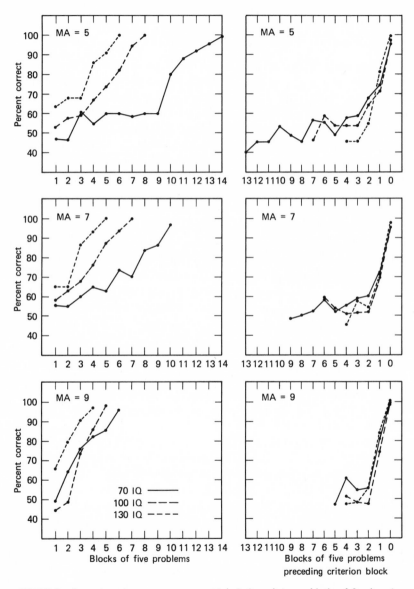

FIGURE 2. Percentage correct responses on trials 2, 3, and 4 over blocks of five learning set problems. Left: conventional acquisition curves; right: backward learning curves.

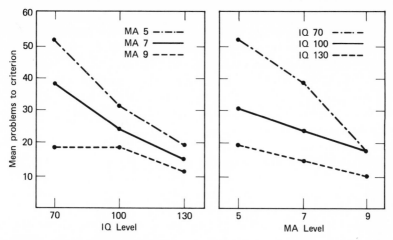

FIGURE 3. Mean problems to criterion as a function of IQ, for each of three MA levels, and MA for each of three IQ levels.

than would be expected from the discovered main effects of IQ and MA. It is of interest to note that the criterion score of this group is exactly the same as that of the group with an IQ of 100 and an MA of nine. In general, the significant interaction suggests a ceiling effect operating at the upper IQ and MA levels of performance.

One-way analysis of variance tests were performed for each IQ and MA level. Employing a one-tailed test, each of these six comparisons was significant beyond the 0.05 level. The least significant p values were found at MA level nine ($p < 0.04$) and IQ level 130 ($p < 0.035$) which further suggests a ceiling effect at the upper levels of both IQ and MA.

The product moment correlations obtaining among all variables, over all Ss, are presented in Table 2. The correlations between mean problems to criterion and IQ and MA were —0.57 and —0.47, respectively, results which are in keeping with the findings of the two-way analysis of variance reported above. In contrast to these substantial correlations was the negligible relation-

TABLE 2

Correlations Among All Variables

	MA	CA	Problems to Criterion
IQ	0.03	—0.71*	—0.57*
MA		0.64*	—0.47*
CA			0.04

* $p < 0.001$.

ship between CA and problems to criterion $(r = 0.04)$. The correlation between IQ and MA was 0.03 which is to be expected since the design provided for this orthogonality. A multiple correlation of 0.73 was found where IQ and MA were used as predictors of problems to criterion. The multiple correlation found when IQ, MA, and CA were used as predictors was also 0.73, indicating that the effect of adding the CA variable as a predictor was negligible. A significance test of the contribution of CA yielded an $F < 1$.

Although no statistical comparisons were made between groups of the same CA, further examination of Fig. 1 reveals some interesting differences. For example, each of the three groups on the upper-left to lower-right diagonal represent CA level seven, although they differ from one another on both IQ and MA dimensions. It is within these groups that the two most extreme LS criterion scores were obtained; the slowest rate of acquisition, 51.8 mean problems to criterion, was found in the group with both the lowest MA and IQ, whereas the most rapid rate, only 10.8 problems to criterion, was found for the group with both the highest MA and IQ. The fact that the children in both groups were the same CA, i.e., seven, suggests that CA, per se, contributes very little to LS performance, and this is substantiated by the statistical evidence presented above.

Upon reaching criterion, each S was asked, "How can you tell where the marble will be every time?" Responses such as "It's always under the same one," "You stick to the same thing [S points to the stimulus object] all the time," and "You keep changing the marble with the same block" were accepted as correct verbalizations of the solution; replies such as "I just knew," and vague remarks such as "You put it there all the time" without reference to the fact that the marble was always under the same block for any given problem, were not acceptable. In general, the responses of those children who could not verbalize the solution were of the "I guessed" or "I don't know" variety rather than a faulty formulation of the solution.

These inquiry data indicated that 33.8% of the Ss demonstrated the ability to verbalize the solution. Although the N's were small, the frequency data were entered into a one-entry per cell MA $\times$ IQ analysis of variance. This analysis revealed that the MA effect was significant $(F_{2/4} = 7.26, p < 0.05)$ but the IQ effect was not $(F_{2/4} = 1.17)$. At MA levels five, seven, and nine, the percentage of children who could verbalize the solution was 11.1, 29.6, and 48.1% respectively.

DISCUSSION

The analysis of the process by which individual Ss acquire LS supports the view of Harlow (1959) that the LS solution is insightful in nature. The two-stage acquisition process found in the present study is reminiscent of the LS findings of Levinson and Reese (1963). These latter investigators, employing the model of Harlow (1959) as extended by Levine (1959) and Bowman (1963), viewed the insightful rapid acceleration near criterion as due to the elimination of specific error factors, i.e., erroneous hypotheses and strategies. Whatever the actual mechanism involved in LS formation, there is general agreement that such learning involves more complex processes, i.e., the ability to generalize, transfer information from problem to problem, form concepts, etc., than are required for the solution of single problems.

It is this complex nature of LS formation that makes it an ideal task for the investigation of such indicators of cognitive functioning as IQ, MA, and CA. Although the data indicate that for all Ss the terminal slopes of the learning curves are similar, the findings clearly demonstrate that the total number of problems required to form the learning set is influenced by both IQ and MA. It would appear, then, that these cognitive factors have their effect in determining the length of the presolution period, i.e., the number of problems required before the abrupt acceleration to criterion.

The magnitude of the relationship between MA and LS performance is similar to that reported by other investigators (Ellis and Sloan, 1959; Koch and Meyer, 1959). The significant IQ effect found is of special interest since the effects of IQ on LS performance have not been thoroughly examined. Indeed, the general relationship between IQ and performance on a variety of learning tasks has remained ambiguous (cf. House and Zeaman, 1960, for a discussion of this problem). A review of studies in which the IQ effect was examined (Girardeau, 1959; House and Zeaman, 1958; Martin and Blum, 1961) suggests that the possibility of finding an IQ effect is enhanced when a complex problem and a broad range of IQ's are employed. The clear IQ effect found in the present study may reflect the fact that these two conditions were met.

The finding that differences between the three IQ groups are less at MA level nine than at the lower levels is in keeping with the findings of Wischner et al. (1962) that the MA-LS relationship does not hold beyond an upper MA limit of eight. Given this relatively high MA, the LS problem becomes comparatively simple for the Ss and, as suggested earlier, with a simple problem the effects of IQ are attenuated or non-existent.

The negligible CA effect found in the present study is consistent with earlier findings (Ellis and Sloan, 1959; House and Zeaman, 1960). The near-zero correlation discovered is a critical finding since the interpretation that IQ and MA independently contribute to LS formation is based on the assumption that CA is unrelated to LS. In view of the negligible relationship obtained between LS and CA, one may conclude that variability in CA was neither a contributing nor a contaminating factor, and that interpretations based solely on IQ and MA are justifiable. This conclusion is quite similar to that advanced by House and Zeaman (1960).

Although CA has frequently been employed as a measure of cognitive level, the typical finding that older children learn faster than younger children does not justify the interpretation that faster learning is a function of CA. (See Zigler, 1963, who has pointed out the error in conceptualizing CA as a psychological variable.) The present study suggests that differences associated with CA actually reflect differences in MA, and that CA will predict learning ability only to the extent that CA is positively correlated with MA. As long as normal IQ Ss are employed, such a positive relationship will obtain. It is only in studies with retarded or superior Ss that the relative effects of CA and MA can be teased apart.

The finding that IQ independently affects LS formation is a troublesome one for developmental thinkers. Developmentalists have generally been content to employ the MA as the best measure of the developmental or cognitive level obtained by the child. While it is true that some (Kounin, 1948; Lewin, 1936) have argued that the IQ reflects certain formal characteristics of cognitive structure, developmental theorists in general have justified their neglect of IQ by pointing to the fact that the IQ in isolation has not been viewed as a very sound predictor of behavior. It is, in fact, difficult, if not impossible, to so employ the IQ. If one is dealing with a 2-year-old child having an IQ of 200 and an 8-year-old child having an IQ of 100, the IQ's alone tell us very little about the nature of the cognitive structures of these children or what they are capable of learning.

The implication of much developmental research is that learning ability increases as the MA increases, with no differences expected between groups of differing IQ's at the same MA level. In the present study this suggested MA-learning relationship was found; however, a significant IQ effect was also discovered. It would appear then that the best predictor of learning is some combination of IQ and MA level, much as has been suggested by House and Zeaman (1960). The role of IQ in this combination becomes understandable if it is viewed as a ratio which represents not only the slope of a life-time learning curve but also the rate of acquisition in many complex learning situations.

Such a position need not be conceptualized as antithetical to the conventional view of MA, and the following theoretical interpretation is suggested. Typically, when MA is taken as a developmental measure of cognitive level, this measure represents the amount of prior learning. To the extent that any new learning involves the combination and generalization of previously acquired habits and skills, MA level would be expected to predict speed of learning. This, in itself, is a researchable area of investigation.

However if, in addition, one takes the microgenetic view seriously, then the role of IQ may also be interpreted within a general developmental framework, as follows. By definition the high IQ child has advanced more rapidly than the average or low IQ child since his MA is higher than his CA. The interpretation advanced here is that if a child's IQ is regarded as an index of the relative speed with which he characteristically acquires new knowledge, then in any new learning situation, IQ should predict the speed with which the child can acquire new skills, strategies, or concepts. Thus we would expect the higher IQ child to solve a new problem more rapidly; for example, he should require fewer problems in the formation of a learning set.

Viewed in this way, the IQ represents more than a mathematical relationship between the child's MA and CA. Since learning occurs over time, one could argue that the faster learner is capable of learning a greater amount of material in a fixed period of time. Therefore, IQ may be interpreted as indirectly determining the child's MA level to the extent that it places limits on the amount of knowledge which he can acquire within that period of time. This role of IQ is intentionally highlighted here since the theoretical significance of this measure does not appear to have been fully appreciated.

It should be emphasized, however, that in the present study, since both IQ and MA are related to the same dependent measure, the data do not bear directly on the theoretical proposition that the relationship between MA and LS reflects the transfer of prior learning, whereas the contribution of IQ in the learning process reflects some capacity or speed factor. This interpretation poses a question for further research; however, it is clear that both IQ and MA have independent effects on the speed with which a learning set is acquired. The fact that these independent effects of IQ and MA have not emerged in previous investigations may reflect the use of more limited IQ and MA ranges, the selection of only one of these variables for manipulation, or the use of tasks which are less demanding than the LS problem.

References

Barnett, C. D., and Cantor, G. N. Discrimination set in defectives. *Amer. J. ment. Defic.*, 1957, **62**, 334–337.

Bowman, R. E. Discrimination learning set under intermittent and secondary reinforcement. *J. comp. physiol. Psychol.*, 1963, **56**, 429–434.

Ellis, N. R. Object-quality discrimination learning sets in mental defectives. *J. comp. physiol. Psychol.*, 1958, **51**, 79–81.

Ellis, N. R., and Sloan, W. Oddity learning as a function of mental age. *J. comp. physiol. Psychol.*, 1959, **52**, 228–230.

Girardeau, F. L. The formation of discrimination learning sets in mongoloid and normal children. *J. comp. physiol. Psychol.*, 1959, **52**, 566–570.

Harlow, H. F. The formation of learning sets. *Psychol. Rev.*, 1949, **56**, 51–65.

Harlow, H. F. Learning set and error factor theory. In S. Koch (Ed.), *Psychology: A study of science.* Vol. II. New York: McGraw-Hill, 1959. Pp. 492–537.

Hayes, K. J., and Pereboom, A. C. Artifacts in criterion-reference learning curves. *Psychol. Rev.*, 1959, **66**, 23–26.

Hayes, K. J., Thompson, R., and Hayes, C. Discrimination learning set in chimpanzees. *J. comp. physiol. Psychol.*, 1953, **46**, 99–104.

House, B. J., and Zeaman, D. Comparison of discrimination learning in normal and defective children. *Child Develpm.*, 1958, **29**, 411–416.

House, B. J., and Zeaman, D. Visual discrimination learning and intelligence in defectives of low mental age. *Amer. J. ment. Def.*, 1960, **65**, 51–58.

Kaufman, M. E. The formation of a learning set in institutionalized and non-institutionalized mental defectives. *Amer. J. ment. Def.*, 1963, **67**, 601–605.

Kaufman, M. E., and Peterson, W. M. Acquisition of a learning set by normal and mentally retarded children. *J. comp. physiol. Psychol.*, 1958, **51**, 619–621.

Koch, M. B., and Meyer, D. R. A relationship of mental age to learning set formation in the preschool child. *J. comp. physiol. Psychol.*, 1959, **52**, 387–389.

Kounin, J. Experimental studies of rigidity. I. The measurement of rigidity in normal and feebleminded persons. *Charact. & Pers.*, 1941, **9**, 499–508.

Kuenne, M. Reported in Harlow (1949).

Levine, M. A model of hypothesis behavior in discrimination learning set. *Psychol. Rev.*, 1959, **66**, 353–366.

Levinson, B., and Reese, H. W. Patterns of discrimination learning set in preschool children, fifth graders, college freshmen, and the aged. USDHEW Project No. 1059, 1963.

Lewin, K. *A dynamic theory of personality.* New York: McGraw-Hill, 1936.

Lyle, J. G. The effect of an institution environment upon the verbal development of imbecile children: The Brooklands residential family unit. *J. ment. Def. Res.*, 1960, **4**, 14–23.

Martin, W. E., and Blum, A. Inter-test generalization and learning in mentally normal and subnormal children. *J. comp. physiol. Psychol.*, 1961, **54**, 28–32.

Shepard, W. O. Learning set in preschool children. *J. comp. physiol. Psychol.*, 1957, **50**, 15–17.

Stevenson, H. W., and Swartz, J. W. Learning set in children as a function of intellectual level. *J. comp. physiol. psychol.*, 1958, **51**, 755–757.

Stevenson, H., and Zigler, E. Discrimination learning and rigidity in normal and feebleminded individuals. *J. Pers.*, 1957, **25**, 699–711.

Wischner, G. J., Braun, H. W., and Patton, R. A. Acquisition and long-term retention of an object-quality learning set by retarded children. *J. comp. physiol. Psychol.*, 1962, **55**, 518–523.

Zigler, E. Social deprivation and rigidity in the performance of feebleminded children. *J. abnorm. soc. Psychol.*, 1961, **62**, 413–421.

Zigler, E. Metatheoretical issues in developmental psychology. In M. Marx (Ed.), *Psychological theory.* 2nd edition. New York: Macmillan, 1963.

Zigler, E., and Williams, J. Institutionalization and the effectiveness of social reinforcement: A three year follow-up study. *J. abnorm. soc. Psychol.*, 1963, **66**, 197–205.

19. THE ROLE OF COMPREHENSION IN CHILDREN'S PROBLEM SOLVING[1]

Sandra L. Bem[2]

Two theoretical positions have been advanced to account for the failure of children younger than 5 years to solve a variety of problems: the production- and the mediation-deficiency hypotheses. This article explores a temporally prior deficiency, a failure of the child to comprehend the nature of the problem, to achieve an adequate representation of the problem's end state, the "problem as solved." This position is supported by evidence that providing children with end state representations enables them to solve problems previously failed. Additional experiments evaluated competing hypotheses concerning the actual problem-solving strategies employed. It is suggested that at least one training procedure previously interpreted as facilitating production or mediation may be reinterpreted as serving the more primitive instructional function of structuring the child's symbolic representation of the problem.

SOURCE. *Developmental Psychology*, 1970, **2**, 3, 351–358.

[1] This article is based on a doctoral dissertation submitted to the Department of Psychology, University of Michigan. The research was supported, in part, by the National Institute of Child Health and Human Development Grant HD 01368-02 to the Language Development Program, University of Michigan, and, in part, by National Science Foundation Grant GS 1452 to Carnegie-Mellon University. The author is grateful to David Birch for serving as advisor and to Daryl J. Bem for making critical comments on the manuscript. The author would also like to acknowledge Ann Taylor of Carnegie-Mellon's Child Development Laboratory and Florence Nydes of Rodef Shalom Nursery School for their assistance in providing subjects.

[2] Requests for reprints should be sent to author, Department of Psychology, Carnegie-Mellon University, Schenley Park, Pittsburgh, Pennsylvania 15213.

At approximately age 5, a change becomes apparent in the young child's problem-solving behavior. Whereas earlier he had been unable to respond appropriately on a variety of experimental tasks, at about age 5, he begins to respond intelligently and correctly, to simulate, as it were, the problem-solving behavior of the adult (Weir, 1964; White, 1965).

Two theoretical positions have been advanced to account for the child's earlier failures. The mediation-deficiency hypothesis (Reese, 1962) postulates an inability on the part of the young child to mediate or regulate his task behavior verbally, despite his ability to understand and to use the relevant words. The production-deficiency hypothesis (Flavell, Beach, & Chinsky, 1966; Moely, Olson, Halwes, & Flavell, 1969) postulates that the young child may fail to produce those words or instructions which could serve as potential mediators of his task behavior; the problem is not that his verbalizations have insufficient mediating or regulating power, but rather that he does not spontaneously produce relevant verbalizations in the first place.

These two hypotheses are not necessarily mutually exclusive. Rather, they suggest a two-stage problem-solving process in which the successful child produces a relevant verbalization which then, in turn, regulates his task behavior. Failure to solve a problem correctly could reflect a deficiency at either of the two stages.

In many problem contexts, however, it seems more appropriate to consider problem solving as a three-stage process: comprehension, production, and mediation. It is during the first stage, comprehension, that the child presumably discovers what verbalization or self-instruction to produce.

Previous investigators have not found it necessary to deal explicitly with the stage of comprehension because their experimental tasks permitted them to presuppose that once the child thought of producing, he would have no difficulty knowing what to produce. This would appear to be true, for example, in the memory tasks used to investigate the production deficiency, where "the problematical element . . . is precisely whether it will occur to . . . [the child] to rehearse [Moely et al., 1969, p 32]," that is, to produce.

The stage of task comprehension would appear to take on greater importance as the problems requiring solution become more complex, as the answer to the question of what to produce becomes less obvious. In such problems, the question of what to produce may thus be a stumbling block to problem solution even if the strategy of producing occurs to the child.

For a large class of problems, discovering what to produce, that is, discovering a strategy for problem solution, is contingent on comprehending the structure of the problem. This, in turn, typically requires the problem solver to achieve an internal representation of the problem's end state, of the problem as solved (cf. information-processing theorists such as Newell & Simon, 1963); that is, the individual usually cannot develop a strategy for problem solution unless he has some representation of the desired outcome in advance.

The present investigation explores the young child's problem-solving difficulties in a task which is sufficiently complex so that the question of what to produce becomes explicitly problematic. The first experiment seeks to demonstrate that a comprehension failure is responsible for the child's inability to solve this type of problem. The subsequent experiments attempt to clarify the nature of the successful strategy adopted by the child once comprehension has been achieved.

EXPERIMENT I

When a 4-year-old child is holding a red block and is instructed to, "Make it so that the red block is on top of the blue block," he is typically able to respond correctly. If he is holding the blue block when this instruction is given, he does not respond appropriately (Huttenlocher & Strauss, 1968).

This suggests that the young child may not understand a relational statement unless the grammatical subject of the instruction corresponds to the logical actor in the external situation. When the block that the child is asked to place is the grammatical subject of the relation (subject instruction), the two do correspond, and the task presents no problem. When the block that the child is asked to place is the grammatical object of the relation (object instruction), that correspondence is absent, and the child seems unable to comprehend the meaning of the instruction. If, as the hypothesis suggests, the child's difficulty with an object instruction does result from his failure to comprehend the nature of the desired end state, then it should be possible to eliminate his difficulty experimentally by providing him with an accurate representation of that end state.

Method

Procedure. Eight middle-class nursery school children whose mean age was 4 years and 2 months (4–2) served as subjects (range 3–4 to 4–6). Three were male and five were female.

The basic task required each child to place one of eight colored blocks (a mobile block) either above or below a second block already fixed by the experimenter on the middle shelf of a ladder so as to construct the configuration specified by the experimenter's instruction. Two classes of problems were given: (*a*) subject instructions, in which the grammatical subject of the experimenter's instruction corresponded to the mobile block; and (*b*) object instructions, in which the grammatical object of the experimenter's instruction corresponded to the mobile block. Two types of relational terms, on top of and under, were used within each class of problem. Thus, in a situation with the blue block fixed and the red block mobile, the child could be given either a subject instruction. "Make it so that the red block is on top of [under] the blue block"; or an object instruction, "Make it so that the blue block is on top of [under] the red block."

Each test consisted of 16 problems, 8 subject instructions and 8 object instructions. Color pairs of blocks were systematically chosen for each instruction so that no color pair would appear twice on any test and so that no two tests would be alike. Each subject attended as many sessions as necessary for his training and testing to be completed. It should be noted that each subject was his own control, and that each subject provided a complete replication of the experiment.

Pretests. Three pretests were administered. Pretest 1 replicated the Huttenlocher and Strauss (1968) experiment by asking the subject to put his block wherever he thought it should go.

Pretest 2 imposed a delay on the subject's response. The subject was instructed to take his time, to think very hard about the instruction, and to wait until he was absolutely certain he was correct before putting his block into the ladder. This kind of delay instruction has facilitated complex problem solving by young children in other task environments (Olson, 1966), and White (1965) has argued that cognitive responses, which tend to be correct, require a longer latency period than do associative responses, which tend to be incorrect.

Pretest 3 attempted to induce the subject to verbalize. The subject was instructed to state aloud, prior to block placement, where he was planning to put his block. This pretest should facilitate the subject's performance if his difficulties are due solely to the fact that it has not spontaneously occurred to him to verbalize.

Comprehension Training. Any subject who did not respond correctly to at least 80% of both subject and object instructions during the three pretests underwent comprehension training. After the subject had been given an instruction, but before he had the opportunity to place his block, the experimenter showed him a ladder in which the blocks had already been correctly arranged. The experimenter's instruction thus took the following form, "Make it so that the red block is on top of the blue block, so that your ladder looks like this. See: red on top of blue." The experimenter allowed the subject to look at the display ladder for a moment, but he removed the ladder and repeated the instruction before the subject was allowed to place his block. Sixteen training trials were administered, and a posttest followed immediately. It should be noted that this comprehension-training instruction was identical to the instruction of Pretest 1 with the sole exception that it also provided the subject with a visual representation of the problem's end state.

Transfer and Retention Tests. Following the three block pretests, but before comprehension training, two transfer pretests were administered. These used toy trucks on a Masonite road and they represent a modification of a task used by Huttenlocher, Eisenberg, and Strauss (1968). The first task required the subject to "make it so that the red truck is in front [in back] of the blue truck." The second task required him to "make it so that the red truck is pushing [pulling] the blue truck."

A posttest on the front-back truck task was administered on the day following the block posttest. One week later, the subject was presented with three final tests, each containing eight instructions. Both the block task and the frontback truck task were included as tests of retention, and the push-pull posttest was administered as a final test of transfer.

Results

Pretests.   Figure 1 displays the results of all block tests for the seven out of eight subjects who required comprehension training. As seen in the composite graph, during Pretest 1, subjects placed their block into the correct slot on 82% of those trials when it corresponded to the subject of the experimenter's instruction, as compared to only 43% of those trials when it corresponded to the object of the experimenter's instruction. This difference was significant[3] ($p = .02$); and it replicated the Huttenlocher and Strauss (1968) finding that it is easier for young children to place an item when it is the grammatical subject rather than the grammatical object of a relation. The Huttenlocher and Strauss results were further replicated in that the average response latency for correct block placement was longer for object instructions (4.36 seconds) than for subject instructions (3.13 seconds). This difference was significant ($p = .02$).

Figure 1 also reveals that subjects did not show any improvement in performance during either Pretest 2 or Pretest 3. The percentage of correct responses did not change significantly when subjects were required to delay before responding or when they were required to state aloud where they were planning to put their block.

Comprehension Training.   As illustrated in Figure 1, comprehension training was successful. Providing subjects with correct end state representations enabled them to solve new problems when representations were not provided.[4] Following comprehension training, there was no longer a significant difference between the percentage of correct subject responses and that

---

[3] All significance levels reported in this article are based on two-tailed randomization tests (Siegel, 1956).

[4] The possibility that the delay and verbalization pretests may have interacted with comprehension training to produce correct posttest performance is weakened by the results of Experiment III, described later, which replicates the success of comprehension training in the absence of such pretests.

of correct object responses. Furthermore, subjects achieved significantly more correct object responses after training than they had on any of the three pretests ($p = .02$ in all three comparisons). On the average, subjects correctly executed 93% of the object instructions after training, as compared to only 43% before training. Finally, Figure 1 reveals that subjects responded perfectly to both subject and object instructions on the retention test 1 week later.

Comprehension training enabled subjects to respond correctly not only on the training task, but on the two transfer tasks as well. Five out of seven subjects responded perfectly on both the front-back and the push-pull post-tests, whereas on the corresponding pretests, they had correctly executed only 60% and 23% of the object instructions, respectively.

EXPERIMENT II

The results of Experiment I suggest that the child's initial difficulty was the result of a comprehension failure. Providing the child with end state representations apparently enabled him to discover what to produce, that is, to initiate a strategy for problem solution. The nature of that strategy needs now to be clarified.

Huttenlocher and Strauss (1968) have proposed that the successful subject uses a linguistic strategy: "the form of E's statement must be coordinated with the extralinguistic situation in order to be understood. . . . S must transform the statement and make . . . [his block] the subject in order to understand it [p. 303]." According to this hypothesis, then, if the child is holding the red block and is given the instruction, "Make it so that the blue block is on top of the red block," he should find it necessary to transform that into its semantic equivalent, "Make it so that the red block is under the blue block."

This hypothesis implies that the subject attempts to interpret the instruction as an action statement directly dictating the placement of the block that he is holding in his hand. If this is the case, then the grammatical subject of the instruction must correspond to that block in order for the subject to respond correctly. Therefore, if subjects have adopted the linguistic strategy after comprehension training, they should find it necessary to perform a semantic transformation on every object instruction, but on no subject instruction.

The linguistic hypothesis is attractive, for it is easy to imagine how the comprehension training in Experiment I might have served as an indirect device for teaching subjects to make the proposed transformation. That is, one effect of training may have been to show subjects the semantic basis for the relevant transformation, for example, that "red on top of blue" is the same as "blue under red"; and in this way, to induce them to adopt the

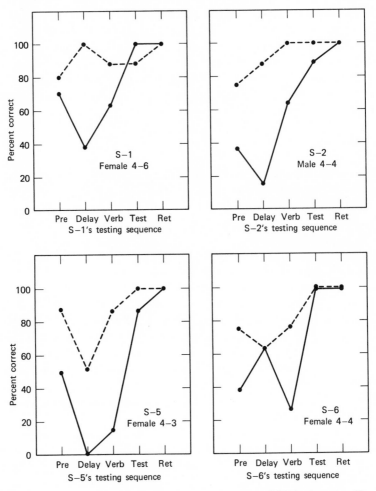

FIGURE 1.   The responses of individual subjects on all tests of block placement. (Pre =
Pretest I; Delay = Delay Pretest; Verb = Verbalization Pretest; Test = Posttest; Ret
= Retention Test; ———— = object instructions; - - - - - = subject instructions.)

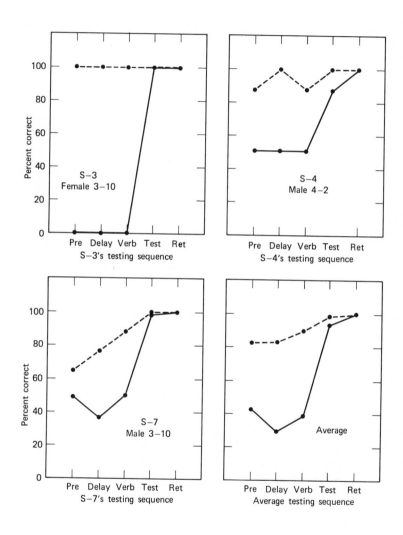

strategy of performing a transformation in order to solve object instructions.

The following procedure was designed to assess whether or not subjects were performing the proposed semantic transformation on object instructions. The procedure rests on the assumption that if a transformation has been performed, the transformed string should be more readily available for verbalization than the nontransformed string.

Method

After each subject had completed comprehension training during Experiment I, he underwent a series of tests for learning and transfer. As described earlier, subjects responded almost perfectly on each of these tests. Subjects were allowed to execute a response, and then they were asked to describe the configuration they had just constructed: "And what does that look like to you?" The experimenter noted whether or not the subject's description represented a transformation of the experimental instruction.

Results

When the subject was asked to describe the pile of blocks he had just constructed, his description tended to be in the same form as the original instruction: 77% of all subjects' descriptions retained the form of the original instruction. Considering only those descriptions which did represent transformations, one finds that transformations were just as likely to follow subject instructions as object instructions. Of the 29 transformations which occurred, 55% followed subject instructions and 45% followed object instructions. This difference was not significant, and, in fact, it was in the direction opposite that implied by the linguistic hypothesis.

A similar pattern of results was observed on the front-back truck task where 83% of the subjects' descriptions retained the form of the original instruction and where an insignificantly greater number of transformations once again followed subject instruction ($p = .13$). Finally, no transformations were observed on the push-pull truck task.

The linguistic hypothesis is clearly not supported by the results of these tests. There is no evidence from subjects' descriptions that they perform a transformation in order to solve object instructions.

EXPERIMENT III

If subjects are not performing a semantic transformation, then what strategy is enabling them to solve object instructions after comprehension training? As noted earlier, the linguistic hypothesis is based on an implicit assumption that subjects interpret instructions as action statements or commands, as if the instruction directly dictated the placement of the block they hold in their hands. An alternative explanation is possible.

It may be that the subject does not tamper with the linguistic input, but instead manipulates the extralinguistic environment, either physically or symbolically, until it matches the end state description inherent in the original instruction. In essence, the child's strategy may be to treat the instruction not as an action statement governing the block he holds, but as a description of an end state. This is called the representational hypothesis.

This hypothesis assumes that the ability to execute object instructions appropriately depends on the ability to interpret those instructions as descriptions of end states. If this is the case, then subjects who are unable to execute object instructions correctly should also be unable to interpret those instructions as descriptions. The following study was designed to demonstrate, first, that a child's inability to execute object instructions correctly is accompanied by a parallel inability to recognize the correct end state in a paired comparison; and second, that the comprehension training which has already been demonstrated to produce successful block placement also produces successful end state recognition. For if subjects do adopt the representational strategy after training, then those subjects who were unable to interpret statements as descriptions prior to comprehension training should be able to do so after comprehension training.

Method

Eleven middle-class children whose mean age was 4 years and 1 month served as subjects (range: 3–5 to 4–6). Seven were female and four were male.

In order to replicate the facilitating effects of comprehension training on block placement, the major procedures of Experiment I were repeated. A no-delay pretest was administered, and any subject who did not respond correctly to at least 87.5% of subject and object instructions underwent comprehension training. The subject was given a series of 16 instructions as usual, but before he could place his block, he was shown a ladder in which the blocks had already been correctly arranged. A posttest followed immediately.

In order to assess the effects of comprehension training on the child's ability to recognize correct end states, description pretests and posttests were administered at the beginning and at the end of this experiment, that is, before the placement pretest and after the placement posttest. These tests also contained 16 trials. Two ladders were presented, one containing the correct and one containing the incorrect arrangement of blocks. The subject was asked to indicate "which ladder has red on top of blue?"

Results

Pretests. The Huttenlocher and Strauss (1968) finding that untrained subjects of this age are generally not able to carry out object instructions was again replicated during the placement pretest of this experiment. The eight unsuccessful subjects placed their block into the correct slot on 84% of those trials when it corresponded to the subject of the experimenter's instruction as compared to only 27% of those trials when it corresponded to the object of the experimenter's instruction $(p = .008)$. In contrast, the three successful subjects correctly executed 96% of both subject and object instructions.

As predicted, those eight subjects who were unable to respond correctly on the placement pretest were also unable to respond correctly on the description pretest. Their general level of performance was not significantly different from chance. On the average, they responded correctly on only 55% of the two-alternative description trials. In contrast, the three subjects who were able to execute object instructions on the placement pretest successfully interpreted statements as descriptions. On the average, they responded correctly on 94% of the description trials. The results of the description pretest thus provide correlational evidence which is consistent with the hypothesis that the ability to execute object instructions does depend on the ability to interpret those instructions as descriptions.

Posttests. Once again, comprehension training was able to induce correct block placement. Following comprehension training, there was no longer a significant difference between the percentage of correct subject responses and that of correct object responses. Subjects correctly executed 95% of the object instructions after training as compared to only 27% before training. This improvement is significant $(p = .008)$; and it replicates the main finding of Experiment I that the young child's inability to execute an object instruction correctly does seem to result from a comprehension failure.

Not only did comprehension training enable subjects to execute object instructions properly, but it also enabled them to interpret statements as descriptions. The eight subjects who required comprehension training responded correctly on 93% of the description trials after training as compared to only 55% before training. This improvement was significant $(p = .01)$.

Now the strategy employed by the successful child can be reexamined. The results of this experiment indicate that in order to execute object instructions correctly, subjects must be able to process those instructions as descriptions. Therefore, subjects appear to employ a representational strategy in order to solve object instructions; that is, they use the end state description which they have extracted from the linguistic input as a guide or template for telling them where to place their block. The initial mismatch between the logical actor and the grammatical subject is thereby rendered irrelevant.

Subjects appear to employ a different strategy for dealing with subject instructions. Because they are able to execute subject instructions before comprehension training, that is, before they have learned to process instructions as descriptions of end states, it seems plausible to suppose that they interpret subject instructions as action statements directly dictating the placement of the block they hold in their hands.

Furthermore, it seems likely that subjects continue to employ separate strategies for dealing with subject instructions and object instructions even after comprehension training, when they could use the representational strategy for both. This hypothesis is supported by latency data, presented in Table 1, which demonstrate that it takes the child about twice as long to execute an object instruction as a subject instruction, even after comprehension training.

DISCUSSION

In the introduction to this article, two hypotheses were discussed which have been advanced in the literature to account for the young child's problem-solving failures. The mediation-deficiency hypothesis postulates that the young child's verbal responses fail to act as mediators. The production-deficiency hypothesis postulates that the child may not spontaneously produce

TABLE 1

A Comparison of Posttraining Response Latencies for Subject and Object Instructions

Task	Subject Instructions (in sec.)	Object Instructions (in sec.)	p
Block task (Exp. I)	4.61	9.00	.02
Block task (Exp. III)	2.69	6.09	.003
Front-back truck task	4.29	7.10	.02
Push-pull truck task	4.42	7.30	.02

verbal mediators. The present studies explore a comprehension deficiency which would be temporally prior to both the mediation and the production deficiencies: The young problem solver fails to comprehend the nature of the problem and, as a result, he does not know what verbalization to produce.

Support for both the production- and the mediation-deficiency hypotheses derives primarily from the ability of particular training procedures to induce successful task performance. The same mode of inference is employed here to support the comprehension-deficiency hypothesis. The success of comprehension training in the present investigation raises the possibility that training procedures which have been interpreted as facilitating production or mediation may, in fact, have been serving the more primitive instructional function of structuring the child's symbolic representation of the problem.

Consider, for example, an earlier study by Bem (1967) in which 3- and 4-year-old children were unable to press a lever exactly that number of times corresponding to the number of lights presented on a display which was then covered. Correct performance in the 4-year-olds was induced as soon as the experimenter explicitly demonstrated the nature of one correct response by generating an instruction in the form of "1, 2, 3, 4 [the experimenter counting the lights] . . . 1, 2, 3, 4 [the experimenter counting his lever presses]." Their difficulties could thus be interpreted as an instance of production deficiency.

Three-year-olds in that experiment continued to fail even after they had been taught to count as they pressed. Because they did not respond correctly even after they had been taught to produce, their difficulties could be interpreted as an instance of mediation deficiency. This interpretation appeared to receive additional support from the success of the subsequent training procedure, fading, explicitly designed to strengthen the mediational properties of the child's verbalizations.

But both 3- and 4-year-olds displayed a sharp discontinuity in their transition from failure to success. For both, the experimental procedures seemed to precipitate a sudden "aha" experience, as if the child suddenly understood the requirements of the task. This observation is more consistent with the hypothesis that the child receives some insight of comprehension than the hypothesis that mediational control, for example, was gradually being acquired.

In light of this observation and the present series of experiments, it now seems more plausible to suggest that the effect of training was actually to alter the child's representation of the problem. The repeated matched pairing of counting and lever pressing in that experiment now appears to constitute a representation of the problem as solved in exactly the same way that the block and ladder configuration does in the present set of experiments. The only major distinction between the two seems to be that the block task emphasizes perceptual representation in space, whereas the lever pressing experiment stresses verbal representation in time.

It may be that still other experiments in the literature will prove amenable to this kind of analysis. In any case, comprehension should be recognized as a conceptually distinct stage in the problem-solving process.

References

Bem, S. L. Verbal self-control: The establishment of effective self-instruction. *Journal of Experimental Psychology*, 1967, **74**, 485–491.

Flavell, J. H., Beach, D. R., & Chinsky, J. M. Spontaneous verbal rehearsal in a memory task as a function of age. *Child Development*, 1966, **37**, 283–299.

Huttenlocher, J., Eisenberg, K., & Strauss, S. Comprehension: Relation between perceived actor and logical subject. *Journal of Verbal Learning and Verbal Behavior*, 1968, **7**, 527–530.

Huttenlocher, J., & Strauss, S. Comprehension and a statement's relation to the situation it describes. *Journal of Verbal Learning and Verbal Behavior*, 1968, **7**, 300–304.

Moely, B. E., Olson, F. A., Halwes, T. G., & Flavell, J. H. Production deficiency in young children's clustered recall. *Developmental Psychology*, 1969, **1**, 26–34.

Newell, A., & Simon, H. A. GPS, a program that simulates human thought. In E. A. Feigenbaum & J. Feldman (Eds.), *Computers and thought*. New York: McGraw-Hill, 1963.

Olson, D. R. On conceptual strategies. In J. S. Bruner, R. R. Olver, & P. M. Greenfield (Eds.), *Studies in cognitive growth*. New York: Wiley, 1966.

Reese, H. W. Verbal mediation as a function of age level. *Psychological Bulletin*, 1962, **59**, 502–509.

Siegel, S. *Nonparametric statistics for the behavioral sciences*. New York: McGraw-Hill, 1956.

Weir, M. W. Developmental changes in problem-solving strategies. *Psychological Review*, 1964, **71**, 473–490.

White, S. H. Evidence for a hierarchical arrangement of learning processes. In L. P. Lipsitt & C. C. Spiker (Eds.), *Advances in child development and behavior*. Vol. 2. New York: Academic Press, 1965.

20. THE EFFECTS OF SEX-ROLE IDENTIFICATION UPON PROBLEM-SOLVING SKILL[1]

G. A. Milton

During recent years, there has been an increased interest in the effects of "nonintellectual" processes upon problem solving and thinking. One area in which such effects can be and have been studied with readily discriminable criterion groups is the area of sex differences. Sweeney (5) has summarized several studies in which problem-solving differences between men and women were observed. He also reports experiments of his own which demonstrate that men solve certain classes of problems with greater facility than do women, even when differences in intellectual aptitude, academic training, and special abilities are controlled.

The present study explores the possibility that the differences in problem-solving skill between men and women may be due, at least in part, to a set of learned behaviors that constitute a culturally defined sex role. A simple extrapolation from the earlier studies of sex differences leads to the hypothesis that the more an individual identifies with the masculine sex role, the greater will be his problem-solving skill.

This hypothesis may be stated more explicitly: (a) There is a positive relationship between masculine identification and problem-solving achieve-

SOURCE. J. of Abnormal and Social Psychol., 1957, **55**, 208–212.

[1] This experiment is one in a series of studies of problem-solving done under Project NR 150-149 and supported by Contract N6onr 25125 between Stanford University and the Office of Naval Research. Work on the contract was under the general direction of Dr. Donald W. Taylor. Permission is granted for reproduction, translation, publication, use, and disposal of this article in whole or in part by or for the United States Government.

ment. (*b*) When an adjustment is made for the between-subjects variance contributed by sex-role identification, sex differences in problem-solving achievement will be reduced. The implication of the hypothesis is, of course, that not only will differences between men and women in problem-solving skill be reduced by an adjustment for masculine role identification, but also that the more "masculine" men will solve problems more readily than "feminine" men and, similarly, that the more masculine women will be better problem solvers than women who have greater identification with the feminine role.

METHOD

Indices of Sex-Role Identification

The concept of sex role refers to a heterogeneous collection of actions that differentiate typically masculine behavior from typically feminine behavior in a particular culture. These characteristics of the sex role may be defined restrictively in terms of overt behavior only, or more broadly in terms of attitudes, interests, needs, and other inferred constructs in addition to overt behavior. The indices of sex role used in this investigation have been determined by primarily empirical means; overt and covert measures were used, the criterion for selection being that they involved nonintellectual factors that differentiate men from women for the general culture from which the experimental sample was drawn.

The Terman-Miles M-F Test (6) was chosen as the primary defining measure of sex-role identification because it measures a broader range of responses than any other sex-role measure cited in the literature. This test consists of a set of items that differentiate men from women in a culture similar to that of the current sample (cf. below). The test elicits responses that not only discriminate men from women, but also seem to assess a culturally defined masculinity-femininity variable within each sex.

Two secondary measures of sex role were also employed. These tests tap a narrower range of sex-role content. One, the M-F scale of the *Minnesota Multiphasic Personality Inventory* (2), consists largely of self-report items referring to feelings and emotions. The other, the *Behavioral Inventory* M-F (4) scale, is part of an unpublished experimental inventory that defines the role in terms of self-reported overt behavior that discriminates between men and women in a college population.

Problems

Twenty problems that had shown significant sex differences in pretest trials were used. The problems were selected and refined by Nakamura (3), and his methods of administration were duplicated in the present study. Item analysis has indicated that the problems involve two types of problem-solving skill, restructuring and straightforward solution. The restructuring problems require the subject to alter his initial set in order to attain the solution; the straightforward problems are solvable by direct means. Ten straightforward and ten restructuring problems were arranged alternately by pairs, according to order of difficulty. One member of each pair involved a numerical solution and the other member was non-numerical. The problems were bound in a booklet with one problem per page so that each problem was presented individually. A working time of four minutes per problem was allowed with a ten-minute intermission after the first ten problems. Problems were scored either correct or incorrect with no partial credits given.

Subjects

One hundred and twenty-nine students from an introductory psychology class at Stanford participated as subjects. Of these, 63 were males and 66 were females. Scores on the mathematical and verbal sections of the College Entrance Examination Board Scholastic Aptitude Test were available for all subjects as a control upon intelligence.

Procedure

Subjects were tested in six groups of 16 to 35 subjects. For all groups, the tests were administered in three sessions. The order of presentation of the tests was arbitrary. The MMPI M-F and the Behavioral scale M-F were presented during the first session; the problem-solving test during the second session, and the Terman-Miles M-F during the third session. Because of the nature of the items on the M-F scales, it was assumed that there would be no interaction with order of presentation; therefore, this arrangement was made purely on the basis of experimental expediency.

RESULTS

The results of this investigation may be divided into two categories. First, sex differences on the problem-solving measure are examined in order to establish that those reported by other investigators (5) are found in the current investigation. The hypothesized relationship between sex role and problem solving is then tested. Both the relationships between sexes and within sexes are examined.

Sex Differences in Problem Solving

The differences between the problem-solving achievement of men and women presented in Table 1 are the data which the hypothesis must partially

TABLE 1

Sex Differences in Problem-Solving Skill

	Men		Women		
Type of Problem	Mean	SD	Mean	SD	t
Problem-solving, total score	9.10	3.68	7.18	3.27	3.12**
Restructuring problems	4.33	2.22	3.38	1.88	2.63*
Straight-forward problems	4.76	2.17	3.80	1.79	2.74**
Numerical problems	5.06	2.27	4.04	1.87	2.78**
Non-numerical problems	4.05	2.15	3.14	1.79	2.59*

* Significant beyond .02 level.
** Significant beyond .01 level.

explain. The differences between men and women are significant with respect to the total problem-solving score and all the sub-scores, but the difference between men and women on one subtest is not significantly greater than that on another subtest. The total score can therefore be used to test the effects of the sex-role measure. These results are similar to those obtained by Nakamura (3) for the same problem on a sample of University of California students.

Effects of Sex-Role upon Sex Differences in Problem Solving

In order to confirm the hypothesis of this investigation, two effects must be demonstrated: that there is a correlation between sex-role identification and problem solving, and that this correlation accounts for some of the differences between men and women in problem-solving skill. The correlations between sex-role measures and problem solving are presented in Table 2.

It is clear that problem-solving skill is significantly related to sex-role identification as measured by the Terman-Miles test. There is a significant relationship both within and across sexes. The evidence concerning the

TABLE 2

Correlation of the Sex-Role and Aptitude Variables with Problem-Solving Skill

Variable	Men	Women	Combined
Terman-Miles M-F	.44**	.26*	.41**
MMPI M-F	.14	.13	.29*
Behavior M-F	.28*	.23	.36**
Verbal aptitude	.44**	.28*	
Math aptitude	.63**	.78**	

* Significant beyond .05 level.
** Significant beyond .01 level.

secondary measures of sex-role is less clear. The correlation of problem solving with the MMPI M-F scale approaches significance only for the combined sex group, and the correlation of problem solving with the Behavioral M-F scale does not appear to be significant for the women.

In order to determine if the differences between men and women in problem-solving score can be accounted for in terms of score on the measures of sex-role identification, a simple analysis of covariance was performed. The rationale of this operation is that if the correlation between the problem-solving score and the sex-role measure is sufficient to reduce significantly the difference in problem-solving score, then sex-role identification as measured by the particular test accounts for a part of this difference. Table 3 presents the results of this analysis for the Terman-Miles test, and Tables 4 and 5 show similar results for the MMPI and the Behavioral Inventory.

The results indicate that the Terman-Miles not only accounts for a significant part of the difference between men and women in problem-solving skill, but also that it diminishes this difference to the point where it is no longer significant. The results with the MMPI and Behavioral Inventory are comparable to those obtained with the Terman-Miles. The difference between

TABLE 3

Analysis of Covariance: Sex Differences in Problem Solving with Adjustment for Terman-Miles M-F Score

Source of Variance	Before Adjustment		After Adjustment			
	df	Sum of Squares	df	Sum of Squares	Mean Squares	F
Total	128	1675	127	1375		
Within	127	1557	126	1366	10.84	
Between	1	118	1	9.32	9.32	0.86

TABLE 4

Analysis of Covariance: Sex Differences in Problem Solving with Adjustment for MMPI M-F Score

Source of Variation	Before Adjustment		After Adjustment			
	df	Sum of Squares	df	Sum of Squares	Mean Squares	F
Total	128	1675	127	1534		
Within	127	1557	126	1529	12.13	
Between	1	118	1	5.86	5.86	0.48

TABLE 5

Analysis of Covariance: Sex Differences in Problem Solving with Adjustment for Behavioral M-F Score

	Before Adjustment		After Adjustment			
	df	Sum of Squares	df	Sum of Squares	Mean Squares	F
Total	128	1675	127	1462		
Within	127	1557	126	1454	11.54	
Between	1	118	1	7.76	7.76	0.67

men and women on the problem-solving measure diminishes when the variance attributable to sex-role identification is controlled.

The hypothesis requires, by implication, that differences in problem-solving skill within a sex must also be partially accounted for by differences in sex-role identification. Table 2 indicates that the Terman-Miles measure was significantly correlated with problem solving within both sexes, but that the other sex-role measures were less clearly related to problem solving.

In order to determine what portion of the variance in the problem-solving task within a sex may be explained on the basis of sex-role identification and the other nonintellectual variables related to sex role, the variables were fitted to a multiple regression equation and the appropriate beta weights were determined for each variable by means of a Doolittle solution. Since the hypothesis requires that differences in problem-solving skill must be explained independently of differences in intellectual aptitude, the verbal and mathematical measures were included in the equation. The results of this analysis are presented in Table 6.

TABLE 6

Beta Weights: Relative Independent Contribution of Each of the Variables to Problem-Solving Score

Variable	Men (N = 63) Beta	Women (N = 66) Beta
Terman-Miles M-F	.297**	.183*
MMPI M-F	.074	.050
Behavior M-F	.066	.126
Verbal aptitude	.224**	.099
Math aptitude	.473**	.848**

* Significant beyond .05 level.
** Significant beyond .01 level.

For both the men and the women, the Terman-Miles test measure of sex-role identification is a significant contributor to the variance in problem-solving scores, even when mathematical and verbal aptitude are held constant. The mathematical aptitude scale contributes a large portion of the variance for both sexes, and the verbal aptitude scale makes a significant contribution for the males. The other sex-role variables make no independent contribution to the variance in problem solving, when the more powerful Terman-Miles test is included in the battery.

DISCUSSION

The results of this study seem to indicate that the differences between men and women in problem-solving skill as reported by a number of investigators are merely part of a more general difference between men and women in role identification. Men have characteristically different behavior, attitudes, emotions, and motivations than do women, and the differences in problem-solving skill reflect or are a part of these differences. To the extent that allowance can be made for these differences in general sex-role identification, the differences in problem-solving achievement seem to disappear.

Moreover, there are differences *within* a sex as to the extent of identification with the appropriate sex role, and these within-sex differences in role also seem to be related to problem-solving skill. Men who identify with the masculine sex role are better problem solvers than are those who identify with a more feminine role, and conversely, women who identify with the appropriate sex role have poorer problem-solving scores than do women who have a more masculine identification. All these comparisons, of course, assume a common level of intelligence.

This interpretation leads to several implications. For example, the acquisition of problem-solving skills may be affected by the same processes which govern the formation of sex-role identification. If the Freudian hypothesis concerning the identification process is correct, then important antecedents of adult problem-solving skill are to be found in childhood. The male child who forms an adequate identification with the male role, given sufficient intelligence and opportunity to learn, will grow up to be a good problem solver. On the other hand, the female child, even though possessing adequate intelligence and opportunity to learn, will probably not develop problem-solving skills (of the sort used in this study) if she forms an appropriate identification with the feminine role, because this type of problem solving is not appropriate to the female sex-role in her culture. This is, of course, a very broad extrapolation from the data of this experiment.

Another interesting implication concerns the possibility for improvement in problem-solving skill. If the sex-role interpretation of the results of this experiment is correct, any attempt to change problem-solving skill will be more effective if corresponding changes are made in certain aspects of the conventional sex-role identification. While it may not be necessary to change the sex-role identification of a subject in order to change his (or her) problem-solving skill, it would seem necessary to neutralize the effects of sex-role identification that relate to the problem-solving process. Practice on problems alone probably would not be effective. Carey (1) has demonstrated an effect similar to that of partially changing the problem-solving attitudes associated with sex-role identification. Through group discussions of women's attitudes toward intellectual activity, she was able to improve their problem-solving scores. This change, though significant, was slight, and it would seem that more than a few discussions are required to change attitudes that appear to be basic to the culturally defined sex role. If one considers that sex-role identification has had an effect on the learning of a subject for the major part of a lifetime, it seems that a change in sex role would require a long period of relearning. Also, if major changes in problem-solving performance are to be achieved, the relearning of sex-role would necessarily be accompanied by a period of relearning of problem-solving skills.

Although this interpretation of the results seems appropriate for a college population, there are logical difficulties in any extrapolation of these results to the more general population. Wherever there are subsections of the general population in which problem solving, as defined in this investigation, is not appropriate to the masculine role, this relationship would not be expected. Since the studies of sex differences in problem solving which were mentioned earlier have been conducted upon college populations, there is little evidence as to how far these conclusions can be generalized.

SUMMARY

The hypothesis of the study was that sex differences in problem-solving skill may be partially accounted for by differences in sex-role identification. The Terman-Miles M-F Test was used as the primary index of sex-role identification. Two other M-F questionnaires were also employed. These scales and a measure of problem-solving skill were administered to 63 male and 66 female university undergraduates. In general, the results indicate that there is a positive relationship between masculine sex-role identification and problem-solving skill both across sexes and within a sex. When allowance is made for this relationship, the difference between men and women in problem-solving performance is diminished.

References

1. Carey, G. L. Reduction of sex differences in problem solving by improvement of attitude through group discussion. Dept. Psychol., Stanford Univer., 1955 (ONR Tech. Rep. No. 9, Contract N6onr 25125).

2. Hathaway, S. R., & McKinley, J. C. *Minnesota Multiphasic Personality Inventory.* New York: Psychol. Corp., 1951.

3. Nakamura, C. Y. The relation between conformity and problem solving. Dept. Psychol., Stanford Univer., 1955. (ONR Tech. Rep. No. 11, Contract N6onr 25125).

4. Pinneau, S. R., & Milton, G. A. The objective measurement of overt behavior. Paper read at Western Psychol. Ass., June, 1954.

5. Sweeney, E. J. Sex differences in problem solving. Dept. Psychol., Stanford Univer., 1953 (ONR Tech. Rep. No. 1, Contract N6onr 25125).

6. Terman, L. M., & Miles, C. C. *Sex and personality.* New York: McGraw-Hill, 1936.

21. PROBLEM SOLVING AND PAST EXPERIENCE

Kjell Raaheim

The present report is a presentation of some of my points of view on the study of thinking. The work I have had the opportunity to do in this field has come out of a close co-operation with P. Saugstad; much of my own research work has, as its point of departure, the investigations previously undertaken by him.

If asked to explain what it is that characterizes the study of problem-solving and what are the main questions set forth by different experimenters, one is placed in a situation of some difficulty. Perhaps all one can do is point to the fact that different research workers have been interested in studying how a human being, or an animal, behaves in situations that may be classified as complex or difficult. These would be situations in which there is no opportunity of following already learned modes of behavior, situations in which much of what is encountered is new or unknown, and in which it is rather easy to make mistakes before the goal is reached—if one succeeds in reaching it. It is not easy to present a more precise definition of problem solving that will be accepted by everyone who works in this field. If one turns to the literature one finds that a number of experimenters maintain that a problem situation is a "difficult" situation in which the individual is motivated toward a "goal," but the "road" to the goal is blocked by an "obstacle." Both the Gestalt psychologists and the psychologists influenced by them speak of a "gap" in the "structure" of the situation and maintain

source. P. Mussen (Ed.), *European Research in Cognitive Development*, SRCD Monograph, 1965, **30**, 2.

that the behavior during the attempt to solve the problem tends toward filling this gap.

I shall argue that the problem situation, although "new" in a sense, is not typically a chaotic situation, but rather one with a fairly strict structure. The situations studied by Köhler, Duncker, and Maier, while considered to be examples of problem situations, seem to be situations in which well-specified rules are set up for the individual's behavior. These rules are laid down in the instructions given to the individual. The goal is pointed out by the experimenter, and the obstacle, or difficulty, may be conceived of as restrictions put upon the individual's choice of implements and modes of attack. The situations are often described as new ones, but often only some of the elements in a given situation deviate from what the individual is familiar with from past experience.

I prefer to describe the problem situation as one "familiar" to the individual: a situation previously experienced or, what, in a number of cases, perhaps, means the same to the individual, a situation that he comes to classify as equivalent to a certain series of previous situations. In the problem situation, however, something essential has taken place, so that the situation here and now is experienced with a *deviation* from what is otherwise a familiar situation or series of situations. The *gap* in the situation, in my opinion, may be best defined with reference to the specific nature of the structure in each case, in such a way that, for each individual, one is forced to define the gap with reference to the specific background and past experience of this specific individual. I shall try, later on, to show how it is possible to determine the way different individuals classify one and the same situation and that this classification is of great importance for their behavior in the problem situation.

The philosopher H. H. Price, in his book *Thinking and Experience* argues that recognition is the fundamental intellectual process. Price remarks that a human being without this ability would find himself in a world that could not be thought of, in which there could be no concepts and, in short, a world containing only new impressions or stimuli to confront the individual. We may agree that, for the existence of higher organisms, it is of the utmost importance for them to have the ability to react to the common features of ever shifting situations, as these situations can be described with reference to some kind of objective criteria. That an organism responds with the same reaction to what are, objectively speaking, rather different stimuli might result either from a lack of ability to discriminate between the stimuli or from a cognitive ability to render equivalent these different stimuli. In recent years, the cognitive aspect of the experience of equivalence has been stressed (Bruner, Goodnow, & Austin, 1956). Also, in recently performed factor-analytic studies of the structure of intellect (Guilford, 1957; Guilford,

Frick, Christensen, & Merrifield, 1957), a number of flexibility factors are reckoned with. Considering both Bruner's work and Guilford's, we come to see that the superior intellect may be thought of as characterized by an ability to relate one and the same situation to a great many different series of previous situations, that is, an ability to make the present experience equivalent to a number of different past experiences. Lack of ability to discriminate may have important consequences in the animal's adjustment to his environment. A cognitive code operation, by which one equates situations otherwise conceived of as different, will, however, leave the individual in a freer position in regard to his adjustment by making him more able to react to minor variations in the situations encountered.

As for my own research in this field, I have hitherto not performed any experiments with children younger than those of the upper grades of elementary school. I have, therefore, personal experience only with the upper levels of development from child to adult. The glimpses to be presented from experiments actually performed with older children may, nevertheless, serve to illustrate my points of view regarding the development and general features of the thought process.

First, I want to give a short description of a rather simple test for measuring the individual's ability to name objects that are *functionally equivalent* to a missing object necessary for the solution of a given problem. I constructed this test as a counterpart to Saugstad's test for measuring a person's ability to name different functions for objects. I have called my own test "The Object Test" (later referred to as the *O* test), and the task confronting the subject is that of listing, within a time limit of 10 minutes, all the objects with which he can replace the object missing in a specified problem situation. Three such problem situations are outlines of which the first is the following: "You are trying to reach a shelf, but it is half a meter too high and you have no ladder. Now write down everything you can think of to stand on in order to reach the shelf."

Scores on this test show a tendency to increase with age and level of education. *O* scores for pupils of different grades of high school are listed in Table 1.

TABLE 1

Mean *O* Scores for Subjects at Different School Levels

High-School Grade	N	Mean	SD
5	16	28.7	10.2
4	65	26.8	7.6
3	20	20.8	8.1
2	22	19.6	5.9

The tasks of the O test, in my opinion, resemble the task of the individual in a problem situation of the practical-construction type. Consider for a moment Maier's well known double-pendulum problem. The subjects are asked to construct two pendulums that will reach the floor at two indicated spots. All the material needed for the construction of the pendulums is given to the subjects, but something essential is missing: there is nothing for hanging up the pendulums. This is a problem situation that I would characterize as a situation in which the deviation consists of a missing part. The situation is familiar to the individual, or equivalent to situations previously experienced, but, since there is a part missing, the success in solving the problem depends on his ability to find replacements for this part by means of the material at hand. What is, for instance, functionally equivalent to a hook in the ceiling? An individual with a high score on the O test probably will be able to perform better in a situation such as this than a person with a low score.

That success in solving problems of the practical type correlates with results on the O test, I have previously shown in a study in which the so-called *pea problem* was utilized (Raaheim, 1960). In this problem the subject was confronted with the task of finding a way to transfer a number of peas in a glass on one table to an empty glass placed on another table 2 m. away, the transfer to be done from behind the first table. At his disposal the subject had three newspapers, a string (1 meter long), and a pair of scissors. One finds that the subjects, so far as adults or older children are concerned, in the large majority of the cases try to construct a tube or channel for transferring the peas. One may argue that they conceive of the problem situation as a situation with a missing tube or channel. If an individual has come that far—in other words, if he is able to conceive of the situation as a meaningful whole with a gap consisting of a missing part—his success in solving the problem depends on his ability to find something with which he can replace the missing part. He will be successful if he finds an object that is functionally equivalent to the missing one, or if he is able to construct a replacement by using the material supplied.

We are here touching upon an important point. The solution process may be conceived of as having two distinct phases. The *last* phase is the one accounted for: the filling of the gap in an otherwise meaningful situation. The *first* phase of the process is the discovery of the meaning of the situation. A vague feeling that there is *some* difficulty, that not everything is as it should be, only represents the point of departure for the solution process. The first link in the solution, in my opinion, consists of analysing exactly what the gap in the structure is, what is the deviation from the otherwise familiar situation, or, even, what is the structure itself like or what kind of meaningful situation do we have here? The gap or the deviation can be conceived of only in terms of a specific structure or in terms of a specific type of familiar situation. With a situation of the "missing part" type, the questions to be answered in solving the problem are: exactly what part is missing in which type of situation? and how may this part be replaced?

In the study previously referred to (Raaheim, 1960), I found that some of the subjects with high O scores, in spite of their superior ability to find replacements, did not solve the problem. A closer examination of their proposals for solution gave indications that their lack of success resulted, not from a failure to construct a tube or a channel out of the newspapers, but from a more general lack of awareness of the fact that a tube was missing in the first place. If the situation for these subjects was at all meaningful, it is conceivable that they looked upon the situation as equivalent to a quite different type of familiar situation, for example, one in which something is poured from one container to another by means of a ladle.

In an investigation with children, I found that, to a much lesser extent than adults, pupils in the lower grades of high school conceived of the pea problem as a situation in which the task was to replace a missing tube or channel. In about half the cases the children wanted something that could help them pour the peas from the one glass over into the other. In Table 2,

TABLE 2

Number and Percentage of Tube-Channel Proposals in Pea Problem by Different Groups of Subjects

High-School Grade	Total N	Tube-Channel	
		Number of Proposals	Percentage
5	16	14	88
4	60	49	82
3	20	12	60
2	22	11	50

the number and percentage of tube channel proposals on the pea problem is listed for subjects from different grades.

It seems reasonable, now, to ask whether it is possible to talk about a problem "as such" without specifying the implements at the individual's disposal. Is it not the situation as a whole, including the different objects with which the situation can be handled that determines the type of solution? As Duncker (1945) argued, it often seems to be the objects at hand that give rise to the attack decided upon. The objects may be thought to "signal" their use or function to the subjects, and such "suggestions from below," as

Duncker preferred to put it, may be considered to play an important part in the analysis of the situation.

One cannot, of course, wholly disregard anything in a complex situation. There are, however, indications that only *some* parts of the total situation are of importance for the individual's conception of the situation as a whole, that is, certain features that the problem situation shares with situations from past experience seem to lead to a classification of the situation in this or that way. In an experiment previously reported (Raaheim, 1961), the subjects were asked to write down what they would prefer to have for the transfer of the peas in the pea problem situation if they were able to choose implements freely. The subjects in one group, while writing down their preferred implement, were given opportunity to see objects actually allowed for the solution, while those in another group had to suggest implements without any knowledge of what was actually to be used later on. There was no difference between the groups as to implements preferred. In this case, the individual's choice of line of attack seemed to be independent of the specific objects at his disposal. While the subjects of both groups were later asked to solve the problem by using newspapers, string, and scissors, their proposals could be looked upon as ways of replacing the part missing in the situation. Although the subjects, pupils from grades 9 and 10 of high school, listed different types of preferred implements, their success in replacing the missing part was found to depend upon the possibilities of the objects actually allowed for solution.

Younger pupils, as already noted, in about half the cases want to have a ladle or similar implement to pour the peas from the one glass over into the other, or, in other words, they conceive of the situation as one with a missing ladle. It is clear that these subjects have a smaller chance of solving the problem than do older pupils and adults who, in the majority of the cases, want a tube, and, then, of course, the only objects at their disposal, or with the greatest possibility of success, can be used to make a tube. This means that, when a situation can be conceived of in different ways, that is, can be coded as equivalent to different series of previous situations, and only one way of classifying it leads to success, the individual who is most flexible will be most successful, if flexibility is taken to be, among other things, the ability to classify a situation in a number of different ways.

Is there any reason to believe that flexibility increases with age? If it does, how are we to get a measure of this ability that will make it possible to equate behavior in one and the same situation to behavior in different series of situations from past experience? Indirectly, one can try to get a measure of this ability by letting the subjects go through flexibility tests of the type used by Guilford and Saugstad. If the subjects are handed an object and asked to write down, or to demonstrate as many different ways of using this object as possible, one gets a measure of this individual's ability to see mirrored in the object different, functionally nonequivalent objects. In a specific form of this kind of test, which I have utilized myself, the subject is shown a common object together with a list of verbs. He is then asked to look at the verbs to see if it is possible for the object to serve the functions indicated by the verbs. In going through the list he is told to write down on a sheet of paper the appropriate verbs and to illustrate the function with an example of how to use the object. This technique has also been suggested by Osgood (1953).

In some previously reported studies, I found that scores of this function-naming test, called the F test, correlate with scores on tests of general intelligence. Guilford et al. (1957) reported correlation coefficients similar to my own, that is about $+.50$. While I found the mean F score in a group of male high-school students from grade 4 to be 14.6, the mean score among pupils from grade 2 was 11.7. The difference, statistically significant at $p < .001$, indicates that the ability measured by the F test increases with age and educational level.

In Raaheim (1961), a comparison was made between results on the O test and the F test and success on two different problem situations. The first problem was the pea problem already described. The second was the so-called *ring problem*, in which the subject is confronted with the task of raising a gold ring that is lying at the bottom of a shaft (3 m. deep), by using a glass tube (3 m. long and with the same diameter as the ring), a piece of wood, a nail, a knife, and a pair of pliers. The two problem situations may be said to be quite different. As has been argued above, the pea problem may be conceived of as equivalent to different sets of previous situations, either a type of situation in which something must be transferred from one place to another by means of some sort of channel or tube or a situation in which something must be poured from one container into another. The ring problem, on the other hand, seems to lead to just a single general mode of tenable premises. For these reasons the individual's behavior in many instances may be said to be pretty "unrealistic."

So it might be with children, for instance. Not only do children make classifications that are "faulty," with the result that they behave in "unrealistic" ways in the situations, but also they sometimes try to use objects for functions that the objects do not possess. We learn from experiments such as that of Luchins with the so-called *Einstellungseffekt* that there is no fundamental difference between the behavior of children and of adults. As a result of an immediately preceding series of similar situations, the subjects classify the problem situations with which they are confronted in the water-jar tasks in a stupid way. Their behavior, consequently, becomes unsuited for the task in question and their mode of attack is as unrealistic as that of smaller children. Such a "blind" organization, without sufficient attention to all details of the situation, I have myself witnessed in an experiment with university students.

The problem situation asked for a way to cross a river when on safari in Africa. Dependent on the distance between the banks, and on the material at disposal (for instance trees of different lengths), the appropriate line of attack is sometimes to build a bridge, sometimes to make a float. The solutions of this written problem, suggested by the students, were seldom based on a careful evaluation of the possibilities in each case. Certain details of the information given seemed to dominate, and the results were pretty unrealistic proposals. Even with a distance of 100 meters the bridge was sometimes suggested. On the other hand, when certain cues in the situation suggested that the current was not strong, the float was proposed even with a distance of only 10 meters and long trees at their disposal. A problem situation presented in writing is not, of course, comparable to a situation in which the subjects are actually at the riverside. But the point is that in using the writing procedure one gets hold of some essential parts of the thought process initiated by the presentation of the material. In a concrete situation, some trial and error may precede the actual solution, and it may be more difficult to get hold of the different ideas that occur to the subjects.

In conclusion, we might state that, in problem situations, adults as well as children behave on the basis of a specific conception of the situation, which is thought to depend on how the situation is seen to deviate from past situations with which it is compared. With both children and adults it is difficult for the observer to get an understanding of how the problem, or difficulty, is conceived of by the specific individual. One cannot hope to reach the whole truth by observing overt behavior. If, thus, a lecturer speaks so fast that his listeners cannot comprehend everything he says, the listeners, who may be trained psychologists, may be wrong in assuming that he is a rather nervous type. The speaker's problem, may, in fact, be better described as that of how to finish his lecture in the allotted time!

References

Bruner, J. S., Goodnow, J., & Austin, G. A. *A study of thinking.* New York: Wiley, 1956.

Duncker, K. On Problem-solving. *Psychol. Monogr.,* 58, No. 5, (No. 270 entire), 1945.

Guilford, J. P. A revised structure of intellect. *Rep. Psychol. Lab., U. Sth. Calif.,* No. 19, 1957.

Guilford, J. P., Frick, J. W., Christensen, P. R., & Merrifield, P. R. A factor-analytic study of flexibility in thinking. *Rep. Psychol. Lab. U. Sth. Calif.*, No. 18, 1957.

Osgood, C. E. *Method and theory in experimental psychology.* New York: Oxford Univ. Press, 1953.

Raaheim, K. Problem solving and the ability to find replacements. *Scand. J. Psychol.*, 1, 14–18, 1960.

Raaheim, K., Problem solving: a new approach. *Acta Univ. Bergensis, Ser. Hum. Litt.*, No. 5, 1961.

22. ELEMENTS OF A THEORY OF HUMAN PROBLEM SOLVING

Allen Newell, Herbert A. Simon, & John C. Shaw

In this paper we shall set forth the elements of a theory of human problem solving, together with some evidence for its validity drawn from the currently accepted facts about the nature of problem solving. What questions should a theory of problem solving answer? First, it should predict the performance of a problem solver handling specified tasks. It should explain how human problem solving takes place: what processes are used, and what mechanisms perform these processes. It should predict the incidental phenomena that accompany problem solving, and the relation of these to the problem-solving process. For example, it should account for "set" and for the apparent discontinuities that are sometimes called "insight." It should show how changes in the attendant conditions—both changes "inside" the problem solver and changes in the task confronting him—alter problem-solving behavior. It should explain how specific and general problem-solving skills are learned, and what it is that the problem solver "has" when he has learned them.

INFORMATION PROCESSING SYSTEMS

Questions about problem-solving behavior can be answered at various levels and in varying degrees of detail. The theory to be described here explains problem-solving behavior in terms of what we shall call *information processes*. If one considers the organism to consist of effectors, receptors, and a control system for joining these, then this theory is mostly a theory of the

SOURCE. *Psychological Review*, 1958, **65**, 151–166.

control system. It avoids most questions of sensory and motor activities. The theory postulates:

1. A control system consisting of a number of *memories*, which contain symbolized information and are interconnected by various ordering relations. The theory is not at all concerned with the physical structures that allow this symbolization, nor with any properties of the memories and symbols other than those it explicitly states.

2. A number of *primitive information processes*, which operate on the information in the memories. Each primitive process is a perfectly definite operation for which known physical mechanisms exist. (The mechanisms are not necessarily known to exist in the human brain, however—we are only concerned that the processes be described without ambiguity.)

3. A perfectly definite set of rules for combining these processes into whole *programs* of processing. From a program it is possible to deduce unequivocally what externally observable behaviors will be generated.

At this level of theorizing, *an explanation of an observed behavior of the organism is provided by a program of primitive information processes that generates this behavior.*

A program viewed as a theory of behavior is highly specific: it describes one organism in a particular class of situations. When either the situation or the organism is changed, the program must be modified. The program can be used as a theory—that is, as a predictor of behavior—in two distinct ways. First, it makes many precise predictions that can be tested in detail regarding the area of behavior it is designed to handle. For example, the theory considered in this paper predicts exactly how much difficulty an organism with the specified program will encounter in solving each of a series of mathematical problems: which of the problems it will solve, how much time (up to a proportionality constant) will be spent on each, and so on.

Second, there will be important qualitative similarities among the programs that an organism uses in various situations, and among the programs used by different organisms in a given situation. The program that a human subject uses to solve mathematical problems will be similar in many respects to the program he uses to choose a move in chess; the program one subject uses for any such task will resemble the programs used by other subjects possessing similar training and abilities. If there were no such similarities, if each subject and each task were completely idiosyncratic, there could be no theory of human problem solving. Moreover, there is some positive evidence, as we shall see, that such similarities and general characteristics of problem-solving processes do exist.

In this paper we shall limit ourselves to this kind of validation of our theory of problem solving. We shall predict qualitative characteristics of human problem-solving behavior and compare them with those that have already been observed and described. Since all of the available data on the psychology of human problem solving are of this qualitative kind, no more detailed test of a program is possible at present. The more precise validation must wait upon new experimental work.[1]

In succeeding sections we shall describe an information-processing program for discovering proofs for theorems in logic. We shall compare its behavior qualitatively with that of human problem solvers. In general, the processes that compose the program are familiar from everyday experience and from research on human problem solving: searching for possible solutions, generating these possibilities out of other elements, and evaluating partial solutions and cues. From this standpoint there is nothing particularly novel about the theory. It rests its claims on other considerations:

1. It shows specifically and in detail how the processes that occur in human problem solving can be compounded out of elementary information processes, and hence how they can be carried out by mechanisms.

2. It shows that a program incorporating such processes, with appropriate organization, can in fact solve problems. This aspect of problem solving has been thought to be "mysterious" and unexplained because it was not understood how sequences of simple processes could account for the successful solution of complex problems. The theory dissolves the mystery by showing that nothing more need be added to the constitution of a successful problem solver.

Relation to Digital Computers

The ability to specify programs precisely, and to infer accurately the behavior they will produce, derives from the use of high-speed digital computers. Each specific theory—each program of information processes that purports to describe some human behavior—is coded for a computer. That is, each primitive information process is coded to be a separate computer routine, and a "master" routine is written that allows these primitive processes to be assembled into any system we wish to specify. Once this has been done, we can find out exactly what behavior the purported theory predicts by having the computer "simulate" the system.

We wish to emphasize that we are not using the computer as a crude

---

[1] Several studies of individual and group problem-solving behavior with logic problems have been carried out by O. K. Moore and Scarvia Anderson (5). The problems Moore and Anderson gave their subjects are somewhat different from those handled by our program, and hence a detailed comparison of behavior is not yet possible. We are now engaged, with Peter Houts, in replicating and extending the experiments of Moore and Anderson with human subjects and at the same time modifying our program to predict the human laboratory behavior in detail.

analogy to human behavior—we are not comparing computer structures with brains, nor electrical relays with synapses. Our position is that the appropriate way to describe a piece of problem-solving behavior is in terms of a program: a specification of what the organism will do under varying environmental circumstances in terms of certain elementary information processes it is capable of performing. This assertion has nothing to do—directly —with computers. Such programs could be written (now that we have discovered how to do it) if computers had never existed.[2] A program is no more, and no less, an analogy to the behavior of an organism than is a differential equation to the behavior of the electrical circuit it describes. Digital computers come into the picture only because they can, by appropriate programming, be induced to execute the same sequences of information processes that humans execute when they are solving problems. Hence, as we shall see, these programs describe both human and machine problem solving at the level of information processes.[3]

With this discussion of the relation of programs to machines and humans behind us, we can afford to relax into convenient, and even metaphoric, uses of language without much danger of misunderstanding. It is often convenient to talk about the behavior implied by a program as that of an existing physical mechanism doing things. This mode of expression is legitimate, for if we take the trouble to put any particular program in a computer, we have in fact a machine that behaves in the way prescribed by the program. Similarly, for concreteness, we will often talk as if our theory of problem solving consisted of statements about the ability of a computer to do certain things.

THE LOGIC THEORIST

We can now turn to an example of the theory. This is a program capable of solving problems in a particular domain—capable, specifically, of discovering proofs for theorems in elementary symbolic logic. We shall call this program the Logic Theorist (LT).[4] We assert that the behavior of this pro-

---

[2] We can, in fact, find a number of attempts in the psychological literature to explain behavior in terms of programs—or the prototypes thereof. One of the most interesting, because it comes relatively close to the modern conception of a computer program, is Adrian de Groot's analysis of problem solving by chess players (2). The theory of de Groot is based on the thought-psychology of Selz, a somewhat neglected successor to the Wurzburg school. Quite recently, and apparently independently, we find the same idea applied by Jerome S. Bruner and his associates to the theory of concept formation (1). Bruner uses the term "strategy," derived from economics and game theory, for what we have called a program.

[3] For a fuller discussion of this point see (9).

[4] In fact, matters are a little more complicated, for in the body of this paper we will consider both the basic program of LT and a number of variants on this program. We

gram, when the stimulus consists of the instruction that it prove a particular theorem, can be used to predict the behavior of (certain) humans when they are faced with the same problem in symbolic logic.

The program of LT was not fashioned directly as a theory of human behavior; it was constructed in order to get a program that would prove theorems in logic. To be sure, in constructing it the authors were guided by a firm belief that a practicable program could be constructed only if it used many of the processes that humans use. The fact remains that the program was not devised by fitting it directly to human data. As a result, there are many details of LT that we would not expect to correspond to human behavior. For example, no particular care was exercised in choosing the primitive information processes to correspond, point by point, with elementary human processes. All that was required in writing the program was that the primitive processes constitute a sufficient set and a convenient set for the type of program under study.

Since LT has been described in detail elsewhere (6, 8), the description will not be repeated here. It will also be unnecessary to describe in detail the system of symbolic logic that is used by LT. For those readers who are not familiar with symbolic logic, we may remark that problems in the sentential calculus are at about the same level of difficulty and have somewhat the same "flavor" as problems in high school geometry.[5]

Design of the Experiments

First we will describe the overt behavior of LT when it is presented with problems in elementary symbolic logic. In order to be concrete, we will refer to an experiment conducted on a digital computer. We take an ordinary general-purpose digital computer,[6] and store in its memory a program for interpreting the specifications of LT. Then we load the program that specifies LT. The reader may think of this program as a collection of techniques that LT has acquired for discovering proofs. These techniques range from the ability to read and write expressions in symbolic logic to general schemes for how a proof might be found.

will refer to all of these variants, interchangeably, as "LT." This will not be confusing, since the exact content of the program we are considering at any particular point will always be clear from the context.

[5] LT employs the sentential calculus as set forth in Chapters 1 and 2 of A. N. Whitehead and Bertrand Russell, *Principia Mathematica* (10)—the "classic" of modern symbolic logic. A simple introduction to the system of *Principia* will be found in (3).

[6] The experiments described here were carried out with the Rand Johnniac computer. The Johnniac is an automatic digital computer of the Princeton type. It has a word length of 40 bits, with two instructions in each word. Its first storage consists of 4,096 words of magnetic cores, and its secondary storage consists of 9,216 words on magnetic drums. Its speed is about 15,000 operations per second. The programming techniques used are described more fully in (6). The experiments are reported in more detail in (7).

Once we have loaded this program and pushed the start button, the computer, to all intents and purposes, *is* LT. It already knows how to do symbolic logic, in the sense that the basic rules of operation of the mathematics are already in the program (analogously to a human's knowing that "equals added to equals give equals" in elementary algebra).

We are now ready to give LT a task. We give it a list of the expressions (axioms and previously proved theorems) that it may take as "given" for the task at hand. These are stored in LT's memory. Finally, we present LT with another expression and instruct it to discover a proof for this expression.

From this point, the computer is on its own. The program plus the task uniquely determines its behavior. It attempts to find a proof—that is, it tries various techniques, and if they don't work, it tries other techniques. If LT finds a legitimate proof, it prints this out on a long strip of paper. There is, of course, no guarantee that it will find a proof; after working for some time, the machine will give up—that is, it will stop looking for a proof.

Now the experimenters know exactly what is in the memory of LT when it starts—indeed, they created the program. This, however, is quite different from saying that the experimenters can predict everything LT will do. In principle this is possible; but in fact the program is so complex that the only way to make detailed predictions is to employ a human to simulate the program by hand. (A human can do anything a digital computer can do, although it may take him considerably longer.)

1. As the initial experiment, we stored the axioms of *Principia Mathematica*, together with the program, in the memory of LT, and then presented to LT the first 52 theorems in Chapter 2 of *Principia* in the sequence in which they appear there. LT's program specified that as a theorem was proved it was stored in memory and was available, along with the axioms, as material for the construction of proofs of subsequent theorems. With this program and this order of presentation of problems, LT succeeded in proving 38 (73%) of the 52 theorems. About half of the proofs were accomplished in less than a minute each; most of the remainder took from one to five minutes. A few theorems were proved in times ranging from 15 minutes to 45 minutes. There was a strong relation between the times and the lengths of the proofs—the time increasing sharply (perhaps exponentially) with each additional proof step.

2. The initial conditions were now restored by removing from LT's memory the theorems it had proved. (Translate: "A new subject was obtained who knew how to solve problems in logic but was unfamiliar with the particular problems to be used in the experiment.") When one of the later theorems of Chapter 2 (Theorem 2.12) was presented to LT, it was not able

to find a proof, although when it had held the prior theorems in memory, it had found one in about ten seconds.

3. Next, an experiment was performed intermediate between the first two. The axioms and Theorem 2.03 were stored in memory, but not the other theorems prior to Theorem 2.12, and LT was again given the task of proving the latter. Now, using Theorem 2.03 as one of its resources, LT succeeded— in fifteen minutes—where it had failed in the second experiment. The proof required three steps. In the first experiment, with all prior theorems available, the proof required only one step.

Outcome of the Experiments

From these three series of experiments we obtain several important pieces of evidence that the program of LT is qualitatively like that of a human faced with the same task. The first, and most important, evidence is that LT does in fact succeed in finding proofs for a large number of theorems.

Let us make this point quite clear. Since LT can actually discover proofs for theorems, its program incorporates a *sufficient* set of elementary processes arranged in a sufficiently effective strategy to produce this result. Since no other program has ever been specified for handling successfully these kinds of problem-solving tasks, no definite alternative hypothesis is available. We are well aware of the standard argument that "similarity of function does not imply similarity of process." However useful a caution this may be, it should not blind us to the fact that specification of a set of mechanisms sufficient to produce observed behavior is strong confirmatory evidence for the theory embodying these mechanisms, especially when it is contrasted with theories that cannot establish their sufficiency.

The only alternative problem-solving mechanisms that have been completely specified for these kinds of tasks are simple algorithms that carry out exhaustive searches of all possibilities, substituting "brute force" for the selective search of LT. Even with the speeds available to digital computers, the principal algorithm we have devised as an alternative to LT would require times of the order of hundreds or even thousands of years to prove theorems that LT proves in a few minutes. LT's success does not depend on the "brute force" use of a computer's speed, but on the use of heuristic processes like those employed by humans.[7] This can be seen directly from examination of the program, but it also shows up repeatedly in all the other behavior exhibited by LT.

The second important fact that emerges from the experiments is that LT's success depends in a very sensitive way upon the order in which problems are presented to it. When the sequence is arranged so that before any partic-

---

[7] A quantitative analysis of the power of the heuristics incorporated in LT will be found in (7).

ular problem is reached some potentially helpful intermediate results have already been obtained, then the task is easy. It can be made progressively harder by skipping more and more of these intermediate stepping-stones. Moreover, by providing a single "hint," as in the third experiment (that is, "Here is a theorem that might provide help"), we can induce LT to solve a problem it had previously found insoluble. All of these results are easily reproduced in the laboratory with humans. To compare LT's behavior with that of a human subject, we would first have to train the latter in symbolic logic (this is equivalent to reading the program into LT), but without using the specific theorems of Chapter 2 of *Principia Mathematica* that are to serve as problem material. We would then present problems to the human subject in the same sequence as to LT. For each new sequence we would need naive subjects, since it is difficult to induce a human subject to forget completely theorems he has once learned.

PERFORMANCE PROCESSES IN THE LOGIC THEORIST

We can learn more about LT's approximation to human problem solving by instructing it to print out some of its intermediate results—to work its problems on paper, so to speak. The data thus obtained can be compared with data obtained from a human subject who is asked to use scratch paper as he works on a problem, or to think aloud.[8] Specifically, the computer can be instructed to print out a record of the subproblems it works on and the methods it applies, successfully and unsuccessfully, while seeking a solution. We can obtain this information at any level of detail we wish, and make a correspondingly detailed study of LT's processes.

To understand the additional information provided by this "thinking aloud" procedure, we need to describe a little more fully how LT goes about solving problems. This description has two parts: (a) specifying what constitutes a proof in symbolic logic; (b) describing the methods that LT uses in finding proofs.

Nature of a Proof

A proof in symbolic logic (and in other branches of logic and mathematics) is a sequence of statements such that each statement: (a) follows from

---

[8] Evidence obtained from a subject who thinks aloud is sometimes compared with evidence obtained by asking the subject to theorize introspectively about his own thought processes. This is misleading. Thinking aloud is just as truly behavior as is circling the correct answer on a paper-and-pencil test. What we infer from it about other *processes* going on inside the subject (or the machine) is, of course, another question. In the case of the machine, the problem is simpler than in the case of the human, for we can determine exactly the correspondence between the internal processes and what the machine prints out.

one or more of the others that precede it in the sequence, or (b) is an axiom or previously proved theorem.[9] Here "follows" means "follows by the rules of logic."

LT is given four rules of inference:

Substitution. In a true expression (for example, "[p or p] implies p") there may be substituted for any variable a new variable or expression, provided that the substitution is made throughout the original expression. Thus, by substituting p or q for p in the expression "(p or p) implies p," we get: "([p or q] or [p or q]) implies (p or q)" but *not:* "([p or q] or p) implies p."

Replacement. In a true expression a connective ("implies," etc.) may be replaced by its definition in terms of other connectives. Thus "A implies B" is defined to be "not-A or B"; hence the two forms can be used interchangeably.

Detachment. If "A" is a true expression and "A implies B" is a true expression, then B may be written down as a true expression.

Syllogism. (Chaining). It is possible to show by two successive applications of detachment that the following is also legitimate: If "a implies b" is a true expression and "b implies c" is a true expression, then "a implies c" is also a true expression.

Proof Methods

The task of LT is to construct a proof sequence deriving a problem expression from the axioms and the previously proved theorems by the rules of inference listed above. But the rules of inference, like the rules of any mathematical system or any game, are permissive, not mandatory. That is, they state what sequences *may* legitimately be constructed, not what particular sequence should be constructed in order to achieve a particular result (i.e., to prove a particular problem expression). The set of "legal" sequences is exceeding large, and to try to find a suitable sequence by trial and error

---

[9] The axioms of symbolic logic and the theories that follow from them are all tautologies, true by virtue of the definitions of their terms. It is their tautological character that gives laws of logic their validity, independent of empirical evidence, as rules of inductive inference. Hence the very simple axioms that we shall use as examples here will have an appearance of redundancy, if not triviality. For example, the first axiom of *Principia* states, in effect, that "if any particular sentence (call it p) is true, or if that same sentence (p) is true, then that sentence (p) is, indeed, true"—for example, "if frogs are fish, or if frogs are fish, then frogs are fish." The "if—then" is trivially and tautologically true irrespective of whether p is true, for in truth frogs are not fish. Since our interest here is in problem solving, not in logic, the reader can regard LT's task as one of manipulating symbols to produce desired expressions, and he can ignore the material interpretations of these symbols.

alone would almost always use up the available time or memory before it would exhaust the set of legal sequences.[10]

To discover proofs, LT uses *methods* which are particular combinations of information processes that result in coordinated activity aimed at progress in a particular direction. LT has four methods (it could have more): *substitution, detachment, forward chaining,* and *backward chaining.* Each method focuses on a single possibility for achieving a link in a proof.

The substitution method attempts to prove an expression by generating it from a known theorem employing substitutions of variables and replacements of connectives.

The detachment method tries to work backward, utilizing the rule of detachment to obtain a new expression whose proof implies the proof of the desired expression. This possibility arises from the fact that if B is to be proved, and we already know a theorem of the form "A implies B," then proof of A is tantamount to proof of B.

Both chaining methods try to work backward to new problems, using the rule of syllogism, analogously to the detachment method. Forward chaining uses the fact that if "a implies c" is desired and "a implies b" is already known, then it is sufficient to prove "b implies c." Backward chaining runs the argument the other way: desiring "a implies c" and knowing "b implies c" yields "a implies b" as a new problem.

The methods are the major organizations of processes in LT, but they are not all of it. There is an executive process that coordinates the use of the methods, and selects the subproblems and theorems upon which the methods operate. The executive process also applies any learning processes that are to be applied. Also, all the methods utilize common subprocesses in carrying out their activity. The two most important subprocesses are the *matching* process, which endeavors to make two given subexpressions identical, and the *similarity test,* which determines (on the basis of certain computed descriptions) whether two expressions are "similar" in a certain sense (for details, cf. 8).

LT can be instructed to list its attempts, successful and unsuccessful, to use these methods, and can list the new subproblems generated at each stage by these attempts. We can make this concrete by an example:

Suppose that the problem is to prove "p implies p." The statement "$(p$ or $p)$ implies p" is an axiom; and "p implies $(p$ or $p)$" is a theorem that has already been proved and stored in the theorem memory. Following its program LT first tries to prove "p implies p" by the substitution method, but fails because it can find no similar theorem in which to make substitutions.

---

[10] See (7). The situation here is like that in chess or checkers where the player knows what moves are legal but has to find in a reasonable time a move that is also "suitable"— that is, conducive to winning the game.

Next, it tries the detachment method. Letting B stand for "p implies p," several theorems are found of the form "A implies B." For example, by substitution of not-p for q, "p implies (q or p)" becomes "p implies (not-p or p)"; this becomes, in turn, by replacement of "or" by "implies": "p implies (p implies p)." Discovery of this theorem creates a new subproblem: "Prove A"—that is, "prove p." This subproblem, of course, leads nowhere, since p is not a universally true theorem, hence cannot be proved.

At a later stage in its search LT tries the chaining method. Chaining forward, it finds the theorem "p implies (p or p)" and is then faced with the new problem of proving that "(p or p) implies p." This it is able to do by the substitution method, when it discovers the corresponding axiom.

All of these steps, successful and unsuccessful, in its proof—and the ones we have omitted from our exposition, as well—can be printed out to provide us with a complete record of how LT executed its program in solving this particular problem.

SOME CHARACTERISTICS OF THE PROBLEM-SOLVING PROCESS

Using as our data the information provided by LT as to the methods it tries, the sequence of these methods, and the theorems employed, we can ask whether its procedure shows any resemblance to the human problem-solving process as it has been described in psychological literature. We find that there are, indeed, many such resemblances, which we summarize under the following headings: set, insight, concept formation, and structure of the problem-subproblem hierarchy.

Set

The term "set," sometimes defined as "a readiness to make a specified response to a specified stimulus" (4, p. 65), covers a variety of psychological phenomena. We should not be surprised to find that more than one aspect of LT's behavior exhibits "set," nor that these several evidences of set correspond to quite different underlying processes.

1. Suppose that after the program has been loaded in LT, the axioms and a sequence of problem expressions are placed in its memory. Before LT undertakes to prove the first problem expression, it goes through the list of axioms and computes a description of each for subsequent use in the "similarity" tests. For this reason, the proof of the first theorem takes an extra interval of time amounting, in fact, to about twenty seconds. Functionally and phenomenologically, this computation process and interval represent a *preparatory set* in the sense in which that term is used in reaction-time experiments. It turns out in LT that this preparatory set saves about one third

of the computing time that would otherwise be required in later stages of the program.

2. *Directional set* is also evident in LT's behavior. When it is attempting a particular subproblem, LT tries first to solve it by the substitution method. If this proves fruitless, and only then, it tries the detachment method, then chaining forward, then chaining backward. Now when it searches for theorems suitable for the substitution method, it will not notice theorems that might later be suitable for detachment (different similarity tests being applied in the two cases). It attends single-mindedly to possible candidates for substitution until the theorem list has been exhausted; then it turns to the detachment method.

3. Hints and the change in behavior they induce have been mentioned earlier. Variants of LT exist in which the order of methods attempted by LT, and the choice of units in describing expressions, depend upon appropriate hints from the experimenter.

4. Effects from directional set occur in certain learning situations—as illustrated, for example, by the classical experiments of Luchins. Although LT at the present time has only a few learning mechanisms, these will produce strong effects of directional set if problems are presented to LT in appropriate sequences. For example, it required about 45 minutes to prove Theorem 2.48 in the first experiment because LT, provided with all the prior theorems, explored so many blind alleys. Given only the axioms and Theorem 2.16, LT proved Theorem 2.48 in about 15 minutes because it now considered a quite different set of possibilities.

The instances of set observable in the present program of LT are natural and unintended by-products of a program constructed to solve problems in an efficient way. In fact, it is difficult to see how we could have avoided such effects. In its simplest aspect, the problem-solving process is a search for a solution in a very large space of possible solutions. The possible solutions must be examined in *some* particular sequence, and if they are, then certain possible solutions will be examined before others. The particular rule that induces the order of search induces thereby a definite set in the ordinary psychological meaning of that term.

Preparatory set also arises from the need for processing efficiency. If certain information is needed each time a possible solution or group of solutions is to be examined, it may be useful to compute this information, once and for all, at the beginning of the problem-solving process, and to store it instead of recomputing it each time.

The examples cited show that set can arise in almost every aspect of the problem-solving process. It can govern the sequence in which alternatives are examined (the "method" set), it can select the concepts that are used in classifying perceptions (the "viewing" set), and it can consist in preparatory processes (the description of axioms).

None of the examples of set in LT relate to the way in which information is stored in memory. However, one would certainly expect such set to exist, and certain psychological phenomena bear this out—the set in association experiments, and so-called "incubation" processes. LT as it now stands is inadequate in this respect.

Insight

In the psychological literature, "insight" has two principal connotations: (a) "suddenness" of discovery, and (b) grasp of the "structure" of the problem, as evidenced by absence of trial and error. It has often been pointed out that there is no necessary connection between the absence of overt trial-and-error behavior and grasp of the problem structure, for trial and error may be perceptual or ideational, and no obvious cues may be present in behavior to show that it is going on.

In LT an observer's assessment of how much trial and error there is will depend on how much of the record of its problem-solving processes the computer prints out. Moreover, the amount of trial and error going on "inside" varies within very wide limits, depending on small changes in the program.

The performance of LT throws some light on the classical debate between proponents of trial-and-error learning and proponents of "insight," and shows that this controversy, as it is usually phrased, rests on ambiguity and confusion. LT searches for solutions to the problems that are presented it. This search must be carried out in some sequence, and LT's success in actually finding solutions for rather difficult problems rests on the fact that the sequences it uses are not chosen casually but do, in fact, depend on problem "structure."

To keep matters simple, let us consider just one of the methods LT uses—proof by substitution. The number of valid proofs (of *some* theorem) that the machine can construct by substitution of new expressions for the variables in the axioms is limited only by its patience in generating expressions. Suppose now that LT is presented with a problem expression to be proved by substitution. The crudest trial-and-error procedure we can imagine is for the machine to generate substitutions in a predetermined sequence that is independent of the expression to be proved, and to compare each of the resulting expressions with the problem expression, stopping when a pair are identical (cf. 7).

Suppose, now, that the generator of substitutions is constructed so that it is *not* independent of the problem expression—so that it tries substitutions in different sequences depending on the nature of the latter. Then, if the dependence is an appropriate one, the amount of search required on the average can be reduced. A simple strategy of this sort would be to try in the axioms only substitutions involving variables that actually appear in the problem expression.

The actual generator employed by LT is more efficient (and hence more "insightful" by the usual criteria) than this. In fact, it works backward from the problem expression, and takes into account necessary conditions that a substitution must satisfy if it is to work. For example, suppose we are substituting in the axiom "p implies (q or p);" and are seeking to prove "r implies (r or r)." Working backward, it is clear that if the latter expression can be obtained from the former by substitution at all, then the variable that must be substituted for p is r. This can be seen by examining the first variable in each expression, without considering the rest of the expression at all (cf. 7).

Trial and error is reduced to still smaller proportions by the method for searching the list of theorems. Only those theorems are extracted from the list for attempted substitution which are "similar" in a defined sense to the problem expression. This means, in practice, that substitution is attempted in only about ten per cent of the theorems. Thus a trial-and-error search of the theorem list to find theorems similar to the problem expression is substituted for a trial-and-error series of attempted substitutions in each of the theorems.

In these examples, the concept of proceeding in a "meaningful" fashion is entirely clear and explicit. Trial-and-error attempts take place in some "space" of possible solutions. To approach a problem "meaningfully" is to have a strategy that either permits the search to be limited to a smaller subspace, or generates elements of the space in an order that makes probable the discovery of one of the solutions early in the process.

We have already listed some of the most important elements in the program of LT for reducing search to tolerable proportions. These are: (a) the description programs to select theorems that are "likely" candidates for substitution attempts; (b) the process of working backwards, which uses information about the goal to rule out large numbers of attempts without actually trying them. In addition to these, the executive routine may select the sequence of subproblems to be worked on in an order that takes up "simple" subproblems first.

Concepts

Most of the psychological research on concepts has focused on the processes of their formation. The current version of LT is mainly a performance program, and hence shows no concept formation. There is in the program, however, a clearcut example of the use of concepts in problem solving. This is the routine for describing theorems and searching for theorems "similar" to the problem expression or some part of it in order to attempt substitutions, detachments, or chainings. All theorems having the same description exemplify a common concept. We have, for example, the concept of an expression that has a single variable, one argument places on its left side, and two argument places on its right side: "p implies $(p$ or $p)$" is an expression exemplifying this concept; so is "q implies $(q$ implies $q)$."

The basis for these concepts is purely pragmatic. Two expressions having the same description "look alike" in some undefined sense; hence, if we are seeking to prove one of them as a theorem, while the other is an axiom or theorem already proved, the latter is likely construction material for the proof of the former.

Hierarchies of Processes

Another characteristic of the behavior of LT that resembles human problem-solving behavior is the hierarchical structure of its processes. Two kinds of hierarchies exist, and these will be described in the next two paragraphs.

In solving a problem, LT breaks it down into component problems. First of all, it makes three successive attempts: a proof by substitution, a proof by detachment, or a proof by chaining. In attempting to prove a theorem by any of these methods, it divides its task into two parts: first, finding likely raw materials in the form of axioms or theorems previously proved; second, using these materials in matching. To find theorems similar to the problem expression, the first step is to compute a description of the problem expression; the second step is to search the list of theorems for expressions with the same description. The description-computing program divides, in turn, into a program for computing the number of levels in the expression, a program for computing the number of distinct variables, and a program for computing the number of argument places.

LT has a second kind of hierarchy in the generation of new expressions to be proved. Both the detachment and chaining methods do not give proofs directly but, instead, provide new alternative expressions to prove. LT keeps a list of these subproblems, and, since they are of the same type as the original problem, it can apply all its problem-solving methods to them. These methods, of course, yield yet other sub-problems, and in this way a large network of problems is developed during the course of proving a given logic expression. The importance of this type of hierarchy is that it is not fixed in advance, but grows in response to the problem-solving process itself, and shows some of the flexibility and transferability that seem to characterize human higher mental processes.

The problem-subproblem hierarchy in LT's program is quite comparable with the hierarchies that have been discovered by students of human problem-solving processes, and particularly by de Groot in his detailed studies of the thought methods of chess players (2, pp. 78–83, 105–111). Our earlier discussion of insight shows how the program structure permits an efficient combination of trial-and-error search with systematic use of experience and cues in the total problem-solving process.

SUMMARY OF THE EVIDENCE

We have now reviewed the principal evidence that LT solves problems in a manner closely resembling that exhibited by humans in dealing with the same problems. First, and perhaps most important, it is in fact capable of finding proofs for theorems—hence incorporates a system of processes that is sufficient for a problem-solving mechanism. Second, its ability to solve a particular problem depends on the sequence in which problems are presented to it in much the same way that a human subject's behavior depends on this sequence. Third, its behavior exhibits both preparatory and directional set. Fourth, it exhibits insight both in the sense of vicarious trial and error leading to "sudden" problem solution, and in the sense of employing heuristics to keep the total amount of trial and error within reasonable bounds. Fifth, it employs simple concepts to classify the expressions with which it deals. Sixth, its program exhibits a complex organized hierarchy of problems and subproblems.

COMPARISON WITH OTHER THEORIES

We have proposed a theory of the higher mental processes, and have shown how LT, which is a particular exemplar of the theory, provides an explanation for the processes used by humans to solve problems in symbolic logic. What is the relation of this explanation to others that have been advanced?

Associationism

The broad class of theories usually labelled "associationist" share a generally behaviorist viewpoint and a commitment to reducing mental functions to elementary, mechanistic neural events. We agree with the associationists that the higher mental processes can be performed by mechanisms—indeed, we have exhibited a specific set of mechanisms capable of performing some of them.

We have avoided, however, specifying these mechanisms in neurological or pseudo-neurological terms. Problem solving—at the information-processing level at which we have described it—has nothing specifically "neural" about it, but can be performed by a wide class of mechanisms, including both human brains and digital computers. We do not believe that this functional equivalence between brains and computers implies any structural equivalence at a more minute anatomical level (e.g., equivalence of neurons with circuits). Discovering what neural mechanisms realize these information-processing functions in the human brain is a task for another level of theory construction. Our theory is a theory of the information processes involved in problem solving, and not a theory of neural or electronic mechanisms for information processing.

The picture of the central nervous system to which our theory leads is a picture of a more complex and active system than that contemplated by most associationists. The notions of "trace," "fixation," "excitation," and "inhibition" suggest a relatively passive electrochemical system (or, alternatively, a passive "switchboard"), acted upon by stimuli, altered by that action, and subsequently behaving in a modified manner when later stimuli impinge on it.

In contrast, we postulate an information-processing system with large storage capacity that holds, among other things, complex strategies (programs) that may be evoked by stimuli. The stimulus determines what strategy or strategies will be evoked; the content of these strategies is already largely determined by the previous experience of the system. The ability of the system to respond in complex and highly selective ways to relatively simple stimuli is a consequence of this storage of programs and this "active" response to stimuli. The phenomena of set and insight that we have already described and the hierarchical structure of the response system are all consequences of this "active" organization of the central processes.

The historical preference of behaviorists for a theory of the brain that pictured it as a passive photographic plate or switchboard, rather than as an active computer, is no doubt connected with the struggle against vitalism. The invention of the digital computer has acquainted the world with a device—obviously a mechanism—whose response to stimuli is clearly more complex and "active" than the response of more traditional switching networks. It has provided us with operational and unobjectionable interpretations of terms like "purpose," "set," and "insight." The real importance of the digital computer for the theory of higher mental processes lies not merely in allowing us to realize such processes "in the metal" and outside the brain, but in providing us with a much profounder idea than we have hitherto had of the characteristics a mechanism must possess if it is to carry out complex information-processing tasks.

Gestalt Theories

The theory we have presented resembles the associationist theories largely in its acceptance of the premise of mechanism, and in few other respects. It resembles much more closely some of the Gestalt theories of problem solving, and perhaps most closely the theories of "directed thinking" of Selz and de Groot. A brief overview of Selz's conceptions of problem solving, as expounded by de Groot, will make its relation to our theory clear.

1. Selz and his followers describe problem solving in terms of processes or "operations" (2, p. 42). These are clearly the counterparts of the basic processes in terms of which LT is specified.

2. These operations are organized in a strategy, in which the outcome of each step determines the next (2, p. 44). The strategy is the counterpart of the program of LT.

3. A problem takes the form of a "schematic anticipation." That is, it is posed in some such form as: Find an X that stands in the specified relation R to the given element E (2, pp. 44–46). The counterpart of this in LT is the problem: Find a *sequence of sentences* (X) that stands in the relation of *proof* (R) to the given *problem expression* (E). Similarly, the subproblems posed by LT can be described in terms of schematic anticipations: for example, "Find an expression that is 'similar' to the expression to be proved." Many other examples can be supplied of "schematic anticipations" in LT.

4. The method that is applied toward solving the problem is fully specified by the schematic anticipation. The counterpart in LT is that, upon receipt of the problem, the executive program for solving logic problems specifies the next processing step. Similarly, when a subproblem is posed— like "prove the theorem by substitution"—the response to this subproblem is the initiation of a corresponding program (here, the method of substitution).

5. Problem solving is said to involve (a) finding means of solution, and (b) applying them (2, pp. 47–53). A counterpart in LT is the division between the similarity routines, which find "likely" materials for a proof, and the matching routines, which try to use these materials. In applying means, there are needed both *ordering* processes (to assign priorities when more than one method is available) and *control* processes (to evaluate the application) (2, p. 50).

6. Long sequences of solution methods are coupled together. This coupling may be *cumulative* (the following step builds on the result of the preceding) or *subsidiary* (the previous step was unsuccessful, and a new attempt is now made) (2, p. 51). In LT the former is illustrated by a successful similarity comparison followed by an attempt at matching; the latter by the failure of the method of substitution, which is then followed by an attempt at detachment.

7. In cumulative coupling, we can distinguish *complementary* methods from *subordinated* methods (2, p. 52). The former are illustrated by successive substitutions and replacements in successive elements of a pair of logic

expressions. The latter are illustrated by the role of matching as a subordinate process in the detachment method.

We could continue this list a good deal further. Our purpose is not to suggest that the theory of LT can or should be translated into the language of "directed thinking." On the contrary, the specification of the program for LT clarifies to a considerable extent notions whose meanings are only vague in the earlier literature. What the list illustrates is that the processes that we observe in LT are basically the same as the processes that have been observed in human problem solving in other contexts.

PERFORMANCE AND LEARNING

LT is primarily a performance machine. That is to say, it solves problems rather than learning how to solve problems. However, although LT does not learn in all the ways that a human problem solver learns, there are a number of important learning processes in the program of LT. These serve to illustrate some, but not all, of the forms of human learning.

Learning in LT

By learning, we mean any more or less lasting change in the response of the system to successive presentations of the same stimulus. By this definition—which is the customary one—LT does learn.

1. When LT has proved a theorem, it stores this theorem in its memory. Henceforth, the theorem is available as material for the proof of subsequent theorems. Therefore, whether LT is able to prove a particular theorem depends, in general, on what theorems it has previously been asked to prove.

2. LT remembers, during the course of its attempt to prove a theorem, what subproblems it has already tried to solve. If the same subproblem is obtained twice in the course of the attempt at a proof, LT will remember and will not try to solve it a second time if it has failed a first.

3. In one variant, LT remembers what theorems have proved useful in the past in conjunction with particular methods and tries these theorems first when applying the method in question. Hence, although its total repertory of methods remains constant, it learns to apply particular methods in particular ways.

These are types of learning that would certainly be found also in human problem solvers. There are other kinds of human learning that are not yet represented in LT. We have already mentioned one—acquiring new methods for attacking problems. Another is modifying the descriptions used in searches for similar theorems, to increase the efficiency of those searches. The latter learning process may also be regarded as a process for concept formation. We have under way a number of activities directed toward incorporating new forms of learning into LT, but we will postpone a more detailed discussion of these until we can report concrete results.

What Is Learned

The several kinds of learning now found in LT begin to cast light on the pedagogical problems of "what is learned?" including the problems of transfer of training. For example, if LT simply stored proofs of theorems as it found these, it would be able to prove a theorem a second time very rapidly, but its learning would not transfer at all to new theorems. The storage of *theorems* has much broader transfer value than the storage of *proofs*, since, as already noted, the proved theorems may be used as stepping stones to the proofs of new theorems. There is no mystery here in the fact that the transferability of what is learned is dependent in a very sensitive way upon the form in which it is learned and remembered. We hope to draw out the implications, psychological and pedagogical, of this finding in our subsequent research on learning.

CONCLUSION

We should like, in conclusion, only to draw attention to the broader implications of this approach to the study of information-processing systems. The heart of the approach is describing the behavior of a system by a well specified program, defined in terms of elementary information processes. In this approach, a specific program plays the role that is played in classical systems of applied mathematics by a specific system of differential equations.

Once the program has been specified, we proceed exactly as we do with traditional mathematical systems. We attempt to deduce general properties of the system from the program (the equations); we compare the behavior predicted from the program (from the equations) with actual behavior observed in experimental or field settings; we modify the program (the equations) when modification is required to fit the facts.

The promise of this approach is several-fold. First, the digital computer provides us with a device capable of realizing programs, and hence, of actually determining what behavior is implied by a program under various environmental conditions. Second, a program is a very concrete specification of the processes, and permits us to see whether the processes we postulate are realizable, and whether they are sufficient to produce the phenomena. The vaguenesses that have plagued the theory of higher mental processes and other parts of psychology disappear when the phenomena are described as programs.

In the present paper we have illustrated this approach by beginning the construction of a thoroughly operational theory of human problem solving. There is every reason to believe that it will prove equally fruitful in application to the theories of learning, of perception, and of concept formation.

References

1. Bruner, J. S., Goodnow, J., & Austin, G. *A study of thinking.* New York: Wiley, 1956.
2. de Groot, A. *Het Denken van den Schaker.* Amsterdam: Noord-Hollandsche Uitgevers Maatschappij, 1946.
3. Hilbert, D., & Ackermann, W. *Principles of mathematical logic.* New York: Chelsea, 1950.
4. Johnson, D. M. *The psychology of thought and judgment.* New York: Harper, 1955.
5. Moore, O. K., & Anderson, S. B. Search behavior in individual and group problem solving. *Amer. sociol. Rev.,* 1955, **19,** 702–714.
6. Newell, A., & Shaw, J. C. Programming the logic theory machine. *Proceedings Western Joint Computer Conference* (Institute of Radio Engineers), 1957, 230–240.
7. Newell, A., Shaw, J. C., & Simon, H. A. Empirical explorations with the logic theory machine. *Proceedings Western Joint Computer Conference* (Institute of Radio Engineers), 1957, 218–230.
8. Newell, A., & Simon, H. A. The logic theory machine: A complex information processing system. *Transactions on information theory* (Institute of Radio Engineers), 1956, Vol. IT-2, No. 3, 61–79.
9. Simon, H. A., & Newell, A. Models, their uses and limitations. In L. D. White (Ed.), *The state of the social sciences.* Chicago: Univer. Chicago Press, 1956. Pp. 66–83.
10. Whitehead, A. N., & Russell, B. *Principia mathematica.* Vol. I. (2d ed.) Cambridge: Cambridge Univer. Press, 1925.

23. THE TEACHING OF THINKING

Hilda Taba[1]

Educators have long said to themselves and to others that the proper business of school is to teach students to think. Yet this objective has remained a pious hope instead of becoming a tangible reality. A variety of factors have militated against developing a serious and well thought out strategy for helping students to become autonomous, creative, and productive thinkers.

Perhaps the most serious inhibiting factor has been the hazy conceptualization both of what is meant by teaching and what thinking consists of. Thinking has been treated as a global process which seemingly encompasses anything that goes on in the head, from daydreaming to constructing a concept of relativity. Consequently, the problem of defining thinking is still before us. The distinctions between the various types of thinking have been defective also. Even the more serious educational thinkers fail to distinguish the strategies of thinking, such as problem solving, from the basic cognitive process and skills, such as generalizing, differentiating, and forming concepts. These processes are the necessary ingredients of problem solving if this strategy is to amount to anything beyond sheer formality.

Implementation of thinking as an educational objective also has been handicapped by several questionable assumptions. One rather widely accepted

SOURCE. *Elementary English*, May, 1965.

[1] Dr. Taba, now deceased, was a Professor of Education at San Francisco State College. This is another paper in the series on "Language and the Higher Thought Processes," to be published jointly as a bulletin by the National Conference on Research in English and the National Council of Teachers of English.

assumption is that reflective thinking cannot take place until a sufficient body of factual information is accumulated. Teaching, which follows this assumption, stresses factual coverage and burdens the memory with unorganized and, therefore, rather perishable information.

An equally unproductive assumption is that thought is an automatic by-product of studying certain subjects and assimilating the end products of someone else's disciplined thought. Some subjects are assumed to have this power independently of how they learn or are taught. Inherently, memorizing mathematical formulae or the steps in mathematical processes is assumed to be better training than memorizing cake recipes, even though both may be learned in the same manner and call for the same mental process—rote memory (15).

The analysis of teaching suffers from similar difficulties. Teaching is still viewed largely as communication of knowledge, and often knowledge is equated with descriptive information—the "what," "who," and "when" questions are the main diet of classroom instruction. As a consequence the current methods of teaching tend to be shaped by this emphasis. Research on teaching has skirted the actual process of teaching and has concentrated instead on such matters as personal characteristics of good teachers and *a priori* criteria for rating effective teaching (6).

It is no wonder, then, that despite the widespread acceptance of thinking as an educational objective little consideration has been given to the ways in which learning to think differ from the ways in which students learn knowledge or content of various sorts.

Recent research is producing changes in both of these areas. Studies of cognition are under way, which promise a more precise analysis of the processes and of the psychological dynamics of the mental activity we call thinking. Some of these studies are concerned with styles of labeling (12), others with strategies of concept formation (2), and still others with what amounts to the styles in strategies of thinking (7, 10). Important as these studies are, as yet their results cannot be easily translated into the methods for modifying the ways of thinking. But at least they are opening up the possibility of a scientific approach to the analysis of thinking.

The development of thinking has received renewed attention also, as exemplified by the recent interest in the work of Piaget and his followers. Piaget's theories regarding the nature of thought and the sequences in the transformation of the patterns or modes of thinking have influenced such enterprises as Bruner's (3) analysis of the process of education and Suchman's (13) experiments with inquiry training.

Some progress is being made in the study of the teaching process also. Recent studies of teaching have focused on teaching as it occurs in the classroom instead of inferring its effectiveness either from *a priori* notions of good teaching or from the characteristics of good teachers. Studies by Hughes (8), Flanders (5), and Bellack (1) focus on describing and cataloguing the teaching acts and on inferring from these descriptions their impact on learning in general, on classroom climate, and on achievement.

This article is a description of a study of classroom interaction designed to examine the relationship between teaching strategies and the development of cognitive processes (16). The study, conducted under a grant from the Cooperative Research Branch of the U.S. Office of Education, focused on several hypotheses. The central hypothesis was that it is possible to train students in the processes of thinking, provided that the trainable cognitive skills could be identified.

The studies of thinking cited above seemed to have one difficulty in common as far as the application of their findings to instruction in the classroom is concerned. The findings regarding the styles of thought fail to shed light on the processes by which these styles are acquired or to describe the skills on which these styles are founded.

Another hypothesis was that under optimal conditions this training would result in an acceleration of the usual developmental sequence, such as the appearance of abstract or formal thought. The studies of the development of thought and intelligence by Piaget and the Geneva school (9^2, 11, 14^3) suggest that the evolution of thought takes place in three stages, essentially: 1) the sensory-motor stage or the preverbal intelligence; 2) the stage of concrete operations or thinking with objects and concrete events, which stage lasts from around two to eleven years of age; and 3) the stage of conceptual or formal thought which is established between eleven years of age and adolescence. There is a question, however, whether training would alter these age placements since the available data recorded the performance of untrained children, or those with only a minimum of training, such as in the study by Ervin (4). It seemed reasonable to assume that if both the curriculum and teaching strategies were addressed to the development of thought, formal thought could appear earlier.

The third hypothesis was that with adequate teaching strategies the possibility of abstract thought would be opened to students who are now considered to have too low an IQ to be capable of higher levels of mental activity.

The study was conducted in elementary classes which were using a curriculum in social studies that systematically stressed the development of an ability to generalize and to use generalizations productively. What remained to be done was to specify the necessary teaching strategies and to train the

2 Chapter 6.
3 Pp. 107–112.

teachers in their use, in order to become adept at these processes themselves, and to learn how to induct children in the mastery of the required cognitive skills.

THE CONCEPT OF COGNITIVE TASKS

In an effort to arrive at teachable and learnable aspects of thought, three cognitive tasks were identified: (1) concept formation, (2) the development of generalizations and inferences through interpretation of raw data, and (3) the explanation and prediction of new phenomena by applying known principles and facts.

Concept Formation. In its simplest form, concept development may be described as consisting of three processes or operations. One is the differentiation of the properties or characteristics of objects and events, such as differentiating the materials of which houses are built from other characteristics of houses. This differentiating involves analysis in the sense of breaking down global wholes into specific properties and elements.

The second process is that of grouping. This process calls for abstracting certain common characteristics in an array of dissimilar objects or events and for grouping these on the basis of this similar property, such as grouping together hospitals, doctors, and medicine as something to do with health care or according to their availability as an index to the standard of living. Naturally, the same objects and events can be grouped in several different ways. For example, hospitals, X-rays, and surgical equipment can be grouped together as health facilities, as type of services, or as indices of standard of living, depending on the purpose of the grouping.

The third process is that of categorizing and labeling. This process calls for the discovery of categories or labels which encompass and organize diverse objects and events, such as evolving the concept of a unit measurement from measuring with a cup, a yardstick, a plain stick, and a rubber band. It also involves the process of super- and subordination; that is, deciding which items can be subsumed under which category.

In classrooms this cognitive task occurs in the form of enumerating or listing, such as identifying a series of specific items noted in a film or reported by a research committee, then grouping similar things, and, finally, labeling the groups.

Interpretation of Data and Inference. Essentially this cognitive task consists of evolving generalizations and principles from an analysis of concrete data. Several subprocesses are involved. The first and the simplest is that of identifying specific points in the data. This process is somewhat analogous to the listing or enumeration preceding grouping. The second process is that of explaining specific items or events, such as why ocean currents affect

temperature, why Mexico employs the "each one teach one" system in erad-
icating illiteracy, or why the way of life in California changed when its
harbors were opened for free trade. This process also involves relating the
points of information to each other to enlarge their meaning and to establish
relationships.

The third operation is that of forming inferences which go beyond that
which is directly given, such as inferring, from the comparison of the data
on population composition with data on standards of living in certain Latin
American states, that countries with predominantly white populations tend to
have a higher standard of living.

Interpretation of data and formulation of inferences takes place in the classroom whenever the students must cope with raw data of one sort or another,
such as comparing the imports and exports of several countries or analyzing
and synthesizing the factors which determine the level of technological development in a given culture by examining the tools and techniques used in
the production of goods.

Application of principles. A third cognitive task is that of applying
known principles and facts to explain new phenomena or to predict consequences from known conditions. For example, if one knows what a desert
is like, what way of life it permits, and how water affects the productivity of
the soil, one can predict what might happen to the desert way of life if
water became available.

This cognitive task requires essentially two different operations. One is
that of predicting and hypothesizing. This process requires an analysis of
the problem and of the conditions in order to determine which facts and
principles are relevant and which are not. Second is that of developing informational or logical parameters which constitute the causal links between
the conditions and the prediction and, in fact, make a rational prediction or
explanation possible. For example, if one predicts that the presence of water
in the desert will cause cities to be built, one needs also to make explicit the
chain of causal links that leads from the availability of water to the building
of cities. These chains may consist of logical conditions, such as that the
presence of water is the only condition to make the soil productive, or from
factual conditions, such as whether the desert soil contains salt or not.

These predictions and explanations are of different orders of generality
and complexity: for example, the prediction that cities will be built as a
consequence of a water supply represents a greater leap than does the prediction that grass will grow.

In order to develop criteria for effective teaching strategies it was necessary to evolve a theoretical construct. In the light of this construct these
processes and their development were viewed.

Space permits the description of only a few principles in this theoretical construct. First, the learning of thinking was viewed as essentially an active transaction between the individual and his environment. The nature of this transaction is only partly controlled by the nature of the immediate stimulus. Partly, it is controlled by whatever mediation is available either in the form of models offered or of guidance that is available. Chiefly, however, the individual must develop for himself both the conceptual schemes and the processes of using them. In other words, the environment and training become available to the individual only to the extent that he performs certain operations on what he receives. These operations cannot be "given" in the ordinary sense of the word. An individual may, for example, imitate a model of the "if-then" reasoning. But this model remains unproductive unless he internalizes and elaborates this process himself.

Second, the development of thought follows a sequence in which the simpler and the more concrete operations must precede and prepare for the more complex and the abstract. The elementary school child, for example, must work out the idea of cause and consequence on concrete material before he can evolve an abstract concept of causes and consequences. It appears also that the elementary school years are the period during which the concrete thinking, or thinking with concrete objects and events, is being transformed into formal thinking or thinking with symbols. For this reason an emphasis on the development of certain basic cognitive skills on this level is crucial.

The idea of a sequential order applies also to the mastery of the skills involved in the cognitive tasks described above. As a matter of fact, the skills as described above could be seen as a series of sequential steps in which each preceding one is a prerequisite for the success in mastering the next one. For example, in interpreting data the differentiation of specific points is a prerequisite to comparing and contrasting these points or to seeing relationships between them. The latter is, in turn, a prerequisite for making inferences, and so on.

Finally, the conceptual schema undergo a constant reorganization. The dynamics of this reorganization can be visualized as a rotation of intake of information into the existing conceptual scheme and the extension or reorganization of the scheme whenever the problem or the information received creates a dissonance because it does not fit the scheme. For example, a child whose concept of relationship of altitude and temperature is that the higher one goes the colder it gets is jarred into modifying this concept when faced with the fact of high altitude combined with high temperature. He now needs to extend this concept to include the concept of geographic zones.

Piaget (11) calls these two processes "assimilation" and "accommodation," and these terms will be used in the discussion that follows. This rotation of assimilation and accommodation seems to describe the psychological dynamics or mechanism for the gradual maturation of thought, and, as such, is extremely important in the strategy of training.

Hunt (9) points out, in addition, that this rotation requires a proper match between the existing conceptual scheme and that which is required by the new information or task. When the requirements of the accommodation are too far beyond the existing conceptual scheme it is impossible for the child to make a leap. When it is too close there is no challenge for reorganization.

TEACHING STRATEGIES FOR COGNITIVE GROWTH

The concepts of the cognitive tasks together with the principles which govern the development of the cognitive skills have interesting implications for the formulation of teaching strategies.

First, the concept of thinking as essentially an active process, in the sense that it can be learned only by doing, sets the process of teaching into a new perspective. If students are to develop a cognitive structure by their own efforts, the usual role of teaching and of the teacher has to be reversed. Instead of teaching consisting primarily of communication of information, with the role of the teacher as a fount of that information, he needs to become an adroit guide of the heuristic process. In this kind of teaching strategy the art of asking questions assumes a crucial role. Questions, furthermore, need a double focus: on the substance of what is being discussed and on the cognitive operations. A question such as, "What materials do we use in building houses?" focuses on the materials and excludes other characteristics of building houses such as tools and labor. This question also asks for enumeration of these materials rather than explanations of why these materials are used. Other questions are addressed to explanation, such as why women in certain primitive tribes carry things on their heads or why some countries fail to use the natural resources they have.

The concept of sequence and of the rotation of assimilation and accommodation suggests, further, that teaching acts, such as the questions, need to be programmed to foster an appropriate sequence of learning. If the learning to apply knowledge to explaining new phenomena involves mastering certain modes of thinking in a certain order, then the questions the teacher asks and the remarks she makes need to follow that order. If there is to be rotation of intake of new information with tasks that require changing the conceptual structure, then the teaching acts need to be organized to stimulate such a rotation. If time and pacing of transitions from one mode or level of thinking into another is essential, then the teaching strategy must manage this pacing. In other words, teaching needs to be addressed first to the objective of thinking; second, seen as a series of acts, each of which has a specific pedagogical function; and, finally, viewed as a strategy or organization of these functions.

In the study described above, *Thinking in Elementary School Children* (16), two groups of teaching functions were identified which seemed to affect the development of cognitive skills, either positively or negatively. First are questions or statements made by the teacher or the students which are psychological or managerial in their function and unrelated to the logic of the content. Statements of this type included approval, disagreement, disapproval, management, and reiteration. Second, are teacher questions or statements which give direction to discussions and are related to the logic of the content and of the cognitive operations sought. This group of functions included focusing, refocusing, change of focus, deviating from focus, extending thought on the same level, lifting thought to a higher level, and controlling thought (16[4]).

Focusing questions or remarks establish both the content topic under consideration and the cognitive operations to be performed. They set the cognitive task. For example, a question by the teacher such as, "If the desert had all the water it needed what would happen to the desert way of life?" establishes the central content topic for discussion and calls for prediction of consequences. However, to prevent students from indulging in associative thinking which follows a single line and opens up new dimensions, a change of focus may be needed. Refocusing may be necessary to bring the discussion back to the original topic.

Extending thought on the same level fulfills the requirement of allowing a sufficient amount of assimilation before thought is lifted to another level, such as making a transition from description of specific points noted in a film, to explaining why certain events took place in the film or from prediction to establishing its validity. This is essentially a strategy in which a number of students are induced to respond to the same question instead of proceeding from an answer by one student to a question to the same one, as is usual. Extension of thought on the same level also assures the participation of the lower students. This engages them in the initial step of the process and thus prepares them for participation in the next step.

Lifting of the level of thought occurs when the teacher or child either gives or seeks information that shifts the thought to a level higher than the previously established one. Thus, making a transition from enumeration to grouping and from grouping to labelling represents lifting of thought. However, pursuing each of these steps by engaging more students or by seeking clarification and elaboration would represent extension.

Controlling thought occurs when the teacher gives what the students should do for themselves, such as suggesting a category or classification or giving

[4] Chapter 7.

explanations of phenomena observed instead of seeking explanation from the children.

The examples below illustrate the function of focusing, extending, and lifting thought:

(1) C Malobi took the money home with her. (Child gives specific information.)

(2) T What did Malobi do with the money? (Teacher seeks specific information.)

(3) C She saved it. (Child extends thought on the level of specific information.)

(4) C She put it underground. (Child extends thought on the level of specific information.)

(5) C She put sticks and tin over it. (Child extends thought on the level of specific information.)

(6) C Before she did that she put it in a little pot. (Child extends thought on the level of specific information.)

In the following example the teacher attempts to lift the level of thought from the giving of information to explanation:

(1) C They carried things in baskets on their heads. (Child gives specific information.)

(2) T Explain why. (Teacher lifts thought to the level of explanation.)

(3) C I suppose they can carry more things that way. (Child gives an explanation.)

The combination of these functions together with the pacing of assimilation and the timing of lifting thought to a new level is what constitutes the teaching strategy. This strategy is determined by recognizing that it takes time to learn the skills involved in these cognitive tasks. They are not in the class of instantaneous learning. Furthermore, presumably there are individual differences in the speed with which these skills can be mastered. Some students may make a clear distinction after a few attempts at enumeration, while others need to "mess around" for a longer time to discover what is at stake and what the model of differentiation is. Teaching strategy, to be effective, must allow variation in pacing each step, determining how long to continue on the plateau of each step, and when to make a transition to the next one.

In order to assess the effectiveness of these pedagogical functions, the verbal remarks of students were rated as to level of thought in each of the three cognitive tasks. In effect, these ratings described the successive cognitive operations involved in each of the tasks described previously. Presumably the process of making inferences is a more complex one and of a higher order than is identification of the points in the information presented, the latter being a prerequisite to the former. In the task calling for inferring from data, a teacher may seek, first, specific information. She may then attempt to lift the level of thought to that of explanation, and follow with questions designed to elicit inference, *etc*. The success in eliciting appropriate responses constitutes the measure of the effectiveness of the teaching strategy.

The charting of this flow of teaching acts and of the level of students' responses describes visually the relationship of the two. For example, when the teacher attempts to raise the level of thought too early in the discussion, this typically results in the children's returning to a lower level and in their inability to sustain discussion at the higher levels of thought. On the other hand, an effective strategy of focusing, extending, and lifting thought, combined with appropriate pacing of extensions and properly matched lifts, will result in a gradual movement toward higher levels of mental operation by the majority of the students. A frequent change of focus produces an alternation between several levels, a lack of sustained thought at any level, and a gradual return to the most primitive one. The same result occurs when the teacher inserts controls of thought by giving students what they should be doing for themselves. Figure 1 illustrates some of these strategies:

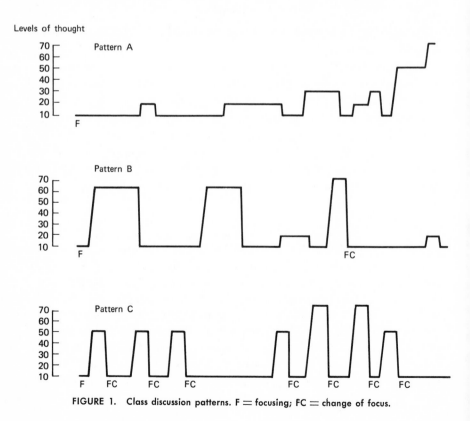

FIGURE 1.   Class discussion patterns. F = focusing; FC = change of focus.

Pattern A represents a strategy in which the transitions are paced appropriately, with the result that the class follows the transitions from one level of thought to the next and sustains the thought on each. In Pattern B the lifting of thought occurs too early, with the result that when the few students who could follow it have exhausted their ideas the class settles down to the lowest level. Pattern C illustrates a discussion in which the focus is lost, and the teacher is forced to keep the discussion alive by constantly changing the topic, without being able to sustain thought on any.

What, then, can be said about the merits of this approach to teaching thinking? First, the specification of thinking as an object of educational effort permits a clearer analysis of the appropriate pedagogical functions necessary to make this objective both more realistic and attainable. A more clearly focused target together with more articulated pedagogical functions may also permit a more effective training of teachers than is possible when both the nature of cognitive processes and of the appropriate teaching strategies for them are vague and obscure.

Second, it seems that a similar analysis of other educational objectives, such as the enhancement of the ego concept, the growth in affective domain, and the development of a creative approach to literature and art, might eventuate in the kinds of description of instructional processes which may provide the material for the development of a generic and a functional theory of learning and teaching.

Finally, such an approach to teaching thinking may reach students who are now relatively untouched by instruction. The results of the study described here indicated a lack of correlation between the performance on the test of Inference in Social Studies and the students' IQ. Analysis of tapescripts suggested that a careful structuring of the sequential steps in mastering the basic cognitive skills and an appropriate timing and pacing of the transitions from one level of thought to another are the chief ingredients to opening the possibility for a higher level of mental functioning to students of low ability (as measured by tests of intelligence). Analysis of a few individual cases indicated the possibility that among the so-called slow students are many who are only slow absorbers. Evidently, when the amount of information to be assimilated is reduced and opportunity is provided for systematic processing of that information, such students can function on abstract levels of thought.

Bibliography

1. Bellack, A., J. R. Davitz, *et al.*, *The Language of the Classroom.* New York: Institute of Psychological Research, Teachers College, Columbia University, 1963.

2. Bruner, J. S., Jacqueline J. Goodnow, & G. A. Austin, *A Study of Thinking.* New York: Wiley, 1956.

3. Bruner, J. S., *The Process of Education.* Cambridge: Harvard University Press, 1960.

4. Ervin, Susan M., "Training and Logical Operation of Children," *Child Development*, 31 (1960) 555–563.

5. Flanders, N. A., *Teacher Influence, Pupil Attitudes, and Achievement.* Prepublication manuscript of a proposed research monograph for the U.S. Office of Education, Cooperative Research Branch, Washington, D.C. 1960.

6. Gage, N. L. (Editor), *Handbook of Research on Teaching.* A Project of The American Educational Research Association. Chicago: Rand McNally and Company, 1963, Chap. 11.

7. Guilford, J. P., "Basic Conceptual Problems in the Psychology of Thinking," *Annals New York Academy of Science*, 91 (1961) 9–19.

8. Hughes, Marie, *et al.*, *Development of the Means for the Assessment of the Quality of Teaching in Elementary School.* (Mimeo.) Salt Lake City: University of Utah, 1959.

9. Hunt, J. McV., *Experience and Intelligence.* New York: Ronald Press, 1961, Ch. 5–9.

10. Peel, E. A., *The Pupil's Thinking.* London: Oldbourne, 1960.

11. Piaget, J., *The Psychology of Intelligence.* New York: Harcourt, 1950.

12. Sigel, I., *Cognitive Style and Personality Dynamics.* Interim report. Merrill-Palmer Institute, 1961.

13. Suchman, J. R., *The Elementary School Training Program in Scientific Inquiry.* U.S. Office of Education, Title VII, Project 216. Urbana: University of Illinois, 1964.

14. Taba, Hilda, *Curriculum Development. Theory and Practice.* New York: Harcourt, Brace & World, 1962.

15. Taba, Hilda, & F. F. Elzey, "Teaching Strategies and Thought Processes," *Teachers College Record*, Vol. 65, No. 6, March, 1964.

16. Taba, Hilda, S. Levine, & F. F. Elzey, *Thinking in Elementary School Children*, U.S. Office of Education, Cooperative Research Branch Project No. 1574. San Francisco: San Francisco State College, 1964.

CHAPTER 4

The Development of Language

SUSAN B. CROCKENBERG, EDITOR

This chapter focuses on the acquisition of language. The readings included cover three distinct research trends. The first concerns linguistic aspects of language, particularly the development of the grammatical and semantic systems. The second has to do with demographic variables such as social class and race and their effect on language development. And the third relates the acquisition of language to cognitive functions such as concept formation, problem solving, regulation of behavior, and discrimination. While these three dimensions of language acquisition do not exhaust the research trends, they do cover the empirical and theoretical work that is developmental and that seems most relevant to research in education.

Another characteristic of the research articles included in this volume is their concern with process variables in contrast with earlier attempts (Davis, 1937; McCarthy, 1930; Templin, 1957), which provided the base from which present studies depart, but were primarily descriptive in nature.

In the area of language acquisition, much of the relevant literature is linguistically oriented, that is, it examines language structure in an attempt to get at the "how" of language acquisition. Because methodology in psycholinguistics, specifically in the collection of grammars, is still in its formative stages, much of the relevant research is not experimental; samples are small, and statistical analyses are used infrequently. Nonetheless, the studies included introduce a number of issues and controversies prominent in the area of language development.

A study by Werner and Kaplan (1950) treats the relationship between semantic and grammatical aspects of language in an investigation of word-meaning discovery through verbal contexts. By observing how children gave signification to artificial words embedded in sentences, two types of immature signification were distinguished with different developmental characteristics. One type declined gradually from age 8 to 13; the other showed an abrupt decrease at about age 11. The authors suggest that this decrease may reflect a more general change in abstracting ability that occurs at that age. The view that semantic meaning is learned by using words in a verbal context is in contrast to a second view that word meanings develop by direct association with referents (the objects or instances to which the words refer). It may be, as the results suggest, that word meanings are learned more effectively through verbal contexts at older ages, while for younger children association of words with referents is a more effective way of conveying meaning. Such differences in learning might well be considered in developing curricula.

Brown and Bellugi (1964), from their analysis of the grammars of two children, suggest three processes to account for the development of increasingly complex grammars: imitation with reduction, imitation with expansion, and induction of latent structure. Their view that imitation is a primary source of progress in grammar is contradictory to the finding that subjects could not imitate grammatical forms that had never appeared in their own spontaneous production (Ervin-Tripp, 1964). Ervin-Tripp argues, instead, that analogic extension (generalization) accounts for the increasing similarity of the child's speech to that of the adult.

The issue of whether imitation is a source of progress in the development of grammatical structures is only one aspect of the larger question of why the child's language system changes with age. The account preferred by McNeill (1966) and Chomsky (1965) is that the child has an innate language-acquisition device that is predisposed to developing the major syntactic structures. This reliance on innate factors derives from the fact that syntactic structures are unmarked in overt speech, that is, syntactic rules cannot be directly observed but must be inferred from overt speech. However, Olson (1968) points out that other aspects of grammar, such as inflections, are unmarked and yet the child learns the rules that guide their use. McNeill's explanation of this phenomenon is that a child constructs a tentative rule that he finds inadequate because it has too many exceptions. So he hypothesizes some higher-order rule, based on the speech of adult models, that better handles the data. Olson then raises this question, "If he can get these relations from an adult model, why can he not get the others from them as well?"

Research by Lovaas et al. (1966) on two autistic children suggests that knowledge of language development in a natural environment is not a necessary condition for designing remedial or compensatory programs. Lovaas found that mute autistic children, trained individually, learned to speak and to use words appropriately through imitation of an adult tutor. In terms of extrapolation to curriculum design it should be noted, however, that the language training these children received was intensive, six hours a day, seven days a week.

While it seems that language development follows a definite pattern from less to more complex sets of rules, a number of authors have observed differences in comprehension and communication ability in children, which they suggest may be attributable to environmental factors associated with social class and race. Carson and Rabin (1960), for example, compared Negro and white children from both north and south on language communication and comprehension. While northern whites were able to communicate better than northern Negroes, northern Negroes rated higher than southern Negroes. The study also indicated that the difference in language ability between the two racial groups is attributable to differences in communication rather than comprehension.

Bernstein's theory of the relationship between social class and language postulates that linguistic codes are the result of the kinds of relationships that typify each class. A restricted code, i.e., one in which language lacks specificity and statements are made without giving reasons, evolves in the lower class as a consequence of a social structure that emphasizes status or roles as the source of behavioral directives. The elaborated code of the middle class is characterized by a number of alternative ways of expressing the same thing and by verbalizations of intent. It reflects a social structure that emphasizes individual differences and environmental circumstances as qualifications of behavior and speech.

Taking off from Bernstein's work, Hess and Shipman (1965) speculate that the correlation between social class and cognitive functioning may be understood in terms of language and communication patterns. Using Negro mothers from four social classes, the authors find differences between social classes in mothers' verbal codes, in their methods of control in situations requiring a disciplinary response, and in concept utilization. Lower-class children perform more poorly on a sorting task, and mothers' use of low-level concepts is significantly correlated with their children's performance. Like Brown and Bellugi (1964) and Ervin-Tripp (1964), Hess and Shipman are concerned with process variables and ask what it is about the environment that depresses the lower-class child's cognitive functioning.

Bernstein's theory of restricted and elaborated codes has also been used to explain differences between social classes in the relative importance they attribute to the use of language in skill and person areas of socialization [Bernstein and Henderson (1969)]. Bernstein argues that the greater emphasis placed on the use of language in interpersonal contexts by the middle class relative to the working class occurs because middle-class social structure necessitates finer social distinctions and a greater degree of explicitness that is best conveyed verbally. On the other hand, the greater emphasis placed by the working class on language use in transmitting skills arises out of differences in the concept of learning held by the two classes. In the middle class an autonomous learning situation is valued; hence linguistic exchange is minimized in skill learning. In the working class the learner is viewed as a passive recipient of knowledge, there is little autonomy, and as a consequence there is greater need for verbal communication. Bernstein points out that there may well be discontinuities between the theories of learning of home and school and that "it may be unreasonable to expect children exposed to such discontinuities to respond to forms of control which presuppose a culture and socialization very different from their own."

Much of the recent interest in the relationship of social class and language is based on the assumption that language and cognition are functionally related. Whorf (1956) argued that the structure of thought is determined by the structure of the spoken language. Basically, this is the assumption underlying Blank's and Solomon's attempt to develop abstract thinking in disadvantaged children through a language-training program. The study used only one measure of abstract thinking, namely scores on the Stanford-Binet, but results did indicate that children given the training showed increases in IQ significantly greater than did control children.

Research on verbal mediation is also relevant to the question of the relationship of language and thought. The work in this area originated in the ideas of Hull (1943) and Pavlov (1955), and has culminated in recent work by the Kendlers (1959, 1961, 1963, 1964) and by Flavell, Beach, and Chinsky (1966). The classic study was done by Kuenne (1946) and investigated the role that verbal mediators play in human discrimination learning. The hypothesis was that, unlike animal or preverbal subjects, older children with the capacity to employ verbal responses would generalize equally well to all other pairs of test stimuli differing from the training stimuli only on the one relevant dimension. Preschool and kindergarten children were trained to select the smaller of a pair of squares and then tested with two pairs of still smaller squares. Only subjects who were able to verbalize the mediating principle evidenced generalization to the smallest pair of squares.

In their series of experiments (one is reprinted in the chapter on conceptual processes), the Kendlers confirmed earlier findings and concluded that before a certain age children do not use verbal mediating responses. Experiments that tested this developmental hypothesis further led to the formulation of a mediation-deficiency hypothesis. Since young children could make the verbal responses on request, their failure to mediate was attributed either to their failure to make the verbal responses at the appropriate time or to the failure of their verbal responses to act as mediators. Flavell, Beach, and Chinsky

(1966) tested these two alternatives. They called the child's failure to make the verbal response on the appropriate occasion "production deficiency," and the failure of the verbal response to mediate "mediation deficiency." The results of their experiment, which involved children at three grade levels, indicated that second-grade subjects produced significantly more detectable verbal coding and rehearsal than kindergarten subjects, supporting the production-deficiency hypothesis. While these results provide a glimmer of the processes involved in the development of verbal mediation, the relationship between verbal labels and other thought processes is still obscure.

Another approach to the relationship of thought and language is taken by Carroll and Casagrande (1958). To test the hypothesis that perception is influenced by grammatical characteristics of the language an individual speaks, the form orientation of Navaho-speaking and English-speaking children was compared. Since the Navaho language has special verb endings for verbs of handling to indicate different shapes, it was expected that Navaho-speaking children would be form-oriented earlier. The results supported this hypothesis; Navaho-speaking children matched pairs of objects on the basis of form earlier than did English-speaking children. A replication of the study with English-speaking children having form experience indicated that these children were very similar to Navaho-speaking children in their form orientation. This finding suggests that at the level of simple discrimination and form orientation, language structure has no more of an effect than does direct perceptual experience. However, it is probable that language is essential for some aspects of thought but not for others. Language structure may have more determinative effects on higher-level thought processes, as Blank and Solomon suggest.

The articles in this chapter provide an introduction to the expanding field of research in language development, but they do not represent a complete set of readings. A bibliography of additional studies is included for readers interested in broader coverage.

References

Readings

Berko, Jean. The Child's Learning of English Morphology. *Word*, 1958, **14**, 150–177.

Bernstein, B. Linguistic Codes, Hesitation Phenomena and Intelligence. In D. B. Fry (Ed.), *Language and Speech*. England: Robert Diaper Ltd., 1962, 31–48.

Bernstein, Basil, & Henderson, Dorothy. Social Class Differences in the Relevance of Language to Socialization. *Sociology*, 1969, **3**, 1.

Blank, M., & Solomon, F. A Tutorial Language Program to Develop Abstract Thinking in Socially Disadvantaged Preschool Children. *Child Development*, 1968, **38**, 379–389.

Brown, R., & Bellugi, U. Three Processes in the Child's Acquisition of Syntax. *Harvard Educational Review,* 1964, **34**, 2, 133–151.

Brown, R., & Berko, J. Word Association and the Acquisition of Grammar. *Child Development*, 1960, **31**, 1–14.

Brown, R., & Fraser, C. The Acquisition of Syntax. In C. N. Cofer and B. S. Musgrave (Eds.), *Verbal Behavior and Learning*. New York: McGraw-Hill, 1963. Also in *Monographs of Society for Research in Child Development*, 1964, **29**, 43–79.

Brown, R., & Lenneberg, E. H. A Study in Language and Cognition. *Journal of Abnormal and Social Psychology*, 1954, **49**, 454–462.

Bullowa, Margaret. The Acquisition of a Word. *Language and Speech*, 1964, **7**, Part II, 107–111.

Carroll, John, & Casagrande, Joseph. The Function of Language Classification in Behavior. In E. Maccoby, F. Newcomb, & E. Hartley (Eds.), *Readings in Social Psychology*. New York: Holt, Rinehart & Winston, Inc., 1958, 18–31.

Carson, A. S., & Rabin, A. I. Verbal Comprehension and Communication in Negro and White Children. *Journal of Educational Psychology*, 1960, **51**, 47–51.

Casler, L. The Effect of Supplementary Verbal Stimulation on a Group of Institutionalized Infants. *Journal of Child Psychology and Psychiatry*, 1965, **6**, 19–27.

Cazden, Courtney B. Subcultural Differences in Child Language: An Interdisciplinary Review. *Merrill-Palmer Quarterly*, 1966, **12**, 185–220.

Chomsky, N. *Aspects of the Theory of Language*. Cambridge, Mass: M. I. T. Press, 1965.

Davis, E. A. The Development of Linguistic Skill. *Institute of Child Welfare Monograph Series*, #4, University of Minnesota Press, 1937.

Deutsch, Martin. The Role of Social Class in Language Development and Cognition. *American Journal of Orthopsychiatry*, 1965, **35**, 78–88.

Entwisle, Doris R. Developmental Socio-linguistics: A Comparative Study in Four Subcultural Settings. *Sociometry*, 1966, **29**, 67–84.

Ervin, S. M., & Foster, G. The Development of Meaning in Children's Descriptive Terms. *Journal of Abnormal and Social Psychology*, 1960, **61**, 271–275.

Ervin, S. M. Changes with Age in the Verbal Determinants of Word Association. *American Journal of Psychology*, 1961, **74**, 361–372.

Ervin-Tripp, Susan M. Imitation and Structural Change in Children's Language. In E. Lenneberg (Ed.), *New Directions in the Study of Language*. Cambridge: M. I. T. Press, 1964, 163–189.

Flavell, J. H., Beach, D. R., & Chinsky, J. M. Spontaneous Verbal Rehearsal in a Memory Task as a Function of Age. *Child Development*, 1966, **37**, 2, 283–299.

Glucksberg, Sam, Krauss, Robert M., & Weisberg, Robert. Referential Communication in Nursery School Children: Method and Some Preliminary Findings. *Journal of Experimental Child Psychology*, 1966, **3**, 4.

Gordon, E. W. Characteristics of Socially Disadvantaged Children: Language, Cognition and Intelligence. *Review of Educational Research*, 1965, **35**, 379–382.

Hawkins, P. R. Social Class, the Nominal Group and Reference. *Language and Speech*, 1969, **12**, 125–135.

Hess, R. D., & Shipman, V. C. Early Experience and the Socialization of Cognitive Modes in Children. *Child Development*, 1965, **36**, 869–886.

Hull, C. L. *Principles of Behavior*. New York: Appleton-Century-Crofts, 1943.

Huttenlocher, Janellen. Children's Language: Word-Phrase Relationship. *Science*, 1964, **143**, 264–265.

Jensen, A. R. Social Class and Verbal Learning. In M. Deutsch, A. R. Jensen, & I. Katz (Eds.), *Social Class, Race, and Psychological Development*. New York: Holt, Rinehart & Winston, 1967.

Jensen, A. R., & Rohwer, W. D. Syntactical Mediation of Serial and Paired-Associate Learning as a Function of Age. *Child Development*, 1965, **36**, 601–608.

Katz, P. A. Effects of Labels on Children's Perception and Discrimination Learning. *Journal of Experimental Psychology*, 1963, **66**, 423–428.

Kendler, H., & Kendler, Tracy. Effect of Verbalization on Reversal Shifts in Children. *Science*, 1961, **134**, 1619–1620.

Kendler, Tracy. Development of Mediating Thought in Children. *Monographs of Society for Research in Child Development*, 1963, **28**, 2, 33–48.

Kendler, T. S. Verbalization and Optional Reversal Shifts among Kindergarten Children. *Journal of Verbal Learning and Verbal Behavior*, 1964, **5**, 428–436.

Kuenne, M. R. Experimental Investigation of the Relation of Language to Transposition Behavior in Young Children. *Journal of Experimental Psychology*, 1946, **36**, 471–490.

Lawton, D. Social Class Differences in Language Development: A Study of Some Samples of Written Work. *Language and Speech*, 1963, **6**, 120–144.

Levin, H., & Silverman, Irene. Hesitation Phenomena in Children's Speech. *Language and Speech*, 1965, **8**, Part II, 67–85.

Lovaas, O. I., Berberich, J. P., Perloff, B. F., & Schaeffer, B. Acquisition of Imitative Speech by Schizophrenic Children. *Science*, 1966, **151**, 705–709.

Luria, A. R. Verbal Regulation of Behavior. In M. A. Brazier (Ed.), *The Central Nervous System and Behavior*. New York: Josiah Macy, Jr. Foundation, 1960, 359–379.

McCarthy, Dorothea. The Language Development of the Preschool Child. *Institute of Child Welfare Monograph Series*, #4. University of Minnesota Press, 1930.

McNeill, David. Developmental Psycholinguistics. In F. Smith & G. A. Miller, *The Genesis of Language*. Cambridge: M. I. T. Press, 1966, 15–85.

Menyunk, P. Syntactic Rules Used by Children from Preschool through First Grade. *Child Development*, 1964, **35**, 533–546.

Miller, W., & Ervin, S. M. The Development of Grammar in Child Language. *Monographs of Society for Research in Child Development*, 1964, **29**, 1, 9–40.

Olson, David R. Language Acquisition and Cognitive Development. Preliminary draft of a paper prepared for International Conference on Social-Cultural Aspects of Mental Retardation, Nashville, June 12, 1968.

Pavlov, I. P. *Selected Works*. Moscow Foreign Languages Publishing House, 1955.

Peisach, Estelle C. Children's Comprehension of Teacher and Peer Speech. *Child Development*, 1965, **36**, 467–480.

Reese, H. W. Verbal Mediation as a Function of Age Level. *Psychological Bulletin*, 1962, **59**, 502–509.

Slobin, D. I. Imitation and the Acquisition of Syntax. Paper presented at Second Research Planning Conference of Project Literacy, 1964.

Spiker, C. C. Verbal Factors in the Discrimination Learning of Children. In J. C. Wright & J. Kagan, Basic Cognitive Processes in Children,

Monographs of Society for Research in Child Development, 1963, **28,** 2, 53–69.

Templin, M. C. *Certain Language Skills in Children: Their Development and Interrelationships.* Minneapolis: University of Minnesota Press, 1957.

Weir, M. H., & Stevenson, H. W. The Effect of Verbalization in Children's Learning as a Function of Chronological Age. *Child Development,* 1959, **30,** 143–149.

Weir, Ruth H. *Language in the Crib.* The Hague: Mouton, 1962.

Werner, H., & Kaplan, E. Development of Word Meaning Through Verbal Context: An Experimental Study. *Journal of Psychology,* 1950, **29,** 251–257.

Whorf, B. L. *Language, Thought and Reality: Selected Writings.* Cambridge: Technology Press, 1956.

Zigler, Edward, Jones, L., & Keyes, Patricia. Acquisition of Language Habits in 1st, 2nd, and 3rd Grade Boys. *Child Development,* 1964, **35,** 725–736.

24. SOCIAL CLASS DIFFERENCES IN THE RELEVANCE OF LANGUAGE TO SOCIALIZATION

Basil Bernstein & Dorothy Henderson*

Abstract. *This paper reports social class differences in the emphasis placed upon the use of language in two areas of the socialization of the child: inter-person relationships and the acquisition of basic skills. The sample of 100 mothers is a sub-sample of 120 mothers who live in a middle class area and 192 mothers who live in a working class area. (The correlation between area and the social class position of the family is 0.74.) The results obtained from the use of a closed schedule show that the middle class mothers, relative to the working class mothers, place a much greater emphasis upon the use of language in the person area; whereas the working class mothers, relative to the middle class mothers, place a greater emphasis upon the use of language in the transmission of basic skills. The results are consonant with the prediction derived from the theory of restricted and elaborated linguistic codes which has also been used to generate a model for the understanding of social learning and forms of cultural discontinuity between the home and the school.*

SOURCE. *Sociology*, 1969, **1**, 3.

* *Biographical note.* Basil Bernstein, born 1924, London; studied at London School of Economics and Political Science, B.Sc.(Econ.). Assistant Teacher, City Day College, 1954–1960; Honorary Research Assistant, University College, London, 1960–1962; Reader in Sociology of Education and Head of Sociological Research Unit, University of London Institute of Education, 1962; Professor of the Sociology of Education, 1967.

Dorothy Henderson, born 1936. Diploma in Sociology, University of London, 1965. Sociological Research Unit, University of London Institute of Education, 1966. Present position, Research Officer.

430

Introduction

One of the most important movements in behavioral science since the war is the convergence of interest upon the study of basic processes of communication and their regulative functions. The one discipline which appears so far least affected is sociology. However, from different quarters there are now signs of growing interest (Grimshaw, 1967; Fishman, 1966; Cicourel, 1964; Garfinkle, 1967; Hymes, 1968). The study of the educationally disadvantaged has also led to a concentration of research into the process of language acquisition, into the relationships between language and cognition and into the social antecedents and regulative consequences of forms of language use.

The Sociological Research Unit at the University of London is engaged upon an exploratory study of forms of familial socialization which affect orientations toward the use of language. We shall present here the results of a closed schedule designed to reveal the relative emphasis which members of social class groups place upon the use of language in different areas of the socialization of the pre-school child. Although this report is confined to a study only of the mothers' *orientation* towards the relevance of language, as this group of mothers have been interviewed twice within a three year period and because two speech samples have been collected from their children when aged five years and seven years, it should prove to be possible to obtain some measure of both the reliability and validity of the mothers' reports.[1]

This report is the first step in the analysis of the section of the second questionnaire given to the mothers which enquired into the orientation of the mother towards various uses of language. As the other sections were concerned with the decision-making within the family, its kinship and community relationships, the procedures of control and role definition, the relationships between home and school, we can relate the orientation towards various uses of language to a range of variables.

In the discussion section of the paper we present a model which gives a sociological explanation of social learning in terms of the mediation of the linguistic process in socialization.

HYPOTHESES

The following hypotheses (derived from Bernstein 1966 and 1968) are to be tested:

1. Both middle class and working class would place greater emphasis upon

[1] The work reported in this paper was supported by grants from the Department of Education and Science and the Ford Foundation to whom, gratefully, acknowledgement is made. Thanks are also given to the Local Education Authorities for their close help and co-operation in the research.

the use of language in inter-personal aspects of socialization than the emphasis placed upon language in the socialization into basic skills.

2. The shift in emphasis in the use of language from the skill to the person area would be much greater for the middle class group.

3. Within the skill area the middle class group would place a greater emphasis upon language in the transmission of principles.

Description of the Sample

The total sample consists of 311 mothers drawn from two areas: one a working class area and the other a middle class area. The r between area and social class of the parents is 0.74. The index of social class was constructed by W. Brandis of the Sociological Research Unit and is based upon the terminal education and occupation of husband and wife. A full description of the Index will be found in Brandis, W. and Henderson, D. (1968). Social class is measured on a ten-point scale 0–9. The sample used in this paper consists of 50 mothers randomly selected from the middle class area and 50 mothers randomly selected from the working class area. It was necessary to limit the sample of this study in order that a detailed analysis could be carried out, and to examine possible social class differences in response to the schedule. In terms of the ten-point scale, the mean social class position of the middle class group is 2.8 and the mean social class position of the working class group is 6.9.

The Closed Schedule[2]

The closed schedule consisted of a list of eleven statements which covered the major aspects of socialization. As the schedule was presented, the interviewer put to each mother the question which was printed above the list of statements: "If parents could not speak, how much *more* difficult do you think it would be for them to do the following things with young children who had not yet started school?" The mother's attention was then directed to the statements and she was asked to assess the difficulty she thought dumb parents would experience in dealing with each situation. A six-point scale was provided: very much more difficult, much more difficult, more difficult, not too difficult, fairly easy, easy. The statements are listed below in the order in which they were presented on the schedule:

1. Teaching them everyday tasks like dressing, and
   using a knife and fork.   (Motor skill)
2. Helping them to make things.   (Constructional skill)

---

[2] The schedule was designed by Marian Bernstein and Basil Bernstein.

3. Drawing their attention to different shapes.   (Perceptual skill)
4. Playing games with them.   (Dummy)
5. Showing them what is right and wrong.   (Moral principles)
6. Letting them know what you are feeling.   (Mother-oriented affective)
7. Showing them how things work.   (Cognitive)
8. Helping them to work things out for themselves.   (Independent-cognitive)
9. Disciplining them.   (Control)
10. Showing them how pleased you are with their progress.   (Dummy)
11. Dealing with them when they are unhappy.   (Child-oriented affective)

Statements 4 and 10 were deliberately inserted as dummy statements designed to move the mother's responses across to "fairly easy" and "easy" and thus mitigate the emphasis placed on "difficulty" in the initial question. In fact, these statements elicited the responses "fairly easy" or "easy" from 72 per cent of the middle class mothers and from 76 per cent of the working class mothers. No other statements shifted both groups to the "easy" points of the scale to this extent. Four of the statements—1, 2, 3 and 7—were concerned with the transmission of skills. Five of the statements—5, 6, 8, 9 and 11—were concerned with aspects of social control. Statements 1, 2, 3 and 7 will be referred to as the *skill* area of statements, and statements 5, 6, 8, 9 and 11 will be referred to as the *person* area of statements. The points of the scale "very much more difficult," "much more difficult" and "more difficult" will be referred to as the "difficult" points of the scale, whilst "fairly easy" and "easy" will be referred to as the "easy" points of the scale. "Not too difficult" will be referred to as the mid-point of the scale.

It will be remembered that the aim of the schedule was to examine the effect of the social class position of the mothers on their perception of the role of language as a socializing process. In order to obtain such information it was necessary to focus the mother's attention upon the relevance of language across a number of different areas. It was thought that mothers would experience great difficulty if they were simply asked to what extent they relied upon language when dealing with their children. We constructed a general situation such that each mother was faced with a problem of comparison. She also had to assess the difficulty of transmitting skills and dealing with inter-personal processes without language. This focussed her attention upon the relevance of the linguistic component of the interaction. At the same time, it was necessary to ensure, as far as possible, that the mother should not feel that the problem was a challenge to her own extra-verbal ingenuity with her child, and so the problem was presented with the general referents *parents* and *young children*. It was equally necessary to preclude the possible use of other linguistic alternatives and therefore we stated the problem in terms of young children who had *not yet started school* and were thus unlikely to be able to read written instructions or explanations.

Method

The analysis was carried out in three stages. In the first stage we examined the population scores, in the second stage we examined the responses of individual mothers within each social class to each statement, and in the third stage analyses of variance were carried out in order to examine the interaction between the social class position of the mothers and their responses within and between the *skill* and *person* areas of statements.

First Stage

The population scores enabled us:

(a) to examine the distribution of maternal responses across the scale for each statement.
(b) to examine the total number of responses across the scale within each area of statements.
(c) to compare the total population scores within each area of statements in terms of "difficult" and "easy" responses.

We were then in a position to compare differences in patterns of response in relation to the statements.

Second Stage

The difference between the number of "difficult" responses and the number of "easy" responses to each statement was examined in terms of the social class of the mothers. This procedure also enabled us to compare the "difficult" to "easy" responses for each statement with reference to social class.

Third Stage

(a) A 2×2 analysis of variance on repeated measures was carried out. This type of analysis enabled us to control for within-person variance as well as for between-people variance and residual variance. Each point on the scale was assigned a score as follows:

Very much more difficult	$+3$
Much more difficult	$+2$

More difficult	$+1$
Not too difficult	0
Fairly easy	-1
Easy	-2

The basic unit of the analysis here was the individual mother's mean response score to the four *skill* statements. This was compared to the mother's mean response score to the five *person* statements. The analysis enabled us to test for significance the differential emphasis upon difficulty in response to each area of statements and its relationship with social class.

(b) A 2×5 analysis of variance on repeated measures was carried out on the maternal responses to each of the statements within the *person* area, in order to find out whether there was a significant interaction effect between the social class of the mothers and the individual statements.

(c) For the same reason a 2×4 analysis was carried out on the maternal responses to the individual statements within the *skill* area.

Results

First, we will deal briefly with the results which were found when the population scores were examined. It must be emphasized that the main justification for this stage of the analysis was to discover whether differences between the responses to the statements, as well as differences between the social class groups, were sufficiently large to justify carrying out a more sensitive analysis on the data. We will then deal at greater length with the results of the second and third stages of the analysis.

1. The Population Responses

The distribution of the population responses across the scale show that the patterns of distributions differ markedly between the *person* statements and the *skill* statements (Table 1). The responses cluster at the "difficult" points of the scale in response to the *person* statements, whereas the distribution is normal, with "not too difficult" operating as the mid-point, in response to the *skill* statements. Since the two areas of statements were clearly eliciting quite different patterns of response, we decided to compare the summed scores across all the statements within each area for each point of the scale. We then found that although both middle class and working class mothers showed a marked move to "difficult" responses within the *person* area in comparison with their responses within the *skill* area, the relative shift was greater in the case of the middle class responses (Table 1). In order to make a more stringent comparison the responses "very much more difficult" and "much more difficult" were summed within each social class and compared with the summed responses "fairly easy" and "easy." We found that the social class

TABLE 1

Distributions of Population Responses to Statements

The Scale[a]		Skill Statements				Person Statements				
		1	2	3	7	5	6	8	9	11
	0	0	1	1	3	12	12	13	19	11
	1	0	4	5	9	12	12	12	8	11
Middle class	2	7	12	11	13	19	12	18	14	15
responses	3	20	21	16	17	5	11	4	8	9
	4	15	7	12	7	2	2	3	0	2
	5	8	5	5	1	0	1	0	1	2
	0	9	4	4	4	4	10	11	11	10
	1	5	5	5	6	13	4	9	7	4
Working class	2	3	7	6	8	11	12	14	13	11
responses	3	23	23	27	20	14	10	11	8	10
	4	5	7	6	10	4	8	4	9	8
	5	5	4	2	2	4	6	1	2	7

[a] Note. 0—Very much more difficult.
  1—Much more difficult.
  2—More difficult.
  3—Not too difficult.
  4—Fairly easy.
  5—Easy.

differences in response within each area of statements were very great. In particular, the shift of middle class responses from the *skill* area to the *person* area in terms of the emphasis upon difficulty was just over 5 to 1, whereas the shift of working class responses from the *skill* area to the *person* area was just under 2 to 1 (Table 2).

2. Individual Responses to Statements

In the next stage of the analysis we examined the *individual* responses within each social class to each statement, in terms of the ratios of "difficult"

TABLE 2

Percentages of Summed Difficult/Easy Responses in Each Area

		% Difficult (0, 1)	% Easy (4, 5)	Total Number of Responses
M.C.	Person statements	48.8	5.2	250
	Skill statements	11.5	30.0	200
W.C.	Person statements	33.2	21.2	250
	Skill statements	21.0	20.4	200

to "easy" responses. Again we found that both middle class and working class mothers had shifted to the "difficult" points of the scale in response to the *person* statements. But *within* the *person* area, middle class mothers placed greater emphasis upon difficulty than did working class mothers (Table 1). Within the *skill* area we found a reversal in the pattern of response on the part of middle class mothers. Middle class mothers were less likely to give an "easy" response to the statement "Showing them how things work" than the working class mothers. Table 1 also shows that more working class mothers than middle class mothers gave a "difficult" response to the statement "Teaching them everyday tasks like dressing, and using a knife and fork."

3. The Analysis of Variance

(a) The results of the 2×2 analysis of variance on repeated measures show that the differential emphasis on difficulty between the two areas is highly significant ($F_{1,98} = 294.53$, $p > .001$). Very much greater emphasis was placed upon difficulty within the *person* area of statements than within the *skill* area of statements. However, the analysis also showed that, although greater emphasis was placed on the difficulty of dealing with the situations described in the *person* area by *all* the mothers, the difference between the responses of the middle class mothers in relation to the two areas of statements was significantly greater than the difference between the responses of the working class mothers ($F_{1,98} = 73.60$, $p > .001$). Middle class mothers placed much *greater* emphasis upon the difficulty of doing the things described in the *person* area than the working class mothers, but they placed much *less* emphasis upon the difficulty of doing the things described in the *skill* area than the working class mothers. This highly significant interaction effect illustrates the polarization of the responses of middle class mothers in relation to the two areas of statements.

We will now turn to the results of the analyses of maternal responses *within* each area.

(b) Within the *skill* area the results show that middle class mothers placed very much less emphasis on language than working class mothers on the difficulty of doing the things described in these statements, and that this difference in response was highly significant ($F_{1, 98} = 228.78$, $p > .001$). This finding replicates the result found by the previous analysis. However, a highly significant interaction effect between the social class of the mothers and responses to individual *skill* statements was revealed by this analysis. Working class mothers placed significantly greater emphasis on difficulty in response to the statement "Teaching them everyday tasks like dressing and using a knife and fork," than did middle class mothers; middle class mothers, on the other hand, placed significantly greater emphasis on dif-

TABLE 3

Summary Table of Mean Scores

	Statements		
	Skill Area	Person Area	Total x̄
x̄ Middle class	.07	1.49	.78
x̄ Working class	.33	.80	.56
Sample x̄	.20	1.04	

TABLE 4

Summary Table of Mean Scores

	Skill Statements				
	1	2	3	7	Total x̄
x̄ Middle class	—.48	.12	.04	.62	.30
x̄ Working class	.48	.28	.36	.36	1.50
Sample x̄	.01	.20	.20	.49	

ficulty in response to the statement "Showing them how things work" than did working class mothers $(F_{3,\,294} = 74.88, p > .001)$.

(c) The 2×5 analysis of maternal responses to the five *person* statements shows that middle class mothers considered that these situations would be more difficult to deal with without language than did working class mothers. This differential emphasis on difficulty in relation to the *person* statements is highly significant $(F_{1,98} = 14.25, p > .001)$. A highly significant main order effect, *irrespective* of the social class position of the mothers, arose out of differences in response to individual statements $(F_{4,392} = 6.49, p > .001)$.

This result shows that individual statements within the *person* area had elicited very different responses from both middle class and working class mothers. We were therefore interested to know how the responses differed *between* the *person* statements. In other words, how were the *person* statements *ranked* in difficulty? The mean scores are presented below as they were ranked in order of difficulty by *all* the mothers in the sample.

Person Statements	Mean Scores
8. Helping them to work things out for themselves.	1.37
9. Disciplining them.	1.32
5. Showing them what is right and wrong.	1.14
6. Letting them know what you are feeling.	.98
11. Dealing with them when they are unhappy.	.91

Summary of Results

Differences in response were shown to be due to (a) the statements within each area, (b) the social class of the mothers, and (c) the interaction between

TABLE 5

Summary Table of Mean Scores

	Person Statements					
	5	6	8	9	11	Total $\bar{x}$
$\bar{x}$ Middle class	1.54	1.36	1.56	1.70	1.28	7.44
$\bar{x}$ Working class	.74	.60	1.18	.94	.54	4.00
Sample $\bar{x}$	1.14	.98	1.37	1.32	.91	

social class and individual statements. We find that middle class mothers consider language less relevant to the situations described by the *skill* statements than do working class mothers. There is one exception. Middle class mothers considered that "Showing them how things work," would be *more* difficult to deal with without language than working class mothers. Conversely, middle class mothers place greater emphasis upon language than working class mothers in response to the *person* statements. However, *all* the mothers considered the *person* situations more difficult to cope with than the *skill* situations.

Methodological Criticisms of the Schedule[3]

The rationale for the construction of the schedule has been given earlier in this paper, nevertheless, a number of methodological issues are raised by the design.

Let us examine the points one by one, and see to what extent each issue is resolved in the light of the analysis.

1. The definition of the problem is lengthy and contains three items of information which the mother has to bear in mind throughout her responses to *all* the statements if the results are to be a reliable measure of her orientation to language in relation to major aspects of socialization.

Very great differences in response were found between the statements which described skills and the statements which described aspects of inter-personal processes, irrespective of the social class of the mothers in the sample. It can reasonably be argued that such differences in the emphasis upon difficulty

[3] We are not here elaborating upon the more complex issues of sub-cultural differences in the interpretation of statements within closed schedules.

would not have been found if the mothers had merely assessed each statement without reference to the role of speech and its absence. We can assume then that the question, despite its complexity, was borne in mind by the mothers throughout their responses. It focussed their attention on the linguistic aspect of their own behaviour with their children.

2. In order to assess the difficulty for dumb parents when doing a number of things with young children, the mother can only refer to her *own* experience in each situation and try to imagine how difficult she herself would find each situation if *she* could not speak. Such an assessment involves an internal three-stage experiment, and this may have been quite difficult for some mothers. However, this point is clearly related to the first point, since it can reasonably be assumed that if the mother bears the problem in mind *throughout* her responses then she is forced to focus upon her *own* reliance upon language.

3. The mother is asked to discriminate *between* degrees of difficulty on a six-point scale, two points of which do not refer to difficulty but to ease. It may be that some mothers found it difficult to use the six-point scale. They had either to keep all the points in mind in response to each statement, or they had frequently to refer back to the scale. If they failed to do this then their responses would be unreliable.

The 2×5 analysis of the mother's responses to the five *person* statements has shown that, although all mothers emphasized difficulty in response to these statements rather than to the *skill* statements, there were significant differences in the emphasis upon difficulty *between* the statements. The fact that the problem emphasized difficulty—"how much *more* difficult do you think it would be?"—may have given rise to greater discrimination between degrees of difficulty. This result strongly suggested that the mothers, irrespective of social class, were indeed discriminating between the "difficult" points of the scale. We decided to examine the data in order to find out whether the percentage of mothers within each social class using *more than one "difficult" point* in response to the control statements and *more than one "easy" point* in response to the *skill* statements differed. We found that there was no difference in the percentage of mothers within each social class using *all three* "difficult" points in response to the *person* statements, and that *all* the percentage differences were minimal in response to the *skill* statements. The major differences between the social class groups occurs in the relative use of only *one* "difficult" point in response to the *person* statements. Eighteen per cent of the middle class mothers used only one "difficult" point in response to these statements whereas 40 per cent of the working class mothers used only one "difficult" point. This could well argue a lack of discrimination between degrees of difficulty as set out in the scale on the part of nearly half the working class sub-sample. One final point should be made in regard to discrimination. Discrimination between the "difficult" points did not relate to the *number* of *person* statements which elicited a "difficult" response, nor to the *number* of *skill* statements which elicited an "easy" response. It is important to stress this point since we suspected that there may have been a greater likelihood of discrimination if a mother was confining herself to the "difficult" part of the scale across all five *person* statements.

We were also interested in the extent of movement *across* the scale. We considered that this, together with the discrimination *within* the scale might justify a six-point scale, since this would reveal the extent to which mothers limited their responses to adjacent points. Seventy-eight per cent of the middle class mothers and 62 per cent of the working class mothers distributed their responses across at least four points of the scale. Examination of the data showed that mothers who moved across four or more points of the scale when responding to the statements were much more likely to use one of the extreme points "very much more difficult" and "easy" than were mothers who moved across less than four points.

We then examined the number of mothers who moved across five or six points of the scale, since this clearly involved the use of one or both extreme points. We found that 48 per cent of the middle class mothers, but only 28 per cent of the working class mothers, moved across five or six points. This may be an indication that the middle class mothers in our sample were better able to use a six-point scale, either because of their ability to bear the six points in mind, or because of their greater readiness to refer back to the scale frequently.

4. There was inadequate randomization of the statements. This is particularly relevant to the close proximity of the statements "Helping them to work things out for themselves" and "Showing them how things work." It was thought that the lexical similarity of these two statements might have prevented the mothers from discriminating between them, despite the fact that they describe rather different activities and orientations. Surprisingly, the analysis of the mothers' responses showed that more working class mothers than middle class mothers discriminated between these two statements. The implication of this finding will be taken up later in the discussion. At present it is sufficient to point out that the social class group which one may have least expected to discriminate between two very similar statements did, in fact, do so. Finally, the fact that the mothers did discriminate between the statements—that they did not exhibit response sets—is shown by the pattern of their responses across the scale. Statements 1, 2, 3 and 4 elicited "easy" responses; statements 5 and 6 elicited "difficult" responses; statement 7 elicited "easy" responses; statements 8 and 9 elicited "difficult"

responses; statement 10 elicited "easy" responses; and statement 11 elicited "difficult" responses. This pattern was consistent for both middle class and working class mothers.

Summary of Criticisms

It is clear that movement from "difficult" responses to "easy" responses was triggered by the two main areas. Discrimination between degrees of difficulty was dependent upon individual statements: there were significant differences in the ranking of the *person* statements in order of difficulty, and the order was the same for both social class groups. Movement across four points of the scale was found to involve the use of one of the extreme points, and there was very little difference in the number of middle class and working class mothers who used the scale in this way. However, more of the middle class mothers moved across five or six points of the scale than did the working class mothers. This raises the substantive question as to the orientation of the working class group; they may not have required such a sensitive scale. We might add that few researchers have carried out such a close examination of their results in terms of their scaling procedures. Our experience suggests that, although on balance our scaling procedure was justified, the following recommendation might provide a more reliable measure. We suggest that in order to over-come some of the scaling difficulties for the mother it is recommended first to ask the general question and then, for each statement, ask the mother whether she thought it on the whole difficult or on the whole easy. We could then present the mother with a three-point scale for degrees of difficulty or a three-point scale for relative ease, depending upon her general response.

Discussion

The results show that the middle class, relative to the working class, place a greater emphasis upon the use of language in dealing with situations within the person area. The working class, relative to the middle class, place a greater emphasis upon the use of language in the transmission of various skills. However, within the skill area the middle class place a greater emphasis upon the use of language in their response to the statement, "Showing them how things work," whereas within the same area the working class place a greater emphasis upon the use of language in response to the statement, "Teaching them every day tasks like dressing, and using a knife and fork."

Can these differences in emphasis be accounted for in terms of differences in the relevance of these two *areas* for the social classes? In other words, does the move to language simply reflect the relevance of the area? Or is it the case that both areas respectively have equal relevance to the social classes but their verbal realization is different? It is unlikely that the middle class relative to the working class value basic skills less and yet it is this group which places a reduced emphasis upon language in the skill area. It would be just as difficult to maintain that socialization into relationships between persons is not of *equal* relevance to every sub-cultural group, although the *form* of that socialization may well vary. On the other hand, the very marked shift by *both* groups towards language in the person area and away from language in the skill area may well reflect the greater importance of control over persons rather than control over the development of skills in the socialization of the very young child. It is therefore unlikely that the shifts in emphasis placed upon the use of language in each of the two areas respectively, by the two social class groups can be explained in terms of the difference in the relevance of the skill area and the person area. It might be that middle class mothers can conceive of a variety of ways, other than linguistic, for the acquisition of skills and for this reason these mothers place less emphasis upon language. Whereas the working class mothers can conceive of fewer alternatives to language for the acquisition of skills. This might seem to be a plausible explanation, but we think that it by no means accounts for the differences between the social classes.

We shall argue that the explanation is to be found in the nature of the social relationship when skills and person relationships are transmitted. If it is the case that in the working class knowledge is transmitted through a social relationship in which the receiver is relatively passive and if, in the middle class, knowledge is transmitted through a social relationship in which the receiver is active, then we might expect the distribution of responses which have been revealed. It may be that motor, perceptual and manipulative skills are acquired by the child in the middle class by his exposure to varied and attractive stimuli which the child explores on his *own* terms. In other words, in the acquisition of motor, perceptual and manipulative skills, the child regulates his own learning in a carefully controlled environment. It is of significance that despite the relatively greater emphasis placed upon language in the skill area by the working class group, the middle class place greater emphasis upon language in response to the statement, "Showing them how things work." It is likely that this statement, for the middle class, raises questions of the transmission of principles, whereas the other three statements within the same area *do not*. If this is the case, then the situation for the middle class child is particularly fortunate. For, on the one hand, he is socialized into elementary skill learning through role relationships which emphasize autonomy *and* he has access to principles.

In the working class group, the concept of learning may well be different and, therefore, the form the social relationship takes when skills are acquired would be of a different order. The concept of learning here seems to be less one of self-regulated learning in an arranged environment and more a concept of a didactic theory of learning implying a passive receiver, in which a mother has little alternative but to tell or instruct a child. Although the emphasis in the working class group, relative to the middle class, is upon language, presumably upon *telling* or instructing, the child is much less likely to receive explanations of principles. Thus it may be that the working class child learns skills in terms only of an understanding of the operations they entail, whereas the middle class child learns both the operations and principles.

Other work of the Sociological Research Unit can be referred to here in support of these hypotheses. Two years prior to the interview in which the present schedule was administered, a sample of 351 middle class and working class mothers (of which the sample used in this paper is a sub-sample) were given a questionnaire in which the mothers were invited to give their views upon a range of experiences relevant to their child's behaviour in the infant school. We found that when middle class mothers were asked to rank in order of importance six possible uses of toys, they ranked more highly than did the working class mothers "To find out about things" (Bernstein and Young, 1967). Further, middle class mothers saw the role of the infant school child as an active role, whereas the working class mothers tended to see this role as a passive one (Jones, 1966). Middle class mothers, relative to working class mothers, indicated that "play" in the infant school had educational significance (Bernstein, 1967).

It would appear then that the difference in the response of middle class and working class mothers to the relevance of language in the acquisition of various skills is more likely to arise out of differences in the concept of learning than out of differences between the social classes in terms of the value placed upon the learning of such skills. The socialization of the middle class child into the acquisition of skills is into both operations and principles which are learned in a social context which emphasizes *autonomy*. In the case of the working class child, his socialization into skills emphasizes operations rather than principles learned in a social context where the child is accorded *reduced autonomy*.

We will now turn to discuss the differences between the social classes in their emphasis upon the use of language in inter-personal contexts. The results are very clear. Where the context is inter-personal, the middle class, relative to the working class, move markedly towards the use of language. Further, the shift in the emphasis upon language from the skill area to the person area is very much greater in the middle class than in the working class. Thus, the verbal realization of affects, moral principles and their application to behaviour, and independence in cognitive functioning, is much more likely to be linguistically elaborated in the middle class than in the working class. This is *not* to say that these aspects of socialization do not have the same significance in the working class, only that (according to the mothers' responses) language is of less relevance in the form of the socialization.

Indeed, *both* classes rank the statements (in the person area) in the same order of difficulty.

It is not possible to infer from the mothers' responses what they actually would say to the child, but again we can refer to evidence obtained from the first interview with the mothers two years earlier. This evidence strongly suggests that:

1. The middle class mothers are more likely than working class mothers to take up the child's attempts to interact verbally with the mother in a range of contexts.
2. The middle class mothers are less likely to avoid or evade answering difficult questions put to them by their children.
3. The middle class mothers are less likely to use coercive methods of control.
4. The middle class mothers are more likely to explain to the child why they want a change in his behaviour. (Bernstein and Brandis, 1968).

Thus, we have good reasons for believing that not only is there a difference between the social classes in their emphasis upon language in contexts of interpersonal control, but there is a difference in the meanings which are verbally realized. It would seem that the internalizing of the principles of the moral order, the relating of this order to the specifics of the child's behaviour, the communication of feeling, is realized far more through language in the middle class than in the working class. The social is made explicit in one group, whereas the social is rendered less explicit in the other. Where the social is made explicit through language then that which is internalized can itself become an object (Mead, 1934). Perhaps here we can begin to see that the form of control over persons in the middle class induces a reflexive relation to the social order, whereas, in the working class, the form of control over persons induces a relatively less reflexive relation to the social order. (See Note.)

The question of the relatively greater emphasis upon the use of language in the inter-personal area raises fundamental questions about the nature of middle class forms of socialization which would take us beyond the confines of an empirical research report. In Bernstein (1966 and particularly 1968) there is an extensive discussion of the social antecedents of forms of language use and socialization. The view taken in these and other papers is that linguistic codes are realizations of social structure, and both shape the contents of social roles and the process by which they are learned. In short, it has been suggested that the use of elaborated codes renders the implicit explicit, whereas the use of restricted codes reduces the possibility of such explicitness. Thus the codes and their variants regulate the cultural meanings which are rendered both explicit and individuated through the use of language. Whilst there is no evidence in this paper that middle class mothers use forms of an elaborated code and working class mothers use forms of a restricted code, Robinson and Rackstraw's analysis (1967) of the answering behaviour of mothers in the main sample indicates grounds for believing that these coding orientations are likely to be found. Further, the works of Bernstein and Brandis (1968) and Cook (1968) show that the forms of control used by the middle class and the working class are consonant with the predictions derived from the sociolinguistic theory. We will have further evidence when Miss Cook's analysis of the speech of the mothers is completed.

We have suggested that in the middle class skills are acquired in such a way that the child has access both to operations and principles. He tends to regulate his own learning in an arranged environment which encourages autonomy in skill acquisition. For this reason the middle class mothers place less emphasis upon the use of language in the statements within the skill area. In the case of the working class child, we have argued that he is socialized more into the acquisition of operations than into principles through a social relationship which encourages passivity in the learner and so reduces autonomy in skill acquisition. Thus the working class mothers, relative to middle class mothers, place greater emphasis upon the use of language when responding to the statements in the skill area. In the case of control over persons, we have suggested that the forms of such control in the middle class arise out of a social structure which is realized through the use of elaborated codes, whereas the forms of control in the sub-group of the working class under examination arise out of a social structure which is realized through forms of a restricted code. As a result, the form of control in the middle class induces a reflexive relation upon the part of the child towards the social order, whereas in the working class the forms of control induce a much less reflexive relation to the social order.

We should point out that a developed reflexive relation to the social order does not necessarily imply role distancing behaviour. In the same way, reduced reflexiveness to a particularistic social order does not necessarily imply that role distancing behaviour will *not* occur in relation to members of a society holding universalistic status.

We can best summarize our interpretation of the results of this analysis and the more general explanation given in this paper, by the use of the following model:

SOCIAL STRUCTURE
↓
EMPHASIS ON LANGUAGE

Orientation	Role/Self-Concept		M.C.	W.C.
Persons	Reflexiveness:	→	High	Low
Skills	Autonomy:	→	Low	High
Implicit Theory of Learning:			Self-regulating	Didactic

The model should be read *horizontally* in relation to the areas of orientation and consequent emphasis on language, and *vertically* in relation to implicit theories of learning and emphasis upon language. For example, if there is a *high* emphasis upon the use of language in terms of orientation to *persons* then this will tend to generate high *reflexiveness* of the self-concept; if the emphasis on the use of language is *low* then this will generate *reduced reflexiveness* of the self-concept. In terms of the orientation to *skills*, a *low* emphasis on language will generate *autonomy* in the self-concept, whilst a *high* emphasis on language in this area will *reduce autonomy* in the self-concept. At the same time, the relative emphasis upon the use of language in these two areas perhaps implies different implicit theories of learning. Where the emphasis upon the use of language is *high* in terms of orientation to persons or *low* in terms of orientation to skills, then the implicit theory of learning is *self-regulating*. Where the emphasis on the use of language is *low* in terms of orientation to persons or *high* in terms of orientation to skills, then the implicit theory of learning is *didactic*.[4] It is important to add that, in this paper, because of the small sample, we have treated the middle class and working class as homogeneous groups. When the total sample is analysed it may be possible to show that there are subgroups within each social class group who respond differently in relation to these two areas. It is quite possible that differential emphasis upon the use of language in terms of the acquisition of skills or inter-personal control is related to differences in the form of the social relationships. A sub-culture may give rise to an implicit theory of learning which is self-regulating in terms of orientation to persons and didactic in terms of orientation to skills, or *vice versa*. The relationship between culture, linguistic codes, implicit theories of learning and differential emphasis upon the use of language is a matter of investigation. An extensive discussion in Bernstein (1968) deals

---

[4] On implicit theories of learning, see Klein, J., *Samples of British Culture* Vol. II, Routledge and Kegan Paul, 1965; Trasler, G. (ed.), *The Formative Years*, B.B.C. Publication, 1968; Hess, R. D. and Shipman, V.C. Early Experience and the Socialisation of Cognitive Modes in Children, *Child Development*, 1965, 36, No. 4, pp. 869–886.

with the relationship between social structure, forms of social relationship, linguistic codes, and different orders of meaning. The hypotheses on which our model is based are derived from this paper.

We can now develop our discussion in regard to possible discontinuities between implicit theories of learning in the home and explicit theories of learning in the school. It is suggested that there may be, for the working class child in the primary school, two sources of discontinuity; one in the area of skill acquisition and the other in the area of inter-personal relations. If, for example, the school emphasizes autonomy in the acquisition of skills but the implicit concept of learning in the home is didactic in relation to skills, this will be a major source of discontinuity. Similarly, if the school is concerned with the development of reflexive relations in the area of inter-personal relations but the implicit concept of social learning in the home operates to reduce reflexiveness in this area, then this will be another source of discontinuity. It may be unreasonable to expect children exposed to such discontinuities to respond initially to forms of control which presuppose a culture and socialization very different from their own.

Earlier in this discussion we referred to the fortunate situation of the middle class child in terms of the results of our analysis. His role relationships emphasize autonomy in the acquisition of skills and reflexiveness in the area of inter-personal relations. He is accorded discretion to *achieve* his social role. On the other hand, the role relationships of the working class child, in terms of our analysis, reduce his autonomy in the skill area and reduce reflexiveness in the inter-personal area. He has much less discretion— his social role is *assigned*.

In this paper we have shown that maternal definitions of the role of language as a socializing process are dependent upon the area of orientation, and that this differential emphasis on the use of language is related to different forms of social relationship within the social structure. Further, we have argued that the differential emphasis on the use of language in relation to certain areas of orientation may reflect different implicit theories of learning which affect the self-concept of the child. We have suggested that these different implicit theories of learning in the home may conflict with the theories of learning in the school, and in this way give rise to major sources of discontinuity between the home and the school.

This analysis has enabled us to construct a model which gives a sociological explanation of social learning through the mediation of the linguistic process of socialization.

Conclusion

We must emphasize that our data consists of mothers' reports not of their actual behaviour, and that these reports have been obtained through the use of a closed schedule. The analysis of the degree and type of discrimination on the part of the middle class and working class mothers gives us reasonable grounds for believing that the scaling procedures and the statements were appropriate. We also believe that the situation constructed was such that the "right" or conventional response was not obvious to the mothers. We have shown that both groups ranked the statements in the person area according to the same gradient of difficulty. However, we cannot present at the moment an analysis of possible differences between the social classes in their interpretation of the statements. We may be able to throw some light on social class differences in the interpretation of the statements when the responses of the mothers to the closed schedule are related to their responses to the other schedules within the language section of the second questionnaire *and* to the results of the analysis of the initial questionnaire.

The findings presented here indicate very clear differences between the social class groups in their relative emphasis upon language. We hope to be able to utilize the model offered in the conclusion of the discussion to show, when the total sample is analysed, *intra-class* differences in the orientation to the use of language in these two areas of socialization. Perhaps the most important conclusion of this paper is to stress the need for small scale naturalistic and experimental studies of the channels, codes and contexts which control the process of socialization.

In conclusion, it is the case that the three hypotheses given in the introduction have been confirmed. The findings have also revealed that working class mothers relative to middle class mothers place a greater emphasis upon language in the acquisition of basic skills. The inferential structure developed in the discussion makes explicit the relationships between macro aspects of social structure and micro aspects of socialization.

NOTE

The diagram below sets out the different relationships between reflexiveness and autonomy which may arise as a result of the cultural meanings realized through language.

The diagram should be read as follows. The vertical and horizontal axes are scaled in terms of the emphasis upon language. The vertical axis refers to degrees of reflexiveness in socialization into relationships with persons and the horizontal axis refers to degrees of autonomy in the acquisition of skills. The four quadrants contain similarities and differences between implicit theories of learning. These control the forms of the socialization into the two basic areas of socialization. Whilst quadrants "B" and "D" would apply to sections of the middle class and working class respectively, the model indicates the probability of intra-class variance both at one point and over time.

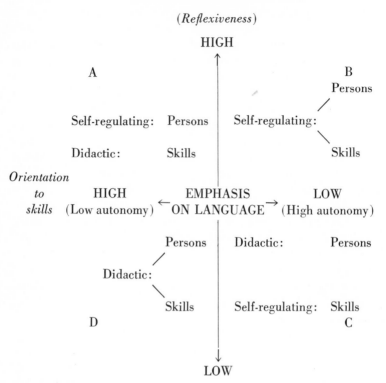

SUB-CULTURE CULTURE
ORIENTATION TO PERSONS

(Reflexiveness)

The model only permits statements about the emphasis upon language; no inferences can be drawn which refer to the nature of the information. In order to examine the latter it would be necessary to know the dominant linguistic code used in each area of socialization. Whilst it is unlikely that individuals limited to restricted codes would hold self-regulating theories of learning (except embryonically) didactic theories of learning may well be held by users of both elaborated and restricted codes. The hypothetical relationships between social structure, family role systems, linguistic codes and person and object verbally realized meanings are set out in Bernstein (1968).

The Concept of Reflexiveness[5]

It is useful to distinguish between two aspects of reflexiveness; a role and an ideational aspect.

[5] We are very grateful to Mr. Michael Young, Lecturer in the Sociology of Education, University of London, Institute of Education, for his comments upon this formulation.

Ideational Aspects. Reflexiveness here refers to the degree to which an individual is able to make explicit verbally the principles underlying object and person relationships. Thus we could have high or low reflexiveness towards objects and/or persons.

Role Aspects. WITHIN ROLE. Reflexiveness here refers to the range of alternatives or options which are accorded to any given role. Thus we could have high or low reflexiveness in terms of the range of alternatives made available.

BETWEEN ROLE. Reflexiveness here would refer to the degree of insulation among the *meanings* made available through role relationships. Roles may be more or less insulated from each other and so may the meanings to which the roles give access. Where the meanings made available through different roles are highly insulated we could say that there is low reflexiveness; where the meanings made available through different roles *reverberate* against each other (low insulation) we could say there is high reflexiveness.

This formulation indicates that the relationship between language and reflexiveness and the cultural and the institutional order is indeed complex.

Bibliography

Bernstein, Basil. 1961. A Socio-linguistic Approach to Social Learning, *Social Science Survey* (ed.) Gould, Julius, London: Penguin.

Bernstein, Basil. 1967. Play and the Infant School, *Where*, Supplement 11, *Toys:* Christmas, 1967.

Bernstein, Basil. 1968. A Socio-linguistic Approach to Socialization, *Directions in Socio-linguistics* (eds.) Gumperz, J. and Hymes, D. Holt, Rinehart and Winston (in press). Also in *Human Context, I*, Dec. 1968 (in press).

Bernstein, B., & Young, D. 1967. Social Class Differences in Conceptions of the Uses of Toys, *Sociology, I*, No. 2, May 1967.

Bernstein, B., & Brandis, W. 1968. Social Class Differences in Communication and Control. In *Primary Socialization, Language and Education Vol. I: Social Class, Language and Communication* by Brandis, W. and Henderson, D. (University of London Institute of Education, Sociological Research Unit Monograph Series directed by Basil Bernstein) Routledge, and Kegan Paul (in press).

Cicourel, Aaron V. 1964. *Method and Measurement in Sociology.* The Free Press of Glencoe.

Cook, J. 1968. Familial Processes of Communication and Control. To be published in the Sociological Research Unit Monograph Series (see above) in preparation.

Fishman, Joshua. 1966. *Language Loyalty in the United States*, Mouton and Co.

Garfinkle, Harold. 1967. *Studies in Ethnomethodology*, Prentice Hall Inc.

Grimshaw, Alan. D. 1968. Socio-linguistics. In *Handbook of Communication* (eds.) Schramm, W., Pool, I., Maccoby, N., Parker, E., Fein, L. Rand McNally and Co. (in press).

Hymes, Dell. 1967. On Communicative Competence. This paper is revised from the one presented at the *Research Planning Conference on Language Development Among Disadvantaged Children*, held under the sponsorship of the Department of Educational Psychology and Guidance, Ferkauf Graduate School, Yeshiva University, 1966. The paper is available from Department of Social Anthropology, University of Pennsylvania, Philadelphia.

Jones, Jean. 1966. Social Class and the Under-Fives, *New Society*, Dec. 1966.

Loevinger, Jane. 1959. Patterns of Parenthood as Theories of Learning, *J. Social and Abnormal Psychol.*, sq, pp. 148–150.

Mead, G. H. 1934. *Mind, Self and Society*, University of Chicago Press.

Robinson, W. P. and Rackstraw, S. J. 1967. Variations in Mothers' Answers to Children's Questions, as a function of Social Class, Verbal Intelligence Test Scores and Sex, *Sociology*, *I*, No. 3.

Winer, B. J. 1962. *Statistical Principles in Experimental Design*, McGraw-Hill, Chs. 4 and 8.

25. A TUTORIAL LANGUAGE PROGRAM TO DEVELOP ABSTRACT THINKING IN SOCIALLY DISADVANTAGED PRESCHOOL CHILDREN[1]

Marion Blank & Frances Solomon

A specialized language program was developed to facilitate abstract think-ing in young deprived children through short, individual tutoring sessions on a daily basis. The role of individual attention in the experiment was controlled through the use of a comparison group which had daily individ-ual sessions without the specialized tutoring. A second comparison group was included which consisted of children who received their usual training in the regular nursery school program. The results show a marked gain in IQ for the groups who received the specialized tutoring and no significant gains for the control groups.

Widespread deficiencies ranging across the cognitive, affective, motiva-tional, and social areas have been found in deprived children. Compensatory programs have therefore aimed at exposing the children to a different and wider range of almost every type of stimulus deemed to be beneficial (e.g., better equipment, parent participation, trips, perceptual training). In essence, this approach assumes that all factors contribute an equal amount to the alleviation of the deficits found in the deprived child.

This paper outlines an approach which offers an alternative to the phi-

SOURCE. *Child Development*, 1968, **39**, 379–389.

[1] This research was supported by U. S. Public Health Service grant K3-MH-10, 749. The authors wish to thank the Bronx River Day Care Center and Miss E. Johnson for their cooperation and participation in this research. A preliminary version of this paper was presented at the meetings of the Society for Research in Child Development, New York, March, 1967. Authors' address: 1300 Morris Park Avenue, Bronx, New York 10461.

losophy of total enrichment. The premise of this approach is that, while total enrichment is not without value, it does not diagnose the key deficits of the deprived child. The usual concept of enrichment is also limited by the idea that exposure to the previously absent stimuli is sufficient for learning.

We feel that exposure to an infinite number of ostensibly enriching stimuli does not necessarily overcome the deficits. Presentation alone does not insure that the child will partake of newly available material. If learning is to occur, the child must involve himself actively with the stimuli so as to comprehend their significance. Active involvement refers, not to motor activity, but rather to the internal mental manipulation of experience. The latter applies to skills involving the ability to organize thoughts, to reflect upon situations, to comprehend the meaning of events, and to structure behavior so as to be able to choose among alternatives.

These skills coincide with many of the characteristics defining the abstract attitude (Goldstein, 1959). Research by the senior author (Blank & Bridger, 1964, 1966, 1967) has led us to postulate that the failure to develop this abstract attitude represents the most glaring deficiency of deprived children. *Their behavior reflects the lack of a symbolic system by which to organize the plentiful stimulation surrounding them.*

The problem then arises of what is the most effective means for developing abstract thinking. We feel that an internal symbolic system can best be achieved through the development of abstract language (Vygotsky, 1962). Certain types of language, such as labeling clear, circumscribed objects (e.g., bottle, table, ball), can be grasped easily through illustration and/or imitation. Therefore, no great effort is required to learn these words. By contrast, words referring to properties which are not immediately evident require much elaboration for understanding. For example, a word such as "top" is much more abstract than a word such as "book." The word "top" can refer to such physically different things as the "top" of one's head, the "top" of one's desk, and the "top" of a building. The word unites these instances only when there is an understanding that "top" refers to the highest point on anything, regardless of how different the "anythings" look. Other examples requiring a similar level of abstraction are time (before, after), direction (underneath, between), and relative judgments (warmer, heavier). It is here that an articulate person, be it mother, teacher, or sibling, is required to offer the necessary corroboration or negation of the child's emerging ideas.

This type of feedback is readily available in the middle-class home, but it is rare in the lower-class home (see Freeberg & Payne, 1967). We therefore propose that this lack of an ongoing, elaborated dialogue is the major experiential deficit of the deprived child (Bernstein, 1960).

Previous attempts to transmit this aspect of learning to disadvantaged children have relied on using the group situation (Bereiter & Engelmann, 1966; Deutsch, 1964; Gray & Klaus, 1965). A serious question arises of whether early language skills can be fostered in a group situation or whether we must in some way mirror the middle-class one-to-one situation. For example, if given a direction to "place the red block on top of the blue one," a child in the group setting can wait to see what the other children do and simply *imitate* their action. Of course, the child *might* listen to the language and associate it with the key features of the performance he just imitated. However, this method relies on the hope that the child will avail himself of this opportunity to learn. Nothing inherent in the situation requires him either to heed or to understand the language in order to fulfil the demands placed upon him.

In the latter example, the child at least had to make a response; in many classroom situations, no overt response is required. It is assumed that, when the teacher instructs, the child makes the appropriate inner response even though he is not required to answer overtly. If the inner response is lacking, he cannot follow the dialogue, and the teaching, no matter how well organized, is lost. By contrast, the one-to-one situation can be easily designed so that the child is required to use his language skills, and then he cannot function on a level lower than the goals set by the teacher. In addition, since goals set in individual instruction are designed for the child's specific capabilities, they are more likely to be appropriate.

Although most educators acknowledge that ideal teaching would be a one-to-one relation, this has been deemed impractical because of the costs involved. The conclusion of excessive costs is based on the implicit assumption that individual teaching would or should occupy most of the teaching day. Little consideration has been given to the possible effectiveness of short periods of daily individual instruction, even though such instruction is widely and effectively used in the initial teaching of language to other language-deficient groups, such as deaf children (Blank, 1965). In addition, the limited attention spans of young children suggest that relatively brief sessions involving frequent reinforcement of new (language) skills would theoretically be the most effective means of teaching.

In summary, our assumptions were:

1. Deprived preschool children do not have a firm language base for thinking. They will develop one only if they are given consistent guidance. This leads to the further assumption that the most effective teaching is based on individual tutoring.

2. Language acquisition, like any new complex skill, may be met with some resistance. To prevent resistance from becoming established, the child should not be permitted to leave a task unfinished. If necessary, the task can be simplified, but the child should still be required to fulfil the demands set

by the teacher. Once these initial difficulties have been conquered, the child is able to experience great pleasure both in using this new tool and in knowing that he has this tool to use.

3. Young children have short attention spans and therefore need relatively brief but frequent reinforcement of new skills (i.e., 5 days a week for 15–20 minutes each day, resulting in a total of about 1½ hours of tutoring per week).

4. The new command of language will allow the child to cope more effectively with an otherwise debilitating environment. Therefore, marked improvements in many aspects of maladaptive behavior should occur.

Based on these considerations, an exploratory program was developed which involved brief daily teaching of language skills for abstract thinking. The central hypothesis was that intervention limited to the development of language for reflection would play such a vital role in cognition that it would facilitate not only language but many other aspects of thinking.

METHOD

Teaching Techniques

Even though we are stressing abstract language, we are not deceived into thinking that the young child is capable of the highest level of concept formation. His concepts must still be bound to direct referents because he needs some tangible evidence of the idea being demonstrated. Nevertheless, the young child can be taught to bring to his level of conceptualization the processes of thinking vital to the development of abstraction.

The first goal of the teaching was to have the child recognize that information relevant to his world was not immediately evident but could be and *had* to be sought from his previous experience. Thus he was taught to question, to probe, to investigate. For example, the teacher put on her coat at the end of a session. The child said, "Why are you going home?" The teacher replied, "How do you know I am going home?" to which the child said, "You're not going home?" This response meant that the child had dropped any attempt at reasoning; he had interpreted the teacher's query to mean that he must negate his earlier inference. To encourage the child to pursue the matter, the teacher said "I *am* going home, but what makes you think I am going home? When you get ready to go home, what do you do?" The child said, "I get my coat." A discussion then followed to solidify the significance of these observations. Thus Socratic dialogue was employed instead of didactic teaching.

Various teaching methods were devised to achieve these goals. A common denominator of all the methods was that the child was confronted with situations in which the teacher used no gestures; to accomplish the task correctly, the child had to understand and/or use language. Another consistent factor was that the child was led to produce an independent response relevant to a situation created by the teacher and to extend the situation set forth by her. This extension focused on having the child discuss situations which did not exist in front of him at the moment but which were relevant to the present situations (e.g., past, future, alternative courses of action, giving explanations of events). By structuring the teaching time in this way, the teacher made maximum use of every opportunity to aid the child in developing his budding ability to think and to reflect. Some of the major techniques used are described below. As the work progresses, we hope to expand and refine this list. It should be noted that each technique is specifically geared to overcome a particular deficiency. This is in contrast to the concept of an enriched environment where the aim is to give a massive dosage that will somehow hit the individual deficiencies. Specifically, the method attempted to develop the following:

(a) *Selective attention.* The young child has few guidelines to assist him in discriminating selectively from the plethora of stimuli which surround him. He tends to be drawn to stimuli which may not be of great cognitive importance but which have potent perceptual qualities (e.g., blast of a horn, a whirling disk). The aim of this technique was to teach the child to recognize essential elements by requiring him to compare objects and make choices among them (e.g., if given a group of different-colored blocks, he was asked to take "two red blocks and one green block"). In this example, the higher-level concept of number helps the child restrain his impulse to respond primitively to the sensory impact of color alone.

(b) *Categories of exclusion.* When the adult gives specific instructions (e.g., "get a crayon"), the child does not need to reflect upon the characteristics of a particular category; he merely responds to direct commands. When the adult gives no direction, the child works aimlessly. When the child can work within the confines of exclusion, however, it means that he has understood the teacher's frame of reference and can independently make appropriate responses. To develop this skill, the child may be asked to make decisions within the confines set by the teacher. For example, the child may be asked to draw something, and he may draw a circle. To encourage the development of exclusion, he would then be asked to draw something "other than a circle."

(c) *Imagery of future events.* The young child can easily describe existing objects and situations. Difficulty arises when he must perceive the meaning of this information relevant to a particular context (see John, 1963). To increase this capacity, the child was required to think through the results of realistically possible but not present courses of action. The child might be first asked to locate a doll that was on the table. After the child completed this correctly, the doll would remain on the table, and the child might be asked, "Where would the doll be if it fell from the table?"

(d) Relevant inner verbalization. We have found that many deprived children will use language to direct their problem-solving only when asked to; they will not spontaneously use language when these external requirements are not imposed. Thus it is not a matter of not having the words but rather a matter of not voluntarily using these words without specific demands. This technique attempts to train the children to develop inner verbalization by retaining words as substitutes for objects. In this method, the child must use language silently and then express it upon request. He might be asked to look at a picture, say the name to himself, and then after the picture has been removed tell the name to the teacher.

(e) Separation of the word from its referent. Young children tend to respond to language automatically without fully recognizing that the word exists independently of the object or action represented. If this separation is not achieved, the child will not generalize the meaning of words beyond the particular contexts in which he hears them. To encourage the ability to reflect upon meaning, the child might be given a command which he must repeat aloud *before* acting out the command—for example, "Jump up two times," "Walk to the door and open it."

(f) Models for cause-and-effect reasonings. Our research (Blank & Bridger, 1966, 1967) has indicated that the perceptual powers of deprived children are intact; they need help, however, in organizing their observations so as to comprehend their significance. To achieve this comprehension, the child can be led to observe common but not frequently noted phenomena (e.g., "What is the weather outside today?" "Can we go out and play today?"). He can then be asked to draw upon his previous experience to determine the reasons underlying these observations (e.g., "Why can't we go out and play?" "Where is the rain coming from?").

(g) Ability to categorize. The place of categorization in thinking has been well documented, and its importance was recognized in this project. To aid the children in this sphere, elementary categories such as food, clothing, transportation, and job functions were taught. Thus, after feeding a doll an imaginary apple, the child was asked to name some other fruits that the doll might eat. Then, utilizing the process of exclusion (*b* above), the child might be asked to name some foods that were *not* fruits.

(h) Awareness of possessing language. Frequently young children are only passive recipients of instruction. This deficiency means that they are unaware that they can independently invoke language to help order their world. This weakness can be overcome by techniques such as asking the child

to give commands to the teacher. The teacher might say to the child, "What shall I do with these pencils?" "Now *you* ask *me* to draw something," "Now tell me what the doll should do this afternoon."

(i) Sustained sequential thinking. Just as musical notes attain their full meaning only when heard within a melody, words attain their full potential only when imbedded in context. This is true even at the elementary level of a simple sentence, and it becomes increasingly important as chains of events extending into time and space must be understood. To be able to see objects, events, and words as located within their appropriate framework, the child has to be taught to maintain concentration and to determine all the possibilities of a course of action. For example, in discussing ways in which material can be altered, the discussion might begin with vegetable dyes (their function, their appearance, etc.). The issue can then be raised as to what can happen to these dyes under various conditions (diluting them with water, leaving them in concentrated form, etc.). In each case, the child is required to apply the necessary change (e.g., add the water) so that he can directly and immediately experience the phenomenon being discussed.

These techniques for achieving higher mental processes are in contrast to the language programs stressing concepts as an end in themselves. In our view, concepts were seen as the necessary preliminary tools for thinking; accordingly, they occupied only a segment of the program. The type of concept taught could not be illustrated by simple direct examples or simple labeling. For example, to call an object a "book" may facilitate communication, but it does not serve to abstract anything more of the object than does a gesture. In addition, the child who can label glibly is often deceptive, since his facile use of words gives the false appearance of understanding. Concepts such as number, speed, direction, temperature, and emotions are suitable for stressing the more abstract functions of language. Techniques for teaching these concepts have been well documented by Bereiter and Englemann (1966).

Common inexpensive objects readily available in the child's environment were the only ones used in the teaching, (e.g., papers, crayons, blocks, toy cars, simple books). The materials were used only as points of departure from which the child could discuss increasingly abstract (non-presently-existing) situations which were relevant to the materials. The same materials, when used alone by the child without supervision, might prove useless in terms of the aims of the study—namely, the avoidance of aimless, scattered, stimulus-bound activity.

Subjects and Procedure

The subjects were selected from a nursery school in a socioeconomically deprived area in New York City. All 22 children from the youngest classes were tested on the Stanford-Binet Intelligence Test (S-B Test) and the Leiter Scale. The children ranged in age from 3 years, 3 months to 4 years, 7 months. Based on these test results, the children were divided into four groups, two tutored and two untutored, matched as closely as possible for IQ, age, and sex. Each child in the first tutored group received individual teaching for 15–20 minutes daily, five times per week; each child in the second tutored group received the same training only three times a week. This tutoring involved taking the child for this short period from his classroom to a familiar room in the school. Each child in one untutored group had daily individual sessions with the same teacher, but no attempt was made to tutor the child. During this time, the child was exposed to the identical materials and was permitted to engage in any activity of his choice. While the teacher was warm and responsive to the child's questions and comments, she did not initiate or extend any cognitive interchange. This group was included to control for the possible role of individual attention alone in facilitating intellectual performance. Another untutored group of seven children remained in the regular nursery school program with no additional attention.

All the tutoring was conducted by a professional nursery school teacher who was trained in the techniques outlined above. The experiment took place over a 4-month period, after which the children were retested. Both the pre- and posttesting were conducted by two research assistants who did not know to which of the groups the children had been assigned and who had had no contact with the children other than at the time of testing.

RESULTS

The pre- and posttest results on the S-B Test are shown in Table 1. Mean IQ increases in tutored groups 1 and 2 were 14.5 and 7.0 points, respectively; in untutored groups 1 and 2, the changes were 2.0 and 1.3 points, respectively. A Kruskal-Wallis analysis of variance indicated that the changes in the four groups were significantly different $(p < .05)$. A Mann-Whitney Test indicated that the rise in the tutored groups was significantly greater than the rise in the untutored groups $(p < .02)$. Although the difference was not significant, the gain by the group tutored five times a week was greater than that of the group tutored three times a week. This suggests that improvements in performance may be directly correlated to the amount of tutoring per week. The lack of a clear difference in gain between the two untutored groups indicates that the element of individual attention from an adult without specialized tutoring was not sufficient to achieve the rise in IQ scores.

The results on the Leiter Scale, though somewhat less marked, are in accord with those on the S-B Test. Thus, tutored groups 1 and 2 showed mean increases of 4.5 and 9.5, respectively, while untutored groups 1 and 2 showed 5.0 and 1.9, respectively. The lower overall gains on the Leiter Scale may also be a reflection of the fact that this test does not require verbal abilities, while the teaching techniques emphasized verbal development. The Leiter scores, however, showed erratic variations. For example, untutored children who remained in the classroom showed spontaneous losses and gains of up to 20 points. This result leads us to believe that the Leiter performance is not a reliable indicator of functioning at this age range.

These IQ changes must also be evaluated in conjunction with the dramatic behavioral changes that accompanied these rises. For example, three of the children were so excessively withdrawn that they had not uttered any coherent verbalizations during their entire time in school. They also exhibited other severe symptoms, such as drooling, "ramlike" head-butting, and bizarre physical coordination. Within 1 month after the program was started, all three were speaking clearly, coherently, and appropriately, and there was a diminution of all symptomatology. No comparable changes were noted in the two children from the control groups who exhibited similar symptomatology.

Even among the children who were relatively well functioning, striking improvements were found. For example, on the S-B Test the pretest response of one girl in describing a picture was "a lady, a horse"; the posttest response was, "The mother is trying to catch the dog with the clothes, the dog takes the clothes, and the mother was trying to get it." This response illustrates the growth from simple labeling to a coordinated, sequential story construction.

The most striking gains in the program were the apparent joy in learning and the feeling of mastery which the children displayed as the tutoring progressed. The untutored children, even those who received individual attention, showed none of these attitudes. This result is extremely important in that it strongly suggests that exposure to materials, a school-like situation, and an interested adult is not sufficient for learning. Both mastery and enthusiasm for learning will come only when the child can be shown how to become actively involved in the learning process.

DISCUSSION

The program outlined above is offered as a means of teaching those language skills necessary for developing abstract thinking in disadvantaged preschool children. We feel that most enrichment programs, and indeed most nursery school programs, are remiss in this area. It is generally assumed that abstract thinking will evolve naturally by school age from having an enriched environment available in the early years. This expectation is

TABLE 1

Pre- and Posttest Stanford-Binet Scores

Sex	Age[a]	Total Hours Tutored	IQ		
			Pre	Post	Change
Tutored group 1					
(5 times/wk.):					
F1	3.8	11	70	98	+28
F2	3.11	11	100	109	+ 9
F3	3.4	13	104	115	+11
M1	3.3	12	111	127	+16
M2	3.11	14	90	109	+19
M3	3.7	14	111	115	+ 4
Mean			97.7	112.2	+14.5
Tutored group 2					
(3 times/wk.):					
F4	3.9	8	89	105	+16
F5	4.7	6	86	98	+12
F6	4.5	7	103	103	0
F7	3.3	6	79[b]	96	+17
M4	3.11	9	94	93	− 1
M5	4.0	5	107	105	− 2
Mean			93.0	100.0	+ 7.0
Untutored group 1					
(5 times/wk.):					
F8	4.1	13	107	111	+ 4
M6	4.4	10	101	99	− 2
M7	4.2	11	80	84	+ 4
Mean			96.0	98.0	+ 2.0
Untutored group 2					
(classroom):					
F9	4.6	—	97	99	+ 2
F10	3.5	—	105	107	+ 2
F11	3.11	—	105	103	− 2
F12	4.2	—	117	114	− 3
M8	4.2	—	115	124	+ 9
M9	4.2	—	88	88	0
M10	3.5	—	93	94	+ 1
Mean			102.8	104.1	+ 1.3

[a] Age at beginning of study.

[b] No basal score was achieved; a basal MA of 2 years was assumed for the calculations, thus overestimating the score.

often met in the case of middle-class children, because the skills not taught by the nursery school are learned in the verbally rich home environment. In the case of the lower-class child, these experiences are not available.

Although the disadvantaged child has not been given the necessary tools for thinking, there are implicit expectations when he enters school that he has a well-formulated abstract attitude. For example, multiple-choice questions are common in reading-readiness tests. Aside from the content, this type of question assumes that the child can evaluate a series sequentially, can refocus attention selectively, and can realize that he must make a definitive choice between alternatives. How is this abstract attitude to emerge? Our research indicates that high-level language skills are central to the development of this kind of thinking. Even at the preschool level, there are tasks for which abstract language is the only means of solution (Blank & Bridger, 1964). Therefore, it is risky to hope that the "fallout" from a perceptually enriched environment will encourage the formation of what is the central core of intelligence.

Even where the language deficits of the deprived preschooler are recognized, they are treated through enlarging the vocabulary, since vocabulary is seen as the basic unit of language. Implicit in this approach is that, as in perceptual training, mere exposure to the basic units will "lubricate" the entire language system. It is our thesis that these children do not simply need more and better words; rather, they need to use the language they already have, as well as any new words they learn, to structure and guide their thinking.

Although this approach benefited the children in this study, its full potential needs further exploration. In addition, it is believed that the program would have to be maintained for a considerable period of time, probably for about 2–3 years, for the gain to be maintained independently thereafter by the child. Reasoning is still difficult for these children, and they need continuing guidance for it to become firmly established. However, considering the amount of time (approximately 60–90 minutes per week per child), the low cost of the materials, and the rapid gains in performance, it seems worthwhile to pursue this program as a technique for facilitating cognitive growth in young children from deprived backgrounds.

References

Bereiter, C., & Engelmann, S. *Teaching disadvantaged children in the preschool.* Englewood Cliffs, N.J.: Prentice Hall, 1966.

Bernstein, B. Language and social class. *British Journal of Sociology*, 1960, **2**, 271–276.

Blank, M. Use of the deaf in language studies: a reply to Furth. *Psychological Bulletin*, 1965, **63**, 442–444.

Blank, M., & Bridger, W. H. Cross-modal transfer in nursery school children. *Journal of Comparative and Physiological Psychology*, 1964, **58**, 277–282.

Blank, M., & Bridger, W. H. Deficiencies in verbal labeling in retarded readers. *American Journal of Orthopsychiatry*, 1966, **36**, 840–847.

Blank, M., & Bridger, W. H. Perceptual abilities and conceptual deficiencies in retarded readers. In J. Zubin (Ed.), *Psychopathology of Mental Development*. New York: Grune & Stratton, 1967, 401–412.

Deutsch, M. Facilitating development in the preschool child: social and psychological perspectives. *Merrill-Palmer Quarterly*, 1964, **10**, 249–263.

Freeburg, N. E., & Payne, D. T. Parental influence on cognitive development in early childhood: a review. *Child Development*, 1967, **38**, 65–87.

Goldstein, K. Functional disturbances in brain damage. In S. Arieti (Ed.), *American Handbook of Psychiatry*. Vol. 1. New York: Basic Books, 1959, 770–794.

Gray, S. W., & Klaus, R. A. An experimental preschool program for culturally deprived children. *Child Development*, 1965, **36**, 887–898.

John, V. P. The intellectual development of slum children: some preliminary findings. *American Journal of Orthopsychiatry*, 1963, **33**, 813–822.

Vygotsky, L. S. *Thought and language*. New York: Wiley, 1962.

26. THREE PROCESSES IN THE CHILD'S ACQUISITION OF SYNTAX*

Roger Brown & Ursula Bellugi

Some time in the second six months of life most children say a first intelligible word. A few months later most children are saying many words and some children go about the house all day long naming things (*table, doggie, ball,* etc.) and actions (*play, see, drop,* etc.) and an occasional quality (*blue, broke, bad,* etc.). At about eighteen months children are likely to begin constructing two-word utterances; such a one, for instance, as *Push car.*

A construction such as *Push car* is not just two single-word utterances spoken in a certain order. As single word utterances (they are sometimes called holophrases) both *push* and *car* would have primary stresses and terminal intonation contours. When they are two words programmed as a single utterance the primary stress would fall on *car* and so would the highest level of pitch. *Push* would be subordinated to *car* by a lesser stress and a lower pitch; the unity of the whole would appear in the absence of a terminal contour between words and the presence of such a contour at the end of the full sequence.

By the age of thirty-six months some children are so advanced in the construction process as to produce all of the major varieties of English simple sentences up to a length of ten or eleven words. For several years we have been studying the development of English syntax, of the sentence-construct-

SOURCE. *Harvard Educational Review,* 2, 1964, 133–151.
* This investigation was supported in whole by Public Health Service Research Grant MH7088 from the National Institute of Mental Health.

ing process, in children between eighteen and thirty-six months of age. Most recently we have made a longitudinal study of a boy and girl whom we shall call Adam and Eve. We began work with Adam and Eve in October of 1962 when Adam was twenty-seven months old and Eve eighteen months old. The two children were selected from some thirty whom we considered. They were selected primarily because their speech was exceptionally intelligible and because they talked a lot. We wanted to make it as easy as possible to transcribe accurately large quantities of child speech. Adam and Eve are the children of highly-educated parents, the fathers were graduate students at Harvard and the mothers are both college graduates. Both Adam and Eve were single children when we began the study. These facts must be remembered in generalizing the outcomes of the research.

While Adam is nine months older than Eve, his speech was only a little more advanced in October of 1962. The best single index of the level of speech development is the average length of utterance and in October, 1962, Adam's average was 1.84 morphemes and Eve's was 1.40 morphemes. The two children stayed fairly close together in the year that followed; in the records for the thirty-eighth week Adam's average was 3.55 and Eve's, 3.27. The processes we shall describe appeared in both children.

Every second week we visited each child for at least two hours and made a tape recording of everything said by the child as well as of everything said to the child. The mother was always present and most of the speech to the child is hers. Both mother and child became very accustomed to our presence and learned to continue their usual routine with us as the observers.

One of us always made a written transcription, on the scene, of the speech of mother and child with notes about important actions and objects of attention. From this transcription and the tape a final transcription was made and these transcriptions constitute the primary data of the study. For many purposes we require a "distributional analysis" of the speech of the child. To this end the child's utterances in a given transcription were cross classified and relisted under such headings as: "A + noun"; "Noun + verb"; "Verbs in the past"; "Utterances containing the pronoun it," etc. The categorized utterances expose the syntactic regularities of the child's speech.

Each week we met as a research seminar, with students of the psychology of language,[1] to discuss the state of the construction process in one of the two children as of that date. In these discussions small experiments were often suggested, experiments that had to be done within a few days if they were to be informative. At one time, for instance, we were uncertain whether Adam understood the semantic difference between putting a noun in subject

[1] We are grateful for intellectual stimulation and lighthearted companionship to Dr. Jean Berko Gleason, Mr. Samuel Anderson, Mr. Colin Fraser, Dr. David McNeill, and Dr. Daniel Slobin.

position and putting it in object position. Consequently one of us paid an extra visit to Adam equipped with some toys. "Adam," we said, "show us the duck pushing the boat." And, when he had done so: "Now show us the boat pushing the duck."

Another week we noticed that Adam would sometimes pluralize nouns when they should have been pluralized and sometimes would not. We wondered if he could make grammatical judgments about the plural, if he could distinguish a correct form from an incorrect form. "Adam," we asked, "which is right, 'two shoes' or 'two shoe'?" His answer on that occasion, produced with explosive enthusiasm, was "Pop goes the weasel!" The two-year-old child does not make a perfectly docile experimental subject.

The dialogue between mother and child does not read like a transcribed dialogue between two adults. Table 1 offers a sample section from an early

TABLE 1

A Section from Adam's First Record

Adam	Mother
See truck, Mommy.	
See truck.	
	Did you see the truck?
No I see truck.	
	No, you didn't see it?
	There goes one.
There go one.	
	Yes, there goes one.
See a truck.	
See truck, Mommy.	
See truck.	
Truck.	
Put truck, Mommy.	
	Put the truck where?
Put truck window.	
	I think that one's too large to go in the window.

transcribed record. It has some interesting properties. The conversation is, in the first place, very much in the here and now. From the child there is no speech of the sort that Bloomfield called "displaced," speech about other times and other places. Adam's utterances in the early months were largely a coding of contemporaneous events and impulses. The mother's speech differs from the speech that adults use to one another in many ways. Her sentences are short and simple; for the most part they are the kinds of sentences that Adam will produce a year later.

Perhaps because they are short, the sentences of the mother are perfectly grammatical. The sentences adults use to one another, perhaps because they are longer and more complex, are very often not grammatical, not well formed. Here for instance is a rather representative example produced at a conference of psychologists and linguists: "As far as I know, no one yet has done the in a way obvious now and interesting problem of doing a in a sense a structural frequency study of the alternative syntactical in a given language, say, like English, the alternative possible structures, and how what their hierarchical probability of occurrence structure is."[2] It seems unlikely that a child could learn the patterns of English syntax from such speech. His introduction to English ordinarily comes in the form of a simplified, repetitive, and idealized dialect. It may be that such an introduction is necessary for the acquisition of syntax to be possible but we do not know that.

In the course of the brief interchange of Table 1 Adam imitates his mother in saying: "There go one" immediately after she says "There goes one." The imitation is not perfect; Adam omits the inflection on the verb. His imitation is a reduction in that it omits something from the original. This kind of imitation with reduction is extremely common in the records of Adam and Eve and it is the first process we shall discuss.

IMITATION AND REDUCTION

Table 2 presents some model sentences spoken by the mothers and the imitations produced by Adam and Eve. These were selected from hundreds in the records in order to illustrate some general propositions. The first thing to notice is that the imitations preserve the word order of the model sentences. To be sure, words in the model are often missing from the imitation but the words preserved are in the order of the original. This is a fact that is so familiar and somehow reasonable that we did not at once recognize it as an empirical outcome rather than as a natural necessity. But of course it is not a necessity, the outcome could have been otherwise. For example, words could have been said back in the reverse of their original order, the most recent first. The preservation of order suggests that the model sentence is processed by the child as a total construction rather than as a list of words.

In English the order of words in a sentence is an important grammatical signal. Order is used to distinguish among subject, direct object, and indirect object and it is one of the marks of imperative and interrogative constructions. The fact that the child's first sentences preserve the word order of their models partially accounts for the ability of an adult to "understand" these sentences and so to feel that he is in communication with the child. It

---

[2] H. Maclay and C. E. Osgood, "Hesitation phenomena in spontaneous English speech," *Word*, XV (1959), 19–44.

TABLE 2

Some Imitations Produced by Adam and Eve

Model Utterance	Child's Imitation
Tank car	Tank car
Wait a minute	Wait a minute
Daddy's brief case	Daddy brief case
Fraser will be unhappy	Fraser unhappy
He's going out	He go out
That's an old time train	Old time train
It's not the same dog as Pepper	Dog Pepper
No, you can't write on Mr. Cromer's shoe	Write Cromer shoe

is conceivable that the child "intends" the meanings coded by his word orders and that, when he preserves the order of an adult sentence, he does so because he wants to say what the order says. It is also possible that he preserves word order just because his brain works that way and that he has no comprehension of the semantic contrasts involved. In some languages word order is not an important grammatical signal. In Latin, for instance, "Agricola amat puellam" has the same meaning as "Puellam amat agricola" and subject-object relations are signalled by case endings. We would be interested to know whether children who are exposed to languages that do not utilize word order as a major syntactic signal, preserve order as reliably as do children exposed to English.

The second thing to notice in Table 2 is the fact that when the models increase in length there is not a corresponding increase in the imitation. The imitations stay in the range of two to four morphemes which was the range characteristic of the children at this time. The children were operating under some constraint of length or span. This is not a limitation of vocabulary; the children knew hundreds of words. Neither is it a constraint of immediate memory. We infer this from the fact that the average length of utterances produced spontaneously, where immediate memory is not involved, is about the same as the average length of utterances produced as immediate imitations. The constraint is a limitation on the length of utterance the children are able to program or plan.[3] This kind of narrow span limitation in children is characteristic of most or all of their intellectual operations. The limitation grows less restrictive with age as a consequence, probably, of both neurological growth and of practice, but of course it is never lifted altogether.

[3] Additional evidence of the constraint on sentence length may be found in R. Brown and C. Fraser. "The acquisition of syntax," C. N. Cofer and Barbara Musgrave, eds., *Verbal Behavior and Learning* (New York: McGraw Hill, 1963).

A constraint on length compels the imitating child to omit some words or morphemes from the mother's longer sentences. Which forms are retained and which omitted? The selection is not random but highly systematic. Forms retained in the examples of Table 2 include: *Daddy, Fraser, Pepper,* and *Cromer; tank car, minute, briefcase, train, dog, and shoe; wait, go,* and *write; unhappy* and *old time.* For the most part they are nouns, verbs, and adjectives, though there are exceptions, as witness the initial pronoun *He* and the preposition *out* and the indefinite article *a.* Forms omitted in the samples of Table 2 include: the possessive inflection *–s,* the modal auxiliary *will,* the contraction of the auxiliary verb *is,* the progressive inflection *–ing,* the preposition *on,* the articles *the* and *an,* and the modal auxiliary *can.* It is possible to make a general characterization of the forms likely to be retained that distinguishes them as a total class from the forms likely to be omitted.

Forms likely to be retained are nouns and verbs and, less often, adjectives, and these are the three large and "open" parts-of-speech in English. The number of forms in any one of these parts-of-speech is extremely large and always growing. Words belonging to these classes are sometimes called "contentives" because they have semantic content. Forms likely to be omitted are inflections, auxiliary verbs, articles, prepositions, and conjunctions. These forms belong to syntactic classes that are small and closed. Any one class has few members and new members are not readily added. The omitted forms are the ones that linguists sometimes call "functors," their grammatical *functions* being more obvious than their semantic content.

Why should young children omit functors and retain contentives? There is more than one plausible answer. Nouns, verbs, and adjectives are words that make reference. One can conceive of teaching the meanings of these words by speaking them, one at a time, and pointing at things or actions or qualities. And of course parents do exactly that. These are the kinds of words that children have been encouraged to practice speaking one at a time. The child arrives at the age of sentence construction with a stock of well-practiced nouns, verbs, and adjectives. Is it not likely then that this prior practice causes him to retain the contentives from model sentences too long to be reproduced in full, that the child imitates those forms in the speech he hears which are already well developed in him as individual habits? There is probably some truth in this explanation but it is not the only determinant since children will often select for retention contentives that are relatively unfamiliar to them.

We adults sometimes operate under a constraint on length and the curious fact is that the English we produce in these circumstances bears a formal resemblance to the English produced by two-year-old children. When words cost money there is a premium on brevity or to put it otherwise, a constraint on length. The result is "telegraphic" English and telegraphic English is an

English of nouns, verbs, and adjectives. One does not send a cable reading: "My car has broken down and I have lost my wallet; send money to me at the American Express in Paris" but rather "Car broken down; wallet lost; send money American Express Paris." The telegram omits: *my, has, and, I, have, my, to, me, at, the, in.* All of these are functors. We make the same kind of telegraphic reduction when time or fatigue constrain us to be brief, as witness any set of notes taken at a fast-moving lecture.

A telegraphic transformation of English generally communicates very well. It does so because it retains the high-information words and drops the low-information words. We are here using "information" in the sense of the mathematical theory of communication. The information carried by a word is inversely related to the chances of guessing it from context. From a given string of content words, missing functors can often be guessed but the message "my has and I have my to me at the in" will not serve to get money to Paris. Perhaps children are able to make a communication analysis of adult speech and so adapt in an optimal way to their limitation of span. There is, however, another way in which the adaptive outcome might be achieved.

If you say aloud the model sentences of Table 2 you will find that you place the heavier stresses, the primary and secondary stresses in the sentences, on contentives rather than on functors. In fact the heavier stresses fall, for the most part, on the words the child retains. We first realized that this was the case when we found that in transcribing tapes, the words of the mother that we could hear most clearly were usually the words that the child reproduced. We had trouble hearing the weakly stressed functors and, of course, the child usually failed to reproduce them. Differential stress may then be the cause of the child's differential retention. The outcome is a maximally informative reduction but the cause of this outcome need not be the making of an information analysis. The outcome may be an incidental consequence of the fact that English is a well-designed language that places its heavier stresses where they are needed, on contentives that cannot easily be guessed from context.

We are fairly sure that differential stress is one of the determinants of the child's telegraphic productions. For one thing, stress will also account for the way in which children reproduce polysyllabic words when the total is too much for them. Adam, for instance, gave us *'pression* for *expression* and Eve gave us *'raff* for *giraffe*; the more heavily-stressed syllables were the ones retained. In addition we have tried the effect of placing heavy stresses on functors which do not ordinarily receive such stresses. To Adam we said: "You say what I say" and then, speaking in a normal way at first: "The doggie will bite." Adam gave back: "Doggie bite." Then we stressed the auxiliary: "The doggie *will* bite" and, after a few trials, Adam made attempts at reproducing that auxiliary. A science fiction experiment comes to mind. If there were parents who stressed functors rather than contentives would they have children whose speech was a kind of "reciprocal telegraphic" made up of articles, prepositions, conjunctions, auxiliaries, and the like? Such children would be out of touch with the community as real children are not.

It may be that all the factors we have mentioned play some part in determining the child's selective imitations; the reference-making function of contentives, the fact that they are practiced as single words, the fact that they cannot be guessed from context, and the heavy stresses they receive. There are also other possible factors: for example, the left-to-right, earlier-to-later position of words in a sentence, but these make too long a story to tell here.[4] Whatever the causes, the first utterances produced as imitations of adult sentences are highly systematic reductions of their models. Furthermore, the telegraphic properties of these imitations appear also in the child's spontaneously produced utterances. When his speech is not modeled on an immediately prior adult sentence, it observes the same limitation on length and the same predilection for contentives as when it is modeled on an immediately prior sentence.

IMITATION WITH EXPANSION

In the course of the brief conversation set down in Table 1, Adam's mother at one point imitates Adam. The boy says: "There go one" and mother responds: "Yes, there goes one." She does not exactly reproduce the model sentence of the child but instead adds something to it or expands it. What she adds is a functor, the inflection for third-person on the verb, the very form that Adam had omitted when he imitated his mother.

One of the first things we noticed when we began to study child speech several years ago was the frequency with which adults imitated children. Indeed they seemed to imitate more often than did the children themselves. We later came to realize that adult imitations are seldom exact reproductions; they are usually expansions. The mothers of Adam and Eve responded to the speech of their children with expansions about thirty per cent of the time. We did it ourselves when we talked with the children. Indeed we found it very difficult to withhold expansions. A reduced or incomplete English sentence seems to constrain the English-speaking adult to expand it into the nearest properly formed complete sentence. Table 3 lists a few sample expansions from the hundreds in the records.

The first thing worthy of attention in the expansions of Table 3 is the fact that the words spoken by the mother preserve the order of the words in the child's sentences. To be sure, words and inflections are added but they are

[4] Brown and Fraser, *ibid.*

TABLE 3

Expansions of Child Speech Produced by Mothers

Child	Mother
Baby highchair	Baby is in the highchair
Mommy eggnog	Mommy had her eggnog
Eve lunch	Eve is having lunch
Mommy sandwich	Mommy'll have a sandwich
Sat wall	He sat on the wall
Throw Daddy	Throw it to Daddy
Pick glove	Pick the glove up

fitted in—before, and after and between the words the child used; they are not generally permitted to disturb the order of the child's words. It is as if these latter were taken as constants by the mother, constants to which some sentence had to be fitted. She acts as if she were assuming that the child means everything he says, all the words and also their order, but as if he might also mean more than he says. From the mother's point of view an expansion is a kind of communication check; it says in effect: "Is this what you mean?"

The second thing to notice about Table 3 is the character of the forms added to the child's utterances. They include the auxiliaries *is* and *will*; the prepositions *in, on, to,* and *up;* the verb forms *is, have, had,* and *having;* the articles *a* and *the;* the pronouns *her, he,* and *it.* For the most part, the words added are functors and functors are of course the words that the child omits in his reductions.

The interaction between mother and child is, much of the time, a cycle of reductions and expansions. There are two transformations involved. The reduction transformation has an almost completely specifiable and so mechanical character. One could program a machine to do it with the following instructions: "Retain contentives (or stressed forms) in the order given up to some limit of length." The expansion accomplished by Adam's mother when she added the third-person inflection to the verb and said "There goes one" is also a completely specifiable transformation. The instructions would read: "Retain the forms given in the order given and supply obligatory grammatical forms." To be sure this mother-machine would have to be supplied with the obligatory rules of English grammar but that could be done. However, the sentence "There goes one" is atypical in that it only adds a compulsory and redundant inflection. The expansions of Table 3 all add forms that are not grammatically compulsory or redundant and these expansions cannot be mechanically generated by grammatical rules alone.

In Table 3 the topmost four utterances produced by the child are all of the same grammatical type; all four consist of a proper noun followed by a common noun. However, the four are expanded in quite different ways. In particular the form of the verb changes: it is in the first case in the simple present tense; in the second case the simple past; in the third case the present progressive; in the last case the simple future. All of these are perfectly grammatical but they are different. The second set of child utterances is formally uniform in that each one consists of a verb followed by a noun. The expansions are again all grammatical but quite unlike, especially with regard to the preposition supplied. In general, then, there are radical changes in the mother's expansions when there are no changes in the formal character of the utterances expanded. It follows that the expansions cannot be produced simply by making grammatically compulsory additions to the child's utterances.

How does a mother decide on the correct expansion of one of her child's utterances? Consider the utterance "Eve lunch." So far as grammar is concerned this utterance could be appropriately expanded in any of a number of ways: "Eve is having lunch"; "Eve had lunch"; "Eve will have lunch"; "Eve's lunch," etc. On the occasion when Eve produced the utterance, however, one expansion seemed more appropriate than any other. It was then the noon hour, Eve was sitting at the table with a plate of food before her, and her spoon and fingers were busy. In these circumstances "Eve lunch" had to mean "Eve is having lunch." A little later when the plate had been stacked in the sink and Eve was getting down from her chair the utterance "Eve lunch" would have suggested the expansion "Eve has had her lunch." Most expansions are not only responsive to the child's words but also to the circumstances attending their utterance.

What kind of instructions will generate the mother's expansions? The following are approximately correct: "Retain the words given in the order given and add those functors that will result in a well-formed simple sentence that is appropriate to the circumstances." These are not instructions that any machine could follow. A machine could act on the instructions only if it were provided with detailed specifications for judging appropriateness and no such specifications can, at present, be written. They exist, however, in implicit form in the brains of mothers and in the brains of all English-speaking adults and so judgments of appropriateness can be made by such adults.

The expansion encodes aspects of reality that are not coded by the child's telegraphic utterance. Functors have meaning but it is meaning that accrues to them in context rather than in isolation. The meanings that are added by functors seem to be nothing less than the basic terms in which we construe reality: the time of an action, whether it is ongoing or completed, whether it is presently relevant or not; the concept of possession and such relational concepts as are coded by *in, on, up, down,* and the like; the difference between a particular instance of a class ("Has anybody seen *the* paper?") and any instance of a class ("Has anybody seen *a* paper?"); the difference between extended substances given shape and size by an "accidental" container (*sand, water, syrup,* etc.) and countable "things" having a characteristic fixed shape and size (*a cup, a man, a tree,* etc.). It seems to us that a mother in expanding speech may be teaching more than grammar; she may be teaching something like a world-view.

As yet it has not been demonstrated that expansions are *necessary* for learning either grammar or a construction of reality. It has not even been demonstrated that expansions contribute to such learning. All we know is that some parents do expand and their children do learn. It is perfectly possible, however, that children can and do learn simply from hearing their parents or others make well-formed sentences in connection with various nonverbal circumstances. It may not be necessary or even helpful for these sentences to be expansions of utterances of the child. Only experiments contrasting expansion training with simple exposure to English will settle the matter. We hope to do such experiments.

There are, of course, reasons for expecting the expansion transformation to be an effective tutorial technique. By adding something to the words the child has just produced one confirms his response insofar as it is appropriate. In addition one takes him somewhat beyond that response but not greatly beyond it. One encodes additional meanings at a moment when he is most likely to be attending to the cues that can teach that meaning.

INDUCTION OF THE LATENT STRUCTURE

Adam, in the course of the conversation with his mother set down in Table 1, produced one utterance for which no adult is likely ever to have provided an exact model: "No I see truck." His mother elects to expand it as "No, you didn't see it" and this expansion suggests that the child might have created the utterance by reducing an adult model containing the form *didn't*. However, the mother's expansion in this case does some violence to Adam's original version. He did not say *no* as his mother said it, with primary stress and final contour; Adam's *no* had secondary stress and no final contour. It is not easy to imagine an adult model for this utterance. It seems more likely that the utterance was created by Adam as part of a continuing effort to discover the general rules for constructing English negatives.

In Table 4 we have listed some utterances produced by Adam or Eve for which it is difficult to imagine any adult model. It is unlikely that any adult said any of these to Adam or Eve since they are very simple utterances and yet definitely ungrammatical. In addition it is difficult, by adding functors alone, to build any of them up to simple grammatical sentences. Conse-

TABLE 4

Utterances Not Likely to be Imitations

My Cromer suitcase	You naughty are
Two foot	Why it can't turn off?
A bags	Put on it
A scissor	Cowboy did fighting me
A this truck	Put a gas in

quently it does not seem likely that these utterances are reductions of adult originals. It is more likely that they are mistakes which externalize the child's search for the regularities of English syntax.

We have long realized that the occurrence of certain kinds of errors on the level of morphology (or word construction) reveals the child's effort to induce regularities from speech. So long as a child speaks correctly, or at any rate so long as he speaks as correctly as the adults he hears, there is no way to tell whether he is simply repeating what he has heard or whether he is actually constructing. However, when he says something like "I digged a hole" we can often be sure that he is constructing. We can be sure because it is unlikely that he would have heard *digged* from anyone and because we can see how, in processing words he has heard, he might have come by *digged*. It looks like an overgeneralization of the regular past inflection. The inductive operations of the child's mind are externalized in such a creation. Overgeneralizations on the level of syntax (or sentence construction) are more difficult to identify because there are so many ways of adding functors so as to build up conceivable models. But this is difficult to do for the examples of Table 4 and for several hundred other utterances in our records.

The processes of imitation and expansion are not sufficient to account for the degree of linguistic competence that children regularly acquire. These processes alone cannot teach more than the sum total of sentences that speakers of English have either modeled for a child to imitate or built up from a child's reductions. However, a child's linguistic competence extends far beyond this sum total of sentences. All children are able to understand and construct sentences they have never heard but which are nevertheless well-formed, well-formed in terms of general rules that are implicit in the sentences the child has heard. Somehow, then, every child processes the speech to which he is exposed so as to induce from it a latent structure. This latent rule structure is so general that a child can spin out its implications all his life long. It is both semantic and syntactic. The discovery of latent structure is the greatest of the processes involved in language acquisition and the most difficult to understand. We will provide an example of how the analysis can proceed by discussing the evolution in child speech of noun phrases.

A noun phrase in adult English includes a noun but also more than a noun. One variety consists of a noun with assorted modifiers: *The girl; The pretty girl; That pretty girl; My girl,* etc. All of these are constructions which have the same syntactic privileges as do nouns alone. One can use a noun phrase in isolation to name or request something; one can use it in sentences, in subject position or in object position or in predicate nominative position. All of these are slots that nouns alone can also fill. A larger construction having the same syntactic privileges as its "head" word is called in linguistics an "endocentric" construction and noun phrases are endocentric constructions.

For both Adam and Eve, in the early records, noun phrases usually occur as total independent utterances rather than as components of sentences. Table 5 presents an assortment of such utterances at Time 1. They consist in each

TABLE 5

Noun Phrases in Isolation and Rule for Generating Noun Phrases at Time 1

A coat	More coffee
A celery[a]	More nut[a]
A Becky[a]	Two sock[a]
A hands[a]	Two shoes
The top	two tinker-toy[a]
My Mommy	Big boot
That Adam	Poor man
My stool	Little top
That knee	Dirty knee

$$NP \rightarrow M + N$$

M → a, big, dirty, little, more, my, poor, that, the, two.

N → Adam, Becky, boot, coat, coffee, knee, man, Mommy, nut, sock, stool, tinker-toy, top, and very many others.

[a] Ungrammatical for an adult.

case of some sort of modifier, just one, preceding a noun. The modifiers, or as they are sometimes called the "pivot" words, are a much smaller class than the noun class. Three students of child speech have independently discovered that this kind of construction is extremely common when children first begin to combine words. [5, 6, 7]

[5] M. D. S. Braine, "The ontogeny of English phrase structure: the first phrase," *Language*, XXXIX (1963), 1–13.

[6] W. Miller and Susan Ervin, "The development of grammar in child language," Ursula Bellugi and R. Brown, eds., *The Acquisition of Language, Child Developm. Monogr.* (1964).

[7] Brown and Fraser, *op. cit.*

It is possible to generalize the cases of Table 5 into a simple implicit rule. The rule symbolized in Table 5 reads: "In order to form a noun phrase of this type, select first one word from the small class of modifiers and select, second, one word from the large class of nouns." This is a "generative" rule by which we mean it is a program that would actually serve to build constructions of the type in question. It is offered as a model of the mental mechanism by which Adam and Eve generated such utterances. Furthermore, judging from our work with other children and from the reports of Braine and of Miller and Ervin, the model describes a mechanism present in many children when their average utterance is approximately two morphemes long.

We have found that even in our earliest records the M + N construction is sometimes used as a component of larger constructions. For instance, Eve said: "Fix a Lassie" and "Turn the page" and "A horsie stuck" and Adam even said: "Adam wear a shirt." There are, at first, only a handful of these larger constructions but there are very many constructions in which single nouns occur in subject or in object position.

Let us look again at the utterances of Table 5 and the rule generalizing them. The class M does not correspond with any syntactic class of adult English. In the class M are articles, a possessive pronoun, a cardinal number, a demonstrative adjective or pronoun, a quantifier, and some descriptive adjectives—a mixed bag indeed. For adult English these words cannot belong to the same syntactic class because they have very different privileges of occurrence in sentences. For the children the words do seem to function as one class having the common privilege of occurrence before nouns.

If the initial words of the utterances in Table 5 are treated as one class M then many utterances are generated which an adult speaker would judge to be ungrammatical. Consider the indefinite article *a*. Adults use it only to modify common count nouns in the singular such as *coat, dog, cup*, etc. We would not say *a celery*, or *a cereal*, or *a dirt*; *celery, cereal*, and *dirt* are mass nouns. We would not say *a Becky* or *a Jimmy*; *Becky* and *Jimmy* are proper nouns. We would not say *a hands* or *a shoes*; *hands* and *shoes* are plural nouns. Adam and Eve, at first, did form ungrammatical combinations such as these.

The numeral *two* we use only with count nouns in the plural. We would not say *two sock* since *sock* is singular, nor *two water* since *water* is a mass noun. The word *more* we use before count nouns in the plural (*more nuts*) or mass nouns in the singular (*more coffee*). Adam and Eve made a number of combinations involving *two* or *more* that we would not make.

Given the initial very undiscriminating use of words in the class M it follows that one dimension of development must be a progressive differentiation of privileges, which means the division of M into smaller classes. There must also be subdivision of the noun class (N) for the reason that the privileges of occurrence of various kinds of modifiers must be described in terms of such sub-varieties of N as the common noun and proper noun, the count noun and mass noun. There must eventually emerge a distinction between nouns singular and nouns plural since this distinction figures in the privileges of occurrence of the several sorts of modifiers.

Sixteen weeks after our first records from Adam and Eve (Time 2), the differentiation process had begun. By this time there were distributional reasons for separating out articles (*a, the*) from demonstrative pronouns (*this, that*) and both of these from the residual class of modifiers. Some of the evidence for this conclusion appears in Table 6. In general one syntactic

TABLE 6

Subdivision of the Modifier Class

(A) PRIVILEGES PECULIAR TO ARTICLES	
Obtained	Not Obtained
A blue flower	Blue a flower
A nice nap	Nice a nap
A your car	Your a car
A my pencil	My a pencil
(B) PRIVILEGES PECULIAR TO DEMONSTRATIVE PRONOUNS	
Obtained	Not Obtained
That my cup	My that cup
That a horse	A that horse
That a blue flower	A that blue flower
	Blue a that flower

class is distinguished from another when the members of one class have combinational privileges not enjoyed by the members of the other. Consider, for example, the reasons for distinguishing articles (Art) from modifiers in general (M). Both articles and modifiers appeared in front of nouns in two-word utterances. However, in three-word utterances that were made up from the total pool of words and that had a noun in final position, the privileges of *a* and *the* were different from the privileges of all other modifiers. The articles occurred in initial position followed by a member of class M other than an article. No other modifier occurred in this first position; notice the "Not obtained" examples of Table 6A. If the children had produced utterances like those (for example, *blue a flower, your a car*) there would have been no difference in the privileges of occurrence of articles and modifiers and therefore no reason to separate out articles.

The record of Adam is especially instructive. He created such notably ungrammatical combinations as "a your car" and "a my pencil." It is very unlikely that adults provided models for these. They argue strongly that Adam regarded all the words in the residual M class as syntactic equivalents and so generated these very odd utterances in which possessive pronouns appear where descriptive adjectives would be more acceptable.

Table 6 also presents some of the evidence for distinguishing demonstrative pronouns (Dem) from articles and modifiers. (Table 6B). The pronouns occurred first and ahead of articles in three-and-four-word utterances—a position that neither articles nor modifiers ever filled. The sentences with demonstrative pronouns are recognizable as reductions which omit the copular verb *is*. Such sentences are not noun phrases in adult English and ultimately they will not function as noun phrases in the speech of the children, but for the present they are not distinguishable distributionally from noun phrases.

Recall now the generative formula of Table 5 which constructs noun phrases by simply placing a modifier (M) before a noun (N). The differentiation of privileges illustrated in Table 6, and the syntactic classes this evidence motivates us to create, complicate the formula for generating noun phrases. In Table 7 we have written a single general formula for producing

TABLE 7

Rules for Generating Noun Phrases at Time 2

$NP_1 \rightarrow Dem + Art + M + N$	$NP \rightarrow (Dem) + (Art) + (M) + N$
$NP_2 \rightarrow Art + M + N$	
$NP_3 \rightarrow Dem + M + N$	
$NP_4 \rightarrow Art + N$	( ) means class within
$NP_5 \rightarrow M + N$	parentheses is optional
$NP_6 \rightarrow Dem + N$	
$NP_7 \rightarrow Dem + Art + N$	

all noun phrases at Time 2 [NP → (Dem) + (Art) + (M) + N] and also the numerous more specific rules which are summarized by the general formula.

By the time of the thirteenth transcription, twenty-six weeks after we began our study, privileges of occurrence were much more finely differentiated and syntactic classes were consequently more numerous. From the distributional evidence we judged that Adam had made five classes of his original class M: articles, descriptive adjectives, possessive pronouns, demonstrative pronouns, and a residual class of modifiers. The generative rules of Table 7 had become inadequate; there were no longer, for instance, any combinations like "A your car." Eve had the same set except that she used two residual classes of modifiers. In addition nouns had begun to subdivide for both children. The usage of proper nouns had become clearly distinct from the usage of count nouns. For Eve the evidence justified separating count nouns from mass nouns, but for Adam it still did not. Both children by this time were frequently pluralizing nouns but as yet their syntactic control of the singular-plural distinction was imperfect.

In summary, one major aspect of the development of general structure in child speech is a progressive differentiation in the usage of words and therefore a progressive differentiation of syntactic classes. At the same time, however, there is an integrative process at work. From the first, an occasional noun phrase occurred as a component of some larger construction. At first these noun phrases were just two words long and the range of positions in which they could occur was small. With time the noun phrases grew longer, were more frequently used, and were used in a greater range of positions. The noun phrase structure as a whole, in all the permissible combinations of modifiers and nouns, was assuming the combinational privileges enjoyed by nouns in isolation.

In Table 8 we have set down some of the sentence positions in which both

TABLE 8

Some Privileges of the Noun Phrase

Noun Positions	Noun Phrase Positions
That (flower)	That (a blue flower)
Where (ball) go?	Where (the puzzle) go?
Adam write (penquin)	Doggie eat (the breakfast)
(Horsie) stop	(A horsie) crying
Put (hat) on	Put (the red hat) on

nouns and noun phrases occurred in the speech of Adam and Eve. It is the close match between the positions of nouns alone and of nouns with modifiers in the speech of Adam and Eve that justifies us in calling the longer constructions noun phrases. These longer constructions are, as they should be, endocentric; the head word alone has the same syntactic privileges as the head word with its modifiers. The continuing failure to find in noun phrase positions whole constructions of the type "That a blue flower" signals the fact that these constructions are telegraphic versions of predicate nominative sentences omitting the verb form *is*. Examples of the kind of construction not obtained are: "That (that a blue flower)"; "Where (that a blue flower)?"

For adults the noun phrase is a subwhole of the sentence, what linguists call an "immediate constituent." The noun phrase has a kind of psychological unity. There are signs that the noun phrase was also an immediate constituent for Adam and Eve. Consider the sentence using the separable verb *put on*. The noun phrase in "Put the red hat on" is, as a whole, fitted in between the verb and the particle even as is the noun alone in "Put hat on." What is more, however, the location of pauses in the longer sentence, on several occasions, suggested the psychological organization: "Put . . . the red hat . . . on" rather than "Put the red . . . hat on" or "Put the . . . red hat on." In addition to this evidence the use of pronouns suggests that the noun phrase is a psychological unit.

The unity of noun phrases in adult English is evidenced, in the first place, by the syntactic equivalence between such phrases and nouns alone. It is evidenced, in the second place, by the fact that pronouns are able to substitute for total noun phrases. In our immediately preceding sentence the pronoun "It" stands for the rather involved construction from the first sentence of this paragraph: "The unity of noun phrases in adult English." The words called "pronouns" in English would more aptly be called "pro-noun-phrases" since it is the phrase rather than the noun which they usually replace. One does not replace "unity" with "it" and say "The *it* of noun phrases in adult English." In the speech of Adam and Eve, too, the pronoun came to function as a replacement for the noun phrase. Some of the clearer cases appear in Table 9.

TABLE 9

Pronouns Replacing Nouns or Noun Phrases and Pronouns Produced Together with Nouns or Noun Phrases

Noun Phrases Replaced by Pronouns	Pronouns and Noun Phrases in Same Utterances
Hit ball	Mammy get it ladder
Get it	Mommy get it my ladder
Ball go?	Saw it ball
Go get it	Miss it garage
Made it	I miss it cowboy boot
Made a ship	I Adam drive that
Fix a tricycle	I Adam drive
Fix it	I Adam don't

Adam characteristically externalizes more of his learning than does Eve and his record is especially instructive in connection with the learning of pronouns. In his first eight records, the first sixteen weeks of the study, Adam quite often produced sentences containing both the pronoun and the noun or noun phrase that the pronoun should have replaced. One can here see the equivalence in the process of establishment. First the substitute is produced and then, as if in explication, the form or forms that will eventually be replaced by the substitute. Adam spoke out his pronoun antecedents as chronological consequents. This is additional evidence of the unity of the noun phrase since the noun phrases *my ladder* and *cowboy boot* are linked with *it* in Adam's speech in just the same way as the nouns *ladder* and *ball.*

We have described three processes involved in the child's acquisition of syntax. It is clear that the last of these, the induction of latent structure, is by far the most complex. It looks as if this last process will put a serious strain on any learning theory thus far conceived by psychology. The very intricate simultaneous differentiation and integration that constitutes the evolution of the noun phrase is more reminiscent of the biological development of an embryo than it is of the acquisition of a conditional reflex.

27. THE FUNCTION OF LANGUAGE CLASSIFICATIONS IN BEHAVIOR*

John B. Carroll & Joseph B. Casagrande

More than fifty years ago George Santayana wrote in his essay *The Sense of Beauty*: "Grammar, philosophically studied, is akin to the deepest metaphysics, because in revealing the constitution of speech, it reveals the constitution of thought and the hierarchy of those categories by which we conceive the world."[1] The world of experience is characterized by a logic that deals with continua; our experiences present themselves to us in almost limitless variations and shadings; and there are no boundaries between the parts of experience except those which are created by our perceptions.

If a language is to be used for efficient person-to-person communication about the world of experience, it must operate with a logic that deals with discrete entities—a logic of criteriality which distinguishes experiences on certain arbitrary and agreed-upon terms. When we give proper names to individual persons, pet animals, and geographical locations, we are respond-

SOURCE. J. Carroll and J. Casagrande, The function of language classifications in behavior. In E. Maccoby, F. Newcomb, and E. Hartley (Eds.), *Readings in Social Psychology*. New York: Holt, Rinehart and Winston, 1958, pp. 18–31.

* The two experiments reported here were conducted as a part of the Southwest Project in Comparative Psycholinguistics, sponsored by the Committee on Linguistics and Psychology of the Social Science Research Council under a grant from the Carnegie Corporation of New York. Experiment I was designed and conducted by Carroll; Experiment II, by Casagrande.

[1] George Santayana, *The Sense of Beauty* (Boston: Charles Scribner's Sons, 1896), p. 169.

ing to an extreme need for discreteness and specific differentiation, but most of the time we are well satisfied to convey our experiences by means of a relatively small number (a few thousand, say) of general categories into which we learn to fit them. As a first approximation we may regard each word of a language like English as the name of a category of experience: *horse, petunia, he, ecstasy, reprimand, green, very,* and *nevertheless* are all categories of experience. Not all categories of experience are symbolized by discrete words; some are represented by grammatical phenomena such as are indicated in the following contrasts: *horse v. horse's; petunia v. petunias; he v. him; ecstasy v. ecstatic; reprimand v. reprimanded; green v. greener; the very old man v. the very idea;* and the classic *dog bites man v. man bites dog.*

If we agree that the categories of a language are "arbitrary" in the sense that they could be replaced by other, equally acceptable ways of categorizing experience, we could begin to inquire to what extent the several thousand languages of the world have similar categories. How many languages have a distinct, generic term for *horse?* How many languages have only a term for what we would call *quadruped,* applying it alike to horses, dogs, wolves, giraffes and adding appropriate qualifying terms? Are there languages which have no generic term for *horse* but only terms for particular breeds and conditions of horses? (We are told that Arabic is such a language.) Or let us take a grammatical problem: do all languages distinguish singular and plural? (No, Chinese does not.) Are there languages which have *more* levels of grammatical number than our two? (Yes; some languages have four "numbers," singular, dual, trial, and plural.) Investigations along these lines are not to be undertaken lightly, for they require an immense sophistication in the techniques of linguistic science. We can nevertheless predict the major outlines of the results. There would be many semantic areas of remarkable (though rarely complete) uniformity among languages, while other areas would tend to show considerable diversity. The linguist Morris Swadesh has surveyed a wide variety of languages in an effort to arrive at a list of concepts for which one would be fairly sure to find a distinct word or word-like form in every language. His final list[2] of 100 such concepts includes things like: personal pronouns: *I, thou, we, he, ye, they;* position and movement: *come, sit, give fly, stand, hold, fall, swim;* natural objects and phenomena: *ice, salt, star, sun, wind;* descriptives: *old, dry, good, new, warm, rotten, cold;* miscellaneous: *name, other, not, burn, blow, freeze, swell, road, kill.* But even in observing this apparent uniformity, we must not be misled into thinking that there are exact semantic correspondences between lan-

[2] Morris Swadesh, "Towards Greater Accuracy in Lexicostatistic Dating," *Internat. J. Am. Linguistics,* 1955, XXI, 121–137.

guages. English *horse,* French *cheval,* and German *Pferd* may have different ranges of application and different semantic overtones; the measurement of such differences is a problem beyond the scope of this paper.[3] Further, we can find rather obvious lacks of correspondence when we look at the different ranges of meaning covered by the English *proceed v.* French *procéder* ("to proceed" but also "to behave or conduct oneself"), or English *experience v.* French *expérience* ("experience" but also "experiment"). It would appear that the categories of one language are sometimes "untranslatable" into another language; even if we ignore such problems as finding the difference between the English and the Russian concepts of democracy, there remain such cases as German *Gemütlichkeit* and French *acharnement* which are presumably incapable of exact rendering in English.[4] Even such a simple concept as that represented by the word *too* is extremely clumsy to express in Amharic, the official language of Ethiopia. In the realm of grammar, Edward Sapir's classic work *Language*[5] will suggest the extent to which languages differ among themselves in grammatical concepts. Although Sapir felt that "no language wholly fails to distinguish noun and verb," his writings suggest that there are few basic concepts which universally find expression in the grammatical structures of languages. This is not to say that there are grammatical concepts which *cannot* be expressed in all languages; in general, any grammatical concept found in one language can be expressed somehow in every language, even if the expression is a little awkward or periphrastic. Languages do differ remarkably, however, in the grammatical concepts which are mandatory: for example, the use of the singular-plural distinction is said to be mandatory in English but completely optional in Chinese. If someone says "I'm going out to hunt bear," he is dispensing with the singular-plural distinction and talking in the pattern of Chinese —which happens to be convenient because he does not know whether he will bag one bear or more than one.

The real question for the social psychologist is this: Is the behavior of a person (aside from his language behavior) a function of the language he happens to speak? Granted that languages differ in the ways we have described, what effects will these differences have on the way a person thinks, the way he deals with other people, or the way he deals with his environment?

The notion that language makes an important difference in behavior has

---

[3] The "semantic differential" technique devised by Osgood may be particularly useful here. See C. E. Osgood, G. J. Suci, and P. H. Tannenbaum, *The Measurement of Meaning* (Urbana: Univ. of Illinois Press, 1957).

[4] The success of translation depends partly on the purpose of translation. See J. B. Casagrande, "The Ends of Translation," *Internat. J. Am. Linguistics,* 1954, XX, 335-340.

[5] Edward Sapir, *Language* (New York: Harcourt, Brace & Co., 1921), Ch. V.

a long history, beginning with the writings of the German philologist W. von Humboldt more than a century ago. In more recent times, the linguist Benjamin Lee Whorf has been the chief exponent of what he termed "linguistic relativity":

> . . . the background linguistic system (in other words, the grammar) of each language is not merely a reproducing instrument for voicing ideas but rather is itself the shaper of ideas, the program and guide for the individual's mental activity, for his analysis of impressions, for his synthesis of his mental stock in trade. Formulation of ideas is not an independent process, strictly rational in the old sense, but is part of a particular grammar and differs, from slightly to greatly, between different grammars."[6]

The linguistic relativity hypothesis is a special case of the culture-personality theory. Substituting terms in Smith, Bruner, and White's précis of culture-personality theory,[7] we may express it this way: Each language creates a special plight to which the individual must adjust. The human plight is in no sense universal save in this fact: that however different the language may be, it has certain common problems with which to deal—time, space, quantity, action, state, etc. But each language handles these problems differently and develops special ways of communicating. These ways of communicating create special needs, special responses, and lead to the development of special modes of thinking.

The alternative to the linguistic relativity hypothesis would be a statement that the behavior of a person is not a function of the language he happens to speak or be speaking, that his modes of categorizing experience and dealing with his world operate independently of language, that language is simply a way of communicating something which is in every way prior to its codification in language.

This paper reports two experiments designed to explore, in a preliminary way, to what extent and under what conditions the linguistic relativity hypothesis can be accepted.

In order to find evidence to support the linguistic relativity hypothesis it is not sufficient merely to point to differences between languages and assume that users of those languages have correspondingly different mental experiences; if we are not to be guilty of circular inference, it is necessary to show some correspondence between the presence or absence of a certain linguistic phenomenon and the presence or absence of a certain kind of

---

[6] B. L. Whorf, *Language, Thought and Reality*, J. B. Carroll (ed.), (New York: John Wiley & Sons, Inc., 1956), pp. 212f.

[7] M. B. Smith, J. S. Bruner, and R. W. White, *Opinions and Personality* (New York: John Wiley & Sons, Inc., 1956), p. 25.

"nonlinguistic" response. This being the case, we must be clear as to what we mean by a nonlinguistic response. Unfortunately, it is extremely difficult to define this rigorously. We might be tempted to do so by saying that a nonlinguistic response is one which can be elicited without the intervention of any symbolic system, but as soon as we realize that the bells, buzzers, lights, levers, and food pellets through which we elicit the behavior of dogs and rats may be regarded as symbolic systems, this definition would serve to exclude large classes of responses which we would still like to call "nonlinguistic." When we come to examine the actual behaviors used in our experiments, we will find that their "nonlinguistic" character resides in the fact that they are neutral, as it were, with respect to the *special* symbolic systems against which they are being tested. For example, in the second experiment to be presented, a child is asked to tell whether a blue rope "goes best with" a blue stick or a yellow rope. Now, by appropriate reinforcement techniques, we could teach the child always to choose on the basis of form or always to choose on the basis of color, and we could do this without using English or Navaho or any other special symbolic systems. Suppose, again, we were studying differences in the arithmetical abilities of children who had learned the decimal system and of children who had learned only the system of Roman numerals. The arithmetical behavior being studied is analogous to our "nonlinguistic" behavior because it is *neutral* to any one special system of arithmetical symbolism in the sense that it is *possible* to operate in either system, though not necessarily with the same efficiency.

As Brown and Lenneberg have suggested,[8] two approaches present themselves for the testing of the linguistic relativity hypothesis. Brown and Lenneberg used the first of these—an *intralinguistic* approach which, capitalizing on the fact that the speakers of a given language manifest differences in their knowledge and use of that language, attempts to show that these differences are correlated with certain other behaviors. In both experiments reported here, we have used the second approach—an *interlinguistic* design in which nonlinguistic behaviors of speakers of two different languages are compared. Use of this second approach entails an advantage and a danger: it may become possible to select linguistic features in two languages which are strikingly and fundamentally different, but it becomes difficult to assure oneself that any observed behavioral correlates are *not* due to irrelevant factors such as dissimilar cultural backgrounds and experiences.

EXPERIMENT I

In the Hopi language, still spoken in the pueblos of northeastern Arizona, the semantic domains of verbs for various kinds of physical activities have

---

[8] R. W. Brown and E. H. Lenneberg, "A Study in Language and Cognition," *J. Abnorm. & Soc. Psychol.*, 1954, XLIX, 454–462.

structures quite different from the corresponding domains in English. In speaking of *breaking,* the Hopi must use verbs depending upon whether there is one fission or many fissions (a distinction not unlike that between "break" and "shatter"). He uses the same verb for *spilling* and for *pouring,* but must use a different verb depending upon whether the material being spilled or poured is liquid or nonliquid. He can use the same verb in speaking of denting an object like a fender and in speaking of pressing a doorbell. The question posed in this experiment was whether these linguistic features would show corresponding features of nonlinguistic behavior in speakers of Hopi when contrasted with speakers of English. The "nonlinguistic" behavior chosen for study was that of sorting or classifying pictures of the actions represented by verbs of breaking, spilling, pressing, and similar physical activities.

Method. Line drawings were prepared, representing various physical actions such as falling, breaking, dropping, etc. These drawings were then assembled in sets of three, or triads, in such a way that, on the basis of comparative linguistic analysis, it could be hypothesized that in each triad native speakers of Hopi would tend to put a different pair of pictures together as contrasted with native speakers of English.

The test was administered individually to 14 Hopi adults (age range 24 to over 66) who were known to be fluent speakers of Hopi. All could speak English with varying degrees of competence, but regarded themselves as more fluent in Hopi. The test was also administered to 28 "Anglos" (as they are called in the Southwest) consisting of 12 adults of comparable degree of education in a rural New England community and 16 graduate students at Harvard University.

The test was introduced as an experiment in "how we think" and started with six pretest items, of which the first is shown as Figure 1(a). The three pictures were presented as physically separated photographs which could be shuffled and arranged at the will of the subject, who was asked simply to decide which two of the three pictures went together. The subjects had no difficulty in seeing that the two pictures of *falling* objects went together. The remaining five pretest items were designed to reveal whether the subjects understood the task and to make it clear that they were to respond on the basis of the action or type of action represented rather than incidental features of any objects depicted. The test proper consisted of 17 "critical" items and five "control" items about which no linguistic hypothesis was formulated. (We shall omit further discussion of the control items because they showed no interesting differences between Hopis and Anglos.)

The subjects were also asked to tell why their choices went together. No suggestion was given that the experiment had anything to do with language, and most of the Hopis responded in English. Occasionally, however, subjects volunteered that it seemed to "work better" to "think in Hopi," and gave their

FIGURE 1. Sample items from Experiment 1.

verbalizations in Hopi. The results, therefore, consist not only of the choices made by the subjects but also (except for three or four cases) the stated reasons for the choices.

Results.   The nature of the results and some of the problems in their interpretation may be first illustrated by presenting data for one of the "critical" items in detail. The pictures for Item 20 are presented in Figure 1(*b*).

The linguistic basis for this item resides in the fact that in Hopi there is a verb *'u'ta* which means "to close an opening," and this is the verb normally used for placing covers on open boxes, closing lids, closing holes in tubes or walls, etc.; in contrast, placing a cover on something for protection against dust or damage is represented by the verbs *na:kwapna* or *nönöma*. In English, however, we tend to use *cover* regardless of whether we are covering an opening or not, and we tend to reserve *close* for the situation where an opening can be more or less exactly fitted with a lid or other special stoppage (also for special cases like *closing a book*). On this basis it was hypothesized that Hopis would tend to put together pictures *A* and *C*, while Anglos would tend to put together pictures *B* and *C*.

In presenting this item to Anglo subjects, it was necessary to explain (without mentioning or suggesting the verbs "cover" or "close") that in picture *C* a woman was placing a wicker plaque over a box of food (the traditional Hopi "*piki*" corn bread).

Table 1 shows the number of subjects in various classifications making each of three possible groupings, together with a classification of the reasons for these choices.

The small numbers of cases make statistical significance testing difficult

TABLE 1

Choices and Reasons for Choices for the Item of Figure 1(b)

Group	"Hopi" Response: A and C Combined		"English" Response: B and C Combined		Neutral: A and B Combined	
14 Hopi adults	3	Both '*u'ta*	2	Both covering	1	Both will be
	1	Neither is	2	(Not given)		tightly cov-
		na:kwapna (N = 4)		(N = 4)		ered
	1	Both are boxes			1	Both being
	1	Both holding				covered
		the lid				(N = 2)
	2	(Not given)				
	(N = 8)					
12 Rural Anglos	4	Both are boxes	4	Both covering,	1	Both covering
	2	Both covering		v. closing or	1	Both more
		with lids		shutting		familiar
	(N = 6)		(N = 4)		(N = 2)	
16 Graduate students	1	Putting on a	8	Both covering,	1	Both (customar-
		flat cover		v. closing or		ily) "used and
	3	(Not given)		shutting		covered" v. one-
	(N = 4)		1	Both putting		time covering
				on top		(N = 1)
			1	Both "dealing		
				with entire		
				structure"		
			1	(Not given)		
			(N = 11)			

if not impossible, but even if we are to make a statistical test, it must be recognized that a given response may mean different things. Thus, at least three Hopis put pictures *A* and *C* together on the ground that both show *'u'ta* "closing an opening," but to at least four Anglos pictures *A* and *C* go together because they show boxes. The most striking result here is the fact that Hopis tend *not* to put pictures *B* and *C* together, while Anglos, particularly educated ones, show a strong tendency to do so. Only four out of 14 Hopis put pictures *B* and *C* together, while 11 out of 16 college-educated Anglos did so.[9] We can look at the reasons for the choices more closely. Only four out of the 14 Hopis mentioned any kind of "covering" in giving their reasons (whatever their choice), while 17 out of 28 Anglos did—a result significant below the 10-percent level.

Although limited, these results suggest that speakers of Hopi tend to organize their perceptions of situations such as those pictured in Figure 1(*a*), in terms of "closing openings" instead of "putting covers on things."

There were several other critical items showing results tending to favor our hypothesis. For the pictures of Figure 1(*c*), it was expected that Hopis would tend to pair *A* and *C* because both represent the action called *leluwi*, "to apply or spread over a surface," while Anglos would pair *B* and *C* because they both show "painting." (Hopi has a word for painting, but its use is restricted to cases where one paints a picture or a design, as distinct from covering a surface with paint.) Six of the 14 Hopis paired *A* and *C*, while only four of all 28 Anglos did so; of these four, two paired on the basis of the fact that both showed the use of a tool versus the use of one's hands; the significance of this result is at just below the 5-percent level by Fisher's test. Actually, a more striking result was unanticipated: Anglos had a strong tendency to pair either *B* and *C* or *A* and *B* because they felt both members of these pairs represented "decorating" versus mere painting or covering. "Artistic creation" was also mentioned as a basis for these choices.

Another item showing interesting results is shown in Figure 1(*d*). As has been mentioned, "spilling" (accidentally) and "pouring" (intentionally) are not distinguished in Hopi; there is a way of translating the idea of "accidentally" but this is handled as a separate expression instead of being built into the verb, as in English. Hopi uses slightly different forms for pouring: *wehekna*, "to pour liquid," and *wa:hokna*, "to pour sand, gravel, or other nonliquid loose things," but the form for dropping something is entirely different: *po:sna*. We found that eight out of 14 Hopis (57 percent) paired pictures *A* and *C*, consonant with the linguistic forms; these figures contrast with the finding that only seven out of 28 Anglos, or 25 percent, made this

---

[9] This result is significant at the 5-percent level by Fischer's exact test of significance in a 2×2 contingency table.

pairing. The probability of chance occurrence of a result as extreme as this, determined by the χ^2 test with continuity-correction, is less than 10 percent. At least 16 of the 20 Anglos who paired pictures B and C explained that there was unintentional, accidental action in both of them, while only two Hopis drew attention to this accidental character of the action. Instead, Hopis rarely seemed concerned about whether the man in picture A *meant* to pour out the peaches, while Anglos frequently queried the experimenter about this.

Admitting the results from all 17 "critical" items as evidence, we present in Table 2 a summary to show the extent to which our hypotheses were

TABLE 2

Total Frequency of Pairing

			"Hopi" Response: A and C	"Anglo" Response: B and C	Neutral: A and B	Total
17 "Critical items"	14	Hopi	69 (29.0%)	126 (52.9%)	43 (18.1%)	238
	12	Rural Anglos	46 (22.6)	119 (58.3)	39 (19.1)	204
	16	Educated Anglos	65 (24.0)	156 (57.5)	50 (18.5)	271
12 "Critical items" with "good hypotheses"	14	Hopi	57 (34.0)	80 (47.6)	31 (18.4)	168
	12	Rural Anglos	31 (21.5)	85 (59.0)	28 (19.5)	144
	16	Educated Anglos	36 (18.8)	122 (63.9)	33 (17.3)	191

favored by the data. There is probably not a truly significant difference between the 29 percent representing the tendency of the Hopi subjects to make the expected "Hopi" response of pairing pictures A and C and the 22.6 percent and 24.0 percent, values for the two Anglo groups, but the trend is at least one of those tantalizingly modest ones which can be characterized only as being "in the predicted direction."

Upon re-examination of the purely linguistic data and consideration of certain unanticipated difficulties which had arisen in the subjects' interpretations of the drawings, it was possible to weed out five items which had gone sour, so to speak, leaving 12 critical items for which the results are presented in the lower part of Table 2. Here we see a sturdier trend in favor of our general hypothesis, although the results are still far from striking. It is not really legitimate to treat Table 2 as a contingency table and apply a χ^2 test, because the events represented there are not necessarily independent; were we to assume that all the choices are independent, however, and were we then to apply a χ^2 test to the lower part of Table 2, we would find that the probability of this χ^2 being exceeded by chance would be less than .01.

The results encourage us to think that not only do we have a promising technique for studying the linguistic relativity hypothesis, but we also have an indication that in further and more extensive trials of this method we may obtain greater assurances that language categories influence at least one variety of nonlinguistic behavior. Several suggestions towards improvement of the experimental methodology may be offered: (1) drawings should be given extensive pretests to insure that they are interpreted similarly by all subjects; (2) the experiment should utilize contrasting groups of monolinguals (rather than bilinguals as we had to use here) ; and (3) subjects should be asked to choose which of two pictures, *A* or *B,* go best with a fixed third picture, *C.* (This procedure is used in Experiment II.)

EXPERIMENT II

This second experiment was an attempt to show that behavior can be influenced by a grammatical phenomenon as well as a purely lexical or semantic phenomenon.

It is obligatory in the Navaho language, when using verbs of *handling,* to employ a particular one of a set of verbal forms according to the shape or some other essential attribute of the object about which one is speaking. Thus, if I ask you in Navaho to hand me an object, I must use the appropriate verb stem depending on the nature of the object. If it is a long flexible object such as a piece of string, I must say *šańléh;* if it is a long rigid object such as a stick, I must say *šańt̨įh;* if it is a flat flexible material such as a paper or cloth, I must say *šańilcóós,* and so on.

The groups of words in Navaho which together regularly take one or another of these verb stems, say the family of words for all long, rigid objects, carry no linguistic marker of their class membership. They comprise what Whorf[10] has called a *covert class,* as distinguished from an *overt class* such as gender in Latin with the familiar *–us, –i, – a, –ae* case and number suffixes. Nor, in the absence of native grammarians, are there any terms in Navaho for these categories themselves. This like many another grammatical rule operates well below the level of conscious awareness. Although most Navaho-speaking children, even at the age of three or four, used these forms unerringly, they were unable to tell why they used a particular form with any particular object. Even though a child could not name an object, or may not have seen one like it before, in most cases he used the correct verb form according to the nature of the object.

Because of this obligatory categorization of objects in Navaho, it seemed reasonable that Navaho-speaking children would learn to discriminate the

10 Whorf, *op. cit.,* pp. 87–101.

"form" attributes of objects at an earlier age than their English-speaking compeers. The finding of American[11] and European[12] psychologists that children tend first to distinguish objects on the basis of size and color might—at least at the level of verbal facility in dealing with these variables—be partly an artifact of the particular language they use. The hypothesis was, then, that this feature of the Navaho language would affect the relative potency, or order of emergence of such concepts as color, size, shape or form, and number in the Navaho-speaking child, as compared with English-speaking Navaho children of the same age, and that Navaho-speaking children would be more inclined than the latter to perceive formal similarities between objects.

This hypothesis was tested using a variety of experimental materials and several different procedures, of which only one will be reported here. Although the test was expressly adapted to Navaho, the design as well as the basic hypothesis could be extended to other languages since nearly all languages have obligatory categories.

The procedure whose results we will report here was called Ambiguous Sets and was actually interposed between several other procedures well after the child had become accustomed to the experimental situation.

Method. Ten pairs of objects (colored wooden blocks, sticks, and pieces of rope) were used, each of which differed significantly in two respects, e.g., color and size, color and shape, size and shape, or shape and Navaho verb-form classification. These pairs of objects were arranged before the child, one pair at a time. After being presented with a pair of objects, the child was shown a third object similar to each member of the pair in only one of the two relevant characteristics, but of course matching neither, and was asked to tell the experimenter which of the pair went best with the object shown to him. For example, one of the pairs consisted of a yellow stick and a piece of blue rope of comparable size. The child was then shown a yellow rope, and the basis of his choice could be either color or the Navaho verb-form classification—since different verbal forms are used for a length of rope and a stick. The ten sets of objects were presented in the alphabetical order of the letters shown in Table 3, with the exception that the first set presented was set *O*, and the last was set *P*.

The subjects were 135 Navaho children ranging from three to about ten years of age, drawn from the vicinity of Fort Defiance and Window Rock, Arizona, on the Navaho reservation. On the basis of a bilingualism test and other criteria of a language dominance, the 135 subjects were divided into five groups: monolingual in Navaho, Navaho-predominant, balanced bilin-

---

[11] Clara R. Brian and Florence L. Goodenough, "The Relative Potency of Color and Form Perception at Various Ages," *J. Exper. Psychol.*, 1929, XII, 197–213.

[12] Alice Descœudres, "Couleur, forme, ou nombre." *Arch. de Psychol.*, 1914, XIV, 305–341.

TABLE 3
Results of the "Ambiguous Sets" Experiment

Set	Attributes Contrasted	Objects in Set			Percent of "a" Choices			
		Comparison model	Alternative choices (a)	(b)	Navaho-dominant Navahos (N = 59)	English-dominant Navahos (N = 43)	P[a]	White American children (N = 47)
O	Verb-stem, color	Blue rope	Yellow rope	Blue stick	70.7	39.5	<.01	83.0
P	Verb-stem, color	Yellow rope	Blue rope	Yellow stick	70.7	39.5	<.01	80.7
H	Verb-stem, color	Blue stick	Yellow stick	Blue cylinder	71.2	44.2	<.01	76.6
N	Verb-stem, color	Blue stick	Yellow stick	Blue oblong block	72.4	44.2	<.01	82.9
I	shape, size	Small blue cube	Medium blue cube	Small blue sphere	79.7	60.5	<.05	72.4
L	shape, size	Small blue cylinder	Large blue cylinder	Small blue oblong	59.4	44.2	>.10	82.9
K	shape, color	Medium blue cube	Medium white cube	Medium blue pyramid	45.7	39.5	>.10	70.2
G	size, color	Medium blue cube	Medium yellow cube	Small blue cube	21.0	23.2	>.10	74.4
J	size, color	Medium blue cube	Medium white cube	Large blue cube	15.2	14.0	>.10	55.3
M	size, color	Medium blue cube	Medium black cube	Small blue cube	59.3	30.2	<.01	74.4

[a] This is the probability that χ^2 as obtained in a 2×2 table comparing the two groups of Navahos would be equalled or exceeded under the hypothesis of no difference.

gual, English-predominant and English monolingual. For purposes of statistical analysis Navaho monolinguals and Navaho-predominants were grouped together (59 subjects), as were the English monolinguals and English-predominants (43). The remaining 33 subjects were classed as "balanced bilinguals" and this group included a number of individuals whose language status was dubious.

The experiment was conducted in Navaho or, with appropriate modifications in the instructions, in English, as indicated. An interpreter was used with Navaho-speaking children, although the experimenter was able to give instructions in Navaho for some of the procedures used. Most of the testing was done in the children's homes—usually Navaho hogans of the traditional sort—and in the presence of parents, grandparents, siblings, and other interested and very curious onlookers.

Although the establishment of contrasting groups of Navaho children on the basis of language dominance was regarded as providing adequate control, a supplementary control group was obtained by testing 47 white American middle-class children in the Boston metropolitan area, with an age range roughly comparable to that of the Navaho children.[13]

Results.   The children were not at all baffled by the ambiguity inherent in the task; their choices were invariably made with little or no hesitation.

The data were analyzed both item by item and by age. In considering the results, shown in Table 3, it must be remembered that it was our hypothesis that Navaho-dominant children would be more likely to make their choices on the basis of similarity in shape and verb-stem classification than on the basis of size or color. Thus, for the first seven sets listed in Table 3, we would expect the Navaho-dominant children to choose the object listed under (a), the "Navaho choice." This prediction is borne out by the data, for the differences between the two groups of Navaho children are all in the expected direction, and five are significant (by a two-tailed χ^2 test) at better than the 5-percent level. The most striking differences come for those sets of objects that involve a contrast embodied in the Navaho system of verbal categories: sets O and P where the contrast is between color and material and verb stem, and sets H and N where the contrast is between color and verb stem, material being the same, comparing objects of the long-rigid class, and of the so-called "round object" class. The less striking differences involve contrasts which are not formally recognized in Navaho grammar since the same verb stem is used in talking about the cubes and pyramids of set K.

In sets G, J, and M our hypothesis would not lead us to predict any difference between the groups; they may be regarded as control items. Both groups

---

[13] This testing was performed by Miss Nancy Despres of the Buckingham School in Cambridge, under the supervision of Carroll.

of children show a marked preference for color rather than size in sets G and J. Set M shows a significant difference between the two Navaho groups, possibly explicable on the basis of the greater potency of color for the English-dominant children, the contrast of the blue and yellow of set G and the blue and white of set J being more marked than that between the black and dark blue of set M.

Table 4 shows that there are important and consistent developmental trends for the seven critical sets involving the contrast between shape or verb form

TABLE 4

Percent of "a" Choices in the First Seven Sets, by Age Level

Age	Navaho-Dominant Navahos		English-Dominant Navahos		White American Children	
	N^a	Percent	N^a	Percent	N^a	Percent
3 } 4	14	64	7	33	{ 8 10	45 69
5	13	57	9	38	10	91
6	12	64	5	34	8	93
7	9	71	9	36	4	100
8	6	74	5	49	5	83
9–10	5	81	8	75	2	93

[a] Note that this N is the number of cases yielding data; each case contributes seven responses, and the percentages are computed on the basis of the total number of responses.

and color—a trend which gives added significance to the differences between the Navaho-dominant and English-dominant groups noted above, since the Navaho-dominant children averaged almost a year younger. In both the Navaho groups (the data for white Americans will be discussed below) the trend is toward the increasing perceptual saliency of shape or form, as compared with color, with increasing age. The curve starts lower and remains lower for English-dominant Navaho children, although it rises rather rapidly after the age of seven. Navaho children stay ahead of their English-speaking age mates, although the two curves tend to converge as age increases.

Thus far discussion has been restricted to the results for two contrasting groups of *Navaho* children. These groups had been established in the hope that maximum possible control would be gained over the variables of race, culture, and environment which might affect the results. All the children tested were from the same rather small area on the Navaho reservation; the parents of nearly every child were both Navaho, except for the few cases in which one of the parents was a member of some other American Indian tribe. To be sure, the cultural variable could be only imperfectly controlled—

the English-dominant children were almost inevitably more acculturated to the local variant of white American culture than were the Navaho-dominant children, but certainly the culture contrast is not as great as between Navaho-speaking children and English-speaking white children, say, from the Eastern United States. However, we may well ask how the performance of these Navaho children compares with that of children speaking English or another language on the same or a comparable test. In an experiment closely similar in materials and procedures to the one reported here, Clara Brian and Florence Goodenough[14] found a marked preference for color over form for American children aged three to six. At age three years six months, 33.6 percent of choices were for form over color; at age four, 24.7 percent for form over color; and at age four years six months, 36 percent (as compared with 64 percent for Navaho-dominant children in this age group and 33 percent for English-dominant children of the same age group). The Brian and Goodenough results are also in substantial agreement with those of Alice Descœudres[15] working with French-speaking children more than 40 years ago. When we compare our Navaho results with those obtained for 47 white American children in the Boston area, we find that the responses of the white American children are more similar to those for the Navaho-dominant children than for the English-dominant children; as we may see from the last column of Table 3, they consistently tend to choose object "a" on the basis of form or shape in preference to color and size. The white children today, however, can hardly be considered a fair control group for the Indian children, for their cultural background of experiences with forms and colors is enormously different. Early and continued practice with toys of the formboard variety is likely to impress the white American child with the importance of form and size as contrasted with a "secondary" quality like color. Further, social class is known to be correlated with tendency to choose form over color,[16] and our white American children tended to be from the upper middle class. Nevertheless, it is interesting to observe in Table 4 that the white American children show the same developmental trend as either group of Navaho children. As a matter of fact, at the earliest age level, the three- and four-year-old Navaho-dominant children outstrip their white American age mates in preferring form to color.

If we consider only the two groups over which we have exercised the maximum control over the variables we presume to be relevant, the Navaho-dominant and English-dominant Navaho children, we have shown that language patterning seems to be correlated with a tendency to match objects on

[14] Brian and Goodenough, *op. cit.*

[15] Descœudres, *op. cit.*

[16] Sylvia Honkavaara, "A Critical Re-evaluation of the Color or Form Reaction and Disproving of the Hypotheses Connected with It," *J. Psychol.*, 1958, XLV, 25–36.

the basis of form rather than color or size. When we also consider the data from white American children, as well as the age trends, we may amend our hypothesis in possibly the following form: The tendency of a child to match objects on the basis of form or material rather than size or color increases with age and may be enhanced by either of two kinds of experiences; (a) learning to speak a language, like Navaho, which because of the central role played by form and material in its grammatical structure, requires the learner to make certain discriminations of form and material in the earlier stages of language learning in order to make himself understood at all; or (b) practice with toys and other objects involving the fitting of forms and shapes, and the resultant greater reinforcement received from form-matching. If our results are accepted as supporting this revised hypothesis, they indicate, we believe, that the potential influence of linguistic patterning on cognitive functioning and on the conceptual development of the child, as he is inducted by his language into the world of experience, is a fruitful area for further study.

28. VERBAL COMPREHENSION AND COMMUNICATION IN NEGRO AND WHITE CHILDREN[1]

Arnold S. Carson & A. I. Rabin[2]

Comparisons of intellectual functioning in Negroes and whites have been of concern to research workers for some time. The classical review and summary by Klineberg (1935) is not yet outdated. For the most part, the superiority of the whites, especially on verbal tasks, has been demonstrated. However, the improvement in intelligence test scores of Negro children who migrated to the North from Southern states has also been shown. Moreover, the degree of improvement tends to be related to duration of residence in the North.

Performance tasks which correlate highly with "general intelligence", such as the Goodenough Draw-A-Man IQ Test, have not yielded significant differences between Negro and white children (Anastasi & D'Angelo, 1952). It would appear that tasks requiring verbal comprehension and verbal expression are the ones that are to a large extent responsible for the significant differences between the groups.

The present study is concerned with the investigation of these two functions, comprehension and expression or communication, in Negro and white children. We propose to study these functions separately, and in relation to each other, in Southern and Northern Negro, and in Northern white, chil-

SOURCE. *The Journal of Educational Psychology*, 1960, **51**, 2.

[1] Based on master's thesis (Carson, 1959) submitted to the Department of Psychology, Michigan State University by A. S. Carson and supervised by A. I. Rabin.

[2] The authors are grateful to G. F. King and C. F. Wrighley for their valuable assistance and suggestions.

501

dren. Our prediction was, in consonance with previous related findings, that when groups are matched for age, grade placement, sex, and level of verbal comprehension, the white children will be superior to the Southern and Northern Negroes in verbal communication; also, that the Northern Negro children will be superior to the Southern Negro children on measures of verbal communication.

METHOD

The Full Range Picture Vocabulary Test (Ammons & Ammons, 1949) was selected as the method of determining the level of verbal comprehension. This test requires no verbal response from the subjects (S). It consists of a series of cards with several pictures on each card. The S is merely required to point to the specific picture each time the examiner reads a word from the vocabulary test.

Two measures of verbal communication were employed for comparative purposes. First, the WISC Vocabulary (Wechsler, 1949) was presented in the standard manner and the responses scored as provided in the manual. Second, the words of the Full-Range Picture Vocabulary Test (FRPVT) which were "defined" by gesticulation were presented as a conventional vocabulary test, requiring oral definition.

The conventional scoring of vocabulary tests is an "all or none" affair. No provisions are made for qualitative differences in definitions or in levels of abstraction, precision and communication. This lack of sensitivity in the conventional scoring of vocabulary tests has been pointed out long ago by Yacorzynski (1940).

In order to provide for scoring of levels of communication with the vocabulary of the FRPVT an adaptation of a method reported in the literature (Rabin, King, & Ehrmann, 1955) was utilized. A description of this Qualitative Vocabulary Scale, of the categories of responses and definitions of the word "wagon" as illustrative of the levels of communication appear below.

Class 1. *Categorization and Synonym*

a. *Categorization.* The categorization responses classified by some definite scheme in terms of its universal characteristics.

Response—"a vehicle"

b. *Synonym.* The synonym response may essentially be used to replace the object or idea with no or little change in the denotative aspects of the stimulus word.

Response—"a cart"

Class 2. *Essential Description.* An essential description response must give the characterizing features of the stimulus word. If the stimulus word is abstract, the response must create mental imagery of the relevant situation. If the stimulus word is concrete (physically tangible), the response must differentiate between the stimulus word and members in its class.

> Response—"It's a wooden thing with 4
> wheels, and it looks like a box."

Class 3. *Essential Function.* An essential function response must describe primary rather than peripheral usage or purpose of an object or an idea.

> Response—"You ride in it out West."

Class 4. *Example.* An example response defines an object or idea in terms of its aspects or members.

> Response—"There's a red wagon kids play with."

Class 5. *Vague Description and Vague Function*

a. Vague Description. A vague description is a response that is not totally irrelevant but does not give the characterizing features of the object or idea.

> Response—"Something that has four wheels."

b. Vague Function. A vague function response describes the peripheral rather than primary usage or purpose of the object or the idea.

> Response—"It bumps into people."

Class 6. *Error.* The error response is totally irrelevant to the stimulus word.

> Response—"The dog 'wagons' his tail."

Class 7. *Don't Know.* A "don't know" response is a statement or a lack of statement designating that the S is unable to verbally define a word *which he had previously designated recognition* for by a gesticulation response.

> Response—"Don't know."

Subjects

The Ss were Southern Negro (SN), Northern Negro (NN), and Northern white (NW) children in the fourth, fifth, and sixth grades. None of the Ss were advanced or behind in their age-grade placement. The SN group comprised all of the Negro children within the age range from 9.5 to 11.5 years who were born and reared in the South and had migrated to Lansing, Michigan within 28 months of the date tested. All of the NW and NN children were born and reared in Ingham County, Michigan. Data was collected on the occupational levels of the NW and NN children in accordance with the *Dictionary of Occupational Titles* (United States Government Printing Office, 1944) classification. Two of the main wage earners in the NW children's families were professional, technical or managerial workers, 4 were clerical or sales workers, 3 were service employees, 9 were mechanical workers, and 12 were manual laborers; respectively, there were 0, 5, 2, 5, and 18 NN main wage earners. It may be noted that the occupational levels of main wage earners from the two samples are similar. Due to the recent relocation of the SN families, the main wage earners' vocations were unsettled and therefore unavailable as data.

Children were tested with the FRPVT at random from the NW and NN groups in order to acquire Ss whose scores could be individually matched

TABLE 1

Grade, Sex, Age, and Mean Picture Vocabulary Test Scores of the Three Groups

Group	N	Grade			Sex		Ages (Months)		Raw Score of FRPVT	
		4th	5th	6th	Male	Female	Mean	SD	Mean	SD
NW	30	16	8	6	16	14	128	10.9	43.67	4.95
NN	30	16	8	6	15	15	125	10.9	43.57	5.74
SN	30	16	8	6	14	16	128	13.5	43.53	5.21

with the scores of children in the SN group. Table 1 summarizes relevant data for the three groups of children.

PROCEDURE

The FRPVT and the two oral vocabulary devices were administered individually to the Ss by the same examiner in single testing sessions. The SN children were tested first followed by random testing of NN and NW children who would qualify for the respective samples. When each SN child was matched with a NW and NN child in terms of the FRPVT scores, the testing was discontinued.

Two independent scorers tallied verbal responses to the FRPVT. These responses were scored according to the classification system described above. The total percentage of interscorer agreement was .79. Complete agreement between the two scorers was obtained after the debatable responses were discussed.

RESULTS AND DISCUSSION

As a preliminary step in the treatment of the data, all Ss were classified into "high" and "low" responders. The Ss whose majority of responses were tallied in categories 1, 2 and 3 were placed in the former classification; the predominance of the remaining four categories characterized the second group. Table 2 reports the incidence of members of each sample in the "high" and "low" categories. The differences in the distribution are statistically significant.

TABLE 2

A Comparison of the Incidence of High and Low Responders on the Qualitative Vocabulary Scale in the Three Groups

Group	High	Low	χ^2	p^a
NW	25	5		
NN	18	12		
SN	7	23	22.54	<.001

[a] One-tailed test.

As predicted, the white children assume the top position. It is also interesting to note that the NN group place in an intermediate position between the white and SN children.

The responses of the three groups were also compared on each of the seven categories comprising our qualitative (levels of communication) scoring system. Table 3 summarizes the levels of significance of the differences between the groups computed by means of the Wilcoxon matched-pairs signed-rank test (Siegel, 1956). Thirteen of the 21 comparisons were significant in the predicted direction. The table indicates that the general prediction is supported to a considerable degree. This is especially true with the extremes of the qualitative categories.

The results of the study demonstrated that NW children, of comparable non-verbal word recognition (or comprehension) abilities, manifest higher levels of verbal communication than NN children, and, in turn, the NN children manifest higher levels of verbal communication than SN children.

All comparisons by means of the WISC vocabulary subtest yield significant differences in the predicted direction (using Wilcoxon's test mentioned above).

Again, global vocabulary scores, as in the case of the more refined treatment of the FRPVT, indicate the superiority of the white children compared with the two Negro samples. Also, the NN group is inferior to the NW but superior to the SN children. This finding is consistent with the results in the previous two tables.

The children's pattern of responding is interesting in that it was unique for each of the groups and may therefore be a clue to differences in characteristic thinking among the three groups. The NW children favor the higher levels of verbal communication (Classes 1, 2, 3). Their percentage of responses decreases sharply in the Example classification and after a slight increase in the Vague classification, their percentage of responses continues to decrease lower than that of the two Negro groups in the Error and Don't Know classifications. NN children favor the Vague type response and manifest a greater percentage of Error type responses than the white children. The SN children's pattern is the only one which manifests a high peak in the Don't Know classification.

The differences among the groups cannot be consistently explained according to one theoretical viewpoint. Differences between the NW and NN children could lend support to the contention that constitutional racial differences in intelligence exist or to the viewpoint that a difference of cultural opportunities accounts for the variance between racial groups. However, there are sufficient possibilities of differences in the cultural milieu of the two samples to question their equivalence of social opportunities. The two groups remain segregated from each other in activities other than those which revolve around school. The NN sample, for the most part, lives in a section of town which is a homogeneous Negro settlement. Their cultural milieu is definitely not characteristic of white middle-class modes of living.

The comparisons of the NN and SN children lend themselves to a more clear-cut interpretation since the cultural variable of geographical residence was considered in the experimental design. It is contended that the superior educational environment and the greater opportunity for cultural advancement of the NN child over the SN child accounts for the significant differences between the two groups.

The present study supports Klineberg's (1947) research findings that geographical residency of the Negro child is an important determinant of vocabulary performance. Coppinger and Ammons' (1952) contention that different norms should be utilized when making intergroup comparisons involving Negroes where the members of the groups have different cultural backgrounds is also supported.

Finally, it should be pointed out that verbal comprehension and verbal communication seem to be two different functions. Although the groups were equated on comprehension, they showed marked differences with respect to communication. The former task requires recognition within a certain context, which is quite different from verbal communication and definition of a word in isolation, and not in context. It would appear that differences be-

TABLE 3

Summary of Levels of Significance Obtained from Comparisons of Ranks on the Qualitative Vocabulary Scale

	Groups																	
	NW vs. SN				NW vs. NN				NN vs. SN									
	(T)	(T')			(T)	(T')			(T)	(T')								
Class	T	T'	z	p	T	T'	z	p	T	T'	z	p						
1	271.0	29.0	3.44	<.0005	289.0	62.0	2.87	<.0025	181.0	72.0	1.76	<.05						
2	327.5	107.5	2.36	<.01	283.5	122.5	1.82	<.05	206.5	171.5	.41	ns						
3	350.0	85.0	2.85	<.0005	233.0	118.0	1.45	ns	326.0	139.0	1.91	<.05						
4	274.5	160.5	1.22	ns	126.5	198.5	.82	ns	301.0	105.0	2.22	<.025[a]						
5	154.5	223.5	.82	ns	147.0	231.0	1.00	ns	202.5	203.5	.00	ns						
6	34.5	316.5	3.57	<.0005	57.5	218.5	2.43	<.01	55.5	295.5	3.04	<.0025						
7	3.0	432.0	4.63	<.0001	95.5	229.5	1.79	<.05	40.5	394.5	3.82	<.0005						

[a] If a two-tailed test were employed, the difference would have been significant in a direction contrary to the current hypothesis.

TABLE 4

Summary of Comparisons of Ranks on the WISC Vocabulary Subtest

Comparisons	Total Ranks			Theoretical			Significance
	NW	NN	SN	Mean	SD	z	
NW vs. SN	432.0	—	3.0	217.5	46.25	4.62	<.0001
NN vs. SN	—	345.5	60.6	203.0	43.92	3.24	<.001
NW vs. NN	334.0	101.0	—	217.5	46.25	2.51	<.01

tween Negroes and whites on conventional intelligence tests, and especially on vocabulary subtests, may be primarily due to failure in verbal communication rather than in comprehension.

SUMMARY

Three groups (30 in each group) of NW, NN, and SN school children, matched for age, sex, grade placement, and level of verbal comprehension, were compared on two vocabulary tests requiring verbal communication. In accord with the original prediction, the white children were superior to the Negro children, and the NN children were superior to the SN children on these two measures. The results were discussed in relation to the possible racial and cultural geographic factors involved.

References

Ammons, R. B., & Ammons, H. S. The Full-Range Picture Vocabulary Test. *Amer. Psychologist*, 1949, 4, 267–268.

Anastasi, Ann, & D'Angelo, Rita Y. A comparison of Negro and white preschool children in language development and Goodenough Draw-A-Man IQ. *J. genet. Psychol.*, 1952, 81, 147–165.

Carson, A. S. Verbal comprehension and verbal communication in Negro and white children. Unpublished master's thesis, Mich. State Univer., 1959.

Coppinger, N. W., & Ammons, R. B. The Full-Range Picture Vocabulary Test: VIII. A normative study of Negro children. *J. clin. Psychol.*, 1952, 8, 136–140.

Klineberg, O. *Race differences.* New York: Harper, 1935.

Klineberg, O. Negro intelligence and urban residence. In T. M. Newcomb & E. L. Hartley (Eds.), *Readings in social psychology.* New York: Holt, 1947. Pp. 24–32.

Rabin, A. I., King, G. F., & Ehrmann, J. C. Vocabulary performance of short-term and long-term schizophrenics. *J. abnorm. soc. Psychol.*, 1955, **50**, 255–258.

Siegel, S. *Nonparametric statistics for the behavioral sciences.* New York: McGraw-Hill, 1956.

United States Government Printing Office, Division of Occupational Analysis. *Dictionary of occupational titles.* Part IV. Washington, D.C.: Author, 1944.

Wechsler, D. *Wechsler Intelligence Scale for Children.* New York: Psychological Corp., 1949.

Yacorzynski, G. K. An evaluation of the postulates underlying the Babcock deterioration test. *Psychol. Bull.*, 1940, **37**, 425–426. (Abstract).

29. SPONTANEOUS VERBAL REHEARSAL IN A MEMORY TASK AS A FUNCTION OF AGE

John H. Flavell, David R. Beach, & Jack M. Chinsky*

A distinction is made between 2 alternative hypotheses for explaining an often-reported deficiency in verbally mediated performance during early childhood: (1) the verbal response is made, but tends not to mediate performance ("mediational-deficiency hypothesis"); (2) the verbal response tends not to be made ("production-deficiency hypothesis"). A study is described which attempts to meet the ideal criteria for a test of the production-deficiency hypothesis. The method used was that of direct observation of S's spontaneous verbalizations, and the hypothesis was confirmed by the findings that kindergarteners are less likely than older children to rehearse stimulus names in a nonverbal serial recall task.

There is considerable research attention currently being given to the possibility that the relation between the child's linguistic and nonlinguistic behavior undergoes important developmental changes during the preschool and early school years (e.g., Kendler, 1963; Luria, 1961; Reese, 1963; Weir & Stevenson, 1959). Reese (1962) has reviewed much of this literature and has also given a name to the principal developmental hypothesis which has animated it. According to this, the "mediational-deficiency hypothesis," there is

SOURCE. *Child Development*, 1966, **37**, 2.

* The writers are indebted to Mr. Lawrence W. Utter, principal at Rochester Public School 49, and his staff for their excellent cooperation in providing Ss and testing facilities for this study. They wish also to thank Drs. Ralph N. Haber, James R. Ison, Emory L. Cowen, and Dean H. Obrecht, and Miss Frances C. Wynns for their advice and assistance during the design and pilot-testing phases. John H. Flavell's present address: Institute of Child Development, University of Minnesota, Minneapolis, Minn. 55455.

a stage in ontogenesis during which the child tends not to mediate or regulate his overt behavior verbally, despite the fact that he is able to understand and correctly use the words in question; subsequently, this discrepancy between linguistic and mediational capacities gets reduced, that is, mediational deficiency tends to disappear with age.

Maccoby (1964) has recently called attention to an apparent ambiguity in the meaning of this hypothesis: "The question is, then, whether they [i.e, these young children] simply fail to use the verbal labels which are presumably available to them, or whether they do use them, but for some reason the words do not serve to mediate the response" (p. 213). It appears that there are really two distinct and separate developmental hypotheses which ought to be entertained here, distinct and separate in the sense that the truth or falsity of one is not logically dependent on the truth or falsity of the other. One of these hypotheses would assert that the younger child does indeed spontaneously produce the potential verbal mediators at the appropriate point in the task situation, just as the older child does, but that these verbalizations for one reason or another fail to have their expected mediational effects on his overt behavior; in brief, they occur when they ought but do not mediate as they ought. The second hypothesis would simply predict that the younger child tends not to produce the relevant words in the first place, and this suffices to explain the apparent nonmediated character of his overt task behavior. It is stipulated that he "knows" the relevant words and that he can and does produce them in some situations; his deficiency here consists solely in the fact that this particular task (or perhaps tasklike situations in general) fails to elicit them.

It is suggested that the expression "mediational deficiency" be restricted henceforth to the first of these two hypotheses, since it is that hypothesis alone which predicts that the young child's operant verbalizations tend to be deficient in mediational power. A new modifier, "production deficiency," is proposed for the second hypothesis, implying as it does that the child's difficulty may not lie in an inability to use the words which he produces in a mediational fashion, but rather in a lack of ability or disposition to produce or emit them on appropriate occasions.

What are the ideal experimental conditions for testing each of these hypotheses? In the case of the mediational-deficiency hypothesis, there appear to be four:

Elicitation. The task situation used ought to be such that most mature human Ss would more or less naturally follow a verbal-mediational approach in trying to cope with it. That is, one should employ a task which is likely to exert considerable verbal mediational "pull" for Ss who are deficient in neither production nor mediational skills.

Mediation. E should be able to distinguish mediated (i.e., verbally mediated) from nonmediated overt responses on this task. Ideally, he ought to be able to make this discrimination for each individual response, rather than simply for the overall pattern of responses, for example, faster versus slower learning, as measured by number of trials to criterion.

Production. E should have some procedure for establishing whether S actually produced any potentially mediating verbalization at each of the various points in the task sequence where such verbalization would have a reasonable chance of mediating something, that is, in at least rough temporal contiguity with the overt task responses just mentioned. The E might insure such production for all Ss by instructing them to make the appropriate verbalization, but if he does, he should also make sure that they are instructed to do so at the appropriate times.

Competence. E has of course to be sure that his younger Ss have about the same receptive and productive command of the words in question that his older Ss do. That is, he should be able to provide evidence that all the children in his sample can use and interpret these words in approximately the same way.

If these four conditions are satisfied, the mediational-deficiency hypothesis can be tested by examining only those task responses for which there was in fact relevant and temporally contiguous verbal production. The hypothesis is then confirmed if older Ss show more responses judged to be mediated than younger Ss do. Only the Elicitation, Production, and Competence conditions need be satisfied when testing the production-deficiency hypothesis. As regards the Production condition, however, there obviously can be no instructions to verbalize, since spontaneous production versus nonproduction constitutes the dependent variable. The hypothesis is supported if older Ss simply verbalize on a greater number of the appropriate occasions than do younger Ss.

A review of existing research would show little unequivocal evidence for or against either of these two hypotheses.[1] This is of course partly a consequence of the fact that the developmental problem here has not been analyzed in terms of a clear distinction between production and mediational sources of variance. More than that, however, the tasks and methodology which have characterized the typical study in this area appear not even to

---

[1] Some of Luria's research (e.g., 1961) comes quite close to satisfying the conditions for a test of the mediational-deficiency hypothesis. He claims to have shown that there is an early childhood phase during which S's own self-commands fail to regulate—indeed, may interfere with—his motor actions, followed by a phase when such commands facilitate organized motor responding. Although we shall not review his procedure in detail here, suffice it to say that it does appear to meet at least the Mediation, Production, and Competence conditions fairly well. There remains the problem, however, of whether to trust his reported findings: a recent, very careful replication study by Jarvis (1963) failed to turn up even a hint of any such deficiency in young American children.

approach the experimental conditions outlined above. To be sure, these conditions are ideal standards, severe and restrictive, and perhaps there is no feasible experimental study which can do better than approximate them. They may, nonetheless, serve the heuristic function of making us rethink our traditional methods of seeking research answers in this area, just as the production-mediation distinction has done with respect to the research questions. Our own rethinking has so far centered on the production- rather than mediational-deficiency hypothesis and has led us to the conclusion that a credible test of it might be made if only one could find a way to assess S's spontaneous verbal production directly, that is, by actually observing it as it happens rather than having to infer its occurrence from task performance or other data. The experiment reported here was thus designed to approximate the requisite Elicitation, Production, and Competence conditions, with particular emphasis on realizing the Production condition through direct observation of S's uninstructed, task-related verbalization.

METHOD

Research Strategy

The initial research step was to find a task which would accord with the Elicitation condition. Such a task ought itself to be wholly nonverbal in character but, at the same time, should tend to elicit a considerable amount of spontaneous verbalization in older Ss. The work of Glanzer & Clark (1963), Ranken (1963), and others suggested that some sort of serial recall task might have such properties. Spiker (1956) observed, moreover, that young children sometimes spontaneously rehearsed stimulus names aloud during the delay period of his delayed-reaction task. A memory task might thus have the further advantage of constituting an experimental setting in which whatever mediating speech is produced would tend to be more overt than in other settings, thereby enhancing opportunities for direct observation. The task finally selected was the following: S sees seven pictures, each depicting a single object, spread out randomly before him. E then slowly points to, say, some randomly chosen three of these pictures in succession. Either immediately or after a 15-second delay, S is presented with a duplicate set of pictures (set out in a different random arrangement, so that spatial position cannot serve as a memory aid), and his task is to point to the same three pictures and in the same sequence that E had pointed to them previously. It was expected that a relatively mature S would try to cope with this task verbally: name to himself each object as it was pointed to, rehearse the resulting list of names (perhaps a number of times if there is a delay period), and then work directly from the list when it came time for him to reproduce the sequence gesturally.

The stimuli to be recalled and the conditions under which their recall was tested were designed with the Competence and Production conditions in mind. The objects shown in the pictures were intended to be familiar ones which even the youngest Ss tested would find easy to label (an attempt was subsequently made to verify this empirically). The names of most of these objects had the further property of entailing rather large and conspicuous mouth movements when pronounced—words like "pipe," "flag," etc. Furthermore, these mouth-movement patterns were relatively distinctive and discriminable, one name from another. Prior to the experiment, one of us (Beach) trained himself to become as expert as he could at lip-reading this specially selected seven-word "language." And finally, S was semiblindfolded during the delay period of all delayed-recall trials, both to give him some sense of being alone and undisturbed (a condition which might facilitate semiovert verbalization) and also to permit E to stare fixedly at his mouth throughout this period without causing embarrassment or discomfort. It was never supposed that these particular procedures would necessarily yield the largest possible fraction of observable speech to total speech produced. One could, for example, imagine testing S in true rather than partial isolation; one could likewise imagine utilizing sensitive throat microphones, and so on. It was hoped, however, that the yield from the present method would be sufficient to make a convincing test of the production-deficiency hypothesis.

Subjects

The Ss were 60 public school children, 10 boys and 10 girls at each of grades K, 2, and 5. The group mean ages were 69, 93, and 129 months, respectively. The Ss were drawn from their classrooms on an essentially random basis, with no attempt to match groups on variables other than grade and sex.

Procedure

The Ss were tested individually, all three authors serving as Es. A testing session lasted 20–25 minutes and was composed of the following sequence of events.

Introduction. The child was told that he would play some games for which he might win little prizes and that we would actually begin things by giving him one of these prizes. He was thereupon offered a choice of two prizes, drawn from a collection of plastic rings, key chains bearing charms, balloons, and toy money. He was then assured that if he tried hard and did his best in the games, he would get some more prizes.

Pretraining on "Same Order." S was instructed to point to each of a series of wooden blocks (a two-block series was used first, then a four-block series) in the same order that E had just pointed to them, regardless of intervening changes in spatial arrangement. The E continuously verbalized what he and S were doing (e.g., "First I point to this one, and then I point, etc.") and concluded by defining "same order" in terms of S pointing first to the same block E had pointed to first, S pointing second to the same block E had pointed to second, etc. This brief pretraining was not expected to teach S a new concept, but rather to prime or set him to use one he doubtless already possessed at some level, as well as to familiarize him with the verbal expressions E would subsequently employ in instructing him to use it.

Habituation to Space Helmet. S was next presented with a brightly colored toy space helmet and was assisted in placing it on his head. Its adjustable plastic visor was covered with white tape, which effectively prevented him from seeing Es or task materials when the visor was in the down position. His visual field was not appreciably darkened, however, both because the tape was essentially translucent and because a considerable amount of light could enter at the top, bottom, and sides of the visor. The S was trained to raise and lower the visor himself on E's command, that is, "Visor up!" and "Visor down!" and was gradually habituated to a visor-down period of 15 seconds. None of the Ss appeared to be particularly disturbed at having to wear the space helmet, lower the visor, etc., although appearances here may of course have been deceiving; some of them were manifestly amused by the whole thing.

Immediate Recall (IR). The Immediate Recall (IR) and Delayed Recall (DR) subtasks constituted the "heart" of the experimental sequence, the ones from which the most important data were expected. Half of the Ss of each grade and sex experienced them in the IR-DR order; the other half in the DR-IR order. The following equipment was used for these two subtasks and for the last, Point and Name (PN) subtask. There were two identical sets of seven colored paintings of objects, each photographically reproduced on a 3×4-inch card. The paintings depicted an apple, comb, an American flag, two yellow flowers on a stem, a moon, an owl, and a pipe. There was a $21 \times 14 \times \frac{1}{4}$-inch board covered with a special black felt which tends to adhere to itself. One of the two sets of pictures was backed with the same felt, thus permitting E to place and displace these pictures freely on the board without fear of slippage, even when the board was held in a vertical position. The third major item was a two-tiered wooden rack, 27 inches long and 10 inches high, covered with ordinary green felt. The rack tilted slightly backward, away from S, permitting the second set of pictures to sit securely in a near-upright position on the two tiers. The final item was an ordinary stop watch used to time the 15-second delay period.

Throughout the experiment, S and the three Es sat in small chairs around a small table. One E (Beach), seated directly across the table from S (about

3 feet away), was occupied almost exclusively with recording any speech he could hear or lip read during the three subtasks. Another E (Chinsky) pointed to the pictures and recorded the child's pointing. The particular pictures pointed to, as well as their sequence, were random for each S, subtask, and trial. The third E (Flavell) did the instructing and other verbal interacting with S, randomly rearranged the pictures on the portable board and stationary rack after each recall trial, dispensed the prizes, etc.

The IR procedure on each trial was as follows: E held the portable· board upright in front of S in such a position that S could not see the stationary rack sitting on the table just behind it. The second E then pointed to a given number of the pictures on the portable board at the rate of one point per 2 seconds. As soon as he had finished, the portable board was removed from view, and S tried to point to the same pictures in the same order on the rack. The E then rearranged the pictures on both board and rack in preparation for the next trial. The IR subtask began with preliminary instructions followed by two practice trials, each involving sequences of two pictures. The first of these trials was purely demonstrational: one E carefully explained the procedure, repeatedly stressing that S's recall was to be ordered, etc., while the other E did both the original pointing and, simulating S, the recall pointing. The second practice trial was indistinguishable from the subsequent test trials, except that S was corrected if he made an error. A minimum of three test trials followed. These involved sequences of first two, then three, then four pictures for grades K and 2, and first three, then four, then five pictures for grade 5. If S should perform correctly on the third of these trials, he was presented with progressively longer sequences until he failed; only a small minority of Ss recalled well enough to require any additional trials on this or the other two subtasks, however. As soon as the IR trials were completed, S was allowed to choose a second prize, regardless of how well he had performed.

Delayed Recall (DR). The procedure for this subtask was identical to the preceding one, except that the space helmet visor was pulled down for a 15-second period between E's and S's pointing. As in IR, S was allowed to choose a third prize after the last DR trial.

Inquiry. S was given a brief break following the third reward (he was encouraged to stand up and stretch if he wished, etc.), during the course of which E casually asked him the following question: "When he pointed to the pictures, you knew you were supposed to try to remember them, so you could point to the same ones afterward. Right? What did you *do* to remember them? I mean, how did you *go about* trying to keep them straight in your head?" Although E sometimes asked additional probing questions on the basis of S's answer, no S was later classified as having reported using a verbal rehearsal strategy unless he had given an unambiguous answer to that effect in response to this initial question.

Picture Naming. Directly following the inquiry, *E* directed *S*'s attention to the rack and asked: "By the way, can you tell me what each picture is a picture of? What's this [points], and this . . . ?"

Point and Name (PN). This subtask was identical to the DR subtask, except that *S* was instructed to name each depicted object aloud as *E* pointed to it, and again to name each one as he pointed to it during the recall period. The fourth of *S*'s prizes was dispensed immediately afterward, and *S* returned to his classroom.

HYPOTHESES

The major prediction was that the second-grade *S*s would produce significantly more detectable verbal coding and rehearsal of the depicted objects across the IR and DR trials than would the kindergarten *S*s. If it turned out that the younger *S*s could readily and accurately name the objects when asked to (Picture Naming), the above finding ought to constitute a reasonably adequate confirmation of the production-deficiency hypothesis, at least within the area of functioning represented by this task. A fifth-grade group was included in the sample only to test a minor hypothesis, derived from Vygotsky's (1962) writings on the development of inner speech. While it was of course supposed that fifth graders would be at least as likely to handle our task verbally as would the second graders, it might be predicted that their verbalizations would be relatively more covert and hence that our observer would see or hear a smaller proportion of the total actually produced. Taking both hypotheses together, one would expect something like an inverted U-shaped curve when observed verbal production is plotted against grade. Like the inclusion of the fifth-grade group, the addition of the third (PN) subtask constituted an excursion from the major focus of the study. We simply wondered if induced labeling would affect either *S*'s recall score or his tendency to rehearse during the delay intervals. There are, of course, additional questions which could be put to the verbalization and recall data of this investigation; most of these will be taken up below.

RESULTS

An examination of the Picture-Naming data is a necessary preliminary to any empirical test of the production-deficiency hypothesis. These data strongly suggest that any production deficiency which may characterize our kindergarten group could not be attributed to an inability to name the stimuli. As would be expected, no second- or fifth-grade S mislabeled any of the seven pictures. Five kindergarten Ss made one minor labeling error each (e.g., moon = "sun," flowers = "roses" (they were not), owl = "eagle" or "bird"). Two Ss (including one of these five) were unable to name one picture each. This constitutes a total of only two serious and five minor naming problems out of 140 picture identifications made by these 20 Ss.

As indicated earlier, one of the Es—previously trained to lip read the seven object names—spent each testing session watching and listening for any verbalization he could detect. He was unable to see either set of pictures from where he sat and thus had no knowledge (unless S verbalized) as to exactly which pictures on a given IR or DR trial were being pointed to (he did know during the PN trials, of course, because S overtly labeled each pointing). While some Ss actually verbalized aloud or half aloud on occasion, most of what E detected was at the level of soft whispering or soundless mouth movements. Anything E observed was immediately coded as belonging to one of three categories. The first category consisted of behavior which was indisputably stimulus labeling: E could either hear a specific word, lip read it with certainty, or both. The second category comprised lip-movement activity which E could with reasonable assurance interpret as labeling, even though he could not positively identify the particular word or words being spoken. An example would be an undecipherable but speechlike-movement pattern which was repeated several times over during a delay period. Lip-movement activity about which E had no such assurance constituted the third category: some of it looked like it definitely did not represent speech activity; some looked like it may have, but E did not feel sufficiently sure to categorize it as such. He occasionally noted other behaviors which may also have attested to covert verbal rehearsal, for example, rhythmic head nodding. However, only observations which could be assigned to the first two categories were treated as speech for data analysis purposes. As things turned out—happily—the results to be presented would have been about the same if we had adopted the more conservative course of accepting only first-category instances as evidence for speech production, since the first and second categories tended to be highly correlated within Ss. For example, the first column of Table 1 would read 18, 9, 4 instead of 18, 8, 3, if only first-category data were considered.

Within a single recall trial, there were between one and three occasions when spontaneous speech could occur, these occasions corresponding to subtask segments. In the case of the DR subtask, speech could occur during the presentation segments (when E points), during the delay segments, or during the recall segments (when S points). The number of possible occasions is reduced to two on IR trials (presentation and recall segments), and to one on PN trials (delay segment). A "verbalization instance" can then

TABLE 1

Number of Ss Showing 0, 1–2, and 3+ Verbalization Instances on Subtasks
IR and DR Combined

Grade	Number of Instances		
	0	1–2	3+
K	18	1	1
2	8	7	5
5	3	4	13
Total	29	12	19

be defined as the occurrence of any detectable speech (first category, second category, or a mixture of both) on one of the available occasions within one trial of one subtask. "Any detectable speech" could thus refer to a single word, or it could refer to the 11 complete rehearsals of a three-picture sequence which one second-grade boy managed to squeeze into the delay period of a DR trial.

Table 1 shows the number of Ss at each grade level who produced a total of 0, 1–2, or 3 or more verbalization instances during the IR and DR trials combined. As predicted, there is a substantial increase in spontaneous verbal production from grade K to grade 2 (χ^2 11.02; $df = 2$; $p < .01$). Much to our surprise, however, production continues to increase from grade 2 to grade 5, and this increase is likewise statistically significant ($\chi^2 = 8.10$; $df = 2$; $p < .02$). As the table shows, much of the change here appears to concern how much verbalization S does, rather than whether he engages in any. The fact that the production curve continues to rise between second and fifth grade seems to render even more improbable any naming-deficiency explanation for a child's failure to verbalize on this task.

Table 2 shows the age distribution of production-nonproduction within

TABLE 2

Number of Ss Showing 1+ Verbalization Instances on Each Segment of
Each Subtask

Grade	Segments and Subtasks					
	Presentation		Delay		Recall	
	IR	DR	DR	PN	IR	DR
K	1	0	2	7	1	1
2	4	7	7	13	5	7
5	11	6	10	16	13	12
Total	16	13	19	36	19	20

each segment of each subtask, including PN. There seems to be a fairly regular grade-by-grade increase on all segments of all subtasks (χ^2s for all columns are statistically reliable), with the exception of the grade 2–grade 5 portion of Presentation-IR. As regards the comparisons among columns, the IR and DR tasks appear not to have differed much in their capacity for evoking verbalization on comparable, that is, Presentation and Recall, segments. One might have expected that the total for column three would be higher than that of either the first two or the last two columns; for one thing, the sheer time available for verbalization was greater on this segment than on the others. Nonetheless, the probability of S making at least one verbalization seems not to have been significantly higher here than elsewhere. The most interesting comparison in the table is that between Delay-DR and Delay-PN. At all grade levels, the PN total is 5–6 Ss higher; indeed, this is the only subtask segment in which more than one or two kindergarten Ss show any verbalization. Some caution is required in interpreting this finding, however. On the one hand, the PN subtask came last in the experimental sequence (a fact which may have had some influence on the recall scores, at least, as will be shown). On the other hand, the observer always knew which pictures E had pointed to on this subtask, and this may have helped him promote to the first or second category certain lip-movement patterns which would otherwise have been relegated to the third category. The following fact may or may not reflect such a scoring bias: there were five Ss who were recorded as showing nothing higher than third-category responses on Delay-DR trials but who went on to produce second- or third-category responses on Delay-PN. These caveats notwithstanding, it is hard to avoid believing that the PN procedure really did boost S's disposition to rehearse the stimulus names during the delay period. There were 17 Ss who produced no detectable verbalization during Delay-DR but did produce some during Delay-PN; there were no Ss who showed the opposite pattern.

Table 3 presents the observed verbalization data taken in conjunction

TABLE 3

Number of Ss Showing Various Patterns of Observed and Reported Verbalization on Subtasks IR and DR Combined

Pattern		Grade			
Observed	Reported	K	2	5	Total
+	+	1	7	15	23
0	0	18	4	0	22
+	0	1	5	2	8
0	+	0	4	3	7

with S's responses to the inquiry question. Reported and observed behavior were consistent for 45 of the 60 Ss and inconsistent for 15. Of the 15, eight showed behavioral evidence of verbalization but did not unambiguously report that they had; they said that they did not know how they had remembered the items, or that they "tried to remember" them, or that they "thought" about them, etc. Interestingly enough, none of these eight produced more than one or two verbalization instances, or to put it differently, no S with three or more instances on IR and DR combined failed to state that he had managed the task verbally. What of the seven Ss who said they had verbalized but did not produce any speech overt enough for E to detect? We found their retrospections very convincing. These two second graders were representative: "When he pointed to them, I just sayed them to myself, when he pointed to them." "Well, I kept saying them in my mind. (Like what did you say?) Well, he'd point to the apple and then to the flag, and I'd keep saying 'apple,' 'flag,' 'apple,' 'flag.'" It would be incredible if our gross detection procedure had not failed to identify as verbalizers at least some Ss who actually were. These seven 0+ children were surely among the false negatives, and there were undoubtedly others in the 00 group. It may be noted in passing that if one uses a disjunctive criterion for verbal production on this task—S either shows it or reports it—the number of producers remains at 2 in kindergarten but rises from 12 to 16 in second grade and from 17 to a unanimous 20 in fifth grade.

While this study was obviously not designed with mediation as opposed to production issues in mind, it would naturally be of interest to see if some of its data turned out to be relevant to these issues. There are two questions here for which one might look for tentative answers. First, does verbalization of the picture names actually assist the ordered recall of the pictures for either older or younger Ss? We had chosen this particular task in the first place on the hunch that Ss beyond a certain level of development would tend to handle it verbally (in an attempt to meet the Elicitation condition), and the evidence just presented suggests that this hunch was probably correct. We had further supposed that a verbal mediational strategy would attain this popularity precisely because it is a useful way of managing this sort of task, but this supposition may have been wrong. The second question is the familiar mediational-deficiency one: if verbalization is in fact a useful strategy here, is it less useful to younger children than to older children?

The recall scores obtained under the PN versus the IR and DR task conditions might give evidence relevant to the first question. If recall under PN turned out to be significantly superior to that under the other two conditions, and if this superiority could not be attributed to subtask order effects, it would suggest that verbalization was facilitative. The S was given a recall score for each of the three subtasks. This score was simply the number of objects contained in the longest object series (test trials only) which he recalled correctly. For example, a kindergarten or second-grade child who pointed to the correct objects in correct sequence on his second trial but not on his first and third would receive a score of 3. Any S who failed all three test trials was arbitrarily assigned a score of 1. Table 4 presents the

TABLE 4

Group Mean Recall Scores by Subtask and Subtask Order

| Grade | Subtask | | Subtask Order | | |
	IR	DR	First	Second	Third (PN)
K	1.75	1.40	1.30	1.85	2.20
2	2.50	2.90	2.55	2.85	3.50
5	3.95	3.70	3.60	4.05	3.95
All Ss	2.73	2.67	2.48	2.92	3.22

mean recall scores for IR and DR (order counterbalanced within each group), and also for the first subtask administered (IR or DR), the second (IR or DR), and the third (PN for all Ss). There is no suggestion in the table that the IR and DR conditions per se led to differences in recall. On the other hand, it does appear that subtask order was a variable, S tending to improve in recall with each successive subtask, regardless of which subtasks occupied the first and second position in the sequence. The analysis of variance shown in Table 5 confirms this impression: subtask order is a significant main effect. It is therefore apparent that no conclusions about verbal facilitation can be drawn from this segment of the data.

TABLE 5

Summary of Analysis of Variance of Recall Scores

Source	df	MS	F	p
Between Ss:	59			
Grade (A)	2	65.51	52.82	<.01
Sex (B)	1	1.61	1.29	—
A × B	2	1.57	1.27	—
Error (b)	54	1.24	—	—
Within Ss:	120			
Subtask order (C)	2	8.16	11.79	<.01
A × C	4	0.90	1.30	—
B × C	2	3.76	5.43	<.01
A × B × C	4	0.80	1.15	—
Error (w)	108	0.69	—	—

Note. For all other Fs, $p > .25$.

Another way to test for verbal facilitation might be to divide each group of Ss into two approximately equal-sized subgroups, based upon how much spontaneous verbalization they apparently engaged in, and then compare subgroup recall scores. This obviously cannot be done with the kindergarten group, since there were only two Ss who showed any detectable verbalization. Neither can it be done with the fifth graders for the opposite reason: all of them either reported that they had verbalized, produced detectable verbalization, or both. The data on the second graders appear more promising in this respect, but there is the question of exactly what basis to use for dividing the group. The division ought to be a plausible one, and it also ought to yield two subgroups of roughly equal Ns. The division which appears to come closest to satisfying these two criteria is that which separates these 20 Ss into those who reported having verbalized during the recall trials $(N = 11)$ and those who did not $(N = 9)$; one might assume that

TABLE 6

Mean Recall Scores of Second-Grade Ss Reporting $(N = 11)$ and Not Reporting $(N = 9)$ Verbalization

Verbalization	Subtask		
	IR	DR	PN
Reported	2.82	3.27	3.45
Not reported	2.11	2.44	3.45

the former subgroup did more verbalizing, at least, than the latter did. Table 6 shows the subgroup recall scores. The 11 recalled better than the 9 on both IR and DR, significantly so in the latter case $(t = 2.59; df = 18; p < .02)$. Had these subgroup differences been simply a matter of differential recall skills, unrelated to the use of verbalization, one would have expected a similar difference on the PN subtask; as the table shows, however, the mean recall scores are identical there. Although this finding is suggestive, it must be regarded as rather slender evidence for the hypothesis.

A mediational-deficiency hypothesis would receive support in our study if either of the following were shown to be true: (1) the PN condition does not facilitate recall as much for kindergarten nonproducers as it does for second-grade nonproducers, or (2) differences in recall scores (on IR and DR) between producers and nonproducers of the same grade should be smaller in the kindergarten than in the second-grade group. Since there really is no good evidence as yet that PN facilitates anyone's recall, and since the comparison suggested in (2) above is impossible in the case of the kindergarten Ss, it is obvious that our data can provide no sort of test for this hypothesis. It would certainly be interesting to establish that verbalization does in fact assist memory on this type of task, and even more interesting to prove that this assistance is less marked in younger versus older children. The present study was manifestly not intended to accomplish either of these things and, not surprisingly, did not succeed in doing so by chance.

DISCUSSION

The results of this study confirm the existence of something akin to a verbal production deficiency in young children, at least within the experimental setting we used to test for it. They do not, however, shed any light whatever on the precise nature and meaning of this deficiency or on the mechanisms responsible for its apparent decline during the elementary school years. Why, exactly, did most of the kindergarten Ss seemingly fail to use naming and rehearsal as a cognitive "trick" to aid their recall? Perhaps for either or both of two reasons.

The failure might have reflected an immaturity that was specifically linguistic in nature, performance on Picture Naming notwithstanding. According to this line of explanation, there is more to language development than just a gradual mastery of its phonology, morphology, and syntax. The child who "has" a language, in the sense of having acquired such mastery, may still not know exactly when and where to use what he has, in rather the same way that an individual may "have" a concept or cognitive rule and yet not think to apply it on every appropriate occasion. While the 5-year-old has learned to translate linguistic competence into verbal utterance in a number of contexts where an adult would do the same—in communicative ones, notably—he may well not have learned to do this in all appropriate contexts. Thus, the genesis of language in its broadest sense may partly entail a progressive "linguification" of more and more situations. Initially, only a limited number of behavioral contexts call forth speech activity, but this number gradually increases as development proceeds. To borrow an expression from Wittgenstein (1958), the number and variety of "language games" the child knows how to "play" is a function of his developmental level, and most kindergarten children have simply not yet acquired the one demanded by our task.

When the present study had been completed, the senior author reported the findings to the school principal and the three teachers whose children had served as Ss. Hoping to get some leads for future research, he brought along two lists of second graders: the five most verbally productive Ss among the seven who showed the $++$ pattern (see Table 3), and the four who showed the 00 pattern. The second-grade teacher was asked to guess which group had used verbal rehearsal in our task. She identified the correct list without a moment's hesitation, and when asked how she knew, she replied to the effect that those were the ones who perpetually talked in class. It may be that these particular children have simply learned to "linguify" a great variety of stimulus situations, situations which do not obviously call for verbal responding (such as our task) as well as those which do.

A second line of explanation would stress a more general cognitive immaturity, one which could make for a deficiency in verbal and nonverbal production alike, depending upon which kind of behavior the task demanded. Verbal coding and rehearsal on a task such as ours could be construed as reflecting or embodying certain intellectual competencies which have nothing intrinsically verbal about them. An S who codes and rehearses is, first of all, responding to the task in an intellectually active fashion. Not content simply to track the picture sequence in a purely—and passively—sensory fashion, he "goes beyond the information given" to transform this perceived sequence into an isomorphic sequence of vocal responses in accordance with what looks like a self-generated cognitive strategy. Second, in continuously rehearsing the stimulus names during the delay period, S is demonstrating a capacity for sustained attentional focusing in the absence of both perceptual and social (i.e., instructional) supports for doing so. Third, coding and rehearsal represents a systematic plan for coping effectively with the task requirements; it is, as such, a kind of problem-solving "algorithm" of S's own devising. And finally, it represents a time-binding, goal-directed effort on his part. He codes for the future when the stimuli are first presented, and he also keeps the past alive by carrying that code forward into the recall period. Viewed in this way, our kindergarten Ss may have failed to talk to themselves for reasons having nothing whatever to do with their level of linguistic development. That is, they may simply have been too young to engage in the kinds of intellectual activities which assume the guise in this particular task, of verbal coding and rehearsal. The work of Piaget and others on this age group would support such a view.

As indicated earlier, the continuing increase in detectable verbalization from second to fifth grade came as a surprise, and appears inconsistent with Vygotsky's (1962) speculations about the progressive internalization of nonsocial speech during early childhood. A recent study by Klein (1963) also provides evidence relevant to Vygotsky's internalization hypothesis. He looked and listened for any detectable speech which 3–7-year-old children produced when left alone in an observation room with cut-out puzzles and drawing materials. He found a significant decrease with age in the ratio of "audible-comprehensible" speech (that which could be clearly understood on tape playback) to total speech (audible-comprehensible plus incomprehensible muttering, soundless lip movements, etc.). There was, however, no such decrease with age in the number of Ss on whom those ratios could be calculated, that is, within that subset of children (about half the total group) who produced any detectable verbalization at all. What both Klein's findings and our own signify for the internalization hypothesis seems to depend upon one's interpretation of "internalized," that is, upon just how far the alleged internalization is thought to proceed in the course of maturation. If soundless or near-soundless lip-movement activity is accepted as "internalized," that is, considered a likely ontogenetic end point, then Klein's first result supports the hypothesis. Our data, in turn, could probably be dismissed as either irrelevant to it or consistent with it: our youngest verbalizers (second graders, largely) were the same age as Klein's oldest and, together with the still older fifth graders, mostly talked at this criterial, barely detectable level when rehearsing. If, on the other hand, "internalized" is taken literally to mean *really covert*—well below what either we or Klein could hope to detect with our gross procedures—the data must be construed differently. Klein's second finding now becomes the relevant one and provides no support for the hypothesis across the 3–7-year span. Our data complement his for the 7–10-year span and likewise fail to show any developmental movement toward complete internalization. One pays his money and takes his choice.

We are presently inclined to guess that there is something to Vygotsky's hypothesis, actually, but that it needs a more complicated restatement. The restated version is that in most or all cases where the intensity level of nonsocial speech changes with age, that change will in fact be in the direction of lesser intensity. However, what the initial level is; how much, if any, developmental reduction will occur (and hence, what the final level will be); what the rate of reduction will be across childhood, and when asymptote will be reached—all of these will vary in as yet unknown ways both with the individual and with the context or setting in which the speech occurs. For example, rehearsal in a memory task may show little if any reduction in level as a function of age, but may vary with what has to be remembered and how much difficulty S has in trying to remember it, and surely will vary among individuals at a given age level (recall Table 3). The import of Vygotsky's hypothesis, or any restatement of it, really amounts to this: an adequate account of the noncommunicative uses of language will eventually have to deal with two major questions. First and foremost, in what contexts do individuals tend to engage in nonsocial speech and to what effect? This is an oversimplified statement of what is usually referred to as the "language-thought" question, the question of the precise role and significance of language in cognitive and other activities. Second, in those situations where speech is produced, what governs its intensity level? This second question has seldom been broached, let alone answered. It may be important to ask and answer it, however, because doing so may provide us with valuable insights concerning the first, ultimately more interesting question.

References

Glanzer, M., & Clark, W. H. The verbal loop hypothesis: binary numbers. *J. verb. Learn. verb. Behav.*, 1963, **2**, 301–309.

Jarvis, P. E. The effect of self-administered verbal instructions on simple sensory-motor performance in children. Unpublished doctoral dissertation, Univer. of Rochester, 1963.

Kendler, Tracy S. Development of mediating responses in children. In J. C. Wright, & J. Kagan (Eds.), Basic cognitive processes in children. *Monogr. Soc. Res. Child. Develpm.*, 1963, **28** (2), 33–52.

Klein, W. An investigation of the spontaneous speech of children during problem-solving. Unpublished doctoral dissertation, Univer. of Rochester, 1963.

Luria, A. R. The genesis of voluntary movements. In N. O'Connor (Ed.), *Recent Soviet psychology*. New York: Pergamon, 1961. Pp. 165–185.

Maccoby, Eleanor E. Developmental psychology. *Ann. Rev. Psychol.*, 1964, **15**, 203–250.

Ranken, H. B. Language and thinking: positive and negative effects of learning. *Science*, 1963, **141**, 48–50.

Reese, H. W. Verbal mediation as a function of age level. *Psychol. Bull.*, 1962, **59**, 502–509.

Reese, H. W. "Perceptual set" in young children. *Child Develpm.*, 1963, **34**, 151–159.

Spiker, C. C. Stimulus pretraining and subsequent performance in the delayed reaction experiment. *J. exp. Psychol.*, 1956, **52**, 107–111.

Vygotsky, L. S. *Thought and Language*. Trans. Eugenia Hanfmann and Gertrude Vakar. Cambridge, Mass. and New York: M.I.T. Press and Wiley, 1962.

Weir, M. W., & Stevenson, H. W. The effect of verbalization in children's learning as a function of chronological age. *Child Develpm.*, 1959, **30**, 143–149.

Wittgenstein, L. *Preliminary studies for the "Philosophical investigations," generally known as the blue and brown books*. Oxford: Blackwell, 1958.

30. EARLY EXPERIENCE AND THE SOCIALIZATION OF COGNITIVE MODES IN CHILDREN[1]

Robert D. Hess & Virginia C. Shipman

This paper deals with the question: what is cultural deprivation and how does it act to shape and depress the resources of the human mind? The arguments presented are: first, that the behavior which leads to social, educational, and economic poverty is socialized in early childhood; second, that the central quality involved in the effects of cultural deprivation is a lack of cognitive meaning in the mother-child communication system; and, third, that the growth of cognitive processes is fostered in family control systems which offer and permit a wide range of alternatives of action and thought and that such growth is constricted by systems of control which offer predetermined solutions and few alternatives for consideration and choice.

The research group was composed of 160 Negro mothers and their 4-year-old children selected from four different social status levels.

The data are presented to show social status differences among the four groups with respect to cognitive functioning and linguistic codes and to offer examples of relations between maternal and child behavior that are congruent with the general lines of argument laid out.

SOURCE. Child Development, December 1965, **36**, 4. © 1965 by The Society for Research in Child Development, Inc.

[1] This research is supported by the Research Division of the Children's Bureau, Social Security Administration; Department of Health, Education, and Welfare; Ford Foundation for the Advancement of Learning; and grants-in-aid from the Social Science Research Committee of the Division of Social Sciences, University of Chicago. Project staff members who made specific contributions to the analysis of data are Jere Brophy, Dina Feitelson, Roberta Meyer, and Ellis Olim. Hess's address: Committee on Human Development, University of Chicago, Chicago, Ill. 60637.

528

THE PROBLEM

One of the questions arising from the contemporary concern with the education of culturally disadvantaged children is how we should conceptualize the effects of such deprivation upon the cognitive faculties of the child. The outcome is well known: children from deprived backgrounds score well below middle-class children on standard individual and group measures of intelligence (a gap that increases with age); they come to school without the skills necessary for coping with first grade curricula; their language development, both written and spoken, is relatively poor; auditory and visual discrimination skills are not well developed; in scholastic achievement they are retarded an average of 2 years by grade 6 and almost 3 years by grade 8; they are more likely to drop out of school before completing a secondary education; and even when they have adequate ability are less likely to go to college (Deutsch, 1963; Deutsch & Brown, 1964; Eells, Davis, Havighurst, Herriels, & Tyler 1951; John, 1963; Kennedy, Van de Riet, & White, 1963; Lesser, 1964).

For many years the central theoretical issues in this field dealt with the origin of these effects, argued in terms of the relative contribution of genetic as compared with environmental factors. Current interest in the effects of cultural deprivation ignores this classic debate; the more basic problem is to understand how cultural experience is translated into cognitive behavior and academic achievement (Bernstein, 1961; Hess, 1964).

The focus of concern is no longer upon the question of whether social and cultural disadvantage depress academic ability, but has shifted to a study of the mechanisms of exchange that mediate between the individual and his environment. The thrust of research and theory is toward conceptualizing social class as a discrete array of experiences and patterns of experience that can be examined in relation to the effects they have upon the emerging cognitive equipment of the young child. In short, the question this paper presents is this: what *is* cultural deprivation, and how does it act to shape and depress the resources of the human mind?

The arguments we wish to present here are these: first, that the behavior which leads to social, educational, and economic poverty is socialized in early childhood—that is, it is learned; second, that the central quality involved in the effects of cultural deprivation is a lack of cognitive meaning in the mother-child communication system; and, third, that the growth of cognitive processes is fostered in family control systems which offer and permit a wide range of alternatives of action and thought and that such growth is constricted by systems of control which offer predetermined solutions and few alternatives for consideration and choice.

In this paper we will argue that the structure of the social system and the structure of the family shape communication and language and that language shapes thought and cognitive styles of problem-solving. In the deprived-family context this means that the nature of the control system which relates parent to child restricts the number and kind of alternatives for action and thought that are opened to the child; such constriction precludes a tendency for the child to reflect, to consider and choose among alternatives for speech and action. It develops modes for dealing with stimuli and with problems which are impulsive rather than reflective, which deal with the immediate rather than the future, and which are disconnected rather than sequential.

This position draws from the work of Basil Bernstein (1961) of the University of London. In his view, language structures and conditions what the child learns and how he learns, setting limits within which future learning may take place. He identifies two forms of communication codes or styles of verbal behavior: *restricted* and *elaborated*. Restricted codes are stereotyped, limited, and condensed, lacking in specificity and the exactness needed for precise conceptualization and differentiation. Sentences are short, simple, often unfinished; there is little use of subordinate clauses for elaborating the content of the sentence; it is a language of implicit meaning, easily understood and commonly shared. It is the language form often used in impersonal situations when the intent is to promote solidarity or reduce tension. Restricted codes are nonspecific cliches, statements, or observations about events made in general terms that will be readily understood. The basic quality of this mode is to limit the range and detail of concept and information involved.

Elaborated codes, however, are those in which communication is individualized and the message is specific to a particular situation, topic, and person. It is more particular, more differentiated, and more precise. It permits expression of a wider and more complex range of thought, tending toward discrimination among cognitive and affective content.

The effects of early experience with these codes are not only upon the communication modes and cognitive structure—they also establish potential patterns of relation with the external world. It is one of the dynamic features of Bernstein's work that he views language as social behavior. As such, language is used by participants of a social network to elaborate and express social and other interpersonal relations and, in turn, is shaped and determined by these relations.

The interlacing of social interaction and language is illustrated by the distinction between two types of family control. One is oriented toward control by *status* appeal or ascribed role norms. The second is oriented toward *persons*. Families differ in the degree to which they utilize each of these types of regulatory appeal. In status- (position-) oriented families, behavior tends to be regulated in terms of role expectations. There is little opportunity for the unique characteristics of the child to influence the decision-making process or the interaction between parent and child. In these families, the internal or personal states of the children are not influential as a basis for decision. Norms of behavior are stressed with such imperatives as, "You must do this because I say so," or "Girls don't act like that," or other statements which rely on the status of the participants or a behavior norm for justification (Bernstein, 1964).

In the family, as in other social structures, control is exercised in part through status appeals. The feature that distinguishes among families is the extent to which the status-based control maneuvers are modified by orientation toward persons. In a person-oriented appeal system, the unique characteristics of the child modify status demands and are taken into account in interaction. The decisions of this type of family are individualized and less frequently related to status or role ascriptions. Behavior is justified in terms of feelings, preference, personal and unique reactions, and subjective states. This philosophy not only permits but demands an elaborated linguistic code and a wide range of linguistic and behavioral alternatives in interpersonal interaction. Status-oriented families may be regulated by less individuated commands, messages, and responses. Indeed, by its nature, the status-oriented family will rely more heavily on a restricted code. The verbal exchange is inherent in the structure—regulates it and is regulated by it.

These distinctions may be clarified by two examples of mother-child communication using these two types of codes. Assume that the emotional climate of two homes is approximately the same; the significant difference between them is in style of communication employed. A child is playing noisily in the kitchen with an assortment of pots and pans when the telephone rings. In one home the mother says, "Be quiet," or "Shut up," or issues any one of several other short, preemptory commands. In the other home the mother says, "Would you keep quiet a minute? I want to talk on the phone." The question our study poses is this: what inner response is elicited in the child, what is the effect upon his developing cognitive network of concepts and meaning in each of these two situations? In one instance the child is asked for a simple mental response. He is asked to attend to an uncomplicated message and to make a conditioned response (to comply); he is not called upon to reflect or to make mental discriminations. In the other example the child is required to follow two or three ideas. He is asked to relate his behavior to a time dimension; he must think of his behavior in relation to its effect upon another person. He must perform a more complicated task to follow the communication of his mother in that his relationship to her is mediated in part through concepts and shared ideas; his mind is stimulated or exercised (in an elementary fashion) by a more elaborate and complex verbal communication initiated by the mother. As objects of these two divergent communication styles, repeated in various ways, in similar situations and circumstances during the preschool years, these two imaginary children would be expected to develop significantly different verbal facility and cognitive equipment by the time they enter the public-school system.

A person-oriented family allows the child to achieve the behavior rules (role requirements) by presenting them in a specific context for the child and by emphasizing the consequences of alternative actions. Status-oriented families present the rules in an assigned manner, where compliance is the *only* rule-following possibility. In these situations the role of power in the interaction is more obvious, and, indeed, coercion and defiance are likely interactional possibilities. From another perspective, status-oriented families use a more rigid learning and teaching model in which compliance, rather than rationale, is stressed.

A central dimension through which we look at maternal behavior is to inquire what responses are elicited and permitted by styles of communication and interaction. There are two axes of the child's behavior in which we have a particular interest. One of these is represented by an *assertive, initiatory* approach to learning, as contrasted with a *passive, compliant* mode of engagement; the other deals with the tendency to reach solutions impulsively or hastily as distinguished from a tendency to *reflect*, to compare alternatives, and to choose among available options.

These styles of cognitive behavior are related, in our hypotheses, to the dimensions of maternal linguistic codes and types of family control systems. A status-oriented statement, for example, tends to offer a set of regulations and rules for conduct and interaction that is based on arbitrary decisions rather than upon logical consequences which result from selection of one or another alternatives. Elaborated and person-oriented statements lend themselves more easily to styles of cognitive approach that involve reflection and reflective comparison. Status-oriented statements tend to be restrictive of thought. Take our simple example of the two children and the telephone. The verbal categoric command to "Be quiet" cuts off thought and offers little opportunity to relate the information conveyed in the command to the context in which it occurred. The more elaborated message, "Would you be quiet a minute? I want to talk on the phone" gives the child a rationale for relating his behavior to a wider set of considerations. In effect, he has been given a *why* for his mother's request and, by this example, possibly becomes more likely to *ask* why in another situation. It may be through this type of verbal interaction that the child learns to look for action sequences in his own and others' behavior. Perhaps through these more intent-oriented statements the child comes to see the world as others see it and learns to take the role of others in viewing himself and his actions. The child comes to see the world as a set of possibilities from which he can make a personal selection. He learns to role play with an element of personal flexibility, not by role-conforming rigidity.

RESEARCH PLAN

For our project a research group of 163 Negro mothers and their 4-year-old children was selected from four different social status levels: Group A came from college-educated professional, executive, and managerial occupational levels; Group B came from skilled blue-collar occupational levels, with not more than high-school education; Group C came from unskilled or semi-skilled occupational levels, with predominantly elementary-school education; Group D from unskilled or semiskilled occupational levels, with fathers absent and families supported by public assistance.

These mothers were interviewed twice in their homes and brought to the university for testing and for an interaction session between mother and child in which the mother was taught three simple tasks by the staff member and then asked to teach these tasks to the child.

One of these tasks was to sort or group a number of plastic toys by color and by function; a second task was to sort eight blocks by two characteristics simultaneously; the third task required the mother and child to work together to copy five designs on a toy called an Etch-a-Sketch. A description of various aspects of the project and some preliminary results have been presented in several papers (Brophy, Hess, & Shipman, 1965; Jackson, Hess, & Shipman, 1965; Meyer, Shipman, & Hess, 1964; Olim, Hess, & Shipman, 1965; Shipman & Hess, 1965).

RESULTS

The data in this paper are organized to show social-status differences among the four groups in the dimensions of behavior described above to indicate something of the maternal teaching styles that are emerging and to offer examples of relations between maternal and child behavior that are congruent with the general lines of argument we have laid out.

Social-Status Differences

Verbal Codes: Restricted Versus Elaborated. One of the most striking and obvious differences between the environments provided by the mothers of the research group was in their patterns of language use. In our testing sessions, the most obvious social-class variations were in the total amount of verbal output in response to questions and tasks asking for verbal response. For example, as Table 1 shows, mothers from the middle-class gave protocols

TABLE 1

Mean Number of Typed Lines in Three Data-Gathering Situations

	Upper Middle $N = 40$	Upper Lower $N = 40$	Lower Lower $N = 36$	ADC $N = 36$
School situations	34.68	22.80	18.86	18.64
Mastery situations	28.45	18.70	15.94	17.75
CAT card	18.72	9.62	12.39	12.24
Total	81.85	51.12	47.19	48.63

that were consistently longer in language productivity than did mothers from the other three groups.

Taking three different types of questions that called for free response on the part of the mothers and counting the number of lines of typescript of the protocols, the tally for middle-class mothers was approximately 82 contrasted with an average of roughly 49 for mothers from the three other groups.

These differences in verbal products indicate the extent to which the maternal environments of children in different social-class groups tend to be mediated by verbal cue and thus offer (or fail to offer) opportunities for labeling, for identifying objects and feelings and adult models who can demonstrate the usefulness of language as a tool for dealing with interpersonal interaction and for ordering stimuli in the environment.

In addition to this gross disparity in verbal output there were differences in the quality of language used by mothers in the various status groups. One approach to the analysis of language used by these mothers was an examination of their responses to the following task: They were shown the Lion Card of the Children's Apperception Test and asked to tell their child a story relating to the card. This card is a picture of a lion sitting on a chair holding a pipe in his hand. Beside him is a cane. In the corner is a mouse peering out of a hole. The lion appears to be deep in thought. These protocols were the source of language samples which were summarized in nine scales (Table 2), two of which we wish to describe here.

The first scale dealt with the mother's tendency to use abstract words. The index derived was a proportion of abstract noun and verb types to total number of noun and verb types. Words were defined as abstract when the name of the object is thought of apart from the cases in which it is actually realized. For example, in the sentence, "The lion is an *animal*," "animal" is an abstract word. However, in the sentence, "This animal in the picture is sitting on his throne," "animal" is not an abstract noun.

In our research group, middle-class mothers achieved an abstraction score

TABLE 2

Social Status Differences in Language Usage (Scores are the Means for Each Group)

Scale	Social Status			
	Upper Middle N = 40	Upper Lower N = 42	Lower Lower N = 40	ADC N = 41
Mean sentence length[a]	11.39	8.74	9.66	8.23
Adjective range[b]	31.99	28.32	28.37	30.49
Adverb range[c]	11.14	9.40	8.70	8.20
Verb elaboration[d]	.59	.52	.47	.44
Complex verb preference[e]	63.25	59.12	50.85	51.73
Syntactic structure elaboration[f]	8.89	6.90	8.07	6.46
Stimulus utilization	5.82	4.81	4.87	5.36
Introduced content	3.75	2.62	2.45	2.34
Abstraction[g]	5.60	4.89	3.71	1.75

[a] Average number of words per sentence.

[b] Proportion of uncommon adjective types to total nouns, expressed as a percentage.

[c] Proportion of uncommon adverb types to total verbs, adjectives, and adverbs, expressed as a percentage.

[d] Average number of complex verb types per sentence.

[e] Proportion of complex verb types to all verb types, simple and complex.

[f] Average number of weighted complex syntactic structures per 100 words.

[g] Proportion of abstract nouns and verbs (excluding repetitions) to total nouns and verbs (excluding repetitions), expressed as a percentage.

of 5.6; the score for skilled work levels was 4.9; the score for the unskilled group was 3.7; for recipients of Aid to Dependent Children (ADC), 1.8.

The second scale dealt with the mother's tendency to use complex syntactic structures such as coordinate and subordinate clauses, unusual infinitive phrases (e.g., "To drive well, you must be alert"), infinitive clauses (e.g., "What to do next was the lion's problem"), and participial phrases (e.g., "Continuing the story, the lion . . ."). The index of structural elaboration derived was a proportion of these complex syntactic structures, weighted in accordance with their complexity and with the degree to which they are strung together to form still more complicated structures (e.g., clauses within clauses), to the total number of sentences.

In the research group, mothers from the middle class had a structure elaboration index of 8.89; the score for ADC mothers was 6.46. The use of complex grammatical forms and elaboration of these forms into complex clauses and sentences provides a highly elaborated code with which to manipulate the environment symbolically. This type of code encourages the child to recognize the possibilities and subtleties inherent in language not only for communication but also for carrying on high-level cognitive procedures.

Control Systems: Person Versus Status Orientation. Our data on the mothers' use of status- as contrasted with person-oriented statements comes from maternal responses to questions inquiring what the mother would do in order to deal with several different hypothetical situations at school in which the child had broken the rules of the school, had failed to achieve, or had been wronged by a teacher or classmate. The results of this tally are shown in Table 3.

TABLE 3

Person-Oriented and Status-Oriented Units on School Situation Protocols (Mothers)

	A. Mean Number			
Social Class	Person-Oriented	Status-Oriented	P/S Ratio	N
Upper middle	9.52 (1–19)	7.50 (0–19)	1.27	40
Upper lower	6.20 (0–20)	7.32 (2–17)	0.85	40
Lower lower	4.66 (0–15)	7.34 (2–17)	0.63	35
ADC	3.59 (0–16)	8.15 (3–29)	0.44	34

	B. Mean Per Cent		
Social Class	Person-Oriented	Status-Oriented	N
Upper middle	36.92	27.78	40
Upper lower	31.65	36.92	40
Lower lower	26.43	40.69	35
ADC	20.85	51.09	34

As is clear from these means, the greatest differences between status groups is in the tendency to utilize person-oriented statements. These differences are even greater if seen as a ratio of person-to-status type responses.

The orientation of the mothers to these different types of control is seen not only in prohibitive or reparative situations but in their instructions to their children in preparing them for new experiences. The data on this point come from answers to the question: "Suppose your child were starting to school tomorrow for the first time. What would you tell him? How would you prepare him for school?"

One mother, who was person-oriented and used elaborated verbal codes, replied as follows:

"First of all, I would remind her that she was going to school to learn, that her teacher would take my place, and that she would be expected to follow instructions. Also that her time was to be spent mostly in the classroom with other children, and that any questions or any problems that she might have she could consult with her teacher for assistance."

"Anything else?"

"No, anything else would probably be confusing for her at her particular age."

In terms of promoting educability, what did this mother do in her response? First, she was informative; she presented the school situation as comparable to one already familiar to the child; second, she offered reassurance and support to help the child deal with anxiety; third, she described the school situation as one that involves a personal relationship between the child and the teacher; and, fourth, she presented the classroom situation as one in which the child was to learn.

A second mother responded as follows to this question:

"Well, John, it's time to go to school now. You must know how to behave. The first day at school you should be a good boy and should do just what the teacher tells you to do."

In contrast to the first mother, what did this mother do? First, she defined the role of the child as passive and compliant; second, the central issues she presented were those dealing with authority and the institution, rather than with learning; third, the relationship and roles she portrayed were sketched in terms of status and role expectations rather than in personal terms; and, fourth, her message was general, restricted, and vague, lacking information about how to deal with the problems of school except by passive compliance.

A more detailed analysis of the mothers' responses to this question grouped their statements as *imperative* or *instructive* (Table 4). An impera-

TABLE 4

Information Mothers Would Give to Child on His First Day at School

Social Status	Imperative	Instructive	Support	Preparation	Other	N
			% of Total Statements			
Upper middle	14.9	8.7	30.2	8.6	37.6	39
Upper lower	48.2	4.6	13.8	3.8	29.6	41
Lower lower	44.4	1.7	13.1	1.2	39.6	36
ADC	46.6	3.2	17.1	1.3	31.8	37
			% of Mothers Using Category			
Upper middle	48.7	38.5	76.9	33.3	87.2	—
Upper lower	85.4	17.1	39.0	19.5	70.7	—
Lower lower	75.0	5.6	36.1	8.3	77.8	—
ADC	86.5	16.2	43.2	8.1	86.5	—

tive statement was defined as an unqualified injunction or command, such as, "Mind the teacher and do what she tells you to do," or "The first thing you have to do is be on time," or "Be nice and do not fight." An instructive statement offers information or commands which carry a rationale or justification for the rule to be observed. Examples: "If you are tardy or if you stay away from school, your marks will go down"; or "I would tell him about the importance of minding the teacher. The teacher needs his full cooperation. She will have so many children that she won't be able to pamper any youngster."

Status Differences in Concept Utilization. One of the measures of cognitive style used with both mothers and children in the research group was the S's mode of classificatory behavior. For the adult version, (Kagan, Moss & Sigel, 1963) S is required to make 12 consecutive sorts of MAPS figures placed in a prearranged random order on a large cardboard. After each sort she was asked to give her reason for putting certain figures together. This task was intended to reveal her typical or preferred manner of grouping stimuli and the level of abstraction that she uses in perceiving and ordering objects in the environment. Responses fell into four categories: descriptive part-whole, descriptive global, relational-contextual, and categorical-inferential. A descriptive response is a direct reference to physical attributes present in the stimuli, such as size, shape, or posture. Examples: "They're all children," or "They are all lying down," or "They are all men." The subject may also choose to use only a part of the figure—"They both have hats on." In a relational-contextual response, any one stimulus gets its meaning from a relation with other stimuli. Examples: "Doctor and nurse," or "Wife is cooking dinner for her husband," or "This guy looks like he shot this other guy." In categorical-inferential responses, sorts are based on non-observable characteristics of the stimulus for which each stimulus is an independent representative of the total class. Examples: "All of these people work for a living" or "These are all handicapped people."

As may be seen in Table 5, relational responses were most frequently

TABLE 5

Mean Responses to Adult Sigel Sorting Task (Maps)

	Social Status			
Category	Upper Middle $N = 40$	Upper Lower $N = 42$	Lower Lower $N = 39$	ADC $N = 41$
Total descriptive	3.18	2.19	2.18	2.59
Descriptive part-whole	1.65	1.33	1.31	1.49
Descriptive global	1.52	0.86	0.87	1.10
Relational-contextual	5.52	6.79	7.38	6.73
Categorical-inferential	3.30	3.00	2.23	2.66

offered; categorical-inferential were next most common, and descriptive most infrequent. The distribution of responses of our status groups showed that the middle-class group was higher on descriptive and categorical; low-status groups were higher on relational. The greater use of relational categories by the working-class mothers is especially significant. Response times for relational sorts are usually shorter, indicating less reflection and evaluating of alternative hypotheses. Such responses also indicate relatively low attention to external stimuli details (Kagan, 1964). Relational responses are often subjective, reflecting a tendency to relate objects to personal concerns in contrast with the descriptive and categorical responses which tend to be objective and detached, more general, and more abstract. Categorical responses, in particular, represent thought processes that are more orderly and complex in organizing stimuli, suggesting more efficient strategies of information processing.

The most striking finding from the data obtained from the children's Sigel Sorting Task was the decreasing use of the cognitive style dimensions and increasing nonverbal responses with decrease in social-status level. As may be seen in the tables showing children's performance on the Sigel Sorting Task (Tables 6 and 7), although most upper middle-class children

TABLE 6

Children's Responses to Sigel Sorting Task (Means)

	Social Status			
Category	Upper Middle $N = 40$	Upper Lower $N = 42$	Lower Lower $N = 39$	ADC $N = 41$
Descriptive part-whole	2.25	0.71	0.20	0.34
Descriptive global	2.80	2.29	1.51	0.98
Relational-contextual	3.18	2.31	1.18	1.02
Categorical-inferential	2.02	1.36	1.18	0.61
Nonscorable verbal responses	5.75	6.31	6.64	7.24
Nonverbal	3.00	6.41	7.08	8.76
No sort	1.00	0.62	2.21	1.05

and a majority of the upper lower-class children use relational and descriptive global responses, there is no extensive use of any of the other cognitive style dimensions by the two lower lower-class groups. In looking at particular categories one may note the relative absence of descriptive part-whole responses for other than the middle-class group and the large rise in nonverbal responses below the middle-class level. These results would seem to reflect the relatively undeveloped verbal and conceptual ability of children from homes with restricted range of verbal and conceptual content.

TABLE 7

Percentage of Four-Year-Old Children Responding in Each of the Categories

	Social Status			
Category	Upper Middle N = 40	Upper Lower N = 42	Lower Lower N = 39	ADC N = 41
Descriptive part-whole	40.0	28.6	18.0	14.6
Descriptive global	70.0	54.8	53.8	31.7
Total descriptive	80.0	66.7	59.0	39.0
Relational-contextual	77.5	66.7	41.0	43.9
Categorical-inferential	52.5	45.2	30.8	24.4
Nonscorable verbal	85.0	88.1	92.3	85.4
Nonverbal	52.5	66.7	82.0	87.8
No sort	12.5	7.1	25.6	19.5

Relational and descriptive global responses have been considered the most immature and would be hypothesized to occur most frequently in preschool children. Relational responses are often subjective, using idiosyncratic and irrelevant cues; descriptive global responses, often referring to sex and occupational roles, are somewhat more dependent upon experience. On the other hand, descriptive part-whole responses have been shown to increase with age and would be expected to be used less frequently. However, these descriptive part-whole responses, which are correlated with favorable prognostic signs for educability (such as attentiveness, control and learning ability), were almost totally absent from all but the upper middle-class group. Kagan (1964) has described two fundamental cognitive dispositions involved in producing such analytic concepts: the tendency to reflect over alternative solutions that are simultaneously available and the tendency to analyze a visual stimulus into component parts. Both behaviors require a delayed discrimination response. One may describe the impairment noted for culturally disadvantaged children as arising from differences in opportunities for developing these reflective attitudes.

The mothers' use of relational responses was significantly correlated with their children's use of nonscorable and nonverbal responses on the Sigel task and with poor performance on the 8-Block and Etch-a-Sketch tasks. The mothers' inability or disinclination to take an abstract attitude on the Sigel task was correlated with ineffectual teaching on the 8-Block task and inability to plan and control the Etch-a-Sketch situation. Since relational responses have been found (Kagan, Moss, & Sigel, 1963) to be correlated with impulsivity, tendencies for nonverbal rather than verbal teaching, mother-domination, and limited sequencing and discrimination might be expected and would be predicted to result in limited categorizing ability and impaired verbal skills in the child.

Analysis of Maternal Teaching Styles

These differences among the status groups and among mothers within the groups appear in slightly different form in the teaching sessions in which the mothers and children engaged. There were large differences among the status groups in the ability of the mothers to teach and the children to learn. This is illustrated by the performance scores on the sorting tasks.

Let us describe the interaction between the mother and child in one of the structured teaching situations. The wide range of individual differences in linguistic and interactional styles of these mothers may be illustrated by excerpts from recordings. The task of the mother is to teach the child how to group or sort a small number of toys.

The first mother outlines the task for the child, gives sufficient help and explanation to permit the child to proceed on her own. She says:

"All right, Susan, this board is the place where we put the little toys; first of all you're supposed to learn how to place them according to color. Can you do that? The things that are all the same color you put in one section; in the second section you put another group of colors, and in the third section you put the last group of colors. Can you do that? Or would you like to see me do it first?"

CHILD: "I want to do it."

This mother has given explicit information about the task and what is expected of the child; she has offered support and help of various kinds; and she has made it clear that she impelled the child to perform.

A second mother's style offers less clarity and precision. She says in introducing the same task:

"Now, I'll take them all off the board; now you put them all back on the board. What are these?"

CHILD: "A truck."

"All right, just put them right here; put the other one right here; all right put the other one there."

This mother must rely more on nonverbal communication in her commands; she does not define the task for the child; the child is not provided with ideas or information that she can grasp in attempting to solve the problem; neither is she told what to expect or what the task is, even in general terms.

A third mother is even less explicit. She introduces the task as follows:

"I've got some chairs and cars, do you want to play the game?" Child does not respond. Mother continues: "O.K. What's this?"

CHILD: "A wagon?"

MOTHER: "Hm?"

CHILD: "A wagon?"

MOTHER: "This is not a wagon. What's this?"

The conversation continues with this sort of exchange for several pages. Here again, the child is not provided with the essential information he needs to solve or to understand the problem. There is clearly some impelling on the part of the mother for the child to perform, but the child has not been told what he is to do. There were marked social-class differences in the ability of the children to learn from their mothers in the teaching sessions.

Each teaching session was concluded with an assessment by a staff member of the extent to which the child had learned the concepts taught by the mother. His achievement was scored in two ways: first, the ability to correctly place or sort the objects and, second, the ability to verbalize the principle on which the sorting or grouping was made.

Children from middle-class homes were well above children from working-class homes in performance on these sorting tasks, particularly in offering verbal explanations as to the basis for making the sort (Tables 8 and 9).

TABLE 8

Differences Among Status Groups in Children's Performance in Teaching Situations (Toy Sort Task)

Social Status	Placed Correctly (%)	Verbalized Correctly (%)		N
A. Identity sort (cars, spoons, chairs)				
Upper middle	61.5	28.2	45.8[a]	39
Upper lower	65.0	20.0	30.8	40
Lower lower	68.4	29.0	42.3	38
ADC	66.7	30.8	46.2	39
B. Color sort (red, green, yellow)				
Upper middle	69.2	28.2	40.7[a]	39
Upper lower	67.5	15.0	22.2	40
Lower lower	57.9	13.2	22.7	38
ADC	33.3	5.1	15.4	39

[a] Per cent of those who placed object correctly.

Over 60 per cent of middle-class children placed the objects correctly on all tasks; the performance of working-class children ranged as low as 29 per cent correct. Approximately 40 per cent of these middle-class children who were successful were able to verbalize the sorting principle; working-class children were less able to explain the sorting principle, ranging downward from the middle-class level to one task on which no child was able to verbalize

TABLE 9

Differences Among Status Groups in Children's Performance in Teaching
Situations (8-Block Task)

Social Status	Placed Correctly (%)	One-Dimension Verbalized (%)		Both Verbalized (%)		N
A. Short O						
Upper middle	75.0	57.5	57.5[a]	25.0	33.3[a]	40
Upper lower	51.2	39.0	43.2	2.4	4.8	41
Lower lower	50.0	29.0	33.3	15.8	31.6	38
ADC	43.6	20.5	22.2	2.6	5.9	39
B. Tall X						
Upper middle	60.0	62.5	64.1[a]	27.5	45.8[a]	40
Upper lower	48.8	39.0	42.1	17.1	35.0	41
Lower lower	34.2	23.7	26.5	7.9	23.1	38
ADC	28.2	18.0	20.0	0.0	0.0	39

[a] Per cent of those who placed object correctly.

correctly the basis of his sorting behavior. These differences clearly paralleled
the relative abilities and teaching skills of the mothers from differing social-
status groups.

The difference among the four status levels was apparent not only on these
sorting and verbal skills but also in the mother's ability to regulate her own
behavior and her child's in performing tasks which require planning or care
rather than verbal or conceptual skill. These differences were revealed by the
mother-child performance on the Etch-a-Sketch task. An Etch-a-Sketch toy
is a small, flat box with a screen on which lines can be drawn by a device
within the box. The marker is controlled by two knobs: one for horizontal
movement, one for vertical. The mother is assigned one knob, the child the
other. The mother is shown several designs which are to be reproduced.
Together they attempt to copy the design models. The mother decides when
their product is a satisfactory copy of the original. The products are scored
by measuring deviations from the original designs.

These sessions were recorded, and the nonverbal interaction was described
by an observer. Some of the most relevant results were these: middle-class
mothers and children performed better on the task (14.6 points) than mother
and children from the other groups (9.2; 8.3; 9.5; [Table 10]). Mothers
of the three lower-status groups were relatively persistent, rejecting more
complete figures than the middle-class mothers; mothers from the middle
class praised the child's efforts more than did other mothers but gave just as
much criticism; the child's cooperation as rated by the observer was as good
or better in low-status groups as in middle-class pairs (Table 11), there was

TABLE 10

Performance on Etch-a-Sketch Task (Means)

	Social Status			
	Upper Middle N = 40	Upper Lower N = 42	Lower Lower N = 40	ADC N = 41
Total score (range 0–40)	14.6	9.2	8.3	9.5
Average number of attempts	12.7	17.2	12.2	15.1
Complete figures rejected	2.3	3.6	3.5	3.4
Child's total score	5.9	4.0	3.4	4.0
Child's contribution to total score (per cent)	40.4	43.5	41.0	42.1

TABLE 11[a]

Mother-Child Interaction on Etch-a-Sketch Task (Means)

	Social Status			
	Upper Middle N = 40	Upper Lower N = 41	Lower Lower N = 39	ADC N = 39
Praises child	4.6	6.9	7.2	7.5
Criticizes child	6.4	5.5	6.4	5.9
Overall acceptance of child	2.2	3.2	3.4	3.6
Child's cooperation	5.6	5.3	4.5	5.1
Level of affection shown to child	4.8	5.4	5.2	5.8

[a] Ratings made by observer; low number indicates more of the quality rated.

little difference between the groups in affect expressed to the child by the mother (Brophy et al., 1965).

In these data, as in other not presented here, the mothers of the four status groups differed relatively little, on the average, in the affective elements of their interaction with their children. The gross differences appeared in the verbal and cognitive environments that they presented.

Against this background, I would like to return for a moment to the problem of the meaning, or, perhaps more correctly, the lack of meaning in cultural deprivation. One of the features of the behavior of the working-class mothers and children is a tendency to act without taking sufficient time for reflection and planning. In a sense one might call this impulsive behavior—not by acting out unconscious or forbidden impulses, but in a type of activity in which a particular act seems not to be related to the act that preceded it or to its consequences. In this sense it lacks meaning; it is not sufficiently related to the context in which it occurs, to the motivations of the participants, or to the goals of the task. This behavior may be verbal or motor; it shows itself in several ways. On the Etch-a-Sketch task, for example, the mother may silently watch a child make an error and then punish him. Another mother will anticipate the error, will warn the child that he is about to reach a decision point; she will prepare him by verbal and nonverbal cues to be careful, to look ahead, and to avoid the mistake. He is encouraged to reflect, to anticipate the consequences of his action, and in this way to avoid error. A problem-solving approach requires reflection and the ability to weigh decisions, to choose among alternatives. The effect of restricted speech and of status orientation is to foreclose the need for reflective weighing of alternatives and consequences; the use of an elaborated code, with its orientation to persons and to consequences (including future), tends to produce cognitive styles more easily adapted to problem-solving and reflection.

The objective of our study is to discover how teaching styles of the mothers induce and shape learning styles and information-processing strategies in the children. The picture that is beginning to emerge is that the meaning of deprivation is a deprivation of meaning—a cognitive environment in which behavior is controlled by status rules rather than by attention to the individual characteristics of a specific situation and one in which behavior is not mediated by verbal cues or by teaching that relates events to one another and the present to the future. This environment produces a child who relates to authority rather than to rationale, who, although often compliant, is not reflective in his behavior, and for whom the consequences of an act are largely considered in terms of immediate punishment or reward rather than future effects and long-range goals.

When the data are more complete, a more detailed analysis of the findings will enable us to examine the effect of maternal cognitive environments in terms of individual mother-child transactions, rather than in the gross categories of social class. This analysis will not only help us to understand how social-class environment is mediated through the interaction between mother and child but will give more precise information about the effects of individual maternal environments on the cognitive growth of the young child.

References

Bernstein, B. Social class and linguistic development: a theory of social learning. In A. H. Halsey, Jean Floud, & C. A. Anderson (Eds.), *Education, economy, and society.* Glencoe, Ill.: Free Pr., 1961.

Bernstein, B. Family role systems, communication, and socialization. Paper presented at Conf. on Develpm. of Cross-National Res. on the Education of Children and Adolescents, Univer. of Chicago, February, 1964.

Brophy, J., Hess, R. D., & Shipman, Virginia. Effects of social class and level of aspiration on performance in a structured mother-child interaction. Paper presented at Biennial Meeting of Soc. Res. Child Develpm., Minneapolis, Minn., March, 1965.

Deutsch, M. The disadvantaged child and the learning process. In A. H. Passow (Ed.), *Education in depressed areas.* New York: Columbia Univer. T.C., 1963. Pp. 163–180.

Deutsch, M., & Brown, B. Social influences in Negro-white intelligence differences. *J. soc. Issues,* 1964, **20** (2), 24–35.

Eells, K., Davis, Allison, Havighurst, R. J., Herrick, V. E., & Tyler, R. W. *Intelligence and cultural differences.* Chicago: Univer. of Chicago Pr., 1951.

Hess, R. D. Educability and rehabilitation: the future of the welfare class. *Marr. fam. Lvg.,* 1964, **26**, 422–429.

Jackson, J. D., Hess, R. D., & Shipman, Virginia. Communication styles in teachers: an experiment. Paper presented at Amer. Educ. and Res. Ass., Chicago, February, 1965.

John, Vera. The intellectual development of slum children: some preliminary findings. *Amer. J. Orthopsychiat.,* 1963, **33**, 813–822.

Kagan, J., Moss, H. A., & Sigel, I. E. Psychological significance of styles of conceptualization. *Monogr. Soc. Res. Child Develpm.,* 1963, **28**, No. 2.

Kagan, J. Information processing in the child: significance of analytic and reflective attitudes. *Psychol. Monogr.,* 1964, **78**, No. 1 (Whole No. 578).

Kennedy, W. A., Van de Riet, V., & White, J. C., Jr. A normative sample of intelligence and achievement of Negro elementary school children in the southeastern United States. *Monogr. Soc. Res. Child Develpm.,* 1963, **28**, No. 6.

Lesser, G. Mental abilities of children in different social and cultural groups. New York: Cooperative Research Project No. 1635, 1964.

Meyer, Roberta, Shipman, Virginia, & Hess, R. D. Family structure and social class in the socialization of curiosity in urban preschool children. Paper presented at APA meeting in Los Angeles, Calif. September, 1964.

Olim, E. G., Hess, R. D., & Shipman, Virginia. Relationship between mothers' language styles and cognitive styles of urban preschool children. Paper presented at Biennial Meeting of Soc. Res. Child Develpm., Minneapolis, Minn., March, 1965.

Shipman, Virginia, & Hess, R. D. Social class and sex differences in the utilization of language and the consequences for cognitive development. Paper presented at Midwest. Psychol. Ass., Chicago, April, 1965.

31. ACQUISITION OF IMITATIVE SPEECH BY SCHIZOPHRENIC CHILDREN

O. Ivar Lovaas, John P. Berberich, Bernard F. Perloff, & Benson Schaeffer

Abstract. *Two mute schizophrenic children were taught imitative speech within an operant conditioning framework. The training procedure consisted of a series of increasingly fine verbal discriminations; the children were rewarded for closer and closer reproductions of the attending adults' speech. We found that reward delivered contingent upon imitation was necessary for development of imitation. Furthermore, the newly established imitation was shown to have acquired rewarding properties for the children.*

With the great majority of children, the problem of teaching speech never arises. Speech develops within each child's particular environment without parents and teachers having to know a great deal about how it occurs. Yet, in some children, because of deviations in organic structure or prior experience, speech fails to develop. Children with the diagnosis of childhood schizophrenia, especially autistic children, often show little in the way of speech development (1). The literature on childhood schizophrenia suggests two conclusions regarding speech in such children, first, that the usual treatment setting (psychotherapy) in which these children are placed might not be conducive to speech development (2); and second, that a child failing to develop speech by the age of 5 years remains withdrawn and does not improve clinically (2). That is, the presence or absence of speech is an important prognostic indicator. It is perhaps obvious that a child who

SOURCE. O. I. Lovaas, J. P. Berberich, B. F. Perloff, and B. Schaeffer, Acquisition of imitative speech by schizophrenic children. Science, 1966, **151**, 705–709.

can speak can engage in a much more therapeutic interchange with his environment than the child who has no speech.

The failure of some children to develop speech as a "natural" consequence of growing up poses the need for an increased knowledge of how language is acquired. A procedure for the development of speech in previously mute children would not only be of practical importance but might also illuminate the development of speech in normal children. Although several theoretical attempts have been made to account for language development, the empirical basis for these theoretical formulations is probably inadequate. In fact, there are no published, systematic studies on how to go about developing speech in a person who has never spoken. We now outline a procedure by which speech can be made to occur. Undoubtedly there are or will be other ways by which speech can be acquired. Furthermore, our procedure centers on the acquisition of only one aspect of speech, the acquisition of vocal responses. The development of speech also requires the acquisition of a context for the occurrence of such responses ("meaning").

Casual observation suggests that normal children acquire words by hearing speech; that is, children learn to speak by imitation. The mute schizophrenic children with whom we worked were not imitative. Thus the establishment of imitation in these children appeared to be the most beneficial and practical starting point for building speech. The first step in creating speech, then, was to establish conditions in which imitation of vocal sounds would be learned.

The method that we eventually found most feasible for establishing verbal imitation involved a discrimination training procedure. Early in training the child was rewarded only if he emitted a sound within a certain time after an adult had emitted a sound. Next he was rewarded only if the sound he emitted within the prescribed interval resembled the adult's sound. Toward the end of training, he was rewarded only if his vocalization very closely matched the adult's vocalization—that is, if it was, in effect, imitative. Thus verbal imitation was taught through the development of a series of increasingly fine discriminations.

The first two children exposed to this program are discussed here. Chuck and Billy were 6-year-old in-patients at the Neuropsychiatric Institute at UCLA. These children were selected for the program because they did not speak. At the onset of the program, vocal behavior in both children was restricted to occasional vowel productions with no discernible communicative intent. These vowel sounds occurred infrequently, except when the children were tantrumous, and did not resemble the pre-speech babbling of infants. In addition, the children evidenced no appropriate play (for example, they would spin toys or mouth them). They engaged in a considerable amount of self-stimulatory behavior such as rocking and twirling. They did not initiate social contacts and became tantrumous when such contact was initiated by others. They evidenced occasional self-destructive behavior (biting self, head-banging, and so forth). Symbolic rewards such as social approval were inoperative, so biological rewards such as food were substituted. In short, they were profoundly schizophrenic.

Training was conducted 6 days a week, 7 hours a day, with a 15-minute rest period accompanying each hour of training. During the training sessions the child and the adult sat facing each other, their heads about 30 cm apart. The adult physically prevented the child from leaving the training situation by holding the child's legs between his own legs. Rewards, in the form of single spoonsful of the child's meal, were delivered immediately after correct responses. Punishment (spanking, shouting by the adult) was delivered for inattentive, self-destructive, and tantrumous behavior which interfered with the training, and most of these behaviors were thereby suppressed within 1 week. Incorrect vocal behavior was never punished.

Four distinct steps were required to establish verbal imitation. In step 1, the child was rewarded for all vocalizations. We frequently would fondle the children and we avoided aversive stimulation. This was done in order to increase the frequency of vocal responses. During this stage in training the child was also rewarded for visually fixating on the adult's mouth. When the child reached an achievement level of about one verbal response every 5 seconds and was visually fixating on the adult's mouth more than 50 percent of the time, step 2 of training was introduced.

Step 2 marked our initial attempt to bring the child's verbal behavior under our verbal control in such a manner that our speech would ultimately stimulate speech in the child. Mastery of this second step involved acquisition of a temporal discrimination by the child. The adult emitted a vocal response —for example, "baby"—about once on the average of every 10th second. The child was rewarded only if he vocalized within 6 seconds after the adult's vocalization. However, any vocal response of the child would be rewarded in that time interval. Step 3 was introduced when the frequency of the child's vocal responses within the 6-second interval was three times what it had been initially.

Step 3 was structurally similar to the preceding step, but it included the additional requirement that the child actually match the adult's vocalization before receiving the reward. In this and in following steps the adult selected the verbalization to be placed in imitative training from a pool of possible verbalizations that had met one or more of the following criteria. First, we selected vocal behaviors that could be prompted, that is, vocal behaviors that could be elicited by a cue prior to any experimental training, such as by manually moving the child through the behavior.

An example of training with the use of a prompt is afforded in teaching the sound "b". The training would proceed in three stages: (i) the adult emitted "b" and simultaneously prompted the child to emit "b" by holding the child's lips closed with his fingers and quickly removing them when the child exhaled; (ii) the prompt would be gradually faded, by the adult's moving his fingers away from the child's mouth, to his cheek, and finally gently touching the child's jaw; (iii) the adult emitted the vocalization "b" only, withholding all prompts. The rate of fading was determined by the child; the sooner the child's verbal behavior came under control of the adult's without the use of the prompt, the better. The second criterion for selection of words or sounds in the early stages of training centered on their concomitant visual components (which we exaggerated when we pronounced them), such as those of the labial consonant "m" and of open-mouthed vowels like "a." We selected such sounds after having previously found that the children could discriminate words with visual components more easily than those with only auditory components (the guttural consonants, "k" and "g," proved extremely difficult and, like "l" and "s," were mastered later than other sounds). Third, we selected for training sounds which the child emitted most frequently in step 1.

Step 4 was a recycling of step 3, with the addition of a new sound. We selected a sound that was very different from those presented in step 3, so that the child could discriminate between the new and old sounds more easily. To make certain that the child was in fact imitating, we randomly interspersed the sounds of step 3 with the sound of step 4, in a randomized ratio of about 1 to 3. This random presentation "forced" (or enabled) the child to discriminate the particular sounds involved, in order to be rewarded. There was no requirement placed upon the child in step 3 to discriminate specific aspects such as vowels, consonants, and order of the adult's speech; a child might master step 3 without attending to the specific properties of the adult's speech. Each new introduction of sounds and words required increasingly fine discrimination by the child and hence provided evidence that the child was in fact matching the adult's speech. All steps beyond step 4 consisted of replications of step 3, but new sounds, words, and phrases were used. In each new step the previously mastered words and sounds were rehearsed on a randomized ratio of 1 to 3. The next step was introduced when the child had mastered the previous steps—that is, when he had made ten consecutive correct replications of the adult's utterances.

One hour of each day's training was tape-recorded. Two independent observers scored the child's correct vocal responses from these sessions. A correct response was defined as a recognizable reproduction of the adult's utterance. The observers showed better than 90 percent agreement over

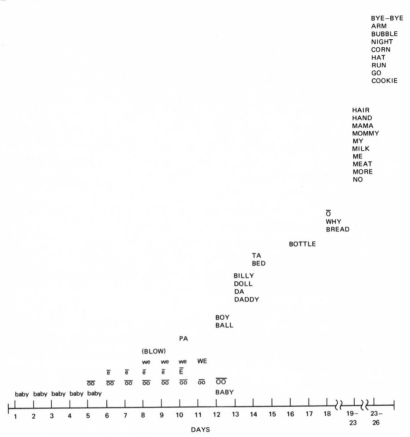

FIGURE 1. Acquisition of verbal imitation by Billy. The abscissa denotes training days. Words and sounds are printed in lower case letters on the days they were introduced, and in capital letters on the days they were mastered.

sessions. When the child's correct responses are plotted against days of training, and the resulting function is positively accelerated, it can be said that the child has learned to imitate.

The results of the first 26 days of imitation training, starting from introduction of step 3, have been plotted for Billy (Fig. 1). The abscissa denotes training days. The words and sounds are printed in lower case letters on the days they were introduced and in capital letters on the days they were mastered. It can be seen that as training progressed the rate of mastery increased. Billy took several days to learn a single word during the first 2 weeks of the program, but a single day to master several words during the last 2 weeks. Chuck's performance was very similar to Billy's.

After 26 days of training both children had learned to imitate new words with such ease and rapidity that merely adding verbal responses to their imitative repertoire seemed pointless. Hence the children were then introduced to the second part of the language training program, wherein they were taught to use language appropriately.

The imitation training took place in a rather complex environment, with many events happening concurrently. We hypothesized that it was the reward, given for imitative behavior, which was crucial to the learning. To test this hypothesis, the adult uttered the sounds as during the training and the children received the same number of rewards as before. However, the rewards were contingent upon time elapsed since the last reward, regardless of the child's behavior.

The data show a deterioration in imitation behavior whenever rewards are shifted from response-contingent to time-contingent delivery. It is concluded, therefore, that reward immediately following correct, imitative behavior (and withholding ofreward following incorrect responding) is a crucial variable in maintaining imitative behavior in these children. The same finding has been reported by Baer and Sherman (3) who worked with imitative behavior in normal children.

Since the child was rewarded whenever he responded like the adult, *similarity* was consistently associated with food. Because of such association, similarity should become symbolic of reward. In other words, imitative behavior, being symbolic of reward, should eventually provide its own reward (Baer and Sherman, 3). To test this hypothesis, both children were exposed to Norwegian words which they were unable to reproduce perfectly when first presented. The adult simply stated the Norwegian word and the child always attempted to repeat it; no extrinsic rewards were delivered. However, occasionally the child was presented with English words which the adult rewarded when correctly imitated. This procedure was necessary to maintain the hypothesized symbolic (learned) reward function of imitation.

The children improved in the imitation of the Norwegian words over time. It is as if they were rewarded for correct behavior. In view of the data pointing to the need for rewards in maintaining imitative behavior, and in the absence of extrinsic rewards, we would argue that the reward was intrinsic and a function of the prior imitation training. There is one implication of this finding which is of particular interest for therapeutic reasons: children may be able to acquire new behaviors on their own. (This finding contrasts with the frequent stereotype of a conditioning product, namely, that of an automaton unable to function independently.)

Currently, three new schizophrenic children are undergoing the same speech training program as Billy and Chuck. After 3 days of training, one of these children achieved a level of imitative behavior similar to that shown by Billy and Chuck after 26 days. It should be pointed out that schizophrenic children are a very heterogeneous group with respect to their speech histories and symptomatology in general, and that Billy and Chuck had failed in development to a profound degree. Insofar as one works with such a diverse population, it is likely that numerous procedures could be helpful in establishing speech.

References and Notes

1. B. Rimland, *Infantile Autism* (Appleton-Century-Crofts, New York, 1964).
2. J. Brown, *Amer. J. Orthopsychiat.* 30, 382 (1960).
3. D. Baer and J. Sherman, *J. Exp. Child Psychol.* 1, 37 (1964).
4. Study supported by grants from Margaret Sabl of Los Angeles. We express appreciation to James Q. Simmons and the staff at the Children's Unit, Neuropsychiatric Institute, University of California, Los Angeles.

32. DEVELOPMENT OF WORD MEANING THROUGH VERBAL CONTEXT: AN EXPERIMENTAL STUDY[1]

Heinz Werner & Edith Kaplan

A. THE TEST

In the main, a child learns the meaning of a word in two ways. One way is direct and explicit, i.e., the adult names a thing or defines a word for the child. The other way is indirect and implicit, through experience with concrete and/or verbal contexts.

This study is concerned with the acquisition of word meanings through verbal contexts. The children participating in this investigation ranged from 8½ to 13½ years of age and were divided into five age groups with 25 children at each age level. The interquartile IQ range was from 101 to 111.

The test was as follows: The child's task was to find the meaning of an artificial word, which appeared in six different verbal contexts. In all, there were 12 sets of six sentences each. The 12 artificial words denoted either an object or an action. For example, the artificial word in the first set of six sentences was CORPLUM, for which the correct translation was "stick" or "piece of wood." The contexts for CORPLUM were as follows:

1. A CORPLUM MAY BE USED FOR SUPPORT.
2. CORPLUMS MAY BE USED TO CLOSE OFF AN OPEN PLACE.
3. A CORPLUM MAY BE LONG OR SHORT, THICK OR THIN, STRONG OR WEAK.

SOURCE. *Journal of Psychology*, 1950, **29**, 251–257.

[1] This study has been carried out under a grant from the Social Science Research Council; a comprehensive report will be published at a later date.

4. A WET CORPLUM DOES NOT BURN.
5. YOU CAN MAKE A CORPLUM SMOOTH WITH SANDPAPER.
6. THE PAINTER USED A CORPLUM TO MIX HIS PAINTS.

B. PROCEDURE

The experimental procedure was as follows: After the child was made thoroughly familiar with the task, he was presented with a card on which Sentence 1 of Series 1 was printed. After the child responded to the first sentence, he was asked how and why the meaning he gave for the word fit into the sentence. He then was presented with the second sentence while the first context was still in view. After having given his interpretation of the word as it appeared in the second sentence (which may or may not have differed from his first response) the child was again asked how and why it fit and also whether it could be applied to the preceding sentence. This procedure was carried out until all six contexts had been presented to the child. The child's responses were carefully recorded.

C. ANALYSIS AND RESULTS

Although correctness was not the major aspect of the study, it may be briefly mentioned that correctness of responses increased significantly from age level to age level.

Our main concern was with the ways children gave signification to the artificial words; we were especially interested in the development of the signification process. For the purpose of analysis, three judges derived 60 criteria from a preliminary inspection of the protocols. These criteria, pertaining to linguistic as well as semantic characteristics, were then employed by the three judges in the final analysis.

Studying the protocols one is impressed with the great variety of processes by which children acquired and generalized word meanings from verbal contexts. Many responses of the younger children indicate *a lack in the differentiation between the meaning of the word and the given verbal context.* Instead of conceiving the word as referring to a circumscribed meaning, many of the younger children regarded the artificial word as carrying the meaning of the whole or part of the context in which it appeared. We may call this type of conception a *sentence-core concept.* For instance, one sentence, containing the artificial word, BORDICK, (faults) was the following: PEOPLE TALK ABOUT THE BORDICKS OF OTHERS AND DON'T LIKE TO TALK ABOUT THEIR OWN. One child, dealing with this sentence, remarked: "Well, BORDICK means 'people talk about others and don't talk about themselves,' that's what BORDICK means." That this child seriously thought that BORDICK meant the whole sentence became clear when he tried to fit this meaning into the context: PEOPLE WITH BORDICKS ARE OFTEN UNHAPPY. The child fitted his sentence-core concept into this context as follows: "People talk about others and don't talk about themselves—they are often unhappy." To the question: "How does this meaning fit?", the child had this answer: "Say this lady hears that another lady is talking about her, so she'll get mad at her and that lady will be very unhappy."

A frequent method of fitting a sentence-core concept, formed for one sentence, into another context was by a process we have termed *assimilation*. The child interprets the context of a new sentence as the same or similar to the context of the previous sentence. Through such assimilation, the concept for the previous sentence now fits into the new sentence. To illustrate, in one series the artificial word is HUDRAY (for which such concepts as "increase," "enlarge" or "grow" are adequate). Sentence 6 of this series read: YOU MUST HAVE ENOUGH SPACE IN THE BOOKCASE TO HUDRAY YOUR LIBRARY. One child said: "Hudray means 'to have enough space.' " He took a part of the context as the referent for HUDRAY. Returning to the previous sentences, he said that the concept, "to have enough space," fit all six sentences. For example, it fit Sentence 1 (IF YOU EAT WELL AND SLEEP WELL YOU WILL HUDRAY): "If you eat well, that is, if you do not overeat, you will have enough room in your stomach and won't get too chubby; if you sleep well, but not too much, you don't get overlazy; so you leave some room for more sleep—so you leave space—like."

Not infrequently, the child derived two independent sentence-core concepts pertaining to two successive sentences. In attempting to apply the second solution to the first sentence, he often combined the two solutions. For instance, for the two sentences:

JANE HAD TO HUDRAY THE CLOTH SO THE DRESS WOULD FIT MARY.
YOU HUDRAY WHAT YOU KNOW BY READING AND STUDYING.

One child gave as respective solutions: "Jane had to 'let out the hem' of the cloth" and "You 'learn by books' what you know." Coming back from the second to the first sentence the child said, " 'Learn by books' fits here. Jane had to 'learn by books' how to 'let out the hem' in the cloth. Jane used an encyclopedia of sewing." For this girl, the first solution "let out the hem" was so completely embedded in the sentence context that it became a part of the sentence and no longer a substitute for HUDRAY. The child could now introduce the subsequent solution ("learn by books") above and beyond the first, original solution. At times, we obtained as many as three independent solutions combined in one sentence.

Another indication that word and sentence were not clearly differentiated at the earlier levels was the frequent manifestation of what we have called *holophrastic gradient*. Here, the concept was not limited to the unknown word, but spread to neighboring parts, thus carrying pieces of the sentence with it; e.g., for the word, LIDBER (collect, gather), one child stated for the sentence: JIMMY LIDBERED STAMPS FROM ALL COUNTRIES, "Jimmy 'collected' stamps from all countries." The concept was extended from "collect" to "collect stamps." Thus the concept, "collect stamps" was applied to another sentence: THE POLICE DID NOT ALLOW THE PEOPLE TO LIDBER ON THE STREET, in the following manner: "Police did not permit people to 'collect stamps' on the street."

Thus far, we have considered only those forms of signification of a word which are based on an intimate fusion of word and sentence (or sentence-parts). In our analysis, we found other forms of signification, in which the concepts, though they did not display sentence-word fusion, were still lacking the circumscribed, stable character of the more mature concepts. We called such products *simple contextual or simple holophrastic concepts*. Here the word meaning was definitely set apart from the context of the sentence; nevertheless, it differed from conventional word meanings in that it bore a wide situational connotation rather than a circumscribed, stable one. The artificial word did not refer, for the child, to a single object or action, but to a more inclusive context. Sometimes the broad situational connotation of the word was explicitly stated by the child, i.e., he employed a whole phrase to express the meaning of the word. In other cases, the child used a single word, seemingly delimited in its meaning, which on probing was found to be far more inclusive than it appeared on the surface. The following may serve as examples of explicitly stated holophrastic concepts.

The artificial word, ASHDER (obstacle), appears in the sentence, THE WAY IS CLEAR IF THERE ARE NO ASHDERS. One child responded: "The way is clear if there are no 'parts of a radio that don't fit in right' (together)." In the mind of this child, the word, ASHDER, referred to a radio-repair situation.

In the case of the sentence: THE POLICE DID NOT ALLOW THE PEOPLE TO LIDBER ON THE STREET, one child's translation of LIDBER was "throw paper around" (i.e., cluttering up the street by throwing paper around).

An illustration of implicit holophrastic concepts is the following, involving the word ONTRAVE (hope): ONTRAVE SOMETIMES KEEPS US FROM BEING UNHAPPY. A child substituted for ONTRAVE the seemingly circumscribed word "want." However, on probing, it became apparent that "want" referred to a broad contextual situation: "If you 'want a bow and arrow set and you get it,' that keeps you from being unhappy."

For this same sentence, another child came to the solution, "mother." " 'Mother' keeps you from being unhappy." However, "mother" actually meant "mother when she gives you things you want."

One may note an important characteristic attached to such situational word meanings; the word has not only a broad situational content, but this content is fluid and lacks closure: i.e., the concept may change in range from sentence to sentence, elements being added or subtracted, etc. This can be seen from the way children quite typically expanded a concept in order to fit it into another sentence. This process of expansion, denoting fluidity of conceptualization, we have termed *contextual* or *holophrastic expansion.* An example of this holophrastic expansion is the following: One child had developed the concept "books to study" for HUDRAY. "Books" became expanded to "throwing books" when the child attempted to fit the concept into the sentence: MRS. SMITH WANTED TO HUDRAY HER FAMILY. The child stated: "Mrs. Smith wanted to 'throw books,' at her family."

Another child, who had arrived at the concept "long" for one sentence, expanded it to "get long hair" in another: THE OLDER YOU GET THE SOONER YOU WILL BEGIN TO SOLDEVE, ". . . the sooner you will begin to 'get long hair.' "

On occasion the contextual expansion was more systematically employed. The child formed a conceptual nucleus, which remained constant throughout the six contexts; and added to this nucleus elements varying with each sentence. We have termed this procedure *pluralization.* For example, one child formed a nucleus for all the sentences of one series containing the artificial word, LIDBER. This nucleus was "collect." In one sentence LIDBER meant "collect ribbons" (ALL THE CHILDREN WILL "collect ribbons" AT MARY'S PARTY); in another sentence, it was "collect autographs" (THE PEOPLE "collected autographs" from THE SPEAKER WHEN HE FINISHED HIS TALK); in a third sentence, it meant "collect information" (PEOPLE "collect information" QUICKLY WHEN THERE IS AN ACCIDENT), and so on.

We should like to mention two other forms of signification of a word, that were essentially based on contextual or holophrastic conceptualization. One we have termed *generalization by juxtaposition;* the other *generalization by chain.*

In the case of juxtaposition, a concept of an object A obtained in one sentence is applicable to a second sentence through the mediation of a concept of an object B that is spatially contiguous to the object A. For instance, a child gave the solution "plaster" for CONTAVISH in the sentence: BEFORE THE HOUSE IS FINISHED, THE WALLS MUST HAVE CON-

TAVISHES. "Plaster" also fit into the sentence, A BOTTLE HAS ONLY ONE CONTAVISH. Here the child used "label" for CONTAVISH, saying, "A bottle has only one 'label.'" Nevertheless "plaster" was retained as the solution because "plaster," as the child explained, "is used to put on the 'label.'" In other words, the concept of an object such as "plaster" could be used as an over-all solution because the juxtaposed object ("label") fit into the sentence. Most likely, the concept was contextual: not just "plaster" but "plaster+."

A similar mechanism seemed to be operative in generalization by chain. This type of generalization probably differs from juxtaposition only insofar as the two objects in question are conceived of as temporally rather than spatially connected (e.g., cause and effect). As an example, "honor" was substituted for SACKOY in one sentence: WE ALL ADMIRE PEOPLE WHO HAVE MUCH SACKOY. In the next sentence, "guts" was the meaning attributed to SACKOY. "You need 'guts' to fight with a boy bigger than you." But "honor" still fit because, as the child explained, "If you have 'guts,' you are 'honored' aren't you?"

Finally, the two main groups of immature signification discussed in this paper may be briefly compared statistically. As will be recalled, in the first group, the word carries with it the whole or parts of the sentence context; in the second group, the word is clearly differentiated from the sentence context, though it still possesses a broad contextual meaning. Table 1 summarizes the occurrence of these two types of contextual word meanings at the various age levels.

TABLE 1

Age	8½–9½	9½–10½	10½–11½	11½–12½	12½–13½
I Sentence-contextual	11.9	9.2	1.8	0.2	0.5
II Non-sentence-contextual	11.7	10.8	7.9	4.6	3.3

The figures represent the mean occurrence per child at each age group. Both forms of word meanings decreased as age increased; however, there is a clearcut difference between the two developmental curves. Signification based on sentence-word fusion (Type I) decreased most sharply between the second and third age levels (around 10–11 years), with practically no occurrence after the third age level. The other type of contextual signification (in which there is no fusion of word meaning and sentence) showed an entirely different developmental trend: it gradually decreased, and even at the 13 year-level there were as many as 3.3 such solutions per child.

The abrupt decrease of Type I, the most immature form of signification, around the 10- to 11-year level suggests a rather fundamental shift in language attitude, toward a task, which, as in our test, is on a relatively abstract verbal plane. This points to important implications which will be treated at greater length in a future paper.

In closing, we should like to mention briefly that there are aspects of language development other than semantic, discussed in this paper, which showed similar abrupt changes at the same age levels. This is particularly true with respect to grammatical structure. The data indicate that there is a growing comprehension of the test sentence as a stable, grammatical structure. Younger children manipulated the sentence as a fluid medium, lacking closure; that is, in the case of giving meaning to the artificial word they frequently altered the grammatical structure of the test sentence. The frequency of such manipulation showed an abrupt drop at the end of the second age level with pratically no occurrence at the fourth and fifth levels.

One of the most significant and little explored problems of language development concerns the relationship between the semantic and grammatical aspects of language. The close correspondence of the developmental curves, indicated by our data, between two seemingly independent aspects of language lends support to those theories that assume a genetic interdependence of meaning and structure.

Author Index

Subject Index

571